Java™ for ColdFusion Developers

Eben Hewitt

Prentice Hall PTR
Upper Saddle River, NJ 07458
www.phptr.com

A Cataloging-in-Publication data record for this book can be obtained from the Library of Congress.

Editorial/Production Supervision: *Faye Gemmellaro*
Senior Managing Editor: *John Neidhart*
Cover Design Director: *Jerry Votta*
Manufacturing Manager: *Alexis Heydt-Long*
Marketing Manager: *Bryan Gambrel/Kate Hargett*
Editorial Assistant: *Brandt Kenna*
Interior Design: *Gail Cocker-Bogusz*

© 2003 Pearson Education, Inc.
Publishing as Prentice Hall PTR
Upper Saddle River, NJ 07458

Prentice Hall books are widely used by corporations and government agencies for training, marketing, and resale.

For information regarding corporate and government bulk discounts, contact:

Corporate and Government Sales: (800) 382-3419 or corpsales@pearsontechgroup.com

All products mentioned herein are trademarks or registered trademarks of their respective owners.

All rights reserved. No part of this book may be reproduced, in any form or by any means, without permission in writing from the publisher.

Printed in the United States of America

10 9 8 7 6 5 4 3 2 1

ISBN 0-13-046180-6

Pearson Education Ltd.
Pearson Education Australia Pty., Ltd.
Pearson Education Singapore, Pte. Ltd.
Pearson Education North Asia Ltd.
Pearson Education Canada, Ltd.
Pearson Educación de Mexico, S.A. de C.V.
Pearson Education—Japan
Pearson Education Malaysia, Pte. Ltd.

For Lil' G—

A perfect instance of Girl.

Love,

Big D

Contents

CHAPTER 4 Programming Structures 67

CHAPTER 6
IDEs

CHAPTER 9 Advanced Object-Oriented Concepts *245*

CHAPTER 15
JSP Custom Tags

Chapter 16 J2EE Case Study: An E-commerce Site

Foreword

Well, someone has finally dared to use the J-word in a book written for the ColdFusion developer community. I couldn't be happier! Eben Hewitt has written a book about *Java* for ColdFusion developers—and it's an excellent book, I'm happy to report.

But wait—*Java*? Hasn't Macromedia spent a great deal of effort reassuring ColdFusion developers that they won't need to learn Java to use ColdFusion? They certainly have—and when the question is phrased as "*Must* I learn Java?," the answer must be "No." But perhaps our question ought to be, "*Should* I learn Java?" Ask a better question and you may get a better answer.

There are any number of very practical reasons that you might want to learn Java. That you're holding *this* book in your hands rather than another indicates that you're probably well aware of them. For many of us, the most compelling reasons are the increased job opportunities and better pay that knowing Java represents.

Like it or not, we developers work in a field where our current knowledge has a finite lifetime of usefulness. In the hyper-accelerated environment of Web technology, new knowledge springs forth daily to replace the old. Our hard-won expertise becomes less valuable daily. Economists even have a term for this; they call it a *wasting asset*. Ouch.

The inescapable fact is that this new knowledge mainly centers on Java, and that fact can be a terrifying one to ColdFusion programmers, who might ask, "*Java? You want me to learn Java—with all its weird, C-like syntax and classes that extend from this and inherit that and are dependent on something else? That Java?*"

Yes—that Java. Java represents a watershed event in the history of software development—the mass adoption of object orientation (OO) as the standard for building software. For 30 years, OO has been being nurtured in a community of dedicated academicians, theorists, and tool-builders.

Building on the best practices that proceeded it, OO provides not only some new languages (e.g., Eiffel, Smalltalk, and Java), but a new way of approaching how we create software. During my career, OO has moved from being a quirky, ivory-tower science project to the dominant paradigm for building commercial software. And Java stands as the unchallenged 800-pound gorilla of OO languages.

Financial considerations aside, I find that developers are very creative people who enjoy the thrill of making scale-modeled universes that *work*! Java represents a new set of tools that can help you built bigger, better, cooler (and yes, more profitable) universes. Learning Java will almost certainly make you a more capable and more secure developer. And, while you don't have to learn Java to continue to use ColdFusion, the new capabilities of ColdFusion MX make learning Java more attractive than ever.

All right; you've decided to take the plunge. If Java is the future, you're ready to embrace it. Why *this* book, though? There's certainly no shortage of Java books around. Some are bigger, some are cheaper, some even have a snazzier cover! Or does it even matter? Having made the decision to learn Java, does the choice of book really make much of a difference?

I believe it does. Learning a new language is not easy. Consider the difficulties encountered for centuries by Egyptologists trying to decipher the picture-language used by ancient Egyptians. Scholars had expended great efforts only to achieve scant results. Then, in 1799, some of Napoleon's soldiers were digging the foundations of an addition to a fort near the town of Rashid in the Nile delta when they came across a six-foot tall stone with hieroglyphs on it.

Had that been all there was to the stone, very little consideration would have been given to it. It dated from about 195 B.C., but such ancient artifacts endowed with hieroglyphs were neither rare nor notable in the Nile valley. The text of the stone was not particularly noteworthy, either. It began with the praises of King Ptolemy V, it was followed by an account of the siege of the city, Lycopolis, and it ended with the establishment of a religion venerating the king. But, today, every schoolchild knows of this stone, which became known as the Rosetta stone. What made this stone special was the fact that the text was inscribed in both the unknown Egyptian hieroglyphs and the familiar Greek language. The scholars' knowledge of Greek thus became a key to learning an unknown language.

You might think of this book as a type of Rosetta stone—one that will help you to decipher Java. It begins with what you know—ColdFusion—and uses this as a key to help you understand Java. I can think of no better way to learn a new language.

Building on this excellent idea, Eben uses clear language, copious examples, insightful theory, and wry humor to achieve his goal—helping us leverage our ColdFusion knowledge into Java expertise.

This book won't teach you everything about Java. No book can. As a friend of mine says, "Saying 'I know Java' is like saying, 'I know science.'" There's plenty of material to work with for years to come. But this book *will* give you a working knowledge of Java basics and a firm foundation on which to increase your knowledge. If you're a ColdFusion programmer looking to learn Java, I can offer no better advice than to buy this book and study it.

Hal Helms

Acknowledgments

The most important scientific revolutions all include, as their only common feature, the dethronement of human arrogance from one pedestal after another of previous convictions about our own centrality in the cosmos.

—Stephen Jay Gould

There are many people whose labor contributed to this book. I am grateful for their thought, energy, and care. I am proud to call them my friends, my family, and my colleagues, and I am pleased to acknowledge their considerable work.

This book was improved tremendously by the labor of its technical reviewers, whose knowledge and perspicuity caught many errors, omissions, and oversights. They worked even through writing their own books, changing jobs, having babies, and moving, and I appreciate their efforts.

Thanks to Scott Stirling. Your careful, diligent readings caught subtle shades in the text that only a watchmaker could see, and I am grateful for your work. You straightened out several technical issues with clarity and detail. You really raised the bar for this book.

Thanks to Ray Camden. I appreciate your help in sorting out the diverse relationships between ColdFusion and Java, and your review work very much improved the communicativeness of the book.

Thanks to Susan Matteson. In working through the code examples, you made sure that everything came together, and you didn't allow any shortcuts. You made sure that the book does what it purports to do, and I'm grateful.

I am grateful to the people with whom it is my pleasure to work at CyberTrails. Thank you to Ted Taylor, Brian Aden, and Brad Senff for being very supportive of this book; I could not have done it without each of you being so understanding and accommodating. Thank you to Deb Klein, who helped get me the best Java training early on—even in tight times.

Thank you to Mike O'Brien and Erin Martin for sweating out the Tomcat warp connector with me. Thank you to David Schoenecker and the Asian Prince for making our department so fun. Thank you to Vic Miller for programming Java and ColdFusion with me and hacking into unchartered territory all the time. The grape soda is on me.

Thanks to Howard Young, Jim Dewar, Richard Moore, Alan Chick, and everyone at CyberTrails who works hard and makes my life inestimably better.

Thank you to Hal Helms for writing such a generous foreword to the book. Your writing and teaching are terrific, and I appreciate your work.

Thank you to entrepreneur and bon vivant John DePoe, for laying the most adventure-filled network on the Navajo Nation with me. Thank you to sys admin Garrick Brooks for taking extra time to introduce me to ColdFusion years ago. You both changed my life and helped make this possible.

Thank you to the fantastic people at Prentice Hall. I am so pleased and proud to work with John Neidhart. Thank you for your patience with me in finishing up this third title in one year with Prentice Hall. I feel so lucky and happy to be working with such a wonderful editor. You kept things rolling through a great number of changes in the lineup. Your moxie, your sense of humor, and your honesty are fantastic. I am grateful to be able to work with you.

Thank you to Editor-in-Chief Mark Taub, Brian Gambrel, Executive Marketing Manager, and to the copyeditors and hard-working salespeople who get the job done.

Thank you to John and Avis Hewitt for teaching me to read and write and for showing me that books are a best thing.

Thank you to Alison Brown. I could not have done it without you. Thank you for taking care of me, for talking to me, and for helping me be a better writer, better programmer, better sweetheart, better father, and better person every day. Throw some *heat*.

There was a definite process by which one made people into friends, and it involved talking to them and listening to them for hours at a time.

—Rebecca West

1

Introduction

Proceed, proceed: we will begin these rites,
As we do trust they'll end, in true delights.

—William Shakespeare, *As You Like It*, 5.4

Java for ColdFusion Developers is the one book any ColdFusion developer needs to get started using Java technologies for programming and Web application development.

1.1 Why *Java for ColdFusion Developers*?

There are many Java books currently on the market. However, many of these books assume that you have already mastered another programming language. This can make it difficult to understand the concepts behind the syntax. Likewise, many of these books are riddled with references to C++, because there are a number of similarities between C++ and Java. This is not useful for a Web developer who is interested in learning programming. This book is therefore riddled with references to ColdFusion, allowing you to learn Java more quickly because the language is contextualized strongly in terms of something you are already very familiar with.

1.1.1 Java Programming First, Java Web Technology Second

While ColdFusion developers may be interested in standalone software application development, they are certainly interested in Web technologies. Therefore, this book does something few other current Java books do: it teaches you Java first, and then the Web technologies that Java features. Many Java books are geared toward those who want to be software developers (for obvious reasons), and they often don't even mention JavaServer Pages (JSP). You therefore would need to get a second book to learn them specifically. This book handles it.

While there are also numerous books on JSP and servlets, they often assume that you already know Java, or that you can write JSPs without knowing Java. I feel strongly that one cannot write more than a toy JSP—let alone architect and build a complete real-world application (the kind clients like)—without knowing any Java. This book handles it.

1.1.2 ColdFusion MX

1.1.2.1 NEW ARCHITECTURE

With the introduction of ColdFusion MX, ColdFusion developers are now facing a new architecture, written in Java, as well as other updates to ColdFusion that work closely with the Java programming language. While it is not necessary to learn Java to continue writing regular ColdFusion applications, there is certainly no better time or excuse to do so. Learning Java and JSP now will enhance and extend your ability to write powerful Web applications.

1.1.2.2 NEW FEATURES

ColdFusion MX has a number of new features, including ColdFusion Components, which define, for example, `<cffunction>` and `<cfargument>`. These allow you to create reusable components that you can call from a ColdFusion template, a Web service, or from Flash. While this is an exciting feature, there is a sense in which the behavior and terminology involved mimics Java (which is underneath the hood). The same can be said for the "finally" statement—that recent addition to CFScript that you may have noticed. Well, it's not a coincidence—it's Java. It just makes sense to learn what is happening behind the scenes.

1.1.2.3 JSP/SERVLET SUPPORT

Because it is written in Java, ColdFusion MX now supports JSP and servlets natively. This means that you will be able to write hybrid applications that combine the rapid application development inherent in ColdFusion with the power of Java technologies such as JavaBeans. ColdFusion MX developers can call JSPs or servlets directly from within a CFML page, or import JSP tag libraries and use them as if they were ColdFusion custom tags.

Moreover, because this book is focused specifically on helping ColdFusion developers, learning Java and JSP will be faster and easier.

1.1.3 Updated for Java 1.4, JSP 1.3, and Servlets 2.4

During the writing of this book, Java 1.4 was released, and JSP 1.3 and Servlets 2.4 are close to a release. This book makes sure you have the most up-to-date information on Java technologies, which have changed significantly even in the last year. This is especially true of the Web technologies.

1.2 Who This Book Is For

This book is for Web developers who are interested in learning Java. It is assumed that you already know HTML and attendant Web technologies and server behavior, and are able to write SQL statements. Many callouts in the text will reference how the Java topic being covered is distinguished from the corresponding ColdFusion topic. For instance, ColdFusion has arrays, and Java has arrays. But ColdFusion arrays start at 1, whereas Java arrays start at 0. Likewise, there are a number of similarities between CFScript (especially in ColdFusion MX) and Java syntax, so that knowledge will help you. Exception handling is similar as well.

This book would also be useful to a Web developer who does not know ColdFusion specifically, but some of the ColdFusion contextualization would of course have little meaning.

Here is one version of how a ColdFusion developer might have previously gone about learning Java and JSP:

1. Spend hours in the bookstore reading endless tables of contents and hours online reading reviews to determine the best Java book to buy.
2. Decide to buy the "serious" Java book because I'm not an idiot, nor quite a dummy; nor do I think I can learn anything complex in 10 minutes. Pick up one that looks big and straightforward that covers the basics.
3. Read 40 pages of *Serious Java*. Realize that I have not been writing software in C++ for the past 10 years and have no background in OOP. Decide, when I'm honest with myself, that it's my fault—not the book's—and that this is okay. Determine that I need another book to serve as background for this one.
4. Buy a UML book because now I know I should learn that first. Consider buying *Beginning Programming* so that I have a true foundation. Instead, get a taco and slink home.
5. Everything in the UML book is too abstract and removed from code. I need something faster. Buy the *Marketing Manager's Guide to Java*. Strangely, it doesn't quite seem deep enough.

6. Realize that all I wanted to know in the first place was how to write JSPs. Buy three JSP books.
7. Read 30 pages of the first JSP book. Buy a 700-page book on JDBC because now I'm "cooking." Spend 14 hours trying to install Tomcat on Windows as a service. Realize that my understanding of Java is insufficient to follow along. Decide that maybe I need an easier book. Buy a Java exam preparation guide because I'm not embarrassed to bring it to the counter.
8. Now disoriented and bloody near disgusted, forget about the whole thing for five months. Take a *Cosmo* self-help quiz to determine if what I really like is *buying* books, not reading them, or just reading programming books, and not programming. Consider a career in the design department where "the money's easy." Fall asleep.
9. Resume reading *Serious Java*. Decide it's high time to ride or get off the horse. Invest $2,500 in a two-day training class. Wear the free t-shirt so that the guys at the batting cage will think I work for Sun.
10. Slowly come to understand Java. Piece it together by writing programs of increasing difficulty, sorting through all of these texts, and talking to people "with a different skill set." Congratulate self on wry navigation of the Java world.

Java for ColdFusion Developers is written with ColdFusion developers in mind. Even if you are a seasoned Visual Basic programmer and the above scenario does not remotely describe your experience, you will find this book concise and very useful.

1.3 What This Book Is Not

This is not a ColdFusion book. This book assumes that you are a knowledgeable ColdFusion developer; as such, it does not teach ColdFusion or new features found in ColdFusion MX. There are many good books for that.

Java is a lot to learn. It would be very difficult to cover all aspects of the language. This book covers significant aspects of the Java language, with an emphasis on the areas that Web developers need to work with most; it does not cover AWT or Swing in much depth. These are aspects of GUI development that you will have no trouble learning on your own after finishing this book. It also does not cover Enterprise JavaBeans in much depth. EJBs are, as their name avows, an advanced aspect of enterprise development, and again, you will be readily prepared to learn them once you've completed this book.

Java for ColdFusion Developers will give you enough information to be comfortable moving into greater depth and specificity on any aspect of Java, whether it is server side, software development, or Web development.

1.4 Overview of Book Sections

This section overviews what you will find in the book.

Chapter 1 provides an overview of Java and explains why knowing Java will be useful to ColdFusion developers.

Chapter 2 introduces the new Java-based ColdFusion MX architecture, and provides a focus and orientation to the world of Java.

Chapter 3 looks at Java data structures, including memory and storage of data on the stack and the heap, data structures, and more.

Chapter 4 delves into programming structures and the basic tools needed to code in Java, including strings and arrays, loops, and conditional logic.

Chapter 5 steps back a bit from syntax and examines the concepts of object-oriented application design and object-oriented programming.

Chapter 6 details the ins and outs of the popular integrated development environments.

Chapter 7 covers objects and classes and how they are used.

Chapter 8 examines exceptions and how Java extends the exceptions concept.

Chapter 9 works deeper into advanced object-oriented concepts including inheritance, interfaces, abstract classes and methods, and reflection.

Chapter 10 shows how to use Java extensions to extend the ColdFusion environment.

Chapter 11 describes Java's Collections interfaces and classes, and shows how and when to implement them.

Chapter 12 adds detailed coverage of database connectivity with JDBC to the discussion.

Chapter 13 brings Java to the server, including the use of servlets and integrating ColdFusion MX and J2EE.

Chapter 14 explains how to extend Web sites with JavaServer Pages; coverage includes JSP tags, directives, scriptlets, and expressions.

Chapter 15 reveals how to write and deploy custom JSP tags, as well as how to import JSP tag libraries into ColdFusion MX.

Chapter 16 caps off our coverage of Java and ColdFusion with an in-depth case study of an e-commerce Web site, complete with all of the code needed for a working application.

Appendix A is a reference for the syntax of comments, directives, scripting elements, standard actions, and implicit objects for JSP 1.2.

Appendix B outlines the classes and interfaces in the JSP 1.2 and Servlet 2.3 specifications.

Appendix C provides a glossary of key terms.

Appendix D provides a useful and interesting list of Java Internet resources.

Appendix E serves as a quick reference guide and resource index.

In the next chapter, we will explore the Java-based ColdFusion MX architecture and get an introduction to Java. By the end of the chapter, we will have written our first Java program.

2

Java Jump Start

This chapter will introduce you to the ColdFusion MX architecture and the Java platform, providing a focus and orientation to the rather large world of Java.

The purpose of overviewing the ColdFusion MX architecture here is to contextualize why it is important for ColdFusion developers to learn Java at this time. From there, we will quickly move into an orientation of the Java language, how it works, and what you need to get started. We will finish the chapter with an examination of how a simple Java program is put together and a couple of useful exercises.

2.1 The New ColdFusion Architecture

The release of ColdFusion MX in the summer of 2002 comes less than a year after its predecessor, ColdFusion 5. In fact, work on MX was begun long before Cold-Fusion 5 was released. There has been a good deal of excitement surrounding Macromedia's MX technology platform, which includes not only ColdFusion, but Flash and Dreamweaver.

NOTE There has been much speculation about the origins of the "MX" moniker. Guesses about its significance include the following: It is an abbreviation of *The Matrix*, which featured a character named Neo (Neo was also the code name of the ColdFusion MX project); it is the ICANN domain abbreviation for the country of Mexico; it stands for Macromedia eXperience or Macromedia's eXperiment. Public speculation about the meaning of MX soon led to the suggestion that it stood for "Macromedia X," where X is the Roman numeral for 10 and 2002 marks the 10th anniversary of Macromedia.

2.1.1 ColdFusion Prior to MX

Prior to ColdFusion MX, the code base for ColdFusion Server was written in C++, which had several ramifications for the product. To begin with, it made it expensive and time consuming to offer ColdFusion on platforms other than Windows. Though ColdFusion 5 was offered for Linux, Solaris, and HP-UX, the code had to be specifically written for each of these platforms.

For the users of ColdFusion, this meant a limitation in the choice of platforms on which they could run ColdFusion. This fact contributed to a sense in the development community that ColdFusion was only for Windows users—a perception that Macromedia has worked to put to rest in recent years. It might have been hard, for instance, for a hosting company running FreeBSD to look seriously at incorporating ColdFusion into its offerings.

NOTE Three of the biggest limitations with CF prior to MX were lack of support for industry standard languages and APIs like the Java servlet and EJB APIs, difficulty of supporting localization/internationalization in CF applications, and general interoperability with Java. Since about 1998, there has been building pressure to make CF interoperate better with Java objects, and then JRun, EJBs, and other J2EE servers like Weblogic and Websphere. CFX and CFOBJECT with Java required Macromedia to use JNI from the ColdFusion process to load the JVM (like how the browers do it), which was very buggy and hard to support across platforms and various JVM versions. Calls to servlets only worked with JRun and CFSERVLET; since it was an out-of-process call, the integration between CF and JRun at that point was just too disconnected to provide the benefits users wanted, like in-process integration and fully shared session objects between CFM pages and Java servlets.

ColdFusion 5 was built with four major subsystems: a p-code just-in-time compiler responsible for preprocessing CFML templates, runtime services for CFML language, support for application services (such as searching and graphing engines), and infrastructure services.

When a `.cfm` template is called for the first time in ColdFusion 5, the JIT compiler converts the template to p-code. It is then cached for further requests, and the cached copy remains valid until the template is modified or the server is restarted. The CFML runtime service then executes the resulting p-code; that is, it does the work specified in the code, such as querying a database, executing a loop, and so on. At this time the infrastructure services may be called upon to perform their supporting role, which includes such functions as opening database connections, interacting with the operating system, or interoperating with various protocols. The results of the template execution are then formatted and sent back to the Web server.

2.1.2 ColdFusion MX Architecture

As you likely know, ColdFusion MX sees the second fundamental rewrite of the core ColdFusion code base in the product's history. ColdFusion MX is written entirely in Java. While you as a ColdFusion developer can continue to write ColdFusion applications without learning Java, there are, as we will see, many benefits to the new opportunities the migration to Java affords.

> **NOTE** ColdFusion was first written in 1995 as a CGI executable. As the product grew, it became clear that this model, which spawned a new process for every request, was not only too slow, but also would not scale. It was rewritten in C++ to integrate with IIS and other Web servers via their proprietary APIs (ISAPI for IIS, NSAPI for Netscape, DSO for Apache), which provided better speed and scalability than the generic CGI.

The manner in which the old architecture incorporated its infrastructure services meant complexity for Macromedia, as well as slight differences among the same product on different platforms. It also meant complexity for ColdFusion users. Increasingly, organizations are moving toward a standard infrastructure not only for their Web environment, but also for a wide range of IT systems. In a world where open, flexible standards and system interoperability are increasingly important, rewriting the ColdFusion Server code base in Java made sense. Benefits to IT departments with a standardized model include reduced complexity of management, reduced costs, and easier integration.

The most fundamental change to the underlying architecture is that its infrastructure services are implemented by an embedded version of JRun 4, Macromedia's J2EE (Java 2 Enterprise Edition) server. Note that this is not a full version of the JRun product.

Here is an overview of how the MX architecture works. Just like ColdFusion 5, ColdFusion MX has four major subsystems. There is a translation engine that parses CFM pages and generates Java code from them. These Java files are compiled by a Java compiler and loaded by the core CF engine, which is implemented on top of the Java servlet API. When a requested template is processed, the compiled code is cached in memory and on disk. Subsequent requests for the same template execute the bytecode that has already been compiled.

2.2 Benefits of Moving to the Java Technology Platform

A major benefit of the new architecture is performance. Because numerous companies have invested time and resources in optimizing the performance of the Java Virtual Machine (which executes Java commands), ColdFusion templates should run faster. This performance benefit was demonstrated at the 2001 ColdFusion Developers Conference, in which a bit of prime number crunching code was run concurrently on both versions of the architecture.

Another benefit to this architecture is that it protects your code and encourages distribution of applications. Instead of encrypting ColdFusion templates with the built-in command line utility `cfencrypt` (which was notoriously weak), developers can now precompile their applications as Java bytecode. This offers developers better protection for their work.

> **NOTE** Despite the fact that ColdFusion MX templates are compiled into Java bytecode, they require a copy of ColdFusion MX Server to run properly. This is because of dependencies on other ColdFusion runtime components.

There are many enhancements to the environment that make ColdFusion MX interesting. Developers can extend their work by importing JavaServer Pages (JSP) tag libraries and even execute JSPs directly from ColdFusion MX. Because Java is under the hood, MX can now fully support the Unicode standard. This means the ability to work in double-byte languages such as Japanese, Chinese, or Korean. ColdFusion MX also means we can take advantage of messaging services and legacy connectors offered by other application servers.

By standing on the Java technology platform, ColdFusion MX represents a big step forward for ColdFusion. While, as noted, it is not necessary to learn Java to continue working with ColdFusion, it is certainly not a bad idea. Knowing the language will give you more power as you continue developing

ColdFusion, it will give you an alternative language if the situation calls for it, and it will give you greater flexibility to meet the demands of tomorrow's integrated systems.

> **NOTE** While one could easily (if one wanted to violate license restrictions) decompile a CF MX app back to Java source, one would not be able to decompile back to the CFML source. To reverse engineer back to CFML source, one would need to reverse engineer the CF-to-Java translation process.

We will leave our discussion of ColdFusion at that. The remainder of this book is devoted to Java, with an emphasis on its Web technologies, since I presume that, as a ColdFusion developer, that's what you're primarily interested in. Where relevant, differences, similarities, or other distinctions are made with respect to how ColdFusion works, in the hope that it will help the Java topic be more quickly and easily understood. These distinctions will generally take the form of notes.

2.3 The Java Platform

This section contains a brief history of how Java came to be, which highlights its most important features today.

2.3.1 Brief History of Java

Not only was the Java programming language not originally called "Java," it wasn't originally a programming language. Java started out as a small, three-person project at Sun Microsystems in 1991. The goal of the project was to produce a language that would work on interactive, handheld home entertainment device controllers and home appliances. At that time, the TV set-top box and on-demand video markets seemed like the most high-profile way to enter the home, which would soon expand, Sun predicted, to include the "smart toasters" that have been right around the corner for 10 years. The project was code-named "Green."

The team of developers, which included James Gosling (now touted as the "father of Java"), saw little interest from their intended market once they had a workable design for their language. Interest in the possibilities of the language may also not have been sparked by its name, "Oak," which was conceived because there was an Oak tree outside Gosling's window. In 1994, however, the team realized that they were creating a language that would fit in perfectly with the way that applications were written and delivered on the Internet.

In 1994, interest in the Internet was booming. The Oak team performed a demonstration of a Web page that included applets before a group of venture capitalists who instantly saw the possibilities. The team wrote a Web browser called HotJava (currently in version 3.0) to display the applet-enabled Web pages.

The marketing people at Sun renamed the language Java (when it was discovered that another computer language was already called Oak), and introduced Duke, a little character in the shape of the old Star Trek emblems, to help show people how much fun it is to write applets. Java was announced in May of 1995, and the first non-beta version of the language was released in 1996.

> **NOTE** There is only a very marginal relation between Java and JavaScript. JavaScript is not part of the Java technology platform, nor is it a subset of Java like CFML and CFScript. Their relation is merely one of some syntactical similarities. JavaScript (originally called LiveScript) was developed by Netscape, and a legal agreement has been worked out between Sun and Netscape with respect to the Java name.

2.3.2 Goals of the Java Language

As the team at Sun was reworking Oak into the programming language that would become Java, several design goals surfaced. Chief among these goals are the following:

1. **Object oriented.** Object-oriented languages have a number of advantages over procedural languages, including code reuse, easier maintenance, and system extensibility.
2. **Security.** Because this was a primary goal from the beginning, Java is very secure. An example of Java's security is applets, which surged in popularity because they are programs that run client side without the ability to harm files on a local disk. It would be very difficult to distribute a Java-borne virus.
3. **Platform independence.** Programs compiled from 100% Java code will run without modification on any operating system that has a Java Virtual Machine, including Linux, Windows, Solaris, FreeBSD, Tru64, HP-UX, OS390, AIX, and so on. This is a significant benefit to the language and a primary reason for its popular implementation.

4. **Multi threading.** Java has the high-performance ability to run multiple system processes at once.
5. **Distributed.** The ability to dynamically download and load libraries and classes over a network.
6. **Code libraries.** There is a tremendous amount of code already written that you can use in your Java work.

We will discuss each of these in detail over the course of the book. One of these goals, however, we will discuss first, because of its relevance to the ColdFusion migration to MX, and because it is fundamental to how Java programs are built and run.

2.3.3 Java's Relation to C, C++, and C#

There are a number of close ties between Java and C, C++, and C#, which may be instructive if you are familiar with any of those languages. Java gets its syntax from C. This was an intentional effort by the designers of the language to make Java easier for programmers to learn. Since so many people already knew and used C, they wanted to facilitate their transition to Java. Many statements and expressions are similar or identical to those in C and C++.

It was also important to solve some of the problems that programmers faced using these languages. For one thing, Java has no implementation dependency regarding primitive data types, whose size is specified in Java. For example, an `int` is always an integer composed of 32 bits. In C++, an `int` could be 16, 32, or 64 bits—the choice is left to the compiler vendor. This could cause unexpected behavior in programs.

C# is a lot like Java; it has garbage collection, single-class inheritance, reflection API, source-code documentation comments and tools, intermediate interpreted language (like bytecode), and so forth. .NET is not cross-platform like Java is.

There are features of Java that address specific shortcomings of these languages as well. For instance, the programmer does not have to worry about memory allocation and deallocation. This is because Java has automatic garbage collection. That is, when the JVM finds that a reference points to something no longer usable, it automatically reclaims the space. Java also removed pointer arithmetic, which made it too easy to accidentally overwrite data. These improvements eliminate worries over memory corruption.

> **NOTE** While ColdFusion developers don't have to worry about memory corruption either, you may be familiar with memory errors that pop up with some frequency while using ColdFusion Studio (especially 4.5).

2.3.4 Compiled or Interpreted

Software applications require an operating system to serve as a middle layer between themselves and the hardware that makes up the computer. For example, your machine might have a Sun SPARC, a DEC Alpha, or an Intel processor. The operating environments that work with this hardware have a different kind of machine language. Machine language, written in binary files represented as a series of 1s and 0s, is what any program that runs on a computer is eventually translated into. Because different types of hardware speak different formats of machine language, programs are often created for only one kind of system. Making it work with another system requires a rewrite for each specific platform you want your program to run on, which is expensive.

Computer programs are either compiled or interpreted, each of which have their benefits.

2.3.4.1 COMPILED PROGRAMS

Writing and running a compiled program consists of the following steps:

1. Programmer writes source code into a text editor.
2. The source code is run through a compiler, which checks the code for errors.
3. If there are errors, the programmer is notified and revises the code. If there are no errors, the program is successfully compiled into an executable binary program, which is platform-specific.
4. The compiled program is run.

The advantages of compiled programs are many. Chief among these benefits is that, as noted above, errors in the program can frequently be found before the program is distributed (don't laugh, now). Also, compiled programs run very quickly, because they are able to interact directly with the computer on which they are running.

> **NOTE** Some research has shown that HotSpot's dynamic JIT has provable performance advantages over compiled code (mainly because HotSpot can optimize dynamically but compiled code can only be optimized at compile time).

2.3.4.2 INTERPRETED PROGRAMS

The primary difference between compiled and interpreted programs is time. Interpreted programs are not compiled before they are executed; their source code is interpreted into machine-readable binary code at runtime, for whatever the current platform is. Their advantage is that they are cross-platform. As you might suspect, however, they have serious drawbacks; among the worst is that they run slowly because they are not precompiled and because all of their error checking is handled on the fly.

2.3.5 Compiled *and* Interpreted: The Java Virtual Machine

Java solves the problems presented by this dichotomy in a unique manner. Programs written in the Java programming language are compiled *and* interpreted. When you write a Java program, you compile the source code into bytecode. Every Java-enabled system includes a *Java Runtime Environment (JRE)*, which is engineered specifically for the given platform. The JRE consists of the Java Virtual Machine, the class files that make up the core of the Java platform, and other supporting files. The Java Virtual Machine is a software engine that interprets previously compiled bytecode into machine-readable instructions. It has no other associated files and is not enough to run a Java application—that requires a Java Runtime.

The Java Runtime, then, is specific to each platform and has variations from platform to platform. The reason that this offers an advantage over programs that are compiled into native code is that once a JRE is created for a platform, any Java program in the world can run on it, because the bytecode is all exactly the same.

This advantage was directly responsible for Java's fast rise to fame. It is what allowed applets to work in Web pages, because Java wasn't required to have a different set of code for each type of CPU connected to the Internet.

To recap, here are the steps required to run a Java program:

1. Programmer writes plain text source code and saves it with a `.java` extension.
2. The source code is run through a compiler (the Java Virtual Machine), which checks for errors.
3. If there are errors, the programmer is notified and revises the code. If there are no errors, the program is successfully compiled into a generic executable Java class file, which contains the executable bytecode. This new file is saved with a `.class` extension.
4. The compiled program is run: The operating system-specific Java Virtual Machine reads the `.class` file, runs a security check, and interprets the bytecode.

As you might suspect, this setup makes initial calls to an application rather slow, but subsequent calls very fast. Significant performance improvements are made with each Java release.

2.3.6 The SDK

The Java Virtual Machine is at the core of this architecture, but it alone is not enough to run Java programs. For that, you need the Java Runtime Environment. However, these tools together are not enough for the programmer to write Java programs. For that, you need the SDK (Software Development Kit). The *Java SDK* consists of a JVM, compiler and other tools, and core APIs. Documentation is a separate download.

> **NOTE** You may wonder what happened to the JDK (Java Development Kit). It has become the SDK—it was merely renamed in November of 1999. The term JDK persisted through Java version 1.1. It can be confusing, because while the name has changed, the versioning has not. Sort of. Because so many changes to the language occurred, version 1.2 became referred to as Java 2 (three days after it was released!). Java is currently in version 1.4, with version 1.5 (code-named Tiger) to be released in the summer of 2003. So Java 1.2, 1.3, and 1.4 are all referred to as Java 2. Perhaps Tiger will be referred to as Java 5 (hey—it was good enough for IntraDev, which just jumped from version 1.0 to version 6). Sheesh.

2.3.7 The JRE

The Java Runtime Environment is what allows access to the Java Virtual Machine and to the supporting system. The JRE offers a way to start up garbage collection in the JVM and to, for instance, write to the output stream. The JRE also features a security manager, which controls the JVM's access to resources on the local machine or network connections.

When Java classes are loaded into the Virtual Machine, a verifier ensures that the bytecodes are all correctly formed and that all security requirements for the application are met. It is in this way that Java applications are able to execute on the client (in the form of applets) in a safe manner. Careless or malicious programmers cannot do as much harm as easily in this circumstance.

2.3.8 The API and Editions

An *Application Programming Interface* is the set of rules for interfacing with a given technology; it is the syntax for using a language. Java's API includes hundreds of class libraries containing prewritten code that you can use to create Java programs.

You can find documentation for all of the APIs at *http://java.sun.com/products*. The APIs are extensive, and they can be daunting (even fruitless) for beginners to read. Later, in the "Gathering Your Tools" section of this chapter, you will find how to get to and read the Java API references.

The Java platform is specialized and packaged into different editions, each of which caters to a different target system, ranging from cell phones to supercomputers.

2.3.8.1 J2EE

Java 2 Enterprise Edition is intended for building large-scale, server-side systems for the enterprise. Everything that is in the Standard Edition is here, plus libraries for supporting enterprise directory services, messaging, and transaction management. We will discuss a number of J2EE technologies in this book, including JSP and servlets, XML, and JDBC.

2.3.8.2 J2SE

Java 2 Standard Edition is the most frequently used development kit, the obvious starting place for learning Java, and the one we focus on in this book. It includes a compiler and a runtime system, and with it you can write and run Java applications. More than one million downloads of JDK 1.4 were made within a month of its release.

2.3.8.3 J2ME

Java 2 Micro Edition is geared for applications that run embedded in consumer products such as cellular phones, PDAs, smart cards, pagers, set-top devices, and car navigation systems. The Micro Edition is the only edition that is subdivided into *profiles*. A profile is a definition of the libraries required for different platforms and the JVM requirements for supporting a given micro platform. For instance, there is one profile for PDAs and another for wireless devices. The edition includes a runtime environment, like the others, but it is a very small footprint runtime. For instance, the smart card runtime consumes only 128 kB of memory.

2.3.8.4 STANDARD EXTENSIONS

The Java platform also features a number of "standard extensions," which are small packages released as add-ons to an edition. For instance, something called JAXP, the Java API for parsing XML documents, has been available as a standard extension. These are not included in the regular JDK download; you must download each one that you wish to use. Very popular or useful extensions often get added into the core of a new edition release. The XML parsing that used to be performed by JAXP has been incorporated into the core platform for Java 1.4.

2.3.8.5 WHAT'S NEW IN JAVA 1.4

Java 1.4 contains a number of new features that are of interest, many of which we examine in this book. Each JDK release focuses on performance improvements. But each also offers a varying number of new features. For JDK 1.4, these include

- New I/O classes offering improved performance, and the ability to lock files and create file memory maps
- Support for mouse wheels in GUI development
- Built-in logging with the java.util.logging package
- Support for secure sockets and HTTPS
- XML support includes SAX and DOM parsing and XSLT transformations (as noted above, these were standard extensions for Java 1.3)
- Incorporation of WebStart, an exciting utility for distributing programs via the Web
- Assertions, which are used to verify design assumptions in your code
- 64-bit addressing for Solaris machines
- Regular expression support, with the pattern syntax used in Perl 5

New JDKs will be shipped approximately every 12–15 months. You can follow new releases and work with beta releases at the Sun website at *http://java.sun.com*. To see in advance where the technology is going, you might look at *http://jcp.org/jsr/stage/jsr.jsp*, which is the homepage for Java Specification Requests. This site offers information about proposed updates to the language, who is involved in the user groups, what the proposed specification will do, and why it is needed.

2.3.9 Execution Environments

There are three execution environments for Java, as you likely know. These are as follows:

1. **Standalone applications**. These range from small command-line programs that output a string, to utility programs, to full-blown GUI applications such as a Web browser, text editor, spreadsheet program, character games, and so on.

2. **Applets**. These are just applications made specifically to run in a Web browser.
3. **Servlets**. Servlets are run on the server side, usually as part of a Web application. These and JSP (JavaServer Pages) are the aspects of the Java language that fulfill the same goals that ColdFusion does.

All of the above are written in the same language, using the same general tools. The SDK contains everything you need to write, test, and run Java applications. If you are writing applets, then you can use either a Web browser or a specific command-line utility (called `appletviewer`) to execute your applets. Servlets are a different deal and will only run in a servlet container such as Apache Software Foundation's Tomcat or Macromedia's JRun, both currently in version 4.

The JVM is one level—everything ultimately runs in a JVM. Then, besides applets and standalone apps, there are various types of components (JSPs, servlets, EJBs, JMX MBeans) that require a particular type of container, which provides calls to execute their lifecycle methods and provides services to the components.

Because knowledge of the Java programming language is necessary for writing each of these, we will begin by getting everything we need to write and execute Java programs. We will spend a good deal of time discussing server-side Java, but not much time on applets. The reason for this is that interest in applets has lagged significantly since the introduction of server-side Java.

2.4 Gathering Your Tools

There are a number of things you'll need to get started writing and running Java programs. The first thing to do is download the most recent Java SDK, which, at the time of this writing, is 1.4.0. You can download the SDK from *http://java.sun.com*. You are likely to see a prominent link to download it on this page. If not, click on Products and APIs, and get the Java 2 Platform, Standard Edition.

> **NOTE** A Java compiler is included with the SDK downloadable from Sun. However, there are other Java compilers on the market, including the Jikes compiler from IBM alphaWorks. Originally a project of the Tom Watson Research Center, it is now exclusively an OSI Certified Open Source project. You may ask, why bother fiddling with another compiler when Sun's compiler ships with the SDK? Jikes offers high performance and includes analysis tools.

2.4.1 Installing the SDK

In order to use Java, your computer must meet the minimum requirements, which are 32 MB RAM and 180 MB hard drive space for 32-bit systems, and 48 MB memory for NT. You can download Java for free from *http://java.sun.com*. Click on Download and follow the instructions for the type of computer you have.

The SDK will come in a compressed file. Extract it to an easily accessible location on your disk. I will extract it to `C:\jdk1.4`. There is no need to restart your machine.

> **NOTE** When `JAVA_HOME` is referred to throughout the book, it means the root directory of your particular Java installation, whether that is `usr/local/java` or `F:\sdk1.4.0` or `C:\jdk1.4` or whatever you have called it.

There are two programs in Java that are central to your development. The first program is the compiler (`javac.exe`). When you write a Java program (class file definition), you save your file with a `.java` extension. You then run the compiler on it, which performs the translation into bytecode. The bytecode is output to a new file that the compiler creates. This file has the name of your Java program, but is saved with a `.class` extension. This is an executable file, which you run by passing the name of the program as an argument to the second important program in the SDK: the Java interpreter (`java.exe`).

Generally, Java developers write programs in different packages. A *package* is a namespace used to minimize name conflicts and to promote organization of code. Each package basically corresponds to a directory on your hard drive. So, for instance, to create a package called "JavaForCF," we just create a regular directory of that name under the place that we are keeping our project class files. We assign a particular class file to a package using the `package` keyword within the class definition. We will discuss packages in greater depth later. For now, create a folder under your `JAVA_HOME` location called "JavaForCF" (for example, `C:\jdk1.4\JavaForCF`); we will put all of our code in here.

At this point, you could compile and run a Java program that you place in the `JAVA_HOME\bin` directory. Because this is where the Java binaries are kept that make Java work, this is obviously not a very safe or portable place to put your code. In order for Java to be able to find your programs and execute them wherever you place them, you need to do a little bit of configuration. The configuration is slightly different for different platforms. Once Java is up and running, however, the rest of the material in the book should work about the same, regardless of platform.

2.4.2 Setting the Execution Path

After you have installed the JDK as discussed above, you need to do just one more thing: You need to set the execution path. The *execution path* is the list of directories that your operating system traverses to find executables. This is an environment variable that will make the location of your Java executables accessible wherever you are in the directory structure.

2.4.2.1 ON WINDOWS XP

Go to Start > Control Panel > System > Advanced > Environment Variables. Find the PATH variable. Double click on it to add `JAVA_HOME\bin` to the beginning of the path (for instance, you might add `C:\jdk1.4\bin;` to this string). Semicolons are used to separate variable entries. Click Apply and Save. Once you open a new command window, it should have the correct path settings. You do not have to reboot.

2.4.2.2 ON WINDOWS 2000 AND NT

Go to Start > Control Panel > System > Environment. In the User Variables window, find the variable called PATH. Double click on it to add `JAVA_HOME\bin` to the beginning of the path (for instance, you might add `C:\jdk1.4\bin;` to this string). Semicolons are used to separate variable entries. Click Apply and Save. Once you open a new command window, it should have the correct path settings. You do not have to reboot.

2.4.2.3 ON WINDOWS ME/98

Find your `AUTOEXEC.BAT` file. Open the file with a text editor and place the following line at the end of it:

```
SET PATH=c:jdk1.4\bin;%PATH%
```

where `c:\jdk1.4` is the path where you've installed Java (what we're calling `JAVA_HOME`).

2.4.2.4 ON UNIX, LINUX, AND SOLARIS

Setting the execution path is different depending on what shell you are using.

If you use the C shell (Solaris default), open your `~/.cshrc` file and add a line such as this:

```
set path=(/usr/local/jdk1.4/bin $path)
```

If you use the Bourne Again shell (Linux default), open your `~/.bashrc` or `~/.bash_profile` file and add a line such as this:

```
export PATH=/usr/local/jdk1.4/bin:$PATH
```

2.4.3 Testing Your Installation

You can perform a quick test to see if you set the execution path correctly. Open a command prompt and type

```
java -h
```

This invokes the Java executable with the "help" option. If a list of arguments prints out, you have done everything correctly. If you get a response such as "The name specified is not recognized as an internal or external command, operable program, or batch file," or "Bad command or file name," or other similar message, something is wrong and you need to go back and check your work. Make sure that there are no spaces in the text when you set the variable as described above.

2.4.4 IDEs

There are a great number of Integrated Development Environments (IDEs) that can make it easier to write, compile, and deploy Java applications. These include Borland's JBuilder, Forte for Java, IntelliJ's IDEA, WebGain's Visual-Café, and many more.

> **NOTE** As a ColdFusion developer, you may be familiar with related products by Macromedia, such as JRun Studio and Kawa. Kawa is an IDE for creating JSPs, EJBs, and Java code. This product is currently in EOL (end of life) in favor of Macromedia's partnerships with other, more popular IDE vendors. JRun Studio 3 is another IDE (like ColdFusion Studio) that uses HomeSite as its codebase. If you are used to using ColdFusion Studio, then you will find that JRun Studio is essentially the same product with the added benefit of seamless access to your Java compiler and a couple of buttons for writing JSP directives. JRun Studio has been discontinued in favor of Dreamweaver MX.

Full-featured Java IDEs are typically expensive. While an HTML or Web app code editor typically costs between $100 and $400, enterprise Java code editors with support for JSP and servlets, easy GUI tools, and XML support often run in the thousands of dollars. There are excellent tools that are less expensive than this, and some are even free. For instance, IntelliJ runs about $300, and there are some excellent free IDEs such as Forte, Eclipse, and NetBeans. We can use a simple text editor to write Java programs for now.

TIP If you use Notepad on Windows 2000 or earlier, remember that your Java source files need to have the file extension `.java`. If you try to save your source code file for "MyProgram," you might end up with a file called `MyProgram.java.txt`, which wouldn't compile. You can solve this problem by including quotes around your file name when you save it or by choosing Save as Type: All Files. You do not need to do this on Windows XP.

Some of the more popular IDE products and how to use them will be discussed in Chapter 6, "IDEs."

2.5 Anatomy of a Simple Java Program

Let's write the simplest possible Java program to begin. When run, this program will output the text string "Hello," along with the value of the `name` variable to the command line.

2.5.1 `Hello.java`

```
/* file: Hello.java
   purpose: print a simple string to the command line
   author: E Hewitt
   created date: 4.12.02
*/
package javaforcf;
// declare the name and visibility of this class
public class Hello {

// main method accepts an array of strings as arguments
public static void main (String [] args) {

// create a new String object with the value of 'Jeremy'
String name = new String("Jeremy");

// print the static text and the variable together
// out to the command line
System.out.println("Hello," + name);
        }
}
```

To run this program:

1. Type the code into a plain text editor, and save it as `JAVA_HOME\JavaForCF\Hello.java` (not `hello.java`, or anything else—the class name must match the file name).
2. Open a command window and `cd` to `JAVA_HOME\JavaForCF`.
3. Type `javac Hello.java`.
4. If the program compiles correctly, a new prompt will appear. There won't be any message from the compiler. A new file will appear in that directory. If there are errors in the code, the compiler will notify you with a line number, the nature of the error, and the total number of errors found. If you get an error saying "error:cannot read: Hello.java," that means that the compiler can't find the program to compile it. Make sure that you have navigated to the same directory in which the `.java` file exists. You can list the contents of a directory at a Windows command prompt by typing `dir`.
5. Once the program has compiled without error, you can run it. To do this, type: `java Hello`. Remember that the Java programming language is case sensitive; typing `java hello` won't work.

The program will output

```
Hello, Jeremy
```

Now let's take a moment to look at the code. For now, we will gloss over some of the concepts and look at them in detail in the upcoming chapters. The first block is an SQL-style comment.

> **NOTE** ColdFusion developers will notice that comment syntax is the same in Java as in CFScript or in SQL. That is, use a `/*` to start a multi-line comment and `//` for a single-line comment. You have likely also noticed that semicolons in Java are used in the same way they are in CFScript. You must end statements with semicolons.

The first significant line of the program is the class declaration: `public class Hello {`. All Java programs need to define a class that will serve as a repository for data and define the behavior that they are capable of (their methods). Your source file can contain only one public class statement. Don't worry about the `public` keyword just yet. It basically means that this class is publicly accessible; that is, any class can use it.

> **NOTE** Curly braces in Java are used much as you use them in CFScript. In Java, you define opening and closing boundaries of class definitions, methods, and code blocks with curly braces.

The name of the class must correspond exactly to the name of your resulting `.java` file. Java is a case-sensitive language. `Hello.java` is not the same as `hello.java`. By the same token, `String = Name;` and `String = name;` create two different variables.

> **NOTE** Unlike ColdFusion, Java is ruthlessly case sensitive. Spaces, however, can be used rather freely. For instance, `main (String [ ] args)` is read by the compiler just as `main(String[] args)` is. You can indent away all you like, willy-nilly. This behavior is the same as in ColdFusion.

2.5.2 The `main` Method

Inside the class code block, you declare your variables and your methods. Java features a special method called `main`, which serves as the core structure for your program's execution. The Java Virtual Machine starts processing any Java program with `main`. So everything that will happen in this program is written inside `main`.

For the first few chapters in the book we will write largely procedural programs. These programs will have their code inside the `main` method of a single class file. A procedural program runs the way a Web page is interpreted—once over, from top to bottom. The advantage to doing this while learning is that it is much easier to analyze concepts as you go. Because Web page processing is familiar and straightforward, like regular reading, it helps you learn faster. Second, there is a good deal to figure out about variables, methods, the API, visibility, and so on, before you can really start using objects in any meaningful way. However, there is a disadvantage to this approach as well, which is that you must make a transition in thinking once we start doing real object-oriented programming. That is to say, the way we will write small programs as we get started is not how larger, object-oriented Java applications are written. But we will cross that bridge when we need to.

The `main` method accepts as arguments an array of strings, which we will call `args`. `main` must always be declared as accepting an array of `String` objects, which you can pass from the command line when you run the program. However, the name of this array is arbitrary. We will call it `args`, since that is the convention.

The first thing we do in the program is create an object of type `String`. Almost everything in Java is an object (primitive data types, such as `booleans` and `ints`, are *not* objects). Creating an object is often referred to as *instantiating* an object, because you are creating a concrete instance of what is otherwise just a definition (the object's class). For instance, Jeremy Allaire is a particular instance of the CTO class. Once you have a `String` object, you need to set its value to something (when a `String` object is created, its value is an empty String—it is not null).

```
String name = new String("Jeremy");
```

There are other ways to set a value for a `String` object; this is the most explicit. What this line says is: Hold a place in memory for a variable of type `String`. I'm going to refer to this string as `name`. Create the `String` object with a value of `Jeremy`.

Next, we call the `System.out.println()` method to print out the value of the string to the command line. The `main` method ends, as does the class definition, and program execution stops.

2.6 Understanding the API

In the last section you recall that we created a `String` object and that (almost) everything in Java is an object. We are able to create an object of type `String` because this class is defined by Sun. The SDK contains hundreds and hundreds of classes developed by Sun that are part of the core packages. `java.lang`, for instance, is the package containing the `String` class. A set of predefined code definitions is referred to as a *library*.

> **NOTE** The concept of core Java libraries is much like the `<cf>` tag library that ships with ColdFusion Server, which offers about 90 predefined tags and more than 250 functions. Together, these make up the core ColdFusion language. But if ColdFusion MX did not come with a `<cfchart>` tag, you could create `<cf_chart>` yourself (which people have done). It would be a drag if you had to make your own `<cfset>` tag, though, as it is such a fundamental aspect of working with code. So Sun includes these extensive libraries for convenience, ease of use, rapid adoption of the language, performance, and standardization.

The API is the collection of these libraries. It defines what you can do with the SDK to make Java programs. The API is very, very large. You can read it online at the Sun site. It can be somewhat confusing at first, if for no other reason

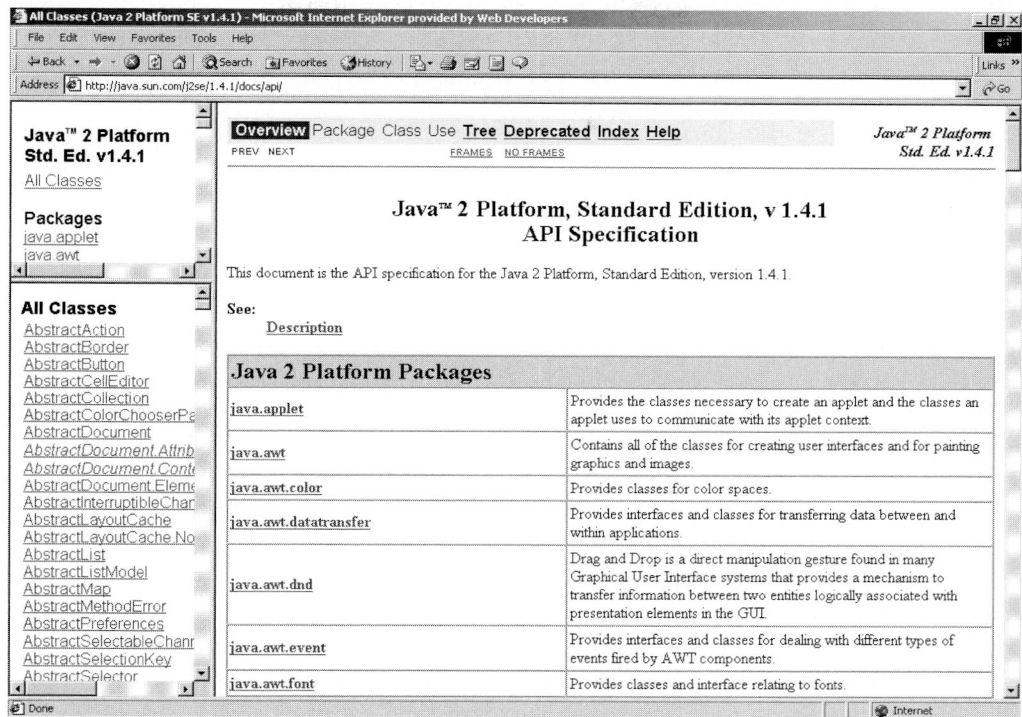

FIGURE 2.1 API documentation.

than that you have to remember where things are (what package the class you want is in) or if the method you want even exists.

To read the API online, go to *http://java.sun.com*. Click on Products and APIs and then Java 2 Platform, Standard Edition. If the site has changed when you read this, you can also search for documentation. This is convenient if you want to check something quickly.

You can also download the documentation (it's about 30 MB) so that you can view it locally. Figure 2.1 shows the Overview page.

2.6.1 Unpacking an Archive

Once you have downloaded the `.zip` file (Windows), you need to unpack it. Go ahead and move it into your `JAVA_HOME` directory. If you don't have a Zip utility, you can unpack the `.zip` file using Java. Java lets you create archive files called jars (Java ARchives); these use the same compression algorithm as Zip does. So you can interchangeably pack and unpack zips and jars with this utility.

To unpack the documentation, open a command prompt and type `cd jdk1.4`. Assuming this directory is where you placed the documentation zip file, you can now type the command `jar -xf j2sdk-1_4_0-doc.zip` (or the name of your documentation's zip file, if different). Now navigate to the `docs` subdirectory and open the `index.html` page. This is the API documentation.

2.6.2 Reading the API

The API documentation was itself generated by a Java tool called `javadoc`. When a library is created, the programmer can specify comments in a special way that allows the `javadoc` tool to read over the file and automatically generate this style of documentation for the code. This is a very useful tool that merits quick consideration in later chapters. The code in the Java library is well commented, and, as noted above, its source code is freely available.

Successfully using the API requires some getting used to. The frame in the upper left-hand corner contains all of the packages in the current release. The larger frame below it contains an alphabetical list of all the interfaces, classes, and exceptions in that package. Clicking on an item displays detailed information on the item in the main frame. This information describes the methods of the class, its constructors, and the error conditions and exceptions it throws. This is just the information you need to write Java programs.

For instance, `java.lang` is one of the most basic packages in Java. It is automatically imported into (made available for use) every Java application. Clicking on the `java.lang` package expands a number of interfaces (which we will discuss later), classes, exceptions, and errors. Click on the `java.lang.Math` class. This class defines certain fields—such as pi—and methods—such as `cos()`—that allow you to easily reference and use common mathematical properties and functions.

> **NOTE** ColdFusion defines a number of these same methods, such as `cos()`, `tan()`, `round()`, and so forth, that work much as they do in Java. You will notice that Java defines more methods, however. Some of this is due to Java automatically defining things like pi for you. Some of it is due to the fact that Java is a strongly typed language, whereas ColdFusion is not.

You may notice a small set of + and – signs that form a rudimentary sort of graphical tree that points from `java.lang.Object` to `java.lang.Math`. This indicates that `java.lang.Math` inherits the properties and behavior of the `java.lang.Object` class. In fact, every class in Java inherits from `java.lang.Object`—both those predefined in the library and those that you make yourself.

> **NOTE** `java.Math` and `java.lang.Math` are different. `java.Math` was added in a later version of Java in order to allow for arbitrary precision decimals and integers to aid in precise rounding. The distinction is not necessarily important here; the point is that it can be hard to find things in the API documentation when you're getting started.

We can test how to use the classes we find in the API by printing out Java's value for pi.

2.6.3 `PItest.java`

```
/* file: PItest.java
   purpose: print the value of PI
   author: E Hewitt
   version 1.0
*/
public class PItest {

public static void main (String [] args) {

System.out.println("value of PI:" + java.lang.Math.PI);
   }
}
```

This program prints the following to the command line:

```
value of PI: 3.141592653589793
```

We could just as easily have replaced the call to `java.lang.Math.PI` in the above program with a simple call to `Math.PI`, and the program would run exactly the same way. That is because the `java.lang` package is automatically included with each Java application, so we don't need to use the fully qualified name.

> **NOTE** Other packages that you use may need to be imported to be referenced in this direct manner. We will look more closely at importing later. But this command in Java is the reason for the introduction in ColdFusion MX of the `<cfimport>` tag.

In the next chapter we will look at what kinds of data Java makes available and write a number of procedural programs to illustrate their use.

2.7 Exercise 1: Download and Install the SDK

It is important to download the SDK and get started using it. If you have little experience with programming, it can be awkward getting started. There is a great deal of talk regarding how powerful Java is. What that means in practical terms is that you have to write out very explicitly everything you want your program to do. Even a very simple Java program can be hundreds of lines of code. So it is important to get set up now.

Once you have installed the SDK, you can test that your installation was successful by typing in and running the `Hello.java` program. Try changing the names of the variable inside the program and recompiling. Try changing the name of the `.java` file. What happens? Why?

2.8 Exercise 2: Using the API Documentation

Download and install the API documentation as described above. Use the `jar` tool to unpack it. Read through some of the package classes and notice how the documentation describes a method's return type and parameters.

3

Java Data Structures

We have not the slightest idea what this equation means, but we may be sure that it means something very important.

—Benjamin Pierce, to his students, regarding a mathematical formula

In the last chapter we took a close look at how a simple program is written and executed in Java. This chapter takes a close look at working with data in Java programs. We will examine memory and storage of data on the stack and the heap, look at the eight primitive data types and operators, variable assignment, and coding conventions used by Java programmers.

3.1 Binary Overview

If you have a good understanding of binary numbers, you can safely skip this section. You may want to take a look at the example program at the end of this section, however. This section offers an overview (or quick refresher if it's been a while) of binary numbers. This is important in Java because of memory management and conversions between types.

Common communications regarding numbers use a base 10 number system, likely because we generally have 10 fingers and 10 toes on which to count. Computers currently store data in terms of binary numbers. The reason for this is that early computers used valves to represent one of two different states (on or off). Though some might object, one could say that computers only had two fingers on which to count. But all of the same mathematical concepts can be represented in a base 2 (or binary) system. Of course, to represent the number 3, one would need two sets of valves, just as a base 10 numbering system has only the digits 0 through 9 (there is no "10" digit—it is made up of a 1 and a 0). Because a bit can store one of two values (0 or 1), computers use 2s and powers of 2 to perform calculations and represent states; they are binary systems.

NOTE The term *bit* was first coined by Claude Shannon (some claim John Wilder Tukey) in 1948. The word "bit" in this context is a kind of word called a *portmanteau*—itself a term coined by Lewis Carroll in the 19th century. Carroll used portmanteau to refer to a word created by conjoining two existing words—something he does frequently in his famous poem "The Jabberwocky." For instance, the word *slithy* in that poem doesn't exist in English; it is a portmanteau of the words "lithe" and "slimy," combined to form a new word meaning both things at once. Shannon's *bit* is a purposeful portmanteau of *binary digit*.

In a binary system, one calculates values by raising 2 to the power of the number of bits. The positions of the digits in a multidigit binary number correspond to powers of 2. Given a number composed of a 1 and all the rest zeros, that number is a power of 2. Table 3.1 gives a quick demonstration of this concept.

TABLE 3.1 Powers of 2 Represented in Binary

POWER OF 2	BINARY
2^0	1
2^1	10
2^2	100
2^3	1,000
2^4	10,000
2^5	100,000
2^6	1,000,000
2^7	10,000,000
2^8	100,000,000
2^9	1,000,000,000

Performing mathematical computations in a base 2 numbering system can be tricky for people who are used to base 10. Table 3.2 shows the first few numbers in base 10 with their corresponding base 2 representations.

TABLE 3.2 Base 10 Numbers and Corresponding Base 2 Numbers

BASE 10	BASE 2
1	1
2	10
3	11
4	100
5	101
6	110
7	111
8	1000
9	1001
10	1010

In binary, 0 and 1 are represented just as they are in a decimal system. In decimal, 10 represents the next number after all of the single digits have been used up (9 being the last). Since 2 has no digit for itself in binary, it gets represented just like 10 does. That is, 2_{base10} is the equivalent of 10_{base2}. A more detailed exploration of alternative numbering systems (such as hexadecimal) isn't really required in order to work well with Java. It does help, however, to be comfortable with at least this much, as we will see when we move on into data types and memory.

Here is an example Java program that you can use to generate base 10 numbers in base 2 format. The output will resemble Table 3.2:

3.1.1 MakeBase2.java

```
/*
File: chp3.MakeBase2.java
Date: April 21 2002
Purpose: outputs the base10 numbers 0 - 10 in base2
Author: E Hewitt
*/

public class MakeBase2 {

    public static void main(String[] args) {

    // simple for loop

    for (int i = 0; i <= 10; i++) {

        // get the Integer wrapper class,
        // call its 'toBinaryString' method

        // create String to hold the converted value
        String s = Integer.toBinaryString(i);

        // print it to the command line
        System.out.println(i + " in base2: " + s);
        }
    }
}
```

If the above program doesn't make sense yet, don't worry. We haven't discussed many of the elements in this program. However, the `for` loop and comments are likely to look familiar to you. It might be a good idea to type this program in, try changing the values, and recompile.

3.2 Data Types in ColdFusion

ColdFusion is referred to as a weakly typed language. That means that it is not necessary for the programmer to make distinctions between different types of data used in a program. For instance, ColdFusion will, as you know, process both of these statements in a roughly equivalent manner:

```
<cfset myNumber = '2'> ~= <cfset yourNumber = 'two'>
```

Of course this does not mean that the following statement returns true:

```
<cfif myNumber eq yourNumber>...
```

It does mean that it is very easy to start using ColdFusion, because it cuts down on the amount of code you have to write, how much you have to remember about the language when you're working, and it decreases necessary effort in outputting, testing, or otherwise referencing the variables. Java, however, uses a number of different data types to store information, all of which must be referenced correctly and cast into different types depending on what you're doing with them.

3.3 Data Types in Java

Java uses different types to store data; it is thus referred to as a strongly typed language. The range of values for these types is based on the number 2 raised to a power equal to the number of bits for each type. An 8-bit number therefore has 2^8 possible values, or 256 values. You may have used a `bit` data type in an SQL database to represent a value such as `isOnSpecial` where 0 means the item is not currently on special, and 1 means it is. Since $2^1 = 2$, we see that a 1-bit number (bit) has a range of possible values of 2—it can be 0 or 1.

However, when determining the range of possible values for a data type in Java, one of the bits in the result is saved to represent the number's sign (whether it is positive or negative). Therefore, an 8-bit number does not represent the 256 values 0 to 255. It represents the values –128 to +127. The highest value possible for an 8-bit number is going to be 2 to the power of the number of bits minus 1, minus 1. For an 8-bit number, this is represented $2^{8-1} -1$, or $2^7 -1$. So, 2^7 is 128, minus 1 is 127. It is necessary to subtract the 1 because zero is counted as positive. This is an important aspect of working with Java that can be hard to remember at first: things generally start at 0, not 1.

You can use this formula to calculate the range of possible values for a given data type: $(-2^{x-1 \text{ to }} 2^{x-1} -1)$.

As mentioned above, Java has predefined data types that allow for only certain values to be stored in them (such as numeric or character values), and those data types have a predefined range expressed in a number of bits, of values they are capable of holding. Different kinds of information are stored in different data types in Java.

3.4 Primitive Data Types

Java defines eight primitive data types, each of which reside in one of four main types. These main types are shown in Table 3.3.

TABLE 3.3 Four Main Primitive Data Types

DATA TYPE	PURPOSE
`Integral`	Storing regular numbers
`Floating Point`	Storing decimal point numbers
`Textual`	Storing single text characters
`Logical`	Storing `boolean` values

These data types are called primitive because they are the only things in Java that are not objects. We will now look at each of them in particular.

3.4.1 Integral Data Types

There are four types of integral data: `byte`, `short`, `int`, and `long`. These data types are used to store numbers requiring between 8 and 64 bits for storing their values. The default value of an `int` variable is `0`. Table 3.4 shows the range, length, and example values for each type.

TABLE 3.4 Integral Data Types

DATA TYPE	RANGE	LENGTH	EXAMPLE VALUES
`byte`	–128 to 127	8 bits	–36 125
`short`	–32,768 to 32,767	16 bits	30,005 –42

(continued)

TABLE 3.4 Integral Data Types (Continued)

DATA TYPE	RANGE	LENGTH	EXAMPLE VALUES
`int`	-2,147,483,648 to 2,147,483,648	32 bits	-100 1,904,800,257
`long`	-9,223,372,036,854, 775,808 to 9,223,372,036,854,775,807	64 bits	-1,493,665,740,948L 119L

One thing you may notice about the `long` data type is that the numbers in the example are followed with an `L`. This notation is used when specifying literal values for a number of type `long`. The compiler can assume that your literal is an `int`, and not a `long`, if you do not specifically indicate this using the `L` as a suffix to your number as shown.

Probably the most commonly used of the integral types is `int`. There are a number of situations that call for a `long`, however, such as representing the population of the earth, the national debt, and so forth. There is generally no need to get too picky about which integral data type to use; even if you expect your numeric value to never exceed, say, 100, you're probably just as well off storing an `int`. A good example is probably human life span: while it might seem clever to represent this value as a `byte`, it is possible for people to live to be older than 127 years (a very few people already have). RAM space is cheap—far less expensive than the time required to go back and retool a program insufficiently typed.

One benefit to the Java types is that their ranges do not change from system to system. This is a stark distinction to C and C++ programs, which are subject to overflow problems when porting from one platform to another. That is, specifying an integer in C or C++ program refers to whatever the length of an integer is on the target platform. On a 16-bit processor an integer is (you guessed it) 16 bits, but it can be 32 bits in 32-bit Windows programs on a more recent Intel processor. That can cause problems for data, which would not be truncated, but rather wrapped—creating potentially disastrous results.

3.4.2 Floating Point Types

Java specifies two floating point data types: `float` and `double`. A floating point type is a number stored with a decimal place. There are a couple of things to note about these types. First of all, the highest and lowest possible values cannot be specified because of the decimal place. The accuracy of the number is variable depending on its magnitude, which could be very large or very small depending on where the decimal is placed. The default value for both floating point type variables is `0.00`.

As with a `long`, you should specify a float by placing an `F` after the literal value; otherwise, the compiler will treat it as a `double`. Table 3.5 shows the range, length, and example values for each type.

TABLE 3.5 Floating Point Types

DATA TYPE	RANGE	LENGTH	EXAMPLE VALUES
float	6–7 significant decimal digits	32 bits	3.8E6F
double	15 significant decimal digits	64 bits	–222 2.0E10 888,777,666,555.444

> **NOTE** If you are interested in the use of "e" in numbers, it is engineering notation for an irrational number representing the base of the natural system of logarithms, having an approximate numerical value of 2.7182818284. It was first used in the mid 17th century and has been calculated to 869,894,101 decimal places. So, 4.5E6 is another way of writing $4.5*10^6$.

Floating point numbers in Java follow the IEEE 754 specification. This standard includes positive and negative signed numbers, positive and negative zeros, positive and negative infinities, and a special value referred to as NaN (Not a Number). NaN is used to represent the result of an invalid operation (such as trying to divide by zero) or another non-numeric result. Java's `Double` and `Float` wrapper classes have an `isNan()` method for testing variables.

It is probably most common to choose `double` when a floating point number is required. This is because a `float`, like a `short`, is often not significant enough for many situations.

It is possible to convert between types in Java, which we will see how to do later. For now, it is pertinent to our discussion of data types and their reserved storage space to note certain behavior, which is noted briefly in `IntCast.java`.

3.4.3 IntCast.java

```
/*
File: chp3.IntCast
Purpose: Show primitive integral conversion
Date: 4 14 02
Author: E Hewitt
*/

public class IntCast {

public static void main (String [] args) {

double y = 3.14;            // make a double
int x = (int)(y);           // convert to int
double z = x;               // assign new double the int's value

System.out.println("y: " + y + ", x: " + x + ", z: " + z);
    }
}
```

When compiled and run, this program outputs

```
y: 3.14, x: 3, z: 3.0
```

The integer, as expected, loses the decimal place. An `int` cannot hold a floating point, but the number can be used as an `int` with loss of precision. Other types of conversion are not possible, however, even if it seems they should be allowed. Making the following modification to the above code produces a program that will not compile:

```
int x = (int)(y);
long z = 3L;
int i = z;
```

The compiler will complain that it found a `long` when it needed an `int`. That means that Java does not want to compile the program and possibly lose important data for the variable. Recall that `z`, as a `long`, is 64 bits, while an `int` holds 32 bits—which should be enough room to store the value "3." Even though zeros (empty place holders) are the only thing populating all of the remaining `int` bits, Java doesn't know that, and throws a compile-time error. Data type conversion will be covered in more detail in later chapters.

There has been some contention in different versions of Java between making floating point variables absolutely precise and increasing performance. On the one hand, it can be very important to have totally precise (reproducible) floating point data. On the other hand, maintaining such precision all the time can result in a severe performance degradation, which is especially costly when typical programs don't require it. For this reason, the `strictfp` keyword was created to protect the integrity of floating point operations. `strictfp` can be applied to a class or method by the programmer; declaring a class or a method as `strictfp` means that all of the instructions carried out inside its body must maintain strict floating point computational processes. For example, a `main` method would be declared `strictfp` like this:

```
public static strictfp void main(String[] args) { ....
```

Such precision is often only necessary for programs in which very careful mathematical precision is important, and is not likely to be a concern.

3.4.4 Textual Type

The textual type `char` is reserved for single Unicode character values. That is, you can assign a variable of type `char` the value "a," but not the value "ab." A value requiring more than one character requires creating a `String`. A `char` value is assigned with single quote marks, in contrast to a `String` object, which is assigned with double quote marks. The default value of a char is the Unicode symbol `\u0000`.

> **NOTE** A `String` is a primitive type in C and C++, but it is a class in Java.

The `char` is an unsigned 16-bit type, and as such it is possible to use mathematical operators (that is, treat it like an `int` in some situations). The ASCII character set corresponds to the first 127 values in the Unicode character set. So in Java we can write a simple loop that prints out the entire English alphabet:

3.4.5 alphabet.java

```
/*
File: chp3.alphabet.java
Purpose: print English alphabet
Author: E Hewitt
*/

public class alphabet {

public static void main(String[] args) {

    char letter = 'a';
    int x, y;
    y = 90;

    for (x = 64; x < y; x++) {

        System.out.print(letter + ",");

        letter++; //increment the counter
}

}

}
```

`alphabet.java` prints the letters a–z with each letter followed by a comma.

3.4.6 Unicode in Java

Because Java fully supports the Unicode character set, it is theoretically possible to represent any Unicode value from within a Java program. However, that does not necessarily mean that your platform (or browser) will be able to render it correctly. This is most commonly a consideration when dealing with internationalization issues.

> **NOTE** Until ColdFusion MX, ColdFusion did not offer native Unicode support, and unless you were writing international applications that required support for languages such as Korean or Chinese, it may not have become much of an issue for you.

Unicode is referred to as a double-byte character set, because it uses 16 bits to store character data, unlike the 8-bit ASCII with only 128 characters. Unicode is therefore capable of storing 65,535 different values, often expressed as hexadecimals from `u\0000` to `u\FFFF`.

3.4.7 UnicodeDemo.java

```
/*
  File: chp3.UnicodeDemo.java
  Author: E Hewitt
  Purpose: demos how to work with Unicode characters
       and shows some useful ones
 */

public class UnicodeDemo {

    public static void main (String[] args){
        // Unicode for a space
        String space = "\u0020";

        StringBuffer sb = new
StringBuffer().append("hello").append(space).append("world");

        // using the Unicode symbols directly
        // in the string
        System.out.println(sb.toString());
        // result: hello world

        // a list of handy Unicode chars
        System.out.println("Yen: \u00a5");
        System.out.println("Pound: \u00a3");
        System.out.println("Cents: \u00a2");
        System.out.println("Paragraph: \u00b6");
        System.out.println("mu: \u00b5");
        System.out.println("1/4th: \u00bc");
    }
}
```

The above program may print out characters correctly or incorrectly, depending on whether your platform supports them. The point is simply to see how to reference the Unicode set under slightly different circumstances.

NOTE It is sometimes necessary to escape Unicode characters, as you have no doubt had to do in ColdFusion with the pound sign: `<cfoutput><font color = ##336699>`.... In Java, Unicode characters need to be escaped too.

For more information on Unicode, visit *www.unicode.org.*

3.4.8 Logical Type

The `boolean` type has two possible values: `true` and `false`, used in evaluation of a logical condition. The default value of a `boolean` variable is `false`.

NOTE In ColdFusion (and in C++ for that matter), numbers can be used to represent `boolean` values: 0 can be equivalent to `false`, and 1 (or other non-zero) is equivalent to `true`. The purpose for this is to ensure that Java programmers do not perform an assignation when they meant to check for equivalency.

The following bit of code demonstrates a simple use of the logical type.

3.4.9 `booleanTest.java`

```
/*
File: chp3.booleanTest.java
Purpose: demonstrate use of boolean type
Author: E Hewitt
*/

public class booleanTest {
  public static void main(String [] args) {

  boolean isCurrent = true;

  if (isCurrent) {
System.out.println("isCurrent is true");
      }
  else {
      System.out.println("isCurrent is false");
    }
  }
}
```

This code simply outputs `isCurrent is true` to the command line. The following code produces an equivalent result: ...`if(isCurrent == true)`.... Two equal signs are used, as in JavaScript, to check for the same value. In addition to assigning a variable of `boolean` type literally, `boolean` variables can also store the results of decisions. For instance, you can write `if(numberOf-Employees > 50)`.

> **NOTE** You cannot use `eq`, `is`, `gte`, or similar expression phrases as you can in ColdFusion. As we will see in a moment, checking for equivalency in Java is somewhat more complicated than it is in ColdFusion because of how objects are stored in memory. We will examine this when we start looking at objects.

3.5 Variable Assignment and Initialization

There are a few conventions used in initializing variables, and some rules.

3.5.1 Naming Requirements

When you create a new variable, your naming of the variable must follow these rules:

- The first character can be a dollar sign ($), an underscore (_), or a letter (A–Z or a–z).
- Characters following the first character can be any of the above or a numeric character (0–9).
- Java is case sensitive (`iscurrent` is not the same as `isCurrent`).
- You cannot name a variable using a Java keyword.

> **NOTE** ColdFusion is not case sensitive—Java is!

3.5.2 Java Keywords

The Java keywords, which are reserved and therefore may not be used to, for instance, name variables, are shown in Table 3.6.

> **NOTE** Many of the keywords, such as `try/catch/throw` and `switch/case` are ColdFusion keywords too. Notice that `import` is a Java keyword that is also now a keyword in ColdFusion MX. A number of these constructs even work in Java similarly to how they work in ColdFusion.

TABLE 3.6 Java Keywords

abstract	boolean	break	byte
case	catch	char	class
const	continue	default	do
double	else	extends	false
final	finally	float	for
goto	if	implements	import
instanceof	int	interface	long
native	new	null	package
private	protected	public	return
short	static	strictfp	super
switch	synchronized	this	throw
throws	transient	true	try
void	volatile	while	

3.5.3 Naming Conventions

Like many other things in the world, the rules are outnumbered by the conventions. Not only does Java have a number of naming and other coding conventions, they are all followed with real consistency throughout the community. Some of the conventions are concerned with topics we have not yet covered. We have touched on creating a String, however. While our example above shows `name = new String("Jeremy");` as the way to create a String (and this is technically correct), one very rarely sees a `String` created in this manner. It is far more common to see this: `String name = "Jeremy";`

(I wrote it the long way to demonstrate how objects of all kinds are commonly created, and to just make the distinction between objects and primitive types).

There are some conventions for naming variables:

- Each variable (identifier) should begin with a lowercase letter.
- If more than one word is used in an identifier, each subsequent word should begin with an uppercase letter, like this: `isCurrent`. Identifier words should not be separated with underscores, spaces, or other text.

The above conventions are routinely followed. Other miscellaneous notes about variable naming are as follows:

- In naming a variable, you can also use any Unicode character that denotes a letter in a language other than English.
- Constants (examined below) are named using all uppercase letters, and an underscore is used to separate each word.
- You (obviously) cannot declare two variables of the same name in the same scope.
- It is legal to put declarations just about anywhere in your code.
- The length of a variable name is not limited by Java.

There are some conventions regarding variable naming that are perhaps less consistently followed:

- It is a bad idea to make two variables that differ only in their case. For instance while you can legally create two different variables, called `String name;` and `String Name;`, this would be very confusing, so it should not be done.
- While it is possible to create an object with the same name as the type, this would be very confusing as well, and it should not be done. For example, given an object of type `Employee`, it is a bad idea to instantiate an object of this type with the variable name `employee`. Instead, try putting "a," "an," or "my" in front of it; for example: `anEmployee`. These are all commonly used.

3.5.4 Creating Primitive Variables and Assigning Value

There are two steps to getting a variable assigned. First you must *declare* it, which means reserving space for it in memory. Then you must *initialize* it, which means assigning a value to it.

To declare a variable, first write the type of variable you want to create. We have so far only examined primitive types, but it works the same when you start creating variables of objects.

Here is an example of declaration:

```
int numberOfEmployees; // a declaration
```

This variable has only been declared, it has not been initialized, and Java will tell you so in an error message at compile time if you don't do anything else with it. You need to assign it a value first. Here is an example of assignment:

```
numberOfEmployees = 48;
```

You can declare multiple variables of the same type at the same time. You just separate the variable names with commas, like this:

```
boolean x, y, z; // declares 3 different booleans
```

Some programmers find multiple declarations like this confusing; some find it intuitive organization. You might want to create a new class at this time to start testing some of this. Here are a couple more examples:

```
char help; // declare
help = 'h'; // initialize

double taxOwed; // declare
taxOwed = 12643.0; // initialize
```

It is also possible to both declare and initialize a variable in the same statement, like this:

```
double taxOwed = 12643.0;
```

This may also look familiar by now (though a string is not a primitive type):

```
String name = "Jeremy";
```

3.5.5 Constants

A *constant* is a variable whose value does not change. A constant is denoted with the keyword `final` in the variable declaration. Constants cannot be overwritten. Attempting to assign a value to a constant will generate a compile-time error. As mentioned above, constants are named with all uppercase letters, and underscores separate words in the variable name. Here is an example:

3.5.6 constants.java

```
/*
File: chp3.constants.java
Purpose: demonstrate constants with final keyword
*/

public class constants {

public static void main(String [] args) {

//declare constant var
final double CIRCUMFERENCE_OF_EARTH = 24901.5;

// print it out to command line
    System.out.println("Earth's circumference: " +
        CIRCUMFERENCE_OF_EARTH);
    }
}
```

The advantage of using a constant is that the programmer can reference the variable in other parts of the program without having to worry about its value or about accidentally changing its value. Declaring a constant in the manner shown in `constants.java` is perhaps not terribly useful. While this variable would be a constant, and would thus make it easier to read the program and protect it from being overwritten, it is declared here inside the `main` method. Constants are generally declared as public, class-level variables; that is, they are accessible by methods defined in other classes.

> **NOTE** ColdFusion does not have constant variables that act in this way.

3.6 Operators

Binary operators are used to perform tasks with two operands. There are operators for arithmetic, incrementing and decrementing, logical operations, and bitwise operations.

3.6.1 Arithmetic Operators

These are as you would expect: +, –, /, and * for addition, subtraction, division, and multiplication. The remainder of an integer operation is given by `mod` (%).

NOTE Instead of writing out MOD as you might in ColdFusion (for example, 10 MOD 3), Java uses the % sign. So 10 % 3 is 1.

It is common to have to modify an existing value. Java offers a concise way to use arithmetic operators. Instead of writing

```
x = x + 1;
```

you can write

```
x += 1;
```

These are equivalent operations. You can also perform other mathematical operations (–, *, /) in this manner.

NOTE ColdFusion does not offer this shortcut.

3.6.2 Incrementing and Decrementing Operators

Increment and decrement operations are something we need to do very frequently. Looping over a result set or an array one item at a time are common examples. Java makes this convenient with special operators that increase or decrease a variable by one.

The straightforward way to do an operation like this is to simply state the variable name and add one to it. For instance:

```
int x = 0;
int y = x + 1;
```

It is more concise, however, to write this:

```
int x = 0;
int y = x++; // value of y is 0
```

By the same token you can subtract like this:

```
int x = 10;
int y = x--; // value of y is 10
```

The above examples make use of what is called *post-increment* and *post-decrement* operations. The adjustment by one is made *after* the current value of the variable is evaluated. Note that you can only use these operators on variables, not only literal numbers themselves. For instance, this is illegal:

```
10++; // illegal!
```

You can also *pre-increment* and *pre-decrement*, as shown here:

```
int x = 10;
int y = --x; // value of y is 9
```

This seems straightforward enough. However, you should use these operators with some degree of caution. This is because they can be confusing and difficult to keep track of. Consider the code in `prepostOps.java`:

3.6.3 prepostOps.java

```
/*
File: chp3.prepostOps.java
Purpose: demonstrate post-increment and pre-increment
*/

public class prepostOps {

public static void main(String [] args) {

int x = 10;
int y = 2;

int z = y + x--;

System.out.println("z is: " + z); // z is 12

z += --x;

System.out.println("now z is: " + z); // z is 20!

// here's why:

System.out.println("x is: " + x); // x is 8

    }
} // eof
```

In prepostOps.java, z is assigned the value of y (2) + x, which is 10 when the operation occurs. Because of post-decrementing, one is subtracted from x only after the operation is performed. So z is 12 (y + x). Immediately after this operation, x becomes 9. Next, we take the current value of z (12) and then subtract one from x (9 – 1 = 8) before performing the addition.

3.6.4 Logical and Boolean Operators

There are logical operators such as < and > for less than and greater than. Boolean operators also exist to express different conditions, such as && for AND, and || for OR. Logical operators are shown in Table 3.7 and boolean operators are shown in Table 3.8.

TABLE 3.7 Logical Operators

OPERATION	OPERATOR	EXAMPLE
Equal to	==	(x == 1)
Not equal to	!=	(x != 1)
Less than	<	(x < 1)
Greater than	>	(x > 1)
Less than or equal to	<=	(x <= 1)
Greater than or equal to	>=	(x >= 1)

NOTE In ColdFusion, you cannot use these same operator symbols because of how ColdFusion expressions work. You are used to writing expressions like this: <cfif x EQ y>.... That is in part because assignment and evaluation in ColdFusion are somewhat conflated (i.e., ColdFusion has no == operator, and = always means assignment).

TABLE 3.8 Boolean Operators

OPERATION	OPERATOR	EXAMPLE

AND	&&	`int x = 3;`
		`int y = 6;`
		`((x = 3) && (y == 6))`

OR	||	`int x = 3;`
		`int y = 6;`
		`(( x < 2) || ( y >= 6 ))`

NOT	!	`int x = 3;`
		`int y = 6;`
		`( !( x == 2) )`

The logical operators, as you would expect, are used in expressions that reduce to a `boolean` value. For instance,

```
int x = 5;
x > 2; // true
x != 5; // false
```

> **NOTE** Java "short circuits" the same way that ColdFusion does. That is, when using `&&` in an expression, if the first part is determined to be false, the second part is never evaluated, because the outcome is already necessarily false. Likewise, when using `||`, if the first part is determined to be true, then the second part is not evaluated, because the outcome is already necessarily true. The syntax of the operators is a little different, but the behavior as you expect it to work in ColdFusion is the same. Note that there is no short circuit `XOR` operation.

Java also supports ternary operations. A ternary expression is written as

```
condition ? action1 : action2
```

If the condition evaluates to `true`, the first action is taken; if `false`, the second action is taken. The ternary operator is shorthand for the following construct:

```
if  (aCondition) trueCode else falseCode  // conditional
    (aCondition) ? trueCode : falseCode // ternary
```

The result expressions must have types that are assignment-compatible. That is, you must be able to assign the value of the result of one expression to the type of the other expression *without an explicit cast*. Casting, which is discussed in detail later, is the practice of sending a value of one type into another type. For example, you can assign an `int` value to a `double` value without requiring an explicit cast. If neither type is assignable to the other, the operation is not valid.

The usefulness of a ternary operator is that it can appear in the middle of an expression; `if` statements cannot. You can use the ternary operator in an expression because it has a value. Though it is more concise to use the ternary operator than the corresponding `if` statement, programmers' use of it varies widely.

> **NOTE** Ternary expressions are represented in ColdFusion as an Immediate If (the IIF function). You may have written something like `iif(y eq 0, DE("Error"), x/y)`. It might seem at first that the corresponding Java expression would be something like: `int x = 8; int y = 4; String msg = "Error"; System.out.println( y == 0 ? msg : x/y);`. This won't compile. Remember that Java is strongly typed; ColdFusion is not. Use of the Immediate If is generally discouraged in ColdFusion, as it can add a slight decrease in performance. This is not the case with Java.

3.6.5 Bit Manipulation Operators

The bitwise operators allow you to manipulate individual bits that make up an integer value (which, you may recall, includes `char`) in accordance with the rules for AND (&), OR (|), and the exclusive or (XOR, represented as ^). For instance, given an integer, you can get the value for the bit in a specified position (whether the bit is a 0 or a 1).

An AND operator results in 1 if both bits are 1. The OR operator results in 1 if either bit is a 1. The XOR operator results in 1 if the bits are of different values.

Note that while the operators for bitwise and logical operations appear the same, Java knows the difference based on the types of the operands involved. If you ask Java to mix, say, a `boolean` and an `int` in an expression, it will refuse.

You can also use >> and << operators; these shift the bit pattern of an integer to the right or left, respectively. The left-hand side of the expression indicates *what* to shift, and the right-hand side of the expression indicates how *far* to shift.

<< Shift bits left and fill with zero bits on the right-hand side.
>> Shift bits right and fill with the highest sign bit on the left-hand side.
>>> Shift bits right and fill with zero bits on the left-hand side.

For example:

3.6.6 bitwise.java

```
/*
File: chp3.bitwise.java
Purpose: demonstrate bit manipulation
Author: E Hewitt
*/

public class bitwise {

public static void main(String [] args) {

int x = 0;

int y = (x & 8) / 8; // prints 0

x = 1;

y = (x | 4) / 4;

System.out.println("result: " + y); // prints 1


int i = 7; // in binary, 7 = 111

/* shifting everything to the right 1 and filling
   the remaining bits with 0 would result in
   11 (base 2), or 3 (base 10)
*/

System.out.println("result: " + (i >>> 1)); //prints 3

// try it again--guess the result

int j = 10; // in binary, 10 is written 1010

System.out.println("result: " + (j >>> 2)); // j now 0010
// answer: convert j to base10 (prints 2)

    }
}
```

While that may seem arcane, these operators can be useful because Java will often have return values declared as `int`s, and these can be manipulated at the most fundamental level.

3.6.7 instanceof

The `instanceof` operator evaluates whether a given reference refers to an object that is an instance of a certain class (or interface). `instanceof` is useful in downcasting a reference, which we will discuss in detail later.

3.7 Overflow

An overflow happens when a result is too large for the type of variable that is meant to hold it; that is, the value assigned is too large to be represented by the type. This can happen for a few different reasons, chief among them is that there has been an implicit conversion of type somewhere, or that an expression has evaluated to a result larger than expected.

Java handles overflow differently for integers than it does for floating point values. If an integer overflows, only the least significant bits are stored. Remember that each Integral data type in Java can represent a certain number of values—half of which are negative and half of which (including 0) are positive. That means that exceeding the highest possible positive value of an integer type will cause an overflow that results in a *negative* number (and vice versa). The following program demonstrates:

3.7.1 Overflow.java

```
/*
File: chp3.Overflow.java
Purpose: demo int overflow
Author: E Hewitt
*/

public class Overflow {

public static void main(String[] args) {

int x = java.lang.Integer.MAX_VALUE;
```

```
// prints 2147483647
System.out.println(x);

// add 1 to max int value. prints -2147483648

System.out.println("overflow: "+ (x += 1));
    }

}
```

`Overflow.java` demonstrates the wrapping that occurs with an integer overflow. Floating point expression overflow, however, does something different. When a `double` or a `float` overflows, the result is positive infinity. When a `double` or a `float` *underflows*; that is, when it becomes a value too small to be represented, the result is 0. Illegal operations (such as dividing by zero) result in NaN (Not a Number). Floating point expressions will not raise exceptions, they will simply conform to one of these predefined modes. See Section 3.10, titled "Java Standard Classes," for more information about how `MAX_VALUE` is used in this program.

If you are really in need of performing unbounded arithmetic on integers or floating point numbers, the `java.Math` package makes available two classes for you to use: `BigInteger` and `BigDecimal`. As you might guess, these perform more slowly than their primitive counterparts, which is why they are defined separately. In general, `ints`, `doubles`, and `floats` will be just fine.

3.8 Operator Precedence

There are rules regarding the order of precedence the compiler will follow when executing a mathematical statement with multiple operators. These are generally the standard mathematical rules for operator precedence:

1. Operators inside parentheses
2. Multiplication and division (left to right)
3. Addition and subtraction (left to right)

This short program simply sets two different variables to the value of a mathematical expression result. The expression uses multiple mathematical operators. Each expression uses identical operators and numeric values. One expression shows left to right precedence, while the other shows parenthetical enforcement of precedence.

```
/*
File: chp3.opPrecedence.java
Purpose: demo operator precedence
Author: E Hewitt
*/

public class opPrecedence {
    public static void main(String[] args) {

    // this program simply demonstrates left to
    // right and parenthetical precedence in mathematical
    // operations

int x = 6 + 6 * 2 / 6 - 4;

System.out.println("x is: " + x); // x is 4

// same thing, but with parentheses
int y = (6 + 6) * (2 / (6 - 4)); // y is 12

System.out.println("y is: " + y);
    }
}
```

NOTE I am writing out these code snippets as complete working programs to encourage you to type in, compile, and run them. This can help you get used to reading Java, and begin to notice different kinds of errors (such as `';' expected`) and subtle behaviors (such as a mathematical result of 0 that might slip through the cracks if you're not careful about types).

3.9 Casts and Conversions

In a strongly typed language it is sometimes necessary to make conversions between one data type and another. Perhaps you need to perform an operation that accepts a value of a particular type, so you need to convert the type. You can legally convert one numeric type to another, as shown in Table 3.9.

The compiler will automatically assign a smaller type to a larger type. Because no data would be lost, this operation is unproblematic. However, data of a larger type will *not* automatically be converted to a smaller type—*even if the*

TABLE 3.9 Numeric Type Conversions

FROM	TO	LOSE PRECISION?
`byte`	`short`	No
`short`	`int`	No
`char`	`int`	No
`int`	`long`	No
`int`	`float`	Yes
`int`	`double`	No
`long`	`float`	Yes
`float`	`double`	No
`long`	`double`	Yes

smaller type is sufficiently large to hold the data—because the compiler cannot know if the data's integrity will be maintained. To perform this kind of assignment, a typecast is required. Take a look at these examples:

```
byte x  = 20;
byte y = 10;
int z = x + y; // okay
```

The above code is fine, because the compiler will automatically make a *promotion*—that is, cast from a smaller datatype to a larger datatype—when it can do so without losing precision.

```
int x = 20;
int y = 10;
byte z = x + y; // compiler error
```

Even though in the above examples a `byte` is ostensibly a big enough type to hold the result of 30, the compiler will not make such an assignment and will instead report "possible loss of precision." This kind of thing can occur in your programs for a number of reasons. Perhaps because of a multiplication operation a variable would exceed its range.

In trying to compile the following code snippet, the error reported could be confusing:

```
byte a = 100;
byte b = 30;

byte c = a + b; // error!
```

Here, the compiler reports that it has found an `int` where a `byte` was required, even though no `int` datatypes are explicitly present in the code. That is because a `byte` cannot hold a positive value greater than 127. If the code doesn't mention anything about `int`s, and the compiler rejects the code, why does the compiler say that it found an `int`? The reason is that when you use primitive data types, Java will automatically convert any integral type to an `int` when mathematical operators are applied to them.

> **NOTE** When mathematical operators are used, Java defaults integral types to `int`.

The compiler will also reject this:

```
int myInt = 37F; // error!
```

Again, the error reported regards a possible loss of precision, saying that a `float` was found where an `int` was required. At the same time, the compiler will reject this:

```
float myFloat = 89773.23; // error!
```

Why the error? That looks perfectly reasonable. The reason for the error is that floating point values default to `double`s if they are not explicitly marked. So both of the following are acceptable:

```
float myFloat = 333.25F; // okay

double myDouble = 456.78; // okay
```

NOTE Floating point values default to `double` unless `float` is specifically stated.

While it may look strange, the following is acceptable too. This is called typecasting:

```
float f = (float) 14.5; // okay
```

A *typecast* is lowering the range of a given value by changing its type. To typecast a variable, write the data type to which you want to cast your value in parentheses before the value:

```
identifier = (typecastTo) (value);
```

For example:

```
int x = 10;
int y = 20;
byte z;
z = (byte) (x + y);   // okay
```

Decimal values will be lost in certain situations, such as this:

```
double d = 30405.9893;

int i = (int) (d); // prints 30405
```

While that means you must be very careful when typecasting, sometimes this is exactly what you want to do. For instance, while the `java.lang.Math` package makes available a `round()` method for returning a `float` as an `int`, you can also do this with a typecast. For instance:

```
float f = 2097.8F;

int i = (int) (f); // yields 2097
```

NOTE In some languages, you can exchange a `boolean` value with the numeric values 0 (for `false`) or 1 (for `true`). You cannot cast from a `boolean` value to any numeric type in Java.

When performing mathematical operations on values of different types, there are certain rules that come into play:

- When more than one value, any of different types, are used in an operation, the operands are converted to a common type before the operation is carried out.
- If any operand is a `double`, the values are converted to `doubles`.
- If any operand is a `float`, the values are converted to `float`.
- If any operand is a `long`, the values are converted to `long`.
- In all other cases, the types are converted to `int`.

The following snippet illustrates these rules:

3.9.1 numericOps.java

```
/*
File: chp3.numericOps.java
Purpose: demos conversion dangers
Author: E Hewitt
*/

public class numericOps {

public static void main(String[] args) {

// get some variables to work with

int i = 50;

double d = 70.75;

short s = 32750;


// do some operations


System.out.println(i + d); // 120.75, type is double


int i1 = s + i;

System.out.println(i1); // 32800, type is int
```

```
// remember that a short's positive limit is 32,767

int i2 = (short) i1; // conversion compiles

System.out.println(i2); // whoa!! prints -32736!

     }

}
```

NOTE Clearly, conversion is something to be handled with care, especially for those of us used to dealing with a language like ColdFusion where a number is a number is a string.

When you cast from one type to another, first make sure that the result will not exceed the range allowed for the target type. While many of Java's improvements over other languages are intended to reduce the number of elusive errors that programmers can make, this remains tricky. For instance:

3.10 Java Standard Classes

In `Overflow.java` (Listing 3.7.1, above), we made use of a constant declared in the `java.lang.Integer` standard class. This class makes available a number of methods to work with integers, and it defines three constant variables, including `MAX_VALUE` (the maximum value for an integer) and `MIN_VALUE` (the minimum value for an integer). There are corresponding classes defined for `long`, `float`, `double`, `boolean`, and so forth in the `java.lang` package. These are all standard classes.

Everything (except primitive type variables) in Java is an object. Objects are defined in terms of the data they make available and the behavior that they are capable of. This is what you do when you write Java programs—you write classes that serve as blueprints for making objects. When you define your own classes, you are also able to make use of the classes predefined for you in the Java language (such as `java.lang.Integer`). When you call on one of these classes, you can refer to the data it defines (such as `MAX_VALUE`), and you can perform the actions that it makes available. For example, `java.lang.Integer` defines a method called `toString()`. This method takes an integer value and returns it as a `String` type:

```
int x = 777;
System.out.println(x); //prints 777

// still prints 777, but now it's a String:
System.out.println(java.lang.Integer.toString(x));
```

> **NOTE** When you see a Java "method" referred to, think "function" in ColdFusion. For instance, the `java.lang.Math` class defines a random method, which produces a pseudorandom double whose value is between 0.0 and 1.0. This corresponds to the `random()` function you've likely used in ColdFusion.

There is a way to shorten these calls to classes defined in the standard packages (or indeed any package). You do so using the `import` statement. We will look more at `import` later, but for now, know that because the `java.lang` package is always available (you don't have to explicitly import it), these two statements are functionally equivalent:

```
String firstName = "Jeremy"; // creates a String object
java.lang.String lastName = "Allaire"; // same thing
```

That is because a `String` object is defined in the `java.lang` package. We will examine objects, classes, packages, methods, and so on in depth throughout the book. For now, it is a good idea to get just this much introduction to them so that the API becomes more accessible, and so that we are free to refer to standard classes in examples. The packages are merely overviewed here, so you can get an idea of where to find things in the API.

3.10.1 `java.lang` and `Object`

`java.lang` and `Object` define all of the primitive data types (`Boolean`, `Double`, `Integer`), `String`, and `Object`. `Object` is at the root of the class hierarchy. That means that all of the objects that you create, or that are defined in Java, inherit the behavior of `java.lang.Object`.

Anytime you create a string, you are creating an object of type `java.lang.String`. You can look at the API and see what kinds of things strings allow you to do by default. For instance, the first method defined for strings is `charAt()`, which returns the character at the given index:

```
String name="Java";
charAt(2); // evaluates to v
```

NOTE In the string "Java," the character at position 2 is "v" because Java generally starts counting at 0, not 1. I say "generally" because this is not the case for database connectivity issues, as we will see.

The `Thread` and `Throwable` classes are also defined here.

3.10.2 java.text

This class has some text formatting classes you might use for working with dates and other special textual types.

3.10.3 java.util

This package contains a huge number of important utilities that you will use frequently in programming Java. The collections (`Arrays`, `LinkedList`, `HashSet`, `HashMap`, etc.) are all defined here. This also contains classes for working with different calendars, currency, dates, locales, properties, and much more.

NOTE Java does not contain structures as defined in ColdFusion. Instead, Java uses a number of specific ways to define name value pairs; these are called *collections*. This is easy to remember because the attribute of the `<cfloop>` tag you use when looping over a structure is `collection = #collectionName#`.

3.10.4 java.io

`java.io` contains classes that allow you to work with input/output; that is, the reading and writing of files.

NOTE When you would write `<cffile>` in ColdFusion, you implement classes in the `java.io` package. Instead of using a different value for the action attribute (such as `action="read"` or `action="write"`), use the `java.io` classes. For instance, to delete a file, you can call the `delete()` method of the `file` object.

Note that Java 1.4 defines a new package called `java.nio`, which stands for New IO. By creating a new package, many of the IO classes could be reworked without compromising backward compatibility.

3.10.5 `java.net`

This contains defined classes necessary for working with networks, such as sockets and URLs.

3.10.6 `java.awt`

AWT stands for Abstract Windowing Toolkit, and this package contains numerous classes for creating graphical user interface elements of software programs, such as buttons and fonts. Much of this functionality has ascended into the `javax.Swing` package, which is currently the preferred way to create software GUIs.

There are a number of packages defined as `javax` packages. These are known as "standard extensions" (which seems like an oxymoron). These include `javax.Swing` (for creating graphical user interfaces) and `javax.sql`, which allows you to connect to and work with databases, as well as `javax.naming` (which enables work with naming and directory services) and `javax.xml`.

We will use and refer to many of the classes defined in these packages throughout the book.

3.11 What's Next

In the next chapter, we will look at Java programming structures. We will cover conditional logic constructs and looping, and look more closely at methods for working with data in arrays and strings.

4

Programming Structures

...these phenomena, in the production of which large masses of men are concerned, do actually exhibit a very remarkable degree of regularity...

—George Boole, *The Laws of Thought*

In the last chapter we covered a lot of ground, gaining the fundamental tools we need to work with data, including binary numbers, primitive data types, and typecasting. We overviewed core Java programming language classes and worked with a number of example programs.

In this chapter, we round out the basic programming tools that you need to get started writing real programs. That means we'll look at using character strings and arrays, loops, and conditional logic. This chapter has a lot of example code so that you can see how these structures work in different situations, and the code comes in the form of small, complete programs, so that you can get used to compiling, running, and modifying the code in its true context.

4.1 Wrapper Classes

As we saw in the last chapter, all of the eight primitive types (`int`, `short`, `boolean`, `double`, etc.) are not objects. In order to work with primitive data type variables as if they were objects, Java provides a wrapper class that defines certain constants and methods. Generally, a *wrapper class* provides behavioral features that enhance the usability of another entity that it "wraps," or contains, without modifying the thing it wraps. In the case of Java primitive data type wrappers, the wrapper embeds the primitive data type as a field and provides methods for retrieving the value in different forms and doing comparisons, as well as constants appropriate to each class of primitive type. For example, in the last chapter we used the `java.lang.Integer` wrapper class for the primitive type `int`. Further examples follow.

> **NOTE** There is one additional wrapper class, called `void`. It has no constructors and cannot be instantiated. It is used as a placeholder to reference a Class object that represents the Java keyword `void`, another primitive type. You may be used, by now, to seeing the `main` method in example programs starting with `public static void main`.... The return type is specified as `void` (meaning that the method does not return a value). That's what is being referred to there. More on `main` later....

Wrapper classes are needed because the use of primitive types is more limited than what one can do with objects. A primitive cannot be passed by reference, for example. We will see in later sections in this chapter how that will be useful when we start reading arguments passed to programs from the command line. Wrappers simply allow primitive data types to be used as full-fledged objects in the language. They all offer such methods as `equals()`, which checks if the value of the specified objects are equivalent, and `compareTo()`, which performs a signed comparison of two objects.

> **NOTE** Objects instantiated from the wrapper classes are immutable; that is, once created, they cannot be modified.

The discussion of wrapper classes starts off this chapter as a bridge to discussing strings and arrays.

4.2 Strings

A string is a discrete series of adjacent characters. A string is distinct from the primitive types in that it is a standard class. A string literal is a set of zero or more characters surrounded by double quotes:

```
String name = new String("JJ");
```

Strings are used very frequently, so Java makes available a shortcut for string creation and initialization, like this:

```
String name = "JJ";
```

This longer version, called a *constructor*, represents the way in which objects are created. The shorter version is called a string literal. String literals are implicitly created as instances of the `java.lang.String` class, and as such, a variable defined as a string holds a reference to a `String` object. Because string literals act as if they were references to an instance of the `String` class, you can do all of the things with strings that you can do with objects, including call methods on them and make copies of them. In general, it is not advisable to create a string using the constructor shown above.

A string is immutable; that is, its value cannot change after it has been created. Strings are stored by the compiler in something called the string constant pool. The constant pool is in the class file produced by the compiler and is a standard part of the Java Class file format. The purpose of this is to give Java programs a performance boost. When the Java Virtual Machine encounters a string variable identifier, it checks the pool to see if it already contains that string. If it does, the JVM can simply return a reference to the current string; this saves it the trouble of having to create a new object, allocate new memory, and garbage collect the string when the program is finished using it.

When you create a string using the new operator (the long version above), this obviates the JVM's search for the string reference in the string constant pool, and will therefore always create a unique object and return a reference to that object.

> **NOTE** In ColdFusion, it is perfectly acceptable to write something like this: `<cfparam name = "name" default = "">`. In Java, you can similarly write `String name = "";`. The thing to note here is that the Java string is not then null. Memory has been allocated for the name `String` object, and it therefore has an address and is not null. This is called an empty string—it's just a string with no contents.

The program `StringLiterals.java` demonstrates the difference with respect to memory that the string literals and `String` objects instantiation can make. It also shows why you should not use == to test for equality with strings.

4.2.1 StringLiterals.java

```
/* File: chp4.StringLiterals.java
Purpose: demo mgmt of string objects and literals
Author: E Hewitt
*/

public class StringLiterals {
```

```
    public static void main(String[] args){

    // create a new string literal

    String name1 = "Jedimaster";

    // create a new string, assign it the value of name1

    String name2 = new String(name1);

    // test for equality

    System.out.println(name1.equals(name2)); // true. okay.

    System.out.println(name1 == name2); // false. hmmm...

    }

} // eof
```

What exactly is happening here? Using the `equals()` method compares the contents of strings; that is, the data stored in them. Using the == comparison operator compares the memory addresses of the two Strings to determine if they refer to the same object. Because `name2` was created using the constructor, a new object was created, which is stored in a new place in memory; hence, the == operator returns false.

The following program illustrates a number of methods that are available for use with strings:

4.2.2 StringMethods.java

```
/* File: StringMethods.java
Purpose: demo methods available for working with strings
Author: E Hewitt
*/

public class StringMethods {

    public static void main(String[] args){
        // create a new string
        String phrase = "Java for ColdFusion";

        // set to uppercase, like CF function
```

```
        System.out.println(phrase.toUpperCase());

        // set to lowercase, like CF function
        System.out.println(phrase.toLowerCase());

        // use \ to escape double quotes

        System.out.println("Does the phrase end with "+
            "\",baby!\"? " + phrase.endsWith(",baby!"));

        // get string length in characters
        System.out.println("How long is that string? " +
            phrase.length() + " characters");

        // add 5 spaces to the end:
        phrase += "     ";

        // get new length:
        System.out.println("new length: " + phrase.length());
        // prints 24

        // trim works like the CF trim functions:

        System.out.println("trimmed length: " +
           phrase.trim().length());
           // prints 19

// try it with a tab escape sequence

phrase += "\t";

System.out.println("with tab: " + phrase.length());
//prints 25

// trim the tab

System.out.println("trim tab: " + phrase.trim().length());

// prints 19
    }
}
```

Let's do a little more with strings by looking at how we can replace different characters.

4.2.3 StringReplace.java

```
public class StringReplaceAndIndex {
    public static void main(String [] args) {

        // concatenate strings another way
        // using +=

        String greeting = "Hello ";

        String person = "Sally";

        greeting += person;

        System.out.println(greeting); // prints Hello Sally

        // notice that length() is a method with Strings
        // not so with arrays, in which it is a field:

        System.out.println("There are " + greeting.length() +
            " characters in the greeting String");

        // find the ordinal occurence of char in String
        // use where you would write Find() in CF
        System.out.println(greeting.indexOf("o"));

        // find last occurrence of char in String
        System.out.println(greeting.lastIndexOf("l"));

        // note that this works a bit like the replace
        // function in CF

        greeting.replace('l', 'x');

        // here's the difference: in CF, the original
        // string would have been modified. not so in Java:
        System.out.println(greeting);

        // we can pretend, though: (see Buffers)
        System.out.println(greeting.replace('l', 'x'));

    }
}
```

This gives us the following output:

```
There are 11 characters in the greeting String
4
9
Hello Sally
Hexxo Saxxy
```

4.2.4 Substrings

Substrings are rather easy to work with if you have some experience handling them in ColdFusion. `Substrings.java` shows how to use the pertinent methods:

4.2.5 `Substrings.java`

```
public class Substrings {

    public static void main (String[] args){
        // create a new string

        String name = "dude";

        // print the first 3 characters
        System.out.println("Hello, " +
            name.substring(0,3));
        // prints Hello, dud

        // try it a different way
        name = "Tony Danza";
        System.out.println("Hello, " +
            name.substring(3,7));
        // prints y Da

        // get first occurrence of T
        // remember it starts at 0
        System.out.println(name.indexOf("D"));
        // prints 5

        // is it case-sensitive?
        System.out.println(name.indexOf("d"));
        // yes. prints -1, meaning "not found"
    }
}
```

The program's output is

```
Hello, dud
Hello, y Da
5
-1
```

4.2.6 Concatenation

A string can be combined with another string with the + operator, like this:

```
String firstName = "JJ";
String lastName = "Allaire";

String fullName1 = "JJ" + ""Allaire"; // literal

String fullName2 =  firstName + " " + lastName; // new object
```

`fullname1` now holds a literal. This is because it was formed exclusively with literals and is therefore a *constant string expression*. On the other hand, if one of the values in the expression had been a string variable, as with `fullname2`, then that would form a new `String` object.

4.2.7 `intern()`

There is a final way to create string literals. `intern()` is a method of `String` that tells the virtual machine to look in the string constant pool for a matching object. If one is found, the `intern()` method returns a canonical representation of that object. If the method does not find a matching object, then it creates a new `String` object and places it in the memory pool. Using the `intern()` method works like this:

4.2.8 `Intern.java`

```
/* File: Intern.java
Purpose: demo intern() method
Author: E Hewitt
*/

public class Intern {

public static void main(String[] args){
```

```
        String name1 = "JJ";

        String name2 = new String ("JJ").intern();

        System.out.println(name1.equals(name2)); // true

        System.out.println(name1 == name2); // true!
        }

    } // eof
```

The reason to use the intern method is because you can use the comparison operator == to test for equality.

Strings are part of the java.lang package, so you can read more about their methods in the API at Sun.com. If you installed the documentation, which is highly recommended, then you can read it locally at JAVA_HOME\docs\index.html. Click on the java.lang package in the top-left frame, and then click on String in the bottom-left frame.

> **NOTE** To really look at the items we're going to discuss in this chapter, we will sometimes need to import classes defined in packages other than java.lang (which is available by default). We will look at importing and packages in the chapter on classes; for now, it just seemed polite to let you know why those import statements are sometimes at the top of the following code listings, and that the basic principle is the driving force behind the <cfimport> tag with which you may be familiar.

4.2.9 StringBuffers

It was mentioned in the previous section that strings are immutable. We have seen string concatenations in action, however. When you modify the value of a string, the compiler constructs a StringBuffer and uses its append() method to concatenate the values. A new String object is returned with the modified value. That means that, despite appearances, someString = someString.toLowerCase() does not modify the same object in memory that it seems to. Therefore, if you think you'll need to modify your string, you may want to create a StringBuffer. Once you have performed the manipulations on it, use the toString() method to bring it back to life as a String object.

4.2.10 `StringTokenizers`

A `StringTokenizer` takes a string and breaks it apart, assigning one token for each word boundary. That is, the string is read as whitespace-delimited.

4.2.11 `myStringTokenizer.java`

```
/* File: StringTokenizer.java
Purpose: Demos using string tokens to get at individual items
in a string
*/

import java.util.StringTokenizer;

public class myStringTokenizer {

    public static void main(String[] args) {

String text = "You clean that fish, Vardaman.";

StringTokenizer st = new StringTokenizer(text);

while (st.hasMoreTokens())
    System.out.println("this token: " + st.nextToken());
    }
}
```

You can also set your own delimiter by passing it into the method that constructs the `StringTokenizer` object (called a *constructor*). This is shown in the next listing, which also demonstrates another method of the `StringTokenizer` class:

4.2.12 `TokenizerChangeDelim.java`

```
/* File: TokenizerChangeDelim.java
Purpose: Demos using string tokens with defined delim
Author: E Hewitt
*/

import java.util.StringTokenizer;

public class TokenizerChangeDelim {

    public static void main(String[] args) {
```

```
String text = "\"You clean that fish, Vardaman,\"|said Pa.";

// the third arg tells whether to return the delimiter
StringTokenizer st = new StringTokenizer(text, "|", false);

while (st.hasMoreTokens())
   System.out.println(st.nextToken());

   System.out.println("tokens now left: " + st.countTokens());
   }
}
```

While these aren't really lists, you might quickly see that elements can be treated in this way, as you might treat a delimited list in ColdFusion. I'm thinking of `ListGetAt()` and `ListChangeDelims()`. Here is the output:

```
"You clean that fish, Vardaman,"
said Pa.
tokens now left: 0
```

Tokenizers are useful for interpreting lists of data. You may have to work with CSV or other like data.

4.3 Loops

Because custom functions are defined in ColdFusion script, you are likely to have written in this subset of the ColdFusion language. If you have, that is terrific, because writing loops in CFScript is almost identical to how you write loops and conditional logic statements in Java.

Because loops and conditional logic are a fundamental aspect of any programming language, there is little reason to do more here than examine the syntax, run some example programs so you can get a feel for it, and then move on.

4.3.1 The `for` Loop

The `for` loop is typically used to execute a code block a given number of times. The number of iterations is either known in advance or can be discerned at runtime. The syntax is like this:

```
for (initialization; test condition; update)
code to execute
```

Optionally, you can use curly brackets around the body of the loop:

```
for (initialization; test condition; update) {
        code to execute
}
```

The body (the code to be executed) will never be executed if the test condition initially evaluates to false.

> **NOTE** The most minimal `for` loop that can be written is: `for ( ; ; ) ;`, which would instigate an infinite loop.

A simple `for` loop looks like this:

```
int i;
int j = 10;

for (i = 1; i < j; i++) {
System.out.println("current value of i:" + i);

}
```

Excepting the `System.out.println` in place of the `WriteOutput`, this syntax is much like you would write in ColdFusion Script. However, Java also supports the use of multiple expressions in the initialization and update sections.

4.3.1.1 MULTIPLE EXPRESSIONS

The `for` loop supports the use of multiple expressions within its initialization section. The test condition section must be composed of an expression that evaluates to a single boolean value. This is legal...

```
for ( int i = 0, j = 1;  ;  ; )
```

...but it is uncommon to see it in practice, as one variable typically will appear in the initialization, test, and update sections of the loop as well as its body.

The following example creates the variable inside the initialization section of the loop, which is not only legal, but common:

```
for (int i = 1; i < 10; i++) {
System.out.println("current value of i:" + i);

}
```

This example also uses a literal value (10) inside the test condition section. When a variable is declared inside the initialization section of the loop in this manner, it is available only to the `for` statement in which it was created, and its body. For instance, this is not allowed:

```
for ( int i = 0; i < 10; i++ ) {
    // some code here
} // end for loop

System.out.print( "i is: " + i ); // error!
```

4.3.2 A Nested `for` Loop

As you would expect, you can nest loops, one inside the other. The following example shows how to create a multiplication table using nested loops.

4.3.3 `NestedFor.java`

```
/*
File: chp4.NestedFor.java
Purpose: demonstrates a nested for loop
   by printing multiplication table for 10
   also demos use of print()
 and escape character \t
Author: E Hewitt
*/

public class NestedFor {
    public static void main (String[] args) {
        int i;
        int j;

        // outer loop
        for (i = 1; i <= 10; i++){

            for (j = 1; j <= 10; j++){

                System.out.print(i * j + "\t");

            if (j == 10) System.out.println();

            }
        }
    }
} // eof
```

The listing NestedFor.java demonstrates a few new things. The first is the use of the print() method, which differs from the println() we have been using in that it does not create a carriage return/line feed. We also slipped in an if statement, which we will look at in the next section, though its meaning should be clear. Third, we concatenate to the result of the multiplication operation a string whose contents are \t. This is the escape sequence for a tab and ensures that the output will be evenly spaced.

There are a number of similar escape characters, as shown in Table 4.1.

TABLE 4.1 Special Character Escape Sequences

ESCAPE SEQUENCE	ITEM	UNICODE VALUE
\b	Backspace	\u0008
\n	Line feed	\u000a
\r	Carriage return	\u000d
\t	Tab	\0009
\'	Single quote	\u0027
\"	Double quote	\u0022
\\	Backslash	\u005c

4.3.4 continue

The continue keyword tells a loop to skip the current iteration if some boolean test returns true. Just as in CFScript, to perform this action, you simply write the keyword continue, as shown here:

```
// demos use of the continue keyword
// note that it's not a great idea to use
// continue in general.
public class LoopContinue {
    public static void main (String [] args) {
```

```
            for (int i=1; i < 100; i=i+1){
                if ((i % 4) != 0) {
                    // if the remainder is not 0
                    // then the number is not a
                    // multiple of 3
                continue;
                }
                System.out.println(i);
            }
        }
    }
```

As you are likely to recognize, it's not wonderful to use `continue`. While there are times when the data you are supplied necessitates it, using `continue` can be a sign of poorly written code. It's a band-aid job you generally shouldn't have to resort to.

4.3.5 The `while` Loop

The `while` loop, like the `for` loop, is a zero/many iterative loop. That means that the test condition is checked before the body is executed; if the test returns false, the loop will run zero times. Just as with `for` loops, the `while` loop in Java is strikingly similar to the ColdFusion Script `while`, as this listing shows:

4.3.6 `while.java`

```
// demos a while loop
public class LoopWhile {
    public static void main (String[] args) {
        int time = 10;
        int start = 1;

        while (time  >= start){
            System.out.println(time);
            // decrement the value
           time--;
        }
        System.out.println("Happy New Year!");
    }
}
```

4.3.7 The `do while` Loop

The `do while` loop, sometimes called a `do` loop, is a one/many iterative variant of the `while` loop. That means that the test condition is checked after the body is executed; if the test returns false, the body will be processed once. It is sometimes useful to be able to ensure that the code inside the loop executes at least once.

4.3.8 `LoopDoWhile.java`

```
public class LoopDoWhile {

    public static void main(String[] args){


int x;
do {

   System.out.println("Starting program...");
   x = (int) 2 + 2;
}

while (x != 4);

   System.out.println(x + " is 4");
 }
}
```

4.4 Arrays

Arrays work somewhat differently in Java than in ColdFusion. To begin with, they start at zero, rather than one. Second, once created, arrays cannot be resized.

All arrays in Java are one-dimensional. You can create multidimensional arrays as you would in ColdFusion by simply storing one array as the cell value of another. Arrays can be manipulated using the `java.util.Arrays` class, which exposes such methods as `equals()`, `fill()`, and `sort()`—all of which we use in upcoming code examples.

Arrays are references to objects. The arrays you create can be populated with primitive types or with references to objects.

4.4.1 Creating Arrays of Primitive Types

There are three steps to creating an array:

1. **Declare it.** Write the array identifier and the type it will hold.
2. **Instantiate it.** Create the array object itself with the new keyword.
3. **Initialize it.** Specify the value for each variable in the array. Before you do this, arrays will be populated with the default value for the declared type.

There are actually two different ways to declare an array:

1. `type [] identifier;`

   This should be familiar from `main(String[] args)`. Remember that spaces don't matter.

2. `type identifier [];`

   An example using this syntax is `main(String args [])`.

The first way is preferred, and it's the one I'll generally use. It is just easier to read and understand code when it is written this way.

Once you have declared an array, the compiler does not yet know how large the array is meant to be. Because it will hold references to objects of certain types, you must declare it to be a certain size (unlike in ColdFusion). When a new array is instantiated, it is populated with the default value specified by the type of data it will hold.

Because arrays themselves are objects, you create a new array using the new keyword and the type of data it will hold:

```
names = new int [10];
```

Arrays can be declared and instantiated in one statement too. The syntax is as follows:

```
type [] identifier = new type [length];
```

Here is an example:

```
char alphabet = new char [26];
```

Notice that you don't use the term "array"; the square brackets indicate that.

If you know in advance the specific values you want the array to hold, there is a way to do all of this work in one statement. That is, you can declare, instantiate, and initialize all at once:

```
type [] identifier = {values_or_expressions};
```

Here is an example:

4.4.2 Creating Arrays of Reference Types

Creating an array of objects requires the same steps as creating an array of primitive types. You still have to declare, instantiate, and initialize them, and the syntax for doing so is the same:

```
type [] identifier;
// or like this:
type identifier [];
```

Reference arrays are instantiated in the same manner as primitive arrays:

```
identifier = new type [length];
```

They can be declared and instantiated on one line, as well:

```
type [] identifier = new type [length];
```

Of course, instantiating an array of object references cannot create the objects themselves.

Arrays that hold references to objects are initialized with a default of null. A simple string example looks like this:

```
String [] names = {"Bill", "Scott", "Larry", "Jeremy"};
```

Let's say that we had an object called `Customer`. This object defines certain properties, such as CustomerID, FirstName, Gender, and so forth. Then let's imagine that to create an object of type `Customer` we could either send it values for FirstName and Gender, or just leave them blank if we don't know them yet. The CustomerID will be created by some internal process. We could create an array of different `Customer` objects like this:

```
Customer [] myCustomers = new Customer [3];
     // create the objects and populate the array
myCustomers[0] = new Customer();
myCustomers[1] = new Customer("Susan", 'F');
myCustomers[2] = new Customer{"Scott", 'M');
```

We could also have done this in one statement if we knew in advance what these values were going to be:

```
Customer [] myCustomers = {new Customer(),
    new Customer("Susan", 'F'),
    new Customer{"Scott", 'M') } ;
```

4.4.3 Arrays Are Objects

As mentioned before, arrays are objects, regardless of whether they hold primitive values or object references. Objects in Java have knowledge of their own states. The length of an array is therefore known to the array. The value of the length of any array is stored in the array object itself. This is necessary so that the JVM knows if you are trying to reference a cell that doesn't exist. Any attempt to reference, say, cell 50 of an array capable of holding only 25 cells throws an exception called an `ArrayIndexOutOfBounds`. Attempting to reference a null pointer results in a `NullPointerException`.

> **NOTE** Arrays in Java have an unalterable capacity. Once you state the number of cells an array will hold, you cannot change it for that array. This can be hard for ColdFusion developers to remember. It means, for instance, that you can't simply create an array without declaring the number of cells, and then add shopping cart items to it. You need to specify a number of cells in Java. As we will see, Java has many more data storage options than ColdFusion does. So it isn't a problem. In fact, it could encourage developers to write more deterministic programs.

Notice the subtle difference in the way that you can access the value of the length of strings and arrays. This is a very important difference, and understanding it now will save you a lot of hassles as you start writing programs. You can access the length of a given string by calling the `String` object's `length()` method. This method takes no parameters and is an action defined by the `String` class. It is called like this:

```
String name = "John";
name.length(); // 4
```

An array, however, stores its length as a public field. Which basically means that you reference it without parens:

```
String daysOfWeek [] = new String [7];
daysOfWeek.length // 7
```

The value is equal to the array length when declared. You will often make use of this property in looping, for example. The thing to notice is that `()` means you're making a method call and the absence of `()` means you are accessing a property. This can be confusing when you're getting the hang of things. The following example may make it easier to see. Let's go back to our `Customer` object:

```
Customer.name // refers directly to the name property
Customer.getName() // calls the method that defines the
                   // behavior for getting the name
```

Because you very likely have to use arrays with some frequency in ColdFusion, there is little reason to extol their virtues here. Let's just look at some Java code examples that show you how to do the kinds of things you normally have to do, such as populating an array, reading and modifying its data, sorting, and so forth. `Arrays1.java` also shows how to declare and instantiate an array.

4.4.4 Arrays1.java

```
/*  File: Arrays1.java
    Purpose: demo use of one dimensional array, performs
    various operations on the array, and outputs values
 */

public class Arrays1 {

    public static void main (String[] args){
        // DECLARE an array that holds numbers
        int [] myArray;

        // INSTANTIATE it; that is, create it
        // to hold a certain number of "cells"

        myArray = new int [5];

        /* loop over the array and output current
         * values. This proves that array values are
         * automatically initialized to 0.
         * Remember that Java arrays start at 0--not 1
         * as they do in CF.
         */

        for (int i = 0; i < myArray.length; i++){
         System.out.print("cell #" + i + ": " + myArray[i]
                    + ", ");
          }

        // now set values into the array.

        myArray[0] = 32799;
        myArray[1] = 6792;
```

```
        // use random() to generate a random number
        // cast to an int type, because random()
        // returns a double

        myArray[2] = (int) (Math.random()*100);

        // just to give us some space
        System.out.println();

        System.out.println(myArray[2]);

        // generate an error by referencing an array
        // index (cell) that is outside the bounds of
        // the array. In this case, that's anything
        // greater than 10. In every case, that's
        // anything less than 0.

        // System.out.println(myArray[140]); // ERROR!

        // create a new array, declaring AND instantiating
        // in one statement instead of two. This one will
        // hold character values and hold 26 values.

        char [] letters = new char [26];

        // create alphabet
        String alphabet = "abcdefghijklmnopqrstuvwxyz";

        for (int i = 0; i <= letters.length-1; i++){
            // set value of current cell to this character
            // in the alphabet

            letters[i] = alphabet.charAt(i);

            //output value of current array cell

            System.out.print(letters[i]);
        }

        // output the current length of the "letters"
        // array. use backslash to escape quote marks
System.out.println();
        System.out.println("length of the \"letters\" array "+
            "is: " + letters.length);
    }
}
```

`Arrays1`, whose interspersed comments should illustrate what's happening, will show you something like this output:

```
C:\jdk1.4\JavaForCF\chp4>java Arrays1
cell #0: 0, cell #1: 0, cell #2: 0, cell #3: 0, cell #4: 0,
42
abcdefghijklmnopqrstuvwxyz
length of the "letters" array is: 26
```

4.4.5 `ArrayLists`

You can work with an array as a delimited list as well. While `java.util.Arrays` defines an `asList` method, we can also use an `ArrayList`:

4.4.6 `ArraysList.java`

```
import java.util.ArrayList;

public class ArraysListTest {

public static void main(String[] arg) {

        // create new object of ArrayList type
        // call it 'a'
     ArrayList a = new ArrayList();
        // add items to the list.
     a.add(0,"thank you");
     a.add(1,"for shopping");

        // we could keep going, the array will
        // resize automatically like a CF array
     System.out.println(a.toString());

    }
}
```

One advantage to using an `ArrayList` is that you can manipulate the size of the internal array that stores the list. An `ArrayList` has a capacity, which is the size of the array that stores the list. The main difference, then, between an array and an `ArrayList` is that you can automatically grow the size of the `ArrayList`. This makes using an `ArrayList` more like using a ColdFusion array, which does not have a preset, unalterable size. An `ArrayList` is really a member of the set of Collections interfaces, and it is important to think of `ArrayLists` as Collections.

4.4.7 ArraysSearch.java

ArraysSearch.java shows you how to search and compare values inside an array.

```
/* File: ArraysSearch.java
Purpose: demo Array searching & comparison
Author: E Hewitt
*/

// import the java.util. package, which
// contains the Arrays class
// to handle sorting, searching, filling, and comparing.

import java.util.*;

public class ArraysSearch {
    public static void main (String [] dude){

        /* you can search a sorted array for a given key
         * returns the key's index. */

        // create a new array of chars
        char [] myArray = {'a', 'b', 'c', 'd', 'e', 'f', 'g'};

        int cIndex = Arrays.binarySearch(myArray, 'e');
        System.out.println(cIndex); // prints 4

        // create a new character array
        char [] a2 = {'l','m','n'};

        // is the new array equal to the old array?
        // equal here means that all elements have
        // same content, in same order
        boolean answer = Arrays.equals(myArray, a2);
        System.out.println(answer); // false

        char [] a3 = {'m','n','l'};
        answer = Arrays.equals(a2, a3);
        System.out.println(answer); // false

        Arrays.sort(a3);
        answer = Arrays.equals(a2,a3);
        System.out.println(answer); // true!

    }
}
```

Running `ArraysSearch` produces this output:

```
4
false
false
true
```

4.4.8 ArraysSort.java

```
/* File: ArraysSort.java
   Purpose: demos SORTING arrays
   Date: May 5 02
   Author: E Hewitt
*/

import java.util.*;

// get the java.util.Arrays class
// to handle sorting, searching, filling, and comparing.
// remember that the name is case-sensitive

public class ArraysSort {
    public static void main (String[] args){
        // declare, initialize, and instantiate
        // all on the same line:

        int [] IDs = {555, 333, 111, 444, 222};

        // print array
        for (int i = 0; i < IDs.length; i++){
            System.out.println(IDs[i]);
        }
        System.out.println("");

        // sort the array
        Arrays.sort(IDs);
        System.out.println(IDs[0] + "\n"); // prints 111

        int start = 2;
        int end = 4;
        Arrays.sort(IDs, start, end); // returns void
        // print the sorted array
```

```
        for (int i = 0; i < IDs.length; i++) {
            System.out.println(IDs[i]);
            }

    }
}
```

Running `ArraysSort` should give you this output:

```
555
333
111
444
222

111

111
222
333
444
555
```

4.4.9 ArraysFill.java

```
/* File: ArraysFill.java
Purpose: demonstrate default values and filling an array with
values.
Author: E Hewitt
*/

import java.util.*;

public class ArraysFill{
    public static void main(String [] args){
        int from = 2;
        int to = 5;
        // create an array
        // fill its data in indexes 2, 3, and 4 with 9s
        // other indexes will default to 0
        int [] a;
        a = new int[10];
```

```
        Arrays.fill(a, from, to, 9);
        System.out.println(a[2] + " " + a[0]); // prints 9 0

        // be careful: java will do the math, not
        // simply print the values concatenated
        System.out.println(a[2] + a[3]); // prints 18

        boolean [] aB = new boolean[10];
        System.out.println(aB[5]);

        // boolean arrays default to false;
        // fill with all trues:
        Arrays.fill(aB, true);
        System.out.println(aB[0] + " " + aB[9]);

        // remember that 9 is the last cell
        // since they start at 0 instead of 1
    }
}
```

This is the output produced by `ArraysFill`:

```
9 0
18
false
true true
```

This program simply demonstrates the default values that populate an array and shows how they can be modified. It also demonstrates the return type of many operations of this sort. Populating data structures in Java often returns a `boolean` indicating the success of the operation, not the value inserted.

4.4.10 Multidimensional Arrays

So far we've looked at only one-dimensional arrays. There are many times, maybe when you're implementing a shopping cart or writing a nifty program that prints a series of characters in some rectangular pattern on the screen, that you need more than one dimension. Multidimensional arrays work in somewhat similar fashion to ColdFusion two- and three-dimensional arrays.

To create a two-dimensional array, just add another set of `[]` into the declaration:

```
type [][] identifier = new type [first_size][second_size];
```

You do not have to instantiate all of the dimensions at once, but if you don't, then you must instantiate the top-level array first. For instance, this is okay:

```
int a [][] = new int[4][]; // okay
```

and so is this:

```
int a[][] = new int[4][5]; // okay
```

but this isn't:

```
int a [][] = new int [][5]; // error
```

Once we discuss conditional logic, we will write a sample program that puts multidimensional arrays to work.

4.5 Conditional Logic

Conditional logic can be represented in Java much as you would represent it in CFScript. There are `if/else` constructs as well as `switch/case` constructs. Let's look at these in turn.

4.5.1 The `if` Statement

There is little difference between how you write an `if/else` block in Java from how you write it in CFScript. While the `<cfelseif>` tag can lead one to believe otherwise, there is no specific `elseif` statement; instead, you use `else if`.

4.5.2 `Retirement.java`

```
/* shows use of if/else if, else
 * works very much as in <cfscript>
 */

// declare a new class called Retirement
class Retirement {

// the main method is the start point for program processing
// it accepts an array of strings called "args" (arguments)
   public static void main(String[] args) {

// create a new integer called age
// because the argument comes in as a string,
// we have to parse it into a corresponding integer value
```

```
// using the parseInt() method of the Integer wrapper class

        int age = Integer.parseInt(args[0]);

// print a different statement based on the value of age

        if (age < 50) {
            System.out.println("You are too young to
            retire.");
        }

        else if (age > 50 && age < 65) {
            System.out.println("You should start thinking
            about retirement.");
        }
        else {
            System.out.println("How's your golf game?");
        }
    }
}
```

The comments in the `Retirement.java` program explain different aspects of the program such as using the Integer wrapper class. The conditional logic itself is very straightforward and requires no explanation—based on the value of `age`, a different statement is printed to the command line.

If you simply compile and run `Retirement.java`, you will get an error such as this:

```
C:\jdk1.4\JavaForCF\chp4>java Retirement
Exception in thread "main"
java.lang.ArrayIndexOutOfBoundsException
        at Retirement.main(Retirement.java:17)
```

This tells you that while Java was executing your `main` method it found itself in a state from which it could not recover. Items in the `java.lang` package throw an `ArrayIndexOutOfBoundsException`, which is something you might see often. The corresponding error that you may have seen in ColdFusion tells you "cannot reference array at index [x]." It means that you have made programmatic reference to an array cell that doesn't exist.

Examining the program, the square brackets (`[]`) indicate an array much like they do in ColdFusion. `Retirement.java` makes reference to a value at index `0` of the `args` array. This is the array of strings that the `main` method always can accept as arguments. You can actually call the array whatever you like, but `args` is often used by convention. For now, it is good to know that you can avoid this error by supplying an age at the command line when you run the program. Just as `javac` demands as an argument the name of the file you want to compile, our retirement program needs an age to test for. Try running the program again, like this:

```
java Retirement 30
```

Then try substituting different ages to see the different messages. Of course, a real program should have complete error handling to account for users entering a negative value, a value over 110, a non-numeric value, and so on.

4.5.3 The `switch` Statement

`Switch/case` usage is similarly quick to pick up. It has one caveat for programmers used to CFScript, however—your test condition must be an integral type (`char`, `int`, etc.). The following program demonstrates two key things. First, it shows how similar using Java switches is to using them in ColdFusion. The syntax is identical. It also shows how you need to do a little working around to accommodate the fact that Java will only switch against integral types.

4.5.4 `SwitchSuperHero.java`

```
/* File: SwitchSuperHero.java
   Purpose: demonstrates how to switch. Remember that you can
     only switch against BYTE, SHORT, INT, or CHAR
*/

public class SwitchSuperHero {
    public static void main (String[] args) {

//supply the code for your superhero
// 101 is Superman
// 102 is WonderWoman
// 103 is Spidey

int Superman = 101;
int WonderWoman = 102;
int Spidey = 103;

int hero = Integer.parseInt(args[0]);
```

```
            switch (hero) {
                case 101 :
                    System.out.println("He is the man of steel");
                    break;
                case 102:
                    System.out.println("She has a magic lasso"
                        + " and an invisible plane");
                    break;
                case 103:
                    System.out.println("Spiderman does whatever a
spider can");
                    break;

// calling with any other number prints this default:
                   System.out.println("I have no knowledge of that
superhero");
            }
        }
}
```

Running and output:

```
C:\jdk1.4\JavaForCF\chp4>java SwitchSuperHero 103
Spiderman does whatever a spider can
```

4.5.5 SwitchWithConvert.java

```
/* same as SwitchWithText, but shows
 * how to cast the arg into a char
 * so it can be switched against.
 * Therefore demos use of the charAt() method.
 * Also allows that program may be run without
 * an argument being passed by embedding the switch
 * in an if/else.
 */

public class SwitchWithConvert {
    public static void main (String[] args) {

     if (args.length > 0) {
           char option;
```

```
        // "option" value from command line arg
        // so we need to convert to char

        option = args[0].charAt(0);

        switch (option) {
        case 'h' :
            System.out.println("I am the help file...");
            break;
        case 'v' :
            System.out.println("This is the verbose option"
                + " that shows you everything as it happens.");
            break;
        case 'o' :
           System.out.println("Currently available options:");
           System.out.println("h --prints the Help file");
           System.out.println("v --runs in Verbose mode");
           System.out.println("o --displays this Option list");
            break;


         default:
            System.out.println("Error: Invalid option.");
            }
         }
         // no args passed
         else {
             System.out.println("You are runnning the program"
                + " without passing arguments.");
         }
    }
}
```

4.5.6 SwitchNoBreaks.java

```
/*    File: SwitchNoBreaks
Purpose: reminds us that switch requires break stmt or else all
of them run
this behavior is precisely how CFScripts handle switches
*/

class SwitchNoBreaks {
```

```
    public static void main (String[] args) {
        // accept an arg from the command line
        // remember that args come in as strings
        int number = Integer.parseInt(args[0]);

        // can only switch against ints
        switch (number) {
            case 1:
                System.out.println("You chose 1");

            case 2:
                System.out.println("You chose 2");

           default: System.out.println("I don't have a message
about that value.");
        }
    }
}
```

Here is the output with the argument `1` supplied:

```
C:\jdk1.4\JavaForCF\chp4>java SwitchNoBreaks 1
You chose 1
You chose 2
I don't have a message about that value.
```

As you can see, just as in CFScript, not using the `break` statement causes all of the conditions to run.

4.6 Example Program: `CheckerBoard.java`

The following program will demonstrate using a two-dimensional array. It populates a checkerboard with red pieces and black pieces where they are supposed to go and prints it to the screen. This incorporates many of the programming structures we've looked at in this chapter, including loops, conditional logic, and two-dimensional arrays.

4.6.1 CheckerBoard.java

```
/*      File: CheckerBoard.java
        Purpose: demo using multidimensional arrays,
                loops, and conditional logic all in one.
                Prints a checker board.
```

```
        Author: E Hewitt
*/

import java.util.*;
public class CheckerBoard {
    public static void main (String [] args) {

        // initialize some vars to loop with
        int x = 0;
        int y = 0;

        char board[][] = new char[8][8];
        // populate red

        for (x = 0; x<=7; x++) {

                for (y = 0; y <=7; y++) {

                        // make red
                        if (x == 0 || x == 1)
                        board[x][y] = 'r';

                        // make empties
                        else if (x > 1 && x < 6)
                                board[x][y] = '.';

                        // make black
                        else
                                board[x][y] = 'b';

                        // print the current cell

                        System.out.print(board[x][y]);

                        // start a new row
                        if (y == 7) {System.out.println();}
                }
        }

        }
} //eof
```

The output looks like this:

```
rrrrrrrr
rrrrrrrr
........
........
........
........
bbbbbbbb
bbbbbbbb
```

This is a useful program to play around with so that you get comfortable using arrays, nested loops, and so forth. You can imagine how this could be extended, once you're writing objects, to create the start of a real checkers game program.

4.7 Example Program: Debt Calculator

While the checkerboard program is a hoot, it is not necessarily very useful. Let's write another program that is a bit more realistic, again with the aim of tying together many of the concepts we have learned thus far. The program we will write is a debt calculator. It will take a few variables, such as the amount of debt you've got, your income, and the interest rate, and the program will figure out how many years it will take you to pay it off. In so doing, it makes use of different variable types (including constants and typecasting), logical and mathematical operations and varying notation, conditional logic, and loops.

Here's a more specific overview. The purpose of the program is to calculate the number of years it will take to pay off a debt with accruing interest. There are a few variables required to perform this calculation: debt, income, expenses, and the interest rate. These are `int`s, except for the interest rate, which is a `final double`.

By subtracting expenses from income, we get an amount available to pay toward the debt (`savings`). The interest is added to the amount of debt and a `while` loop is set up to determine the number of years required to pay off that debt with that amount of savings at that interest rate. The interest compounds while the savings never gets any bigger, which creates a variety of possible payment scenarios. There are certain cases in which the debt will effectively never get paid off; in these cases, the program informs the user that they may be enjoying themselves, but they can never pay it off. In other cases, the debt could conceivably get paid off, but it might take longer than 50 years to do so. In these situations it is possible that, given the human life span, the user may die before paying off the debt completely. So we notify the user of this possibility after showing the effect of the first 50 years of payment.

Here is the code:

4.7.1 DebtApp.java

```
/*
File: DebtApp.java
Purpose: demonstrates a semi-realistic debt calculating
         program
Author: E Hewitt
*/

public class DebtApp {

    public static void main(String[] args){

    // declare vars
    int income, expenses, debt, interest, savings, payment;

    byte years;

    // initialize vars

    income = 115000;
    expenses = 82000;
    debt = 149000;

    // interest rate won't change in here

    final double INTEREST_RATE = 7.25;

    // this will hold the current year

    years = 1;

    // we'll put toward the debt what we have
    // left over from salary after expenses are paid

    savings = income - expenses;
    payment = savings;


if (expenses >= income ||
```

```
        ((INTEREST_RATE / 100 * debt) > (income - expenses))) {

      System.out.println("You are living the life. But...");
      System.out.println("Your debt will never be paid off.");
}


else {
          System.out.println("You started $" + debt +" in debt");
          System.out.println("You pay $" + payment + " against
the debt each year");

// make a new line spacer just for readability
          System.out.println();

// as long as there is more debt, calculate what
// remains to be paid

while ( debt > payment) {

// cast the interest to an int so we can work with it
// more easily, and pennies don't matter

   interest = (int) ((INTEREST_RATE / 100) * debt);

// debt is debt + interest

   debt += interest;

   System.out.println("You are paying $" + interest + " in
           interest alone.");
   System.out.println("Total debt including interest: $" +
debt);

// debt is debt - this payment

   debt -= payment;

   System.out.println("You still owe $" + debt +" in year "+
years);

// spacer
System.out.println();
```

```
// tell them if it is just fruitless

    if (years >= 50) {

       System.out.println("Your payments can't keep up with
              your interest.");
        System.out.println("At this rate, it will probably
               take longer than you've got.");
            break;
            }

    // increment years
    ++years;

          }
       }
    }
}
```

Here is the output with these particular numbers:

```
C:\jdk1.4\JavaForCF\chp4>javac DebtApp.java

C:\jdk1.4\JavaForCF\chp4>java DebtApp
You started $149000 in debt
You pay $33000 against the debt each year

You are paying $10802 in interest
Total debt including interest: $159802
You still owe $126802 in year 1

You are paying $9193 in interest
Total debt including interest: $135995
You still owe $102995 in year 2

You are paying $7467 in interest
Total debt including interest: $110462
You still owe $77462 in year 3

You are paying $5615 in interest
Total debt including interest: $83077
You still owe $50077 in year 4
```

```
You are paying $3630 in interest
Total debt including interest: $53707
You still owe $20707 in year 5
```

That is the end of the output, as the user's payments can now overcome the debt and pay it off.

Let's take a moment to look at some of the more interesting aspects of the program. The `(int)` cast will automatically lose the decimal places introduced by the interest `double`. That is just fine here, because we don't want to deal with pennies, and it will make our output more attractive and readable. It is important to remember that the cast is necessary because the constant `INTEREST_RATE` is a `double`, and the compiler will worry that you will lose precision you might need without a cast—both `interest` and `debt` are `int`s.

You may find it fruitful to work with this program a bit. Try modifying it in different ways to get used to how things work. For instance, you could add a savings account into the mix that also grows interest, which helps reduce the debt more quickly. You could modify the program to accept values such as the current debt and salary as arguments from the command line. Then, if the program receives no arguments, print out a help menu (the set of arguments the program accepts). To get an idea of what a help menu looks like, try typing `javac` at the command line. `javac` prints a list of argument options.

4.8 Command Line Input

Generally, arguments are sent to programs run on the command line by simply typing them after the name of the program you're about to run. The program will likely expect them in a certain order. For instance, think of modifying the `DebtApp` program to accept debt, expenses, and income values: the program will expect the values in a certain order. We could modify the program to accept first income, then expenses, then debt. Instead of hardcoding these values inside the program, which requires you to retype inside the code (which could be dangerous), and then recompile the program (which takes time), you could pass them in as arguments. Here is how we had it written inside the `DebtApp` class:

```
...
        // initialize vars

        income = 115000;
        expenses = 82000;
        debt = 149000;
...
```

Now at first glance, it might seem okay to write the following:

```
// initialize vars

income = args[0];
expenses = args[1];
debt = args[2];      // won't work!
```

That's because Java needs `ints` for each of those values, and although we are correctly referencing the cells in the `args` array, these are strings. So we have to parse them; this should do the trick:

```
// convert Strings to ints
income = Integer.parseInt(args[0]);
expenses = Integer.parseInt(args[1]);
debt = Integer.parseInt(args[2]);
```

Then recompile the program and call it, supplying values for each of the three arguments, like this:

```
C:\jdk1.4\JavaForCF\chp4>java DebtApp 115000 117000 105000
You are living the life...
But your debt will never be paid off.
```

The program runs and prints the output. But now you can call it again with different values, and you don't have to recompile.

4.9 Using Methods: Toward Object-Oriented Programming

While the next chapter is really devoted to understanding OOP and planning OOP applications, this chapter would not be complete without a discussion of methods. This will give us a flavor for objects.

So far we have only discussed procedural programs; that is, programs that work from top to bottom, like a browser reads HTML. Once we're inside the `main()` method, the program executes top to bottom with no break or redirection. It has been very straightforward.

This approach has been very useful, but one can quickly see that it is not very extensible. Creating programs that had all of their code behavior written inline would be a nightmare to update later, and it would be extraordinarily difficult to reuse any of your code.

As in ColdFusion, there are a number of reasons to define methods to handle specific tasks. It encourages you to organize your code, and it makes it easier for you and others to read your work when well-named methods handle discrete, clear tasks.

Using class-specific methods also encourages object orientation. Just because we're writing Java code doesn't mean our code is object oriented. Methods allow you to define methods that get and set data in an object (`get` is approximately like `SELECT` and `set` is approximately like `UPDATE`). Many objects define `private` data, which means that only methods defined in the object's class can modify it.

4.9.1 Method Naming Conventions

Like data and classes in Java, there are naming conventions for methods. Typical conventions are as follows:

- Do not use an underscore.
- Use verbs or verb phrases to describe the operation the method represents.
- Start your method name lowercase and then use an uppercase first letter for each subsequent word in your method name.

The following are examples of well-named methods:

- `getPrice()`
- `square()`
- `setProductID()`

By contrast, the following are poorly named methods:

- `price()`
- `Square()`
- `set_product_id()`

Let's take a look at how you define methods, and how you call them.

4.9.2 Declaring Methods

Methods are all defined the same way, whether they are built in or are defined by the programmer. Any class you write can define zero or more methods. What can be difficult to remember when making the transition to Java from a non-object-oriented background is that the order in which you define your methods is indifferent. This is perhaps similar to writing a user-defined function library in ColdFusion—you can create a page called `lib.cfm` and write all of your application functions in there, then `<cfinclude>` it. When you call the function determines when it is processed in the application. This is how it works in Java.

All methods are defined in the same manner:

```
modifiers   return_type   method_identifier ([arguments]) {

     method_body
}
```

You can open the method body with curly braces on the first line or on their own line. It doesn't make a difference. Just do what you find more easily readable. Let's take a look at each of the parts of the method declaration.

The modifier first defines the *access type* for the method; the access type declares what the visibility of the method is. Possible values are `public`, `private`, `protected`, or `default`.

The second kind of modifier defines the *method type*. Possible values are `static`, `final`, and `abstract`.

Next, the method declaration states its *return type*. A method will typically perform some calculation or modify an object, and then it may return something. It might just perform some operation and not return a value at all. It might also return the result of a calculation, or return a modified object. A method can return only one value. As with a ColdFusion UDF, use the return keyword to send the value back to the calling method. The return type specifies the type of the value that the method will return, for instance, `char`, `String`, `int`, or the name of an object type such as `File`. `return` specifies a single value, or an expression, which will be evaluated before being returned. The keyword `void` indicates that the method does not return anything. The parentheses surrounding the return value or expression are optional. For example, both of the following are legal:

```
return (x * x); // okay
return x*x; // okay
```

Because a method returns only one value, the following is illegal:

```
return(x*x, y+2); // illegal
```

Next comes the *method identifier*. This is simply the name that you want to call the method.

Inside the parentheses you define the argument list that the method will accept. A method can accept zero or more arguments, each of which must be of a specified type. Arguments, as in ColdFusion functions, are changeable information that get passed into a method so that some processing can be done with them. If a method accepts no arguments, the parentheses are necessary anyway.

Arguments are supplied by writing first the type and then the identifier. Each set of type-identifier arguments must be separated by a comma:

```
public void setAge(int age) { ...

public void checkTicket(String event, java.util.Date
       eventDate, int seatNumber) { ...
```

We will look at parameters supplied to methods in more detail later, when we discuss objects and classes.

4.10 Visibility

Visibility is similar to "scope" in ColdFusion and other languages such as Visual Basic. Everything in a program is not visible to every other thing all of the time. That is a prescription for chaos in code maintainability, encapsulation, and readability. In order to ensure the integrity of your data and the operations you perform on them, you declare classes, methods, and data as having certain visibility. You do that using access modifiers.

4.10.1 Access Modifiers

Access modifiers are composed of Java keywords that describe how something is stored or how it runs. Access modifiers are used in declaring variables (data *fields*), methods, and classes. They determine what level of access the item will allow. That is, an access modifier determines where other methods or classes must be located to make use of this method or class. Possible values for access modifiers are `private`, `protected`, and `public`.

`private:` Any programmatic feature declared `private` will not be visible to other classes. This is the strictest level of access. Fields in a class should generally be declared private to ensure that they are only accessed or modified by methods defined to do so. A method that is private can only be called from other methods in the same class.

`protected:` A protected item restricts a method or class to use only by its subclasses.

`public:` Whatever is declared public is visible to the world; that is, the field or method or class can be called from any other class. Most methods are public, and the methods we will write in the next few chapters will generally be public.

NOTE "Default" is not a possible value for an access modifier. It is not a keyword, but a concept for describing the access permissions when no access modifier is specified. By default, features have package-level visibility. We will look more at packages later, but essentially a package is a directory in which a class resides. To declare a feature with package visibility, you don't need to use any modifier.

There are three possible values for the type modifier: `static`, `final`, and `abstract`.

4.10.1.1 `static` METHODS

A `static` *method* is a method that does not operate on an object. It is associated with the class that defines it and does not need an object to do its work. For instance, the `equals()` method of the `String` class requires an object on which to operate—making a comparison requires a thing to compare with another thing. On the other hand, consider the `max()` method defined in `java.lang.Math`. This method takes two numeric arguments and returns the greater value:

```
public static int max(int a, int b)
```

`max()` is declared `static` because it doesn't get called on a particular object; you can just call it when you need it.

`static` methods are useful for doing two things. The first, as mentioned, is when the method doesn't need access to the state of an object because you can supply the parameters explicitly, as with `max()`. The second reason to declare a method `static` is when it only needs access to the `static` fields of the class.

4.10.1.2 `final` METHODS

Methods are declared `final` in order to prevent an extended class from overriding the method. An important feature of OOP and Java is that the programmer can define certain functionality in a parent class, and then write classes that inherit its properties and extend its functionality. The programmer can override a method by defining it in a different way than the parent does. Declaring a method `final` prevents this.

The benefit to declaring a method `final` is that you can be certain of its implementation. You can declare classes, as well as methods, `final`. A class declared `final` cannot be extended at all, which limits its usefulness. On the other hand, you may not want people to have a large degree of flexibility when implementing your authorization classes, for example. One way to balance the need for security and extensibility is to leave the class open and mark the methods as `final`.

> **NOTE** The `java.lang.String` class is `final`. It can never be subclassed. If it could be subclassed, you could create your own `String` methods—say, `setCharAt()`—that could rewrite `String` objects. This would open a serious security hole, because you could, for instance, write an applet that gained access to otherwise restricted system files, thereby destroying the "sandbox" applets run in.

4.10.1.3 `abstract` METHODS

Abstract things lack concreteness. That is, you cannot create an object from an abstract class, just as you cannot find a concrete instance of something abstract in the world, such as the economy. There is no such *thing* as the economy; pretending like there is helps us organize things that are real, such as Alison's 50 pounds British sterling and Zoe's 100 shares of Macromedia stock. There is no "animal"; but there are individual lions, tigers, and bears. Abstract classes in Java operate under a similar principle. To translate the above reasoning into Java basically means that you cannot do this: `new Economy();`.

Any class with abstract methods must itself be declared `abstract`. This helps someone reading your code to quickly discover that the class is `abstract` without having to search all of the methods.

If this all seems a bit abstruse right now, that's okay. It is good to just know why you are writing all of those Java keywords when you make a new class or write a new method. We will look at all of this again when we discuss classes and objects.

4.11 Composition of the `main` Method

Let's take a moment to look at the now familiar `main` method and break it apart to see how it is composed. The purpose of the `main` method is to have a starting place for programs to execute. So far all of the code we have written has been confined to one class file. As our programs grow in complexity, we will define different classes distributed in different files to handle particular aspects of the programs' work.

```
public static void main(String[] args)  {
    ...
}
```

The main method is declared public. That means that it is accessible by other classes. It is also static. Remember that static methods are called on a class, not on an object. main is necessarily static because at the start of a program's execution, no objects exist. main starts, and the code written inside its body instantiates the objects and calls the methods required to execute the program.

In the argument list, (String[] args), we see that main accepts one argument: an array whose cells hold String objects. Referencing the cells of this array gives you access to the arguments passed in from the command line.

The purpose of the main method is to start program execution, so a program may have only one main method.

> **NOTE** It is legal to have one main method per class. Sometimes programmers will write a main method into every class for unit testing. Instead of having to run the entire application, you can find bugs in confined parts of a program by simply calling the main method to execute the class you want to test.

4.11.1 Calling Methods

Let's write a couple of programs that offload some of the program's work into methods.

4.11.2 Square1.java

```
/* this program tells you the square of a hardcoded int and
   demonstrates how to write a program that
   calls a method other than main.
*/

class Square1 {

// execution starts here
    public static void main (String [] args) {

// define a number to square
    int number = 3;
```

```
// 'answer' holds the result of the method call
// to square(), which calculates the square of the number
// passed to it as an argument

    int answer = square(number);

// now we call the 'show' method to display the result
show(answer);

     }  // the program processing really ends here.
        // the remainder of the program just defines these
        // methods we're calling

// square() method accepts an int and returns an int
    public static int square(int x) {
        return x * x;
    }

// show() method accepts an int and prints it out
    public static void show(int result) {
        System.out.println("The answer is " + result);
    }
}
```

`Square1.java` can be compiled and run to produce this output:

```
The answer is 9
```

As you can see, defining methods changes the structure of your program a bit. While the comments in the program should explain what's happening fairly well, the main thing to notice is the end of the program. After calling `show(answer)`, we close the `main` method with a }, stopping execution of the program. Our methods, `square()` and `show()`, are defined below that. This is perhaps similar to defining a file called `lib.cfm` that holds several custom functions for a ColdFusion application, and including them in the template that you need to call them from.

The `square()` and `show()` methods as defined in `Square1.java` are *class-level* methods. They do not have an object associated with them. They are defined as part of the class itself.

The `square()` method is defined with this code block:

```
public static int square(int x) {
        ...
}
```

The method is declared public, which means that it is accessible anywhere that the class is accessible.

The static access modifier indicates that the method is a class-level method and that the method is not associated with an object. Such methods are invoked on behalf of the class and are meant to perform general sorts of tasks. For instance, our square() method is static for a couple of reasons. First, we don't have any objects (we'll get to those later). However, even if this program did create some objects, we could still reasonably declare a square() method as static because it might not make sense to associate it with an instance of an object. A static method only has access to the static fields and other static methods of its class. non-static members must be accessed via an object, and static methods do not have an available object reference.

Populating the return position of our method declaration is int, indicating that the method will return a value of type int.

Then we name the method square and open a parens for the arguments.

Arguments are written as (type identifier). So, this method accepts an int called x. If x existed previously in the program, we could just refer to the identifier, as we recall from using the println() method of System.out:

```
String msg = "Hello, dude.";

 System.out.println(msg);
```

The body of the method defines the statements that do the work of the method. We could have written a more verbose square() method to demonstrate how statements might work in a method body:

```
public static int square(int x) {

// statements making up the method body:
    int y = x * x;

    return y;
}
```

This makes a nice way to demonstrate the difference between the return statement and the method body, but otherwise there is certainly no advantage to adding this unnecessary complexity.

It does, however, bring up an important point. As with loops, variables declared inside a method are only available to that method. For instance, this is illegal:

```
...       } // end main

    public static int square(int x) {

int y = x*x;
return y;
    }

    public static void show(int ans) {
        System.out.println("The answer is " + ans);
        System.out.println("y is: " + y); // ERROR!
    }
```

The compiler does not have access to the value of `y` because it was declared inside the body of the `square()` method.

Here is a slightly revised version of the `Square` program. It now accepts an argument to be squared and features a touch of handling in the event that no argument is passed. If the argument is an integer, processing continues normally.

4.11.3 Square2.java

```
/* just like Square1, but accept an arg from cmd line
   as int to square
   also demonstrates use of Integer.parseInt
*/

public class Square2 {

    public static void main(String[] args) {

/* add some conditional logic in case user
   does not supply an argument
   so our program doesn't just
   inelegantly fail
*/

if (args.length == 0) {

// no argument supplied
```

```
        String msg = "Please supply a number for me to square.
        Thank you.";

        System.out.println(msg);

    } // end if



    else {


    // convert passed number to an int.
    // we had to move this guy down here so it's inside the else
            int number = Integer.parseInt(args[0]);

    // make a new int to hold the result of
    // calling the square method on the number
            int answer = square(number);

    // print to the command line
            show(answer);


    } // end else

        } // end main

    method declarations same...

    }
```

This revised version of `Square1` is just a little more realistic and combines a few of the things we've learned in this chapter. What would be nice is if we could determine what type of item is being passed into the method. We can do that, and if you type an argument that cannot be converted to an `int`, Java will throw a `java.lang.IllegalNumberFormat` exception. In order to deal with this, we would want to catch and throw the exception, which we will do later.

While we have not discussed objects much yet, the following simple program will perhaps help demonstrate how putting the work of your program into discrete methods can be valuable, and how simple it can be to use methods.

This program, called `SquareAndCube`, simply takes an integer and does two different things with it: the `square()` method squares it and the `cube()` method cubes it.

4.11.4 SquareAndCube.java

```
/* File: SquareAndCube.java
Purpose: demonstrate using a method other than main,
defining two different methods that each perform
different tasks with the same value.
Notes: Must be passed an int
Author: E Hewitt
*/

public class SquareAndCube {

    public static void main (String [] args) {

        int number = Integer.parseInt(args[0]);

        int theSquare = square(number);
        int theCube = cube(number);

        showSquare(theSquare);
        showCube(theCube);
    }

    // the square method returns the square
    public static int square(int x) {
        return x*x;
    }

    // the cube method returns the cube
    public static int cube(int x) {
        return x*x*x;
    }

    // the showSquare method will display
    // a string and the result of the square() method
    public static void showSquare(int ans) {
        System.out.println("The square is: " + ans);
    }

    // the showCube method will display
```

```
        // a string and the result of the cube() method
        public static void showCube(int ans) {
            System.out.println("The cube is: " + ans);
        }

    }
```

Here is the output from running the program.

```
C:\jdk1.4\JavaForCF\chp4>java SquareAndCube 6
The square is: 36
The cube is: 216
```

While `SquareAndCube` defines no objects, it does encapsulate the operations of the program into small methods that perform simple tasks. This is good practice for the upcoming discussion of objects. A primary challenge of writing a Java program is often determining what methods you will need, but once you've done that, it is perhaps a relief to find that the methods themselves are often fairly simple.

4.12 What's Next?

By now, we have seen the basic programming components of the Java programming language. You are able to make simple but realistic programs using many of the same programming constructs you are used to using in ColdFusion. Perhaps the only significant difference so far has been that you are writing programs instead of Web applications. Many of the tools we have used are the same—loops, conditional logic, and so forth.

In the next chapter we will look at object-oriented programming and design principles and notation. This will allow us to begin planning OOP projects and start us really thinking in terms of objects. Now we will start to see stark distinctions between what OOP programming in Java means and how you may be used to writing ColdFusion applications. If you are chiefly used to writing ColdFusion, this stage can require a paradigm shift in how you think about making applications.

5

Object-Oriented Application Design

In this chapter we will step back from the syntax of the Java language. At this point you should have enough knowledge of Java basics to write simple applications. But so far, we have not actually written an object-oriented application, and we have not done anything that we couldn't do more easily in ColdFusion.

This chapter is devoted to determining what objects are, what object-oriented programming and object-oriented application design are, how these concepts relate to building programs, and why they are important. We will also see how to plan and represent your programs' features using the Unified Modeling Language.

You probably have strong systems analytical skills given your background in ColdFusion. However, if UML is new to you, I strongly suggest you read this chapter—especially since we will also be introducing objects and classes at a conceptual level that we will rely on later.

5.1 Objects

ColdFusion 5 introduced user-defined functions, which allowed us to write functions much as we would in JavaScript. In the Java programming language, functions are often referred to as methods. One way of making a distinction between them is that a function can be declared (as in ColdFusion) in a vacuum of sorts—it needn't always refer to any other thing or be part of any other thing (such as an object or a class). ColdFusion allows us to write user-defined functions that stand on their own, and the language defines many such functions.

Specific objects (or classes) define specific methods, and you can only use them when you have access to them. When you call a static method like `Integer.parseInt()`, you are *not* using an instance of the Integer class. Static methods are methods of classes, not objects. No integer object is necessary to call its static methods, and even if you have an instance, a static method is always called on the class, not the object.

Probably the easiest way to start thinking about object orientation is to think of things in the world, since programs are generally written to represent real things in the world. While you probably do this already in ColdFusion, this is also where the major difference between ColdFusion and Java comes into play. For example, if you were designing a ColdFusion application for a car manufacturer, you would likely create a database design, modelling your database in such a way that you would be able to represent everything your program needed to know about cars. Different tables would hold data about different aspects of the model. The car table might need to hold information about the make, model, year, color, and so on. A database design defines a representation of something in the world that will be interrogated by your program. A good design can answer all of the questions that will be asked of it in a timely fashion.

While databases are frequently used in Java programs, there is another layer of abstraction to help you model your data at the programmatic level: the object.

One way that might help you start thinking in terms of objects is to think about how you are used to representing data in a database. Instead of defining only the fields (that is, the data that your object contains), you also define what the object is capable of doing (the methods). This is where things start to depart dramatically from working with ColdFusion. Generally, the database defines the data and the CF code defines what you do with it. In Java, the data and what can be done with the data are both stored in objects. Classes are templates for making objects.

NOTE There are, of course, object-relational databases and object-oriented databases that store data in a hierarchical manner. One such popular database is PostgreSQL, which is an object-relational database—sometimes called a relational database capable of object-oriented extensions. That means that the database holds data, but that the concept of the table is extended as a class. Classes contain attributes (the columns), which are defined as a set (the table). The difference is that classes can inherit from other classes, which makes the model not only relational but also logically hierarchical. You can also define functions inside the database itself using either an internal language or an external language (such as C).

PostgreSQL is gaining more interest among ColdFusion users. It began as a project of the University of California at Berkeley in the late 1970s. There, a team created one of the early relational databases in a project called Ingres. The Ingres code base was peddled by a company named Ingres that tried to break into the database market. In the late 1980s, a team led by Michael Stonebraker developed the code into an object-relational database, which was also turned into a commercial product called Illustra. Informix later purchased the Illustra company and merged the code into its database product. As the academic project continued, the code base for PostgreSQL remained distinct. It is currently open-source and free. You can download PostgreSQL from *www.postgresql.org*.

A car, a person, and a ball are all objects. These objects all have certain things that you can do only with them. For instance, a car object might define methods for start, accelerate, and brake. When trying to determine how to write your program in Java, you need to determine what objects you need to represent the problem domain that your program addresses.

5.2 Why Software Projects Fail

Seventy percent of software projects fail. Seventy. There are a number of reasons for this. Some of these reasons are just as insidious in Web application projects. Understanding and avoiding these pitfalls is crucial to the success of your project.

5.2.1 Inadequate Gathering of Requirements

Gathering requirements is very important to a project. Because it sounds almost too obvious to state, many programmers even overlook this stage for smaller projects. In my view, conducting smart interviews of the important players in the problem domain in order to arrive at the true requirements for a system is *the* key to a successful project. The inability to gain access to these players is a major reason why software projects fail. It can be perceived that a program is being written, so shouldn't the programmer have everything she needs to get the job done? Executives, bank tellers, teachers, consultants, janitors, baseball fans—whoever is of central importance to the project *must* be included in this discovery phase. Find out who they are. Write down a list of questions specific to their role in the problem space. Write down their answers. Compile all of this information to help you when you start writing use cases, scenarios, and planning your program's structure.

This can be a painful stage in the project. People who are non-programmers, but who are a key part of the problem domain, can find it difficult to describe their goals, their role, or the forms they use clearly and precisely enough for you to easily translate these into facets of the program. Interviewing people in groups often gets everyone (but you, the programmer) involved in a hot and heavy debate about company policies; this is a terrible waste of time (imagine a Dilbert cartoon). On the other hand, interviewing players separately can create confusion about system dependencies and interoperability. This may mean that you end up hearing a lot of redundant information and have trouble circling in on certain issues. One way to solve this is to locate certain areas of the project, and interview a couple of the players in those areas of the problem domain. Then go back and write up what you've found out in ways that we will describe below. Go back to your interviewees and have them look at it. Have them tell you if it is accurate in describing the interaction. Generally this will prompt one or two things that were forgotten or glossed over to get teased into the foreground. Then perform this process for the remaining areas of the project. Meet with a couple of key people once it is written up to get sign-off on the project requirements. The "requirements of a project" is another way to talk about the "project scope": the number and complexity of requirements indicate its scope. This brings us to reason number two that software projects fail.

5.2.2 Scope Creep

You must be vigilant and protect your project and define clearly and specifically what exactly the project will entail. That means that you decide what a person is within the scope of your application, and present this material to the client for sign-off. If the client agrees that a person (within the world of your application) does not need to have a middle name, but only a middle initial, and then wants to change this later, you need to rewrite the definition of the database, the code that accesses the data, and the business logic that goes along with it, and then probably the code that presents it. This happens with frequency, and is a vexing issue in Web and software development. It is vexing because it is rather unreasonable and most likely unprofitable to try to define such minutiae before the contract is even signed or the project bid is won. Dealing with these issues is not particular to Java to be sure, or even software development. And while this lack of definition is no one's "fault" and can draw out the project, it is not scope creep. Scope creep is the demon child of this lack of definition and the developer allowing the client to drive the project.

Scope creep is the phenomenon in software development when the scope of the project gradually becomes larger and larger than was originally envisioned. Generally clients are responsible for trying to sneak in seemingly innocuous features that leave developers trying to please the client or to finally just get the project done. It can happen because a new version of some highly anticipated software was just released, and your team wants to incorporate the snazzy new features that the product makes available, or (usually) just does in a different way.

5.2.3 "Wouldn't it Be Cool if We..."

You have no doubt heard someone, at some time, say, "Wouldn't it be cool if we did X," where X represents some smooth new thing the program should do (if it's a Web project, it might involve Flash or XML). Though related to scope creep, this phenomenon is different—and even more deadly to your projects. "Wouldn't it Be Cool if We..." is a killer.

"Wouldn't it Be Cool if We..." is a frequent reason that software projects fail. It means a number of things. It means that your scope creeps. Your timeline increases. Your costs increase. Your code bloats. You run serious risks of breaking good, working code—because generally what would be cool is something new that the programmer has little experience in.

The client never cares. The client, 9 times out of 10, could not care less if you parse XML with SAX or DOM. And SAX is *not* cooler than DOM. Or vice-versa. It doesn't matter.

The reason the client doesn't care is because she generally doesn't even know. In my experience it is rarely the client and almost always the programmers who invite themselves into more work, more confusion, and more problems with "Wouldn't it Be Cool if We...." Clients rarely pay for, appreciate, or even know about "Wouldn't it Be Cool if We...." However, somebody is paying for your time—whether or not you're making money.

In American business, the average employee costs a company twice his salary to employ. That is, if your salary is $25 per hour, it costs your company $50 per hour for you to work at that company. They have to pay for janitorial services, air conditioning, 401(k), lights, insurance, and so forth. "Wouldn't it Be

Cool if We..." not only hurts projects and clients, it hurts companies. When a company has too many "cool" projects that aren't profitable, it goes out of business.

If there's something really cool that you want to do ("Flash MX now allows us to use embedded video..."), then suggest it at the first definition meeting. If you haven't decided on it by then, wait until next time. If there is a "good reason" that you need to do something cool halfway through a project, here's a test: If what you want to do is actually worth doing, then you should be able to explain to the client what you want to do and why it is worth changing horses in midstream. If clients think it is cool too, they will pay for it to be done the cool way. If the client won't pay for it, why should your boss?

Of course, none of these problems stated above suggest a direct development methodology. They simply illustrate the need for having a plan and sticking to it.

5.3 Software Development Processes

Perhaps the best way to help keep your project from failing is to work with a process or a methodology. There are a number of stages to typical software development, many of which may be similar to how you currently design Web applications.

Object-oriented application design exists to improve the productivity of each of these stages and to help make the most reliable system. There are many different software design methodologies floating around. These include the waterfall model, the iterative process, the rational unified process, and extreme programming.

5.3.1 The Waterfall Methodology

The waterfall methodology is not used as frequently as it used to be. In this method, the development process had several stages, each one with very distinct boundaries. The stages might look familiar:

1. Gather requirements
2. Analyze requirements
3. Design system
4. Write system code
5. Test system
6. Maintain system

The output of each stage becomes the input for the next stage. So in the above process, writing the code produces the output of the code base, which serves as the input for the next stage, testing the code.

Like many things in computing, this model is inherited from the world of industry. The waterfall model has its origins in the world of building construction. With this model, the stages are all predefined. The customer must sign off at each stage to ensure that everything completed so far is acceptable. Nothing is worse than completing a loosely defined project and having the client reject it or simply say, "I just thought it was going to be... I don't know... *different*."

This process works well in theory. It also works well for projects with more than a few developers, when it is hard to keep everybody informed of every aspect of the spec along the way. This approach encourages definition and makes sure that things are well documented. It also encourages communication with the client, which is a good thing.

In practice, this process can lead to serious problems if you are working on a project that has new requirements for you or poses challenges you may not have tackled many times before. The reason is this: The waterfall method necessitates a denial of certain fundamental psychological truths about people: We make mistakes. We change our minds. Things happen. We forget something. The "artist's rendering" may not be drawn precisely to scale. What's worse is that you don't find this out when gathering requirements. You might catch a couple of things in the analytic stage. How many more snags lurk ahead, only to be discovered when you've already written 2,000 lines of code?

Another serious problem with the waterfall method is that testing happens very late in the process. This means that testing is not so much testing as it is a rote exercise in hoping for the best. If your test fails, you've got to take a completed system and rework it. Depending on what your test turns up, this could be a terrible detriment to your project.

The shortcomings of the waterfall method begot the iterative process.

5.3.2 Iterative Process

Iterative is like recursive. It means that as you develop, you go through the entire process repeatedly. Instead of deciding up front how everything is going to work and then doing exactly that until you hit a brick wall, you define things as well as you can, then do a little work, then check to make sure your analysis still makes sense, revise it if you need to, go back and do a little more work, and so on.

The stages—and the sequence in which they occur in an iterative process—are just the same as the stages in the waterfall method. But in an iterative process, you allow yourself to go back to a previous stage and modify your work there. The clear advantage here is that your work, analysis, and design are all always based on your most current knowledge of the most complete model of the system—not an artist's sketch from a far-off hill.

This process, as you can imagine, takes time. It takes longer to do some things two or three times than to do them once. The idea is that if you don't follow an iterative process, you're going to end up doing things over again in some way, and in all likelihood after you've rolled out the product. Then you're still taking the time, but now you've got disappointed users and angry clients.

5.3.3 Rational Unified Process

5.3.3.1 HISTORY OF RATIONAL UNIFIED PROCESS

In the early 1990s, Jim Rumbaugh was head of a team at the research labs at General Electric. One of the products of its work was a 1991 book called *Object-Oriented Modeling and Design*. Meanwhile, Grady Booch had been working on Ada systems with Rational Software and published books of his own on object-oriented methodologies. In 1994, Rumbaugh left to join Grady Booch at Rational. The idea was to merge their methodologies, which were composed of many complementary ideas.

At the same time, Ivar Jacobson had broken ground in the world of object-oriented modeling approaches by introducing the concept of use cases. The books *Object-Oriented Software Engineering* (1992) and *The Object Advantage* (1995) are good examples of his work. By 1995, Jacobson had joined Rational, and began working with Booch and Rumbaugh. The three renamed their work UML (Unified Modeling Language) and soon came to be referred to as "the three amigos."

In 1996, the Object Modeling Group (OMG) was formed. The purpose of the OMG was to ensure methods standardization and keep the work non-proprietary. In 1997 Rational released version 1.0 of the UML documentation to the OMG. Other organizations released their methods as well, and the OMG went about the arduous task of merging the proposals into a standard.

The three amigos' recent thought on the Rational Unified Process (RUP) is explained in *The Unified Software Development Process* (1999).

5.3.3.2 THE RATIONAL UNIFIED PROCESS IN A NUTSHELL

The RUP defines a number of different terms, some of which we have been tossing around with abandon in this chapter. These are examined specifically in Table 5.1. Each of the terms is part of the picture wherein workers do things for customers. Each thing that is done is measurable in some way—either in relation to other artifacts (deliverables) or its place in a workflow, or because of the value it represents to a customer.

Here are the basic guidelines for running a project following the RUP:

1. Determine the members of the team.
2. Determine the system to build.
3. Create a use case model. Create the user interface in prototype.
4. Create an analysis object model.
5. Create diagrams to represent classes, states, sequences (conventional UML activities that we'll discuss below).
6. Determine the best architecture for the system. Assign classes to packages, and packages to modules.
7. Test your system against the model described in your use cases.
8. Transition to the live system.

TABLE 5.1 Terms in the Rational Unified Process

RUP TERM	GENERAL TERM	DEFINITION
Activity	Task	A unit of work, performed by a worker, that creates a deliverable artifact.
Activity step	Subtask	A measurable, distinct step that is part of an activity.
Artifact	Deliverable	An artifact is a deliverable that is of use to a customer.
Iteration	Iteration	A planned sequence of activities that results in a milestone (a tested release).
Phase	Stage	The duration of a workflow.

(Continued)

TABLE 5.1 Terms in the Rational Unified Process (Continued)

RUP TERM	GENERAL TERM	DEFINITION
Worker	Role	An agent in the development process who performs activities.
Workflow	Activity	A sequence of activities, wherein each is generally dependent on the prior, that produces a result of value to an actor.

NOTE As a ColdFusion developer, you might be familiar with the term "Workflows" from Macromedia Spectra. The concept there refers to a number of loosely coupled tasks, which can either be done in parallel or in a sequence of dependencies. Same basic idea here. In fact, it could be said that Spectra was a crucial step on the road to CFMX. Consider that Spectra was an "object-based development" platform consisting of ContentObjects, which have properties and methods and are concrete instances of ContentObject Types. Sounds like objects and classes to me. Spectra was, among other things, an attempt to bring to ColdFusion the advantages of flexibility and separation of logic/presentation inherent in object-oriented platforms such as Java.

Perhaps the main difference between RUP and the waterfall method is that RUP creates a set of deliverables all along the project, and these deliverables are foregrounded.

There are a number of advantages to following the RUP. First of all, it is architecture-driven. This may seem strange given that determining the architecture is the sixth step in an eight-step process. However, so much time is spent in analysis determining how classes will interact with each other and what their responsibilities are, the code practically writes itself by the time you're done.

A common disadvantage cited with respect to the RUP is that it is tied to only one supplier, and that makes people nervous. It means that you have to figure into your budget the cost of acquiring the many tools you'll use to do the project. Moreover, the specification is more than 1,700 pages long. Reading that much is a lot of work and makes the process of developing software sort of take the focus away from the "real" work—creating a product for your customer. RUP is very detailed and complex. Many developers find understanding it an overwhelming task. There is support available for a fee from Rational, and there is training.

Many developers cite the formality of the RUP as a stifler of communication. It is rather likely that a team's communication would be greatly enhanced if every member had a complete understanding of the RUP. However, this is very often not the case. People have different backgrounds, different jobs in a project, are different stakeholders, etc. Short of this, communication in RUP can be very difficult.

There is, however, a lot that we can take away from the RUP, and we will therefore discuss use cases, classes, state diagrams, and the like in this chapter.

5.3.4 Extreme Programming

This is a style of programming that has received increasing interest since it was put forth by Kent Beck in *Extreme Programming Explained* (2000). XP is really two things: It is a set of guidelines about how to program, and these guidelines are based in a unique philosophy of programming.

The two chief goals of XP, as with many programming methodologies, are to improve the reliability of the programs you create and to improve your productivity as you write code.

There are two assertions of XP that have probably garnered the most attention: Program in pairs, and write the test cases first.

Programming in pairs means that the code for a project is written in teams of two. One programmer drives (writes the code), while the other thinks about the larger picture. This means that your team can achieve a meaningful balance between focusing on the details of the implementation and the overall program, including how the current piece fits in. Other benefits of this approach include the ability to really talk through the current challenges you might be facing—it doesn't allow you to sweep minor annoyances under the rug quite as easily. It also keeps the project moving, because you cannot so easily move into corners of the program in ways that others will later find arcane.

Writing the test cases first addresses a common problem in software projects. Many software projects fail in part because the testing phase is inadequately addressed. Testing is often an afterthought or is the last item on the list of priorities. When the deadline draws near, projects are often pressed right up until the last minute to get the product out the door. When this happens, the tests can be hastily administered. Lamentably, many flaws found at this stage are often time-consuming and expensive to fix. Writing the test cases first means that you are writing code to the test, knowing what you'll have to pass. It is harder to overlook things like this, and this can even promote a more user-centric design.

The obvious disadvantage to XP is that it is not as mature, understood, or widely accepted as its predecessors from the 1980s and 1990s. It is difficult enough to get a complex project in on time and on budget, especially if new technology is involved. If there is resistance to this particular methodology by any of the members, you could have real problems. Because it is frankly stranger than other, more traditional methodologies, it could take some effort to get such a project moving.

One can quickly see why managers might discourage this manner of working: it seems less productive to have two people doing one job. What is perhaps less obvious is that it requires very knowledgeable, experienced programmers to really be able to do it and take advantage of its features. XP was not really envisioned for teams of more than 10 or 12. For very large projects, this method is not really workable.

Finally, XP does not produce any documentation. There is little provision for it, and as corporations find documentation increasingly important as their turnover rates rise, it is important to have a solid documentation structure in place for a project of any complexity. With XP, you're on your own.

Other key aspects of XP include the following:

- **Refactoring.** Refactoring means evaluating your code and rewriting it for readability, performance, and efficiency. It means reworking a system to make it simpler. By having a testing framework already in place, this makes code refactoring rather clear.
- **Simplicity.** This is a key aspect of XP. Anything that is not immediately necessary to the system working is not implemented. Of course, the simpler your system is, the less bug-prone it is, the easier it is to change, and so on.

5.3.5 Do It Your Way

There are certainly a wide range of attitudes when it comes to programming methodologies and how seriously people take them. The 1980s boom of programming methodologies was partly a response to a perceived increase in project failures.

There are a number of good books on various methodologies, especially UML, each with a slightly different approach, focus, and degree of detail. I encourage you to check a few of these out, and yet start now using everything that you already know about project management, discovery, and development. I have found that what one OOP designer means by "use case" is not precisely what another means. That's okay; we're working with (literally) about 45 different methods or method fragments for object-oriented application design

(OOAD). You may find, depending on the kinds of systems you're used to building, that you have a hybrid approach of your own that works rather well.

The main thing, of course, is to stay focused on your project and its goals. It could be that the project is simple enough that you don't need to do much planning and can sit down and start writing code. You could be dealing with a sufficiently complex project that you spend two months just doing requirements gathering. These are different kinds of projects. Don't think that you need to go through some painstaking process of writing numerous scenarios when the project is relatively familiar and well understood. So please take the remainder of this chapter at face value and assume that some projects require more, or less, or simply different kinds of planning. If OOAD starts to cramp your style and you never sit down to write any code, something is amiss. Take a step back, and come at the project from another angle.

That said, it is a good idea to start relatively small and familiar as we begin discussing these concepts; it will be easier to get a handle on them this way.

5.4 Case Study: Bookstore

Polonius: What do you read, my lord?
Hamlet: Words, words, words.

—William Shakespeare, *Hamlet*, 2.2.192

Let's take a moment to look at a case study—a brief description of a problem domain that we can refer to consistently throughout the chapter and the rest of the book. This will help us understand object-oriented analysis so that we can design stable, sensible, extensible systems. It also presents the system that we will use to create many examples.

The fictional Words, Words, Words bookstore (WWWBooks) is expanding. It has hired you to create a processing system that will replace its current paper-based system. The store's buyer orders books from publishers. The books come in, and need to be added to inventory and shelved. All books are classified by their section (nonfiction, poetry, home improvement, etc.). They are also classified in terms of pricing: books can either be full price, on sale, or on the close-out table. The discount for sale items can vary.

The store also sells non-book items such as shirts, bookmarks, writing material, magazines, and coffee mugs.

WWWBooks has an owner, a few managers, booksellers, and a buyer.

Once an item has been selected for purchase, the bookseller enters the order in the system. The customer can choose to have the order wrapped and shipped to someone else. Once entered, the ordered items must be removed from inventory. If inventory drops below a threshold level, a message is sent to the buyer, who may choose to reorder. The managers want to be able to track the best booksellers, and they may choose to award the best salesperson of the month.

In the second phase of the project, WWWBooks also wants to add the ability to sell books online.

We will refer to different facets of this case study throughout the book and use it for code examples when it makes sense.

5.5 Introduction to OOAD

Object-oriented analysis and design is the process for modelling a system to be built. The idea is to describe the situation as it exists in real life, and then apply analytical techniques to translate this into a system that describes the program you will write.

OOAD is more art than science. It requires strong analytical skills. There are not always "right" answers, but, as in life, there are often answers that are more right than others. It is subjective, however, and depends not only on who is designing the system, but also on what the purpose is, what other systems exist in support or in tandem, who the users will be, and many other factors.

The purpose of designing your system with OOAD is to determine, before you start coding, what all the parts of your system are precisely and what they need to be able to do. Your program acts as a director, asking the objects you've identified for information, and then sending messages to workers who perform tasks based on that information.

As mentioned earlier, classes are like little object factories. Objects are the work of the program. When you write a program, you define classes that are called on to make objects that fit its definition. Objects have *attributes*. Attributes are the qualities of the object or class—the data about it. These attributes could be name, size, publisher, number of pages, and so on. They also have methods—the things that they can do.

Objects can call on other objects with which they need to interact to get their work done. This is just like in a company where, for instance, the Web developer needs to interact with the designer to integrate the code with the layout, and then a box administrator is required to address it and put the site up.

5.5.1 Object Identification and Testing

There are a number of ways to identify what things should be objects in your system. Perhaps the best way to begin to design a system is to describe what exactly it needs to be able to do. You can then get an easy start by looking at your text and pulling out the nouns and verbs. The nouns represent objects and the verbs represent methods.

Let's look at our WWWBooks case study to see what objects we can find. It seems clear that we need a `Customer` object. Those are familiar creatures (hopefully!) who generally have a name, billing information, and possibly contact information. A necessary condition for being a customer is that you have purchased something. Because a customer can purchase more than one thing at a time, and on multiple occasions, we need to isolate each set of purchases as an order. An order needs to know who ordered it as well as what products it comprises. So we should probably have a `Product` object. Products are sold by booksellers, who are employees. Here is where things generally get interesting. Do we need to represent employees in the system at all? Yes. They are a necessary part of the sale, and the managers want to track the best salespeople. That means that an order needs to know not only who the customer was, but who the seller was. Okay. So what is so interesting about the employee object? Well, managers manage employees, but they are employees too. They are different. They can do things, such as view the top booksellers of the month, that regular employees cannot. They do, however, share a significant number of attributes with regular employees, such as a name, an address, an ID number, a hire date, and a salary. The question then becomes how to best represent that in your system. Do you make a `Bookseller` object and a `Manager` object? That doesn't seem quite right. Then you've got to replicate all of the data that booksellers and managers share. If later you decide that you want to expand your "middle initial" attribute to allow for employees' complete middle name, you've got to do it in two places. And what about the owner?

Poor design of the database is one of the chief causes of bloated code, slow performance, and maintenance difficulty in Web applications. Similarly, it is very important to choose the right objects when designing your Java programs. There are ways to determine if what you have chosen to represent as an object is going to work well in your system. This is called object testing. Once you have selected good candidates for objects in your system, consider the following:

1. *Does the object exist in the problem domain?* When designing the WWW-Books system, we have a `Customer` object. The customer's favorite color or place of employment are not really relevant to the transactions the program will perform.
2. *Is the object required to answer the questions the program will ask?* While the customer might pay with a debit card that is an extension of a bank account, we don't really need to know the customer's bank account

number (as any customer would tell us!). The bank account is outside the problem domain. It does not add to the knowledge that we require to answer the questions the program will ask.

3. *Can the object maintain independent existence?* How do you know whether an object should be defined independently as its own object, or whether it should merely be a characteristic of another object? For instance, should the manager object exist independently, or should we just define some kind of "isManager" bit? The customer and the order are clearly independent entities, even though they are related. Should the customer's address be a separate object from `Customer`? Employees have addresses too. Maybe it is best to create a separate `Address` object, and anything in the world of the system that has an address (customers, booksellers, buyers, managers, owner) can use this `Address` object. Then any relevant changes can cascade throughout the system. The answer is not absolutely clear. A customer at a brick-and-mortar bookstore would generally have no need to give an address to the store. However, a customer buying online would. In the case of the online order, the site visitor can enter two addresses: a billing address and a shipping address. A shipping address is just a certain type of address. Does it make sense to define an entirely different object for the shipping address? That seems like a drag to maintain, and it would require so much extra work writing to begin with. That might be okay if there were some big advantage in performance or functionality, but I can't see what that would be. Also, if we think about it a little more, a shipping address is more or less an aspect of the order, is not necessarily related to the customer, and doesn't necessarily repeat. Probably we should just decide to store the bloody shipping address, if there is one, with the `Order` object, and go to lunch.
4. *Objects have attributes and operations.* All objects must have data that they store as attributes, and operations that they perform. If you cannot define both of these for your object candidate, then you've probably got a characteristic of another object, not an object. For instance, just looking at the nouns in our case study, we might think initially that we need an inventory object. However, inventory is kind of one of those deals like the economy. It doesn't really exist. There are only actual products, and at any given time each product has zero or more of itself in the store. That number is the inventory.

Some related questions arise. What about books and products? Eighty percent of the store's total sales are from books. And a book (as something that can be sold) is a product. However, since such an overwhelming number of books are sold as opposed to the other items, we might want to think about making a separate `Book` object and a separate `Product` object. After all a book has an ISBN, which other products don't have. And books get classified by their genre, and other products don't have a genre. However, this is where it is important to look at what you are structurally needing to represent. It could be that an ISBN is not necessarily any different from a product number. It could also be that genre is just a fancy way of saying "category." Again, this probably depends on the size of the store, the number of employees, expected growth, and many other factors.

Once you have described your problem domain, use these tests to determine if you've got a list of objects that makes sense. For now, let's decide on the following objects for WWWBooks:

- `Customer`
- `Employee`
- `Product`
- `Order`

We can reexamine these choices as needed. If these are going to be our objects, we need to determine what their attributes are (the data fields) and what their operations are (their methods).

5.5.2 Modeling Object Attributes and Operations

Attributes can be fields such as `customerID`, but they can also be objects, such as the `Customer` object. Let's look at the fields and methods we might choose for each of our system objects. We represent an object by writing its fields (properties), one per line, and then its methods, one per line. Methods are indicated by their trailing `()`. The act of graphically representing an object as a step in planning an application is referred to as *object modeling*.

The `Product` object might look like this:

```
productID
product
productName
price
discount
etc...

getProductID()
getPrice()
addToInventory()
removeFromInventory()
```

The `Customer` object might look like this:

```
customerID
customerName
billingAddress

getCustomerID()
getCustomerName()
getBillingAddress()
setBillingAddress()
```

The `Employee` object might look like this:

```
employeeID
hireDate
salary

getEmployeeID()
getHireDate()
getSalary()
```

And here is a possible representation of the `Order` object:

```
orderID
orderDate
customerID
employeeID
shippingAddress

getOrderID()
getOrderDate()
getStatus()
getOrderEmployeeID()
getShippingAddress()
placeOrder()
cancelOrder()
```

NOTE These are just some reasonable possibilities. One possible improvement to this design is to store the ZIP code and other parts of the address in separate fields. There are a lot of good choices for different designs, and there is no need to get bogged down at this stage.

Note that an attribute can be a reference for another object. Instead of referencing, for instance, the `employeeID` as we do in the `Order` object, we could have the `Employee` object itself be an attribute of the `Order` object. This would give us access to all of the data in the `Employee` object through the `Order` object.

5.6 Use Cases

Once you have defined what objects should be in your system, you need to describe how the user will interact with the system. This is most commonly done with use cases.

5.6.1 What Are Use Cases?

A use case is a high-level description of a discrete user interaction with an aspect of a software system. Collecting a complete set of use cases should describe your system entirely.

Use cases drive the analysis, design, implementation, and testing phases:

- In the *analysis* stage, use cases help ensure that you are representing the system correctly to your customer.
- In the *design* stage, use cases help you see your project completely. This means you can refine, refactor, and reduce your project's operative agents.
- In the *implementation* stage, use cases help you to concentrate on the code you're writing so that you don't write anything you don't need to, and so you do write all of the code sufficient to cover every user-based eventuality that your system could generate.
- In the *testing* stage, use cases help to measure that you have written to spec, and they speed up the time required to test. Because the system must make the use cases possible, it is very easy for QA to test if they work—the tests are built into the system.

Use cases support you at every step of the way on a project. They are a cornerstone of good OOAD.

In order to really start writing use cases, there is another term we should understand: the *actor*. An actor is either a real person or another system that interacts with the system being designed. This could be a Web service, a user in a role (such as a secretary logged in as content updater or a manager logged in as administrator), another program, or an intelligent agent. The (ever-evaporating) distinction between people and machines is totally useless to a use case. Something that interacts with your system just needs a description of what that interaction is, what the outcome is supposed to be, and what happens if all does not go as planned.

It is sort of easy to generate use cases once you understand them, so we won't belabor it. Consider our WWWBooks case study. What are some of the things a user will need to do with that system?

- A user can login to the system and is assigned a role for that session.
- A user in the employee role enters a new order.
- A user in the manager role requests a graph indicating bookseller performance for the month.
- And so on.

Note that the customer never directly acts with the system. This would be modified, of course, if implemented on the Web. Writing out all of your use cases tends to force you to answer questions that you might otherwise wait until later (or never) to deal with. Later in this chapter you will see how to create a use-case diagram.

5.7 Creating UML Diagrams

In planning a software application, you generally need to create use cases and user scenarios, class and package diagrams, and perhaps sequence diagrams. We will cover all of these in this chapter so that you will be ready to plan your own applications. The discussion will also serve as a circumambulatory way to approach creating complex Java classes, as we will in Chapter 7.

There are many software packages designed to help developers plan software applications. These packages allow you to create all of the different kinds of diagrams we discuss in this chapter, and more. These include:

- Rational Rose
- Microsoft Visio
- Platinum ERWin

5.7.1 Rational Software

As you might guess, Rational Software makes several products that help developers create their software architecture drawings. Some of these packages are expensive (several thousand dollars) for beginners or small companies. If you aren't sure that you'll have many OOP projects, the Rational products might be needlessly complex. It's not a bad idea to start simple and increase the power of your tools as required. It can also require a large investment of time just to learn how to work with the Rational tools. However, some of the more sophisticated features of Rational Rose really go the extra mile. The Rational programs don't stop at representing your application. Rational knows that you're writing the representation in order to write real code—and its programs will translate your diagrams directly into the appropriate Java code. That's a huge time saver.

5.7.2 Microsoft Visio

One easy and inexpensive way to get started drawing UML diagrams is Microsoft Visio. This program costs only a couple hundred dollars, is easy to start using, and contains libraries that help you quickly create and organize your diagrams.

There are different editions of Visio. The Professional Edition has the right features to work with most small- to medium-sized projects. It allows you to create more than a dozen different kinds of UML diagrams, as well as six different database schema diagrams, flowcharts, and other items such as organization charts, schedules, and network maps.

In the end, of course, you'll choose what you're comfortable with and what's in your budget. You don't need to use any of these packages to write or plan Java programs. But they can make doing so much easier. You can use a word processor or even an HTML editor to make a basic bordered table to write class diagrams. It gets trickier with the other kinds of diagrams, and this solution is not very easy to modify.

5.7.3 Pencil and Paper

You can also draw out your diagrams with paper and pencil. For this kind of work it is very efficient to use pencil and paper or a large posterboard. This entire package costs about one dollar and is in many cases as fast or faster than using the software packages mentioned above. Once you need to share it digitally, you can scan it in and save it as an image. The obvious downside is that it becomes rather cumbersome to modify. This is, however, a surprisingly common practice and an efficient, workable solution.

In the next several sections, we will look at the more common UML diagrams, what they're for, and how to create them.

5.8 Class Diagrams

The purpose of a class diagram is to visually and simply represent the important aspects of your classes in a compact manner. The diagram of a class has three main parts: the class name, the attributes, and the methods. It also includes the visibility modifiers and, sometimes, datatypes.

> **NOTE** A constructor is a special method that is called when you create an instance of a class using the new keyword. Since a constructor is a method, include it as such in your class diagram.

Let's create the Employee class for our WWWBooks case study with Visio. To create a class diagram in Visio, choose File > New > Software > UML Model Diagram. This opens a new blank drawing along with a special tool bar that has many different components. You'll see several submenus in this tool bar that store the different components needed for each type of diagram. You'll notice submenus for UML Sequence, Activity, Collaborations, and so forth. You can choose the appropriate submenu for the kind of diagram you want to create, and the things you'll need for each drawing will appear. In general with components in Visio, you can drag and drop them onto your page, and then double-click on them to edit their properties. Visio refers to these components as *stencils*.

The Visio 2000 class editor is shown in Figure 5.1.

If you do not see Java Data Types in the UML Navigator in Visio, you can make it appear (and remove others you may not want) by choosing UML from the Main Toolbar > Options and then clicking the UML Document tab. Check the boxes next to the datatype you want to have available.

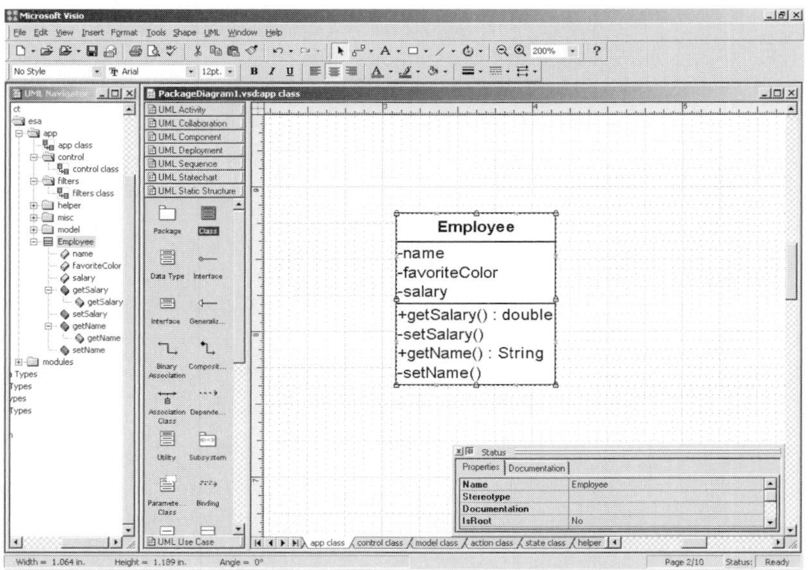

FIGURE 5.1 Visio 2000 class editor.

5.8.1 Changing the Class Name

Under the UML Static Structure menu, you should see Class at the top. Drag a class onto the page and double-click on it. A UML Class Properties dialog box appears, which allows us to edit the properties on the class. In the Name field, type Employee. The name of the class changes at the top of the diagram.

5.8.2 Access Modifiers

In a class diagram, the access modifier is noted next to the attributes and methods defined. Access modifiers for your data and operations will play an increasingly important role in our discussion of classes. Therefore, let us take a quick detour to recap what we know about access modifiers.

An access modifier (also called *visibility modifier*) is either `private`, `protected`, or `public`. You represent these visibility modifiers like this:

```
- (private)
# (protected)
+ (public)
```

Table 5.2 shows the different access levels and their descriptions. While we have discussed these access modifiers previously, they can be tricky to remember as they do not exist in ColdFusion. Covering them here reinforces their importance in your design.

TABLE 5.2 Description of Access Levels for Attributes and Operations

ACCESS LEVEL	DESCRIPTION
`default`	`default` is *not* a keyword that you explicitly use. If you don't type one of the other three modifiers, you get an access level of `default`. `default` basically means "package"—only code within the same package can access it. The following items can be `default`: classes, instance variables, methods, static variables, static methods, constructors, inner and nested classes, and interfaces.
`private`	`private` data is private to the class. Only other parts of the class can access data marked `private`. An instance variable marked `private` can only be accessed by methods inside its own class (with the exception of inner classes). You can mark the following items `private`: instance variables, methods, static variables, static methods, constructors, and inner and nested classes.

(Continued)

TABLE 5.2 Description of Access Levels for Attributes and Operations (Continued)

ACCESS LEVEL	DESCRIPTION
`protected`	`protected` items extend `default` in a way; they are accessible at the `default` level *and* to any subclasses *including those* in a package different from the one in which the superclass (the parent class) resides. It is therefore less restrictive than `default`. You can mark the following items `protected`: instance variables, methods, static variables, static methods, and interfaces.
`public`	The least restrictive access level, data marked `public` are accessible by any code that has a valid reference to the object marked `public`. You can mark the following items `public`: classes, instance variables, methods, static variables, static methods, constructors, inner classes, and interfaces.

> **NOTE** The introduction of ColdFusion components (CFCs) in ColdFusion MX allows you to specify access modifiers—this is only true for CFCs.

5.8.3 Adding Attributes

On the left-hand side of the screen, you'll see the UML Navigator. The UML Navigator appears when you open a new UML drawing file. It shows your model as a hierarchy, including the datatypes available. These are C++, BASIC, IDL, and Java.

In the UML Class Properties dialog, choose the Attributes tab and click New. In the Attribute field, type `employeeID`. You may need to expand the column width for the Type column in order to read all of the choices. You will notice that the type `Employee` is now available as an object. Let's choose `int`. Next, choose the visibility for the attribute.

Let's choose `protected` for our `employeeID` so that it is only visible to methods in the same package and subclass. If an application grows and you start defining things in many different packages, we would just need to make sure that we balance between the modularity, security, and dependability that comes with restrictive access, and the convenience and organization that comes with a more open access modifier.

We can leave the rest of the items (multiplicity and initial value) alone. Add the remaining attributes the same way. `hireDate` for now will be a protected Date object, and `salary` will be a protected `double`. To add another attribute, click New again. To view your work so far, click OK.

5.8.4 Adding Methods

Methods are added in much the same way as attributes. Click the Operations tab to add methods, and type the name using the Java naming conventions; you don't need to include the `()`. Click in the Return Type column header to choose what datatype the operation will return. `getEmployeeID()` returns an `int`. `get-HireDate()` returns a `Date` object of the `java.util` package; `getSal-ary()` returns a `double`, and we'll mark it as such in the dialog box. If you are writing it out or using a program other than Visio, the return type is marked with a colon, like this: `getSalary() : double`. We will leave all of these methods public so that they are accessible from anywhere. Now that we have created the accessor (get) methods, let's create the manipulator (set) methods.

The methods `setHireDate(java.util.Date hd)` and `setSalary-(double s)` are created in the same way that our accessor methods were, with a couple of differences. To begin with, we do not specify a return type, since these manipulator methods won't return anything (you could have a manipulator return a boolean specifying whether the operation was successful, or an error code). It also takes an extra step to specify the parameters that a method accepts. Let's choose to specify that these two manipulator methods are protected, so that only methods defined in the same package as the Employee class or subclasses of the Employee class can change the value of the hire date and the salary.

In order to add a parameter to a method, you have to take an extra step. In Visio, in the UML Navigator, double-click on the method to which you want to add a parameter. The UML Operations Properties dialog box appears. Click the Parameters tab and click New. Type the name of the parameter you want to add. For salary, this might be simply "s." Then choose the datatype that will get passed to the method. Note that Visio allows you to specify only the eight primitive datatypes by default; you have to set up different data types (such as `java.util.Date`) separately.

So now our class diagram looks something like this:

```
Employee
-employeeID
#hireDate

#salary
+getEmployeeID() : int
+getHireDate() : String
+getSalary() : double
#setHireDate(java.util.Date)
#setSalary(double)
```

The Java code corresponding to this class diagram looks like this:

5.8.5 Employee.java

```
import java.util.Date;

public class Employee {

    private static int employeeID;
    protected Date hireDate;
    protected double salary;

    // default constructor
    public Employee() {
        employeeID = (int) (Math.random() * 1000);

    }

public int getEmployeeID() {
        return employeeID;

    }

public Date getHireDate() {

        return hireDate;
    }

public double getSalary() {

        return salary;
    }

protected void setHireDate(Date hd) {

        hireDate = hd;
    }

protected void setSalary(double s) {

        salary = s;
    }

}
```

Once we have created the UML class diagram, it is rather straightforward to write the code that makes up the class, as you can see above.

> **NOTE** Creating and manipulating the various UML document types in Visio is very similar to this process, so we won't belabor interacting with that particular software package as we identify more diagrams.

While we go into depth on writing classes in Chapter 7, I wanted to introduce this process now for a couple of reasons. First, classes are the fundamental aspect of OOP. It is not easy right out of the gate to start writing classes, so it's good to get some practice. I think it helps demystify the process a little. Also, it is most realistic to approach it from a design standpoint, rather than a syntactical standpoint—that's what you'll be doing when you start writing more complex Java programs. Finally, it's more fun; look what we already know how to do:

5.8.6 MakeEmployee.java

```
import java.util.Date;

public class MakeEmployee {

public static void main(String[] args){


// create a new Employee object

Employee myEmp = new Employee();

// call the getEmployeeID method on our new object
System.out.println("Employee created with ID: " +
        myEmp.getEmployeeID());

// set its salary
myEmp.setSalary(75000.00);

// get and print the salary

System.out.println("Salary: " + myEmp.getSalary());

    }

}
```

Using only the skills you have already acquired, we can put together a Java class with its own data and operations, create an object of that type in *another* class, and create and view its data. This represents the first truly object-oriented program we've written so far.

Class diagrams are the basis of just about all OO methods. You will likely use them more frequently than any other kind of UML diagram. Don't get bogged down with them too early on. Instead of writing out all of your class diagrams with the full notation, you might try instead writing a little code, and then writing out some class diagrams once you've got a grip on the project. Then they can aid you in late architectural issues, optimization, and refactoring.

5.9 User Scenarios and Use-Case Diagrams

A *user scenario* is a step-by-step description of a discrete user interaction with your system. It is a sequence written out as a simple paragraph. You can have different scenarios of varying degrees of generality to cover everything in your system. For instance, our WWWBooks online store example would probably have a user scenario for Check Out. The Check Out scenario would look something like this:

```
Customer views items in the catalog. Customer adds items to
shopping cart. When the customer clicks Check Out, forms are
presented for entering billing information and shipping infor-
mation. The system sends the credit card information to the
authorization server. The customer is notified of his or her
order number on screen and advised of the shipment tracking
section of the site.
```

User scenarios are useful in the project discovery stage, and they help you derive your use cases.

A use case is a description of a set of scenarios, all with a common goal. There is not really a standard specification in UML for describing use cases. For this reason, one sees a good number of slightly varying descriptions. Some will include, for instance, the preconditions for a use case (the preconditions are the things that need to be true before the use case can take place, such as "customer has more than one item in shopping cart" or "user is logged on in the SU role"). There also cannot really be hard and fast rules about what the limit of a use case is; that is, how much ground it covers. There are practical limits to be sure.

Use cases and use-case diagrams were introduced by Jacobson in 1994. It is important to remember that the use case and the use-case diagram are separate entities. You do not need to draw the diagram to get the benefit of the use case. Either way, use cases involve actors in some kind of relation to the system, interacting with some aspect of the system.

5.9.1 Actors

Actors perform use cases. An actor can be thought of as a user in a role that performs an interaction. The actor can be a person or another system. Actors in our WWWBooks case study would include Customer, Manager, and Bookseller.

The number or variance of individuals within a role does not matter to the system. It makes no difference to Java if it is Fred or Murray purchasing something at the store. They are both users, yes, but they are in the same role—Customer—and customers all act exactly the same with respect to the system. Actors may play more than one role. It can be difficult, but you must try to think of users as always being in a role, instead of as being individuals.

Actors are the key to good software design. Determining the roles that will interact with your system is the foundation of writing solid systems. Everything is about the user. Before you start writing use cases, determine who your actors are and what they need. The use cases should fall out of this. Determine your actors' goals, and figure out different ways of fulfilling those goals.

Now, on the other hand, use cases will not necessarily result from an actor determination. Often actors represent the user role that requests a particular service from a system. The identity of the appropriate actor is not always entirely clear. That's okay. Try to think of who derives benefit from the use case. This can be another way of thinking of appropriate actors.

Actors are represented in a diagram as human stick figures, though they are not always. A likely example of a non-human actor is an intelligent agent or Web service.

There are discussions in the OOAD community about how detailed to get in a user scenario or use case. Some argue that more detail helps you see problems early on and optimize your design. Others say that you can get bogged down in the details writing use cases all day and that this will impede and confuse the work. A good general rule is that you can vary the degree of detail as appropriate. If a use case is fairly complex, you might break it up into two or more use cases. If the use case involves a good deal of risk, you'll probably want to specify things in greater detail. Anyway, I suggest keeping things relatively simple for a while.

5.9.2 When to Use Use Cases

Use use cases every time you design a new system. Every time you revise or add a significant section to an existing system. All the time.

Use cases force you to focus on the user of the system (see Figure 5.2). They help keep you from running down tempting programmatic paths that don't do anything to help the system or the user.

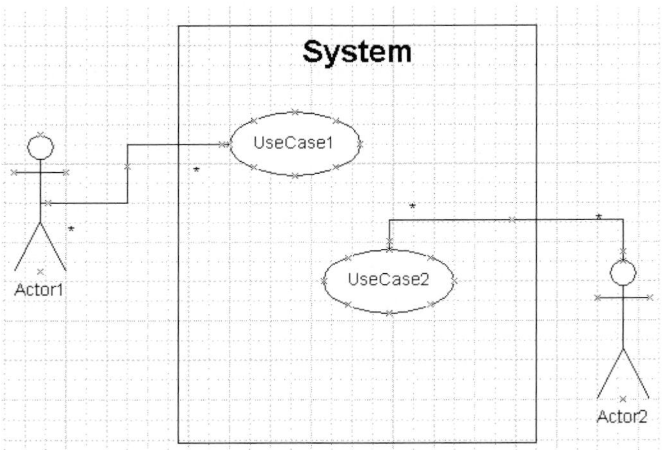

FIGURE 5.2 Use-case outline.

When you start designing your system, write it out in user scenarios. Name the different interactions. Use cases are generally the second thing you create when designing your system, after user scenarios. Writing the class diagrams is somewhat of an iterative process that in theory might be the first thing you do, but in practice I've found it occurs in tandem with the creation of use cases.

5.10 Collaboration Diagrams

Collaboration diagrams and sequence diagrams (discussed in the following section) are the two ways of representing interaction between different classes in UML. Objects in a system interact in order to provide the services defined by the application. Interaction diagrams represent objects in relation to one another.

In a collaboration diagram, objects are represented by rectangles. You draw arrows representing messages between each object. Each arrow is labeled to indicate the nature of the message and the order in which the message is sent.

5.10.1 When to Use Collaboration Diagrams

Use collaboration diagrams early in designing your system so that you can have a picture of how objects will interact. This can help you to refine your understanding of each aspect of the system. Perhaps you will find things that can be trimmed from the design because of redundancy, or more often, things that can be abstracted up to change the definition of your classes. A collaboration diagram is shown in Figure 5.3.

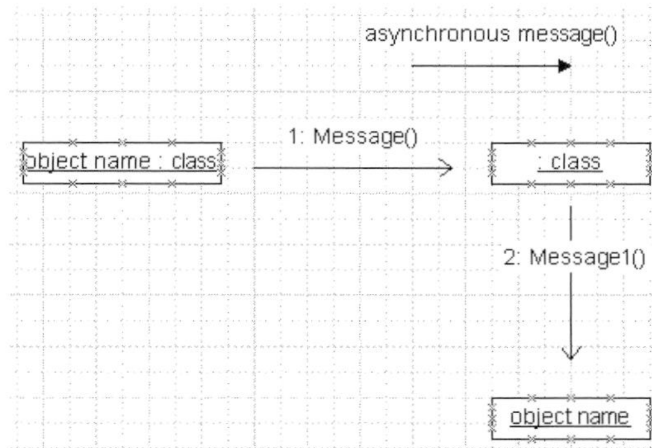

FIGURE 5.3 Collaboration diagram.

The diagram can be used to represent objects in the real world and their spatial relation to one another, and give you an overview that emphasizes the relationship of your system to things in the real world, which is a nice advantage. A chief criticism of collaboration diagrams, however, is that they can't represent very complex operations. This is a general criticism about all graphical systems of representation, really. Once you have more than a few objects, it can quickly get very difficult to read them. This forces you into partial representations of your system that are continued elsewhere.

Collaboration diagrams are generally the third item you create, after user scenarios and use cases.

5.11 Sequence Diagrams

Sequence diagrams are rather like collaboration diagrams, in that they represent the same information. The focus of a sequence diagram is not spatial, as it is with a collaboration diagram, however. Its focus is on the communication between objects in process. A sequence diagram is shown in Figure 5.4.

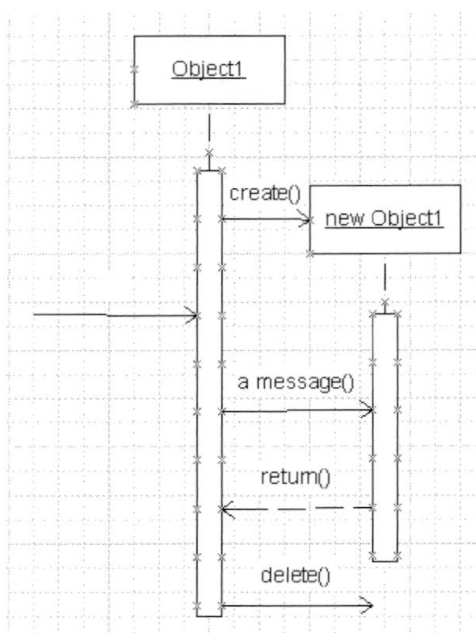

FIGURE 5.4 Sequence diagram.

Each object is represented by a vertical bar. Time elapses from the top to the bottom. Because of this, they can be more straightforward to read than collaboration diagrams. Also, message numbering is optional because the message placement on the page indicates its ordinality.

5.11.1 When to Use Sequence Diagrams

Sequence diagrams are most useful for representing complex interactions within a system. Sequence diagrams are generally written after collaboration diagrams.

5.12 Package Diagrams

A package, as stated previously, is a directory in which classes reside. Packages are represented in UML via the package diagram. You can use them to represent dependencies between packages and show the classes contained in a package. A package diagram is shown in Figure 5.5.

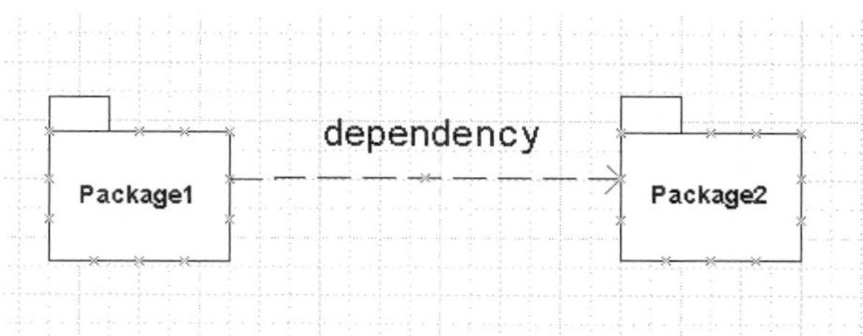

FIGURE 5.5 Package diagram.

Package diagrams help you get a high-level overview of how your system will be put together. Writing these is a very iterative process, like the class diagrams. You don't always know ahead of time how you will implement a certain feature, whether you'll do it using this or that technology. Package diagrams can help you see what you can share, what you can reuse, and how you might organize your classes for reuse in other systems.

That covers the primary, fundamental aspects of how you can use UML to help plan your system. Now we move away from UML and look at two more key features of OOP: encapsulation and inheritance. In this chapter we will define these terms, overview why they are important and how they work, and prepare you for later chapters.

5.13 Encapsulation

Encapsulation is an important aspect of OOP. In general, it means combining the data and the methods in the same object. The purpose of this is to make sure that unrelated, unforeseen functions cannot access or manipulate data in arbitrary ways—it means controlling not only what will happen, but exactly how it will happen. The primary means of ensuring that your programs are encapsulated is to employ an object's interface and its implementation separately.

An *interface* is a primary means of object communication. Every class defines specific interfaces for how they must be properly instantiated. The interface describes completely how messages sent to an object can invoke its behavior.

> **NOTE** Any methods included as part of the interface must be declared `public`.

The interface of the `Employee` object above consists of two things: how to instantiate an `Employee` object; and how to send a parameter to that object, have it perform its work, and send a value back.

In general, only methods are part of the interface, not attributes. That should be obvious upon consideration: The interface describes how to interact with an object, not what is being interacted with per se. Methods that are hidden are not part of the interface.

As we have seen in previous examples, the way that Java and OOP are defined replicates structures in the real world in order to achieve similar benefits of organization and efficiency. In order to understand the need for interfaces, it is important to consider the implementation of a class. When a class is implemented; that is, when it is sent an external message in order to invoke some behavior, the sender of the message should not rely upon the inner workings of the class, how it performs its calculations, or arrives at its results—it just wants the results in the expected format. The benefit of this kind of design is that the underlying code can change, and it will not break the relationship. The concept of code that is written to expose an implementation that is independent from the manner in which messages are sent to and from its objects is called *encapsulation*.

Many things in the real world act this way—their functionality is encapsulated so that interacting with them is easy. Consider a toaster and a laptop computer. You plug in your toaster and it produces a fluffy piece of golden toast—it does what a toaster does with the electricity from the outlet. Same thing with the computer. You plug it in and it does what a computer does. There is little relation between a toaster and a computer, except they both require electricity to run. The power plant produces electricity for consumption by electrical devices; all you have to do is plug a device into the outlet. The outlet is the interface. You don't need to know anything about the power plant or how it works, and neither does your toaster. The power plant is the implementation—it is the way that power gets produced. It doesn't matter if it is coal-generated power or nuclear-generated power. Electricity is electricity. So any appliance that conforms to the interface can use the result of the implementation. You just need to have a plug that fits the socket. An outlet designed for a two-prong plug will not accommodate a three-prong plug.

Let's look at an example of how this works in Java:

```
private int num;

// public interface

public int getNum(int num) {

num = doubleIt(num);

return num;

//private implementation

private int doubleIt(int num) {

return num + num;
}
```

In this example, the implementation is hidden. The `doubleIt()` method, which returns the supplied number doubled, is private. It is not directly accessible to be sent a message from outside this class. Any code wanting to use this method must instead call the `getNum()` method—it must use the public interface. This way we can easily change the implementation of this method without breaking any code we write to access it. For instance, the code currently doubles the supplied number by adding it to itself. So, 5 + 5 = 10. However, we could later decide we wanted a more sophisticated way of doing this, say, by using * 2 (as in 5 * 2 = 10); because we have used encapsulation to shield the implementation from the interface, none of our existing code that interacts with this class will break.

5.14 Inheritance

Inheritance in OOP means that one class can define certain attributes and behaviors, and another class can inherit those attributes and behaviors. The benefits of inheritance are manifold, but one of the primary benefits is extensibility. It promotes good system design and maximizes your possibilities for code reuse.

Classes can be subclassed. You can create a class that inherits the properties and abilities of a parent class. A common and intuitive example is found in the animal kingdom. The class `Animal` might be the parent class of the `Dog` class and the `Cat` class and the `Monkey` class. The `Animal` class would hold attributes and operations that are common to all animals, such as `gestation-Period`, `numberOfLegs`, `AVG_LIFE_SPAN`, `getWeight()`, and so on.

The `Cat` class, a subclass of the `Animal` class, would hold information and define methods particular only to `Cat` objects. As always, you need to consider the purpose and scope of your application. Does `Cat` always mean a domestic cat, or might it include cougars and tigers? You might define your classes—and their data's visibility—differently when creating an application for a zoo than for an animal shelter. Consider naming in the same vein—"Cat" is probably better for the shelter application, and "Feline" might be more appropriate for the zoo.

Subclasses can also be subclassed themselves. For instance, with a `Cat` subclass of `Animal`, you could create four subclasses—`Russian Blue`, `Per-sian`, `Bombay`, and `Siamese`. They would share all of the same properties of the `Cat` class and then define their own distinct properties specific only to that kind of cat. See Figure 5.6.

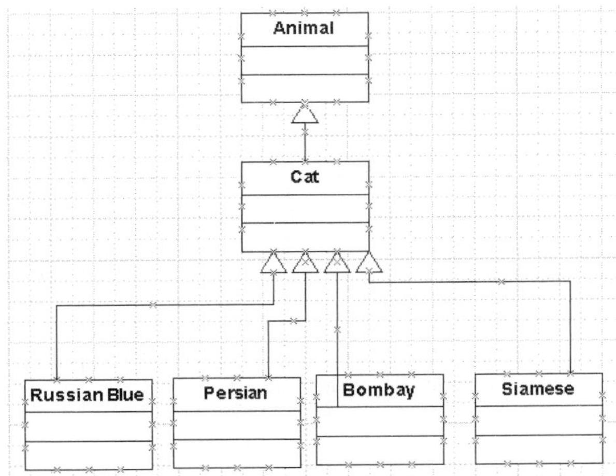

FIGURE 5.6 Inheritance between classes.

Consider this. In our WWWBooks case study, we've got employees and managers. We want to organize our application to optimally represent these two entities. It would cause us to write a lot of unnecessary code if we defined employee and manager separately. On the other hand, in the real world, a manager actually is also an employee of the company; as such, managers share a lot of attributes with employees. But they are a special kind of employee, like

Russian Blue is a special kind of domestic cat, which in turn is a special kind of animal. Perhaps, therefore, when we create our application, we should offload all of the manager data and operations into its own `Manager` class, and make it a subclass of `Employee`. Maybe both of them should be subclasses of `Worker`.

A parent class is defined in UML with an arrow pointing from the subclass to the superclass (from the child to the parent).

It is good to start thinking about what aspects of your program can be abstracted up. Perhaps a more realistic example is in order. Consider our WWWBooks case study. It probably makes sense to have a `placeOrder()` method that works for employees, managers, and customers, instead of trying to define this separately for each. Then what works in the system in the store will also work on the Web site, because you've incorporated inheritance into your design. And if you changed merchant banks, all of your order placement code would still work after you change the code in it that hits the bank, because you've used encapsulation.

5.15 Software and Hollywood Movies

The current climate in IT sees companies going out of business and laying off thousands of people every week. There is a lot of pressure to rush projects just to get them out the door. It is easy to think that there is a lot of code you've already got lying around that can be cut and pasted, and not plan sufficiently for the details of this system. The methods described in this chapter are fairly complex and require some ramping up. Sometimes we get away with it, sometimes not. Users suffer in a poorly planned system. Software must be planned.

Software lacking well-thought-out use cases is generally difficult to use. It is like a punishing art film where nothing happens. The audience is left out so the director can pursue a vision filled with mixed metaphors and cocked camera angles. Such films are boring. They're dreadful. Nobody goes to see them. Everybody hates them.

There is certainly a prominent place for art. Punishing your audience is something you can make a lot of money doing if you're in a punk rock band. This is less lucrative in the software industry.

Designing a successful system doesn't just mean designing a system that works. It means making a system that gives your user everything she needs, when she needs it. It is not confusing. It is not confused itself. And you can always get there from here.

The way to make such systems is to make them like a Hollywood movie. More specifically, a Steven Spielberg movie.

Whether or not you like his movies doesn't matter. Spielberg thinks of his audience above everything else. He is only interested in his audience. He views his job as giving the audience a roller coaster ride—he means to keep them absolutely riveted from start to finish.

Spielberg has a formula for making movies that are like roller coasters. He follows it every time. He maps out every second of the movie from start to finish, drawing it from multiple angles just as if it were an animated film. The actual filming is almost an afterthought, because it is just the real-life description of his plan. The films are obsessively manipulative.

He calls this style of filmmaking "hyperintensity." For the software developer and Web application developer, programs should have hyperintensity. Anticipate every need of the user at every moment she is engaged with your program, and be there with a message, an image, an option. Use signposts to guide your user through the system as if it were a ride. Get the user to do what you want (complete a test, create a document, purchase a product) as if you were making a hyperintensive Hollywood movie.

The only way to achieve this kind of success is to map your user scenarios, use cases, class diagrams, and sequence diagrams carefully and thoroughly. Using sound OOAD will make sure that your users' goals are always in your mind, and everything you do with the system is intended to help them successfully achieve those goals.

5.16 What's Next?

We will continue to work with interfaces and inheritance throughout the book. We will further our understanding of these concepts as we start working closely with classes in Chapter 7 and see many examples of the design work covered in this chapter.

In the next chapter, we will investigate a few different integrated development environments for Java. There are a great number of such products, some free and some very expensive. They can undermine newcomers with their complexity and general fussiness—but they can reap wonderful benefits for the prepared developer.

6

IDEs

Now we turn to the final element in the Getting Started section: integrated development environments (IDEs). Working on Java projects of any size or complexity requires having a good development environment. Because programs in Java participate in packages, require working with what are often large and complex libraries, and can have fussy compilation and deployment settings, you really need to have an environment to work in.

Of course Java programs are plain text, so the only real requirement is a plain text editor. If you only need to knock off a simple program to test something out, typing out your code in Notepad or Emacs and then compiling it from the prompt should work fine. But this quickly becomes tiresome and obviously inappropriate for any kind of project. There are many popular IDEs out there for working with Java. In this chapter we will cover some of the more popular IDEs, including Dreamweaver MX, Sun ONE Studio 3, Borland JBuilder, and IntelliJ IDEA.

There are of course many other IDEs that will do well. These include WebGain VisualCafé, Sybase PowerJ, IBM VisualAge for Java, Metrowerks CodeWarrior, and Oracle JDeveloper.

If you are using a Macintosh, Mac OS X includes an IDE with its Developer Tools that can be used to create and compile Java files. Metrowerks CodeWarrior is also available for the Mac.

There are a few of these IDEs, such as Sun ONE Studio and JBuilder, that were written in Java themselves. This is great because, as with Sun ONE Studio 3 (formerly Forte for Java), the code is available open source. You can learn about user interface design, modularity, and architecture right from the source. On the other hand, it can be rather slow to start up and slow to operate if you don't have enough system resources. If this concern is greater for you than platform neutrality, you might try one of the binary compiled choices, as they will run somewhat faster.

6.1 Macromedia Editor Changes and Java IDEs

In this section we will take a look at some of the many changes in Macromedia editors of late and what the Java development scene is like with these tools. The remainder of the chapter will examine some of the benefits and disadvantages of the various Java IDEs out there.

There are some Macromedia editors that have been rolled into other products, some that are bundled with others, and some that no longer exist. It is a bit confusing if you haven't paid careful attention; they've made a lot of changes.

6.1.1 ColdFusion Studio

We used to use ColdFusion Studio to do all of our ColdFusion work. ColdFusion Studio is at "end-of-life"—it will no longer be updated. Because of the shared code base between Studio and HomeSite, the products have been rolled into one, now called HomeSite+. This product now only ships as an added bonus when you purchase Dreamweaver MX. The clear signal from Macromedia is for ColdFusion developers to switch from Studio to Dreamweaver MX. While you can still (as of this writing) purchase ColdFusion Studio 5, you won't be able to for long.

6.1.2 Studio Functionality Included in Dreamweaver MX

A short time before the merger between Allaire and Macromedia, Macromedia began scouting for the level of interest ColdFusion developers had in Dreamweaver and other visual editors. When the merger was announced, everything suddenly became clear: It was the company's intention to roll Studio into Dreamweaver. The initial developer reaction was, in general, not favorable. Studio was a terrific product because you could write code by hand, but you could still have your work simplified by features such as RDS and tag insight. So Macromedia has now taken strides to make sure that the key functionality Allaire ColdFusion developers enjoyed in Studio is still available. Here are the features maintained in Dreamweaver MX from Studio:

- ColdFusion Studio-like source code editor view
- Web services browser
- RDS datasource browser
- Tag Dialog support, including new CF MX tags
- Code Insight support
- Tag Inspector
- Preview from Browser view
- Code Snippets
- CFC (ColdFusion Component) browser with available methods
- CFC creation wizard
- Integrated page debugging and CF debug output

6.1.3 HomeSite+

HomeSite+ combines the functionality of HomeSite and ColdFusion Studio. It is not available as a separate product, so you must buy the Windows version of Dreamweaver MX to get HomeSite+. Allaire's award-winning HomeSite has been the industry's most popular editor for HTML Web sites for years. This product will continue to be sold as a standalone HTML editor. HomeSite has actually shipped for free along with Dreamweaver since Dreamweaver 1.0, including the Dreamweaver 4/UltraDev 1 release. Of course, HomeSite doesn't contain any extensions for working with ColdFusion, let alone Java. The basic division is between FrontPage types who want to create Web sites visually and hand coders who don't want a program generating their code. HomeSite is for the latter group, and Macromedia has incorporated many of the features that hand coders want into Dreamweaver.

6.1.4 Where's the Java Support?

One reason to discourse at such length on non-Java-related issues such as the features in the current versions of HomeSite, CF Studio, and Dreamweaver is to highlight something important: There is no explicit support for Java in these editors. You need another IDE for that, which is the focus of the remainder of this chapter.

You are a ColdFusion developer who is now facing an expansion of your role. It is important now more than ever to work with Java in your Web applications. Web apps are expanding onto the desktop in a more mature and serious way than they did in 1995 with the introduction of applets. The Web, as I see it evolving, is becoming a primary distribution channel for full-blown programs instead of a final destination for HTML-based hybrid Web apps. In the last 10 years, it has grown from a massive encyclopedia to what's becoming a unified interactive platform.

The IDEs for Java are very different from what you may be used to. Now, your team may be small or large. You may be doing the design, the programming, the content, or all of it. You may have a very specific, isolated function within a group of 20 developers.

Macromedia makes JRun, the fastest Java Web application container on the market. But JRun Studio has been discontinued as of May 2002. JRun Studio was just the obvious choice for ColdFusion Studio users wishing to create JRun-based Web applications because, like HomeSite, it shares the same code base and acts very much the same. The basic difference is which tags are supported and the fact that JRun Studio included a compiler. JRun Studio 3 is shown in Figure 6.1.

But the Java IDE market is very competitive, and established players have a very solid market share. Developers weren't buying JRun Studio. So if you want to do JRun/JavaServer Pages development with Macromedia tools, you will have to use Dreamweaver MX, which supports JSP development. JRun Studio 3 will not integrate to much advantage with JRun 4.

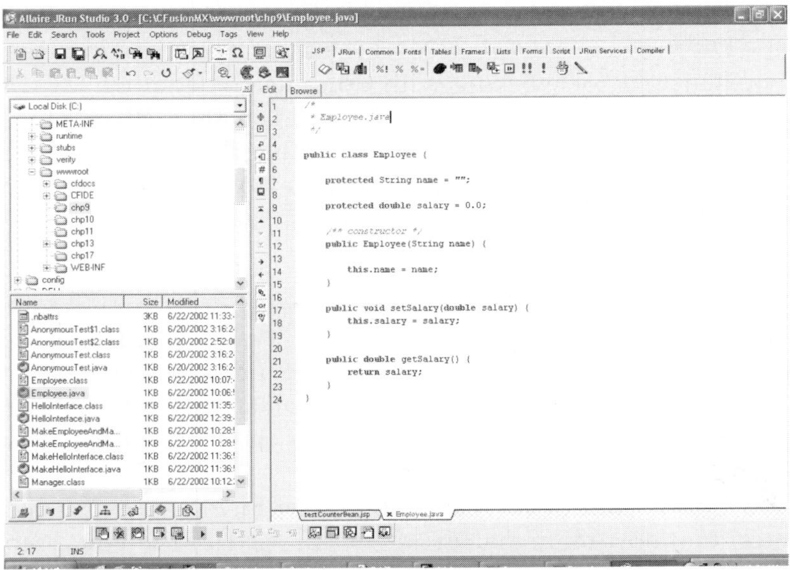

FIGURE 6.1 The discontinued JRun Studio 3.

Macromedia also recently discontinued another Java IDE product, and you may be wondering what happened to it. Allaire purchased the Kawa Java IDE a couple of years ago, and it has seen little acceptance in the market. This product is in end-of-life and the only upgrade path is to choose another IDE, such as JBuilder or VisualCafé.

6.2 Projects

IntelliJ IDEA, Dreamweaver MX, Sun ONE Studio 3, and JBuilder 7 all insist you create a project when you write code. If you are going to write anything in one of these IDEs, it must be part of a project. That can make writing small-class files for testing impractical in these programs—it can take longer to set up the project than to just write out your code in a plain text editor. Of course, the way around this is to create a test project in which you store files that aren't part of anything else, which is what I recommend doing.

NOTE Projects in Dreamweaver MX are called "sites."

Coming from the world of ColdFusion, the notion of projects is probably not entirely foreign. We could set up projects in ColdFusion Studio since version 4. This may not be something you did with any frequency in developing ColdFusion apps, however. That is for two reasons. First, despite the wizard, it is not necessarily easy to set up projects in ColdFusion studio. Second, there was simply no advantage to setting up a project that outweighed the overhead of doing so. This is not a fault of Studio. This is rather due to the nature of the ColdFusion language, especially in version 5 and prior: `.cfm` files do not depend on each other in the same way. Of course there are includes, which depend on each other, but this is not structurally similar to the way that OOP works. Moreover, prior to ColdFusion MX, you don't import packages to make your apps work.

Now, with ColdFusion MX, there is greater need for projects to help you manage your code. You now not only import libraries, but you might work with custom tags and create hybrid applications that feature both ColdFusion and JSP or servlets. So we see the "projects" feature foregrounded in Dreamweaver MX, along with the other IDEs covered here that focus on pure Java code.

If you aren't used to projects, they can cause consternation. It is nice to open up an editor and zip something off. Get used to them—fast. They aren't going anywhere, and trying to work around your IDE's projects feature is an exercise in futility. But once you are in step with using projects in your editor of choice, you will be able to take better advantage of your IDE's feature set.

Now let's take a tour of some of the top editors out there so that you can choose the one that makes sense for you. As you can see, even a simple Java program requires writing a good deal of code. As our programs expand in functionality, they will get rather long. I encourage you to get an IDE for Java. It will help you learn Java faster and keep some of the tedium out of writing common code. So let us look at the major benefits and disadvantages of some popular Java IDEs: Dreamweaver MX, Sun ONE Studio 3, JBuilder 7, and IntelliJ IDEA.

6.3 Dreamweaver MX

Dreamweaver MX is kind of a cross between FrontPage and HomeSite. It allows you to visually develop Web sites in various scripting languages. It is a mature product that now is composed of the best of many different code editing products from Macromedia. *Dreamweaver is not a Java IDE.* It is included in this discussion because it supports JavaServer Pages and is an editor that you are likely to use now that ColdFusion Studio has been discontinued. It changes your development landscape a little.

6.3.1 Overview

There is no Macromedia product intended for you to use to write Java programs as we do in this book. Kawa used to be that product, but it has recently been discontinued. Dreamweaver MX is intended for HTML and scripting languages such as ColdFusion, PHP, and ASP. There is reasonable XML support as well. The Dreamweaver MX Code Editor view is shown in Figure 6.2.

In theory (that is, in marketing material), Dreamweaver MX supports JavaServer Pages. It is indeed sufficient if you are going to write simple JSPs that do not use JavaBeans or custom actions. Writing custom actions in JSP (similar to custom tags in ColdFusion) requires creating Java class files, which Dreamweaver won't do.

6.3.2 Where to Get It

Dreamweaver MX is available from *www.macromedia.com*. There are two ways to get the software: bundled as part of Studio MX and standalone.

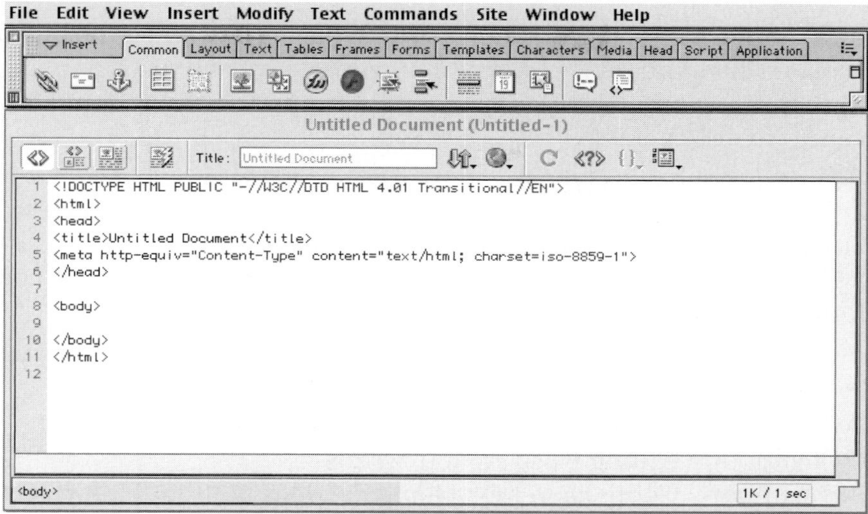

FIGURE 6.2 Dreamweaver MX in Code Editor view.

6.3.3 System Requirements

Dreamweaver MX is available only on Windows and Macintosh. The system requirements for each follow:

6.3.3.1 WINDOWS

- Pentium II, 300 MHz or higher
- Windows 98, 2000, NT, ME, or XP
- Netscape Navigator or Internet Explorer 4.0 or higher
- 96 MB RAM, 128 MB recommended
- 275 MB hard disk space
- Requires Microsoft Data Access Components (MDAC) 2.6

6.3.3.2 MACINTOSH

- Power Mac G3 or higher
- Mac OS 9 or Mac OS X 10.1 or higher
- Netscape Navigator or Internet Explorer 4.0 or higher
- 96 MB RAM, 128 MB recommended
- 275 MB hard disk space

6.3.4 Major Features

Because Dreamweaver MX is not a Java IDE, we'll look briefly at what features it has available compared with code editors you're probably used to using.

First, there are a number of things that got lost in the move from HomeSite 5 to Dreamweaver MX (DMX):

- DMX does not have keyboard shortcuts for snippets.
- DMX does not have Code Collapsing (which is great when debugging HTML tables and browser compatibility issues).
- DMX does not allow you to customize your toolbars as you could in HomeSite/Studio.

On the other hand, Dreamweaver MX has some new features that might up the difference:

- DMX supports Mac OS 9 and Mac OS X 10.1; HomeSite/Studio did not.
- DMX supports editing Flash Action Scripts.
- DMX supports ColdFusion MX; HomeSite does not (but HomeSite+ does support it).

Another nice feature of Dreamweaver MX is that you can switch between different setups, depending on what you're used to. You can have the new Dreamweaver MX workspace, which holds project information on the right-hand side with all of your tools docked. Or you can use the old Dreamweaver 4 layout, in which everything floats. Users coming from an Allaire background can have the HomeSite/coder style that leaves their directories on the left, where they're used to having them, and doesn't clutter the space quite as much.

6.4 Sun ONE Studio 3 (Forte for Java)

Sun ONE Studio 3 is a terrific editor and an excellent place to start as you search for an appropriate IDE. You may have heard of Forte for Java. This was an IDE created originally by NetBeans. Now that Sun is engaged heavily in promoting its Sun ONE (Open Network Environment) platform, it has folded many of its technologies and services under one umbrella. Throughout this book (and on the Sun Web site), you will see the terms Sun ONE Studio 3 and Forte for Java used interchangeably.

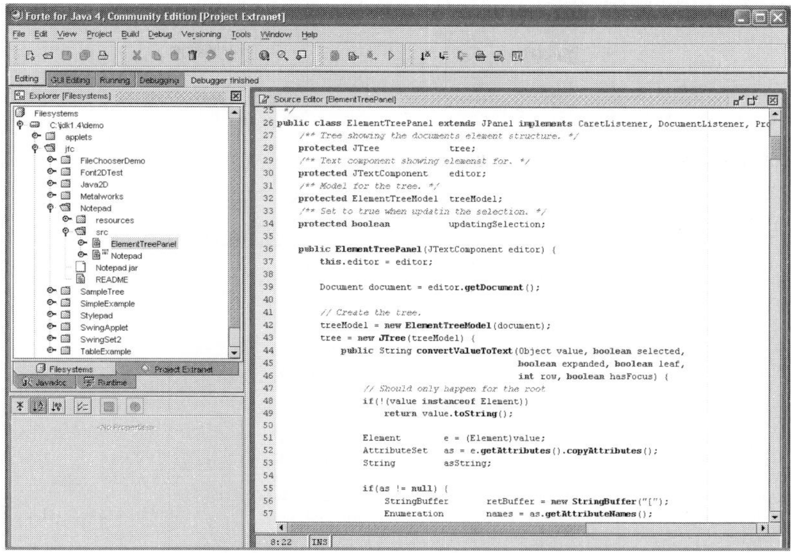

FIGURE 6.3 Sun ONE Studio 3 (Forte for Java).

6.4.1 Overview

Sun ONE Studio 3 is an excellent starting place for beginning Java developers. The Community Edition, shown in Figure 6.3, is free and has numerous features built in (including a version of the Tomcat container for running servlets and JSPs). It can be installed on Solaris, Windows, and Linux. The IDE is intuitively organized and offers a terrific price to feature set ratio—getting many of the advanced features, especially Web app features, in other IDEs can be expensive.

There are some disadvantages to working with this IDE. Sun ONE Studio 3 consumes a surprising amount of resources. It is slow to start up and can be slow to execute commands, even on a comparatively powerful workstation.

Overall, you will certainly want to download Forte and poke around. Even if you do not ultimately make it your editor of choice, it is a must-see attraction on the road to Java.

6.4.2 Where to Get It

You can download Forte for Java for free from *wwws.sun.com/software/Developer-products/ffj/buy.html*. An open source version of Forte for Java and other languages is also available from *www.netbeans.org*.

6.4.3 System Requirements

System requirements below are for the Community Edition. They are significantly higher for the Enterprise Edition.

6.4.3.1 FOR WINDOWS

- Windows NT 4 SP6, Windows 98, Windows 2000 SP2
- Pentium II 350 MHz minimum, 450 MHz recommended
- 128 MB RAM minimum, 256 MB recommended
- 110 MB hard disk space

6.4.3.2 FOR LINUX

- Red Hat Linux 6.2
- Pentium II 350 MHz minimum, 450 MHz recommended
- 128 MB RAM minimum, 512 MB recommended
- 128 MB paging/swap space
- 110 MB hard disk space

6.4.3.3 FOR SOLARIS

- Ultra 10 minimum, Ultra 60 360 MHz UltraSPARC II, or SunBlade 100 500 MHz UltraSPARC IIe recommended
- 128 MB RAM minimum, 512 MB recommended
- 128 MB paging/swap space minimum, 512 MB recommended
- 110 MB hard disk space

6.4.4 Major Features

These are the major features of the Community Edition of Sun ONE Studio that distinguish it from other IDEs.

- **Complete feature set, free.** This IDE is both free and it has many of the features you'll need as you're getting started in both Java programming and Java Web applications.
- **Web app support.** It allows for rapid development of JSPs, servlets, and tag libraries, all of which are created with templates. It's easy to build `.war` (Web application archive) files and deployment descriptors.
- **XML support.**
- **Templates.** Forte comes with a number of templates, which can be used to create beans, classes, forms, JSPs, forms in Swing, servlets, and more.

- **Easy database access.** This is achieved with Transparent Persistence using JDO (Java Data Objects).
- **Interoperability with JNDI, LDAP, RMI, and CORBA.**
- **Form editor.** It is easy to visually create forms for AWT (Abstract Windowing Toolkit), Swing, and JavaBeans. If you have used Visual Basic, it's not quite that easy, but a wizard simplifies this otherwise tedious code writing task. Compare this feature with the Design view in JBuilder.

Upgrade to the Enterprise Edition to get support for features such as J2EE (EJBs), parallel development with code management software on Windows and Linux, iPlanet integration, and Web services creation.

6.4.5 Tips and Tricks

Here are a few tips and tricks that might make working with Sun ONE Studio 3 easier or enhance your understanding of the environment.

- Some users object to the way that the IDE windows interoperate. By default, the interface is divided into several different panels, and it can be hard to keep track of all of them in your task bar. You can change this setting by choosing the Single Window version on installation. If you change your mind later, you can run the setup wizard again by going to Tools > Set Up Wizard.
- If you experience performance problems, you'll find that Forte performs faster with fewer modules installed. In the setup wizard, choose a custom module set, and install only what you think you'll need.
- This is a nice time saver as you work through example programs: In Forte there is a shortcut for writing `System.out.println();`, which can be time consuming to type over and over. On a new line in the editor, simply type `sout` and hit the space bar. Forte takes care of the rest.

6.5 JBuilder

JBuilder is an IDE developed originally by Inprise, but it is now distributed by Borland. In addition to support for Windows, Linux, and Solaris, JBuilder runs very nicely on Mac OS X.

6.5.1 Overview

JBuilder is inexpensive (under $10) for the Personal Edition. The Personal Edition is meant mostly for learning, and it is not licensed for commercial projects. The Personal Edition has few of the features that you will need for

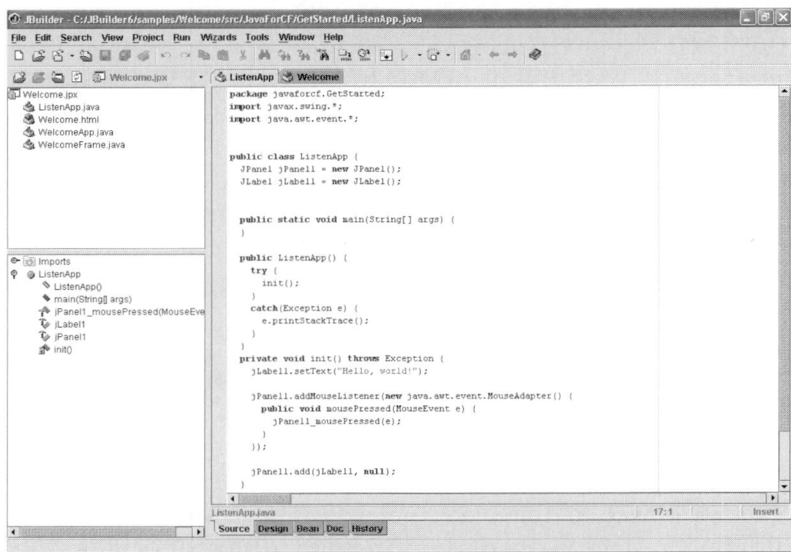

FIGURE 6.4 JBuilder interface.

writing complex applications or Web applications that use XML, JSP, servlets, and so on. The JBuilder interface is shown in Figure 6.4.

One particularly nice aspect of JBuilder is that it is a very mature product. This means that many of the kinks have already been worked out, and you should find this a reliable platform from which to develop. The current version (7) supports the JDK 1.4. Also, JBuilder can be a good choice because it is a very popular tool—there are a lot of shops out there using JBuilder.

Despite the fact that the features are very scaled back for the Personal Edition, JBuilder includes a number of introductory sample applications, which you may find helpful. But if you think you will be doing anything more than writing simple GUI applications for personal use that don't require a database, you won't find much support in the Personal Edition of the software. If you've got the budget (a few thousand dollars) for the Enterprise Edition, then JBuilder is a terrific product that takes a lot of the boring, time-consuming repetition out of writing Java apps.

6.5.2 Editions

JBuilder 7 is available in three editions: Personal, SE, and Enterprise. The Personal Edition costs less than $10, while the SE version ($399) and the Enterprise Edition (ranges from $2,999 to $3,999) are more expensive.

6.5.3 System Requirements

The minimum system requirements are as follows:

- 256 MB RAM, 512 MB recommended
- 700 MB disk space

6.5.3.1 FOR WINDOWS

- Pentium II 233 MHz or higher
- Windows 2000 SP2, XP, or NT 4 (SP 6a)

6.5.3.2 FOR LINUX

- Pentium II 233 MHz or higher
- Red Hat Linux 6.2 or 7.2 with default GNOME or KDE desktop managers

6.5.3.3 FOR SOLARIS

- UltraSPARC II or higher
- Solaris 7 (2.7) or 8 (2.8)

6.5.3.4 FOR MAC OS X

- G3 350 MHz or higher
- Mac OS X 10.1
- Some JBuilder J2EE services not available (application servers not available on this platform)

6.5.4 Where to Get It

You can download a trial version of JBuilder or purchase another version from *www.borland.com/products/downloads/download_jbuilder.html*.

6.5.5 Major Features

Below are some of the major features of JBuilder:

- **Easily create complex Swing GUI interfaces.** Swing is Java library that helps you create GUI components such as buttons and text areas for forms. They are highly configurable, and, while not necessarily difficult, they can be complex to write. You can switch to Design View to access toolbars that allow you to create these components visually. This is a great way to get started writing GUIs. If you are familiar with Visual Basic, you will find the Properties Editor very intuitive. You can draw Swing buttons, frames, text areas, slider controls, and more with the click of a mouse. Then edit each component's properties and switch to Source View to see the Java code that JBuilder generates. While you may be leery of editors that generate a lot of code, I think you'll find JBuilder's code to be sensible and even well commented.

- **Sensible views and navigation.** You can easily find what aspect of your program you're looking for with JBuilder's Structure Pane. The Structure Pane shows the structure of the currently selected file. It is organized as a hierarchical tree with all of the class's members and fields displayed. You can click on any structure item and the item will be highlighted in the Source View. Another handy thing in the Structure Pane is the Imports and Errors folder. The Imports folder holds the names of any packages you have declared imports for. Clicking the package name takes you to the specific `import` statement in your program and highlights it. This is a folder generated by JBuilder as part of a project. The Errors folder holds syntax errors. The Web view displays the output from running JSPs, servlets, SHTML, and HTML (JBuilder Enterprise only). Note that the functionality of the Structure Pane is also available in other IDEs.
- **Code Insight.** JBuilder allows you to access data members and methods for the current context. It offers parameters accepted for the method, and it drills down to source code for the current variable. The Enterprise Edition will evaluate variables and expressions inside tool tips, which is very helpful.
- **Code Templates.** These are like snippets in ColdFusion Studio and HomeSite.
- **Compare Files.** If you've used the split view in ColdFusion Studio or HomeSite, you'll find that JBuilder takes it one step further: You can compare two different files in a split view. This is something you are likely to want frequently in Java development.

6.5.6 Tips and Tricks

Here are a few tips and tricks that might make working with JBuilder easier or enhance your understanding of the environment.

- **Be careful with your JDK when using JBuilder.** If you move applications from one machine to another, you may find that they do not act the same way. Some things that work in JBuilder suddenly don't work when you open them in other editors. This is sometimes due to the fact that JBuilder will install and use its own JDK by default, and the version (currently 1.3.1) may not be what you're used to. You can change the JDK you're using by going to Tools > Configure JDKs. You can add your own by clicking Add and browsing to the home directory of the JDK you want to use.

- **JBuilder recognizes 25 different file types.** These include C and C++, WML, XML, and DTDs. JBuilder also supports syntax highlighting for Java, HTML, JSP, C, C++, SQL, XML, XSL, XSD, XSP, DTD, and IDL.

The SE and Enterprise versions offer much more functionality, especially for Web applications, working with databases, and Enterprise JavaBeans. The Enterprise version, for instance, includes a set of UML options for working with the document types we learned how to create in the last chapter.

To find out more, you can register your copy of JBuilder and participate in forums devoted to JBuilder at *www.borland.com/newsgroups*. You might also check out *http://community.borland.com* and get on a listserv at *www.borland.com/contact/listserv.html*.

6.6 IntelliJ IDEA

IntelliJ IDEA is an excellent Java IDE made in Prague, Czech Republic. The name of the IDE is IDEA, and the name of the company that currently makes it is JetBrains, formerly IntelliJ. IDEA is only available for purchase via the intellij.com Web site as an electronic download.

6.6.1 Overview

IDEA is a mature product with a midrange price (a few hundred dollars). This is an IDE for serious Java hand coders. It offers a lot of the functionality you'll need in development, but it does not give you the easy drag and drop Visual Basic style option that some of the previously mentioned editors do. Its combination of functionality and comparatively low price make it a popular choice in Java shops. In fact, many developers at Macromedia used IntelliJ IDEA to write Java code for ColdFusion MX. IntelliJ IDEA's interface is shown in Figure 6.5.

One downside to IntelliJ, like many of the other Java IDEs mentioned here, is that it does not have robust JSP support. It supports the Java code you might write in a JSP, but it does not support the XML-based JSP tags or their attributes very well. In general, if you want that, you'll find that it will either cost you an arm and a leg or you'll have to use two different editors—one, such as Dreamweaver MX, for JSPs, and another IDE for writing Java code. The obvious problem with using two editors is that your development software can get into a war over their projects. Now, if you have designers who just design, programmers who just program, developers who write JSPs, and the three will only meet once in the project, then that's not too much of an issue.

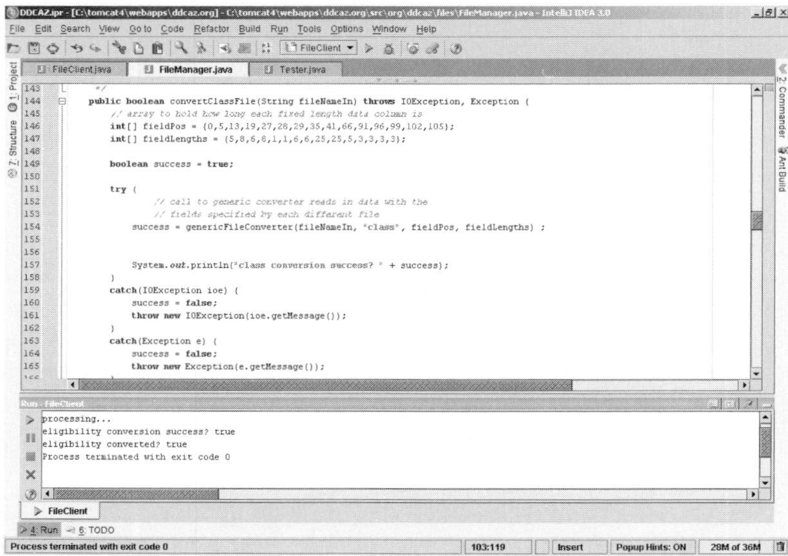

FIGURE 6.5 IntelliJ IDEA.

Another downside to using IDEA is that support on the IntelliJ Web site is rather poor. This is the sole product of a small European company. And while the product is excellent, there is very little information on the Web site about the company or the product.

6.6.2 System Requirements

IDEA will work on Windows, Linux, Mac OS X, and UNIX, and it has minimal system requirements. You only need about 20 MB hard disk space available on your machine. If this is an issue, IDEA can be a good choice, as many of the other editors we've discussed have a lot of overhead.

6.6.3 Where to Get It

You can only get IntelliJ IDEA by downloading it from *www.intellij.com/idea*.

6.6.4 Major Features

IntelliJ IDEA has many of the code editing and compilation features of the other IDEs we've discussed so far. There are a number of other features that might set it apart.

- **JavaDoc generation.** JavaDocs are built into the Java programming language and offer a way to automatically generate documentation of your code that looks just like the Java API by writing comments in your code in a specific manner. Running the JavaDoc utility creates the HTML documentation pages for you. IDEA helps you do this with a built-in feature.
- **Error highlighting.** This is probably my favorite feature of IDEA, as it's the one that I find increases productivity most. Error highlighting means that you see a red highlight under the code when, for instance, you reference a variable that you have not declared or try to send a parameter of the wrong type into a method—even methods you've defined. This feature is almost scary. It reads and understands your code as you type it, and it knows the Java libraries cold. This alone is almost worth the price of admission, in my view.
- **Version control.** IDEA supports CVS integration and Visual Source Safe integration.
- **Refactoring.** Refactor your code easily with a reference correction or with a variety of refactoring methods, all of which are fully supported. This is one of the more user-friendly features in IntelliJ IDEA.
- **Edit Java, JSP, XML, HTML, and text files.** This is achieved with syntax highlighting.
- **Fast shortcuts.** Every single feature in IDEA can be accessed with the keyboard. There is no need to use the mouse. Also, every shortcut is customizable.
- **Many familiar features supported.** These include customizable editor, code completion, and life templates. Among these, I have a couple of favorites: Automatic indention of the closing curly brace is very helpful in keeping code organized, and I also like the import assistant, which automatically inserts necessary package import statements.

Note Be careful when copying over files from one directory to another if you have already defined a project for that directory. When you open the project again, the IDE will not be able to find your project. This can be very dangerous if you copy a directory to another location and keep the old directory. The `.ipr` (IDEA Project) file will be in two locations, and you can unwittingly edit files you do not think you are editing. This can be terribly confusing. If you need to copy directories in this way as some kind of versioning, delete the `.ipr` and rebuild the new project under another name.

6.7 Putting Your IDE to Work

Please do not allow something that has been mentioned in this chapter as a major feature of one IDE to sway you entirely toward that product. Almost all of the features mentioned here are shared among the different IDEs. Sometimes they are easier to use, more prominent, or more powerful. They all have debuggers. They all have inspectors. They all have wizards. In the end, choosing an IDE will be entirely a matter of personal preference—what others around you are using, how serious you think you'll need to be, and what your budget is.

In the next couple of sections, we will take a quick look at some common things you need to do to work in these various IDEs, such as setting up a project, using the built-in templates to reduce the amount of code writing you need to do, and working with the interactive debugger.

6.7.1 Getting Started with a Project in IntelliJ IDEA

Once you have downloaded and unpacked the compressed IDEA file, you'll want to create a folder to extract it to (strangely, the decompressor won't create one for you). Call it `IntelliJ_IDEA`. Go into the `<IDEA_HOME>/bin` folder to find the executable `idea.bat` file. Double clicking here will launch the program. The first time you run the program, it will ask for your username, which you are assigned when you purchase IDEA. Enter this and the key number, and you will be prompted to set up a project.

Now let's create a project that we can use to store the programs we'll write in the remainder of this book.

1. Enter a name for the project. Type `JavaForCF`.
2. The default location for the project will be the name of the project as an `.ipr` file. For instance, if you've installed IDEA in a folder under your root directory on Windows, this will be `C:\Intellij_IDEA\JavaForCF.ipr`.
3. You can change the JDK you want to use with IDEA in the JDK field. Older versions of IDEA will not work well with JDK 1.4; you can specify another JDK here if you wish.
4. Select the compiler output path. When you write source files, the compiler can place them in a different directory from the source files. This is recommended so that when you deploy your application you don't send the source with them. It also helps keep things organized. Choose `C:\IntelliJ_IDEA\JavaForCF`, then we'll make a separate package as we move through each chapter. You'll want to make sure you

package your files, which we'll start doing in the next chapter, so that your classes are organized in that directory.

5. Next, we specify the project path. This is where the working files for the project will be. In general, you'll want to store your source files somewhere other than under the JDK directory. For now, we want to have the source files next to the class files. The project path by default will have the path name of the directory into which you installed IDEA. If you created a folder called `IntelliJ_IDEA` in the Windows root, the default value is `C:\IntelliJ_IDEA`. Let's specify a subfolder for this project. Click the ellipses (`...`) button next to the Project Path field to get a file browser. Find your `<IDEA_HOME>` folder, right click on it, and choose New Folder. Type `JavaForCF`, then click OK.
6. The next screen informs us of the locations for source paths for this project. The JDK is included here, as is the directory we just created with a subdirectory called `src` for "source". Click Next, and allow IntelliJ to create the `src` folder if it asks to. So, you'll write all of your source files for Java classes in `<IDEA_HOME>\JavaForCF\src`. For me, that is `C:\IntelliJ_IDEA\JavaForCF\src`. Click Next.
7. This step asks you to specify the class path entries where other Java class files required for your project can be found. When you write an extensive Java application, you might require, for instance, a particular XML parser or a tag library created by a third party. These are usually packaged into `.jar` (Java archive) files, which use the same compression algorithm as `.zip` files, and are then distributed. You can place such `.jar` files directly under your JDK. This is an easy way to add extensions to your projects. You don't have to modify classpath settings, and they can be used by any application you make. This is the reason that you see all these `.jar` files in this step of the project setup wizard under `<JAVA_HOME>/lib/ext/`. Right now, we don't have any other `.jars` to add, so just click Finish. IntelliJ will create the project and show you a tip of the day.

Now your project is set up in IntelliJ, and you can start working. Click the Project tab, which will reveal your project directory structure. Let's do a test file quickly to make sure that all of the paths are correctly resolving and that you can compile and view the results of your work.

You should see your project tree in the left-hand side of the screen in the Project tab. Right click on the folder in which you want to place your class file or create a new folder.

Let's make a folder called chp6 by right-clicking on the <IDEA_HOME>\JavaForCF\src folder. Choose New > Folder from the context menu and name it chp6. Then, right click on your new chp6 folder. Choose New > Class. You will be prompted for the class name. Type TryIdea and click OK. Something like the following code is created for you:

```
/*
 * Created by IntelliJ IDEA.
 * User: eben
 * Time: 11:33:04 PM
 * To change template for new class use
 * Code Style | Class Templates options (Tools | IDE Options).
 */
package chp6;

public class TryIdea {
}
```

Notice that the package name has automatically been created for you. Now you can enter the data for your class.

Inside the class curly braces, write a main method, type System.out, and wait one second. You will see a menu pop up with all of the available methods of the out object. This is similar to the Tag Insight function you're used to in ColdFusion Studio and HomeSite. Choose println() and type a message to print. Now compile your test program by clicking the icons with the 0s and 1s in it. This will compile all modified files in a project. If you are not sure what a button does, mouse over it for a moment, and you'll see a tip in the bottom left-hand corner of the screen. IDEA will compile your class and display any errors in a bottom window.

To run your project, click the green arrow. If you have not yet compiled your class, this will do it for you.

> **NOTE** You may have difficulty once you have multiple, unrelated example files set up in the same project. That is because the main method is the entry point for a Java program—no matter if it is one file or one thousand files. The project will (rightly) assume that the files in packages under the same directory should all belong to one application.

You should be asked to create a default application configuration. Just click the + button and choose the file in which the main method resides. Right now, this is chp6.TryIdea. You can specify additional parameters for the Virtual

Machine here, and in the Program Parameters you can supply any arguments to send to the `main` method. After you have specified the file containing the `main` method, click Run, and you will see the output of the program at the bottom of the screen.

My program just prints `Hello, sweetheart!`, so my output looks like this:

```
C:\jdk1.4\bin\javaw.exe-classpath
C:\jdk1.4\jre\lib\rt.jar;C:\jdk1.4\jre\lib\ext\dnsns.jar;C:\jd
k1.4\jre\lib\ext\ldapsec.jar;C:\jdk1.4\jre\lib\ext\localedata.
jar;C:\jdk1.4\jre\lib\ext\sunjce_provider.jar;C:\IntelliJ_IDEA
\JavaForCF chp6.TryIdea
Hello, sweetheart!
Process terminated with exit code 0
```

If you see something similar, you're good to go. If you get errors, check your program syntax. Check that you have correctly set up the project and that you have specified the correct JDK. Modify any project-specific settings, including the JDK being used, in File > Project Properties.

6.7.2 Setting Up a Project in JBuilder

In order to work in JBuilder, you need to create a project. In this section, we will see how to do this.

To create a new project, choose File > New Project from the main menu. You will begin a wizard. Type `JavaForCF` for the project name. Choose the home directory to be `<JBUILDER_HOME>/JavaForCF`. Click Next.

You can use the JDK that ships with JBuilder or specify a newer JDK to use. The output paths should be populated more or less like this:

```
JDK: java 1.3.1 -b24
Output Path: C:/JBuilder6/JavaForCF/classes
Backup Path: C:/JBuilder6/JavaForCF/bak
Working Directory: C:/JBuilder6/JavaForCF
```

Click Next to get to the final step, which allows you to specify general project settings. You can add settings such as the name you would like to appear in the JavaDoc comments generated at the top of the source code. Click Finish and you're off.

To test if everything is pointing in the right direction, let's write a quick test file. But this time, instead of writing a little Hello World file like we did with IDEA, let's use the Design View feature of JBuilder to generate a little GUI interface without writing any code.

6.7.3 Creating a File in JBuilder

With the JavaForCF project open, click the white paper icon to create a new file. The Object Gallery will appear, which allows you to choose among different files you can create. You are pretty much limited to class files and applets when using the Personal Edition. Choose Class File, and a wizard appears.

Choose a package for the class. Because we have not created any subfolders, we should specify `javaforcf.chp6` as the package. The default (project) package is `javaforcf`. Adding the `chp6` package in our code will automatically create this folder for you when you compile the class.

In the Class Name field, type `TryJBuilder`.

A Base Class of `java.lang.Object` is fine.

In the options area, choose the options you want for this class. I will leave all of the default options, such as Public, Generate `main` Method, Generate Header Comments, and so on, checked. Click OK and the class code will be started for you. JBuilder 6 creates this code:

```
package javaforcf;

/**
 * <p>Title: </p>
 * <p>Description: </p>
 * <p>Copyright: Copyright (c) 2002</p>
 * <p>Company: </p>
 * @author E Hewitt
 * @version 1.0
 */

public class TryJBuilder {

  public TryJBuilder() {
  }
  public static void main(String[] args) {
    TryJBuilder tryJBuilder1 = new TryJBuilder();
  }
}
```

As you can see, this is rather more code generated than what IDEA made for us, which may or may not be useful, depending on what you're doing. Now we have this basis for a class.

6.7.4 Creating a New Application

JBuilder makes it easy to start creating applications that consist of GUI components. An application needs a window in which to reside, and it can be complicated code to write, but it's rather standard stuff once you've done it a couple of times. So let's start by having JBuilder do it for us first, then we'll know how it's done.

To create a new application, click File > New and choose the Application icon. This starts the New Application Wizard.

First we are asked to enter the application class details. Once we have completed the wizard, the application will consist of the main application class and a Frame class. Then we'll use the visual designer to add elements to it.

Enter `javaforcf.chp6` in the Package Name field.

Next, enter `TryJBuilder` for the Class field value. Click Next.

In the last step, the wizard asks us for details regarding the Frame class, as shown in Figure 6.6. We can leave the class name Frame1 and enter My GUI App in the Title field. In the options area, you'll see several check boxes asking you what components you would like JBuilder to generate the code for. Let's choose all of them: Generate Menu Bar, Generate Toolbar, Generate Status Bar, and Generate About Dialog. Center Frame On Screen is already checked. Click Finish.

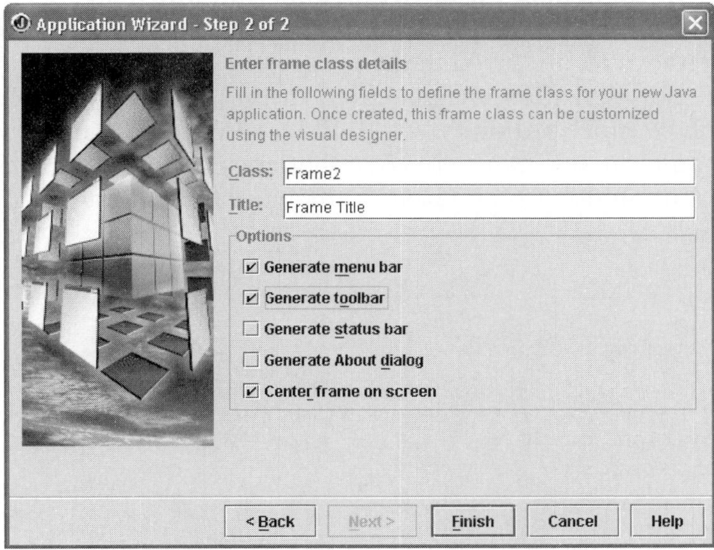

FIGURE 6.6 The JBuilder Application Wizard.

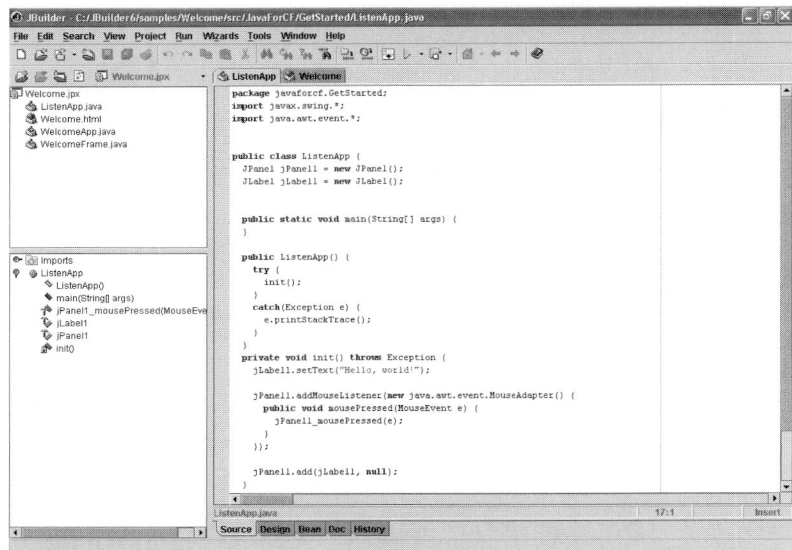

FIGURE 6.7 JBuilder editor after the code has been generated.

After a quick moment, the IDE will return to source editor mode, with the Structure Pane showing all of the fields and methods it created, as shown in Figure 6.7. Click on an item in the Structure Pane, and the relevant code will be highlighted in the editor. You'll notice too that a few icon `.gif` files were automatically written for you and used in the program.

Here is the code that JBuilder generated in the two-step wizard. This not only illustrates how much tedious work JBuilder can take care of for you, but it shows you the amount and nature of code that goes into creating a GUI application in Java. You can use this as a basic framework for creating user interfaces in Java programs.

6.7.5 `Frame1.java`

```
package javaforcf.chp6;

import java.awt.*;
import java.awt.event.*;
import javax.swing.*;

/**
 * <p>Title: </p>
 * <p>Description: </p>
```

```
 * <p>Copyright: Copyright (c) 2002</p>
 * <p>Company: </p>
 * @author E Hewitt
 * @version 1.0
 */

public class Frame1 extends JFrame {
  JPanel contentPane;
  JMenuBar jMenuBar1 = new JMenuBar();
  JMenu jMenuFile = new JMenu();
  JMenuItem jMenuFileExit = new JMenuItem();
  JMenu jMenuHelp = new JMenu();
  JMenuItem jMenuHelpAbout = new JMenuItem();
  JToolBar jToolBar = new JToolBar();
  JButton jButton1 = new JButton();
  JButton jButton2 = new JButton();
  JButton jButton3 = new JButton();
  ImageIcon image1;
  ImageIcon image2;
  ImageIcon image3;
  JLabel statusBar = new JLabel();
  BorderLayout borderLayout1 = new BorderLayout();

  //Construct the frame
  public Frame1() {
    enableEvents(AWTEvent.WINDOW_EVENT_MASK);
    try {
      jbInit();
    }
    catch(Exception e) {
      e.printStackTrace();
    }
  }
  //Component initialization
  private void jbInit() throws Exception  {
    image1 = new
ImageIcon(javaforcf.chp6.Frame1.class.getResource("openFile.
gif"));
    image2 = new
ImageIcon(javaforcf.chp6.Frame1.class.getResource("closeFile.
gif"));
    image3 = new
ImageIcon(javaforcf.chp6.Frame1.class.getResource("help.gif"));
```

```
    //
setIconImage(Toolkit.getDefaultToolkit().createImage(Frame1.
class.getResource("[Your Icon]")));
    contentPane = (JPanel) this.getContentPane();
    contentPane.setLayout(borderLayout1);
    this.setSize(new Dimension(400, 300));
    this.setTitle("My GUI App");
    statusBar.setText(" ");
    jMenuFile.setText("File");
    jMenuFileExit.setText("Exit");
    jMenuFileExit.addActionListener(new ActionListener()  {
      public void actionPerformed(ActionEvent e) {
        jMenuFileExit_actionPerformed(e);
      }
    });
    jMenuHelp.setText("Help");
    jMenuHelpAbout.setText("About");
    jMenuHelpAbout.addActionListener(new ActionListener()  {
      public void actionPerformed(ActionEvent e) {
        jMenuHelpAbout_actionPerformed(e);
      }
    });
    jButton1.setIcon(image1);
    jButton1.setToolTipText("Open File");
    jButton2.setIcon(image2);
    jButton2.setToolTipText("Close File");
    jButton3.setIcon(image3);
    jButton3.setToolTipText("Help");
    jToolBar.add(jButton1);
    jToolBar.add(jButton2);
    jToolBar.add(jButton3);
    jMenuFile.add(jMenuFileExit);
    jMenuHelp.add(jMenuHelpAbout);
    jMenuBar1.add(jMenuFile);
    jMenuBar1.add(jMenuHelp);
    this.setJMenuBar(jMenuBar1);
    contentPane.add(jToolBar, BorderLayout.NORTH);
    contentPane.add(statusBar, BorderLayout.SOUTH);
  }
  //File | Exit action performed
  public void jMenuFileExit_actionPerformed(ActionEvent e) {
    System.exit(0);
  }
```

```
  //Help | About action performed
  public void jMenuHelpAbout_actionPerformed(ActionEvent e) {
    Frame1_AboutBox dlg = new Frame1_AboutBox(this);
    Dimension dlgSize = dlg.getPreferredSize();
    Dimension frmSize = getSize();
    Point loc = getLocation();
    dlg.setLocation((frmSize.width - dlgSize.width) / 2 +
loc.x, (frmSize.height - dlgSize.height) / 2 + loc.y);
    dlg.setModal(true);
    dlg.show();
  }
  //Overridden so we can exit when window is closed
  protected void processWindowEvent(WindowEvent e) {
    super.processWindowEvent(e);
    if (e.getID() == WindowEvent.WINDOW_CLOSING) {
      jMenuFileExit_actionPerformed(null);
    }
  }
}
```

The code and comments are all JBuilder's. Now try running the program to see how it works. To run the program, click the green arrow with the tool tip that reads Run Project. The running program is shown in Figure 6.8.

You'll notice that a menu bar is generated that holds two options: File and Help. Each of these holds one option, respectively: Exit, which closes the application, and About, which displays information from the comments.

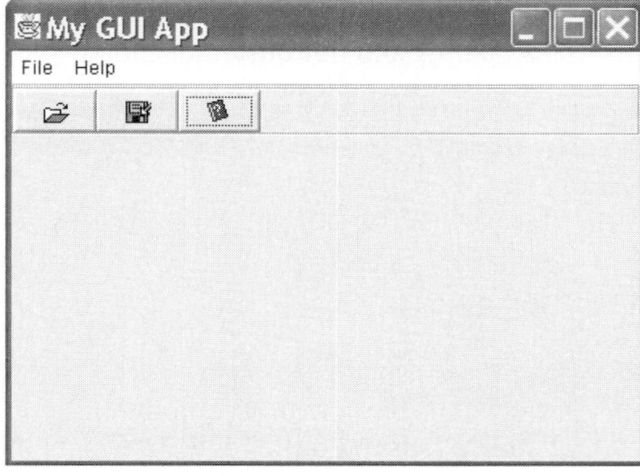

FIGURE 6.8 Result of executing the Frame1 application.

Then there are three buttons with tool tips that explain what each does. Clicking on these buttons has no effect at this point—you have to add code to make them do something.

You will notice too that the window has the look and feel of whatever platform you're on. This figure was generated on a Windows XP machine, so yours may have a different look to it.

As an exercise, try changing some of the text on the JButtons and run the program again.

Choose File > Exit. The application window will close and the program will stop running.

6.7.6 Using Design View in JBuilder

At the bottom of your open source file you should see a few tabs: Source, Design, Bean, Doc, and History. These are the View tabs. Choose the Design tab.

At the top of the editor now are new toolbars that will allow us to easily add components (such as buttons) to our program. Many of these, such as the XML, EJB, and Database, tabs are reserved for the Enterprise version of the product. We will use the Swing tab to test it.

The Java Swing library is relatively new, in some ways replacing the older AWT (Abstract Windowing Toolkit). It comprises a good deal of GUI components such as buttons, text fields, and labels. We will discuss Swing in a later chapter so you can write it by hand. For now, we will just add a simple button to our program to see how Design View works and what kind of code it generates.

> **Note** You must have defined a frame (window) before you can really use Design View to much advantage. You can add a button to your program with no frame defined, and it will compile and run without error, but you won't see anything. Don't worry about frames and buttons at this point—we're just demonstrating certain aspects of JBuilder right now, with the side benefit of getting a sneak preview at more exciting aspects of Java programming.

Choose the first button in the Swing menu, which is labeled OK. Holding your mouse over the button will reveal a tool tip stating that this component is of type `javax.swing.JButton`.

> **Note** `javax` means Java extensions. Swing components were originally made available as an optional extension to the regular Java libraries. They are now in the core libraries.

Click the JButton button and move your mouse into the main frame. The mouse will become a crosshair that you can use to draw the button.

Immediately to the right of the Help button that JBuilder made for us, draw a small square.

The Property Inspector should be on the right-hand side of your screen. We will use this to edit certain properties.

First, in the Name field, type `msg` and hit Enter. This will be our Message button. In the Property Inspector, scroll down to the Text field and type `message`.

Next, in the Title field, type `A Button Program` and hit Enter. This will change the relevant source code line to `this.setTitle("A Button Program");`.

Click the Events tab in the Property Inspector. We want to make something happen when the button is clicked. Right now, the button will appear, but nothing will happen when it is clicked. Edit the `mouseClicked` field, and a default event that should fire when the mouse is clicked will be named `msg_mouseClicked`. Hit Enter.

Now we'll turn to the source code by clicking the Source tab. The skeleton for the method has been added, but there is no functionality yet. So find the place in the code where the Property Inspector added your `mouse event` method. It will look like this:

```
void msg_mouseClicked(MouseEvent e) {

}
```

Inside the `msg_mouseClicked` method we will write the code for what should happen when the button is clicked. Type the following code so that your method looks like this:

```
void msg_mouseClicked(MouseEvent e) {
    Graphics g = getGraphics();
    g.drawString("Hello, sweetheart!", 150, 150);
    g.dispose();
}
```

Now run your program again. Running the program saves the file, compiles it, and executes the class. When you click the button, a message will appear, as shown in Figure 6.9. Choose File > Exit to end the program.

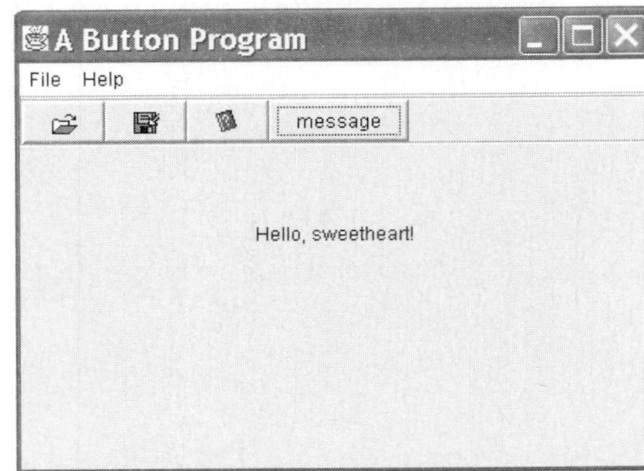

FIGURE 6.9 The final button program once the button has been clicked.

6.7.7 IDE Debugging in Forte

Forte, like other the other editors discussed here, has a debugger that works quite well. You are likely familiar with this process from using ColdFusion Studio's debugger. You will be relieved to find that the terminology is the same and that debugging Java programs is a very similar process.

You can inspect variables, set breakpoints, and step through your program. To set a breakpoint in Forte, go to Debug > Add Breakpoint. To set a variable value for a watch, go to Debug > Add Watch. Then type the name of the variable you want to see, and it shows up in the watch window. To step through an application, go to Debug > Trace Over or Debug > Trace Into. The Forte debugger is shown in Figure 6.10.

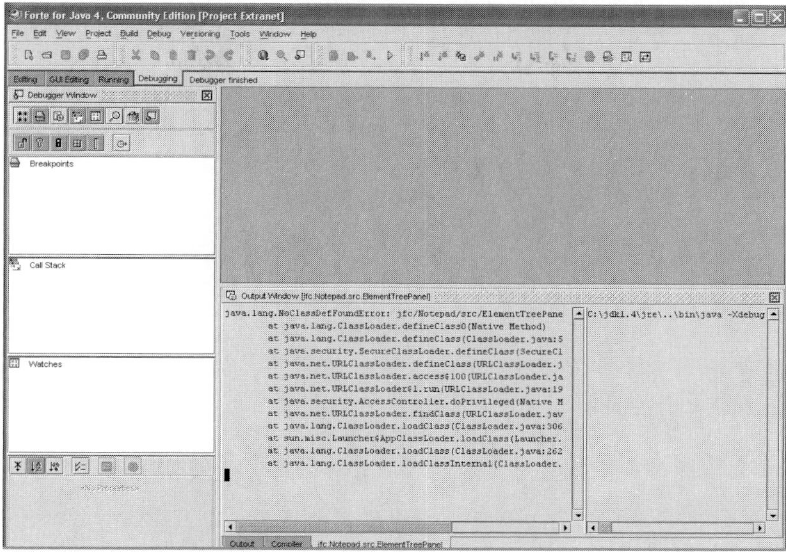

FIGURE 6.10 The Forte debugger in action.

6.8 What's Next

Now that we know Java syntax, have written a few programs, understand what to think about while planning an application, and have an environment in which to work, we can swing into action. The next section of the book, starting with Chapter 7, "Objects and Classes," will start us doing more exciting things with classes and object-oriented programming, including full-fledged GUI software programs using serialized objects, files, and databases. So get an IDE that you like and let's hit the road.

7

Objects and Classes

In this and following chapters, we examine the nature of objects and types of objects and how they interact with one another.

Classes are factories for objects. Once a class defines the kind of data it can hold and the operations it is capable of performing, a particular object can be made. For instance, "Ludwig" is an instance of the "person" class. Once instantiated (once a particular instance of a class has been brought into existence), the object often needs to relate to other objects similarly constructed in order to have a meaningful existence. Once the object can no longer fulfill the obligations of meaningful service to the organization of objects to which it belongs, it is taken out of service. Understanding the concepts presented in this chapter is crucial to excelling at Java development, as the object is the foundation of Java.

In Java, as in life, the rules regarding the creation of objects follow clearly defined and relatively simple patterns. In this chapter, we engage the complexities of the hierarchical relations involved in objects performing their functions. These relations or relational descriptors include packages and documentation, constructors, abstractions, inner classes, exceptions, and finality—few of which have meaningful corresponding terms or concepts in ColdFusion. For that reason I have tried where possible to approach the subject cautiously and from different angles up to this point.

7.1 Packages

We will begin with packages for three reasons. First, they should be somewhat familiar at this point because they have been mentioned previously. Second, working with packages is very straightforward. Finally, we will use packages to organize much of the remainder of our work, so understanding how they are used is necessary.

Applications are organized into *packages*, the fundamental organizational unit in Java. A package is simply a directory, itself composed of Java classes, interfaces, and other packages.

Use packages in a manner similar to how you use directories for storing files on your computer. Package names are hierarchical, corresponding to physical directories on your hard drive. You may create as few or as many packages as you like for your applications. Use your best judgment to decide when it makes sense to create a new package. Think about portability, code reuse, and the audience and purpose of your application.

You have encountered packages many times already. For this book, I have a root package called `JavaForCF`. Inside this package is one package for each chapter in which we write code examples, such as `chp6`. Classes in the standard API created by Sun are generally in the `java` package, and they have a subgroup when it makes sense. Packages are referenced using dot notation. So, for instance, the `java.sql` package contains classes relevant for creating connections to databases. The `java.nio` package contains new classes for input and output. That means that there is a folder called `java` that has a folder called `nio` inside it that contains the source files.

> **NOTE** Where is this folder? Installing the JDK on your system includes an archive called `src.jar`. This archive contains all of the source files used to create the JDK. You can view the source file for any given Java class by unpacking the `src.jar` archive. To unpack the archive, navigate to the JDK directory via a command prompt. Then type this command: `jarv xf src.jar C:/jdk1.4/src/java/sql/Statement.java`. This command will create the new directories `src`, `java`, and `sql`. You can then open and view the `Statement.java` file. This is the object used for executing static SQL statements and returning the results. Depending on your file associations, you might need to replace the file name `src.jar` with `src.zip` in the above command.

You will readily see the importance of using packages if you have worked with XML at all. Because XML allows you to define your own tags, just as Java allows you to define your own classes, you must have some way of indicating the uniqueness of your work to distinguish it from the work of others. That is, you have to avoid name conflicts. In XML, you do this with namespaces. In Java, you use packages.

Packages can be nested. For instance, the `String` class is in the `lang` package, which is nested in the `java` package: Any reference to `String` is really an implicit reference to `java.lang.String`.

Sun recommends using your Internet domain name for your packages, because these are already known to be unique. Generally, packages are created with the domain name as a subpackage of the name extension. For instance, packages created by Apache Software Foundation can be found inside the `org.apache` package. Here's another example: I have registered the domain CoreColdFusion.com. I might create packages for this book and this chapter in `com.corecoldfusion.javaforcf.chp7`.

7.1.1 Designing Packages

Creating unique names is the real reason for package nesting. The compiler honors no relationship whatsoever between `com.corecoldfusion.javaforcf` and `com.corecoldfusion.javaforcf.chp7`. They are organized in your mind, perhaps, but otherwise they are totally unrelated.

However, packages should be designed with care. Think of the access you want to allow, and plan for it. Classes in a package have total access to each other's non-private members. Anything not explicitly marked `private` opens your class members up for unexpected reference by unrelated classes.

Group your packages logically. This will help other programmers find your code. There is no added benefit to obscurity when placing classes in packages.

7.1.2 The `package` Object

There is a `package` object in the `java.lang` package is not used in creating or working with packages. You don't need to reference it when defining packages for your classes. It is useful for discovering metadata about a package, such as version information about a package's implementation and specification.

This can be useful to you as a programmer. For instance, you may need your program to inspect the `package` object for version information and then implement certain functionality depending on the result. You could also need this information in order to work around bugs that may exist in a certain package.

You gain access to this information by calling the `main` methods of the `package` object, which are shown here:

```
public String getName()
```

returns the name of this package.

```
public String getSpecificationTitle()
```

returns the title of the specification implemented by this package. If unknown, returns `null`.

```
public String getSpecificationVersion()
```

returns a string describing the version of the specification implemented by this package. If unknown, returns `null`.

```
public String getSpecificationVendor()
```

returns a string naming the owner and maintainer of this specification implemented by this package. If unknown, returns `null`.

```
public boolean isCompatibleWith(String desiredVersion)
```

returns a boolean indicating whether the package is compatible with the version indicated.

7.1.3 Working with Packages

There are two kinds of classes that a class can use: classes in their own package, and public classes in other packages. If you want to use a public class in another package, you have two options:

- Add the full package name to every reference you make to the class. For instance:

```
package chp7;

public class Test {

    public static void main(String [] a) {

        java.io.File myFile = new java.io.File("Dude.txt");
    }
}
```

- Import the package and reference the class name directly:

```
package chp7;

import java.io.File;

public class Test {

    public static void main(String [] a) {

        File myFile = new File("Dude.txt");
    }
}
```

Importing the `packageName.className` as shown above allows the shortcut reference to only that class, not other classes in the same package. You can use multiple import statements for the same package or different packages, like this:

```
import java.io.BufferedReader;
import java.io.BufferedWriter;
...
```

If you are going to import more than one or two classes in the same package, use the wildcard character to import all of the classes in a package, like this:

```
import java.io.*;
```

When importing a package, you can import the package name with a trailing `*` to indicate that you want to import all of the classes in that package.

> **NOTE** Using the `*` to indicate the import of all classes in a package does NOT import nested packages. For instance, importing `java.util.*` will import all classes located directly in that package, but not the `java.util.jar` or `java.util.zip` subpackages.

You can only import classes. You cannot import objects.

The only time you need to worry about your imports is when you have two classes that have the same name in different packages. A common example of this kind of conflict is with two different Date classes provided by the JDK.

There is one in `java.sql` and another in `java.util`. So while the following will compile,

```
import java.util.*;
import java.sql.*;
```

you won't be able to reference the `Date` class in this program without the package name, like this:

```
Date hireDate; // Error!
```

because the compiler won't know if you mean `java.util.Date` or `java.sql.Date`. If you need to use both Date classes, you don't have a choice but to explicitly reference each one:

```
java.sql.Date hireDate = new java.sql.Date();
java.util.Date fireDate = new java.util.Date();
```

7.1.4 Packaging a Class

It is easy to add classes to a package: Create a directory. You do so using the `package` keyword at the top of your class definition:

```
package chp7;

public class Test {
      //... code here
}
```

This command must be the first non-comment line of code in your class definition.

It is not necessary to put your class into a package. If you do not include a `package` command in your source file, the classes therein are added to the default package. The default package has no name. If the directories don't exist, some IDEs will create the packages for you and place the resultant class in there. The compiler won't check directories, however, when source files are compiled, and the virtual machine may not be able to find the resulting class file. For that reason, put your source files and class files in the same directory structure.

7.2 Documentation with JavaDoc

You can automatically create documentation for your applications using special Java comments in your source files, and you can then extract them with the `javadoc` tool. This has many advantages: Instead of having to go through a separate process of documentation (which people are less likely to do anyway), allowing the documentation to emerge directly from comments in the program itself means the docs are more likely to be up to date, complete, and standardized. Because the pages generated are HTML pages, they are immediately available for distribution in a common format. All of the HTML documentation for the Java API was generated using JavaDoc.

The `javadoc` tool comes with the standard JDK, and it is easy to use.

> **NOTE** This is the third tool we have looked at so far, `javac` for compilation and `java` for program execution being the others. You can view other tools available in the standard JDK by peeking into the `<JAVA_HOME>/bin` directory.

There are two requirements for creating this documentation: You must add the comments to your file, and then you must run the `javadoc` tool to extract the comments and create the HTML files from them.

The `javadoc` tool extracts comments for the following:

- Packages
- Public classes and interfaces
- Public and protected methods
- Public and protected fields

Private items are not included. It is a good idea to comment all of these items in your code. Write your comments immediately above the items in the code.

7.2.1 Creating JavaDoc Comments

You notate comments that you want to be picked up by `javadoc` like this:

```
/**
some comments
*/
```

Putting the extra `*` after the first comment line means that the compiler will rightly ignore your comment as a regular comment, but `javadoc` will know to pick it up. Note that any JavaDoc comments must be outside a method.

Generally, it is a good idea to include information about the creator, creation date of the file, and other information just as you would comment a ColdFusion custom tag:

```
/**
 * <p>Title: SomeClassFile</p>
 * <p>Description: This file prints <b>'Hello!'</b> to the
command line</p>
 * <p>Copyright: Copyright (c) 2003</p>
 * <p>Company: WWWBooks</p>
 * @author E Hewitt
 * @version 1.0
 */
...class definition here...
```

Notice that in the comments there are two kinds of symbols used: HTML paragraph tags and the @ symbol. You can write any HTML in here, though the use of heading tags is generally discouraged because it can conflict with the JavaDoc formatting and distort the layout.

7.2.2 JavaDoc Tags

The @ symbol inside a JavaDoc comment denotes a tag. There are several tags you can use, and they display different kinds of information in the generated document. A description of each follows:

7.2.2.1 `@author` *`author`*

Documents the author of the class. Use one `@author` tag for each author. You might need to use the `-author` option during the `javadoc` execution for the `@author` field to be included.

7.2.2.2 `@deprecated` *`description`*

Indicates that the class, method, or variable is deprecated and should not be referenced in the future. The description text should indicate what to use instead of the deprecated item, for example:

```
@deprecated Use <code>anotherMethod(String s)</code>
```

The description message may indicate other information about the nature of the deprecation; it can be used for classes, variables, and methods.

7.2.2.3 `@docRoot` *`path`*

Specifies the path to the root directory of this documentation.

7.2.2.4 `@exception exceptionName and explanation`

Identifies an exception that a method throws and describes in what circumstances the exception might occur. Can only be used for methods.

7.2.2.5 `{@link` *`name text`*`}`

Inserts a link inline to another item with related information. `name` indicates the name of a class or method to which the link will be added. The `text` is displayed.

7.2.2.6 `@param` *`name`*

Identifies a parameter for a method. Can only be used in documenting a method.

7.2.2.7 `@return` *`value`*

Identifies a method's return value. Can only be used in documenting a method.

7.2.2.8 `@see` *`link`*

Adds a hyperlink to more information, for example:

```
@see href
@see packageName.className#member text
```

The first way of writing this is to specify as `href` an absolute or relative URL. The second form specifies the name of a class in a package and, optionally, the name of a member. The *`text`* parameter is also optional.

7.2.2.9 `@serial` *`link`*

Adds a hyperlink in the "see also" section. More information on this tag appears below.

7.2.2.10 `@serialData` *`description`*

Comments the data written by the `writeObject()` and `writeExternal()` methods.

7.2.2.11 `@serialField` *`name type description`*

Comments an `ObjectStreamField` component.

7.2.2.12 `@since` *`versionNumber`*

Adds a `since` element. Its value should be a description of the release that first introduced this feature. For example, `@since version 1.3.1`. Can be used for documenting classes, variables, and methods.

7.2.2.13 `@throws exceptionName and explanation`

Has the same usage and meaning as the `@exception` tag.

7.2.2.14 `@version` *`description`*

Identifies the version of a class. Example:

```
@version version 1.0
```

You may need to explicitly specify the `-version` argument when using the `javadoc` utility.

7.2.3 Package Comments

You can create comments regarding your packages by adding a file named `package.html` to each package directory. All of the text you write between the `<body>` tags will be extracted when you run the `javadoc` command (we'll see how to do this in a moment).

7.2.4 Overview Comments

It is often useful to supply a general comment on all source files. To do this, create a file called `overview.html` in the parent directory for all application source files. As with the `package.html` file, anything between the `<body>` tags will be extracted. The comments are shown to the user when Overview is selected from the nav bar.

7.2.5 Doclets

Documentation using `javadoc` is a wonderful feature of the JDK. But all of the documentation conforms to the same look and feel as the docs that come with the JDK itself for describing classes in the Sun packages.

While you can specify your own stylesheet for use with `javadoc`, you may wish to include a more customized interface for your comments. If you have this kind of specialized requirement, doclets provide a way for you to create very customized documentation. See the online documentation on doclets at *www.sun.com* for more information.

7.2.6 Extracting Comments

In order to extract the JavaDoc comments you've written into your files, you use the `javadoc` command. Using the `javadoc` tool for extraction creates new HTML files in appropriate folders based on your comments. To do this, follow these steps:

1. Navigate to the directory that contains the source files you wish to create documentation for. You must be in the parent directory for all of the application's source files (usually `com`). This directory also contains the `overview.html` file if you wrote one.
2. If this is a single package, run the `javadoc` tool by issuing the command `javadoc -d docsDirectory packageName`. The `docsDirectory` here is the name of the directory you want to create the HTML files in.
3. If you have multiple packages, run this command: `javadoc -d docsDirectory packageName1 packageName2....`
4. If all of your files are in the default package, you can issue this command: `javadoc -d docsDirectory *.java`.

Note that you can use many different options when running the `javadoc` tool. To see what the options for this tool are, you can simply run `javadoc`. This will give you an error message that says you've not supplied the correct parameters, and it will therefore also show you all of the correct parameters, as shown in the next section.

7.2.7 JavaDoc Usage

Usage for the `javadoc` tool is shown below:

```
    usage: javadoc [options] [packagenames] [sourcefiles]
[classnames] [@files]
```

Some of the notable arguments available are shown below:

`-overview <file>`	Read overview documentation from HTML file
`-public`	Show only public classes and members
`-protected`	Show protected/public classes and members (default)
`-package`	Show package/protected/public classes and members
`-private`	Show all classes and members
`-help`	Display command line options
`-doclet <class>`	Generate output via alternate doclet
`-docletpath <path>`	Specify where to find doclet class files
`-sourcepath <pathlist>`	Specify where to find source files

```
-classpath <pathlist>         Specify where to find user class files
-exclude <pkglist>            Specify a list of packages to exclude
-subpackages <subpkglist>     Specify subpackages to recursively load
-source <release>             Provide source compatibility with specified release
-extdirs <dirlist>            Override location of installed extensions
-verbose                      Output messages about what javadoc is doing
-locale <name>                Locale to be used, e.g., en_US or en_US_WIN
-encoding <name>              Source file encoding name
```

Some notable arguments include the ability to specify your own stylesheet for the documentation. If you don't specify one, your JavaDocs will look like the Sun JDK docs.

Let's write a simple class just to make some comments and see how they are generated into HTML documentation by JavaDoc.

7.2.8 `Comments.java`

```
/*
 * Comments.java
 *
 * Created on June 6, 2002, 9:09 AM
 */

package chp7;

/**
 * The <code>Comments</code> class is <i>very</i>
 * sophisticated. It's like a TS Eliot poem:
 * there are more comments than code!
 * @author  eben hewitt
 * @version 1.0
 */
public class Comments {

    private String msg = "This is the Comments class.";

    /**
      * Public default constructor.
      * Creates a new Comments object.
      */
    public Comments() {
    }
```

```
    /**
    * @param args the command line arguments
    */
    public static void main (String args[]) {
        Comments myComments = new Comments();
        System.out.println(myComments.showMsg());
    }

    /**
     * This method gets the msg String and returns it.
     * @return The value of <code>msg</code>, which is a
     * String message to the user
     */
    public String showMsg() {
        return msg;
    }

     /**
      * @deprecated This method is deprecated because it
      * breaks encapsulation.<br>
      * It has been replaced by showMsg().
      * @see Comments#showMsg() showMsg().
      *
      */
     public void printMsg() {
        System.out.println(msg);
    }
}
```

7.2.9 Generating the `Comments.java` JavaDoc

There are generally two ways to create the JavaDoc. You can do so at the command line, or you can use your IDE of choice. Here's how you would do it for `Comments.java` in Forte (Sun ONE Studio):

1. Once you've written the comments and you're ready to create the JavaDoc, right click anywhere in your source code file. A context menu appears. Choose Tools > Generate JavaDoc.
2. Forte generates the comments and asks if you would like to view them in a browser. If you have not specified a directory, Forte will automatically create the folders and files under a subdirectory of Forte, like this:

   `C:\forte4j\bin\projects\javadoc\index.html.`

   Since this obviously isn't very workable, remember to use the `@docRoot` tag to specify a directory.

Here's what we type at the command line if you prefer this method:

1. At the command prompt, navigate to the directory that contains the package you want to document.
2. Type `javadoc -d docsOutputDirectory nameOfPackage`. To generate the docs for the Comments file in the `chp7` package that we just wrote, I type this:

```
C:\jdk1.4\JavaForCF>javadoc -d C:\MyJavaDocs chp7
```

The utility lets you know what it's doing, and after a moment, your directory will be created and you can view your documentation. Open the `index.html` page, and a link to the `Comments` class documentation will be presented. See Figure 7.1.

In ColdFusion it is very important to comment your work. While the `javadoc` utility makes it very easy to generate sophisticated and usable documentation, it also requires more effort: It forces you to comment everything that's public. It's a good practice to get into. We can't do it in the code examples in this book because of space considerations, but do comment your work.

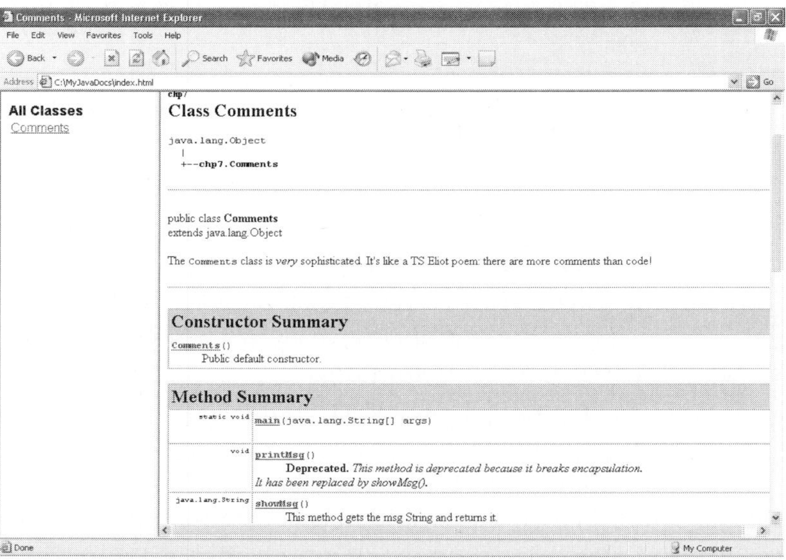

FIGURE 7.1 Generated JavaDoc comments.

7.3 Field Defaults and Field Initializers

Local variables do not have a default value. They cannot be used until they are initialized. By contrast, class fields are automatically initialized to the default values for their types. As you may recall from Chapter 3, fields are set to `0` or `null` or `false` by default, depending on their type. It is a good idea, however, to set your instance fields to something you can use and not just leave them with their defaults.

As you might imagine, initializing a class field value looks like this:

```
public int i = 3;
public static boolean b = true;
```

The syntax here is useful if you want to have all of a class's constructors set your instance field to the same value. You can initialize objects through initialization expressions for fields and in constructor code. Classes have class initialization methods that are like constructors. The difference is that constructors allow you to define the body of those methods, and class initialization methods don't.

The way to initialize class fields is with something called a *static initializer.* A static initializer is the keyword `static` followed by code in curly braces.

You declare a class field much as you would declare a local variable. The chief difference is that field declarations do not belong to any method. For that reason, they cannot be executed like statements. The main thing to remember about class fields is that they are associated with the class itself, not with an object, so they must be initialized before a constructor is called.

7.3.1 `final` Instance Fields

An instance field can be defined as `final`. If you want to do this, you must initialize the instance field when you construct the object (see "Constructors" below). That makes sure it has a value, and the value cannot be modified again in the lifetime of the object.

Instance fields are declared `final` using the `final` keyword:

```
class MyClass {
     private final int ID;
}
```

In general, it is a good idea to mark as `final` whatever you can. If you think you'll never need a mutator method for the field, then the field is probably a good candidate to be `final`. However, be careful that the value really will never need to change. While "name" seems like a reasonable choice for `final`, there are numerous reasons for a name to change: people get married, have their names legally changed, get divorced, decide to start using their middle initial, and so on.

7.3.2 `System.out.println()`

Here is an example to illustrate the usage of class fields. Because we have used it so frequently, it is important to understand what is happening when you use `System.out.println()` to print something out to the command line. What exactly is going on? Now that you know more about classes and methods, it may be apparent: In the `java.lang` package is a class called `System`, which cannot be instantiated. It has three class fields: err (the standard error output stream), in (the standard input stream), and out (the standard output stream). These refer to `PrintStream` objects. A `PrintStream` object is defined in the `java.io` (input/output) package. The `PrintStream` object takes a method called `println()`.

7.3.3 Signatures and Headers

Methods are a key aspect of Java programming. They look similar to the ColdFusion functions we're used to, and in some cases they act similarly. There are even certain Java methods that are just about the same as ColdFusion functions, such as `#abs(a)#` and `java.lang.abs(int a)`. However, because Java is object oriented, defining methods can be a far more complex task than writing ColdFusion UDFs. We have been working with Java methods throughout the book, and in different sections in this chapter we will look at the aspects of Java methods that distinguish them as an object-oriented language.

The *signature* of a method is composed of its name along with its parameter list. The header of a signature is composed of the signature, any modifiers (such as `public` or `static`), and the list of exceptions thrown. The HTML Java API documentation consists of such headers.

We need to have signatures in Java, and not in ColdFusion, because Java is object oriented and ColdFusion isn't. Signatures help us keep things straight, which can be difficult given *polymorphism*—the subject of the next few sections.

7.4 Polymorphism

Polymorphism is Greek for "many shapes." There are two main aspects of Java that make the language polymorphic: overloading and overriding. They both define different ways of referring to the different methods that use the same name. This sounds rather complicated, but it is really rather straightforward.

Java is not the only language that implements polymorphism. This is an aspect of numerous object-oriented languages. The concepts are difficult to explain without reference to other advanced concepts we have not covered yet. So if you find this a bit confusing, try the examples and keep reading, and then reread this section later.

7.4.1 Overloading

Overloading a method means using the same name for more than one method in the same class, supplying each with different argument lists. For example, here are some overloaded methods of the `String` class:

```
compareTo(Object o) // compares this String to another Object
compareTo(String anotherString) // compares two Strings
                                // lexigraphically
```

Overloading is an important concept in Java and is similar to behavior implicit in ColdFusion functions. Consider a familiar function, such as `ListGetAt()`, which returns the element in a given position in a list. When invoking this function, you can choose to send it as two parameters or three:

```
ListGetAt(list, position [, delimiters])
```

The `delimiters` argument is optional. If you do not supply an explicit value for it, the function assumes the delimiter to be a comma. While the implementation of this code is hidden from ColdFusion developers, the result is similar.

Of course, to the ColdFusion developer, there is only one `ListGetAt()` function, and it has three arguments, one of which is optional. But the implementation of that method is totally shielded from the developer. If you wanted to achieve the same effect in Java, you would use overloaded methods. That is, your `List` class would contain two methods, overloaded (something like this):

```
ListGetAt(String list, int position) {
    ...//def here
}
```

and

```
ListGetAt(String list, int position, char delims) {
    ...// def here
}
```

Then Java will use the correct method based on the argument list sent it. If a method is invoked with an argument list that does not match any of your method definition's argument list, a `NoClassDefFoundError` exception is thrown.

> **NOTE** As long as we've brought it up, the Java API has numerous built-in methods for manipulating strings, finding characters, and so on. Java data types are obviously different from those in ColdFusion. While Java does have arrays like ColdFusion does, what about the lists and structures? Lists in Java are in the Collections API (`java.util`). Structures don't exist per se, but name-value paired data is worked with in many different ways in Java, including vectors, hash tables, Maps, properties, and more. These are all in `java.util` as well if you're eager to peek. Don't worry about running out of ways to store name-value pairs in Java. We will talk about all of these in Chapter 11, "Collections and Regular Expressions."

It is perfectly legal to specify a different return type for overloaded methods. Specifying a different return type for a method is not sufficient to make it overloaded. You must also specify a different argument list.

Here is a more complete example of overloading:

7.4.2 DemoOverload.java

```
package chp7;

public class DemoOverload {

    public int getIt(int i) {
        return i;
    }

        // overloads getIt method
    public String getIt(int i, String s) {

        String y = Integer.toString(i) + " " + s;
```

```
        return y;
    }

    public static void main(String[] a) {

        int x = 10;

        DemoOverload o = new DemoOverload();

            // prints 10
        System.out.println(o.getIt(x));

        System.out.println(o.getIt(x, " is a good number"));
    }
}
```

You can compile and run this example. Add your own methods, and change the definitions of these methods to get used to working with overloading. There are numerous examples of overloading in the Java API. For instance, the `compareTo()` method of the `Integer` wrapper class is overloaded:

```
public int compareTo(Integer anotherInteger) {
   int thisVal = this.value;
   int anotherVal = anotherInteger.value;
   return (thisVal<anotherVal ? -1 : (thisVal==anotherVal ? 0
: 1));
    }
```

This compares two objects numerically. The version shown below accepts an object, and throws a `ClassCastException` if the value passed is not of type Integer.

```
public int compareTo(Object o) {
     return compareTo((Integer)o);
    }
```

Let's drop these into a class and see how they behave:

7.4.3 Overload2.java

```
package chp7;

/* demos overloading using API methods
 * Integer.valueOf().
 * The first method returns the integer passed.
```

```
 * The second returns the int in the radix passed.
 */

public class Overload2 {

    public static void main(String[] ar) {

        String s = "100";

        int r = 2;

        Overload2 o = new Overload2();

        System.out.println("The int: " + Integer.valueOf(s));

        System.out.println("The int in base " + r + ": " +
                                   Integer.valueOf(s, r));

    } // end main

}// eof
```

`Overload2` prints the following:

```
The int: 100
The int in base 2: 4
```

7.4.4 Overriding

There is another aspect to polymorphism: overriding. We have mentioned inheritance, and we will talk about it in more depth later in this chapter. When a method is inherited from a superclass, the subclass can change the implementation of that method. The act of a subclass redefining the implementation of a method it has inherited from a superclass is called *method overriding*.

In the case of an abstract class (which we'll also talk about at the end of this chapter), the subclass *must* define the implementation of the method. The main difference between an overloaded method and an overridden method is that overriding does not allow you to change the return type.

Here is an example of method overriding. This example defines two classes—`Parent` and `Child`. The `Parent` class defines a simple string `s`, and it defines one method for retrieving that string, `getS()`. The `Child` class also defines a `getS()` method, therefore overriding the `Parent` class's `getS()`. They have the same name, but they do different things.

7.4.5 Parent.java

```
package chp7;

// Parent is superclass of Child
// it just defines a string and an access method, getS()

public class Parent {

        String s = "I am Darth Vader (Parent). ";

        String getS() {
             return s;
        }
}
```

7.4.6 Child.java

```
package chp7;

/**
 * demonstrates overridding
 * the getS() method of Parent
 */

 // "extends" means that Child inherits from
 // the Parent class
public class Child extends Parent {

        // this value is part of the Child class
    String s;

        // overrides Parent's method
    String getS() {

            // the "super" keyword calls the parent
            // of current class. That is, "super"
            // refers to the value after the "extends"
            // keyword
        s = super.s + " I am Luke (child). ";

        return s;
    }

        public static void main(String [] ar) {
```

```
            // make a new baby
        Child luke = new Child();

            // call the Child's overriding method
        System.out.println(luke.getS());
    }
}
```

Here is the output of running `Child`:

```
I am Darth Vader (Parent).  I am Luke (child).
```

NOTE These listings honor Ray Camden's custom tag example using these same characters in his book *Mastering ColdFusion*. If you have written nested custom tags in ColdFusion, you may find it easier *conceptually* to understand working with inheritance in Java.

Overloading occurs in the compiler at compile time. The compiler chooses which one you mean by finding the corresponding argument type to what you called for. By contrast, overriding occurs at runtime. It happens when one class extends another, and the subclass has a method with the same signature as a method of the superclass.

You will never see static methods associated with overriding. That's because you use overriding when an object could belong to a certain class or a subclass of it. Because static methods do not deal directly with objects, the runtime doesn't have to bother trying to sort out which method is meant to be invoked.

7.4.7 `private` Methods

`private` methods can be called only from methods in the same class. It is common for us to define private data and then define `public` methods to set or access that data. While most methods are public, it is not uncommon to find `private` methods.

`private` methods are useful when you want to break up functionality into multiple methods. Maybe you need a helper to perform certain operations, and the `public` would not be able to call the helper by itself coherently.

All you need to do to create a `private` method is to exchange the keyword `public` for `private` in the method definition, like this:

```
private doSomething(int a) {
    ...// code here
}
```

The chief reason to define a method as `private` is that the programmer can be assured that nothing outside the defining class is accessing it. That means you can drop it or change it without worrying about what you might break somewhere else. You don't have that assurance with a `public` method.

7.5 Constructors

A constructor is a way of creating an object. The most common way to do this is using the `new` keyword, as we have done a number of times already:

```
Type ObjectName = new Type(arguments);
```

When you write this statement, the runtime determines if there is enough memory space to create your object and the data that it will hold. If there is enough, the object is created and set to its initial state. If there is not enough space, then the runtime looks for space it can reclaim and runs the garbage collector to reclaim it. The garbage collector destroys items with no references, as they could no longer be necessary to a program's life. If there is still not enough free space, an `OutOfMemoryError` exception is thrown.

Once an object is created, its variables must be initialized. That is the purpose of constructors. For example, given an `Employee` class, we could perhaps create a new `Employee` like this:

```
Employee anEmployee = new Employee("Bill");
```

The class type is declared, a name is given to the instance of the object, and `new` is invoked to create a new object of type `Employee`. Using the `new` keyword tells the class to call the constructor whose argument list matches the given argument list. Because we're passing one argument—a string representing the employee's name—we need to have one constructor in our class definition that accepts a sole string as an argument. If we don't, the Java Virtual Machine will throw a `NoClassDefFoundError` exception.

7.5.1 Overloading Constructors

Often, classes will have more than one constructor. An object can be created with a different initial depending on which constructor is used. The type and number of arguments determines which constructor will be used to create the object. Defining multiple constructors with the same name but different parameter lists is called *overloading*. There are many classes in the API with overloaded constructors. The `String` class defines 11 different string constructors. Here are a few of them, all of which create a string:

```
String() // one
String(bytes[] bytes) // two
String(char[] value) // three
```

NOTE Defining multiple methods or constructors with the same name but different parameter lists is called *overloading.*

7.5.2 No-arg and Default Constructors

No-arg constructors are constructors that do not accept arguments. You can explicitly write a no-arg constructor in your code. If you do not, then Java writes in a no-arg constructor that does nothing. That constructor is called the *default constructor.*

The default constructor is provided only in the event that no other constructors exist.

7.5.3 Static Constructors

Constructors cannot be declared static, and so Java gives us a way to perform static initialization. To declare a static constructor, you use the keyword `static` followed by the body of the method you're defining.

NOTE You can declare multiple static constructors, but the Java compiler will combine all of them into one method. The reason for this is to ensure that the static constructors are compiled in the same order in which they are written in the source code.

The following program illustrates the fact that static constructors get executed immediately upon the class loading—even before the `main()` method. You can use this to advantage in program design—perhaps to display a tip to your users on start up, like in Forte and IntelliJ.

```
/*
 * StaticConstructorTest.java
 * Created on June 8, 2002, 3:07 PM
 */

package chp7;

/**
 * @version 1.0
```

```
 */
public class StaticConstructorTest {

    static String s;
    static int stringLength;

    // first part of static constructor
    static {
        s = "I am s in the FIRST constructor";

        System.out.println(s);

    }

    public static void main (String [] arg) {
        System.out.println("Now here's the MAIN method.");
    }

    // second part of constructor will execute before main
    static {
        s = "I am s in the SECOND constructor.";

        System.out.println(s);
    }

}
```

7.6 `static` Methods

`static` methods are methods that do not operate on objects. You call them on a class. They do not need objects to carry out their tasks and therefore have no implicit parameter—there is no `this`. Our square class in Chapter 4 defined a couple of `static` methods:

```
    public static int square(int x) {
        return x * x;
    }

        public static void show(int ans) {
           System.out.println("The answer is " + ans);
    }
```

As you can see, there is no object required to carry out this operation, so none is created. All of the methods in the `java.lang.Math` class are `static` methods. When you think about it, it makes a lot of sense: they just perform generic operations, such as calculating the result of one value to the power of another or the smaller of two passed values. The following example makes a call to `Math.random()`, a famous static class:

7.6.1 MakeRandom.java

```
package chp7;

public class MakeRandom {

    public static void main(String[] args) {
        MakeRandom sn = new MakeRandom();
        System.out.println("The number is: " + sn.getNumber());
    }

    public double getNumber() {
            // Math.random is a static method
        return Math.random();
    }
}
```

Because `static` methods don't work with objects, they also don't allow you access to instance fields. There is no instance. Say you've got a class called Human. Allowing `static` methods access to instance fields would be like asking a `static` method to tell you the hair color of Human. Not going to happen.

On the other hand, `static` methods do have access to static fields in their class. In order to get the static field value, you need to call the method on the name of the class. The following overblown example shows how this works:

7.6.2 FieldTest.java

```
package chp7;

public class FieldTest {

    static int num;

    static int makeNumber() {
        int r = num;
        num++;
        return r;
    }

    static int id = makeNumber();
```

```
    public static void main(String[] args) {

        System.out.println(FieldTest.id);
    }
}
```

You cannot call non-static methods from inside static methods, although you can do the opposite. You will find people on occasion who claim that static methods are not object oriented because you're not sending a message to an object to do your work. That may be the case, but they're certainly used to good effect in the API, which is good enough for me.

7.6.3 factory Methods

Classes usually provide a public constructor for the creation of objects. Classes can also provide a public *static factory method*. A static factory method returns an instance of the class, and it can be used in addition to or instead of constructors. For example, the boolean wrapper class defines a static factory method that takes a primitive boolean value and transforms it into an object reference. That static method looks like this:

```
public static Boolean valueOf(boolean b) {
   return (b ? Boolean.TRUE : Boolean.FALSE);
}
```

NOTE Here the Immediate If is used to determine the field to return. The Immediate If is used the same way in ColdFusion, but it has a different syntax altogether: Its structure in ColdFusion is like this: `#IIF( Hour(Now()) GT 12, DE("It is after noon"), DE("It is morning"))#`.

It can be advantageous to use static factory methods for a couple of reasons. For one, they can save space because they don't have to create a new object every time they are invoked. That means you won't have unnecessary objects causing confusion and degrading performance. Also, they are not limited in the same way constructors are. A class can only create one constructor with a given signature. If it seems like a good idea to write more than one constructor with the same signature, then you might do well to offload the work into static factory methods whose names indicate the distinct nature of their usefulness.

7.7 The `this` Reference

The `this` keyword allows you to specify the current object, whatever it might be. This obviates the need to store a separate copy of every variable and method for each instantiation of a class. The `this` reference always refers to the current object. Let's say it another way. When writing `this.name`, `this` refers to the current object's copy of `name`.

When you invoke a new object method from the same object, there is no need to prefix a `this` reference. The `this` reference is included implicitly by Java:

```
public class Test {

void someMethod() {
     anotherMethod();
     }

void anotherMethod() {
     // method definition here...
     }
}
```

In the above code, `anotherMethod` is invoked without an object reference. This code would compile because when the compiler encounters an unreferenced method, it first looks in the local class for one that matches it. If it finds a matching method, the keyword `this` is prefixed to the method call implicitly.

So the above code is actually the equivalent to writing the following:

```
public class Test {

void someMethod() {
     this.anotherMethod();
     }

void anotherMethod() {
     // method definition here...
     }
}
```

Again, you don't need to (and shouldn't) write this out in this manner; Java does it for you in such cases.

> **NOTE** You can only use the object reference `this` inside a non-`static` method. Try to think of why that might be. To figure it out, we'll have to remember what a `static` method is. A `static` method is a class-level method; that is, it is associated with the type and not a specific object: It doesn't make any sense to refer to `this` when there is no object.

7.7.1 `this`, the Implicit Parameter

While it sounds straightforward enough, `this` can be tough to get your mind around, and there is another common occurrence of the `this` keyword, which we'll examine now. As you know, one job of methods is to set values in objects. In order to set those values, the object must have a variable defined to hold that data; those variables, as you'll recall, are referred to as data fields or fields. You often will use `this` in conjunction with method parameters to set field values.

Let's say we have a class with a field named `hireDate`. We write a method that accepts a parameter called `hireDate`. `hireDate` will then refer to the parameter, and not to the object instance's data field of the same name. `this` refers to the *implicit parameter*—that of the object being constructed. Using `this` effectually hides the parameter, and it allows us to refer to the data field. It is therefore very common to see the implicit parameter used in the following fashion.

You may remember our Employee code from Chapter 5; the setter methods look like so:

```
protected void setHireDate(Date hd) {

hireDate = hd;
}

protected void setSalary(double s) {

salary = s;
}
```

We can use `this`, instead, to accomplish the same task with less confusion:

```
public void setHireDate(Date hireDate) {

this.hireDate = hireDate;
}
```

```
public void setSalary(double salary) {

this.salary = salary;
}
```

7.7.2 Calling Other Constructors with `this`

There is another use for `this`. Constructors create objects, and an object can have a different constructor based on what the programmer wishes to do with the object at that time. For example, as we know, there are two constructors for the `java.lang.boolean` wrapper class: `Boolean(boolean value)` and `Boolean(String s)`. You can quickly see how it is often the case that writing different constructors could involve writing code that is common to the different constructors more than once. This can be tedious to write and difficult to debug and maintain. `this` offers a solution by allowing one constructor to call another.

If a constructor's first statement is prefixed with `this(...)`, the constructor will call another constructor within the same class.

> **NOTE** Having one constructor call another in this way is called "explicit constructor invocation."

Here's how it works. Let's say we're going to add a clearance level to our `Employee` object that indicates something about the employee's security clearance. We can create a separate constructor that just sets the security level. The following two listings, `MakeEmployee1.java` and `Employee.java`, show this:

7.7.3 `MakeEmployee1.java`

```
package chp7;

import java.util.Date;

public class MakeEmployee1 {

    public static void main(String[] args){

// create a new Employee object

Employee1 myEmp = new Employee1(444, "Medium");
```

```
System.out.println("Employee created with ID: " +
    myEmp.getEmployeeID());

// set its salary

myEmp.setSalary(75000.00);

// get its salary

System.out.println("Salary: " + myEmp.getSalary());

        // test if our this() constructor call worked.
        // we know it works because we have not set this
        // variable
        // anywhere but in the this("Low") constructor call.
        // We know both constructors are called because
        // we get our employee ID set too.

System.out.println("Clearance Level: " +
                myEmp.getClearanceLevel());
    }
}
```

Notice that we have modified how the Employee object is constructed here, so looking back on the Chapter 5 example will likely only be confusing. Instead of randomly generating an EmployeeID, which is obviously not a great idea, we are supplying it explicitly. We now have two constructors for the Employee object that you can call. The first option is to supply only an EmployeeID. That constructor will then call the second constructor, passing it a value for the ClearanceLevel parameter. The idea is that when the second constructor is called by this(...), then it will automatically supply that value. This is admittedly a mildly contrived example, but it demonstrates how this works in this context:

7.7.4 Employee1.java

```
package chp7;

import java.util.Date;

public class Employee1 {

    private int employeeID;
    private Date hireDate;
    private double salary;
```

```
    // added for this constructor calling demo
    private String clearance;

    // two constructors. one in which only the EmpID is set,
    // and another in which the EmpID and the
    // SecurityLevel are set

    // default constructor creates only EmpID
    public Employee1(int employeeID) {

            // call the other constructor
            // must be first statement in constructor

            this(employeeID, "Low");

        }

        public Employee1(int employeeID, String clearance) {
           this.employeeID = employeeID;
           this.clearance = clearance;
        }

        public String getClearanceLevel() {
return clearance;

    }

    public int getEmployeeID() {
return employeeID;

    }

public Date getHireDate() {

return hireDate;
}

public double getSalary() {

return salary;
}


public void setHireDate(Date hireDate) {

this.hireDate = hireDate;
}
```

```
public void setSalary(double salary) {

this.salary = salary;
}

}
```

Run this example two different ways, and you'll get two different results. Calling this constructor

```
      // create a new Employee object

Employee1 myEmp = new Employee1(444, "Medium");
```

provides both the `EmployeeID` and the `ClearanceLevel`. So only that one constructor is called, and the output is this:

```
Employee created with ID: 444
Salary: 75000.00
 Clearance Level: Medium
```

The `ClearanceLevel` specified is used directly in the constructor that expects to be passed both parameters.

If we ran this program exchanging that line in the `MakeEmployee1` file with this line...

```
// create a new Employee object

 Employee1 myEmp = new Employee1(555);
```

...then the output is

```
Employee created with ID: 555
Salary: 75000.00
 Clearance Level: Low
```

That's because we call the first constructor, which calls the second constructor, passing the string `ClearanceLevel` on in.

Any expressions used as arguments for this kind of explicit constructor invocation must not refer to fields or methods in the current object because there isn't really a current object yet—it hasn't been constructed.

This is a useful way of handling code common to multiple constructors.

7.8 Stack and Heap Memory

In this section we will look at how variables are stored in memory in Java. We are examining memory in Java at this point so that you can understand at a lower level what happens when you create and manipulate the objects that make up your programs.

Primitive data types have just one value to store. For instance:

```
int i = 1;
```

The appropriate amount of space is allocated given the data type, and the variable is stored in memory just as it is.

Objects must be stored differently because they are more complex. They often hold multiple values, each of which must be stored in memory. The association between each value and the object must be maintained throughout its life. An object reference variable must then hold a reference to those values. This reference represents the location where the object and its metadata are stored.

There are two kinds of memory used in Java. These are called stack memory and heap memory. Stack memory stores primitive types and the addresses of objects. The object values are stored in heap memory. An object reference on the stack is only an address that refers to the place in heap memory where that object is kept.

Say you've got two `Test` objects, and you assign the first to the second, like this:

```
Test test1 = new Test();
Test test2 = new Test();

test2 = test1;
```

What you're actually doing when you write this is assigning the address of the `test1` object to the `test2` object. Assume that `test1`'s memory address was `0x33d444` and that `test2`'s address was `0x99f775`. After performing the above assignment, `test2` now holds this address in stack memory: `0x99f775`, which refers to the same object as `test1`. The `test2` object on the heap still exists, but it cannot be accessed. That's because this reassignment overwrote the old address that `test2` was keeping on the stack. This kind of reassignment makes two stack references to the same object on the heap.

It is useful to know that these two different kinds of memory exist in Java. Stack memory is the program's memory, and heap memory resides outside of the program.

As a Java programmer, you do not have to directly address memory allocation and recovery of memory space, which is a common headache for C++ programmers. When you need a new object, Java allocates the required memory. When you are done with an object, the memory is reclaimed for you automatically via Java's garbage collection facility.

Garbage collection runs as a thread in the background, looking for objects that no longer have a usable reference. When it finds them, it destroys them and reclaims the memory.

The implementation of garbage collection varies between Java Virtual Machines. They generally follow the same process, however. First, the garbage collector gets a snapshot of all running threads and all loaded classes. Then, all objects that are referred to by this thread set are marked as current. The process stops when all objects that it is possible to reach have been marked and the rest have been discarded.

In order to help the Virtual Machine, it is a good idea to remove your references to unneeded objects. This is often done by simply setting your reference to `null`:

```
Test t = new Test();
t.someAction();
// all done
t = null;
```

7.8.1 Finalizers

Constructors create objects. Most OOP languages provide methods for you to clean up after yourself. That is, they provide a way for you to destroy the objects you've created after you no longer reference them. Such methods are called *finalizers*.

> **NOTE** ColdFusion does not have finalizers for the same reason it doesn't have constructors: No objects are created. Memory is allocated in ColdFusion for what CF developers refer to as objects, such as the `application` object, the `session` object, and the `query` object. And good ColdFusion programming practice dictates that you shouldn't have a bunch of stuff lying around memory resident, so when you're done with a session variable but you still have an active session, you can set references you don't need to `null`.

Because all objects in Java extend `java.lang.Object`, which defines a `finalize()` method, any object can call `finalize()`. The `protected void finalize()` method returns nothing and does nothing. The `finalize()` method may never be invoked more than once by a JVM for an object.

The typical example for when to use finalizers is when you're working with file input/output. When you open a connection to a resource, such as a file, you might not have a chance to close it before an exception is thrown. In this case, you've got invalid processes consuming system resources unnecessarily.

Finalizers are generally regarded as the sort of thing to do in a last-ditch effort to save system resources. This is because they do not necessarily run as soon as it is possible. That means that the programmer cannot be certain when exactly they will run. Finalizers should therefore be used sparingly. We will see alternatives in Chapter 8, "Exceptions."

7.9 Putting Things Together

In this section, we simply write an example program that demonstrates many of the concepts we have discussed in this chapter. This example is a modified version of an example written by Sun, called `Clock`. A `Clock` object is created, which has hour, minute, and second values. A method displays the current time once the `Clock` is created using either its default no-arg constructor or another constructor that defines a custom time setting. When the `Clock` object's `tick()` method is called, the second value increments by one, possibly changing the hour and minute values on the clock. We need two listings for this example—one that creates the `Clocks`, holds their values, and defines their methods, and another that instantiates the `Clocks`:

7.9.1 MakeClocks.java

```
package chp7;

// based on Sun's Clock class
// here I've only consolidated using the getTime method
class MakeClock {

public static void main (String args[]) {

            // no-arg constructor
Clock c1 = new Clock();

            // set initial time on clock two
Clock c2 = new Clock(59, 59, 1);

System.out.println("Initial time:");
System.out.println(c1.getTime());
```

```
                System.out.println(c2.getTime());

System.out.println("Time after increment: " );

                c1.tick();
                    System.out.println(c1.getTime());

                c2.tick();
                    System.out.println(c2.getTime());

    } // end main
}
```

7.9.2 Clock.java

```
package chp7;

public class Clock {

// declare private vars, which means that only methods of the /
// current class can use them

private int second, minute, hour;

// clock method sets values
// use 'this' to refer to the declared class-level vars above

public Clock(int s, int m, int h) {

     this.second = s;
     this.minute = m;
     this.hour = h;
     }

// constructor method sets defaults
public Clock() {

     this.second = 0;
     this.minute = 0;
     this.hour = 0;
}

public void setSecond(int s) {

     if (s >= 0 && s < 60) {
        this.second = s;
     }
```

```
        else {
           System.out.println("Invalid seconds value, not set.");
        }
    }


    public void setMinute(int m) {

        if (m >= 0 && m < 60) {
           this.minute = m;
        }
        else {
           System.out.println("Invalid minutes value, not set.");
        }
    }
    public void setHour (int h) {

        if (h >= 0 && h < 24) {
             this.hour = h;
        }
        else {
             System.out.println("Invalid hours value.");
        }
    }

    public void setTime(int s, int m, int h) {
        setSecond(s);
        setMinute(m);
        setHour(h);
    }

    public void tick() {
        second++;

        if (second==60) {
            second = 0;
            minute++;

               if (minute==60) {
                  minute=0;
                   hour++;

                      if (hour==24) {
                          hour = 0;
                         }
                  }
```

```
        }
}

public int getSecond() {
    return second;
}

public int getMinute() {

     return minute;
}

public int  getHour() {
     return hour;
}

public String getTime(){
      String s = Integer.toString(getHour()) + ":" +
                Integer.toString(getMinute()) + ":" +
                Integer.toString(getSecond());
            return s;
        }

} // end class
```

The output is as follows:

```
Initial time:
0:0:0
1:59:59
Time after increment:
0:0:1
2:0:0
```

7.10 What's Next

In the next chapter, we will take a momentary break from class-specific discussion to look at exceptions. There is much more to working with classes in Java, however, and the topic will be resumed in all its glorious sophistication in the following chapter.

8

Exceptions

The primary aim of the critic is to see the object as it really is not.

—Oscar Wilde

In this chapter, we will examine some things that are familiar to ColdFusion programmers, such as the difference between exceptions and errors, and the `try`, `catch`, and `throw` statements. We will also look at how an OOP language like Java extends the exception handling concept to include checked and unchecked exceptions, the `finally` statement, and assertions.

8.1 Exceptions

From our work in ColdFusion, we know what exceptions are, when to use them, and what's important about them. They help us write user-friendly code. They keep us honest about what sorts of things can happen in a production environment, and they help us handle such eventualities gracefully. This section should be pretty easy to grasp, as it is one of the places where ColdFusion and Java sort of see eye to eye.

We often talk about "handling exceptions" and "catching exceptions." While these are accurate terms, it is probably not a bad idea to shift our thinking a bit. Exception handling is a form of *flow control*, like a `<cflocation>`, `<cfabort>`, or even a `switch` statement. A `switch` statement says, "if this is the case at this time, then go here." Making this kind of shift in thinking will help us to think of exception handling as an integral part of our programs, and it will help us consider, and make provisions for, the kinds of events that could be triggered in our systems. The idea is that if the program enters a problematic state, you can reroute control to a part of the program that can recover from the injury.

You can only reroute program flow to specific blocks of code, which are designated to handle exceptions. If you have no such blocks, program execution will terminate, and the runtime will deliver its exception message.

You are likely familiar with `<cftry>`, `<cfthrow>`, and `<cfcatch>`. For instance, we might have a custom tag that performs some database lookup. We could wrap this action in a `try/catch` block and specify the kind of exception that we want to look for, like this:

```
<cftry>
  <cfquery name= "#attributes.queryname# datasource =
     "#request.dsn#">

      SELECT something
      FROM somewhere;

  </cfquery>

  <cfcatch type="Database">

     <cfthrow message="Something bad happened during query
               execution.">
  </cfcatch>

</cftry>
```

We should be able to cover working with exceptions in Java rather quickly, as both the concepts and the syntax are very similar. Here we go.

8.1.1 throw

In Java, as you might guess by now, we work with an `Exception` object. The `Exception` object is created as an object of any class that extends the `java.lang.Exception` class.

> **NOTE** We will talk about this more in the next chapter. For now, `extends` is a Java keyword that means "inherits from." In our overloading example earlier, the `Child` class `extends` the `Parent` class.

There are 24 exceptions defined in the `java.lang` package, some of which we have come across already. You may have encountered the `ArrayIndexOutOfBounds` exception, which indicates that you've tried to access an array cell that doesn't exist.

There are two ways to cause an exception:

- The program attempts to perform an illegal action, inadvertently causing an exception.
- The program explicitly creates an exception when it encounters a `throw` statement.

We are unfortunately familiar with the first cause. The second cause works much as it does in ColdFusion. We explicitly generate `exceptions` by using a `throw` statement, which can be handled by a `catch` statement. It takes the following form:

```
public static void main(String[] a) {

    public void myMethod() throws Exception {

        try {

            throw new MyException();
        }

        catch (RuntimeException re) {
            // handling code
        }

        finally {
            // do this whether exception is thrown
            // or not
        }
    }
}
```

There are a number of things to remark on in this structure. First, the `throw` statement throws an exception that must be an object of the Throwable class or one of its subclasses. Above, we create and throw our exception in the same statement.

Methods can throw any `Throwable` object. You can create your own exception class or choose one from the Java API. This is a matter of program design and should be determined on a case-by-case basis.

When an exception is thrown, the Java Virtual Machine stops execution and retraces backward through the methods that the thread has called, trying to find a point at which the exception can be handled. If it cannot find a handler block, then the JVM prints the best error message it can and the thread is killed.

The Throwable class defines the basic behaviors for exceptions and errors. A created Throwable object contains a stack trace with information about every method that the current thread has executed through. As with the ColdFusion tag, <cfthrow message="my message">, Throwable allows you to specify a string containing the message to send the user when the exception is thrown.

There are around 70 direct subclasses of java.lang.Exception. These include common favorites such as ClassNotFoundException, IOException, NoSuchMethodException, and others that are more specialized, such as those for working with MIDI data. You can (and should) take a moment to look in the API to peruse the kinds of exceptions and errors that are defined there. Doing so now will help you to get familiar with the kinds of exceptions that are available to you, thus encouraging their use in your code. Moreover, it will help you see what kinds of custom exceptions you may need.

8.1.2 try and catch

It is often rather difficult to actually recover from an exception situation. Depending on what your program is doing, you are likely to want to simply try for a useful message, as in the ColdFusion example above. Here's how you do it:

8.1.3 DemoException.java

```
package chp8;

/**
 * Purpose: demonstrate throwing an catching exceptions
 * @author  eh
 * @version 1.0
 */
public class DemoException {

            // declare that this method throws an Exception
            // and state the kind of exception
        public void myMethod() throws Exception {

            // this method does nothing but throw the
            // Exception object
            // ~= <cfthrow message = "This is a custom error">

            throw new Exception("This is a custom error");
        }

    public static void main(String[] a) {
```

```
        DemoException de = new DemoException();

        try {
            // this method just throws the error
            de.myMethod();
        }

            // you catch the Exception object,
            // because that is what the myMethod throws
        catch (Exception e) {

            // once you've got the exception object
            // you can call its methods like any other obejct.

            e.printStackTrace();
        }

    }
}
```

The output of running this program is

```
1 java.lang.Exception: This is a custom error
2        at chp7.DemoException.myMethod(DemoException.java:22)
3        at chp7.DemoException.main(DemoException.java:31)
```

It is unfortunately common for us to see messages like this one. Such is our lot in life. And Java messages—especially those generated by servlet containers—can look really daunting to ColdFusion developers. But Java exception messages are as helpful as ColdFusion messages if you know how to read them. They're often very simple. Let's take the above message apart to see what it's made of.

First, we see the Exception type that was thrown, followed by our custom message. The following two lines are related. In the second line, we are looking at this structure:

```
packageName.ClassName.methodName(SourceFileName.java: line
number).
```

The line number here indicates where the error was thrown from. In the `DemoException.java` source file, we shouldn't be surprised to discover that line number 22 consists of the following code:

```
22 throw new Exception("This is a custom error");
```

The third and final line of the exception message has the same structure (remember `main` is a method). This line indicates that line 31 in the `DemoException.java` file contains another culprit. And it is indeed the method that was invoked when the exception got thrown:

```
31 de.myMethod();
```

Here are a few notes before we move on:

- Your `catch` statement always needs to declare a parameter that provides the kind of exception it is prepared to handle and the name you'll use to refer to the `Exception` object in your `catch` code block. The scope of this variable is obviously only the `catch` block, as that is where it gets defined.
- The `Exception` constructor is overloaded. That is, there are two constructors for exception: one that takes a `String` argument to display a custom text message and another no-arg constructor.
- Your `Exception` message can be a variable.

8.1.4 causes

Java version 1.4 made the `cause` available, and there is no real equivalent for this in ColdFusion. As previously mentioned, when an exception is thrown, it contains a snapshot of the execution stack. It can also contain a `cause`, which is another `Throwable` object that caused this exception to get thrown. As you can quickly see, there are many regresses possible here, as a `cause` can not only be a cause, but have a cause itself. So `causes` are a generally referred to as a facility for chaining together exceptions.

There are two reasons to use `causes`. The first is an architectural issue. You generally will separate the outer abstraction layers from the low-level inner workings of your program. An exception can be caused at a lower program level that is unrelated to the outer layers, but gets propagated outward anyway because of the design of the program. Cause chaining acts like a wrapper, allowing you to maintain the integrity of your layer separation effectually; that is, if you change your implementation, you don't have to change the exception structure in your API, because a low-level exception will pass a `cause` up to a higher-level exception so that it can be handled more appropriately.

There are two ways to use a `cause` by associating it with a `Throwable`. The first is by calling the constructor that accepts a `cause` as an argument. The second way to do it is by calling the `initCause(Throwable)` method. The `initCause()` method is `public`, so it allows any `Throwable` object to have an associated `cause`:

```
try {
            obj.something();
        }

        catch (LowLevelException lle) {

            // instead of printing the "low level" error,
            // we'll pass it on to a "high level" one,
            // i.e., chain the cause

throw new HighLevelException(hle);
```

8.1.5 Multiple `catch` Clauses

As in ColdFusion, you can define multiple `catch` clauses, each specifying a different type of exception you anticipate being thrown. You can do that in Java as well, and in the same manner. The concept is not really different from using one `catch` clause, so we'll just look at an example to see what different kinds of exceptions it might make sense to throw given the same `try` block.

A typical need in applications is to connect to databases and retrieve information from them. While this is made very easy in ColdFusion with the `<cfquery>` tag, Java requires rather more work. You have to load a database driver, connect to the database, create a statement and execute it, and then drop the connection. It's all of the same things that you have to do in ColdFusion—we're just used to that being handled for us.

> **NOTE** There certainly are ways to make working with databases easy in Java and especially JavaServer Pages. We'll see how to handle this in another way in later chapters.

Let's say we've got a class that connects to a database. Here we'll write the `makeConnection()` method that loads the driver and connects to the database via the driver. Because this is such a complex process with many steps, there are a lot of things that can go wrong. So we will employ multiple `catch` statements to handle the different kinds of exceptions:

```
...     //we'll put an error message here
String msg;
...
public void makeConnection()
    throws ClassNotFoundException, SQLException, Exception {
```

```
        try
            {
                // load Driver class
                Class.forName("sun.jdbc.odbc.JdbcOdbcDriver");

                // connect to the ODBC datasource
                conn =
DriverManager.getConnection("jdbc:odbc:JavaForCFDB",
"username", "mypassword");
        }
               // in case driver can't be found
        catch (ClassNotFoundException ce)
        {
                msg = "Hey! I can't find the driver";
                throw new ClassNotFoundException(msg);
        }
               // in case of error connection to database
        catch (SQLException se)
        {
            msg = "Hey! I can't connect to the database";
            throw new SQLException(msg);
        }
               // in any other exceptional case
        catch (Exception e)
        {
            msg = "An exception was thrown";
            throw new Exception(msg);
        }

} // end makeConnection()
```

8.1.6 What About `<cfrethrow>`?

In ColdFusion we can rethrow an exception using the `<cfrethrow>` tag. This is very useful, especially when your program is performing an operation on another resource. In these cases, it is usually a good idea to shut down your connection to those resources, whether they are files, printers, or what have you, and then rethrow the exception so that it can be dealt with.

Java does not make use of a keyword such as “rethrow.” To perform a rethrow in Java, just use the same syntax used to throw new exceptions:

```
try {
...
        catch (FileNotFoundException fe) {
                closeResources();
                throw fe ;
        }
}
```

8.1.7 finally

The `finally` keyword is used *after* all of your `catch` clauses to indicate a code block that should run no matter what; that is, whether an exception was thrown or not. Obviously, the `finally` clause cannot execute if the execution thread dies.

> **NOTE** ColdFusion has no `finally` clause. During a couple of the beta versions of CFMX, the CFML included a `<cffinally>` tag. It was dropped from the language prior to the final release of CFMX.

The following code demonstrates how this works:

8.1.8 DemoFinally.java

```
package chp8;

public class DemoFinally {

      public static double tripleIt(String s) {

            try {
                double d = Double.valueOf(s).doubleValue();

                return d * 3;
            }

            catch (NumberFormatException ne) {
                System.out.println("Number Format Problem!");

                return -1.0;
            }

            finally {
                System.out.println("Hello from finally");
            }
      }
```

```
        public static void main(String[] ar) {
          DemoFinally df = new DemoFinally();
          System.out.println(df.tripleIt("hi dude")); //error!
    }
}// eof
```

The `tripleIt()` method accepts a string, converts the value to a `double`, and multiplies it by three. When the `tripleIt()` method is supplied with a real number, such as 6, we see this output:

```
Hello from finally
18.0
```

When it is supplied with a non-numeric value, we get this output:

```
Number Format Problem!
Hello from finally
-1.0
```

This tells us a couple of things. First, the `finally` clause gets executed no matter what. If we supply an incorrect type, we return an arbitrary error code of -1.0. The `finally` clause is always executed after the `try` block. When you pass `tripleIt()` as a number in a string, the `try` puts a `double` in the current method frame as a return value for the calling method. Then the `finally` block does a `System.out.println()` in the context of the same method frame. Then the `tripleIt()` method pops off the stack, and the `main` method's `System.out.println()` is called to print out the `double` returned from the `try` in the previous method. If you put a `System.out.println()` in the `try` block too, you'll see that `finally` is always executed after the `try`. If we supply a non-numeric value, such as "hi dude," we get the exception output, then the `finally` block, and then the error code returned by the method. This allows you to replace the error code in the `finally` block, so that you don't have to rely on the operation performed inside the method where things are going wrong.

Let's look at part of a more realistic example regarding an instance when you might actually need to use `finally`. First of all, it is a good idea to use `finally` whenever you've got `try` blocks that might need some cleaning up if they throw an exception. These typically include connections to a database that should get closed, or connections to files that should be closed.

The `java.io.FileWriter` class is a convenience class that helps you write create and write character text files.

8.1.9 MakeFileWriter.java

```
package chp8;

// import java.io to get access to the IOException
import java.io.*;
// we'll use this to write the file
import java.io.FileWriter.*;

public class MakeFileWriter {


        // method to write file
    public void makeFile(String fileName) throws IOException,
Exception {

        String theFile = fileName;

        FileWriter fw = null;

        try
        {
                // create the file object
            fw = new FileWriter(theFile);

                // write the data
            fw.write("Dude, I am some important data");

        }
        catch (IOException ioe){

            ioe.printStackTrace();
         }

        catch (Exception e){

            e.printStackTrace();
         }

         finally
         {
                 // close the connection
            fw.close();
         }
```

```
        }

            // main
        public static void main(String[] args) throws IOException,
                Exception {

            MakeFileWriter fw = new MakeFileWriter();

                fw.makeFile("C:\\myData.dat");

            System.out.println("The file was written");

        }
    }
```

We have not covered input/output operations directly. But for now, you can see how this creates a new file and writes some character data to it. If the file specified does not exist, then it is created and the data is written. If the file does exist, then the new data overwrites any existing character data in the file.

What is important about the previous listing is to show that the `finally` block contains the method to close the connection to the file. That way, if any exception is thrown, the `close()` method can still execute. Without `finally`, the connection to the resource could have been left open.

As you can see if you run this example, the above listing is the rough equivalent to this sort of thing in ColdFusion:

```
    <cfset theData = "Here is some important stuff.">

    <cftry>

         <cffile action = "write" file="C:\myData.dat"
                 output="#theData#">

          <cfif NOT cffile.FileWasWritten>
                <cfthrow message = "Error! The file wasn't
                        written">
          </cfif>

    <cfcatch type = "Any">
    <cfoutput>
           <cfloop index = i from = 1 to =
                  #ArrayLen(cfcatch.tagContext)#>
              <cfset c = #cfcatch.tagContext[i]#>
                  <br>
                  #i# #c["ID"] #c["LINE"]# #c["COLUMN"]#
```

```
        </cfloop>
    </cfoutput>
    </cfcatch>
    </cftry>
```

8.1.10 Exceptions in Constructors

There are really only two limitations on the exceptions that a constructor can throw:

- A constructor can throw any exception that is not thrown by its superclass constructor.
- A subclass constructor cannot catch an exception thrown by a superclass constructor it calls. The reason is because a call to the superclass constructor has to be the first statement in the subclass constructor. While we haven't talked about inheritance yet, this is similar to how any call to another constructor in the same class using `this` (...) must be the first item on the constructor's agenda too.

There is no way for a constructor in a subclass to catch an exception thrown by the constructor of a superclass. Therefore, the subclass constructor must declare all of the same checked exceptions as its superclass does in its constructor's `throws` clause.

8.1.11 Errors and Checked and Unchecked Exceptions

Errors are like exceptions in that they indicate problems with program execution. However, exceptions indicate a problematic state from which the program can recover. Errors, on the other hand, indicate a problematic state from which the program cannot recover. They represent an abnormal state that the program should never enter. That is the basic conceptual difference between exceptions and errors. An `Error` is a subclass of `Throwable`, and its subclasses should not be declared in a `throws` clause. That is the basic practical difference for the programmer between exceptions and errors.

Instances of the `java.lang.Error` class represent malfunctions in the program's environment that indicate that the program cannot continue to work. The distinction between errors and exceptions creates another distinction: *checked* and *unchecked exceptions*.

Exceptions are checked. The compiler checks to see whether checked exceptions are handled in the code. Exceptions represent issues that can possibly be recovered from or that can be reasonably anticipated to occur. A common example is a `ClassNotFoundException`, which occurs when you try to load a class using its string name, and it can't be found. A related and equally common error is the `java.io.FileNotFoundException`. In working with the compiler at the command line, you've probably seen the `ArrayIndexOutOfBoundsException`; this is thrown when you run a program that expects arguments, references the args `String` array directly, and then throws the exception when it doesn't get any. In these kinds of operations, you can reasonably expect to have to deal with such shenanigans, and Java encourages you to do so.

Errors are unchecked. Unchecked exceptions are subclasses of `Error` and the `RuntimeException` classes. "Unchecked" means that the compiler does not check to see if all of its code is caught or declared in a method's `throws` clause. If Java didn't make this distinction, everything would have to be checked, and your execution would be far slower, your development slower, and your code would be absolutely riddled with generally unnecessary exception handling.

The difference between checked and unchecked exceptions only exists at compile time. When you compile your source, the compiler checks to see that particular exceptions are either caught or declared. Once compiled, the Java Virtual Machine just executes the bytecodes—the checked exceptions have already been checked.

8.1.12 Assertions

Assertions have been in programming languages for some time, and while they're not properly exception handling, they are a key part of the debugging process, and can even help you circle in on problems once you've deployed an application.

The `assert` statement was introduced with Java version 1.4. It is used to debug applications as they are being written. It helps you do this by verifying assumptions in your code. An assertion is written to state something that you, the programmer, believe should always be the case at the that point in your program. An assertion is written using the `assert` keyword and then a boolean expression representing what you believe should always evaluate to true at that point.

The `assert` statement does nothing so long as it evaluates to true. If the expression evaluates to false, a `java.lang.AssertionError` is thrown. By default, assertions are not enabled.

> **NOTE** Prior to JDK 1.4, the `java.lang.Assertion` error did not exist.

It was possible to use assertions previously in Java, and, in fact, an assertion is just a simple replacement for this code:

```
if (x < 10) throw new java.lang.AssertionError("Oh no! x is
   less than 10!");
```

What has been added is the ability to specify whether the statements should be executed. We will see how to do this in a moment.

Assertions look like this:

```
assert booleanExpression;
```

or

```
assert booleanExpression : errorMessage;
```

...where booleanExpression is what you expect to be true. In the second form, errorMessage allows you to write an expression to be passed to the AssertionError's constructor. It allows you to indicate a custom message regarding the nature of the error.

> **NOTE** The error message expression that gets passed to the constructor does not have to be a string. It can be any value, such as int or char, which are sometimes used to represent error codes.

Note that writing assert false will always fail. This can be useful if you've got a situation where all of your possible states are explicitly outlined. You could use an assert to throw an error in any other event:

```
package chp7;

public class AssertTest {

public static void main(String[] arg) {

    int i = 1;
    System.out.println("i is: " + i);
    assert i == 1 : "i is not 1!";

}

}
```

Assertions have been available in other OOP languages, and so many Java programmers have tried to homegrow them. Now that assert is a keyword in

Java 1.4, Sun has made an effort to avoid breaking code that may already exist, and you therefore need to supply an argument to the compiler in order to use assertions in your code. Compile programs using assertions like this:

```
javac -source 1.4 AssertTest.java
```

Remember that assertions are disabled by default, even if they have been compiled at compile time. You must explicitly turn on assert checks. To do this for one program, use `java`'s `-ea` option, which stands for "enable assertions":

```
java -ea AssertTest
```

Your assertion error will be thrown.

8.2 What's Next

In this chapter we covered throwing and catching exceptions and looked at a new feature in the JDK 1.4—the assertion.

In the next chapter, we'll continue our work with classes. We'll go deeper into how to extend your classes via interfaces and inheritance, and we'll look at some more sophisticated aspects of objects, such as cloning and reflection.

9

Advanced Object-Oriented Concepts

This chapter continues the examination of classes and objects from Chapter 7. We now have enough skills to do a surprising number of things in Java. There are few real programs you will encounter, however, that do not make use of the advanced concepts that we will address in this chapter. These include inheritance, interfaces, abstract classes and methods, and reflection.

It is important that you feel you have a pretty good grasp of the concepts from earlier chapters, because things get rather more complicated in this chapter. What the object-oriented concepts presented here open up, however, is a very rich world.

Trying out the code examples, modifying them, and trying them again is a good idea. It can seem like a lot of terminology that is difficult to remember at this point, and the difficulty is exacerbated by the fact that so many of the concepts are hopelessly intertwined with the other concepts. So we will just pretend we didn't know it was supposed to be hard, and we'll work through each concept step by step.

Once we get to the end of this chapter, you will really understand the fundamentals of the Java programming language and related object-oriented concepts. The remainder of the book will simply be learning further implementation of the concepts outlined so far. For instance, dealing with I/O, JDBC (Java database connectivity), and servlets are just different things that these concepts make available. So while that means that these concepts are very important to understand, it also means that it gets much easier after this. And the difficulty may really be in keeping the terminology straight.

9.1 Inner Classes

Inner classes are an advanced topic. They are not totally intuitive. Nor are they regularly necessary if you're mostly writing Java for the Web. The primary use of inner classes is in GUI development. They are covered here in the interest of completeness and flexibility.

Inner classes are also sometimes called nested classes. Simply put, an *inner class* is a class that has its definition inside of another class. Inner classes have complete access to the code in the outer class definition, including its private fields and methods.

When you compile a source file containing a class with an inner class definition, two `.class` files are created.

> **NOTE** There is an interesting thing about compilation and organization that comes up when you start working with inner classes. Only public Java classes need to go into separate files. You can therefore define many different classes inside one source file.

What do inner classes do for you? In a sense, they allow you to scope your classes, because the inner class becomes a member of the outer class. That is, the inner class acts as a property of the outer class just like its regular fields or methods.

Objects in an inner class have access to even the private variables in instances of the outer class. Typically, inner classes are useful when you want to define helpers—that is, classes that have a very specific purpose and require another class (the outer class) to be employed. The most common place for these is in GUI development. For instance, to create a useful window with menus and buttons in Java, you need to create listeners that handle events (such as a mouse press, a button click, etc.). These items are often handled in inner classes, as registering a mouse drag must have somewhere (like a panel that is listening for the drag) to be registered so you can do something like draw a line.

There are four kinds of inner classes:

- Regular inner classes
- Method-local inner classes
- Anonymous inner classes
- Top-level nested classes

We will look at these in turn now.

9.1.1 Regular Inner Classes

A regular inner class is defined inside another class, like this:

```
class AnOuterClass {

  class AnInnerClass {}
}
```

In order to instantiate an inner class, you must first have an instance of the outer class. You cannot instantiate an object of an inner class without first having an object of the outer class. Generally, an object of the inner class is created by the outer class. One advantage to using inner classes is that they can be hidden from other classes in the same package. A class can define more than one inner class.

Another chief reason to use inner classes is that each inner class can inherit an implementation independently. This is, in a way, the answer to the fact that Java classes cannot allow multiple inheritance as C++ allows.

> **NOTE** An inner class method can access data in its own fields and data fields in objects of the outer class that created it.

Inner classes, unlike regular classes, can be declared `private`. When you construct objects of the inner class, these objects are not instance fields of the outer class—they are local to methods of the outer class.

The obvious benefit of inner classes is that they support encapsulation. Because only the outer class can call the inner class, you can go an extra step toward locking down access to your objects.

Objects of an inner class exist relative to objects of the outer class. Creating an object of the inner class from a non-static method of the outer class is relatively straightforward:

```
AnInnerClass ic = new AnInnerClass();
```

If you are in a static method of the outer class, you don't have an implicit reference to an object (no `this`). If you are in another class altogether, you don't have an object to work with either. You can still create an inner class instance in these cases, but you have to do it differently:

```
public class InnerClassTest {
  public static void main(String[] arg) {
     OuterClass oc = new OuterClass();
     // use this instance to create inner class instance
```

```
        OuterClass.InnerClass in = oc.new InnerClass()
      }
    }
```

Here is an example of using an inner class. This file allows you to make a string. It then converts the string into a `char` array, loops over the `char` array, and finds the letters closest to the beginning and end of the alphabet.

9.1.2 OuterClassTest.java

```
// demonstrate using an inner class

class OuterClass {

            // declare a char array to hold letters
            // that make up the string we pass in
        char letters[];

            // constructor
OuterClass(String s) {
letters =  s.toCharArray();
}

            // a method of the outer class
void getValues() {
            // instantiate inner class
InnerClass innerObject = new InnerClass();

                char lowest = innerObject.lowestChar();
                char highest = innerObject.highestChar();

     System.out.println("Lowest letter: " + lowest);
     System.out.println("Highest letter: " + highest);
}

            // here's the inner class
            // whose job it is to do the real work
class InnerClass {

                    // loop through char array to find
                    // the character closest to beginning of
                    // alphabet
     char lowestChar() {
          char x = letters[0];
               for(char i = 0; i < letters.length; i++)
```

```
                    if (letters[i] < x)
                         x = letters[i];

                    return x;


      }
                    // loop through char array to find
                    // letter in the string closest to the END
                    // of the alphabet
      char highestChar() {
          char x = letters[0];
               for(char i = 0; i < letters.length; i++)
                    if (letters[i] > x) x = letters[i];

                    return x;
      }

   }

}

class OuterClassTest {

     public static void main(String[] ar) {
                    // create a string
                    // we will find the lowest and
                    // highest letters in it
                    // note that capital letters come first.
                    // that is, C is 'lower' than c.

          String s = "CFMX";

                    // pass string to the outer class object
          OuterClass outerObject = new OuterClass(s);

                    // call the getValues method
                    // defined in the outer class
                    // even though its implementation is
                    // defined in the inner class
          outerObject.getValues();
      }
} // eof
```

The output is like this:

```
Lowest letter: C
Highest letter: X
```

9.1.3 Method-Local Inner Classes

The second type of inner class is a method-local inner class. As the name suggests, it gives you a way to define an inner class inside a method:

```
class AnOuterClass {

void someMethod() {
class AnInnerClass {

// inner class definition here

} // end inner class definition

// instantiate inner class. This must come after the code that
// defines the inner class

AnInnerClass mi = new AnInnerClass();

} // end someMethod
} // end outer class
```

The primary difference between a regular inner class and a method-local inner class is that the inner object defined method-local cannot use the local variables of the method that contains the inner class definition. Only in the event that local variables or arguments are declared `final` can an object of an inner class have access to them.

9.1.4 Anonymous Inner Classes

The final place that you will see inner classes defined is perhaps surprising: inside a method invocation argument. Because anonymous inner classes are defined inside a method, all restrictions apply to them that apply to method-local inner classes.

> **NOTE** As with regular inner classes, when you compile a source file containing a class with an anonymous inner class definition, a separate class file is created for it.

Anonymous inner classes are declared and instantiated at the same time. They are instantiated using the new operator in conjunction with the name of a class or interface that already exists. The most common place to see the use of anonymous inner classes is in the code for Swing GUI controls. The aim is to keep the code that handles an action in the same place where you create a control. Creating an anonymous inner class looks like this:

```
button.addActionListener(new ActionListener() {
   public void actionPerformed(ActionEvent e) {
         showStatus("button pushed");
         }
    } // end anonymous inner class
); // end the addActionListener method call
```

The `addActionListener()` method takes only one argument—one of type `ActionListener`. So our argument to the method is a single generated instance of an anonymous inner class.

Here is a complete example of anonymous inner classes in use:

9.1.5 AnonymousTest.java

```
// show use of anonymous inner classes

import java.applet.*;
import java.awt.*;
import java.awt.event.*;

public class AnonymousTest extends Applet {

     // declare a button
Button myB;

     // initialize applet
public void init() {

     // create a new button an add
     // to pane
add(myB = new Button("Push Me"));

     // we need to explicitly declare our
     // interest in things that happen to the
     // button. We do this by adding an action
     // listener to the button
```

```
myB.addActionListener(new ActionListener() {
     public void actionPerformed(ActionEvent evt) {
          showStatus("I needed that!");
          }

      }); // end addActionListener arg list

  } // end init
} // eof
```

NOTE In an applet, the `init()` method is called after the applet instance is initially created by the browser.

To test this, create a simple HTML page that calls the applet, like this:

9.1.6 ShowAnonymousTest.html

```
<html>
<head>
<title>Anonymoous Test</title>
</head>

<body>

<applet align="center" code="AnonymousTest.class" width="200"
height="200"></applet>

</body>
</html>
```

You can call the applet using the `appletviewer` utility that comes with the JDK. At the command line, type something like this:

```
C:\>appletviewer
CFusionMX\\wwwroot\\chp9\\ShowAnonymousTest.html
```

NOTE We cover applets in some detail in Chapter 10. If you're having difficulty calling the applet, consult that chapter.

9.1.7 Top-Level Nested Classes

A top-level nested class is a class defined within another. The difference between these and inner classes is that a top-level nested class can be instantiated without an instance of the outer class. The top-level nested class is defined just like a regular inner class, but it is modified with the keyword `static`.

The reason to create a top-level nested class instead of a regular Java class is that it allows you to force the nested class to belong to the outer class nominally without it being a true member of the outer class. That is, once you have created an instance of the top-level nested class, it has no other relationship to any outer class instances.

A top-level nested class can be instantiated provided you have access to the outer class without requiring outer instance references. You create a top-level nested inner class like so:

```
public class AnOuterClass {

  public static class AnInnerClass { }

}
```

Call it like this:

```
AnInnerClass in = new AnOuterClass.TheInner();
```

In general, it is best to use named top-level classes when your class definition is more than a few lines long.

9.2 Inheritance

We have discussed the benefits of inheritance in object-oriented programming in previous chapters. One of the best ways to be successful as a Java programmer is to understand your problem space and appropriately assign the members a place within a hierarchy that achieves a balance between encapsulation and access.

> **NOTE** Java handles inheritance somewhat differently than other object-oriented languages you may be familiar with. C++ and Lisp both allow multiple inheritance, meaning that a class can have more than one immediate parent. In Java, as in Smalltalk, this is not allowed. A Java class may have only one immediate parent class. Some of the same utility that multiple inheritance allows, however, can be achieved using *interfaces*, which we discuss in the next section.

Inheritance allows you to create a class that defines characteristic fields and behaviors that are common to more than one type of related thing. Once you have defined the general class, other classes can define more specific fields and methods that are appropriate only to them.

The typical example to illustrate inheritance conceptually is the animal kingdom. All animals share certain characteristics. Different kinds of animals share more specific kinds of behavior. For instance, you could define a method for animals called `move()`. Then every subclass of animal that you define would inherit the ability to move. A `Fish` subclass could define it more specifically for swimming, and a `Cat` subclass could walk and pounce. You could have a `Human` subclass that defined data fields for language, eye color, and so on, and all humans would inherit the ability to access a language, and they would all have an eye color.

> **NOTE** A subclass is a more specific version of a superclass. A specific kind of animal is a Cat, and a Cheetah is a specific kind of Cat. Cheetahs can do everything Cats can do, and they have all the properties of Cats. Cats can do everything animals can do, and they have all of the properties of animals.

Another common way to think of inheritance is with shapes. You can define a general shape, and you can then make `Triangle`, `Circle`, and `Square` classes to make objects of.

The way that you use inheritance in Java is by writing the general class (the superclass) and then writing the specific class (the subclass). You specify that the subclass should inherit from some other class by using the keyword `extends`, like this:

```
class ASubClass extends ASuperClass {...}
```

In our WWWBooks example, we had employees and managers. Managers are employees, but they are a specific kind of employee. Why redefine FirstName, LastName, SSN, and so on for both of the classes when they will always both need them? It is probably better to define such shared items in the `Employee` class, and do this:

```
class Manager extends Employee {}
```

It is just at this moment when we encounter the real art of Java programming. The second we type the above line of code, we realize that these aren't the only two players in this problem space. There are also `Customers`. And

`Customers` have a FirstName and a LastName, but they do not have an SSN (that we can know about). Maybe the thing to do is to define a `Person` class. Let `Person` define names, phone numbers, and so forth. Then do this instead:

```
class Person {
    // define firstname, lastname
...
}
class Customer extends Person {
    // get all the Person stuff and allow Customer to have
    // Orders
...}

class Employee extends Person {
    // get all the Person stuff and all Employee to have a
    // salary and hireDate
...}

class Manager extends Employee {
    // get everything from Employee and also define
    // a final field: QUARTERLY_BONUS = salary * 1.5;
...}
```

There is no hard and fast answer to this question. Maybe it is a good idea. Maybe it doesn't do enough for you to make it worth the extra effort of keeping track of it. It depends on what your problem space is and what the goals of your program are.

You may specify only one superclass for any subclass. This is illegal:

```
class Manager extends Person, Employee {...} // WRONG!
```

This differs from C++, which does allow this (it's called multiple inheritance).

A subclass does *not* inherit the private members (fields and methods) of a superclass. Variables declared `private` are accessible only by other members of their own class. This may sound like a serious restriction, but it makes perfect sense: It forces you to design for encapsulation. All you have to do to access a private field in a superclass is use an accessor method to retrieve that data.

Now let's take a look at an example.

9.2.1 MakeEmployeeAndManager.java

```
public class MakeEmployeeAndManager {

    public static void main(String[] args) {

            // make employees
        Employee emp1 = new Employee("Rod");

        Employee emp2 = new Employee("Tod");

            // set salaries for employees
        emp1.setSalary(18000.00);
        emp2.setSalary(25000.00);


        System.out.println(emp1.name + "'s salary: $" +
emp1.getSalary());

        System.out.println(emp2.name + "'s salary: $" +
emp2.getSalary());

            // make Manager. Pass name up to the superclass
(Employee)
            // for construction
        Manager mgr1 = new Manager("Ned");

            // set salary. Use Employee method to do this--
            // the setSalary method is NOT defined in Manager
class

        mgr1.setSalary(125000);

            // setBonus is defined in Manager class.
            // you can't do this with Employee objects
        mgr1.setBonus(250000.50);

        System.out.println(mgr1.name + "'s combined salary and
bonus: " +
            (mgr1.getSalary() + mgr1.getBonus()) );
    }
}
```

9.2.2 Employee.java

```
/*
 * Employee.java
 *
 */

/**
 *
 * @author  eben
 * @version
 */
public class Employee {

    protected String name = "";

    protected double salary = 0.0;

    /** constructor */
    public Employee(String name) {

        this.name = name;
    }

    public void setSalary(double salary) {
        this.salary = salary;
    }

    public double getSalary() {
        return salary;
    }
}
```

9.2.3 Manager.java

```
public class Manager extends Employee {

    private double bonus;

    /** constructor for Manager just passes
        along required info to superclass */
    public Manager(String name) {
        super(name);
    }
```

```
    void setBonus(double bonus) {
        this.bonus = bonus;
    }

    public double getBonus() {
        return bonus;
    }

}
```

The output of running the MakeManagerAndEmployee program is as follows:

```
Rod's salary: $18000.0
Tod's salary: $25000.0
Ned's combined salary and bonus: $375000.5
```

You have used the properties and methods defined in the superclass (`Employee`) in the subclass `Manager`. Managers are Employees, but they are a special kind of Employee. So Managers get everything that Employees get—a `name` and a `salary`—but they also get a bonus. There is no reason to replicate the definition of methods for setting and getting names in Manager, and there is no reason to allow all Employees to set and get bonuses when only a specific kind of Employee (the Manager) will need to use those methods. Thus, inheritance keeps your code clean, simple, easy to manage, and encapsulated.

Notice that Managers might have bonuses, but they might not. So the Manager *constructor*—the special method that creates `Manager` objects—simply calls `super();` that is, the constructor of its superclass `Employee`. If the above listings are hard to follow, it's because we've not covered some of these topics yet. That is the purpose of the following several sections of this chapter.

9.2.4 Constructors and `super`

If the subclass constructor does not explicitly call the superclass constructor with `super`, then the superclass's no-arg constructor is implicitly called prior to any code being executed in the subclass's constructor. You must make the call to `super` the first line in the subclass constructor. Notice what this means: When a subclass is compiled, the compiler will throw an error if a call to `super` is made and the superclass does not have a no-arg constructor. That's because a default no-arg constructor is automatically added by the compiler to any class that doesn't define any constructors. This is only the case, however, when no constructors are explicitly defined.

In the following example, we will build on the knowledge of working with exceptions that we gained in the last chapter. Recall that an `Exception` is an object. It can be subclassed, and we can define data in that subclass and pass it to more subclasses. We can also pass a message back up the tree for the superclass to handle.

Here we will create a subclass of `Exception`, and then we'll create related subclasses of that to handle the particular kind of exceptions that we want to throw.

9.2.5 AgeExceptionTest.java

```
package javaforcf.chp9;


/**
 * <p>Title: AgeException</p>
 * <p>Description: Demos creating your own exceptions and
 * using inheritance</p>
 * @version 1.0
 */

class AgeException extends Exception {

  int age;

  AgeException(String msg) {
    super(msg);
    }

    // no-arg constructor
  AgeException() {
    super();
    }

}

class TooYoungException extends AgeException {

  int ageLimit;
  TooYoungException(int age, int ageLimit) {

    super("You are too young!");
    this.age = age;
  }
```

```
}

class TooOldException extends AgeException {

  int ageLimit;
  TooOldException(int age, int ageLimit) {

    super("You are too old!");
    this.age = age;
  }
}

public class AgeExceptionTest {

  static void trySomething(int age, String action) throws
TooYoungException, TooOldException {

    System.out.println("You are trying to " + action + " at
age " + age + "...");

    if (age < 16)
      throw new TooYoungException(age, 16);

    else if (age > 65)
      throw new TooOldException(age, 65);
  }


public static void main(String[] args) {

  int age = 14;
  String action = "drive";
  String conclusion = "We can be in Vegas by midnight!";

  try {

    trySomething(age, action);
    System.out.println("I love to " + action + ".");
  }

  catch (TooYoungException tye) {
    System.out.println(tye.getMessage());
  }
  catch (TooOldException toe) {
```

```
      System.out.println(toe.getMessage());
    }
    finally {
      System.out.println(conclusion);
    }
  }

  }
```

9.3 Abstract Classes and Abstract Methods

There are many occasions when the following situation presents itself: You would like to define a class that can be subclassed, but allowing direct instantiation of the class would not make sense. This generally happens when you've got some behavior that you'd like to make common, but you don't have enough data for the class to be instantiated itself. Enter abstract classes.

9.3.1 Abstract Classes and Methods

An *abstract class* cannot be instantiated. It can define methods that subclasses will use. But you can't make an object of it. Things that are abstract are the opposite of concrete things (if you believe in opposites). What is abstract is not yet made, but it exists on a conceptual level in order to be made apparent. What is concrete exists already and is usable. Concrete classes have methods that are concrete. That is, they define exactly what they are supposed to do, and then they do that same thing in every single case.

With abstract classes, on the other hand, the idea is defined, but the implementation is not defined. The implementation must come from other classes that extend the abstract class. The usefulness of abstract classes is apparent when you need to define certain behavior for objects of a certain type, but you have specific behavior for different subclasses that you want to implement.

> **NOTE** If what you want to do is define methods without providing any implementation of them, you should really write an interface, as described above.

The way to ensure that your subclasses indeed override the methods you want is by defining them as abstract.

Abstract methods do not have a body. They have a return type, and they have parameters—just no body. Any class containing even one abstract method must itself be declared `abstract`. Any subclasses then must also be abstract, unless they implement every abstract method of the superclass.

NOTE You cannot declare constructors or static methods abstract.

Abstract methods are useful when the required behavior of a method is defined, but the implementation is not. Abstract methods give you the flexibility to leave the implementation up to subclasses. Consider the ubiquitous `Vehicle` example. That might be a case where you would define an abstract Vehicle with an abstract `makeSound()` method. Your `Car` class could then implement it with a honk, and a `Bicycle` class could implement it with one of those cute little metal ringers. An `Animal` class could work the same way: A `Cat` subclass could implement `makeSound()` to generate meows, and the `Dog` subclass would implement it to make barks.

NOTE As long as a class does not define abstract methods, its subclasses can be either abstract or concrete. If a class defines abstract methods, they must have a concrete implementation in a subclass.

You cannot create objects of a class that contains even one abstract method. That's because a class that contains even one abstract method must itself be declared `abstract`. Abstract classes by definition are not complete, and they must be implemented in a subclass. You create objects of the subclass type.

NOTE If a class defines even one abstract method, the entire class must be declared `abstract`. You may define concrete methods in an abstract class, however, and subclasses can use them directly.

Let's look at a simple example of this. Here we will make an abstract class called `Vehicle`, which will define certain kinds of properties and behaviors appropriate to vehicles, such as `currentSpeed`. The `setSpeed()` method will be concrete, and it will just accept a double value. We will then create two subclasses of `Vehicle`: `Car` and `SpeedBoat`. These subclasses provide different implementations of the `getSpeed()` method. The reason for this is that the speed of cars in measured in miles per hour in some places and kilometers per hour in others. For now, our cars can only drive in the United States and England. The value passed into `getSpeed()` will be calculated differently depending on where the car is.

9.3.2 Vehicle.java

```
package javaforcf.chp9;

/* Vehicle demos the use of abstract method
 * and inheritance
*/

abstract class Vehicle {

  protected double currentSpeed;
  protected String locale = "";
  protected String measurement = "";

  // default constructor
  Vehicle() {

  }

  // concrete method
  // doesn't get overridden here
    public String drive() {
      String s = "Now driving";
      return s;
    }

  // abstract method
  // notice that declaring abstract method
  // disallows use of {}

  public abstract double getSpeed();

}
```

9.3.3 Car.java

```
package javaforcf.chp9;

public class Car extends Vehicle {

      // constructor overload
        Car() {
          super();
          currentSpeed = 0.0;
          locale = "US";
        }
```

```
        public void setSpeed(double d) {

          this.currentSpeed = d;
        }

        public double getSpeed() {
          double s = this.currentSpeed;
          if (this.getMeasurement() == "MPH") return s;

              // convert to kilometers
          return s = s * 0.6;

        }

        public String getMeasurement() {
          if (this.locale != "US") return "KPH";
          return "MPH";
        }

        public String getLocale() {
          return locale;
        }


      public static void main(String[] args) {

        // create an object of the subclass
        Car myCar = new Car();

        System.out.println(myCar.drive() + " in " +
  myCar.getLocale());
        myCar.setSpeed(100.0);
        System.out.println("Current speed: " +
              myCar.getSpeed() +  " " +
              myCar.getMeasurement());
      }

  }
```

The example is a bit contrived, but it illustrates certain things. The output of compiling and running `Car` with "England" as the value of the `locale` variable produces this:

```
Now driving in England
Current speed: 60.0 KPH
```

Using "US" as the locale produces this output:

```
Now driving in US
Current speed: 100.0 MPH
```

We can also extend the `Vehicle` class further to demonstrate the usefulness of having the `getSpeed()` method declared `abstract`. The speed of boats is measured in knots, not in miles or kilometers. So we can pass it a value in MPH and it will convert it to knots and tell us so, acting in a way appropriate to boats:

9.3.4 SpeedBoat.java

```
package javaforcf.chp9;

public class SpeedBoat extends Vehicle {

      // constructor overload
        SpeedBoat() {

        // call superclass
          super();
          currentSpeed = 0.0;
          locale = "water";
        }
      public void setSpeed(double d) {

        this.currentSpeed = d;
      }

     public double getSpeed() {
        double s = this.currentSpeed;

          // do conversion for nautical miles
        return s = s * 1.1507794;

      }

   public static void main(String[] args) {

     SpeedBoat myBoat = new SpeedBoat();

     System.out.println(myBoat.drive() + " in " +
myBoat.getLocale());
```

```
        myBoat.setSpeed(100.0);
        System.out.println("Current speed: " +
              myBoat.getSpeed() +  " knots");

    }
}
```

Running `SpeedBoat` produces this output:

```
Now driving in water
Current speed: 115.07794 knots
```

We could, of course, have declared `Boat` a subclass of `Vehicle`, and extended `SpeedBoat` and `Yacht` instead. Then `Yacht` would have to declare properties such as `SizeOfBar` and `NumberOfTrophies`, and methods such as `getGuestList()`.

9.4 Interfaces

An interface is a lot like an abstract class. The chief difference is that an interface cannot have any code in it. You might think of it as the class-level version of an abstract method. Remember that an abstract method is declared like this:

```
public abstract double getSpeed();
```

It just ends with a semicolon and no code. An interface is similar, and it has a usefulness like an abstract method's.

The real purpose of interfaces is to prevent multiple inheritance. Other programming languages, including C++, allow you to subclass from more than one immediate parent. It would be like writing this in Java:

```
public class A extends B, C ...
```

You don't need to do this in Java, and you cannot. You *can* inherit from more than one class, of course, just by virtue of the fact that you can inherit from a class that is itself a subclass. Then you get everything from the parent and the grandparent. But you can only have one immediate superclass. If you organize your class hierarchy correctly, then this shouldn't be a problem. Sometimes systems get very complex, however, and you would like to be able to do this sort of thing.

An *interface* is a special kind of class declaration that allows you to declare constants and method declaration, but not the implementation of the methods. An interface can contain no code.

The bare structure of an interface looks like this:

```
public interface MyInterface {

      void myMethod();
}
```

As you can see, it is much like a class, but you write "interface" instead of "class."

> **NOTE** All methods in an interface are `public` by default. You therefore do not need to specify a public accessibility modifier.

When you want to use an interface in a class, you use the `implements` keyword where you would put extends if this were an implementation of an abstract class:

```
public class SomeClass implements SomeInterface
```

You can implement an interface and extend a superclass in the same class:

```
public class SomeClass extends ParentClass implements
    SomeInterface
```

Interfaces are useful when you want to define what a class must do, but not how it should do it. Abstract methods, covered in the last section, are examples of this—they provide a signature and not the implementation. This forces any subclasses to define the implementation for the abstract methods inherited.

An interface can be implemented and used by any number of classes. A single class can implement as many interfaces as it likes. Interfaces provide another key aspect of polymorphism, because one interface gives you multiple methods.

> **NOTE** If you have ever written a ColdFusion CFX tag in Java to extend ColdFusion, you have used the Allaire interfaces.

Interfaces must be declared `public`, or the access modifier must be omitted. Declaring an interface as `public` means that omitting the access modifier causes the access level to be set to `default`, which, as you may recall, means package-level access.

Every class that implements an interface must implement *all* of its methods, each of which are implicitly `public`. Because there is no implementation in an interface, there cannot be instance variables. Any variables in an interface must essentially be constants. These are implicitly `public`, `static`, and `final`, and must be initialized.

An interface has the following structure:

```
accessModifier interface name {
  type aVariable = value;
  returnType methodName(argumentList);
}
```

The way to implement an interface is to use the `implements` keyword in your class definition. In the class that implements the interface, you must write the bodies of the interface's methods. These methods must be declared `public`, and their signature must exactly match the signature of the `interface` method.

In this example, we'll look at probably the simplest interface and implementation one could make.

9.4.1 MakeHelloInterface.java

```
    // use implements keyword to specify interface
public class MakeHelloInterface implements HelloInterface {

    public static void main(String[] args) {

        MakeHelloInterface mhi = new MakeHelloInterface();

        System.out.println(mhi.sayHello());
    }

        // implement this method from the Hello interface
    public String sayHello() {

            // this is a constant, and is initialized in
            // the interface
        return HELLO;
    }

}
```

9.4.2 HelloInterface.java

```
public interface HelloInterface {

        // a constant field
    final String HELLO = "Howdy ho, neighbor!";

        // method to be implemented
   public String sayHello();
}
```

As we see above, you can call a method declared in an interface on an object. It is important to note that the same object can also be used to store references to any object that implements another interface.

If a class declares that it implements an interface, but does not implement all of the methods of the interface, it must be declared `abstract`. You cannot create objects of that abstract class, but this can still be a useful approach, as the abstract class may be subclasses, and the remaining implementation can take place in the subclass.

9.5 final

Inheritance and method overriding are very powerful, as we have seen. However, there are many occasions during which you do not want to allow classes to be extended and methods to be overridden. You disallow such things with the `final` keyword.

There could be a number of reasons for wanting to disallow class extension or method overriding.

9.5.1 final Disallows Inheritance

In order to prevent a class from being inherited, use the `final` keyword in its definition:

```
public final class Class
```

When you declare a class as `final`, all of its methods become implicitly `final` as well.

NOTE As you may infer, you cannot declare a class both `abstract` and `final`. These concepts are at opposite ends of the spectrum: `abstract` says, "I have no implementation whatsoever. I only exist as a concept. You will have to do everything for me in a subclass." `final`, on the other hand, says, "There will never be any other versions of me. I am implemented completely. I'm the last one, and I'm as good as it gets."

The `java.lang.Class` class, which we discuss below, is `final`. The `Class` class has no public constructor, because `Class` objects get automatically constructed by the Java Virtual Machine when classes are loaded. Using `final` means that this is illegal:

```
public final class MyClass {
  //...
}

class SubClass extends MyClass { // Error! Cannot extend final
  //...
}
```

This can protect the integrity of your work and help keep your application secure and working as you expect. Here is another example:

9.5.2 finalTest.java

```
package javaforcf.chp9;

public final class finalTest {

  public static void main(String[] args) {

  finalTest obj  = new finalTest();

  System.out.println(obj.getClass().getModifiers());
  }
}
```

Running this program simply returns the `int` 17, the modifier for a `public final class`.

9.5.3 `final` Disallows Overriding

In keeping with behavior typical of `final`, declaring a method `final` disallows its being overridden. This works just as you would imagine. Let's look at a quick example:

9.5.4 `FinalMethod.java`

```
package javaforcf.chp9;

  // class is not final.
  // we're going to extend it
public class FinalMethod {


  // the multiply method is final
  // mutliplies two ints
  final int multiply(int i, int j) {
    return i * j;
  }

  public static void main(String[] args) {

    FinalMethod obj  = new FinalMethod();

      // okay. returns 15
    System.out.println(obj.multiply(3,5));

  }
}
```

The above class, `FinalMethod`, is not itself `final`. It contains a single `final` method.

9.5.5 `FinalMethodExtender.java`

```
package javaforcf.chp9;

public class FinalMethodExtender extends FinalMethod {

  public static void main(String[] args) {
```

```
        // instantiate
      FinalMethodExtender fme = new FinalMethodExtender();

        /* call the method defined in the superclass
           we don't define this here, the method is inherited
           because of the extends keyword in the class dedinition
           */
      System.out.println(fme.multiply(7,8));

        // prints 56
    }
  }
```

The above class runs fine and prints `56`. We can inherit and use the `multiply()` method normally, even though it is `final`.

We will now see what happens when we try to override this method in `FinalMethodExtender`. What if we just wrote the following?

```
public double multiply(double d, double e) {
  return d * e;
}
```

That is not overriding the method. It has a different signature, and overriding requires that the signatures match. Defining a couple of doubles and running that program would work fine. Note that if you do not create the double fields, you will get a compiler error, but it won't be because of finality. It will complain that the method call is ambiguous—it doesn't know whether you mean the `multiply()` method from the superclass or this class. Why would that be? Because, as you'll recall from the second chapter, the JVM can perform this natural widening conversion. In order to really test this, we need to create a real override:

```
public int multiply(int i, int j) {

  System.out.println("Result: ");
  return i * j;
}
```

Now, compiling and running the class will get this result:

```
final method multiply(int, int) in class
javaforcf.chp9.FinalMethod cannot be overridden by method
```

```
multiply(int, int) in class
javaforcf.chp9.FinalMethodExtender.
```

9.6 Reflection

Reflection is a powerful aspect of Java. Reflection is what allows a program to inspect the abilities of a Java class at runtime. Reflection is used chiefly to build RAD tools for Java programmers. Because it is a complex topic and is of less interest to the typical Java application developer, it will only be mentioned here. You can safely skim this section and return to it later if you have a need for it.

The `java.lang.reflect` package is the package that contains the classes and interfaces necessary to obtain this reflective information. Its primary purpose is to allow access to information regarding the constructors, fields, and methods of loaded classes. Once you have inspected these classes, you can use the reflective items to perform operations on their counterpart objects.

Related to reflection are two classes in the `java.lang` package that we will briefly look at now. These are the class named `Class` and the class named `Object`.

9.6.1 `final` Fields

Using `final` on variables essentially creates a constant. As with other things `final`, you cannot change the value of a `final` variable throughout the life of your program. Use this modifier to declare constants.

9.6.2 `FinalFields.java`

```
package javaforcf.chp9;

public final class FinalFields {

  final double VERSION = 1.0;

  public static void main(String[] args) {

  FinalFields obj  = new FinalFields();

  System.out.println(obj.VERSION);

  }
}
```

Trying to write something like…

```
obj.VERSION = 2.0;
```

…gets you the following compiler error:

```
variable VERSION is declared final; cannot be assigned
```

There are a number of methods in the API that are declared `final`. Some of these, such as methods in `java.lang.Class`, we will look at below.

9.6.3 The Class Named `Class`

In one of the more strikingly beautiful aspects of the Java programming language, every object that you create has some knowledge of itself. This information is kept in an object of type `Class`.

The `Class` class is important because it aids in the loading of classes. One `Class` object is made available for each class loaded into the Java Virtual Machine. It holds objects for any Java class, interface, primitive wrappers, or any Java type.

This class does not have a constructor—you only need to call the `getClass()` method for any instance, like this:

```
System.out.println(someClass.getClass());
```

The following program demonstrates some of the methods made available by the `Class` class.

```
package javaforcf.chp9;

public class TestClass  {


     void printClassName(Object obj) {
         System.out.println("The class of " + obj +
             " is " +
             obj.getClass().getName());
     }

     void printSuper(Object obj) {
         System.out.println("The superclass is " +
            obj.getClass().getSuperclass());
     }
```

```
    void printPackage(Object obj) {
        System.out.println("The field is " +
           obj.getClass().getPackage());
    }

    void printInterface(Object obj) {
        System.out.println("Is this class an interface? " +
            obj.getClass().isInterface());
    }

   public static void main(String [] arg) {

     TestClass obj = new TestClass();

     obj.printClassName(obj);
     obj.printSuper(obj);
     obj.printPackage(obj);
     obj.printInterface(obj);

   }
}
```

Running this program renders the following output:

```
The class of javaforcf.chp9.TestClass@720eeb is
javaforcf.chp9.TestClass
The superclass is class java.lang.Object
The field is package javaforcf.chp9
Is this class an interface? false
```

There is an aspect of the `Class` class that is often useful for Java developers, especially those wishing to connect to a database. This method is called `forName()`. The `forName(String className)` method of `Class` returns the `Class` object associated with the class or interface named in the parameter. This will make more sense when we get to the discussion of Java database connectivity; for now, it is just interesting to know that when you load a database driver to connect to a database, you're going to use `Class.forName("driverNameString")` to do it. For example, here is the string used to load a particular driver to use with the MySQL database:

```
// load driver
          Class.forName("org.gjt.mm.mysql.Driver");
```

You'll notice that the string we're passing is the qualified package name. Think back to ColdFusion 5 when the ability to specify a connect string was added. This gave ColdFusion developers the ability to specify different attributes to be sent along to the database to be used in creating the connection. To get to a database in Java, we have to do a similar deal. But we must also explicitly load the driver. We're used to the ColdFusion Administrator handling that for us when we create a datasource; but using `Class.forName("myDriver")` is how we do it in Java: it's an object like everything else.

9.6.4 The Class Named `Object` and `clone()`

Every object in Java inherits from `java.lang.Object`. Because every class extends `Object`, a variable that is of type `Object` can refer to any object. For the same reason, a number of useful methods are made available by `Object`.

There are two general categories of methods in `Object`: utility methods and methods that support threads. Threads are discussed in a later chapter, so for now we will just glance at the more common utility methods.

```
public boolean equals(Object o)
```

This method indicates whether another object is equal to this one and checks for equality of the values. So given a value `x`, `x.equals(x)` will return `true`. For any reference values, `equals()` returns `true` if and only if the two values refer to the same object. The `String` class overrides the equals method to return `true` if the two compared strings have the same contents.

```
protected Object clone() throws CloneNotSupportedError
```

The `clone()` method returns a clone of this object. A *clone* is a new object that is a copy of the object on which the method was invoked. Using the `clone()` method on an object copies not only the structure of an object but its current values at the time it was invoked.

```
protected void finalize() throws Throwable
```

When the garbage collector has determined that there are no more references to this object, it calls the object's `finalize` method to destroy it.

```
public final Class getClass()
```

returns the object's runtime class.

```
public toString()
```

returns a string representing the object. Whenever you concatenate strings using the + operator, the `toString()` method is invoked implicitly.

The remainder of the methods in `Object` relate to threads, which we will look at later. The methods relating to threads in the `Object` class are all declared `final`. They can, and often should, be overriden.

The following example simply puts some of the methods of the `java.lang.Object` package to work. It also incorporates some of the techniques we've learned in the last couple of chapters, including exception handling and interface implementation. We will also override the `toString()` method of `Object`.

Specifically, the `clone()` interface allows us to duplicate objects. In order to clone an object, you need to do two things: override the `clone()` method made available by `Object` and implement the `Cloneable` interface, which is empty.

9.6.5 TestObject.java

```
package javaforcf.chp9;

public class TestObject implements Cloneable  {

      int i;
      int j;
      String s = "Hello, ";

    // throw the required exception
  public Object clone() throws CloneNotSupportedException {
      return super.clone();
  }

    // override toString method
  public String toString() {
       return s + i + " and " + j;
  }


public static void main(String [] arg) {

  TestObject original = new TestObject();
    original.i = 8;
    original.j = 7;

    try {
        // clone the object
      Object aClone = original.clone();
```

```
            // show the properties using our toString
            // method which will automatically get called
            // prove that the clone and the original have the same
            // data
            // and same method available to them
          System.out.println(original);
          System.out.println(aClone);


      // get the value of the field
      // prints 8
      //System.out.println(original.i);

      // prints: class javaforcf.chp9.TestObject
      // same for calling getClass() on the clone
      System.out.println(original.getClass());


        // are they really of the same class?
        // prints true
      System.out.println(  aClone.getClass() ==
           original.getClass());


      // what is the hashcode for this object?
      // returns something like 7474923
      System.out.println(aClone.hashCode());


        }
        catch (CloneNotSupportedException cnse) {
              System.out.println(cnse);
        }
    }

    }
```

Running this program produces an output such as this:

```
Hello, 8 and 7
Hello, 8 and 7
class javaforcf.chp9.TestObject
true
3242435
```

An empty interface is one that defines no methods or variables; it just indicates that the class that implements it can be cloned. Trying to invoke `clone()` on an object that doesn't implement this interface causes the `CloneNotSupported` exception to be thrown. If you remove the "`implements Cloneable`" statement from the class definition and recompile it, you'll see the exception we've caught:

```
java.lang.CloneNotSupportedException:
javaforcf.chp9.TestObject
```

9.7 What's Next?

In this chapter we have covered advanced concepts in classes and objects. Using inheritance, interfaces, and reflection will really help you honor encapsulation and maximize your ability to reuse code. The more object oriented your applications are, the more sensible they will be. The more sensible your applications are, the more extensible. Ask yourself this question as you design an application architecture or hierarchy: What modification would make this more like the world? That is, does this object definition or this class hierarchy structure really act like the real objects that I'm representing? Sometimes it is difficult to match data representations and interactions with the real world. It can be difficult, for instance, in the way that designing a complex relational database system is: maybe it is easy enough to determine what a customer or a product is, but representing a product's options such as size and color might require join tables to resolve certain many-to-many relationships. And join tables are admittedly scarce in the real world. So it isn't a precise correlation. But it is a simple matter of adopting a discourse that stands in place of things in the world, much like the way that we talk about the economy.

In the following chapter, we cover ways to extend ColdFusion with Java technology. These include importing Java custom tag libraries into ColdFusion MX, writing and calling applets, and writing CFX tags in Java. ColdFusion makes available a special set of interfaces for working with ColdFusion custom tags written in Java.

10

Extending ColdFusion with Java

You now have much of the basic knowledge required to write Java programs of any complexity. A good portion of the remainder of your work is to become as familiar with the API as you can. The concepts you already know regarding classes and objects and OOP principles are all you need to understand the API and implement it. *Classes relate hierarchically to make objects that hold data and define operations.* That is it.

The principles are the same whether you're using a `JPanel` object or an `Employee` object or a `String` object. So in order to begin programming more complex applications, the main thing to do is dive into the API and find out what is available and start working with different items, applying and exercising the principles you already know.

In this chapter, we cover how to use Java extensions to your ColdFusion environment. There is a lot you can start doing now to leverage the capabilities of Java from within ColdFusion MX and earlier versions. Here we will look at using the `<cfobject>` tag to invoke Java objects directly from within a ColdFusion template. We will cover incorporating Java applets into your ColdFusion templates and writing CFX custom tags that allow you to invoke compiled Java classes as custom tags.

In ColdFusion MX, `<cfservlet>` and `<cfservletparam>`, which have been used to invoke JRun servlets, are now deprecated owing to the integration between these products.

We will discuss servlets and JSPs in later chapters, and determining how to invoke them from ColdFusion is a topic more appropriate there. In the chapter devoted to writing custom tags (also known as custom actions) in JSP, we will also discuss another way of extending ColdFusion with Java: the ColdFusion tag introduced in CFMX, `<cfimport>`.

This chapter represents the only real ColdFusion usage we will cover in this book, as it is assumed that you know ColdFusion rather well. However, even many advanced ColdFusion developers have little or no experience with using Java from within ColdFusion, which is the reason it is covered here.

> **NOTE** This chapter assumes that you have ColdFusion MX installed and running. You can download a 30-day free trial version from *www.macromedia.com*. After the 30 days is expired, the server automatically converts to a single-IP development version. You may use the development version indefinitely, but only localhost can send requests to ColdFusion.

10.1 Configure ColdFusion Server Settings for Java

In order to begin working with Java in any of the ways available, we first need to configure the ColdFusion server. To do so, open the ColdFusion MX Administrator, and click Java and JVM. The Settings window is shown in Figure 10.1. There are a few settings here that require attention.

- **Java Virtual Machine Path.** This setting allows you to specify the location of the Java Virtual Machine you wish to use. Because ColdFusion MX is Java-based, this box will be pre-populated with `<COLDFUSION_HOME>/runtime/jre`. ColdFusion used to install JDK 1.3 into its directory structure.
- **Initial Memory Size (MB).** This determines the amount of memory the JVM should use.
- **Maximum Memory Size (MB).** This defaults to the amount of RAM on the system.
- **Class Path.** Here you indicate the directories and JAR files that contain the Java classes ColdFusion will use.
- **JVM Arguments.** Here you specify any additional arguments to send to the JVM. This might include, for instance, a directive to enable assertions.

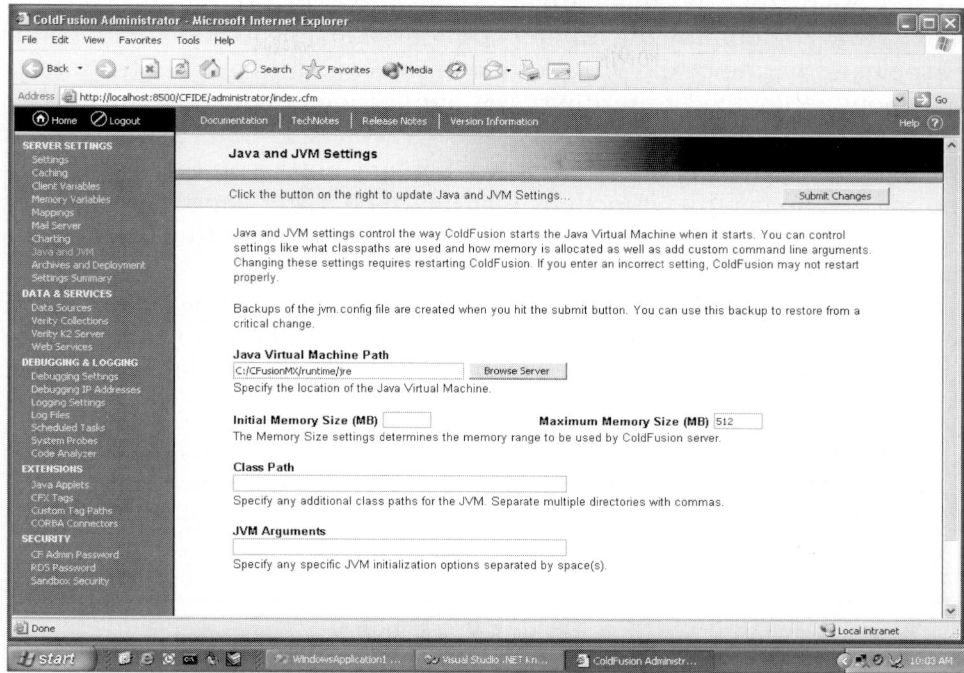

FIGURE 10.1 Java and JVM settings in the ColdFusion MX Administrator.

> **NOTE** Previous versions of ColdFusion had a setting allowing you to indicate whether to load the JVM automatically when ColdFusion was started. This setting is obsolete; because ColdFusion is Java-based, it must always start the JVM.

> **NOTE** It is okay to have multiple versions of the JVM installed concurrently on the same machine.

In the next section, we will write a simple Java class and invoke it from within a ColdFusion template.

10.2 Using `<cfobject>`

Any compiled Java class can be called from within a regular ColdFusion template using the `<cfobject>` tag, as long as it is available to the class path as specified in the ColdFusion Administrator settings.

There are many ways to incorporate Java into your ColdFusion Web applications. How you employ the different options available to you will depend on the scope and nature of the project and the personnel involved. The third part of this book is devoted to writing Web applications exclusively in Java with JavaServer Pages, servlets, and Enterprise JavaBeans. Using `<cfobject>` will likely mean that you have a Web app written in ColdFusion that needs to perform one or two complex functions that might be better handled in Java, or it may mean that you need to interoperate with some other software installed on the server, and a Java object is the way to do it.

This tag is used to invoke not only Java objects, but also COM objects, CORBA objects, and Web services. In this chapter we will only discuss its use with Java objects. For a look at the attributes of the `<cfobject>` tag, see Table 10.1.

> **NOTE** There is an alternative to using the `<cfobject>` tag. To invoke an object from within a `<cfscript>` block, you use the `CreateObject()` statement. We will look at examples using both syntaxes.

TABLE 10.1 `<cfobject>` Tag Attributes

ATTRIBUTE	DESCRIPTION
type	For use with Java objects, specify `type="Java"`. Other values are COM and CORBA.
action	Create: specifies the creations of a Java or BEA WebLogic Environment object.
class	The Java class to use.
name	String name for the instantiated component.

Here is the flow of execution when invoking Java objects in a ColdFusion template: First, call `<cfobject>` or `CreateObject()` to create an instance of the object. Note that calling an object using the `<cfobject>` tag and the function version `CreateObject()` does *not* call the constructor for that object. In order to call the constructor, you need to use ColdFusion's `init()` method. This method replicates the functionality of the Java keyword `new`. ColdFusion will make an implicit call to the default constructor if you call a public method before calling `init()`.

Once you have created an object instance, you can refer to its fields and methods using <cfset>, and you can then output their results using <cfoutput>. At the end of template execution, the object is implicitly released.

10.2.1 Invoking and Instantiating a Java Object

Here is the syntax for creating an object using the tag version:

```
<cfobject type="Java" action="create" class="MyClass"
name="myObj">
```

Here is the syntax for creating an object using <cfscript>:

```
<cfscript>
     myObj = CreateObject("Java", "MyClass");
</cfscript>
```

Invoking the object in this way only loads the object's class into memory—it does not create an instance of the object. So you now need to create an instance of the object, and you have two ways you can do it.

The first way to do this is to simply call any of the object's public fields or methods. Doing so automatically forces a call to the default constructor. Your other option, of course, is to call one of the object's constructors.

You can call a constructor defined within the class with `init()`, which is a ColdFusion function for this purpose. It means that you cannot have an `init()` method defined in your Java class. Calling `init()` when you have an identically named method in your Java class will cause an exception to be thrown.

> **NOTE** You can call Enterprise JavaBeans using the <cfobject> tag. However, this practice is generally not recommended, and it requires extra work with your application servers.

10.2.2 Setting and Retrieving Field Values

To set the value of a field in a Java object you have invoked, use the <cfset> tag:

```
<cfset myObj.someField = "somevalue">
```

To retrieve the value of a field and assign a ColdFusion variable to its value, you leave out the quote marks around the field name:

```
<cfset var = myObj.someField>
```

10.2.3 Calling Object Methods

You similarly use the `<cfset>` tag to call the methods of a Java object:

```
<cfset someValue = myObj.getItem()>
```

10.2.4 Using `JavaCast()`

The `JavaCast()` function is used for scalar and string arguments for use with overloaded constructors. This function converts the data type of a ColdFusion variable to pass it as an argument to an overloaded method of a Java object.

You use the `JavaCast()` function after you have created an object with the `<cfobject>` tag, but before you call one of its methods. Use `JavaCast()` only for overloaded methods that accept arguments of more than one data type. Its purpose is to determine which constructor you mean to call when sending a different data type is the only distinguishing factor between constructors.

> **NOTE** A quick reminder if you're having trouble keeping the terminology straight: Overloading a constructor or method means creating multiple methods or constructors with the same name but different signatures.

The `JavaCast()` function converts a ColdFusion variable into one of the following types:

- `boolean`
- `double`
- `int`
- `long`
- `String`

The `JavaCast()` function takes two parameters: `type`, representing the type into which you want to cast the variable, and `var`, representing the ColdFusion variable to be cast. It has the following syntax:

```
JavaCast(type, var) // both required
```

ColdFusion, as you know, is a weakly typed language. That makes it very easy to start using ColdFusion, but a little tricky when integrating with strongly typed languages such as Java. You may not always get entirely predictable results when using this function.

Here is a simple example using the `<cfobject>` tag and the `JavaCast()` function. First, we'll define a quick Java class, and then we'll write a ColdFusion template that we can use to instantiate it.

10.2.5 CFObjTest.java

```
/* used with CFOBjectTest.cfm
 * to demonstrate working with Java
 * classes from inside CF templates
 */

public class CFObjTest {

    public String message;

    //default constructor
    public CFObjTest() {

        message = "No message specified.";
    }


        // set the message
    public void setMessage(String s) {
        message = s;
    }

    // retrieve message
    public String getMessage() {

        return message;
  }
}
```

10.2.6 CFObjectTest.cfm

```
<!---
File: chp10/ObjTest.cfm
Purpose: demonstrate <cfobject>
Call an overloaded constructor
Send a message into the object and
have it print the message the number
of times specified.
```

```
--->
<!DOCTYPE HTML PUBLIC "-//W3C//DTD HTML 4.01 Transitional//EN">

<html>
<head>
<title>&lt;cfobject test&gt;</title>
</head>

<body>

Loading object...
<cfobject type="JAVA" action="create" name="ATest"
class="CFObjTest">

<br>
<br>

<!---set message to be printed--->
<cfset setIt=ATest.setMessage("Well hello, Mr. Fancy Pants.")>

<!--- retrieve the message from the object--->
<cfset msg = ATest.getMessage()>

<cfoutput>
Here is your message: <br>
<b>#msg#</b>
</cfoutput>

</body>
</html>
```

> **NOTE** If you need to restart ColdFusion manually, you can do so by executing the program at `C:\CFusionMX\runtime\bin`. This will bring up the JRun launcher, and you can start the server from there.

10.2.7 Running the Test

There are a few things you may need to do to run this test. First, add a directory that we can run ColdFusion tests out of, and set the server's class path to find that directory. I will make mine `C:\CFusionMX\wwwroot\chp10`, (the comma will automatically be added for you).

Then we will put the ColdFusion template `CFObjTest.cfm` in this directory on the server, and we'll put the `ObjTest.java` file in the same directory. Compile the Java class. Call the following URL in your browser: *http://localhost:8500/chp10/CFObjTest.cfm*.

Here is your output to the browser:

Loading object...

Here is your message:

Well hello, Mr. Fancy Pants.

It's a lot of work, but getting such an inspiring message back is worth it.

Let's look at another quick example that uses the `JavaCast()` function. I would not recommend calling Java objects from ColdFusion in this way with much intensity or frequency. If you think you'll need to do that, do your work in JSPs or servlets that have containers made specially to run them. Actually, ColdFusion MX Enterprise and Development versions will execute JSPs directly, which is more stable.

10.2.8 Testing the `JavaCast()` Function

```
<!---
File: JavaCastTest.cfm\
Purpose: demonstrate use of JavaCast function
--->

<!DOCTYPE HTML PUBLIC "-//W3C//DTD HTML 4.0 Transitional//EN">

<html>
<head>
<title>Test 2</title>
</head>

<body>

<!---load class--->
<cfobject type="JAVA" action="create" name="ATest"
    class="JavaCastTest">

<!---call object's overloaded method, using JavaCast to
determine which method will be called--->
```

```
<cfset msg = ATest.getVar(JavaCast("String", 007))>

<!----output the result--->

<cfoutput>#msg#</cfoutput>

</body>
</html>
```

This file simply loads the object of class `JavaCastTest`, and it then uses the `JavaCast()` function to determine which method it will call. Below we create the simple class file it uses. This test shows the full extent and purpose of this function—it settles disputes in translation from a weakly typed language to a strongly typed language.

10.2.9 JavaCastTest.java

```
public class JavaCastTest {


public String getVar(String s) {
  message = "I am a String";
  return message;
  }

// overloaded
public String getVar(int i) {
message = "I am an int";
  return message;
  }
}
```

Compile and run this just as the previous example. Here is your output to the browser:

```
I am a String
```

There used to be more uses for this tag and function, as Java support was not as strong, and other functionality that could be exposed to ColdFusion as objects now have been incorporated into ColdFusion MX. For instance, parsing XML from within ColdFusion previously required programs such as Microsoft's XML parser. You could use the `<cfobject>` tag to access XML nodes it parsed and traverse the tree. Now, you can use the `<cfxml>` tag. But that is another subject.

10.2.10 An Advanced <cfobject> Example

Here we look at a code listing that addresses a common problem in ColdFusion. We will read in the contents of a file line by line. This task is generally accomplished using <cffile>. However, the <cffile> tag reads a file into memory all at once. Your environment may require a more judicious use of memory, particularly if you are reading in a large file containing a lot of data.

The typical way of reading in a file line by line would be to create a `FileReader` object, pass that object to a `BufferedReader`, and call its `readLine()` method to read in the file. This poses a subtle and interesting dilemma.

When the `BufferedReader.readLine()` method reaches the end of a line, it returns a `null` value. So when using this method from within ColdFusion, we face a problem: ColdFusion does not have `nulls` like Java does. ColdFusion instead will return an empty string—which means that we cannot determine the difference between a blank line within the file and the end of the dataset (the end of the file).

This example therefore has the added benefit of demonstrating further use of subclassing. In order to work around this, we need to subclass Java's `BufferedReader`. This file will differentiate between a blank line and the end of the file.

The Java source code and ColdFusion template for this example were written by Daryl Banttari, senior consultant at Macromedia, and they are used by permission.

10.2.11 CFBufferedReader.java

```
//CFBufferedReader
// Purpose:
//   Since ColdFusion automatically turns "null" Strings into
//   empty strings,
//   it is necessary to extend BufferedReader so that we can
//   detect
//   the null string returned from readLine().
//// Use:
//   CFBufferedReader works exactly like
//   java.io.BufferedReader,
//   but adds an isEOF() method to indicate whether the last
//   call
//   to readLine detected the end of the file.
//// Author:
//   Daryl Banttari (Macromedia)
//// Copyright: (c)2001 Macromedia
```

```
import java.io.*;
//   Define this class as a subclass of java.io.BufferedReader

public class CFBufferedReader extends java.io.BufferedReader {
// variable to hold the EOF status of the last read
// default to false; we'll assume you're not at eof if
// we haven't read anything yet
     private boolean eof = false;

     // our class constructors will simply pass the arguments
     // through to our superclass, BufferedReader:
     public CFBufferedReader(Reader in, int sz) {
          // "super" is an alias to the superclass.
          // calling super() in this fashion actually
       // invokes the superclass' constructor method.
                  super(in, sz);
     }
     public CFBufferedReader(Reader in) {
          super(in);
     }

     // here we extend the readLine method:
   public String readLine() throws java.io.IOException {
          String curLine;
          // call the "real" readLine() method from the
superclass
                  curLine = super.readLine();
                  // now set eof to "is curline null?"
          // note that there are two equals signs between
"curLine" and "null"
          eof = (curLine == null);
                  // return curline to the caller "as is"
                  return curLine;           }
     public boolean isEOF() {
 // simply return the current value if the eof variable
                  return eof;        }
}
```

Now compile `CFBufferedReader.java` in the Chapter 10 directory. We will call it using `<cfobject>` and the following ColdFusion template: `Java-File-Test.cfm`. This file will read itself in and replace < characters with `<`.

10.2.12 JavaFileTest.cfm

```
<!DOCTYPE HTML PUBLIC "-//W3C//DTD HTML 4.01 Transitional//EN">
<html>
<head>
<!---Author: Daryl Banttari--->
        <title>Java File Example</title>
</head>
<body>
<!--- get our filename from the CGI environment --->
<cfset fn = cgi.cf_template_path>
<!--- create a Java FileReader object to read this file --->
<!--- note that java.io.FileReader is a native Java class.--->

<cfobject type="Java" class="java.io.FileReader" name="fr"
action="create">
<!--- when calling Java from CF, the constructor is called
"init()" --->
<cfset fr.init(fn)>

<!--- now pass the FileReader object to our extended
BufferedReader --->
<cfobject type="Java" class="CFBufferedReader" name="reader"
action="create">
<cfset reader.init(fr)>
<!--- read the first line from the file --->
<cfset curLine=reader.readLine()>

<!--- now loop until we reach the end of the file --->
<cfloop condition="not #reader.isEOF()#">
        <!--- display the current line --->
        <cfoutput>#replace(curLine,"<","&lt;","ALL")#<br>
        </cfoutput>
        <!--- flush the output buffer (cf5 only) --->
        <cfflush>
        <!--- each call to readLine( ) reads the /next/ line,
          until the end of the file is reached, at which point
      isEOF( ) starts returning "true" --->
        <cfset curLine=reader.readLine()>
</cfloop>
</body>
</html>
```

Now call `JavaFileTest.cfm` like this: `http://localhost:8500/chp10/JavaFileTest.cfm`. The file will call the object, read in the file, replace the characters as mentioned, and output the file to the browser. If you had a Web site on which you wanted to display ColdFusion source code without it being processed by the CFAS, you could return it to the browser for readers using these files.

10.3 CFX Custom Tags

Another popular way to gain the power of the Java language while working within the ease of the ColdFusion environment is to write CFX custom tags.

To write a CFX custom tag, you write the Java code that will create the object you want to use. Then you register the code with the ColdFusion Administrator so that ColdFusion knows what code base to run when you invoke the tag.

Before writing your own custom tags, it is not a bad idea to look at the CFX tags that Macromedia ships with the CFMX server. You can find these source files in `<CFMX_HOME>\cfx\java\distrib\examples`. This directory contains several examples, ranging from a simple "Hello, World" tag, to one that creates custom graphics for you.

It is a little extra work to turn regular Java classes into CFX tags. The first thing you need to do is write a Java file that imports the Allaire interfaces for using CFX tags, and then implement the `CustomTag` interface in your class definition. This archive in ColdFusion 5 and prior is located at `<CF_HOME>\java\classes\cfx.jar`. In CFMX, this `.jar` file is located in `<CFMX_HOME>\lib\cfx.jar`. In the ColdFusion Administrator, add this `.jar` to your class path as shown in the previous section. Once you have added it to your class path, use the JRun launcher to restart the server.

The `cfx.jar` file makes three interfaces available to you:

- `Request` represents a request made of a CFX tag, including parameters passed to it as attributes.
- `Response` represents a response that the CFX tag creates to return to the client.
- `Query` represents a query that the CFX uses. With this object you can extend the functionality that the `<cfquery>` tag makes available.

We will look at what these interfaces expose in a bit. For now, let's write the simplest possible CFX tag to make sure that everything is working.

10.3.1 SimpleMessage.java

```
/* custom CFX tag. prints a message */

import com.allaire.cfx.*;
import java.util.*;
import java.text.DateFormat;

public class SimpleMessage implements CustomTag
{

Date now = new Date();
DateFormat f = DateFormat.getDateInstance(DateFormat.FULL,
Locale.US);


   public void processRequest(Request request, Response
               response)

      throws Exception
   {

      f.format(now);
      String name = request.getAttribute( "NAME" ) ;
      response.write( "Hello, " + name + "!  " +
   "Today is " + f) ;
   }
}
```

10.3.2 CallCFX.cfm

```
<html>
<head>
<title>CFX example</title>
</head>

<body>

<!---call the CFX_SimpleMessage tag--->

<CFX_SimpleMessage NAME="DoodleHead">

<cfoutput>#msg#</cfoutput>

</body>
 </html>
```

If you cannot compile the source file, it is almost certainly because the compiler cannot find the .jar file to import the Allaire interfaces. You can compile from the command line, specifying the path to the cfx.jar and the full path to your SimpleMessage.java file, like this:

```
>javac -classpath %CLASSPATH%;c:CFusionMX\lib\cfx.jar
   C:\CFusionMX\wwwroot\chp10\SimpleMessage.java
```

Once you have compiled the Java source, you can call this tag directly as shown using CallCFX.cfm. The registration process in the ColdFusion Administrator is not required if your tag is in the same directory as the calling page. Otherwise, you can put it under the CustomTags subdirectory of CFusionMX_HOME.

NOTE If you have loaded a CFX tag and then modified its source and recompiled it, you may notice that ColdFusion does not read the new tag. This is because it caches CFX tags when the server is first started. Try deleting the class file, shutting down the ColdFusion Application service, and then recompiling. Restart the application server, and it should read your modified class.

You'll notice in the custom tag a few Java items that are specific to using CFX tags. First, we have to import the package com.allaire.cfx, which has the interfaces we must implement in order to use the CFX functionality in our pages. Second, our Java class must implement the CustomTag interface. This implementation must account for HTTP request and response in a manner similar to servlets. We named the method that does the work processRequest. This is not arbitrary, and you must name the main method in a CFX Java file processRequest, and it must accept request and response as parameters. The remainder of the definition is straightforward Java.

10.3.3 The Java CFX Objects

Here let us examine the three Java objects available for use within CFX tags.

There are three objects made available to CFX developers: Request, Response, and Query, which are outlined in Tables 10.2 through 10.4.

The Request object aids in retrieving information sent from the HTTP request, including attributes and query information. The Response object allows you to send information back in the response generated; typically it is used to write text to the output stream. The Query object defines methods that allow you to manipulate database queries passed into the tag from the calling template.

TABLE 10.2 The CFX `Request` Object

METHOD	DESCRIPTION
`attributeExists`	Determines whether the attribute specified was passed into the tag
`debug`	Determines whether the tag contains the `DEBUG` attribute
`getAttribute`	Gets the value of the passed attribute
`getAttributeList`	Gets all attributes passed into the tag
`getIntAttribute`	Gets the value of the passed attribute as an `int`
`getQuery`	Gets a query passed into the tag
`getSetting`	Gets the value of a setting global to custom tags

TABLE 10.3 The CFX `Response` Object

METHOD	DESCRIPTION
`addQuery`	Adds a query to the calling template
`setVariable`	Sets a variable in the calling template
`write`	Outputs text to the calling page
`writeDebug`	Outputs text to the debug output stream

You can use CFX tags to improve on or extend existing CF tags, and in fact one of the sample files included with CFMX does that with `<cfquery>`. CFX tags used to have the benefit of processing more quickly than complex logic written in regular ColdFusion, because they were compiled. Now that all ColdFusion code is compiled and Macromedia has introduced CFCs (ColdFusion Components), there is less reason to use CFX tags. ColdFusion Components are essentially an easy front-end wrapper for writing Java classes; CFXs let you

TABLE 10.4 The CFX `Query` Object

METHOD	DESCRIPTION
`addRows`	Adds a new row to the `Query` object
`getColumns`	Gets the names of the columns in the query
`getData`	Gets an element of data from the query
`getName`	Gets the name of the query
`getRowCount`	Gets the number of rows returned by the query
`setData`	Sets an element of data within the query

write straight Java. You may find that in certain cases you have Java code that you would like to use from within ColdFusion and that it is easier to deploy a CFX than to rewrite it as a component. The advantage of working with CFXs as opposed to calling `<cfobject>` is that you needn't riddle your ColdFusion template with a good deal of code that interacts with the object; a CFX tag makes a neater, cleaner, and more compact interface. A primary objective of working with Java code on the Web is to keep a clear separation of the worker classes in the logic layer and the presentation layer. We will find out more about this when we write servlets and JSP. CFXs encourage this separation.

10.4 Applets

In this section we will look at how to write and use Java applets. Applets are small applications that run on the client. The early success of Java was due in large part to a successful demonstration of an applet running on a client machine via a Web page.

There is some debate at this time regarding the usefulness of applets. They can be cumbersome to download, and the browser wars have made it difficult to deploy mission-critical applets and be sure that your users are able to use them seamlessly.

Rich user interfaces and client applications can now be built using Flash. The most recent version of Flash brings Action Scripting to the forefront, and it features improved database access and XML processing over previous versions. While Flash requires a browser plugin too, and it is arguably not easier to write than an applet is, Flash applications on the client are becoming more popular and useful, especially when integrated with the server-side Flash Gateway for Macromedia JRun or CFMX.

Applets started the excitement surrounding Java, and then moved out of the limelight as Java moved to the server. While servlets have been available for a couple of years, they are tedious to write and are poor choices for pages that need to write out to the browser, for reasons we will see later. JavaServer Pages were introduced in 1999 and quickly garnered a lot of the interest previously reserved for applets. In an interesting twist, there is now a significant trend for moving complex application functionality back onto the client. Programmers will do this with Flash, with applets, and with related Java technology such as Java WebStart, which we will examine in this book. So it is appropriate to look at least briefly at applets.

10.4.1 Applet Basics

Applets are regular Java classes that extend the `Applet` class. Because of this, you can do just about anything that Java allows you to do from within an applet that runs in its own space on the client. That makes applets arguably the most powerful way to execute programs on the client.

There are a few steps to getting an applet running on a client:

- Write a Java class that extends the `java.applet.Applet` class and imports the packages you need.
- Write an HTML page that calls the applet using the HTML `<object>` tag.

Using the HTML `<object>` tag, you specify the size and location of the applet on the page, as well as the class file to be used. The browser then loads the plugin, which contains its own Java Virtual Machine.

In the beginning, you could only view an applet by viewing the Web page in Sun's HotJava browser. This browser is currently in version 3.0 and is still available for free download. However, it is not a full-featured browser, it is slow, and it has little support for the kinds of developments in the language (such as CSS) that users have come to expect.

Applets moved into the big time when they were adopted by Internet Explorer and Netscape browsers. Using a virtual machine embedded in the browser itself, applets could be embedded in an Web page using the HTML `<applet>` tag. As of HTML 4.0, the W3C has deprecated this tag in favor of

`<object>`, which is more general. Note that older browsers may not recognize the `<object>` tag. Browser manufacturers have not updated their Java Virtual Machines for a version later than Java 1.1. This poses obvious difficulties to developers interested in deploying applets with functionality defined in later versions of Java.

So Sun devised a plan to propagate the use of applets without being at the mercy of Netscape and Microsoft to keep current. This plan became the Java Plugin. You are likely familiar with this plugin if you have used the `<cfform>` controls `<cftree>`, `<cfgrid>`, and so forth in ColdFusion 5 or later. This 5 MB download allows both Internet Explorer and Netscape to execute applets using this runtime, which should always be up-to-date. Another benefit to the plugin is added user control over the execution environment; see Figure 10.2. The plugin allows users to switch between different versions of Java Virtual Machines, for instance.

Eventually, Sun determined that limiting the plugin to working with the newer `<object>` tag was dissuading developers from using applets. As of now, the fate of applets is admittedly up in the air.

> **NOTE** You should already have the plugin installed. It comes with the JRE. If for some reason you don't, you need to download it from Sun to execute the examples in this section. If you do have it installed, you can open the plugin outside a browser and review the options it makes available to you. On Windows machines, you access it by double-clicking the icon in the Control Panel.

FIGURE 10.2 Sun Java plugin options.

There are basically two options for writing applets. You can extend `java.applet.Applet`. You can also choose to write applets using Swing components, which are sophisticated GUI elements located in the `javax.swing` package. In order to write applets using Swing components, you instead extend `javax.swing.JApplet`. We will write both versions here.

10.4.2 Viewing Applets

There are two ways to view an applet you write: via a Web page and with the `appletviewer` utility that ships with the JDK. Let's write a quick applet and view it in the `appletviewer`, and then in a browser. Note that both ways of viewing an applet require an HTML page.

10.4.3 SimpleApplet.java

```
/*  File: SimpleApplet.java
Purpose: print a message
*/

import java.applet.*;
import java.awt.*;

public class SimpleApplet extends Applet {

public void paint(Graphics g) {
g.drawString("Hello, sweetheart!", 50, 25);
}
```

10.4.4 Using the appletviewer Tool

Compile your source file into a class file in the `chp10` directory. We will test the applet using the `appletviewer` tool that ships with the JDK. Here is a simple file we can use:

10.4.5 ShowSimpleApplet.html

```
<!DOCTYPE HTML PUBLIC "-//W3C//DTD HTML 4.0 Transitional//EN">

<html>
<head>
<title>Applet Test</title>
</head>
```

```
<body>

<applet align="center"
     code="SimpleApplet.class" width="200" height="100">
</applet>


</body>
</html>
```

Now we can call the applet's HTML page using the JDK `appletviewer` tool, like this:

```
C:\>appletviewer
CFusionMX\\wwwroot\\chp10\\ShowSimpleApplet.html
```

This is the full path to the file on my Windows XP machine. Note that you need not include the drive. Adjust the command for the location of your HTML file. This should launch the viewer program and display the applet, as shown in Figure 10.3.

FIGURE 10.3 The `appletviewer` tool showing the `SimpleApplet` applet.

10.4.6 Using the Java Plugin and HTML Converter

It can be difficult to use the Java plugin, but it is required if you want to deploy an applet in a live Web page. You need to convert the HTML file that displays the applet so that the browser will invoke the plugin when it is supposed to. It is unrealistic to try to create these tags by hand; it is easier to use Sun's HTML Converter tool.

10.4.7 Advanced Applets

Let's have some fun. Using what we already know about Java, we can go to the API and look through the AWT and Swing packages and find things to put into an applet. While writing applets is not particularly complicated, as you can see, this is a good way to practice what you will need to do when writing real Java programs—find what's in the API, and determine how to implement and extend its functionality on your own.

Here we'll make an applet that accepts input from the user in the form of a simple freehand drawing program. The applet will use packages that should be available to the greatest number of browsers and not require the plugin.

Here is the code for an applet that allows the user to draw on the screen:

10.4.8 DrawingApplet.java

```
/* File: DrawingApplet
   Purpose: allows user to draw on an applet
   in several different colors.
*/

import java.applet.*;
import java.awt.*;


public class DrawingApplet extends Applet {

// set color for pen
    private Color penColor = Color.black;

// name drop down box to choose pen color
    private Choice colorPicker;
// end x and y coordinates to keep track
// of where the mouse is
private int endX;
    private int endY;

// handles things to do when applet starts
    public void init () {

// set the background color to white
        setBackground (Color.white);
```

```
// Choice creates a drop down box
// like an HTML <select>
        colorPicker= new Choice();

// add each item to the Choice
// like specifying <option> in HTML
colorPicker.addItem ("black");
        colorPicker.addItem ("blue");
colorPicker.addItem ("green");
colorPicker.addItem ("orange");
colorPicker.addItem ("pink");
        colorPicker.addItem ("red");
        colorPicker.addItem ("yellow");

// choose the foreground (text) color
// and background color of the button
        colorPicker.setForeground (Color.black);
        colorPicker.setBackground (Color.lightGray);

// add the instance
        add (new Label ("Pen Color: "));
        add (colorPicker);

        }


// the following two operations are deprecated
// but they will work fine, and it is very complicated
// to use newer libraries for this, which force you
// to implement listener interfaces for everything.
// so since we're not going heavily into GUIs...

// define what happens on mousedown
    public boolean mouseDown (Event e, int x, int y) {

endX = x;
endY = y;

return true;
     }

// define what happens on drag
  public boolean mouseDrag (Event e, int x, int y) {
```

```
      Graphics g = getGraphics();
      g.setColor (penColor);
      g.drawLine (endX, endY, x, y);
      endX = x;
      endY = y;

      return true;

    }

  // here we set the pen color based on the
  // user choice in colorPicker
    public boolean action (Event event, Object arg) {

    if (arg.equals ("black"))
          penColor = Color.black;
    else if (arg.equals ("blue"))
          penColor = Color.blue;
    else if (arg.equals ("green"))
          penColor = Color.green;
    else if (arg.equals ("orange"))
          penColor = Color.orange;
    else if (arg.equals ("pink"))
          penColor = Color.pink;
    else if (arg.equals ("red"))
          penColor = Color.red;
    else if (arg.equals ("yellow"))
          penColor = Color.yellow;

        return true;

    }

  }
```

Compile this code and write a quick HTML page like `ShowDrawing-Applet.html` that displays the applet. Then run it in the `appletviewer`. You can draw on the applet with your mouse, and use the Choice box to change pen colors. Here I have made what I believe to be a lovely picture of my cat Doodlehead; see Figure 10.4.

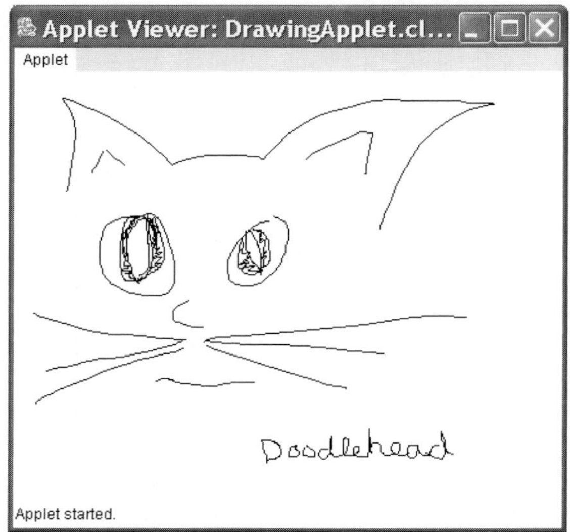

FIGURE 10.4 The `DrawingApplet` class in action: my cat Doodlehead.

10.4.9 ShowDrawingApplet.html

```
<html>
<head>
<title>Applet Test</title>
</head>

<body>

Draw something here:
<br>
<br>

<applet align="center" code="DrawingApplet.class"
     width="300" height="300">
</applet>

</body>
</html>
```

10.5 Using Applets with `<cfapplet>`

The purpose of the `<cfapplet>` tag is to allow you to extend what you can do in a `<cfform>` and to use applets anywhere else you like in an application. There are three steps to using an applet:

1. Write the applet, likely using members of the `javax.swing` package.
2. Register it with the Java Applets section of the ColdFusion Administrator.
3. Call it using the `<cfapplet>` tag inside or outside of a `<cform>`.

10.5.1 Registering Your Applet

Here's how to register a Java applet in the ColdFusion Administrator:

1. Go to Extensions > Java Applets.
2. Click Register New Applet.
3. Fill out the form with the required information.

Figure 10.5 shows what the ColdFusion Administrator needs for you to register your applet and make it available for use.

Once you're done, click Submit and your applet will be available for referencing. Note that these settings, as with many ColdFusion tags, are replicated closely in the `<cfapplet>` tag, and they can be supplied there.

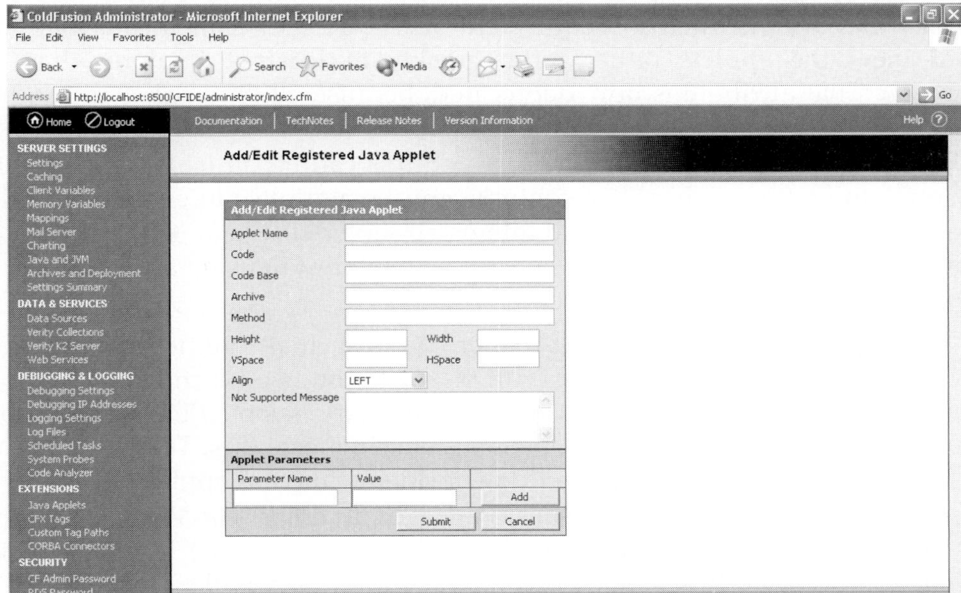

FIGURE 10.5 CFMX Java applet registration screen.

10.6 Working with Browsers and the Java Plugin

If you have attempted to use any of the ColdFusion `<CFFORM>` controls or participate on a ColdFusion news list, you have likely encountered some difficulty. Often, the controls will not display or users will receive an error message regarding the browser's inability to find the necessary files. In some cases, the applet will appear to load, but it will never quite load; however, upon viewing the source of the `.cfm` page, you can find that all of the code for the applet and its accompanying data (as in the case of `<cfgrid>`) has been sent to the client.

In order to use any of the Java form controls, the user is required to download the Java plugin software. This is a 5 MB download that only needs to be downloaded once, but it can be confusing for users. So, consider the connection speed your users are likely to have if you are thinking of deploying an app with one of these controls. These form controls are sometimes considered too unreliable to use in a public environment, and their use has commonly been restricted to intranets, where browsers and downloads can be controlled to an extent.

For ColdFusion 5, these controls were bundled in a single `.jar` file. Prior to that, the control applets were downloaded differently. As you may recall, the `ENABLECAB` attribute of these form controls allowed all of the Java classes that the controls required to be loaded by a Microsoft Internet Explorer `.cab` file (cabinet files are the Microsoft equivalent of a `.jar` file). This meant that you could view the applets rather more quickly in Internet Explorer than in Netscape. That attribute is now deprecated, because all browsers will use the `.jar`.

The reason that working with these controls can be difficult is not due to any error in craftsmanship. The controls, and Java applets in general, are victims of the browser wars. Increased interest in server-side Java, which we cover shortly, was also accompanied by a decrease in interest in using applets. Here is an outline of some of the difficulties:

- The Java support that is built into browsers such as Internet Explorer and Netscape Navigator is based on JDK 1.1. If you use functionality in your applets such as Swing classes or the regular expression API, your end users won't have these installed on their systems in most cases. The workaround here is to have the Swing `.jar` downloaded with your applet.
- The Java plugin, which ColdFusion uses, will replace the Virtual Machine that comes in the browsers with one by Sun (JavaSoft). Again, if your users have not downloaded this plugin before, they will have to endure a 5 MB download before your program starts downloading.

The second most reliable thing to do is insist that your users download the plugin, and give them rather detailed instructions on what they need to do to make sure that it works, and what to do in case they cannot view your applet. The most reliable thing to do is to avoid using applets at all, except in an intranet environment where your sys admin can control the capabilities of each user's browser.

10.6.1 Passing Parameters into Applets

You can pass parameters defined on your HTML page into applets using the `<param>` tag. They take this form:

```
<param name="somestring" value="thevalue">
```

These tags must be nested inside the `<applet>` opening and closing tags. Then, inside the applet code, you access the value of the parameter using `getParameter()` with the name as the argument. It returns a string if there is a parameter with the given name, but it returns null otherwise. Usage is like this:

```
String s = getParameter("Username");
```

Here is an example program that displays values passed into an applet from parameters.

10.6.2 ParamApplet.java

```
/**
 * <p>Title: ParamApplet</p>
 * <p>Description: Outputs parameters passed to the applet
 *  inside an oval.</p>
 *
 * @author E Hewitt
 * @version 1.0
 */

import java.applet.Applet;
import java.awt.*;

public class ParamApplet extends Applet {

public void init() {

       setBackground(Color.white);
}
    public void paint(Graphics g) {
```

```
        String s = getParameter("name");

        String sD = getParameter("number");


        String message = "Hello, " + s + ". Your number is: " +
               sD;

        g.drawOval(20,20,250,100);
        g.drawString(message, 60, 70);
    }


}
```

Remember that when using appletviewer (or a browser, for that matter), you must call the HTML page that displays the applet directly. This can be hard to remember when we've just gotten used to running Java programs by calling them directly. Here's an accompanying HTML page:

10.6.3 ShowParamApplet.html

```
<html>
<head>
<title>ParamApplet Test</title>
</head>

<body>

<applet align="center" code="ParamApplet.class"
    width="300" height="300">

    <param name = "name" value="Eben">
    <param name = "number" value="3.14">

</applet>


</body>
</html>
```

The output is shown in Figure 10.6.

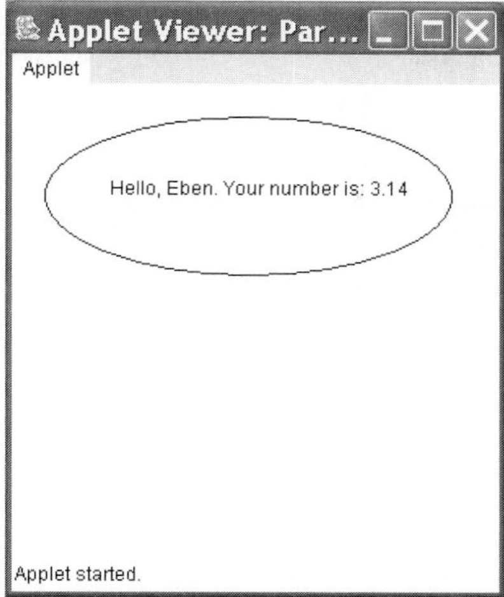

FIGURE 10.6 Displaying values passed into an applet from an HTML page.

10.6.4 Setting Applet Parameters Dynamically in ColdFusion

You can set parameters that you pass to Java applets, just as you might hope. Let's replace our static HTML page with a ColdFusion page that sets CF variables to pass into the applet. The applet code itself need not change.

10.6.5 `ShowParamApplet.cfm`

```
<html>
<head>
<title>ParamApplet Test</title>
</head>

<body>

<cfset name = "Fabio">
<cfset number = 9.9>

<applet align="center" code="ParamApplet.class"
width="300" height="300">

<param name = "name" value="<cfoutput>#name#</cfoutput>">
<param name = "number" value="<cfoutput>#number#</cfoutput>">

</applet>
```

```
</body>
</html>
```

The output of loading the CFM page in Netscape 6 is shown in Figure 10.7.

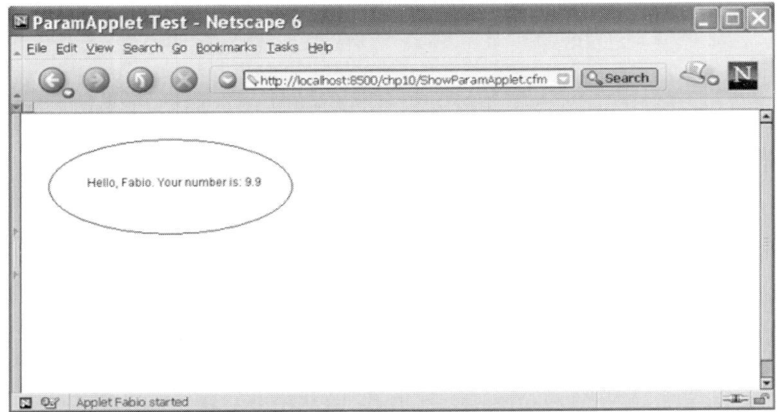

FIGURE 10.7 Sending ColdFusion parameters into an applet and outputting them.

10.6.6 Applets, Java Applications, and WebStart

Note that a chief difference between applets and regular Java programs is that they do not have access to the local file system. This is the only way that applets could be distributed with any manner of security. Applets operate in their own little sandbox so that they can be trusted. While it is certainly not impossible, it is difficult to write and distribute a virus in Java because of the security measures that are built into the language. But it means that there are certain things we cannot do. For instance, much to my dismay, I cannot execute a method that captures my drawing from the `DrawingApplet` and saves it to a file. I could *write* that method—the applet would compile; it just would refuse on the basis of its inability to access local system resources. That is a major difference between applets and applications.

In the last two years there has been a very interesting development that takes the notion of applets one big step further. This development, which we examine later in this book, is called Java WebStart. WebStart allows you to distribute full-blown programs from the Web and execute them on the local machine. With the user's permission, you can gain access to system files, printers, and the network. Java WebStart requires surprisingly little configuration on the server to get up and running.

10.7 Swing and AWT

In this section, we will take a cursory look at writing GUI applications. A graphical user interface is the portion of your program that a user interacts with directly. The Abstract Windowing Toolkit and Swing extension classes are what you use to create GUIs in Java.

Swing and AWT are very large topics. In fact, these two packages alone define more than half of the Java API. They can be difficult to work with, because their class hierarchies are complex. We do not have world enough and time here to cover these topics closely, as this book is more geared toward Java for the Web programmer.

We will look at these topics briefly, however, for two reasons. First, they are an important part of the Java world. Any program you write in Java Standard Edition will run from one of three primary places:

- The command line, as most of our programs have thus far
- Via a Web-based client such as a `.jsp`, a `.cfm` page, or a Web service
- With a graphical user interface

Even if you are not interested in becoming a software engineer, there is a second reason to understand the AWT and Swing APIs: using them is often a requirement for writing applets. So this section will test our ability to use what we already know about Java's object-oriented structures to put an unfamiliar package to use.

You already know that there are other ColdFusion form controls that require the 5-MB Java plugin to run, because they run as applets on the client, and they are written in Java. These are not written entirely from scratch, however. With a little knowledge of the API and some effort, you can write your own `<cfslider>` control, for instance. Think of the `<cftextinput>` control—you'll find its corresponding Swing class in `JTextField`. We are all familiar with the wonder and excitement that is `<cftree>`. These controls were rewritten for ColdFusion 5 to implement new Swing libraries.

In this section, we will create our own version of the `<cftree>` control, using the libraries already available in `javax.Swing` and `java.awt`.

10.7.1 `MakeTree.java`

```
package javaforcf.chp10;

/* uses TreeConrol and TreeFrame
  to create a tree control similar
  to <cftree>.
```

```
  Requires classes from AWT and Swing
  libraries.
  */

import javax.swing.UIManager;

public class MakeTree {

    // main
  public static void main(String[] args) {

    try {
        // sets the look of the icons used
        // this is the JLF (Java Look and Feel),
        // and it might look familiar from the Forte IDE

      String s =
UIManager.getCrossPlatformLookAndFeelClassName();

      // alternatively, you can get the look and feel
      //  for user's system like this:
      // String s = UIManager.getSystemLookAndFeelClassName()

            UIManager.setLookAndFeel(s);
    }
    catch(Exception e) {
      e.printStackTrace();
    }
      // instantiate the object
    new TreeControl();
  }

 }
```

10.7.2 TreeControl.java

```
package javaforcf.chp10;

  // abstract window toolkit
  // we need this for the Frame class
import java.awt.*;
  // swing libraries allow complex user interfaces
  // that are easy to use
import javax.swing.UIManager;

public class TreeControl {
  boolean packFrame = false;
```

```
  // public constructor
  public TreeControl() {

    TreeFrame frame = new TreeFrame();

    /* a java.awt.Frame makes a top-level
    window with a title and a border */

    //Validate frames that have preset sizes
    //Pack frames that have useful preferred size info, e.g.,
from their layout

    /*
    if (packFrame) {
      frame.pack();
    }
    else {
      frame.validate();
    }
    */

    /*
      here we center the window. To do this
      we need to get the screen size, then
      get the size of our frame.
    */
    Dimension screenSize =
Toolkit.getDefaultToolkit().getScreenSize();
    Dimension frameSize = frame.getSize();

      /* next subtract the width of the frame
       from the width of screen, and divide by two.
       do the same for height
       that centers your frame.
      */
    frame.setLocation((screenSize.width - frameSize.width) / 2,
           (screenSize.height - frameSize.height) / 2);

           // you must show the frame explicitly
    frame.setVisible(true);
  }

}
```

10.7.3 TreeFrame.java

```
package javaforcf.chp10;

// tools for making windows,
// controls, and event listeners
// and handlers
import java.awt.*;
import java.awt.event.*;
import javax.swing.*;
import javax.swing.border.*;
import javax.swing.event.*;
// API's built in tree control
import javax.swing.tree.*;


public class TreeFrame extends JFrame {

  /*
    FIELDS
    */

  // container to hold controls
  JPanel contentPane;

  // tree
  DefaultMutableTreeNode top =  new
DefaultMutableTreeNode("Root Directory");
  JTree jTree1 = new JTree(top);
  JScrollPane treeView = new JScrollPane(jTree1);
  DefaultTreeCellRenderer treeRenderer = new
DefaultTreeCellRenderer();

  // menu bar and items
  JMenuBar jMenuBar1 = new JMenuBar();
  JMenu menuFile = new JMenu();
    // "Close" item in File menu
  JMenuItem menuFileClose = new JMenuItem();

  //create the editor pane
  JEditorPane jEditorPane1 = new JEditorPane();
  JButton jButton1 = new JButton();

    // items for tree
    // directory
  DefaultMutableTreeNode dir1 = null;
```

```
  // files
DefaultMutableTreeNode file1 = null;
DefaultMutableTreeNode file1_sub1 = null;
  // second directory
DefaultMutableTreeNode dir2 = null;
  // files
DefaultMutableTreeNode file2 = null;
DefaultMutableTreeNode file2_sub1 = null;

/*
  CONSTRUCTOR
  */

public TreeFrame() {
    // root event class for selecting AWT events
  enableEvents(AWTEvent.WINDOW_EVENT_MASK);

  try {
     initialize();
  }
  catch(Exception e) {
    e.printStackTrace();
  }
}

/*
  METHODS
 */

// initialize components
public void initialize() throws Exception  {

  // our container for UI controls
  contentPane = (JPanel) this.getContentPane();
  contentPane.setLayout(null);

    // sets the title in the window
    // like HTML <title> tag
  this.setTitle("Start of <cftree>");
    // set window size (width, height)
  this.setSize(new Dimension(525, 200));
    // add menu bar
  this.setJMenuBar(jMenuBar1);

  // make tree and add event listeners
  makeNodes(top);
```

```
jTree1.getSelectionModel().setSelectionMode(TreeSelectionModel
.SINGLE_TREE_SELECTION);
      // show the handle on directories?
    jTree1.setShowsRootHandles(true);
      // allow editing of (typing over) the labels?
    jTree1.setEditable(false);

    jTree1.addTreeSelectionListener(new
javax.swing.event.TreeSelectionListener() {
      public void valueChanged(TreeSelectionEvent e) {
        jTree1_valueChanged(e);
      }
    });

      // set specs on tree viewing pane

treeView.setVerticalScrollBarPolicy(JScrollPane.VERTICAL_SCROL
LBAR_ALWAYS);
      // in the javax.swing.BorderFactory

treeView.setViewportBorder(BorderFactory.createRaisedBevelBord
er());
      // coordinates for drawing the tree viewer rectangle pan
      // start from left, from top, width, height
    treeView.setBounds(new Rectangle(10, 10, 235, 110));

    //initializes menu items and creates event listeners
    menuFile.setText("File");
    menuFileClose.setText("Close");
    menuFileClose.addActionListener(new
java.awt.event.ActionListener() {
      public void actionPerformed(ActionEvent e) {
        menuFileExit_actionPerformed(e);
      }
    });


    // set up message panel

    jEditorPane1.setBorder(BorderFactory.createEtchedBorder());
      // coordinates for message panel
    jEditorPane1.setBounds(new Rectangle(250, 20, 260, 50));
    jEditorPane1.setFont(new java.awt.Font("Dialog", 1, 10));
    jEditorPane1.setBackground(Color.white);

    //add items to content pane
```

```
      jMenuBar1.add(menuFile);
        // add "Close" option under File menu
      menuFile.add(menuFileClose);
      contentPane.add(treeView, null);
      contentPane.add(jEditorPane1, null);

}

  // add nodes to tree
  // to make this like <cftree>
  // we would read in the directory structure
  // from the system
  public void makeNodes(DefaultMutableTreeNode top) {

      dir1 = new DefaultMutableTreeNode("Directory 1");
      top.add(dir1);

      file1 = new DefaultMutableTreeNode("Dir 1, File 1");
      dir1.add(file1);
      file1 = new DefaultMutableTreeNode("SubDirectory");
      dir1.add(file1);

      file1_sub1 = new DefaultMutableTreeNode("SubDir 1, File
1");
      file1.add(file1_sub1);
      dir2 = new DefaultMutableTreeNode("Directory 2");
      top.add(dir2);

      file2 = new DefaultMutableTreeNode("Dir 1, File 1");
      dir2.add(file2);
      file2 = new DefaultMutableTreeNode("Dir 2, File 2");
      dir2.add(file2);
      file2 = new DefaultMutableTreeNode("Dir 2, File 3");
      dir2.add(file2);
   }

  //File|Exit event
  void menuFileExit_actionPerformed(ActionEvent e) {
   System.exit(0);
  }

    // make text appear when item is selected
  void jTree1_valueChanged(TreeSelectionEvent e) {
     String rootText = "The root Directory";
     String nodeText = "This is a Directory";
     String childText = "This is a File";
```

```
      // find last selected.
     DefaultMutableTreeNode node =
(DefaultMutableTreeNode)jTree1.getLastSelectedPathComponent();

     TreePath pathnode =
(TreePath)jTree1.getLeadSelectionPath();
     if (jTree1.isVisible(pathnode)) {

        // display the
      if (node.isRoot()) {
          jEditorPane1.setText(rootText + " level: "
            + node.getLevel() + " parent: " +
node.getParent());
        }
          // isLeaf is a method of
          // javax.swing.tree.DefaultMutableTreeNode
        else if (node.isLeaf()) {
            jEditorPane1.setText(childText  + " level: "
            + node.getLevel() + " parent: " +
node.getParent());
        }
        else if (node.isNodeAncestor(top)) {
          jEditorPane1.setText(nodeText  + " level: "
            + node.getLevel() + " parent: " +
node.getParent());
        }

     }
   }

  // allows us to shut down program
  // overide this method of JFrame
  // constant integers represent different states
  protected void processWindowEvent(WindowEvent e) {
    super.processWindowEvent(e);
    if (e.getID() == WindowEvent.WINDOW_CLOSING) {
      // shuts down program
      System.exit(0);
    }
  }

 }
// eof
```

Running the `MakeTree` class calls the controls that make the frame and the Swing classes that make the tree. The files are commented inline to help clarify how the tree gets constructed (see Figure 10.8). As you may have inferred, perhaps the best thing you can do at this point to excel at Java programming is to become familiar with the API. Knowing your way around the API will help you determine quickly what kinds of structures are already available to you and what kinds of things you have to build yourself.

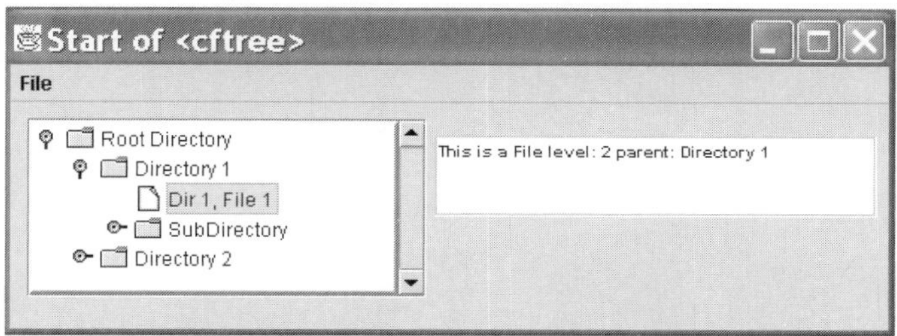

FIGURE 10.8 Running the proto-`<cftree>` application.

10.8 What's Next?

In this chapter we covered ways to extend ColdFusion with Java. You can write ColdFusion CFX custom tags using the ColdFusion interface for Java. You learned how to call Java objects from inside ColdFusion and use `<cfobject>` and the native ColdFusion function `JavaCast()` to differentiate between Java data types.

Applets may or may not have a significant future. For now, people are using them to write stock ticker applications and perform graphics manipulation. It is expected that Java WebStart, which we examine later in this book, will become the client-side venue of choice for client-side Java applications because of its superior power and its imperviousness to the browser wars.

In the next chapter, we cover `Collections`. The interfaces in the `java.util.Collection` framework provide different ways of representing objects in groups. Java collections include lists, maps, sets, and vectors. For the moment, you can think of collections as Java's way of handling name-value pairs. That is, they're what you use in Java when you're wishing you had a ColdFusion structure.

11

Collections and Regular Expressions

This chapter introduces a set of interfaces in the API known as Collections. The `java.util.Collections` interfaces and classes are meant to be implemented in situations requiring logically related sets of name-value pairs. In this chapter we will overview Collections and discuss the most popular and useful of them by turn.

It is easy to determine when and why you would want to implement a collection in Java: When you find yourself wishing you had a ColdFusion structure or a list, then use one of the collections. Collections are more complex than ColdFusion structures and lists, however. That is, ColdFusion defines only one type of thing for holding name-value pairs: the structure. There are many different kinds of Java collections, including Hashmaps, Linked Lists, Vectors, Maps, Hashtables, and so on. These are all very similar, but have slight variations, and some collections are better suited for certain situations than others. Also, some of the collections are regular classes, and some are interfaces, and must be implemented as such. If you need a refresher on interfaces, refer back to Chapter 9.

Having discussed Collections, we will look briefly at an interesting aspect of Java: preferences. The Preferences API, new with Java 1.4, provides a simple way to store primitive data preferences that persist over time. You might think of them as a combination of ColdFusion's Session and Application scopes. Their job is to store data for change notification, user preferences, or application settings. Since writing this kind of thing is such a frequent part of a developer's life, it is nice to have such a structure put together for us.

We finish up with a quick look at how you can use regular expressions in Java to perform pattern matching on objects.

We begin this chapter with synchronization. Not only is it important in its own right, but it is difficult to say much about Collections without running into it. This chapter unlocks the secrets of Java synchronization by way of a key concept in ColdFusion.

11.1 Synchronization and `<cflock>`

Synchronization is Java's way of keeping shared objects from getting corrupted when competing operations are being performed on them. This should be a familiar concept from ColdFusion and from database design.

In ColdFusion you store, for example, variables in the Session scope. Any time you read or write data from the Session, Application, or Server scopes in ColdFusion you must lock those variables. That's because data stored in these scopes is memory resident. While that makes them very fast to access, it also makes them vulnerable to data corruption if two competing operations were to access the same data at the same time and perform some conflicting operation.

In order to prevent this kind of corruption, you lock your variables using the `<cflock>` tag. This should be a familiar operation:

```
<cflock scope="session" timeout="20">
        <cfset Session.BankAccount.Balance = getbalance.Amount>

....perform a withdrawal, and a deposit

        <cfoutput>#Session.BankAccount.Balance#</cfoutput>
</cflock>
```

Now what if the above code were not locked? Another thread (process) could modify the balance between data retrieval and display and the data would be inaccurate. `<cflock>` answers this problem in ColdFusion. The keyword `synchronized` handles it in Java.

The `synchronized` keyword locks Java objects. When a processing thread encounters a synchronized block of code, one of two things happen: It determines that no other process is currently accessing the code block, so it obtains a lock. Alternatively, it may discover that another process is currently inside that code block, in which case it will wait for that process to complete.

> **NOTE** Sometimes these locks are called *monitors*.

Once a process is through executing its business inside the synchronized block, it releases the lock it held so that other processes may access it.

11.1.1 Thread Safety with `synchronized`

Adding the `synchronized` keyword to a method will cause the operation to which you prefix it to be locked. The structure is like this:

```
synchronized public void someMethod() {...}
```

Notice that this is *syntactically* different from ColdFusion, in which you lock *data* that accesses a memory-resident scope (`Session.someValue`). In Java, you lock the *operation* you want to keep thread-safe (`synchronized someMethod()`). The Java syntax is closer, perhaps, to something you may be familiar with from working with relational databases: isolation implemented with locks. Database isolation prevents two competing data reads or modifications from happening at once, just like we've been talking about. Locks in a database ensure that one user's changes to some data do not access it, possibly getting a "dirty" or "phantom" read. While it looks as if it is the method itself that is synchronized, that wouldn't really make sense when you think about it. Only objects are actually synchronized, because objects are the repository for data. There are a couple of rules that are easy to remember about synchronization:

- Multiple threads can execute the same method at the same time—as long as they are all operating on different objects.
- Multiple threads cannot concurrently execute different synchronized methods if they are operating on the same object.

Note that there are times when it is not possible to declare a method as synchronized—generally when someone else created the class. The way around this is to synchronize the object directly, using this statement:

```
synchronized(anObject) {
     //...code to be synchronized
          }
```

Let's have a quick look at implementing thread safety with the following example. This example will demonstrate not only how to keep your data safe using the `synchronized` keyword, but it will help us get a little practice with implementing interfaces, as we learned how to do in Chapter 9. The following example implements the `Runnable` interface, which is an abstract method of `java.lang.Thread`.

11.1.2 SynchTest.java

```
/*
 * SynchTest.java
 *
 */

package chp11;

public class SynchTest implements Runnable  {

   private Account a = new Account();

   public static void main (String[] args) {

       SynchTest sT = new SynchTest();

            // create two threads

       Thread first = new Thread(sT);
       Thread second = new Thread(sT);

            // start them running
       first.start();
       second.start();

       System.out.println("transaction complete...");
     }

        /* This class uses the Runnable interface,
         * so we must implement the abstract run() method.
         * We want to synch the modifying and accessing of
         * the account. No other thread can enter the method
         * until all code inside it is executed.
         */
    public void run() {

         // starting balance
        double startBalance = a.getBalance();

            for (double i = 0; i < 10000 ; i++) {

                    // all code inside here is locked
                synchronized(this) {
```

```
                    // add money
                    a.deposit (100);

                    // subtract money
                    a.withdraw (100);

// this method causes the thread to pause temporarily and let
// other threads execute
                    Thread.yield();

                    if (startBalance != a.getBalance())
                       System.out.println("threads collided");
                }
            }

    }
}
```

This code synchronizes the object passed into it while the deposit and withdraw operations are performed. If the account object were not locked, then there would be an opportunity somewhere among our 10,000 iterations of the loop for one of the threads to make a lone deposit or withdrawal operation—which would mean the balance would not be reconciled, and the error message would be printed.

`Account.java` is the simplest possible account, which has a starting balance of $50, and methods for making a deposit and a withdrawal.

11.1.3 Account.java

```
package chp11;

public class Account {

    private double balance;

        // constructor sets balance at $50
    public Account() {
        balance = 50;
    }

    public double getBalance() {
        return balance;
    }
```

```
    public void deposit(double dep) {
        balance += dep;

    }

    public void withdraw(double withdraw) {
        balance -= withdraw;

    }
}
```

This brief overview shows you how to lock operations that you need to be thread safe. Some Collections can be synchronized, which gives us reason to discuss this here. Depending on your project, there can be many subtle and important aspects of dealing successfully with threads. Consult the API for more information regarding threads.

In the following section we will recall how to use ColdFusion structures in order to set the table for our discussion of Collections.

11.2 ColdFusion Structures

Let's quickly review structures in ColdFusion so that useful comparisons with Java Collections are not lost. Despite their usefulness and their centrality to ColdFusion, developers often do not learn much about structures until late in their learning process.

Structures are used in ColdFusion to store data in name-value pairs. ColdFusion stores a lot of information internally as structures. All ColdFusion variables in the following scopes are stored as structures:

- `application`
- `attributes`
- `cfcatch`
- `cferror`
- `cffile`
- `cgi`
- `cookie`
- `form`
- `request`
- `session`
- `thistag`
- `url`

You can therefore reference variables in any of these scopes using dot notation or array (bracketed) syntax.

11.2.1 Creating and Populating ColdFusion Structures

Structures are created like this:

```
<cfset stMyStruct = StructNew()>
```

or like this:

```
<cfscript>
stMyStruct = StructNew();
</cfscript>
```

Once you have created a structure, you can populate it like so:

```
<cfset BaseballTeam = StructNew()>
<cfset BaseballTeam.teamHome = "Arizona">
<cfset BaseballTeam.teamName = "Diamondbacks">
<cfset BaseballTeam.managerName = "Bob">
```

11.2.2 Retrieving Structure Values

The properties of a structure are known as *keys*. In the above structure there are three keys: `teamHome`, `teamName`, and `managerName`. Each key has one value. You can then output the value of a specified key in three different ways:

```
<cfoutput>
The name of the team is: #BaseballTeam.teamName#
<br>
The manager is: #BaseballTeam[managerName]#
<br>
This team lives in: #StructFind(BaseballTeam, teamHome)#
</cfoutput>
```

Structures can hold other complex data types, including other structures. Structures are popular devices in ColdFusion, as they perform faster than using lists or arrays.

Just as you might use a structure in ColdFusion to store information about items in an online shopping cart, developers often will use one of the collections, such as a vector, for this purpose in a JavaServer Page.

> **NOTE** Even structures in ColdFusion are sometimes referred to as collections. You may recall that in ColdFusion there are several types of loops that one can employ using `<cfloop>`. The way to loop over a structure to output or manipulate its data is to specify the structure name using the `collection` attribute of the `<cfloop>` tag. Coincidence? Nope.

Let's turn now to structures to understand how to use them and how to choose among them.

11.3 Collections Overview

Collections represent a group of related objects. The objects may or may not be ordered. The SDK does not offer a direct implementation of this interface; the interface is implemented using one of the subinterfaces.

Collections have changed significantly over the years. Just as the way that Java handles user interface events and graphics has changed so much between AWT and Swing, collections have seen significant changes and additions. There are far more kinds of collections than there were in Java 1.0—at that time there were a total of four. Now in Java 1.4 there are closer to 20.

The original collections are important to discuss briefly for two reasons. First, you will see a lot of code implementing these collections. Some are still central to application development, and some have been usurped by more efficient collections developed since. The second reason is that, just as with ColdFusion structures, Java uses them internally within the compiler and the runtime system.

Here are the four original collections:

- `Enumeration` is an interface that specifies what methods to implement when iterating over a set of related references. `Enumeration` objects are useful to move through a set of elements one at a time.
- `Hashtable` is a class that allows you to store and retrieve object references from a collection using keys. This has perhaps the most in common with ColdFusion structures. The `Hashtable` is nearly identical to the newer `Hashmap`, but `Hashtable`'s methods are `synchronized`.
- `Stack` is a class that stores object references that are accessed in LIFO (last in, first out) style.
- `Vector` is a class that stores arrays of object references. An advantage to using a `Vector` is that its internal array can be expanded to accommodate more data if necessary. `Vectors` are also synchronized and incur a

good deal of overhead in their use. While commonly found in legacy code, Vectors are declining in popularity, given the overhead and many alternatives.

We will elaborate on these collections and the other collection types they begot in the remainder of this chapter.

11.3.1 Properties

Since the JDK 1.0 we have also had access to an object holding system properties via the properties class. Properties is a subclass of java.util.Hashtable, which is derived from the obsolete java.util.Dictionary class. Properties can be saved to a stream or loaded from a stream, and each property value is accessible as a string. The information stored in the system properties set details Java settings, all of which are available to regular applications, but only a few of which are available to applets (for security reasons).

Listing Props.java demonstrates how to access system properties, which you can use in your programs to base settings on.

11.3.2 Props.java

```
/*
 * File: Props.java
 * Purpose: displays system properties
 */

package chp11;
import java.util.Properties;
import java.util.Enumeration;

public class Props {

    public static void main (String [] a) {

            // get a properties object
        Properties p = System.getProperties();

            // returns an enumeration object
            // which can be iterated over
        Enumeration e = p.propertyNames();

        while (e.hasMoreElements()) {
            String key = (String) e.nextElement();
            String value = p.getProperty(key);
```

```
                System.out.println(key + ": " + value);
            }
        }

    }
```

The output when run is as below. Your output will vary based on your settings:

```
C:\jdk1.4\bin\javaw.exe                              -classpath
C:\jdk1.4\jre\lib\rt.jar;C:\jdk1.4\jre\lib\ext\dnsns.jar;C:\jdk
1.4\jre\lib\ext\ldapsec.jar;C:\jdk1.4\jre\lib\ext\localedata.
jar;C:\jdk1.4\jre\lib\ext\sunjce_provider.jar;C:\IntelliJ_IDEA\
JavaForCF chp11.Props
java.runtime.name: Java(TM) 2 Runtime Environment, Standard
Edition
sun.boot.library.path: C:\jdk1.4\jre\bin
java.vm.version: 1.4.0-b92
java.vm.vendor: Sun Microsystems Inc.
java.vendor.url: http://java.sun.com/
path.separator: ;
java.vm.name: Java HotSpot(TM) Client VM
file.encoding.pkg: sun.io
user.country: US
sun.os.patch.level:
java.vm.specification.name: Java Virtual Machine Specification
user.dir: C:\IntelliJ_IDEA
java.runtime.version: 1.4.0-b92
java.awt.graphicsenv: sun.awt.Win32GraphicsEnvironment
java.endorsed.dirs: C:\jdk1.4\jre\lib\endorsed
os.arch: x86
java.io.tmpdir: C:\DOCUME~1\eben\LOCALS~1\Temp\
line.separator:

java.vm.specification.vendor: Sun Microsystems Inc.
user.variant:
os.name: Windows XP
sun.java2d.fontpath:
java.library.path:
C:\jdk1.4\bin;.;C:\WINDOWS\System32;C:\WINDOWS;C:\jdk1.4\bin;C:
\WINDOWS\system32;C:\WINDOWS;C:\WINDOWS\System32\Wbem;C:\jdk1.4
\bin;
java.specification.name: Java Platform API Specification
java.class.version: 48.0
```

```
java.util.prefs.PreferencesFactory:
java.util.prefs.WindowsPreferencesFactory
os.version: 5.1
user.home: C:\Documents and Settings\eben
user.timezone:
java.awt.printerjob: sun.awt.windows.WPrinterJob
file.encoding: Cp1252
java.specification.version: 1.4
user.name: eben
java.class.path:
C:\jdk1.4\jre\lib\rt.jar;C:\jdk1.4\jre\lib\ext\dnsns.jar;C:\jdk
1.4\jre\lib\ext\ldapsec.jar;C:\jdk1.4\jre\lib\ext\localedata.
jar;C:\jdk1.4\jre\lib\ext\sunjce_provider.jar;C:\IntelliJ_IDEA\
JavaForCF
java.vm.specification.version: 1.0
sun.arch.data.model: 32
java.home: C:\jdk1.4\jre
java.specification.vendor: Sun Microsystems Inc.
user.language: en
awt.toolkit: sun.awt.windows.WToolkit
java.vm.info: mixed mode
java.version: 1.4.0
java.ext.dirs: C:\jdk1.4\jre\lib\ext
sun.boot.class.path:
C:\jdk1.4\jre\lib\rt.jar;C:\jdk1.4\jre\lib\i18n.jar;C:\jdk1.4\
jre\lib\sunrsasign.jar;C:\jdk1.4\jre\lib\jsse.jar;C:\jdk1.4\jre\
lib\jce.jar;C:\jdk1.4\jre\lib\charsets.jar;C:\jdk1.4\jre\classes
java.vendor: Sun Microsystems Inc.
file.separator: \
java.vendor.url.bug: http://java.sun.com/cgi-bin/bugreport.cgi
sun.cpu.endian: little
sun.io.unicode.encoding: UnicodeLittle
sun.cpu.isalist: pentium i486 i386
Process terminated with exit code 0
```

What the above code provides for you is a way to, for instance, create a more flexible program that uses variables for system-dependent properties. This could help ease cross-platform support and can be useful in cases where you develop on, say, Windows, and deploy to a Linux server. For example, different file systems use different characters for file path separators; Linux uses a / while Windows uses a \. So instead of calling files with these items hardcoded, you could use the `file.separator` property instead:

```
p.getProperty("file.separator");
```

Properties is a subclass of the Hashtable collection and is an ideal choice for storing configuration files. Developers have often used it for user preferences as well. In JDK 1.4, the API includes a preferences object, available as java.util.prefs.Preferences, to act as a front end for persistent data stores.

> **NOTE** Note that the properties object maintains strings in key-value pairs much like a ColdFusion structure.

The following example shows a way to interact with the properties as you might define them in a program.

11.3.3 AppProps.java

```
package chp11;

import java.util.*;
import java.io.*;

public class AppProps {

    public static void main(String [] a) {

        // get the user home directory property
    String dir = System.getProperty("user.home");

    Properties useroptions = new Properties();

        // make a new file in the user.home directory
        // on my Win XP machine this is
        // C:\Documents and Settings\eben\
    File configfile = new File(dir +
     System.getProperty("file.separator") +  "AppProps.conf");

    try {
            // get an input stream
        useroptions.load(new FileInputStream(configfile));

    }
    catch (IOException ie) {
        System.out.println(ie.getMessage());
    }
```

```
            // set some properties
      useroptions.setProperty("favoriteColor","blue");
      useroptions.setProperty("preferredFont","Verdana");

    try {
            // output stream to send file data
            // add a comment to the top of the file
        useroptions.store(new FileOutputStream(configfile),
"AppProperties");

        System.out.println("Your favorite color is: " +
                useroptions.getProperty("favoriteColor"));
    }
     catch (IOException e) {
         System.out.println(e.getMessage());
     }
     }
}
```

This program generates this output to the console:

```
Your favorite color is: blue
```

More importantly, if you navigate to your `user.home` directory, you should find a file there called `AppProps.conf`. Open it in a text editor, and you should see output similar to the following:

```
#AppProperties
#Sun Jun 23 18:53:07 GMT-07:00 2002
favoriteColor=blue
preferredFont=Verdana
```

If this file did not exist already, Java created it for you. Notice that you can modify the file to set another property, and that it will not overwrite or harm any other properties that may be set in the file; it will just append them to the properties list. Properties are surprisingly useful and easy to use.

11.4 General Collections Methods

JDK 1.2 added to the collections significantly. It can be difficult to keep them straight, because their names (`TreeMap`, `Map`, `HashMap`, `HashTable`, `HashSet`) are so similar.

The `Collection` interface defines generic methods that you can use with any of the specific collection types. These are listed in Table 11.1.

TABLE 11.1 Generic Methods that Work with All Collections

METHOD	PURPOSE
`add(Object o)`	Inserts the specified element into the collection. Returns `true`.
`addAll(Collection c)`	Adds all of the elements in the specified collection to this collection. Returns `true`.
`clear()`	Removes all elements from this collection.
`contains(Object o)`	Returns a boolean `true` if the specified element is contained in this collection.
`containsAll(Collection c)`	Returns `true` if all of the elements specified are in this collection.
`equals(Object o)`	Compares the object specified to determine equality.
`hashCode()`	Returns the hashcode for this collection.
`isEmpty()`	Returns `true` if there are no elements in this collection.
`iterator()`	Returns an iterator for iterating through the objects in the collection.
`remove(Object o)`	Returns `true` if the element has been successfully removed from the collection.
`removeAll(Collection c)`	Removes all of the elements in this collection. Returns `true`.
`retainAll(Collection c)`	Retains only the elements specified in the passed collection. All others are removed.
`size()`	Returns the number of elements in this collection.
`toArray()`	Returns an array containing all of the elements in this collection.

11.5 Collections Interfaces

While you can always look in the API under `java.util` (which is always a great idea), the following tables will help give you a concise reference of what is available and what each is used for.

Table 11.2 overviews the `List`, `Map`, and `Set` interfaces. It shows you what they are used for, what classes in the API implement them, and how long they've been in the language.

TABLE 11.2 `Collections` Interfaces in `java.util`

INTERFACE	PURPOSE
`List`	• An ordered collection, also known as a *sequence*. • Like a CF list in that they allow precise control over the location of the ordinal placement of an item in the list. • Duplicate elements are allowed. • Provides a special iterator called a `ListIterator` that allows insertion and replacement of items. • Implementing classes are `AbstractList`, `ArrayList`, `LinkedList`, `Vector`. • Since Java 1.2.
`Map`	• Maps keys to values, as a CF structure. • Cannot contain multiple keys with same name, and each key can map to only one value. • Implementing classes are `AbstractMap`, `Attributes`, `HashMap`, `Hashtable`, `IdentityHashMap`, `RenderingHints`, `TreeMap`, `WeakHashMap`. • Subinterface: `SortedMap`. • Since Java 1.2.
`Set`	• A collection that contains no duplicate elements. • Implementing classes are `AbstractSet`, `HashSet`, `LinkedHashSet`, `TreeSet`. • Subinterface: `SortedSet`. • Since Java 1.2.

These interfaces, as we can see from the number of classes implementing each, are the parents of many related collections. So now that we have a sense of the collections landscape, let's look at some of the original collections in greater detail.

11.5.1 The Collection Life Cycle

The fundamental interface from which these derive is the `Collection` interface. Its methods were outlined above. Once you have created a collection of a certain type, then you can add objects to it using the `add()` method. Note that `add()` returns a boolean specifying whether the collection item was added. If the item is a duplicate, it will not be added to the collection and will return `false`.

You can loop over the collection to read, write, or modify each element one by one using an `Iterator` or an `Enumeration`.

11.5.1.1 `Iterator` AND `Enumeration`

A class implementing the `Iterator` interface can step through a collection item by item. The `Iterator` was introduced in Java 1.2 to replace the `Enumeration`. There are two chief ways in which an `Iterator` improves upon the `Enumeration`:

- The caller can remove elements from the collection in a clear, well-defined manner. This was not easily possible with `Enumeration`.
- Method names have been improved.

Preferring `Iterator` to `Enumeration` is recommended. The methods of an `Iterator` are as follows:

- `hasNext()` returns `true` if the `Iterator` has more elements
- `next()` returns the next element in the iteration
- `remove()` removes the last element the `Iterator` returned

You can call an iterator's `next()` method to look up the elements in the collection one by one. Use caution when employing the `remove()` method, because it will remove the element that the last call to `next()` returned. So, you must call `next()` and only then call `remove()`.

11.5.2 `AbstractCollection`

`java.util.AbstractCollection` is an abstract class. It was added in JDK 1.2 to aid developers implementing the `Collection` interface. Recall that interfaces can contain no method implementations; they just define what must be implemented. This meant that developers had to redefine certain useful methods over and over again. This was a lot of work for little return.

So the makers of the JDK created `AbstractCollection` as a partial implementation. It is an abstract class and as such it contains implementations for routine methods, but leaves the core methods abstract for you. Because the class is abstract, you can override the implementations it provides if you have a specialized need, but otherwise you aren't forced to do all of that work. The advantage to this choice is that it achieves an excellent balance of power, flexibility, and efficiency.

11.6 Collection Classes

A great variety of collection types exist, and these types are good at different things. Your classes need a way to store the data that they work with, and different storage formats have different advantages and disadvantages. Some are ordered and some unordered, some offer faster retrieval while others offer precise location mechanisms. Others enforce capacity limits, and some do not.

There are too many collections to cover them exhaustively here, and that isn't really necessary for working with them successfully. In subsequent sections, we will examine different concrete implementations of the collections that you can use to store data. We will list the primary characteristics of the collection type and then see an example.

11.7 Lists

Java lists allow you to perform the same kinds of operations that ColdFusion lists do. Lists have these chief characteristics:

- Lists store their data in an ordered fashion known as a sequence.
- Because the data is ordered, you can refer to individual elements by position. Position is an integer index.
- Lists allow duplicate elements. This is in contrast to other types of collections, such as sets, which do not allow duplicates.
- Lists are zero-based like Java arrays. This is in contrast to a ColdFusion list, the first element of which has an index of 1.

11.7.1 `LinkedList`

The `LinkedList` is much like an `ArrayList` (discussed below). It offers a way to store objects each in their own link. A link stores a reference to the prior and next links in the sequence. Therefore data is stored in a linked list as ordered without ordinal index assignment. This makes the `LinkedList` much faster when you need to remove data from, or insert data into, the middle of the list.

The following listing demonstrates this collection:

11.7.2 LinkedListTest.java

```
package chp11;

import java.util.LinkedList;
import java.util.*;

public class LinkedListTest {

    public static void main(String[] a ) {

        LinkedList employees = new LinkedList();

            // add items to the linked list

        employees.add("Colonel Pickering");
        employees.add("Eliza Doolittle");
        employees.add("Henry Higgins");

            // get an iterator. Notice that this is a method
            // of the LinkedList class, not a new object
        Iterator it = employees.iterator();

        for (int i = 0; i < 3; i++) {

            System.out.println(it.next());
        }
    }
}
```

The similiar operation in ColdFusion would use a list. That's because there are no key names for the values in the collection:

```
<cfset employees = "Colonel Pickering, Eliza Doolittle, Henry
Higgins">

<cfloop from = "1" to = "3" index="i">
<cfoutput>#ListGetAt(employees,  i,  ",")#<br></cfoutput>
</cfloop>
```

This could be written in ColdFusion script as well, in a syntax that is closer to Java:

```
<cfscript>
employees = "Colonel Pickering, Eliza Doolittle, Henry
Higgins";

for (i = 1; i lte 3; i = i + 1) {

this = ListGetAt(employees, i, ",");
WriteOutput(this & "<br>");
}

</cfscript>
```

The output in all of the above cases is:

```
Colonel Pickering
Eliza Doolittle
Henry Higgins
```

Note that `this` is a keyword in Java and JavaScript, but not ColdFusion.

11.7.3 ArrayList

An `ArrayList` is an implementation of the `List` interface that provides a resizeable array. Here are the chief characteristics of the `ArrayList`:

- They are not synchronized. If you want a synchronized version, use a `Vector`.
- `ArrayLists` have a capacity, which is the number of cells required to store the elements in the list.
- An `ArrayList` is resizeable. The capacity will grow automatically when you add elements to the list.
- If you need to add a large number of elements to the list all at once, you can increase performance by using the `ensureCapacity()` method.

Note that there is a ColdFusion function called `ArrayResize`, whose purpose is to resize an array to the specified number of elements. You use this in ColdFusion only when you require an array with more than 500 elements. This function is similar to the `ensureCapacity()` function in Java, in that it is only used when adding large amounts of data.

11.7.4 ArrayListTest.java

```
package chp11;

import java.util.ArrayList;
import java.util.Iterator;

public class ArrayListTest {

    public static void main(String [] a) {
            // create arraylist
        ArrayList vegetables = new ArrayList();

        vegetables.ensureCapacity(5);

            // populate it
        Iterator it = vegetables.iterator();

        String[] names = {"carrots", "yams", "beans"};


        for (int i = 0; i < names.length; i++) {
            vegetables.add(i, names[i]);
        }

        System.out.println("List size: " + vegetables.size());
            // get second element in the array:
        System.out.println(names[1]);
            // get second element in the ArrayList:
        System.out.println(vegetables.get(1));

        String otherveg = "beans";

        boolean result = otherveg.equals(vegetables.get(2)) ?
             true : false;

            // returns true
        System.out.println("Are the items in pos. 2 equal? " +
             result);

    }
}
```

The output of this program is:

```
List size: 3
yams
yams
Are the items in pos. 2 equal? true
```

NOTE The similar operation in ColdFusion would use a regular array. Remember that ColdFusion arrays start at 1, not 0.

It is preferable to use a `LinkedList` when you need to update items in the middle of a list, and your list contains a large number of elements. Otherwise, the performance increase you get is negligible, and you can use an `ArrayList`.

11.7.5 Sorting

It is useful on occasion to sort the data you have stored in a list type collection. You can do this using the Collection `sort()` method, as shown below.

11.7.6 `SortTest.java`

```
package chp11;

import java.util.*;

public class SortTest {

    public static void main(String[] a) {

            // create new list of the specified
            // size

        ArrayList employees =
            new ArrayList(Arrays.asList(new String[6]));

        String defaultName = "Jason";
        Collections.fill(employees, defaultName);

            // now all 5 employees elements are filled
            // with "Jason"

            // add some other employees
```

```
        employees.set(1, "Quentin");
        employees.set(3, "Caddie");
        employees.set(5, "Benji");

            // implicit toString() called
        System.out.println("Unsorted: " + employees);

            // sort them
        Collections.sort(employees);

        System.out.println("Sorted: " + employees);

    }
}
```

The output is as follows:

```
Unsorted: [Jason, Quentin, Jason, Caddie, Jason, Benji]
Sorted: [Benji, Caddie, Jason, Jason, Jason, Quentin]
```

11.7.7 Vector

A `Vector` is used to store an array of object references that can grown automatically as needed. Originally, `Vector` was a direct descendant of `java.lang.Object`. With the many aspects of Java that were redesigned in version 1.2, `Vector` was changed to extend `java.util.AbstractList`.

The Java standard classes use vectors extensively. For instance, in GUI applications using `PopupMenus`, vectors are under the hood to store these objects in `java.awt.Component`.

`Vector` has a number of constructors, each of which are more or less useful depending on the problem at hand. Here are the `Vector` constructors:

- `Vector()` Constructs an empty vector. Its internal data array has a size of 10.
- `Vector(Collection c)` Constructs a vector containing all of the elements of the collection specified, in the order their iterator returns them.
- `Vector(int initialCapacity)` Constructs an empty vector with the initial capacity specified.
- `Vector(int initialCapacity, int capacityIncrement)` Constructs an empty vector with the initial capacity and capacity increment as specified.

11.7.7.1 ACCESSING AND SEARCHING VECTOR ELEMENTS

The object references in a vector are stored as an array. That means you can retrieve their values using an `int` index. Like arrays, the `Vector` index starts at 0. There are a number of methods made available to allow you to find specific elements and search through a vector:

- `firstElement()` returns the object reference for the element at index 0.
- `indexOf(Object o)` searches for the first occurrence of the specified object, similar to how you might use `ListFind()` in ColdFusion. `ListFind()` returns a number indicating the element's ordinal place in the list. By the same token, `indexOf()` returns an `int`.
- `subList(int fromIndex, int toIndex)` returns a `List` containing the portion of the list elements residing between the specified indices.
- `lastIndexOf(Object o)` returns the index of the last occurrence of this element in the vector.

In the listing below, we add some elements to a vector, reference and remove one of them, and then send the vector to a string.

11.7.8 VectorTest.java

```
package chp11;

import java.util.Vector;
import java.util.StringTokenizer;

public class VectorTest {

    public static void main (String [] a) {

    Vector v = new Vector();

    for (int i = 0; i < 5; i++) {
        v.add(i, new Integer(i+100));

        System.out.println(v.get(i));
    }
        // remove the element at 2
    Integer goner =  (Integer) v.remove(2);

        // prove it
    System.out.println("Item removed: " + goner);

        // entire vector as a string
    StringTokenizer st = new StringTokenizer(v.toString());
```

```
        System.out.println("number of tokens: " +
            st.countTokens());

           // print out these in token list
        while (st.hasMoreTokens()) {

            System.out.println(st.nextToken());
        }
        v.removeAll(v);
        System.out.println("is it empty now? " + v.isEmpty());
        }
}
```

The `VectorTest.class` program outputs the following:

```
100
101
102
103
104
Item removed: 102
number of tokens: 4
[100,
101,
103,
104]
is it empty now? true
```

As you can see, you can use the `collection` methods `add()` and `remove()` with vectors.

Vectors cannot contain primitive values. We use this example as a reminder of this fact. We cannot simply store an `int`. We must create an `Integer` object to add it, and then unwrap it to reference it.

11.7.9 Stack

The `Stack` object is a special kind of vector (it extends `Vector`). Its purpose is to provide an easy mechanism for last in, first out (LIFO) processing. This structure allows you to add elements to and remove elements from only the top of the stack. Inserting an element is called a *push,* while retrieving an element is called a *pop*. Just think of a deck of cards being dealt.

The main usefulness of `Stack` is for building lists that do not require frequent or heavy access. There are two ways that you can work with `Stack`. The first is with an iterator; the preferable way is with special methods for stacks:

- `push(Object o)` pushes an object onto the top of the stack.
- `pop()` removes the object at the top of the stack.
- `peek()` looks at the first object on the stack.
- `search(Object o)` looks for an object inside the stack. If the specified item is found,
- `empty()` tests if the stack is empty.

As with `Vector`, you must remember to appropriately wrap and unwrap your primitives. Following is an example using a stack:

11.7.10 StackTest.java

```
package chp11;

import java.util.Stack;

public class StackTest {

    public static void main (String [] a) {

            // create stack
        Stack s = new Stack();

            // add items to stack, which
            // requires Objects
        s.push(new Double(1.00));

        s.push(new Integer(99));

            // which is on top?
        System.out.println(s.peek());

        Integer d1 = (Integer) s.pop();

        Double d2 = (Double) s.pop();

        System.out.println("d1: " + d1 + " d2: " +  d2);
    }
}
```

The output looks like this:

```
99
d1: 99 d2: 1.0
```

The `java.util.Stack` discussed above is a subclass of `Vector`, a type of collection. These are used exclusively for data storage. There is another stack that is important in Java, the Call Stack. The Call Stack is used in the Java Virtual Machine for handling memory internally. Both stacks use the same kind of first in, last out data access.

11.7.11 Choosing a Data Storage Structure

You should be able to accomplish many of the data storage tasks you will commonly need using the `List` classes. It is not generally preferable to use vectors anymore, though you will see them a lot in legacy code. Remember that vectors are single threaded, and they can therefore be a source of bottlenecking in your applications. It is often smarter to use another type, even if you require synchronization. Also recall that vectors will expose an `Enumeration` object, and that it is preferable to use `Iterators` now.

The legacy `Hashtable` class also returns an `Enumeration` object instead of an iterator. A `Hashtable` is very much like a `HashMap`. Methods of the `Hashtable` are synchronized. Because synchronizing at the method level instead of the object level creates greater overhead, you should probably use a `HashMap` instead if you do not require synchronization.

The `List` classes have many advantages, including easy resizing, element ordering, and the ability to easily insert and remove elements. The chief disadvantage with using lists is that you cannot store primitive values in them; storing wrapped primitives in them requires that a good deal of complexity and length be added to your work and hampers readability.

If you need to store only primitives, an array is the best choice. If you need to store any object type, a `List` is the best choice.

11.8 Sets

Most of the straightforward kinds of collections storage can be done in lists. The `Set` is a kind of expansion of `List` that allows you greater control over the elements contained in it. A `Set` is a `List` that does not allow duplicate elements. Because ColdFusion has no precisely corresponding storage mechanism, you might think of this as a primary key in a relational database table—it is just a uniqueness constraint.

The Set classes include: SortedSet, TreeSet, and HashSet, which we will discuss here in turn. Any Set implements these methods, among others:

- add() adds an element to the set. Returns boolean regarding success of the operation. Returns false if an attempt is made to add a duplicate element to the set.
- contains(Object o) returns boolean true if the set contains the element specified.
- equals(Object o) compares the object specified with this Set.
- remove(Object o) removes the object from the Set. If not present, returns false.
- size() returns an int representing the cardinality of the Set.

The Set is meant as an implementation of a mathematical abstract set. That means that logical (mathematical) operations standard to set theory (such as intersection, union, and so forth) can be performed on them.

Two sets are considered equal if they contain all of the same elements. It does not matter what order the elements are in; simple presence of all of the same elements is enough for them to be equal.

11.8.1 TreeSet

The TreeSet has certain features that distinguish it from other kinds of sets:

- Elements are stored in *ascending order.*
- You need to implement the java.lang.Comparable interface for your objects in order to perform sorting.

> **NOTE** The Comparable interface imposes an order on each implementing class in order to sort them alphabetically. Lists and arrays can be sorted automatically using Collections.sort() and Arrays.sort().

SortedSet is an interface implemented by only one class in the JDK: the TreeSet. The chief purpose of the SortedSet is to allow you to extend the collections yourself. So we will demonstrate an example of TreeSets in the SetsTest.java listing.

11.8.2 HashSet

A HashSet implements the set interface, storing its data as an instance of HashMap. The following things are characteristics of HashSet:

- The HashSet is not synchronized. That means you need to add your own synchronization if multiple threads might access the set concurrently. If you do not have an object available externally with which to wrap the set, then you should wrap your set using the Collections.synchronized() set method.
- Sets operate on each element container (or "bucket") in even distribution. That means that you should not set the initial capacity of your set too high, or performance will be hindered unnecessarily.

A HashSet is often faster performing than a TreeSet. This is because the data in a TreeSet is ordered, and a HashSet's data is not.

NOTE A ColdFusion structure's data is unordered, like a HashSet.

11.8.3 Set Theory Operations

In set theory there are several kinds of relationships that can be defined between the elements of different sets. You may be familiar with some of these from working with relational databases. The three most commonly used in programming are probably *union* (which is actually an SQL keyword carried over from set theory), *intersection*, and *difference*.

11.8.3.1 UNION

A *union* of two sets creates a third set that is composed exclusively of the unique elements common to both sets. Say you had two sets of letters. The first set is composed of vowels, and the second set is composed of the first five letters of the alphabet:

Vowels = {a,e,i,o,u}

FirstFiveLetters = {a,b,c,d,e}

The union of these two sets is:

Union = {a,b,c,d,e,i,o,u}

The letter a is common to both sets, and is therefore not repeated in the union. The union of all winged creatures and all non-winged creatures is the set of all creatures.

The Java method `Collection.addAll()` will produce a union. That is, it adds all of the elements in the specified collection to this set if they are not already in it.

11.8.3.2 INTERSECTION

An *intersection* is different from a union. Performing an intersection on two sets creates a new set that contains all of the elements of both sets. An intersection using the letter sets above contains only one element: a.

The Java method `Collection.retainAll()` produces an intersection. That is, it retains only the elements in this set that are contained in the collection specified.

11.8.3.3 DIFFERENCE

The difference set of two sets contains varying results depending on the order in which you compare the two sets. For example, the difference between Vowels and FirstFiveLetters is {e,i,o,u}. The difference between FirstFiveLetters and Vowels is {b,c,d,e}.

The way to get a difference set in Java is to call the `Collections.removeAll()` method.

11.8.4 The Barber Paradox

I can't resist repeating this favorite set theory story, which illustrates the paradoxical nature of sets. Suppose there is a barber, who perhaps lives in Seville. This barber shaves all the men in the town who do not shave themselves. The paradox is clear: if he does not shave himself, he must shave himself. If he does shave himself, then he is not one of the people he shaves. In practical terms there are very easy ways to resolve the paradox. For instance, the barber could be a woman. But in purely theoretical terms it is interesting.

Let's write a quick example that populates two collections and compares their values, printing sets for the union, intersection, and difference of the values.

11.8.5 `SetsTest.java`

```
package chp11;
import java.util.*;
public class SetsTest {

    public static void main (String[] a) {

        String one="1";
```

```
        String two = "2";
        String three = "3";
        String four = "4";
        String five = "5";
        String six = "6";
        String seven = "7";
        String eight = "8";
        String nine = "9";

        // create a hashset to hold
        // prime numbers less than 10
    TreeSet primes = new TreeSet();

    primes.add(two);
    primes.add(three);
    primes.add(five);
    primes.add(seven);

        // create another hashset to hold
        // odd numbers less than 10
    TreeSet odds = new TreeSet();

    odds.add(one);
    odds.add(three);
    odds.add(five);
    odds.add(seven);
    odds.add(nine);

    System.out.println("Primes: " + primes);
    System.out.println("Odds: " + odds);

    TreeSet difference = new TreeSet(odds);
    difference.removeAll(primes);
    System.out.println("Difference: " + difference);

        // get the intersection of the sets
    TreeSet intersect = new TreeSet(primes);
    intersect.retainAll(odds);
    System.out.println("Intersection: " + intersect);

            // get the union of the sets
    TreeSet union =  new TreeSet (primes);
    union.addAll(odds);
    System.out.println("Union: " + union);

    }
}
```

The output is like this:

```
Primes: [2, 3, 5, 7]
Odds: [1, 3, 5, 7, 9]
Difference: [1, 9]
Intersection: [3, 5, 7]
Union: [1, 2, 3, 5, 7, 9]
```

11.8.6 Summary of Sets

Sets are collections of unique objects. Use them only if your storage scheme requires uniqueness. You need to implement the `java.lang.Comparable` interface when using a `TreeSet`, because this interface defines `compareTo()`, which `TreeSet` uses to put your objects in order. Remember that it is important not to change values once you have added them to a set. Changing a value could violate the uniqueness in your set.

11.9 Maps

The `Map` replaces the `Dictionary` class. `Dictionary` used to be the superclass of any implementation that paired keys with values in the manner of a ColdFusion structure. There are many different kinds of maps, but only two that are used with much frequency. The most popular maps are `HashMap` and `TreeMap`, which we will look at here.

The following things are true of `Maps`.

- `Maps` store key-value pairs called *entries*.
- Each key must be unique within a `Map`, and any entry may point to only one value.
- The key and the value can be of any object type. That is, you cannot store primitive types.
- The `Map` interface offers three collection views: as a set of keys (`keySet()`), as a collection of values (`values()`), or as a set of key-value mappings (`entrySet()`).
- It is a good idea to override `equals()` so that only the value is compared, not the object reference.

`Maps` are very flexible, and as such, are used frequently. `Maps` do not implement the `Collection` interface. If you want to use the methods it provides, you can locally convert your `Map` to a `Set` with `Map.entrySet()`.

11.9.1 Comparator

Some Collections, such as the TreeMap and TreeSet, implement the Comparator interface. A comparator is a function that compares two objects, returning a negative value if a comes before b, or zero if they are considered equivalent in the sort order, or a positive value if a comes after b. The comparator takes two arguments: the objects to be compared.

11.9.2 HashMap

Here are things that are the case about HashMap:

- HashMap stores its keys in an *unsorted* fashion.
- Because its data is unsorted, operations perform very quickly.
- HashMap replaces Hashtable. Hashtable is a legacy class that should no longer be used, though you are likely to see it in legacy code.
- Permits null values and null keys.
- It is unsynchronized.
- The class does not guarantee any order of data, or that the data order will stay consistent over time.

One nice thing about a HashMap is that it features a loadFactor, which you can specify in its constructor. The loadFactor, as in an SQL Server database, allows you to specify how full the capacity should become before the HashMap should automatically grow in size. It is a better idea in terms of performance to create an initial capacity that you think will be big enough for your HashMap.

> **NOTE** There is a special kind of HashMap called a WeakHashMap, which is nearly identical to the HashMap class. The only real difference is that WeakHashMap calls the garbage collector to remove a key that is no longer in use. Therefore, the only common use for WeakHashMap is for caches of data, which need not persist reliably.

HashMaps use the put() and get() methods familiar from FTP to insert and retrieve data. Here is an example to demonstrate the use of HashMaps:

11.9.3 HashMapTest.java

```
/*
 * HashMapTest.java
 *
 */
```

```
package chp11;

import java.util.*;

public class HashMapTest {

    public static void main (String [] a) {
            // constructor uses Float for loadFactor
        HashMap map = new HashMap(5, 4.0F);

            // is map empty?
        System.out.println("Is map empty? " + map.isEmpty());

            // print map size
        System.out.println("map size: " +  map.size());

            // add an item in the form 'key','value'
            // this is equivalent to
            // StructInsert() in CF
        map.put("width","50");
        map.put("height", "25");
        map.put("robots", "all");
        map.put("revist-after","30 days");

            // now delete the 'robots' key
        map.remove("robots");

            // ternary operator like IIF() in CF
        String s=map.containsKey("width") ? "true" : "false";
            // print answer
        System.out.println("Is width a key? " + s);
        System.out.println("Its value is: " +
                map.get("width"));

        String x = map.containsValue("30 days") ? "yes" :
                      "no";

        System.out.println("map contains 30 days? " + x);
    }

}
```

11.9.4 TreeMap

Here are things that are the case about TreeMap:

- TreeMap stores its keys in a *sorted* fashion. This contrasts with HashMap.
- Because data is sorted, all operations are slower than with HashMap.
- Keys stored in a TreeMap must implement the Comparable interface.

There are several methods useful in working with TreeMaps, as shown below:

- firstKey() returns the first key; that is, the key with the lowest value.
- lastKey() returns the last key (the one with the highest value).
- containsKey(Object key) returns true if the collection contains the key specified.
- containsValue(Object value) returns true if the collection contains the value specified.
- size() returns the number of keys in the map.
- comparator() returns the comparator used to order this map.

The following class covers new items regarding HashMaps and TreeMaps and demonstrates a useful implementation of an anonymous inner class.

11.9.5 TreeMapTest.java

```
/*
 * TreeMapTest.java
 * demonstrates Comparator use, and
 * anonymous class use, as well as
 * transferring data from a HashMap into a TreeMap
 */

package chp11;

import java.util.*;

public class TreeMapTest {

    private String value;

 public static void main(String[] ar) {

        // create new Map to store key-values
      HashMap characters = new HashMap();

        // add characters from Faulkner novel
        // out of order
```

```
        characters.put(new TreeMapTest("Vardaman"), "fish");
        characters.put(new TreeMapTest("Anse"), "dad");
        characters.put(new TreeMapTest("Addie"), "dead");


           // anonymous inner class Comparator
           // to put characters into new
           // tree map sorted
        TreeMap tm = new TreeMap(new Comparator() {
           public int compare(Object a, Object b) {
               return ((TreeMapTest)a).value.
                      compareTo(((TreeMapTest)b).value);
               }});

               tm.putAll(characters);
               System.out.println("sorted characters: " + tm);

    }

           // constructor
       TreeMapTest(String value) {
           this.value = value;
       }

           // override toString
       public String toString() {
           return "\n" +  value;
       }
}
```

The output produced by this example is as follows:

```
sorted characters: {
Addie=dead,
Anse=dad,
Vardaman=fish}
```

11.10 Using Regular Expressions

Regular expressions are descriptions of textual patterns that enable string matching. You have likely used at least a simple regular expression. Perhaps the most common character in a regular expression is the wildcard character (*). So if you have ever entered `*.cfm` to view only the ColdFusion markup files in a directory, you have used regular expressions. You may or may not have had occasion to use regular expressions with ColdFusion functions.

Regular expressions are a useful tool, and we will cover them here briefly as the JDK 1.4 makes them easy to use; the new classes are a package under `java.util`.

11.10.1 Regex in CF

Using a regular expression in ColdFusion boils down to implementing one of two functions: `REFind()` and `REFindNoCase()`. These functions are prefixed with `RE`, which stands for regular expression.

`REFind()` performs a case-sensitive search that returns the position of the first occurrence of a regular expression in a string, beginning with the position specified. If no occurrences are found, returns `0`.

`REFindNoCase()` is a case-insensitive version of `REFind()`. Here are a few examples showing the different kinds of usage of this function:

A simple regex:

```
<cfoutput>#REFindNoCase("a+c", "abcaaccdd")#</cfoutput>
```

Using POSIX syntax:

```
<cfoutput>#REFindNoCase("[[:alpha:]]", "aBBccDdeeE")#
</cfoutput>
```

11.10.2 Metacharacters and Pattern Matching

Table 11.3 shows the most common metacharacters used in regular expression matching.

TABLE 11.3 The Most Common Metacharacters Used in Regex

METACHARACTER	MEANING
`\d`	Any digit (0–9)
`\D`	Any non-digit
`\s`	A whitespace character
`\S`	Any non-whitespace character
`\w`	Letters, numbers, and underscores

(continued)

TABLE 11.3 The Most Common Metacharacters Used in Regex (Continued)

METACHARACTER	MEANING
\W	Any non-\w characters
.	Any single character
^	Nothing before this character
$	Nothing after this character
+	One or more
*	Zero or more
?	Zero or one

It can be very difficult to get your mind around how regexes work without seeing some examples (or after seeing some, for that matter). So, Table 11.4 provides some examples:

TABLE 11.4 Regex Examples

REGULAR EXPRESSION	STRINGS THAT MATCH
A*B	B, AB, AAB, AAAB, ...
A+B	AB, AAB, AAAB, ...
A?B	B *or* AB
[XYZ]B	XB, YB, *or* ZB
[A-C]B	AB, BB, *or* CB
[3-5]X	3X, 4X, *or* 5X

(Continued)

TABLE 11.4 Regex Examples (Continued)

REGULAR EXPRESSION	STRINGS THAT MATCH
`Item\s\d`	Item 1, ... (but not Item5 or ItemX)
`(X|Z)Y`	XY *or* ZY
`(hi\s){2}`	hi hi
`(hi\s){1-3}`	hi, hi, hi *or* hi hi hi

It used to be that performing regular expression matching in Java was a rather elaborate process. One had to use `StringTokenizers` to match text in substrings using `charAt()`. The JDK 1.4 makes it easier, having introduced a new package called `java.util.regex`. There are two classes in this package that help you work with regex.

11.10.2.1 `public final class` PATTERN

A `Pattern` object is a compiled instance of a string representing a regular expression. The `Pattern` object can then be used to create a `Matcher` object to match character sequences against the regular expression.

11.10.2.2 `public final class` MATCHER

The `Matcher` object interprets patterns in order to match a character sequence. You create a matcher by invoking the pattern's `matcher` method. There are three kinds of match operations you can perform:

1. `matches()` tries to match the complete input sequence against the pattern.
2. `lookingAt()` tries to match the input sequence, starting at the beginning, against the pattern.
3. `find()` scans the input sequence looking for the next subsequence matching the pattern.

A typical sequence for matching a regular expression then looks like this:

```
pattern p = Pattern.compile("a*b");
Matcher m = p.matcher("aaaaab");
boolean b = m.matches();
```

Let's look at an example. Let's create a source file that will have find all instances of "Allaire" and replace them with "Macromedia." This perhaps is not an advanced regex example, but it demonstrates what is important here: how to use these two classes in conjunction to perform any regex matching you need to do.

First, we create a file called `MyData.dat` that contains the following information:

Allaire is a company with an office in Boston.
Not only does Allaire make ColdFusion, but now
Allaire has great parties.

We will use the regex engine to replace all instances of "Allaire" with instances of "Macromedia."

> **NOTE** This example also uses instances of the `java.io.File` class and the `java.io.BufferedReader` and `java.io.BufferedWriter` class. You can work with files and directories using objects in these classes when you would choose `<cffile>` in ColdFusion. This example takes an existing file and reads its data in, then writes a new file with the updated information. Look in the API for more on this subject.

You will want to change the location of the file and match the path to one suitable for your system.

11.10.3 RegexTest.java

```
// performs a search to find and replace
// pattern instances using regex
package chp11;

import java.util.regex.*;
import java.io.*;


public class RegExTest {

    public static void main(String[] args)
        throws Exception {

            // create file object
        File inFile = new File("C:\\MyData.dat");
        File outFile = new File("C:\\UpdatedData.dat");
```

```
            // get an input stream
            // to read a file in
        FileInputStream inputStream =
            new FileInputStream(inFile);

            // get an output stream
            // so we can write the file
            // back out.
        FileOutputStream outputStream =
            new FileOutputStream(outFile);

            // the BufferedReader performs
            // efficient reading-in of text
            // from a character source
        BufferedReader readerIn = new BufferedReader(
            new InputStreamReader(inputStream));

        BufferedWriter writerOut = new BufferedWriter(
            new OutputStreamWriter(outputStream));

            // write pattern and compile it into
            // a pattern object.
            // Your regex goes here:
        Pattern p = Pattern.compile("Allaire");

            // use the matcher to find occurences
        Matcher m = p.matcher("");

        String s = null;

        while((s = readerIn.readLine()) != null) {
            m.reset(s);

                //Replace characters
            String result = m.replaceAll("Macromedia");
            writerOut.write(result);
            writerOut.newLine();
        }
            // close connections
       readerIn.close();
       writerOut.close();

       System.out.println("Operation performed successfully.");
    }
}
```

The output is:

```
Operation performed successfully.
```

Upon opening the file, you should see all instances of "Allaire" replaced with "Macromedia."

With the new regex package, performing regular expression matching now gives you a power closer to that of sed or awk or Perl for this kind of operation.

11.11 What's Next

In the next chapter, we cover Java database connectivity, or JDBC. This standard is based somewhat on Microsoft's Open DataBase Connectivity, and is the technology that allows Java programs and Java Web applications to connect to databases, retrieve record sets, and manipulate the data. Performing such operations in Java requires writing a good deal more code than it does in ColdFusion, as every aspect of the operation requires its own objects, each with its own methods and properties.

12

JDBC

This chapter introduces JDBC, the Java database connectivity technology. JDBC offers developers a standard library for accessing databases and working with queries. This chapter assumes that you have knowledge of relational database design and know how to write at least basic SQL queries to select, insert, update, and delete data from a database.

JDBC standardizes the mechanisms for connecting to databases so that you can use the API with MySQL, Microsoft SQL Server, Oracle, or any other database that implements JDBC with your Java programs.

Working with databases in Java requires a good deal more manual effort on the part of the developer than it does from within ColdFusion. There is no ColdFusion Administrator to handle establishing the datasource—this must be done programmatically in Java. While initially the amount of code required to retrieve a result set may seem intimidating, much of your code can be reused.

The JDBC is currently in version 3.0, and now with Java 1.4, all of the API is included with the JDK; you do not need to download JDBC extension classes to work with databases. The only other thing you will need to work through the examples in this chapter is access to some kind of database system. We will demonstrate examples using Microsoft Access and MySQL, though the examples will work with little modification in enterprise RDBMSs such as Oracle, Microsoft SQL Server, or DB2. You can download a free version of MySQL from *www.mysql.com*.

Using JDBC, you have the full power that you are used to enjoying from within ColdFusion applications. You can use it to connect to enterprise DBMSs, object-oriented databases, Excel spreadsheets, FoxPro databases, plain text files, and more.

12.1 Using JDBC

JDBC is made up of more than 20 classes in the `java.sql` package. JDBC is based on (and works similarly to) Microsoft's ODBC (Open Database Connectivity). A chief difference is that it is implemented in Java, not C, and has the advantage of hindsight, which makes it simpler.

JDBC supports transaction management, precompiled statements, stored procedure calls, and use of metadata such as number of rows returned by a query.

Connecting to a database and using the result set works the same way whether you are writing a desktop application with a GUI or a Web application written with JavaServer Pages. There are several steps required to perform any interaction with a database:

1. Load the driver for this database
2. Establish a connection to this database
3. Create a `Statement` object
4. Execute the statement
5. Do something with the result set
6. Close the connection

We will cover these now in turn.

12.1.1 Loading the Driver

In ColdFusion, you can create a datasource in the ColdFusion Administrator before you start working with a database in your templates. Alternatively, you can connect to a database using the ability (introduced in ColdFusion 5) to create a datasource on the fly, directly inside your template code. In Java, there is no Administrator, so you must always specify how you are going to make a connection directly in your Java code.

A driver is a software program that talks to a particular database server. There are many different drivers available for each kind of database. In order to use a particular driver to connect to a database, you need to download or purchase the driver, install it on your class path, and load the class. The class will create an instance of the driver and register it with the JDBC driver manager.

There are two related concepts implicit here. The first is that you need to be able to load a class without knowing its name when you compile the code. The second is that you need to load a class without creating an instance of it, so that the class itself can do this when necessary. The `Class` class allows us to do both of these things.

The `Class` class is a direct descendant of `java.lang.Object`. Instances of the `Class` class represent classes and interfaces running in a Java program. The `forName()` method returns the `Class` object associated with the class (or interface) within the name you specify as a string. Supply this name to the method as a fully qualified class name (that is, include all of the package names). The call to `Class.forName()` can throw a `ClassNotFoundException`, and it is a good idea to throw this exception and place a handler inside a catch block, like this:

```
try {
    Class.forName("packageName.driver");
}
catch(ClassNotFoundException cfne) {
    System.err.println("Cannot find driver: " + cfne);
}
```

When a regular Java program is compiled, the compiler identifies the classes that the program uses. It then creates instructions for the JVM to load those classes at execution time. JDBC allows a number of different drivers to be loaded, and the driver name is therefore not known at compile time—only at execution time. How do you know what string to pass to the `forName()` method? This depends on which driver you use.

Most database driver vendors will distribute the driver in a `.jar` file. There are a number of ways to ensure that extensions can be found:

- You can place the `.jar` file in your class path, or in `<JAVA_HOME>/jre/lib/ext`. You can place any `.jar` files or other extensions to Java in this folder under the JDK, and they will be available to the system when you restart the JVM.
- You can also use the `-classpath` option for the compiler and JVM, adding the path name to the `.jar` file.
- Another option is to add the full path name of your driver library to the `$CLASSPATH` variable in your startup file (this is `autoexec.bat` for Windows).

A complete listing of available JDBC drivers can be found at Sun's Web site at *http://industry.java.sun.com/products/jdbc*. Currently there are around 200, and all major databases are supported. These drivers are divided into four types: Type I, II, III, and IV. Each of the four driver types have somewhat different personalities and uses, and we will look at these in turn.

12.1.1.1 TYPE I DRIVER: JDBC-ODBC BRIDGE

The Type I driver is actually a bridge between a Java application and an existing ODBC connection. This type of driver is the only one to ship with the JDK, which means that if you have a current ODBC database connection, you can start using it right away without having to fetch another driver. This driver was provided by Sun initially because (obviously) there were no drivers existing for JDBC when it was first introduced, and ODBC was a popular driver mechanism.

The advantage of the Type I driver is that it is easy and quick to use, because it ships with the JDK and it allows you to use any existing ODBC connections you may have. The disadvantage of this driver type is that it requires three tiers in which to operate: the Java application including the JDBC bridge, the ODBC connection, and the database itself. This means that it is a very slow connection and is not suitable for a production environment.

Connecting with a JDBC-ODBC Bridge • Let's briefly look at how we can connect to a database from a Java application using an existing ODBC datasource. I have an Access database on a local machine called `JavaForCF.mdb`. In the Windows Control Panel I have created an ODBC datasource called "javaforcf." Because the JDBC-ODBC bridge comes with the JDK, it is free, and I do not need to get any other package to start using this connection. I can simply load this driver using a statement like this:

```
        // load the class for this driver
Class.forName("sun.jdbc.odbc.JdbcOdbcDriver");

        // create a new connection object, specifying
        // the name of the datasource
Connection con =
DriverManager.getConnection("jdbc:odbc:javaforcf","", "");
```

This Access database has a table called `Items`. This table has columns called itemid, itemname, price, and so forth. Shortly, we will see a complete example of how to reference these columns to retrieve data.

12.1.1.2 TYPE II DRIVER: NATIVE API/JAVA DRIVER

This type of driver takes commands in JDBC and converts them to native calls specific to the DBMS. These conversions communicate directly with the database. The advantage of this type of driver is that it is faster than a Type I driver. However, it still requires specific files to be loaded on every client, which makes it generally unsuitable for production.

12.1.1.3 TYPE III DRIVER: JDBC-NET PURE JAVA DRIVER

The JDBC-Net Pure Java Driver takes commands in JDBC and converts them into a database-independent network protocol. This gets sent to a middleware server that translates the network protocol into a protocol specific to the DBMS in use. This in turn is sent to the specific database that is being accessed. The advantage of this system is its flexibility. It gives the developer a good deal of control over fine-grained aspects of the connection. The disadvantage is that because the translation must occur twice (once when the connection is established, and again when the results are returned), this is not the fastest possible way to connect, and it requires more work.

12.1.1.4 TYPE IV DRIVER: NATIVE PROTOCOL PURE JAVA DRIVER

The Type IV driver is written entirely in Java and communicates with the database directly. JDBC commands entered are converted into the database's native protocol on the fly, eliminating the need for a middle tier completely. These types of drivers are the fastest available and are generally preferable for production environments. Some can be downloaded for free and others are available for a fee. Prices for such drivers, which implement different feature sets and offer different speeds or support packages, can range from free (such as Microsoft's Type IV driver for SQL Server) to a couple thousand dollars for third-party drivers. Many excellent ones are free, however.

Another advantage to using Type IV drivers is that they are easy to deploy, because all you need is the vendor's Java class file in your class path. To makes things easier, the driver should include example applications that demonstrate the URL and class name required to load and use the JDBC driver in your applications.

Here is an example of connecting to a popular (and free) Type IV driver for the MySQL database:

```
        try {
            // load driver
            Class.forName("org.gjt.mm.mysql.Driver");
            // make connection
          con = DriverManager.getConnection("jdbc:mysql://
                     localhost/javaforcf","","");
        }
        catch (ClassNotFoundException cnfe) {
            error = "Class not found: can't find driver";
            throw new ClassNotFoundException(error);
        }
        catch (SQLException sqle) {
            error = "SQL Exception: can't connect to DB";
            throw new SQLException(error);
        }
        catch (Exception e) {
            error = "Exception: unknown";
            throw new Exception(error);
        }
    } //end connect
```

Note that writing this code in your database will simply load the driver and make a `Connection` object. Nothing else that you would notice happens. That is, no object is returned.

12.1.1.5 SPECIFYING THE DRIVER WITH PROPERTIES

You can also specify the driver to use in a properties file. You may recall our using these to store a favorite color parameter value in Chapter 11. You can set a system-level property by passing it in at the command line for your application, like this:

```
java someProgram -Djdbc-driver=package.drivername
```

You can retrieve the value for the driver like this:

```
String myDriver =  System.getProperty("jdbc-driver");
```

Once you have retrieved the driver name, you can pass it to the `Class.forName()` call.

You can also load the properties from a properties file, which is read at runtime. Using the `getProperty()` method, we get a string back. Here is a fragment of how this works:

```
...
Properties p = new Properties();
p.load(new FileInputStream("JDBC.prop"));

// get values for the keys in which we're interested
String driver = p.getProperty("jdbc-driver");
String url = p.getProperty("JDBC-url");

Class.forName(driver);
Connection con = DriverManager.getConnection(url);
...
```

12.1.2 Establish a Connection

Once the driver has been loaded, you must obtain a connection. You do this by writing a URL that specifies the location of the database to connect to, including username and password, and then passing the string to the `getConnection()` method of the `java.sql.DriverManager` class, like this:

```
Connection con;

String url ="jdbc:mysql://localhost/
 databaseName","usernameHere","passwordHere";

con = DriverManager.getConnection(url);
```

Note that there are two alternate ways to use the overloaded `getConnection()` method:

```
getConnection(String url)
```

which accepts only the location of the database, and

```
getConnection(String url, Properties info)
```

where `info` is a list of arbitrary string tag-value pairs that you can send in as connection arguments. This is similar to `connectstring`, introduced in ColdFusion 5.

The connection represents the established possibility of interacting with a database. Without a connection, there is nothing you can do with the database. So the `Connection` object is used to handle the input and output generated in your database interactions.

URLs that refer to databases you want to connect to using JDBC are prefixed with `jdbc:` as the protocol, in the place of, for instance, `http:`. You should specify a port number as well if that is in use. The format of the URL will depend on what driver you use. We have seen examples using Access and MySQL. Here are varying examples for PostgreSQL, Oracle, and Sybase:

```
String hostName = "data.mycompany.com";
String database = "myDB";
String port = "5678";

     // a Postgres URL with username and password
String a PGURL = "jdbc:postgresql:" + hostName + ":" + port +
"/" + database + ";user=myUserName;password=myPassword";
     // an Oracle URL
String  anOracleURL = "jdbc:oracle:thin:@" + hostName + ":" +
     port + ":" + database;

     // a Sybase URL
String aSybaseURL = "jdbc:sybase"Tds:" + hostName + ":" + port
      + ":" + "?SERVICENAME=" + database;
```

The `Connection` class contains the methods required to control the database connection. You make the connection URL as a string and pass it to an instance of the `Connection` class to establish the connection.

> **NOTE** The `getConnection()` method throws an SQLException, which means you need to use a try/catch block around your `DriverManager` object business.

In ColdFusion, you automatically get information about the querying process returned to you in the form of the `CFQuery` object. This allows you to do things such as check the number of records your query returned by referencing `#queryName.recordcount#`. If you want such information in a Java application, you need to specify that explicitly. At this stage in your app, you create a `DatabaseMetaData` object, which is returned by the `Connection` object's `getMetaData()` method.

12.1.3 Create a `Statement` Object

Once you have a connection, you need to make the statement that you want to send off to the database for processing. The `Statement` object allows you to store the SQL statement and then execute it. A statement looks like this:

```
Statement stmt = con.createStatement();
```

12.1.4 Execute the Statement

Once you have a `Statement` object, you need to send it to the database. Then write the SQL you want to send to the database as a string. Then call the `executeQuery()` method of the `Statement` object, passing the SQL string to it as a parameter. This operation will return a `ResultSet` object. The `ResultSet` contains the data retrieved by the execution of the query.

Here an important distinction is made. In ColdFusion, you can write whatever SQL statements you like, and the database will execute them just the same, as long as the statement is between `<cfquery>` tags. In Java, you use different methods to execute a query `SELECT` statement and an `UPDATE` statement.

`SELECT` statements use the `executeQuery()` method of the `Statement` object. If you want to update the information in the database (that is, write an `UPDATE`, `INSERT`, or `DELETE` statement), then you need to use a different method: the `executeUpdate()` method.

12.1.4.1 PREPARED STATEMENTS

The `prepareStatement()` method allow you to execute a precompiled query in an efficient manner. You use a `prepareStatement()` when you want to run a parameterized query; that is, a query where the bulk of the statement is always the same, but the statement has one or more variables that change the result set somewhat. The advantage is that Java can store all of the parts of the query that do not change and only rebuild the variable element of the statement. For instance, you use a `prepareStatement()` in Java when you would write this kind of statement in ColdFusion:

```
<cfquery...>
   select * from items
   where itemid = #itemid#;
</cfquery>
```

In place of the ColdFusion `itemid` variable above, use a question mark (?) in Java to specify a placeholder for a variable:

```
String theSQL = "select * from items where itemid = ?;";
```

Each time you use a prepared statement, you need to replace the ? placeholder with the actual value you want to pass into the query. To do so, you write a `setSomething()` call to replace the marker with the value; the "something" is the type of value to be sent in.

In order to update data in the database, that is, to UPDATE or DELETE data, use an `executeUpdate()` method. For example, when you would write the following in ColdFusion:

```
<cfquery...>
   UPDATE items
   SET title='something'
   WHERE itemid=#itemid#;
</cfquery>
```

Write the SQL string as above, using the ? in place of the variable you want to pass to the statement. Then call the `executeUpdate()` method in place of the `executeQuery()`, as shown in the code example below.

Here is a method that gets called to retrieve the single item in the database matching the ID passed as a parameter. This is a very typical operation when you need to, for instance, view the detail of a product in an online store or view a single news article out of a list, and so forth.

```
public ResultSet viewOneItem(String itemID) throws
   SQLException, Exception {

   ResultSet rs = null;
   try {

        PreparedStatement getArchived;

        String s = new String("select itemName,
          itemText, createdDate from items where
          itemID = ?");

        getArchived = con.prepareStatement(s);

        getArchived.setInt(1, Integer.parseInt(itemID));
                rs = getArchived.executeQuery();
// a second ? would have index of 2.
// SQL is 1-based like CF, not 0-based like Java
```

```
        }
        catch (SQLException sqle) {
             sqle.printStackTrace();
             error = "SQL Error:";
             throw new SQLException(error);
        }
        catch (Exception e) {
             e.printStackTrace();
             error = "An unknown exception occured while executing
                       query";
             throw new Exception(error);
        }

        return rs;
    }   // end viewOneItem
```

Creating a PreparedStatement object is a very expensive process. So once a PreparedStatement is closed, a driver that is compliant with JDBC 3.0 (the most recent as of this writing) will place the statement in a local cache instead of discarding it. This way, the application can retrieve the statement already cached if it attempts to create the same query later. This obviously saves time- and resource-consuming authentication at the database and network traffic.

12.1.5 Process the Result Set

The ResultSet object returned by an executed query exposes a next() method which allows you to move through the results one row at a time. There are also various get methods that take a column index or column name as an argument and return the result as a variety of data types. As you might imagine, these methods include getInt() to return the column data as an int type, getString() to retrieve the value as a string, and so on.

Generally in ColdFusion one will get a result set from a query and then output it in a loop of some sort. The <cfoutput> tag can implicitly loop over a result set, and you can explicitly perform this using a <cfloop> and specifying a query attribute.

> **NOTE** There is a convention in SQL that result sets start with the index 1, not 0. This is of course contrary to Java convention for arrays, collections, and other data types, and as such can be difficult to remember.

In Java, a `while` loop is often used to iterate over a result set:

```
   // assume item object
item.connect();
   // run some query
ResultSet rs = item.doTheQuery();

while (rs.next()) {
  // do something ...
}
```

You cannot simply start referencing individual values within a query as you can with ColdFusion. Without traversing the result, you are likely to get an error informing you that the result set is at the end.

12.1.5.1 HANDLING NULLS

It is quite rare to find a database that does not contain null values. Consider what we know about Java primitives. They do not have a null equivalent the way an object does. This is a problem if the implicit conversion performed by Java is incongruent with the meaning inhering in your data scheme. That is, what if an integer value was left null in your database? Because Java has no null equivalent for primitive types, the result is generally converted to 0. This could be discordant with the rest of your result set if the 0 has meaning or is used in a test.

The workaround for such issues is to use the `wasNull()` method to check whether the previous value in the result set was null. If it was, you can convert it to some other, meaningless value:

```
int numbers rs.getInt("nums");
if (rs.wasNull()) {
       // convert to safe value
    numbers = -123
}
```

12.1.5.2 HANDLING AUTO-GENERATED KEYS

In previous versions of JDBC, developers needed to execute a `SELECT` statement against the database if they needed to know the primary key they just generated after performing an insert. This is a common issue in ColdFusion applications: for example, you insert a new user into the `Users` table, then you need to get its newly generated primary key to make an appropriate insert into a `UsersRoles` join table. As of JDBC, Java developers do not have to return to the database for such an operation.

> **NOTE** Note that some of the JDBC 3.0 features discussed are optional and as such are implementation dependent. Your driver or your database may not support such features. I know it sounds awful, but you'll have to consult your specific documentation on such matters. (At least I won't suggest you "contact your network administrator" to get the answer!)

Here's how you do it; it's easy:

```
// insert new row, then specify column to be returned as key
int rowcount = executeUpdate("INSERT into Users (username)
        VALUES ('doodlehead'), "userID");

// now the userID for this user is available
ResultSet rs = stmt.getGeneratedKeys();
```

12.1.6 Close the Connection

Once you have performed the database operation, then you must close the connection to the database to save unnecessary consumption of resources. However, if you plan on hitting the database again, then it is best to wait until you are completely finished before calling this method. This is because every interaction with the database requires an open connection, and opening a connection is a very expensive operation. You close a connection like this:

```
connection.close()
```

If you do not release the resources consumed by your connection explicitly using `close()`, the system will eventually release them automatically. Closing the statement will always close the accompanying `ResultSet`. A `Statement`, however, may be reused, so explicitly closing the result set will help conserve resources.

You can write an explicit `disconnect()` method that you can call in your application to help this process. It would look something like this:

```
        // assume prior definition of Connection con
    public void disconnect() throws SQLException {
        try {
            if ( con != null )
            {
```

```
                //close connection
                con.close();
            }
        }
        catch (SQLException sqle) {
            error = ("SQLException: unable to close
                            connection");
            throw new SQLException(error);
        }
    } // end disconnect()
```

Now that you have the basic steps down, let's look at a complete example. Here we'll query the items listed in the fledgling WWWBooks bookstore database. So far, they have only a few Shakespeare plays. This listing will connect to a local Access database called `javaforcf` (which has an ODBC connection already established for it), create a statement to find all of the item names along with their IDs and prices, and display the results on the command line.

12.1.7 SelectTest.java

```
package chp12;

// a simple query to connect to
// an Access database with an ODBC
// connection established on the local
// system

import java.sql.*;

public class SelectTest {
   // no-arg constructor
public SelectTest() { }

public void queryDatabase() {

    Connection con = null;
    ResultSet rs = null;

try {
    // connect
    Class.forName("sun.jdbc.odbc.JdbcOdbcDriver");
    con = DriverManager.getConnection("jdbc:odbc:javaforcf");

    // a simple query
    String queryString = "SELECT * FROM items;";
```

```
    Statement stmt = con.createStatement();
    rs = stmt.executeQuery(queryString);

    System.out.println("ID  ItemName   Price");
    System.out.println("__  ________   _____");

  while(rs.next()) {

    System.out.print(rs.getInt("itemID") + "   ");
    System.out.print(rs.getString("itemname") + "\t");
    System.out.print(rs.getString("itemprice"));
    System.out.println();
  }


}
catch (ClassNotFoundException cnfe) {
     System.out.println("Class not found exception thrown:
       Could not locate DB driver");
}
catch (SQLException sqle) {
     System.out.println("SQL Exception: problem reported by
       DB" + sqle);
}
catch (Exception e) {
     System.out.println("An unknown error occurred while
       connecting to DB");
}
finally {
    try {
       if (rs != null) {
          // close the result set
          rs.close();
      }
       if (con != null) {
         // close connection always
         con.close();
       }
    }
    catch (SQLException sqle) {
       System.out.println("Unable to close DB connection");
    }
  }

} /// eoq
```

```
public static void main (String args[]) {

      SelectTest st = new SelectTest();
      st.queryDatabase();
    }

}//eof
```

The result looks something like this:

```
ID  ItemName   Price
__  ________   _____
1  King Lear    15.00
2  Measure for Measure  24.50
3  Hamlet       29.95
4  Twelfth Night        23.50
```

There is not a built-in, straightforward way to determine the number of rows returned by a result set. This is somewhat maddening for ColdFusion developers who find such an operation so easy (`#cfquery.recordcount#`). The best way to do this is to iterate through the result set to generate a count. You can set a variable and do a `var++` with each iteration of the result set, and then output this number if need be (such as how many items a search query found).

12.2 Metadata

The JDBC specification features a `ResultSetMetaData` object that can be used to get metadata regarding a result set.

The following code example from the API creates a result set and then creates a `ResultSetMetaData` object. It uses the `MetaData` object to determine how many columns are in the result set and whether the first column can be used in a `WHERE` clause.

```
ResultSet rs = stmt.executeQuery("SELECT a, b, c FROM
    TABLE2");
ResultSetMetaData rsmd = rs.getMetaData();
int numberOfColumns = rsmd.getColumnCount();
boolean b = rsmd.isSearchable(1);
```

To find out more about what methods are available to a `ResultSetMetaData` object, I encourage you to visit the `java.sql` package in the API and work with this class further.

12.3 Transactions

You may recall from ColdFusion working with the `<cftransaction>` tag, which allows you to create a logical group of statements to be sent to a database. They are meant to *all* be executed, and if one or more cannot be executed, any executed statements must be undone. That is, having specified a series of SQL statements as a transaction group, the entire group can be rolled back if necessary. They also allow you to undo an operation if an exception occurred during a database query. Transaction blocks are defined like this in ColdFusion:

```
<cftry>
<cftransaction action = "begin">
    <cfquery name = q" datasource = "#request.dsn#">
          INSERT INTO Products (productName, price)
          VALUES ('#form.productName#', 75);
     </cfquery>

<cfcatch type="DATABASE">
   <!--- roll back the insertion if an exception occurred--->
   <cftransaction action="rollback">
...
</cfcatch>
etc....
```

The way to create a transaction in Java's JDBC is to use the `Connection` object. Once the driver is started, the `Connection` object by default will automatically commit every change after execution of a statement. The way to turn this off when using commits or rollbacks is to invoke this method of the `Connection` object:

```
     // save this value
boolean saveCommitValue = con.getAutoCommit();
     // turn automatic committing off
con.setAutoComit(false);
```

The way to rollback to a prior state in the event of an exception is just as you might expect:

```
     // undo the partial update
con.rollback();
```

What may appear interesting to a ColdFusion developer here is that the `rollback()` method is tied to the `Connection` object.

NOTE The fact that everything that happens in Java must be tied to an object can be hard to get your mind around as a CF developer. It's okay—in fact, it will make your ColdFusion development much better. Really. There is a difficulty associated with having everything tied to objects, and that is that you must know what objects take what methods. The only solution to this stumbling block is to read the API. When you create objects in a Java IDE, type a dot after the object name and pause for a moment—the IDE should bring up a list of available methods for your current object. This is also a good way to get more familiar with the language. Just remember that in ColdFusion, the processing is done by a Web browser, and as such, is top to bottom. In Java (even in JSPs in an important way), processing is only top to bottom within the `main` methods. You've written enough `main` methods to know that this is hardly the point. Most of Java happens when objects create and use other objects in an asynchronous manner. Your `main` method is generally quite short and non-descript. But things may not appear out of the blue. This is a long-winded way of explaining that you can just write `<cftransaction>` in the middle of a page before a query in ColdFusion, but you must call a method on an object in Java to do that work. Now, once you start working with the JavaServer Pages Standard Tag Library, you'll be able to implement transactions in your JSPs, just as easily as you can in ColdFusion.

Using JDBC 2.0-compliant drivers, you must rollback or commit at some point. It is an all-or-nothing proposition. In Java using JDBC 3.0 you can define *savepoints* in your applications. Savepoints work somewhat like labels do; they allow you to specify a database state to which you may later like to return. Say you are writing an application that performs some inserts and then some updates. You may wish to break the application logic out in order to allow the inserts to occur, but not keep the updates. The following snippet demonstrates how a savepoint can be used to handle such an operation.

```
Statement stmt = con.createStatement();
int rowcount = stmt.executeUpdate("INSERT into Users (username,
privilege) VALUES ('Chico',1)");

     // savepoint allows us to return here and
     // undo only to this point
     // that way we don't lose the insert we just did
Savepoint sp = con.setSavePoint("sp1");

rowcount = stmt.executeUpdate("DELETE from Users");
```

```
        // this undoes the delete statement, not the insert
    con.rollback(sp1)

        // now it is permanent
    con.commit;
```

12.4 Stored Procedures

You are likely aware that one way to increase performance in your database-intensive applications is to offload as much work as you can to the database. Databases can perform many calculations, create aggregate values, sort, and perform very advanced kinds of queries. Even if you are only writing simple queries, it is probably not a bad idea to have your database doing more for you, and a good way to do that is to write stored procedures.

But perhaps the chief reason that stored procedures are popular among developers is that they allow you to group a number of SQL statements together, more accurately and efficiently representing a real business process (that is, procedure). Stored procedures run fast because they are kept on the database server, compiled into a native state.

There are two ways to work with stored procedures in Java. The first is easy: you simply call and execute your procedure using `executeUpdate()`. The alternative is to write the procedure following SQLJ conventions. The purpose of SQLJ is to define an industry standard for embedding SQL statements into Java methods and enhance the work possible using stored procedures. The advantage to using SQLJ is that your code is more portable, because you actually write a standalone Java application to hold your stored procedure. You write normal connection, statement, and execution code in this class, and then compile it into a `.jar` (Java Archive) file. You then place the `.jar` on the database server. Because a special syntax is required for these things, you should visit *www.sqlj.org* to find out more.

12.5 Example GUI Application: Database Query Viewer

In this section, we write an application with a graphical user interface that retrieves a result set from a database and displays the data in a resizable table. Users of `<cfgrid>` will find this application somewhat familiar. While this simple example does not allow the user to edit the cells of the query result set from within the grid, or re-sort the data by doubleclicking the column name headings, such functionality could be added with existing classes in the API.

> **NOTE** This example can be used with drivers other than Type I drivers. In order to use a query result set in this way with a Type I driver (such as the JDBC:ODBC bridge), you must manually cache the result set to scroll through the results. You can use this example as is with SQLServer, Sybase, MySQL, and so forth. Just download the required driver.

For the example to work, you must have the driver on your class path. Remember that if you are using IDEs such as IntelliJ or Forte, they have their own JDKs built in, and they might not be using the JDK you think they are to execute your programs. You can update these settings within each IDE, usually on a per-project basis.

This application defines a few text fields that allow the user to type in a host name, which is the string to be passed to the `Connection` object. The `driver` field accepts the fully qualified path to the driver you use to connect to this database. The `username` and `password` fields accept values that may be required to connect to this database. In the `query` field, type the SQL statement just as you would in your CF code. For instance: `SELECT * FROM Products`.

Once you have the required information entered, click the "Show Results" button. The application will hit the database and retrieve the records. It will then build a table to display the column names and values for each row in a grid.

The application is divided into a Model-View-Controller kind of architecture. This dictates that the data in an application must be separate entirely from the resulting view of that data. The MVC architecture has rarely been used in ColdFusion, because the broad tag-based language makes it easy to write low-level application code directly intertwined with the HTML showing the results. If you have worked with ColdFusion Components, these encourage a strong separation of the presentation and logical layers. In another way, if you have worked with the Fusebox architectural model for ColdFusion, you have these same goals in mind.

The files are commented to make it easy to follow along. I am grateful to my colleague Vic Miller for his contributions to this application.

12.5.1 DBMain.java

```
        /*
            File: DBMain.java
            Purpose: this simply starts the program
        */
public class DBMain {
```

```
    public static void main(String [] ar) {
            // instantiate a new controller object
        DBController controller = new DBController();
            // make the display
        controller.makeDefaultDisplay();
    }
}
```

The DBMain class simply holds the main() method to instantiate a new DBController object. Once you have a Controller object, you call the make-DefaultDisplay() method to show the GUI elements of the application so the user has something with which to interact.

12.5.2 DBController

```
/*
        File: DBController.java
        Purpose: route messages between the display DBDisplay,
        which shows the panels holding buttons and text fields,
        and the DBWorkHandler, which goes to the database and
        returns a result set for display
      */

import javax.swing.*;
import java.sql.*;

public class DBController {

        // declare variables
    private DBResultSetModel resultSetModel;
    private DBWorkHandler worker;
    private DBDisplay display;

        // constructor
    public DBController() {
            //Make a DBWorkHandler object
        worker = new DBWorkHandler();
    }

    public void makeDefaultDisplay() {
            /*
```

```
                *Make a new display and pass a copy of the
                  controller into display
                *so that the display object can send input to the
                  controller which will
                *react to that input
                */
           display = new DBDisplay(this);

               // tell the application to stop its process
               // when the window is closed
         display.setDefaultCloseOperation(JFrame.EXIT_ON_CLOSE);

               // show the display on the screen
           display.show();
       }
               // this method accepts the necessary params
               // to pass to the DBWorkHandler object. The
               // getQueryResults method in there will do the
               // heavy lifting
       public void getResults(String driverName,
                              String hostName,
                              String query,
                              String username,
                              String password) {
           ResultSet rs;

               //get the result set and build a model out of it
           rs = worker.getQueryResults(driverName, hostName,
                           query, username, password);
           resultSetModel = new DBResultSetModel(rs);

               //call the method in Display to show the model
           display.showModel(resultSetModel);
       }
   }
```

The above listing, `DBController`, routes messages where they are supposed to go in the application. The `makeDefaultDisplay()` method, which we call in the previous listing, instantiates a new object of type `DBDisplay`. This class is defined in the next listing. The only other main thing the application does is get a result set, so the controller passes that handler off as well.

12.5.3 DBDisplay.java

```
/*  File: DBDisplay.java
    Purpose: as this is a GUI application,
    this class shows all of the action as it happens.
    the text fields, button, and results table are
    organized for display. The window gets its title
    and dimensions set here. An ActionListener reacts
    to events that happen in the GUI (such as the button
    being pressed)

*/

import javax.swing.*;
import java.awt.*;
import java.awt.event.*;
import javax.swing.table.*;
import java.sql.*;

public class DBDisplay extends JFrame {

        /* add fields for username, password, or DB */
        // name elements ending with their type
    private JTextField hostField, driverField,
            queryField, usernameField;

        // this will put stars over the
    private JPasswordField passwordField;

        // button to send query to DB
    private JButton showResultsButton;

        // get a place to put things
    private Container contentPane;
    private JPanel tablePanel;

        // Hold a reference to the controller
    private DBController controller;

        /** Constructor */
    public DBDisplay(DBController control) {
            // Get the controller
        controller = control;
```

```
            // Set the title and the dimensions
        setTitle("Query Tool");
        setLocation(250, 150);

            // get the content pane
        contentPane = getContentPane();
            // add the panels to it
        contentPane.add(makeControlPanel(),
BorderLayout.NORTH);
            // let the panel determine how
            // to place items in the layout
        pack();
    }

         // create a holder for the various
         // panels that hold the text entry fields
    private JPanel makeControlPanel() {
        JPanel panel = new JPanel(new GridLayout(0,1));

             // add the little panels to the
             // control panel
        panel.add(makeHostPanel());
        panel.add(makeUserPassPanel());
        panel.add(makeQueryPanel());
        panel.add(makeButtonPanel());
        panel.setBorder
(BorderFactory.createTitledBorder("Query DATA"));

        return (panel);
    } //end of makeControlPanel

        // this panel will hold the host/database name
        // field and the name of the driver.
        // The driver must be on your classpath
    private JPanel makeHostPanel() {
        JPanel panel = new JPanel();
        panel.add(new JLabel("       Host:"));
            // the JTextField takes an int param
            // specifying number of columns
        hostField = new JTextField(15);
        panel.add(hostField);
        panel.add(new JLabel("    Driver Name:"));
        driverField = new JTextField(15);
        panel.add(driverField);
```

```
        return (panel);
    }
        // this panel holds text fields
        // for username and password
    private JPanel makeUserPassPanel() {
        JPanel panel = new JPanel();
        panel.add(new JLabel("    Username:"));
        usernameField = new JTextField(15);
        panel.add(usernameField);

        panel.add(new JLabel("    Password:"));
        passwordField = new JPasswordField(15);
        panel.add(passwordField);

        return (panel);
    }

        // place query panel in control panel
    private JPanel makeQueryPanel() {
        JPanel panel = new JPanel();
            // length 40
        queryField = new JTextField(40);

        panel.add(new JLabel("Query"));
        panel.add(queryField);
        return(panel);
    }

        // show results button
    private JPanel makeButtonPanel() {
        JPanel panel = new JPanel();
        showResultsButton = new JButton("Show Results");
            // add an actionlistener to the button
        DisplayActionHandler buttonListener = new
DisplayActionHandler();
        showResultsButton.addActionListener(buttonListener);
        panel.add(showResultsButton);
        return(panel);
    }

        // show warning for bad queries
    private JLabel makeErrorLabel() {
```

```
        JLabel label = new JLabel("no results or error",
JLabel.CENTER);
        label.setFont(new Font("Serif", Font.BOLD, 17));
        return (label);
    }

        // Show the table made from the query results
    public void showModel(DBResultSetModel resultSetModel) {
        JTable table = new JTable(resultSetModel);
        JScrollPane scrollPane = new JScrollPane(table);

        // add the scrollpane to the contentpane
        contentPane.add(scrollPane, "Center");

        pack();
    }

    // Action Listener Inner Class
    private class DisplayActionHandler implements
ActionListener {

        String username = "";
        String password = "";

        public void actionPerformed(ActionEvent actionEvent) {
                // test if the user has typed something
                // into the fields necessary for connecting to
                // the DB
          if(driverField.getText().length() != 0
                   && hostField.getText().length() != 0
                   && queryField.getText().length() != 0) {
            String driverName = driverField.getText();
            String hostName = hostField.getText();
            String query = queryField.getText();

         if (  usernameField.getText().length() != 0) {
            String username = usernameField.getText();
         }

         if (passwordField.getPassword().length != 0) {
            char[] passwordCA = passwordField.getPassword();
            String password = passwordCA.toString();
         }
```

```
                controller.getResults(driverName, hostName, query,
                        username, password);
            }
              // if user leaves any of the necessary fields blank
              // show an alert
            else {
                JOptionPane.showMessageDialog(null, "Please type
                        in some info dude, duh, I mean hello",
                        "Error Message",
                     JOptionPane.ERROR_MESSAGE);
            }
        }
    }
} // eof: DBDisplay.java
```

The job of `DBDisplay` (the listing above) is to create panels and text fields and a button, and handle the events that the user creates when interacting with the application. When a result set is required, the app calls the `WorkHandler`, whose job it is to connect to the database and get a result set. Figures 12.1 and 12.2 show the GUI so far.

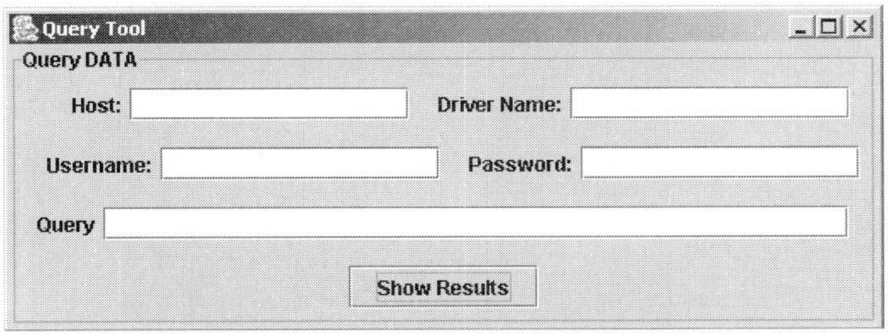

FIGURE 12.1 The initial view of the application on startup.

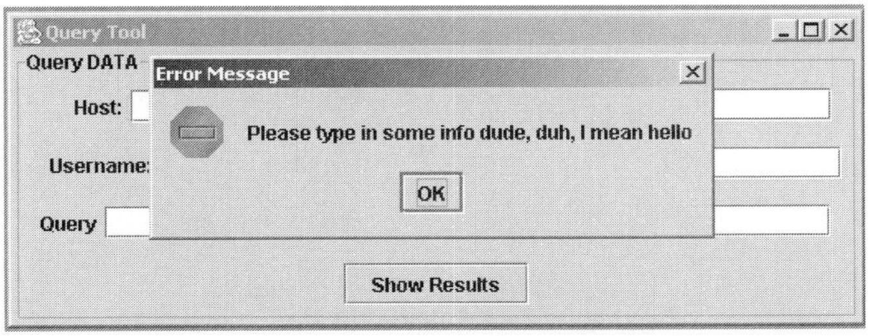

FIGURE 12.2 An error message is displayed when the user neglects to enter all required information.

12.5.4 DBWorkHandler.java

```
        /*
           File: DBController.java
           Purpose: route messages between the display DBDisplay,
           which shows the panels holding buttons and text
           fields,and the DBWorkHandler
        */

import java.sql.*;
import javax.swing.table.*;
import java.util.*;

public class DBWorkHandler {

    private Connection connection;
    private ResultSet rs;

        // no-arg constructor
    public DBWorkHandler() {

    }

    public ResultSet getQueryResults(String driverName,
                                     String hostName,
                                     String query,
                                     String username,
                                     String password)  {

        try {

            Class.forName(driverName);

            Connection con =
DriverManager.getConnection(hostName,
                        username, password);

                // create a statement
            Statement s;
            s = con.createStatement();
                // hit the database
            rs = s.executeQuery(query);
```

```
                // return the result set from the DB
            return (rs);
        }
        catch (ClassNotFoundException cnfe) {
            System.err.println("Error loading driver: " +
cnfe);
        }
        catch(SQLException sqle) {
            System.err.println("Connection error: " + sqle);
        }
                return (null);
    }

}
```

In DBWorkHandler.java, the database is hit, and exceptions are caught that relate to that operation. The DBController class hands off the result set to the DBResultSetModel class, which will handle the data for display and get it sent back up to the DBDisplay when it is ready.

12.5.5 DBResultSetModel.java

```
/*
  File: DBResultSetModel.java
  Purpose: get the results and metadata
*/
import java.sql.*;
import javax.swing.table.*;
import javax.swing.*;

public class DBResultSetModel extends AbstractTableModel{
        // vars
    private ResultSet rs;
    private ResultSetMetaData rsmd;

        // constructor
    public DBResultSetModel(ResultSet inrs) {
        //accept the result set
        rs = inrs;

            // make the result set metadata
            // from the result set
```

```
        try {
            rsmd = getResultSet().getMetaData();
        }
        catch(SQLException sqle) {
            System.out.println("Constructor SQL Error: " +
                    sqle);
        }
        catch(Exception e) {
            System.out.println("Constructor Error: " + e);
        }

        // we have to override these methods
    }
    public int getColumnCount() {
        try {
            return rsmd.getColumnCount();
        }
        catch(SQLException sqle) {
            System.out.println("getColumnCount SQL Error: " +
                    sqle);
            return 0;
        }
        catch(Exception e) {
            System.out.println("getColumnCount Error: " + e);
            return 0;
        }
    }

    public String getColumnName(int columnNum) {
        try {
         return rsmd.getColumnName(columnNum + 1);
        }
        catch(SQLException sqle) {
            System.out.println("getColumnName SQL Error: " +
                  sqle);
            return "";
        }
        catch(Exception e) {
            System.out.println("getColumnName Error: " + e);
            return "";
        }
    }

    public int getRowCount() {
```

```
        try {
            ResultSet temprs = getResultSet();
            temprs.last();
            return temprs.getRow();
        }
        catch(SQLException sqle) {
            System.out.println("getRowCount SQL Error: " +
               sqle);
            return 0;
        }
        catch(Exception e) {
            System.out.println("getRowCount Error: " + e);
            return 0;
        }
    }

    public Object getValueAt(int rowNum, int columnNum) {
        try {
            ResultSet temprs = getResultSet();
            rs.absolute(rowNum + 1);
            return rs.getObject(columnNum + 1);
        }
        catch(SQLException sqle) {
            System.out.println("getValueAt SQL Error: " +
               sqle);
            return null;
        }
    }

    public ResultSet getResultSet() {
        return rs;
    }
} // end of app
```

Figure 12.3 shows the results of a query in our application.

Again, this application works with GUI programming constructs that we have not covered. In the event that you are interested in this kind of development, this example gives you an idea of what is required to create such interfaces. You can run this example locally, with no Internet connection, because it is a standalone executable program. You can use this example to create text

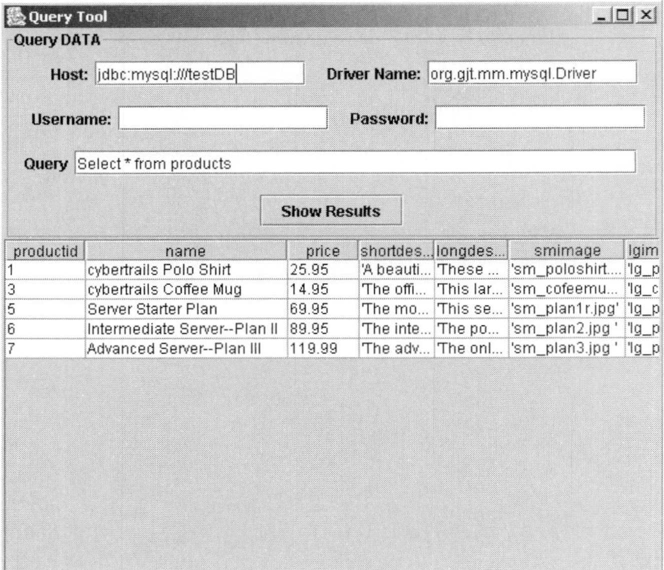

FIGURE 12.3 The application with a query result set in the display.

fields and buttons to enhance and extend your work with applets. Finally, this is a fun tool that can even be useful in development, or can be extended to create a front end to command line database systems or text files that you may be working with as you develop.

12.6 What's Next

Now that you know how to work with databases, we will make the jump into writing Java-based Web applications for the remainder of the book. There are only a few tags native to JavaServer Pages, and, drawing on your knowledge of ColdFusion, we should be up and running quickly.

13

Servlets and CFMX/ J2EE Integration

This chapter introduces Java on the server. We have seen already in Chapter 10 how to integrate ColdFusion and Java with CFX custom tags, applets, and so forth. That chapter, however, had its distinct focus on ColdFusion elements. Moreover, much of the functionality covered in that chapter was possible already with ColdFusion 5.

This chapter puts the focus squarely on Java. After comparing ColdFusion and Java server-side technology, we will cover everything you need to set up a Java Web site, including setting up a servlet container and database server. We will also cover servlets and how to use new CFML functions and capabilities to integrate variables and functionality between your JavaServer Pages (covered in the next chapter) and ColdFusion MX templates.

We will also put together a complete servlet application that interacts with a JSP to password-protect pages.

Note that this chapter cannot offer complete coverage of servlets. This is a very big subject, and we will rely somewhat on the Java knowledge we've gained throughout the book to start putting servlets to work. JSPs will be covered in greater detail in this chapter.

13.1 Using Java Technology to Create Web Sites

The ability to execute Java code from within ColdFusion is not new to ColdFusion MX. Previously, this functionality was available to developers using the `<cfobject>` or `<cfapplet>` tags, and via CFX tags. Use of these technologies to bring Java functionality into ColdFusion has been accepted and popular for years. However, there are times when the requirements of your project demand that a Java Web technology be used. Perhaps your client has existing systems written in Java or prefers to use open source, freely available technology. In these cases, using Java technology to create your dynamic sites may be the best solution.

Java provides a number of ways that you can create dynamic functionality within Web pages. JavaServer Pages (JSP) and servlets are increasingly popular ways of doing this. JSP and servlets are capable of performing everything that ColdFusion is capable of and more. Because the entire Java programming language is available to the developer, very sophisticated Web applications can be built using these technologies. JSP and servlets allow the developer to interact with HTML, relational databases, JavaBeans, and Java code to create dynamic Web pages. Here we will overview servlets and JSP in turn.

13.1.1 Overview of Servlets

Servlets, in version 2.3 as of this writing, were introduced by Sun to extend the power of the Web server. Much of the initial excitement surrounding Java was due to the fact that small applications (applets) could be downloaded and executed securely on the client. (Note that there is no theoretical limit on the size of the program executable as an applet). Applets were secure because they were executed inside the Java Virtual Machine and had no potentially dangerous access to the underlying operating system. The popularity of applets began to suffer, however, as they eventually succumbed to the browser wars between Microsoft and Netscape. If you have experienced difficulty in ColdFusion 5 using `CFGRID`, `CFTREE`, or `CFSLIDER`, you can understand how applets began to reveal certain limitations. The applet plugins for different browsers were incompatible, which undermined one of the fundamental propositions of Java—that programs are platform-independent. Moreover, the trend in Web development was decidedly toward server-side functionality. ColdFusion, Perl, and ASP had been working in this arena for years with great success. So Sun introduced the *servlet*.

An applet is a small application. Servlets, then, act as small servers. A servlet is a Java program that is executed on the server when the Web server receives a request mapped to that servlet. Like applets, servlets are essentially regular Java classes. The primary differences are that servlets require a Web server environment in which to run, and they extend `javax.servlet` and `javax.servlet.http`. The `javax.servlet` package contains all of the classes and interfaces that are used by servlets. The `javax.servlet.http` package contains all of the interfaces required to create HTTP-specific servlets.

Servlets are part of the Java 2 Enterprise Edition and must be downloaded separately to be used with the Standard Edition.

13.1.2 Overview of JSP

JavaServer Pages, in version 1.2 as of this writing, were introduced by Sun in 1999. JSP is a tag-based language with an XML syntax. There are nine JSP tags, as compared with 85 in ColdFusion. This attests nothing, however, to the scope of the language or how long it might take to become comfortable with JSP. This is for a variety of reasons. First, JSP serves as a high-level abstraction of servlets. Writing a JSP is somewhat like writing a ColdFusion template, in that you write tags that call certain functional units and return a result or forward to another page. The JSP engine is a servlet that is mapped to the `*.jsp` extension. When a `.jsp` page is called in a browser, that page is translated into a servlet, which is saved into a temporary directory; at that point the servlet is processed.

There is little one can do using the few standard JSP tags alone. In order to leverage the full power of JSP, one generally writes JavaBeans and implements custom tags (which in JSP are called Custom Actions). A JavaBean is rather like a ColdFusion Component. It is a regular Java class that defines getter and setter methods—for instance, `setPrice()` and `getPrice()`—for the object in its domain. The Bean is then invoked from the JSP to do the heavy lifting. The purpose of this kind of architecture is to maintain a strict separation between a Web site's logic and its presentation layers.

The remainder of this chapter will be devoted to comparing these technologies with those of ColdFusion, installing and configuring a servlet container, and introducing standard JSP.

13.2 Compare ColdFusion and Java Web Technologies

There are many advantages to using ColdFusion over Java Web technologies. Increasingly, however, the current trend in Web development is toward Web services; that is, the ability to interact with data objects on remote hosts. (This is now very easy to do in CFMX and is getting to be easier to do with Java.) It is useful, therefore, to compare ColdFusion and JSP and servlets to determine when and how to use them.

> **Note** We will not cover specific details of writing servlets here. You can do everything on the server with a JSP that you would want to do in a servlet, and since the introduction of the JSP Standard Tag Library and the proliferation of other tag libraries, it is much faster to work with JSPs.

First, let's recall the advantages to using ColdFusion for dynamic Web development.

a. Because ColdFusion is tag-based, it is easy to learn. It is instantly familiar to developers who know only HTML. The tags hide much of the complexity of sophisticated Web transactions, such as querying a database. Setting up the environment consists largely of clicking Next.
b. ColdFusion is fast to develop. Because ColdFusion is easy to use, you can create rather sophisticated Web applications quickly. Fast turnaround times are often crucial for Web projects, and this makes ColdFusion attractive. ColdFusion was intended from the beginning to be used exclusively for Web applications. Java is a full-blown programming language like C++; it consequently inherits all of that time-consuming, error-prone baggage, and it frankly can take a good deal of labor to produce a very modest result with Java Web technologies until you get the hang of it.
c. ColdFusion has many built-in features. What you pay for when you buy ColdFusion is largely the prefabricated tag libraries, the extended technologies such as Crystal Reports and Verity interaction, and the Web-based ColdFusion Administrator. Features such as query-of-queries and probes can make our work in ColdFusion a simple matter of assembly. This allows you to focus on the client or the problem space, instead of putting together the pieces. As clients repeatedly tend to ask for very similiar kinds of functionality, this is a real benefit.
d. ColdFusion has a high level of abstraction. JSP has a high level of abstraction too, but only for a *very* small subset of functionality. JSPs are intended in many cases to call JavaBeans or custom actions to handle the

low-level functionality. The Beans have to be written, and that requires knowing everything that we have discussed throughout this book.

e. ColdFusion is more mature. It has been revised multiple times in the seven years since it was introduced and is in many ways a refined product. Of course, the total re-architecting of CFMX must modify that statement somewhat. JSP, on the other hand, is very young, which makes its place in the market uncertain.

The above advantages to using ColdFusion are significant. However, there are many reasons to choose JSP or servlets over ColdFusion.

a. JSP and servlets are powerful. Because the complete Java language is available to you as you write JSP and servlets, there is a thinner line between applications and Web applications. This tendency in JSP and servlets will allow developers to extend the functionality of their applications as far as they need to, without having to call on another language to perform the difficult work. While one can write extensions to ColdFusion using Java, JSPs have all of that functionality natively and don't require the developer to move into potentially uncharted waters and incorporate another technology.
b. Java offers greater performance under certain conditions. This was first demonstrated publicly at the 2000 Dev Con when a JRun engineer called a framed HTML page that showed a Java-based page and a ColdFusion page in a race to calculate prime numbers. Here an interesting distinction must be made. The ColdFusion 5 page performed faster initially in that comparison, but as the calculation wore on, the Java page sped ahead. Calculating thousands of prime numbers is a fairly resource-intensive task, and Java was better able to handle the complexity. However, certain tests since the release of CFMX show that pages with many complex ColdFusion operations may have performed faster under ColdFusion 5.
c. Java is open. ColdFusion is controlled entirely by Macromedia, while many companies and individuals contribute directly to Java. For instance, IBM developed the entire `Calendar` class added to the language in version 1.1. Numerous companies and organizations from IBM to Apache create drivers, packages, tag libraries, even their Java parsers. That means that the language progresses in a very different manner than does ColdFusion. In 1998, Sun established the Java Community Process, an open forum consisting of more than 300 organizations and developers from across the world. Its sole purpose is to evolve the Java platform. This ensures that Java is driven by those in the computer industry and not a corporation with a strong profit motive. Unlike ColdFusion, all of

Java source code is freely available under the Sun Community Source License. You can read about this process at *http://jcp.org/*.

d. Java is platform independent. When you purchase a ColdFusion license, you do not have easy portability between platforms; your license is platform specific. You may have to rewrite some code. As platform independence is one of the key missions of Java, this is less of a concern. That means more freedom for the developer.
e. Java is popular. Even people who are not in the IT industry (who may be many of your clients) have heard of Java. This can make your clients feel comfortable; it builds confidence in their investment. This is perhaps even more important with respect to the development community. With nearly 60% of developers using Java in some way, there is a good deal of support, code, tutorials, lists, and Web sites to help encourage Java development. Java has a very good name in the developer community and has been integrated into some of the most robust systems in the IT industry.
f. Java is scalable. The same program runs on a Solaris 64-bit processor or an Intel x86 machine. Your applications can improve to handle more complex data for greater performance among even the fastest systems.
g. Java supports a tremendous range of devices. With ColdFusion, you are generally either writing Web sites to be viewed on a Web browser or using the `<cfcontent>` tag to display dynamic cards on Web-enabled cellphones. Java comes in three editions (J2EE, J2SE, and J2ME) that allow your work to communicate across an unprecedented number of devices. Java applications are available to not only Web browsers, but watches, toasters, the Sony PlayStation, ATMs, Smart Cards, car consoles, and more. As the Internet reaches into these areas, and it quickly is, gaining a firm foundation in the Java platform now will put your work at the forefront.

13.2.1 The End of the Web Site

This last point above may seem somewhat trivial—that Java supports a number of different devices. After all, if we're ColdFusion developers, we're necessarily making Web sites. Now, we might extend our site to be viewable on a wireless device such as a mobile phone, but even after the years this technology has been available, it is still somewhat slow to catch on among Web clients. We are seeing some corporations spending money to make wireless-capable sites, but few garden-variety Web clients have shown interest in this technology. The market isn't quite there yet.

That hides a more interesting point, however. This market may never quite surface. That may be because the Web site is coming to an end, after only 11 years.

In its place will be a more complete automation of tasks and information flow between devices of all types—phones, cars, home security systems, cash registers, appliances, gasoline pumps, watches, video games, lawn maintenance devices, and so forth. Connecting the information made available from these sources will demand a somewhat changed model. The Java programming language is currently in use to provide functionality for all of these systems. Sun's assertion that "the network is the computer" is quickly finding new meaning. Java is a language that can natively harvest, route, process, and display information from all of these devices. Java brings us closer to this kind of ability to mine data for rich views and create truly complete experiences for users. This kind of experience will, in my view, begin replacing the traditional Web site. Of course, I could be wrong.

My aim here is not to convince you of server-side Java's merits and charms. My aim is to provide a high-level overview of comparing these rather different technologies. This is useful so that we can look in some detail at how to get started using JSP.

13.3 ColdFusion MX J2EE Capabilities

To complete the comparison of ColdFusion and J2EE (Java 2, Enterprise Edition), let's first clear up some misconceptions about this integration and what it affords the ColdFusion developer:

- The same ColdFusion application can include a mix of ColdFusion templates, servlets, and JSPs.
- ColdFusion pages can *include* servlets and JSPs.
- ColdFusion pages can *forward* control to servlets and JSPs.
- Pages written in CFML or JSP can share data in persistent scopes such as session and application.
- ColdFusion pages can import a tag library written in JSP and use the tags in it. We will see how to do this shortly.
- You *cannot* write Java programming language code directly in a ColdFusion template.
- ColdFusion MX templates are *not* JSPs.
- ColdFusion MX does *not* Java use types for variables.

In Chapter 10 we saw how to integrate ColdFusion with Java technology using CFX tags and Java applets. We will now look at how to write a JavaServer Pages tag library and use it in your JSP and ColdFusion applications. But first we need to figure out JSP. Along the way, we will also look at how to perform the include, forward, and referencing capabilities mentioned above.

13.4 Java Web Servers

Once upon a time there was a software program known as the Java Web Server. This Web server was used to create dynamic funtionality on the fly for Web clients. It has been discontinued, as Sun has favored developing the IPlanet Web Server. (Note that ColdFusion MX runs on IPlanet.)

There are a number of popular Java Web application servers in use today. These include, but are not limited to, the following:

- **Apache Jakarta Tomcat 4.** The reference implementation was written in Java by the organization responsible for Apache Web Server. It is free and open source.
- **Macromedia JRun 4.** The Enterprise and Professional versions of this container have been collapsed for version 4. JRun is a popular, affordable solution with easy administration and a very useful tag library included. JRun is also underneath ColdFusion MX, running the show.
- **New Atlanta Servlet Exec.** A limited-functionality version is available for free at *http://newatlanta.com*.
- **Gefion Lite WebServer.** A compact, free Web server derived from Tomcat, available at *http://www.gefionsoftware.com*.
- **JBoss 3.** Available from *jboss.org*, this server acts as an Enterprise JavaBeans (EJB) container.

> **NOTE** ColdFusion MX Enterprise version now acts as a JSP and servlet container. That means that you can write a JSP, place it under CFMX's `wwwroot`, and it will be processed correctly. This can be a good way to test your JSPs in a familiar environment.

Sun's Java Web Server used to be a moderately used servlet container. It is no longer under development, however, and is not available for download. You may see reference to it in other sources, however, so it is mentioned here. We will use Tomcat for many of our examples, but the pages we'll write should work the same on any container.

13.4.1 Apache Jakarta Tomcat 4

The Apache Software Foundation makes the most popular Web server in the world. It also maintains the reference implementation for JSP and servlets via an agreement with Sun Microsystems. One of Apache's projects is called Jakarta, and its job is to create Java-related work. Apache's flagship product originated as an early implementation of the Java Servlet API called JServ. It is now known as Tomcat, a JSP and servlet container.

Tomcat is itself written in Java and is a free download. You can use Tomcat under the Apache license and even contribute to its development. You may sometimes come across the term Jasper; Jasper is simply a specific name for the JSP processing element of Tomcat.

Like ColdFusion MX, Tomcat has its own HTTP server built in. So you can download it and start testing JSPs immediately without needing to connect to an external server. This makes it easy to use in development. However, Tomcat integrates well with both Apache and IIS, and can be run simultaneously with other Java servers (such as JRun) without issue.

13.5 Installing Tomcat

Installing Tomcat is getting easier all the time. The current version (4.1.3 Alpha) makes it even easier than it was when I began writing this book.

There are different versions of the Tomcat software available at any given time. These likely include beta releases and a version called FCS. FCS stands for "First Customer Shipment," and indicates that the software has passed beta stage and is ready for a production environment.

It is probably best to stick with a production-quality release. Apache makes it clear on its Web site at *http://jakarta.apache.org* what the current production-quality release is.

To download Tomcat, go to the Apache Web site. Follow the links to the binary downloads section. For a Windows system, choose the most recent `jakarta-tomact-4.x.xx` file. You can optionally get the *src* version that has everything in the compiled version, along with all source code, written in Java. You will have to compile this version yourself, however.

Included in the download is the servlet API, which contains the official reference implementation of the servlet and JSP API.

Once you have downloaded the files, you need to unpack them. Create a folder on the top level of your disk called `tomcat4` and unpack the files there. You can use the following commands to unpack your files:

```
cd tomcat4
jar -xf jakarta-tomcat-4.0.4.zip
```

> **NOTE** The Java JAR utility and the WinZip utility use the same algorithm for compressing file collections. You can therefore use them interchangeably to unpack your downloads. To find out how to pack and unpack files using the JAR utility, please see the Quick Reference appendix of this book. That reference shows you how to do common tasks such as this in an easy-to-look-up manner.

Now that Tomcat is downloaded and unpacked, there are a few steps to perform to configure Tomcat to listen for JSP and servlet requests.

JSP and servlet servers are different from ColdFusion servers. They need to be configured more than ColdFusion servers do; there is comparatively less about the process that is automatic. The process has improved a great deal and is now much easier than it used to be. With previous versions of Tomcat it was common to have to edit the Windows registry directly, manually install ISAPI filters into your Web server to run it as a service, and so on. Setting up a new Web application required manually editing XML files. Things are far more streamlined now with Tomcat 4.

> **NOTE** Tomcat 4.1.3, in alpha version as of this writing, includes a Web-based administration console similar to the ColdFusion Administrator. This allows you to create new Web applications for deployment, edit JDBC settings, add users for authentication, and more.

Once you have downloaded Tomcat, simply follow the instructions in the wizard in the installer application. Tomcat 4.1 (normal installation) consumes about 28 MB of hard disk space. The installer should detect your JDK 1.4 and notify you. Agree to the license.

Then choose the type of install you want. The normal installation includes the following items:

- Tomcat
- JSP development shell extensions
- Tomcat Start Menu group
- Tomcat docs
- Example Web apps

To complete your installation, you *may* need to set two environment variables, depending on your system and your version of Tomcat. Tomcat 4 on Windows XP does not require this, but Tomcat 3.2 does. Otherwise, you can go on to the next section, "Testing the Tomcat Installation."

The variables are JAVA_HOME, which indicates the root directory of the JDK, and TOMCAT_HOME, which is the root directory of your Tomcat installation. (You should have JAVA_HOME set already.)

13.5.0.1 SETTING ENVIRONMENT VARIABLES ON WINDOWS 2000

Environment variables are name-value pairs that are used to configure your system environment and provide pointers to different resources on your computer. Programs that run on the Windows platform often install such variables automatically. Here we need to do this manually.

1. Select Start > Settings > Control Panel > System.
2. Choose the Advanced tab.
3. Click Environment Variables.
4. In the lower pane (System Variables), a number of Variable/Value pairs will likely be visible. Click New.
5. In the dialog box that appears, you will see two fields: Variable Name and Variable Value. Type JAVA_HOME for the Variable Name. For the Variable Value, type the name of the root directory of your JDK. For instance, my value for this is C:\jdk1.4. Click OK.
6. Now perform the same steps to create a TOMCAT_HOME variable. Click New. For the Variable Name type TOMCAT_HOME. For the Variable Value type the location of the Tomcat directory. For instance, my value for this is C:\tomcat4.

13.5.0.2 SETTING ENVIRONMENT VARIABLES ON LINUX

Preparing the environment variables setting on Linux is rather similiar. Assuming you have already installed the JDK, you need to set the JAVA_HOME environment variable. For instance, in the bash shell, use the following command:

```
JAVA_HOME=/user/java/jdk/jdk1.4; export JAVA_HOME
```

You may need to replace java/jdk/jdk1.4 above with the location of your JDK install.

Next, enter the variable TOMCAT_HOME and its value. The value of this variable is the root directory of your Tomcat installation. In the bash shell, type:

```
TOMCAT_HOME=/var/tomcat; export TOMCAT_HOME
```

You may need to replace var/tomcat above with the location of your Tomcat install.

Tomcat should now be installed properly. To test your installation, go to the next section.

13.5.1 Testing the Tomcat Installation

Once your installation is complete, you need to start the service (if you installed it as a Windows NT/2000/XP service), or manually start Tomcat.

On Windows, you can start and stop Tomcat by clicking the appropriate icon on your Start menu.

On Linux, you can start and stop Tomcat by executing <TOMCAT_HOME>/bin/startup.sh or shutdown.sh.

By default, Tomcat listens for requests on port 8080. Therefore, open your Web browser to http://localhost:8080. If everything went correctly, you should see the Jakarta project start page for Tomcat, as shown in Figure 13.1.

> **NOTE** ColdFusion MX and Tomcat run on different ports and have their own internal servers; you can run them both on the same machine at the same time without problems.

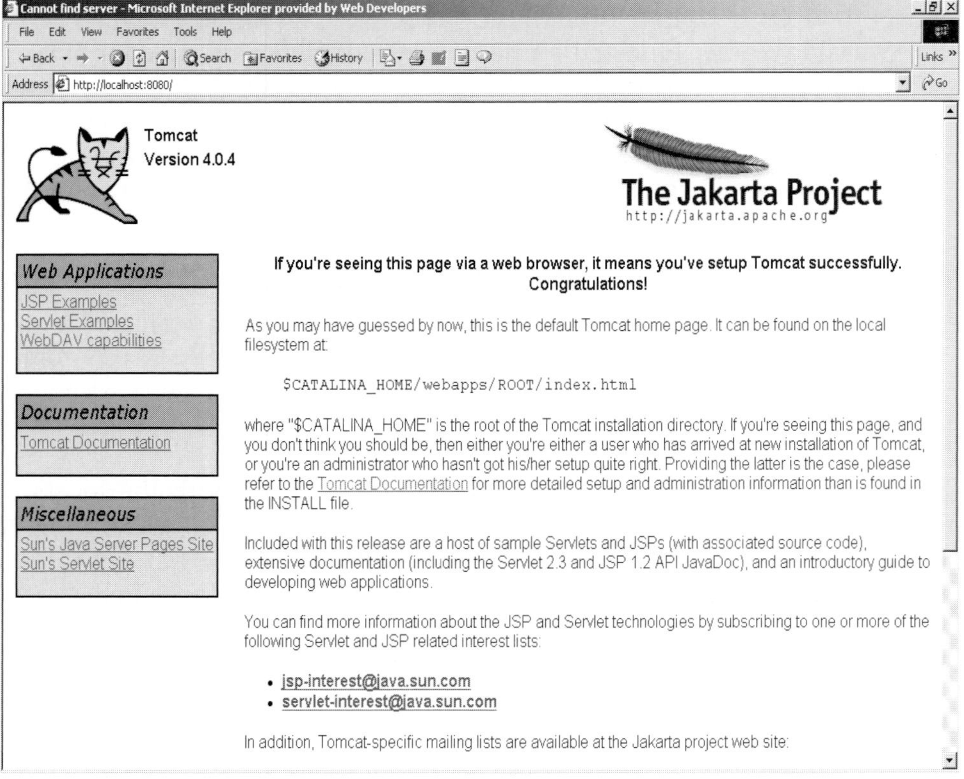

FIGURE 13.1 Tomcat home start page.

The Tomcat home page is an HTML page, however. So the fact that you can view this page does not necessarily mean that your machine is processing JSPs properly.

To make sure that you can process `.jsp` requests, execute at least one of the sample applications included with Tomcat. To test one, click the JSP Examples link under the Web Applications menu on the Tomcat start page. For example, you might click on the Date example. This will run a page that displays the current date.

You can also view the JSP source code that generates the HTML output by clicking the Source link next to the example. Because the source is included as plain text, your browser will probably attempt to display as much of the page as it can. You therefore need to use your browser's View Source function to see the JSP code.

13.5.2 Troubleshooting the Tomcat Installation

The installation process has been greatly simplified, and you are not likely to run into any snags. If you do, however, here is what you can do about them.

13.5.2.1 INVALID PORT

The most common issue occurs when another process is already using the default Tomcat port, port 8080. When Tomcat starts up, it attempts to bind to this port, and if it can't do it, Tomcat will not run.

The easiest solution to this problem is to change the port on which Tomcat runs. To do this, open the file `<TOMCAT_HOME>/conf/server.xml` and search for the string 8080. Change this to any other port that isn't in use and is greater than 1024. That's because those ports require superuser access for binding and because a number of these ports are likely to be used by other processes already (80 for HTTP, 25 for mail, 23 for FTP, etc). Note too that, depending on what else you have installed on your machine, ports 8100 and 51000 are used by JRun, and 8500 by ColdFusion MX.

In order to test JSPs now, you will need to refer to the new port number in the URL you are processing.

13.5.2.2 OUT OF ENVIRONMENT SPACE

On rare occasion, an "out of environment space" error can occur when running the batch files in Windows 9X and ME operating systems. It simply means that you need to allocate more space for the server to use.

To correct this, right-click on the STARTUP.BAT and SHUTDOWN.BAT files. Click on Properties then on the Memory tab. For the "Initial Environment" field, enter a value; 4096 should suffice.

13.5.3 Testing a JSP from ColdFusion

If you have an Enterprise or Developer version of ColdFusion MX installed, you can use it as a servlet/JSP container. Before we discuss JSPs in detail, let's write a quick JSP to demonstrate how you can use ColdFusion MX for testing.

Open a text editor, Dreamweaver MX, Sun's Forte 4, or other editor. Enter the following code:

13.5.4 `Test.jsp`

```
<%-- File: hello.jsp
    Purpose: write a test JSP.
    Sets a String variable
    and outputs it to the browser. Uses
    comments, scriptlet, and an expression.
--%>

<% String n = "Eben"; %>

<html>
<body>
Hello, <%= n %>!
</body>
</html>
```

Save this file to `<CFusionMX_HOME>\wwwroot\chp13\test.jsp`, and make sure that your ColdFusion service is started. To view this page in your browser, you can call *http://localhost:8500/chp13/test.jsp*. The output is:

```
Hello, Eben!
```

Before we move on to discussing the JSP tags, directives, and expressions, we will look at how to set up a Web application for Tomcat.

> **NOTE** Don't close the shell window that pops up when you start Tomcat. This window must be open for as long as you want to run Tomcat applications. Also, when you are done with Tomcat, you should not simply close this window. Navigate to the appropriate icon, `.bat`, or `.sh` file and run shutdown to exit normally. Failure to do so can corrupt your Tomcat installation.

13.6 Configuring JSP Web Applications

In ColdFusion development, when we talk about our applications, we generally mean the sites we're making. The application often consists of a number of `.cfm` templates, and may include other resources such as XML files, Verity collections, and so forth. You have the freedom to quickly crack out a single `.cfm` page and test it. You do not need to configure any special Web application to run it.

While you can do that in JSPs that you view in ColdFusion MX, in other containers you need to set up a Web application for each site you make. In this regard, it is similar to how you might make a project in an IDE. In Tomcat, you can do this manually or do it via the new Tomcat Administration Application, which is similiar to the ColdFusion Administrator.

13.6.1 The Tomcat Administration Application

The Administration tool is a Web application written in JSP that allows you to configure different settings regarding your Web applications. It also makes it very easy to create new Web applications. In this section we will walk through creating a new Web application that we can put JSPs into for testing.

There are a couple of steps required to configure a new Tomcat JSP application with the Administrator:

1. Create a new context
2. Create a physical directory
3. Create a `web.xml` file and other useful directories

We will walk through these steps now. To begin, open the Tomcat Administrator (shown in Figure 13.2).

1. In the Admin area, choose Service > Host.
2. To create a new Web application, you make a new context. To do this, click the Host (localhost) link. This will create the new context on the localhost server.

> **NOTE** Many Java Web application containers allow you to create multiple "servers"—a somewhat confusing bit of terminology that simply means a discrete instance of the container that can maintain its own settings.

3. You must fill out four key items on the Context Addition screen to create the app:
   - **Doc Base:** `javaforcf`. This is the name of the physical directory that serves as the root of this application.

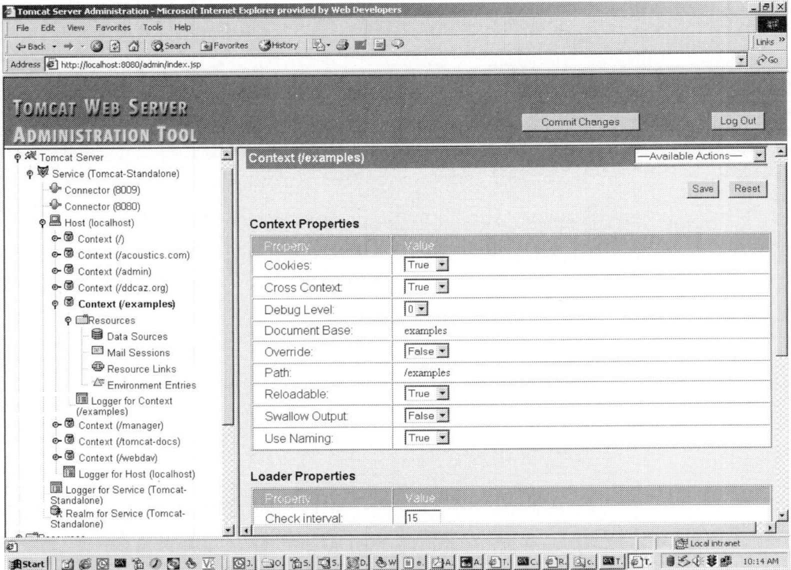

FIGURE 13.2 Tomcat Web Administration tool.

- **Path:** `/javaforcf`. This is the name of the path that will be called in the browser to reference this Web application. So, to call documents in our test directory, we type this address: *http://localhost:8080/javaforcf/filename.jsp*. Note that JSP file names are case sensitive, because Java is.
- **Working Directory:** `work\Standalone\localhost\javaforcf`. This is the path name of the temporary directory that will store the Java class files that are generated by the servlets that are generated by your JSPs. This is the code that will be created the first time a JSP is accessed, and then the classes will be executed after that.
- **SessionID Initializer:** `org.apache.catalina.session.StandardManager`. This is the fully qualified name of the Java class the container will use to initialize sessions.

Once you have entered these values, click Save and Commit Changes. Your context will be created. We now need to create the physical directory we referenced in creating this Web application.

13.6.2 Create the Web Application Directory

This is the directory that will hold all of our files for this Web application. Just like ColdFusion and IIS use `wwwroot` as the home base for the files they serve, Tomcat has a home base too. This is the `Webapps` directory, located under your `<TOMCAT_HOME>` root. In this folder, create a folder called `javaforcf` (since that is the name Tomcat will look for, as it corresponds with what we entered in the Administrator application).

There is a particular directory structure that Tomcat requires to hold the components of a Web application. Generally, the first step in creating an application is to create this directory structure. You create this directory structure in the Tomcat `webapps` directory; see Table 13.1 to see what it looks like.

TABLE 13.1 Tomcat Directory Structure

DIRECTORY	PURPOSE
`/javaforcf`	This is the root directory of the application. All JSP and HTML files should be in this directory. Create subdirectories as you see fit to organize your site; that is, you probably put graphics in a folder called "images" or style sheets in a folder called "styles."
`/javaforcf/WEB-INF`	Contains the Web Deployment Descriptor, an XML file that contains information about the different resources that make up the application, where they can be found, and how they are structured. This directory often contains Java classes and `.jar` files, as nothing in this directory or any subdirectory can be accessed directly by a client.
`/javaforcf/WEB-INF/classes`	Servlets and utility classes go here.
`/javaforcf/WEB-INF/lib`	Contains `.jar` files that the Web application requires. For example, you would put a JDBC driver, a custom tag library, an XSL transformer, or other extensions, here.

13.6.2.1 `WEB-INF`

Next, you need to create another folder to hold the Java classes you write and use in this application. Tomcat expects this folder to be called `WEB-INF`. Developers will often create folders underneath this folder that contain the packages with any Java classes they might use under this directory. That's because this directory is *not accessible* directly from the Web. That protects your classes and other resources from errant viewing by site visitors.

13.6.2.2 `web.xml`

Next, you need to create the application's deployment descriptor. This file, called `web.xml`, describes information regarding the configuration of the application. It can contain the following elements:

- Servlet definitions
- Servlet initialization parameters
- Session configuration parameters
- Servlet/JSP mappings
- MIME type mappings
- Security configuration parameters
- An ordered list of welcome files
- A list of error pages
- Variable definitions regarding tag libraries and other resources, and environment variables

We will see how to use many of these elements in `web.xml`. Even if your application uses no servlets, tag libraries, or other resources, you still must create one.

The most minimal `web.xml` file looks like this:

```
<?xml version="1.0" encoding="ISO-8859-1"?>

<!DOCTYPE web-app
    PUBLIC "-//Sun Microsystems, Inc.//DTD Web Application
      2.3//EN"
    "http://java.sun.com/dtd/web-app_2_3.dtd">
<web-app>
</web-app>
```

We can use this for now until we start adding elements, which we'll do along the way. There are a couple of things to be aware of regarding deployment at this point:

- You do not need to do anything special once you have created a `.jsp` file to use in your application. Simply place it in the application and call it in a browser. This is contrary to the behavior of servlets, each of which must be explicitly accounted for in the deployment descriptor.
- You can modify a JSP and reload it in the browser without having to restart the server. This is similar to ColdFusion.
- Be careful to get the syntax absolutely correct in the `web.xml` file. Minor textual errors in this file can prevent Tomcat from starting. An easy way to make sure that your XML file is well-formed is to open it in Internet

Explorer. Its built-in style sheet will display the page using its internal style sheet if everything is syntactically valid. If there is an error, the browser will notify you of it.

- If you modify web.xml, you must restart Tomcat for changes to take effect. This is different from JRun 4, which now has "hot deployment."

To test our new Java Web application, we need to put a JSP into it. Take the test.jsp file that we called from ColdFusion MX earlier and place it into the <TOMCAT_HOME>/webapps/javaforcf directory. Open a browser and type *http://localhost:8080/javaforcf/test.jsp*. You should see:

```
Hello, Eben!
```

If you get a 404 message, it generally means one of two things: you may have clicked the Save button, but not the Commit Changes button, when creating the application. Or, you may not have restarted Tomcat. These both mean that Tomcat does not know about your application.

13.7 Creating a Tomcat Web Application Manually

All of the steps you go through above in creating the directory structure are exactly the same when you create your application context manually. You still need to do those, and they are just as described above. If you are using a different version of Tomcat, one that does not include the Administrator application, or if you just want to know what's happening under the hood, you need to replace that step in which we created the context in the Web-based Administrator application with this one:

Find the file <TOMCAT_HOME>/tomcat4/conf/server.xml. Open this file in a text editor, and find this comment:

```
<!--  Tomcat Manager Context -->
```

This comment comes after the host for this container has been defined, and you can add new contexts of your own here. To add the javaforcf context, add this entry:

```
<Context path="/javaforcf" docBase="javaforcf"
         debug="0" privileged="true"/>
```

This specifies the same information essentially that we supplied in the Web-based Administrator application eariler. The path attribute says what to look for in the URL after the host and the document base to use. So any time we type *http://localhost:8080/javaforcf/...*, the container will match this context and start looking for documents in the specified document root.

13.8 Servlets

Because ColdFusion is tag-based, and JSP is tag-based for the most part, it is most appropriate to cover JSPs. They are easier to write, deploy, and maintain than servlets. They are capable of everything that servlets are, and they are more familiar to ColdFusion developers. So we will work almost exclusively with them.

However, because eventually every JSP becomes a servlet, and because they continue to be a very important force in the world of J2EE, we should at least introduce them. Here we'll look at a basic "Hello, world" servlet that just prints text to the browser. Then we will look at working with servlet mappings. Finally, because it is such a commonly required task, we'll write a complete application that uses a servlet to authenticate a user against a database and store his or her username in the session object if the login is successful. Because of your background in ColdFusion and what we've learned about Java throughout the book, we'll learn enough about servlets here to go a long way.

Once you grasp the basic concept of servlets and see how to deploy them, it is easy to start writing them. They are easy to write because they are more or less regular Java classes that extend `HttpServlet`. The main caveat regarding servlets is that they are a very poor choice for outputting presentation layer items; that is, content, graphics, or HTML.

Let us write a servlet now and see if we can't get it to appear in a browser.

First, we create the Tomcat directory structure as specified above. We create an optional directory called `src`, which we will use to write all of our servlets and Java source files in. Then, we can output the compiled class files into the `WEB-INF/classes` directory using a setting in our IDE. They can also be compiled directly or moved into the `classes` directory. This keeps you from having to deploy all of your source files along with the rest of your application.

13.8.1 TestServlet

```
/* File: Hello.java
 * Purpose: demonstrate use and deployment of
 * servlets
 */
import javax.servlet.*;
import javax.servlet.http.*;
import java.io.*;
public class Hello extends HttpServlet {
    public void doGet(HttpServletRequest request,
                      HttpServletResponse response)
            throws ServletException, IOException {
```

```
        // if this is an HTTP GET request, forward
        // it in effect to doPost(). They will just
        // do the same thing
        doPost(request, response);
    }

    public void doPost(HttpServletRequest request,
                       HttpServletResponse response)
            throws ServletException, IOException {

        // make a string representing the user passed

        String user = request.getParameter("user");

        // if no user is specified, this value will be used
        if (request.getParameter("user") == null) {
            user = "world";
        }

        // set the content type
        // this will be ignored if included
        // in another servlet or JSP
        response.setContentType("text/html");

        // get an out stream so we can print to the
        // browser
        PrintWriter out = response.getWriter();
        out.println("<HTML><BODY>");
        out.println("<h1>Hello, " + user + "!</h1>");
        out.println("</BODY></HTML>");
    }
} // eof
```

> **NOTE** It is not necessary to add all of your servlets to the `web.xml` file. You only need to add servlets to this file for two chief reasons: to specify initialization parameters for those servlets that require additional information and to provide alternate URL mappings for your servlets.

Now restart Tomcat, and in your browser call this URL: *http://localhost:8080/javaforcf/servlet/Hello*.

Because no parameter was specified, the output is:

```
Hello, world!
```

If you now call this address, *http://localhost:8080/javaforcf/servlet/Hello?user=kitty,* you will see your parameter used in the output instead:

```
Hello, kitty!
```

Servlets do not require any file extension for the same reason that you do not need to specify one when executing a desktop Java application at the command line using the `java` command.

13.8.2 Servlet Mappings and Custom URLs

You will likely have noticed that we reference "servlet" in the URL, despite the fact that there is no directory named `servlet` under our `classes` directory where we placed the class file. This is a virtual mapping built into the container that allows you to execute any servlet without having to add an entry to the `web.xml` file.

Examine the following code:

```
<servlet>
   <servlet-name>MyServlet</servlet-name>
   <display-name>A Test Servlet</display-name>
   <description>Says hello</description>
   <servlet-class>packagename.classname</servlet-class>
</servlet>

<servlet-mapping>
   <servlet-name>MyServlet</servlet-name>
   <url-pattern>*.do</url-pattern>
</servlet-mapping>
```

Using these elements, we can create a new entry in the `web.xml` file that states the name of the servlet, a description and display name (which are arbitary text), and then a class that makes up that servlet. You can optionally include a `<servlet-mapping>` element, which says, "every time you come across this particular pattern in a URL request made of this server, execute the servlet with this name." So using this entry above, we make the `MyServlet` servlet execute every time we encounter a URL containing any text that ends in `.do`, which is a somewhat common practice.

In the next section, we'll make a complete database-driven authentication servlet, which will demonstrate many of the fundamental things we should know about servlets before moving into JSPs.

13.9 A Database-Driven Authentication Servlet

In this section, we will write a complete authentication application. The application is usable almost right out of the box for incorporating into your own Java applications (or your CFMX applications for that matter). The only things you'd need to change are the database name and driver name in the utility class.

The application requires the following components:

- **An HTML page**, which will simply contain a login form. The only interesting thing about this form is where the `<form>` tag's `action` attribute points. As mentioned above, we can define servlets to map to any arbitrary string extension we like. Because this book is called *Java for ColdFusion Developers*, we'll create a mapping in Tomcat's `web.xml` file to have any URL resource containing a `.jfcf` extension map to our servlet. So the HTML `<form>` tag action attribute looks like this: `action="Login.jfcf"`. Notice that no file named *anything.jfcf* actually exists. When the user submits the form, the mapping invokes the servlet to determine whether the username and password combination supplied is in the database.
- **An Access database called JavaForCF.** This database contains a table called `users`. The `users` table has two columns: `username` and `password`. This is the database that stores our list of users allowed in the secure area. Of course, you do not need to use an Access database; if you use a different database, change the reference to the driver and change the database name.
- **A `DBUtil` class.** This is a regular Java class. We have offloaded the database interaction (loading the driver, connecting, getting a result set, and disconnecting) to this utility class. This serves a couple of purposes. First, we can add methods to it and easily reuse the class. Second, it keeps our servlet clean and object oriented.
- **A `Login` servlet.** This servlet will do three things. First, it instantiates a `DBUtil` object to hit the database. Second, it uses the result to determine if the user should be authenticated. If the user is in the database, the servlet forwards the request onto the `secure.jsp` page. If the user is not in the database, the servlet redirects the user to the login screen. Third, if the user is good, then the username is placed into the session object. This will be tested on the `secure.jsp` page.

- **`Secure.jsp`**. This is the page that we want to keep secure. This page simply tests to see whether the user is in the session object. If this value is present, then the user authenticated correctly and is shown the menu. If this value is `null`, then the user tried to bypass the servlet, has not authenticated, and is told to go login.

Now that we know what we need in this application, let's look at the code listings.

13.9.1 web.xml

```
<?xml version="1.0" encoding="ISO-8859-1"?>

<!DOCTYPE web-app
    PUBLIC "-//Sun Microsystems, Inc.//DTD Web Application 2.3/
/EN"
    "http://java.sun.com/dtd/web-app_2_3.dtd">
<web-app>
<servlet>
<servlet-name>Login</servlet-name>
<servlet-class>com.javaforcf.utils.Login</servlet-class>
</servlet>
        <servlet-mapping>
            <servlet-name>Login</servlet-name>
            <url-pattern>*.jfcf</url-pattern>
        </servlet-mapping>
</web-app>
```

The `web.xml` file was not mentioned in the list of resources above, because it is not application-specific. We do need to modify the file as shown in this listing, however, to create the mapping.

13.9.2 Login.html

```
<!DOCTYPE HTML PUBLIC "-//W3C//DTD HTML 4.01 Transitional//EN">

<HTML>
  <HEAD>
    <TITLE></TITLE>
  </HEAD>
  <BODY onLoad="document.loginform.username.focus()">
  <h2 align="center">Please login</h2>
  <p align="center">
```

```
    <form action="auth.jfcf" method="POST" name="loginform">
    username: <input type="text" name="username">
    <br>
    password: <input type="password" name="password">
    <br>
    <input type="submit" value="login">
  </p>
    </form>

  </BODY>
</HTML>
```

Notice the `action` attribute of the `<form>` tag. There is no file on my server called `auth` with a `.jfcf` extension (or any other extension for that matter). The `web.xml` file invokes the mapped servlet, which is called `Login`, any time a request is made for a file ending in `.jfcf`.

> **NOTE** Remember that servlets are just regular Java classes that extend `HttpServlet` and override its `doGet()` and `doPost()` methods. So, you don't reference them with any file name extension.

FIGURE 13.3 The initial login screen.

13.9.3 DBUtils.java

```
/* File: DBUtils.
 * Purpose: Utility class to let us reuse database
 *  connection code.
 */

package com.javaforcf.utils;

import java.sql.*;
import java.util.*;

    public class DBUtils  {

       Connection con;

       //************authenticateUser()
    public boolean authenticateUser(String username,
                                    String password) {

            ResultSet rs = null;
            boolean isAuthenticated = false;
        try {
            connect();

            PreparedStatement authenticateUser;
           String s = new String("SELECT username,
               password FROM users WHERE username = ?" +
               " AND password = ?");
            authenticateUser = con.prepareStatement(s);
            authenticateUser.setString(1, username);
            authenticateUser.setString(2, password);
            rs = authenticateUser.executeQuery();


        while (rs.next()) {
            isAuthenticated = true;
            }

        disconnect();
        }
        catch (ClassNotFoundException cnfe) {
            System.err.println(cnfe.getMessage());
        }
        catch (SQLException sqle) {
            sqle.printStackTrace();
        }
```

```
        catch (Exception e) {
            System.err.println(e.getMessage());
        }

            return isAuthenticated;
    }   // end authenticateUser

        // ************ CONNECT
    public void connect()
        throws ClassNotFoundException,
             SQLException, Exception {

        try {
            // load driver
            Class.forName("sun.jdbc.odbc.JdbcOdbcDriver");
            // make connection to Access database
            con =
DriverManager.getConnection("jdbc:odbc:javaforcf");
        }
        catch (ClassNotFoundException cnfe) {
            System.err.println(cnfe.getMessage());
        }
        catch (SQLException sqle) {
            sqle.printStackTrace();
        }
        catch (Exception e) {
            System.err.println(e.getMessage());
        }
    } //end connect

            //********* DISCONNECT
    public void disconnect() throws SQLException {
        try {
            if ( con != null )
            {
                //close connection
                con.close();
            }
        }
        catch (SQLException sqle) {
            sqle.printStackTrace();
        }
    } // end disconnect()
} // eof
```

This file defines the code to authenticate the user in the database. If you want to use a different database, you can define that here. You might consider expanding the flexibility of this class by overloading the method to accept a database connect string and driver name as parameters. By offloading this aspect of the work to a utility class, we can maximize the ease of reuse and flexibility of this application; perhaps you don't want to even use a database for authentication. As alternatives, you could define a method to read in an XML file, traverse its elements, and determine authentication that way, or you could use LDAP.

13.9.4 Login.java

```
/* File: Login.java
 * Purpose: Servlet to perform login authentication
 *  with a username and password passed in from a form.
 *  This hits an Access database and checks if it has a record,
 *  if so, sets the username into the session object.
 */

    // package this one up
package com.javaforcf.utils;

import javax.servlet.*;
import javax.servlet.http.*;
import java.io.*;

public class Login extends HttpServlet {

    public void doGet(HttpServletRequest request,
                        HttpServletResponse response)
                throws ServletException, IOException {

        // if this is an HTTP GET request, forward
        // it in effect to doPost(). They will just
        // do the same thing
        doPost(request, response);
    }

    public void doPost(HttpServletRequest request,
                       HttpServletResponse response)
                throws ServletException, IOException {

                // access the session object, create
                // a session if it doesn't exist
        HttpSession session = request.getSession(true);
```

```
        String username = request.getParameter("username");
        String password = request.getParameter("password");

            // create a variable to hold where we should
            // redirect the user
            // This will be checked twice--
            // first if the user didn't fill out the form, and
            // again if the username/password combination
            // specified does not have a match in the database.
            // It will be set to a different value depending on
            // the validity of the login

        String redirect;

            // do database lookup
        DBUtils db = new DBUtils();

        boolean isAuth = db.authenticateUser(username,
password);

            // login good, add user to session and redirect to
            // secure page
        if (isAuth) {
           session.setAttribute("USER", username);

           redirect = "/secure.jsp";

        }
            // bad login
        else {
            redirect = "/login.html";
        }

            // go to either the secure page or form page
        ServletContext context = getServletContext();
        RequestDispatcher dispatcher =
           context.getRequestDispatcher(redirect);
           dispatcher.forward(request, response);
    }
} // eof
```

This is our servlet that invoked the `DBUtil.java` class and passes the request parameters from the form into our `authenticateUser()` method. If the method returns `true`, the servlet forwards to the `secure.jsp` page. We will cover JSPs in full in the next chapter.

13.9.5 secure.jsp

```
<%--File: secure.jsp
    Purpose: show menu to authenticated user, demonstrate
    interaction with servlet, introduce basic JSP concepts.
--%>

<%@page contentType="text/html"%>
<html>
<head>
    <title>Some secure page</title>
</head>
<body>

<%
    String thisUser = (String) session.getAttribute("USER");
    if (thisUser != null) {
%>

<h1>Welcome, <%= thisUser %></h1>
<br>
Here are your secret things:
<ul>
    <li>one</li>
    <li>two</li>
    <li>three</li>
</ul>

<%-- user did not authenticate. --%>

<% // close the if statement brace
    }
    else {
%>
<h2>You must be logged in to access this page</h2>
<a href="login.html">Go to login</a>
```

```
<%-- close the else brace--%>

<%
    }
%>
</body>
</html>
```

There is a lot to talk about in this JSP. Since we have not formally introduced JSPs yet, we'll just give it an overview. The neat thing about this JSP at this point is that it introduces a number of the important elements of JSPs. Here are the main things that stand out about this page:

- **The comments.** `<%-- I am a JSP comment --%>` This style of comment works exactly like a ColdFusion comment `<!--- something --->`. It is not visible to the browser, but it is returned as whitespace in the HTML source.
- **The directive** starts with `<%@...`, and the JSP directive tells the client what to expect about this response. In this example, it sets the MIME type for the current page scope to `text/html`.
- **The scriptlet** is the section of the JSP that is enclosed within `<% ... %>`. Scriptlets allow you to write Java programming language code directly on the JSP. So the `String thisUser...` statement and the `if` statement are standard Java code that declare and initialize a new string and test its value, just like you would in a Java class. Notice that we can also use Java-style comments (//) within these blocks as well.

We will cover JSPs formally in the next chapter.

> **NOTE** See the HttpServlet API reference in the appendix of this book for more information on the methods and exceptions available to you when writing servlets. Because things such as sessions and HTTP requests are very familiar to the ColdFusion developer, we do not discuss them in depth here, but the API should get you going.

Figures 13.4 and 13.5 show the results of an unsuccessful and a successful login, respectively.

FIGURE 13.4 Attempting to bypass the login.

FIGURE 13.5 Login successful.

13.10 ColdFusion MX and J2EE Integration

This section contains a couple of notes with regard to ColdFusion MX that will help us understand the connection between CFMX and the J2EE technologies it employs.

Note that what we have done above is manually create the `web.xml` file. CFMX also uses such a file, but it creates the file automatically when we place a JSP into a folder under the `CFMX/wwwroot` and execute it for the first time. A CFMX-generated `web.xml` looks slightly different, like this:

```
<?xml version="1.0" encoding="UTF-8"?>

<!DOCTYPE web-app
    PUBLIC "-//Sun Microsystems, Inc.//DTD Web Application
    2.3//EN"
    "http://java.sun.com/dtd/web-app_2_3.dtd">

<web-app>
    <session-config>
        <session-timeout>
            30
        </session-timeout>
    </session-config>
    <welcome-file-list>
<welcome-file>
            index.jsp
</welcome-file>
<welcome-file>
            index.html
</welcome-file>
<welcome-file>
            index.htm
</welcome-file>
</welcome-file-list>
</web-app>
```

The `welcome-files` serve the same purpose as the welcome file list in IIS, so that the directory can be accessed without a complete filename and extension.

We find something interesting in the ColdFusion MX Web root: it also contains a `WEB-INF` folder, and it also contains a `web.xml` file. What do you notice about this snippet from `<CFMX_HOME>\wwwroot\WEB-INF\web.xml`?

```
<servlet>
<servlet-name>CFCServlet</servlet-name>
<display-name>CFC Processor</display-name>
<description>Compiles and executes CF web components
</description>
<servlet-class>coldfusion.xml.rpc.CFCServlet</servlet-class>
</servlet>
<servlet-mapping>
<servlet-name>CFCServlet</servlet-name>
<url-pattern>*.cfc</url-pattern>
</servlet-mapping>
<servlet-mapping>
<servlet-name>CFCServlet</servlet-name>
<url-pattern>*.cfc/*</url-pattern>
</servlet-mapping>
```

The ColdFusion Components (CFCs) you write are translated into servlets. The CFMX application server picks up any `.cfc` extension in your application path and executes it as a servlet. So, while you create your own servlets that are specifically mapped to a class, CFCs are all mapped to the `CFCServlet` class in the `coldfusion.xml.rpc` package.

13.10.1 ColdFusion Page Contexts

Because CFML pages are Java servlets underneath, all ColdFusion pages expose an object called the `JavaPageContext`. To take advantage of this page context, use the new `GetPageContext()` CFML function. There are a number of fields and methods that this context makes available. You can access, for instance, the `include()` function and the `forward()` function. These functions are one way to integrate JSP and CFML pages.

To use the `include()` function to include a JSP within your ColdFusion page, call it from within CFScript:

```
GetPageContext().include("somePage.jsp");
```

To use the `forward()` function, which is similiar to the JSP `<jsp:forward>` tag or the `<cflocation>` tag, use `<cfscript>` again. This example passes a parameter name and value to the forwarded page:

```
GetPageContext().forward("somePage.jsp?theID=5");
```

13.10.2 Sharing Scopes Between CFML and JSP

You can share three scopes between JSP and CFML: the request, session, and application scopes. You cannot share variables in other scopes, such as URL, FORM, or CFFILE, because JSP does not have a corresponding definition for such scopes.

This example demonstrates how you can use parameters defined in a CFML page and pass them to a JSP page.

13.10.3 application.cfm

```
<!---
File: application.cfm
Purpose: we have to create a named application
 in order to be able to reference shared scopes
 with JSP
--->

<cfapplication name="myApp" sessionmanagement="yes">
```

13.10.4 scopetest.cfm

```
<!---File: scopetest.cfm
Purpose: show sharing between
scopes and moving between JSP and CFML pages--->

<!DOCTYPE HTML PUBLIC "-//W3C//DTD HTML 4.01 Transitional//
    EN">

<HTML>
  <HEAD>
    <TITLE></TITLE>
  </HEAD>
  <BODY>

<h1>CFML Page</h1>

<cfscript>
request.cfRequestVar = "I am a CF request var";
  session.cfSessionVar = "I am a CF session var";
  application.cfApplicationVar = "I am a CF application var";
</cfscript>
```

```
<cfoutput>#request.cfrequestvar#</cfoutput><br>
<cfoutput>#session.cfsessionvar#</cfoutput><br>
<cfoutput>#application.cfapplicationvar#</cfoutput><br>

<hr>

<cfscript>
 GetPageContext().include("scopetest.jsp?somekey=somevalue");
</cfscript>

   </BODY>
</HTML>
```

13.10.5 scopetest.jsp

```
<%--
File: scopetest.jsp
Purpose: set some application and session variables,
then forward to a CFML page
--%>

<%@page import="java.util.*" %>

<!DOCTYPE HTML PUBLIC "-//W3C//DTD HTML 4.0 Transitional//EN">
<html>
<head>
<title>some JSP</title>
</head>
<body>

<h1>JSP Page</h1>

<%
// set a variable with the name USER and the value Eben
// into the JSP session scope
    session.setAttribute("JspUser", "Eben");

// set a variable into the application scope
application.setAttribute("JspDB", "javaforcf");
%>
```

```
JspUser: <%= session.getAttribute("JspUser") %>
<br>
<br>
JspDB: <%= application.getAttribute("JspDB") %>
<br>

<br>CF application: <%=
((Map)(application.getAttribute("myApp"))).get("cfApplication
Var")%>

<hr>

<jsp:include page="athird.cfm">
<jsp:param name="name" value="dude" />
</jsp:include>

</body>
</html>
```

13.10.6 athird.cfm

```
<!---
File: athird.cfm
Purpose: display a parameter passed to the page
that was created in a JSP (scopes.jsp).
--->

<!DOCTYPE HTML PUBLIC "-//W3C//DTD HTML 4.0 Transitional//EN">
<html>
<head>
<title>a third cfml</title>
</head>
<body>

<h1>A different CFML Page</h1>

Request: <cfoutput>#name#</cfoutput>

</body>
</html>
```

The thing you'll notice right off the bat is that the Java data type used to store CFML request, session, and application variables is a `Map`. You know that because we cast the object to this type when calling it. Remember that `Map` is a kind of Collection, which is why we need to import `Java.util.*;`.

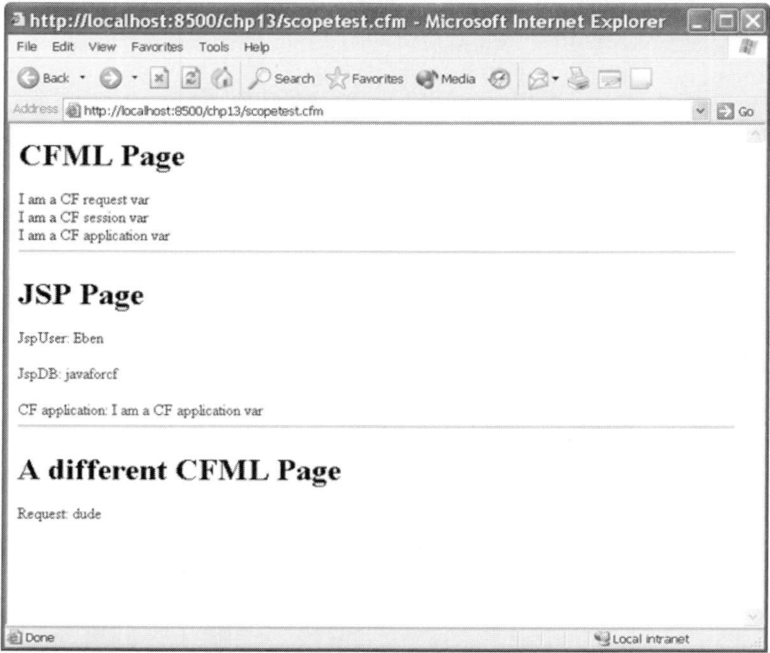

FIGURE 13.6 Sharing scopes and moving between JSP and CFML.

Calling *http://localhost:8500/chp13/scopetest.cfm* should produce the output shown in Figure 13.6.

13.11 Configuring MySQL Database Server

In this section, we will walk through the few simple steps required to set up MySQL on your machine. We will create a database to use in conjunction with this database server. You do not need to set up MySQL. You can use any database you like. Just make the necessary adjustments in the application code we will write. You can use Microsoft Access using the JDBC/ODBC bridge for development, but you'll need to download a driver and install it if you want to use another production-quality RDBMC. Skip this section if you already have MySQL or want to use another database server.

The following instructions are for Windows XP Professional and shouldn't be wildly different for other platforms. Here are the steps:

1. Download the dataserver from *www.mysql.com*. Get the most recent production-quality release. The current one is 3.23, but 4.0 is in alpha and may be ready by the time you read this.
2. Extract the file to `C:\MySQL`.
3. Run `setup.exe` and move through the wizard. Once you have installed it, you need to set up a database.
4. To work with your databases in a GUI environment, go into `MySQL\bin` and click MySqlManager.exe. Otherwise, you can run MySQL from the command line. Navigate into the `MySQL\bin` directory and run `mysql`.
5. You may need to register your MySQL server so you can connect to it. This process is similar to the MS SQL Server registration. I will use these settings:

   Server: `eben`
   Host: `localhost`
   Port: `3306`
   LoginID: `admin`
   Password: `admin`

If you want to install it as a service, which is a good idea on Windows NT or 2000, then open a shell and type this:

```
C:\MySQL\bin>mysqld-nt --install
```

You should see this message:

```
Service successfully installed.
```

Now MySQL should be up and running on your system. You can use standard SQL commands to create and modify your database. To see syntax specific to MySQL, look up the comprehensive online documentation at *www.mysql.com*.

13.11.1 Installing a JDBC Driver

In order to use MySQL with Tomcat, you need to get a JDBC driver that works with this database system. I will use a Type IV driver that can be downloaded for free at *http://mmmysql.sourceforge.net*. You can also use, for example, the Microsoft Type IV driver for SQL Server, which is a free download.

To install the driver, open the `.jar` using WinZip. Extract it to *C:\jdk1.4\jre\lib\ext*. This will make sure that it is always accessible to the JDK without having to bother with the class path. The other place you can install it if you want to use it with just this one Web application, is to place it under `javaforcf/WEB-INF/lib`.

It will create a folder called something like `mm.mysql-2.0.14`, depending on your version. You should restart Tomcat so it picks up your new extension, and you should be ready to access a database from the Web.

13.12 What's Next?

In the next chapter, we will look at JSPs, which should be very easy to handle at this point. We have all of the important tools at our command now. We can ride on much of what we know about architecting ColdFusion applications, but with an object-oriented twist. This can be a very difficult proposition for developers coming from languages such as ColdFusion, PHP, or Perl, where you don't have much in the way of objects or components.

JSPs rely heavily on JavaBeans and custom tags (also called custom actions). These things are really just Java classes at heart, like servlets are. That's why we have spent so much time on Java fundamentals in this book. It may be that your primary or even exclusive interest here is in server-side Java for Web applications. But because we have approached this topic from the ground up, you are very well prepared to start writing comprehensive, object-oriented JSP applications almost immediately.

14

JavaServer Pages

This chapter covers JavaServer Pages (JSP). JSP, introduced in September of 1999, represents the second model for running server-side Java. We will begin with an overview of the tools required to extend the functionality of your Web sites using Java technology.

Because ColdFusion MX itself is Java-based, you can call JSPs directly using ColdFusion as the application server, which we saw how to do in the previous chapter.

In this chapter we cover JSPs. This will be easier to do than it sounds. There are only nine tags in the JSP library, compared with 90 in ColdFusion. Of course, there is a good reason for this.

Now that you have your environment set up, we will learn JSP tags, directives, scriptlets, and expressions. This won't actually take very long, because JSP itself is really only a small front end to Java.

14.1 Overview of JSP

JavaServer Pages do not exactly replace servlets. They offer a different direction in Java development on the server. JSPs were compared with ColdFusion in some detail in the last chapter, so we won't dwell on that now. JSPs offer a tag-based, XML-compatible way to create dynamic Web sites. They give you a flexible way to incorporate complete Java classes in the form of JavaBeans and custom actions.

ColdFusion consists of three basic elements: tags, functions, and components (CFCs). JSPs have four: tags (often called "actions"), scriptlets, directives, and beans. While JSP is in a sense a tag-based language, little of the functionality comes from the tags. In ColdFusion, much of what you do is in the tags already defined in the standard ColdFusion library. Historically, you might extend into writing a CFX tag if you needed some extra functionality that the tag library did not define.

Since ColdFusion 5 there has been a significant focus on helping developers write custom code. ColdFusion 5 saw the introduction of user-defined functions, and ColdFusion Components are now available in CFMX. JSP is far less concerned about providing an extensive, ready-made library to developers as it is with allowing maximum freedom. This can be both frustrating and rewarding: frustrating, because you have to write more code to get things done, and it can increase your development cycle time greatly (though we will see ways around this in the next chapter); rewarding, because you have a very open, extensible architecture to write exactly what you need in an object-oriented way.

14.1.1 JSP Syntax

A tricky thing for ColdFusion developers to pick up is how these different elements are represented. In ColdFusion, everything pretty much looks like this: `<cftagname>`; ColdFusion tags, even the CFX tags, all start with "cf," which tells the processor to execute them differently than the HTML tags it also encounters.

JSP, on the other hand, has slightly different syntaxes to represent each of the different language elements referred to above. We'll now look at these in turn.

14.2 Scripting Elements

There are three types of scripting elements: scriptlets, declarations, and expressions.

14.2.1 Scriptlets

Scriptlets allow little Java code blocks to be written directly in your JSP. You can perhaps remember the definition of scriptlets because they are small Java code scripts (the way applets are small applications and servlets are small servers). A scriptlet takes another syntax, one that looks more like ASP:

```
<% SomeClass s = new SomeClass(param); %>
```

There are certain things to notice about scriptlets. The code you write inside a scriptlet is pure Java code. You can instantiate objects, write methods, and you end your statements in a semicolon. Scriptlets cannot span multiple pages; that is, they must start and end on the same JSP. Scriptlets have page-level scope—that means that a variable declared in one scriptlet is still visible later in the page. It also means that the same variable is not available across multiple requests. In this regard, its variables act like ColdFusion local variables (those in the `VARIABLES` scope).

A difficult aspect of scriptlets to keep in mind is that you cannot write HTML directly into them. So if you are performing a loop, for instance, and want to print out something to the browser, you must close the scriptlet but not the loop, do your business in HTML, and open a new scriptlet to close the loop!

```
<%
   for (int i = 0; i < 5; i++) {
%>
<h1>here is some text</h1>
<%
   }
%>
```

It looks odd at first, perhaps, but it makes perfect sense.

> **NOTE** There is an XML syntax for using scriptlets: `<jsp:scriptlet>` `</jsp:scriptlet>`. This is not widely supported, however. ColdFusion MX and Tomcat 4, for example, will not honor the XML syntax for scriptlets.

While it is very easy to start writing a good deal of scriptlet code into your JSPs, this practice is strongly discouraged. It severely detriments the readability and maintainability of your page. It makes it difficult for content or HTML developers to work with, and endangers your code. That Java code should instead be offloaded into beans (which are just a special kind of Java class we'll look at later in this chapter) or into other Java classes or custom actions. Doing so promotes strong object-oriented architecture, just as you might imagine that it is now preferable to have ColdFusion Components doing the real work of the page instead of interspersing small bits of HTML and CFML on into perpetuity. Scriptlet use should be kept to a minimum.

Nonetheless, scriptlets are useful, and they have their place, which we'll see in examples in the remainder of the book.

14.2.2 Declarations

Declarations are equivalent to the member variables and functions of a regular Java class. You write a declaration like this:

```
<%! %>
```

For example, in order to declare a `String` variable to reference later in the JSP, you can write this:

```
<%! String animal = "kitty" %>
```

This will create the `String` variable.

> **NOTE** It is rare to see declarations in practice, probably because the use of scriptlets has been so strongly discouraged and because they offer only a small, specific subset of what you can do in a scriptlet. They aren't necessary, and they can be confusing.

Of course, declarations cannot reference any variable that has already been declared.

14.2.3 Expressions

Expressions in ColdFusion and in Java are any legal statement in the language that evaluates to a single valid value of any data type. In JSP, an expression is more limited. The expression is still a statement that evaluates to a single value, but the data type of the expression result must be a string. The result of the expression is sent to the output stream using `JspWriter out.println()`. It looks like this:

```
<%= aVariable %>
```

This expression is the equivalent of this statement:

```
...
out.println(aVariable);
...
```

This kind of code is fairly common. Pretend we have a database containing news articles that we want to display in the browser. Each news article has an `author`, a `createdDate`, and a `title`. In this pseudo-example, we take a parameter passed via a form or URL called `typeID` (remember that JSP, unlike CF, is case-sensitive; it inherits this characteristic from its mother). Then we call on the `connect()` method of a Java object called `item` to connect to a database. Then, we call the `item` object's `viewArchive()` method, passing it the `typeID` string variable. This method then hits the database, returning a result set for us to loop over. We write a `while` loop to iterate over the result set, assigning page-local variables the value of the columns retrieved from the database.

```
...
<%    // get result and set vars
    String typeID = request.getParameter("typeID");
    item.connect();
    ResultSet rs = item.viewArchive(typeID);
      while (rs.next()) {
            String itemID = rs.getString("itemID");
            String itemName = rs.getString("itemName");
            String createdDate = rs.getString("createdDate");
            String createdBy = rs.getString("createdBy");
  %>
```

Later in this same page, we can output the values of these new variables, incorporated with lovely HTML.

```
...
<tr>
<td align="left">

<a href="some.jsp?itemID=<%= itemID %>" class="title1">
<%= itemName %></a>

<br>
<span class="greytext">date: <%= createdDate %></span><br>
<span class="greytext">author: <%= createdBy %></span><br>
</td>
</tr>
<%
// close the while loop
}
%>
...
```

Notice how the parameters used in builing a dynamic URL are string expressions, just as you might write this in ColdFusion:

```
<a href = "some.cfm?itemID=<cfoutput>#queryname.itemID#
</cfoutput>"...
```

14.3 Directives

Directives are interpreted in page preprocessing. Before the JSP or its resulting servlet is executed, the page directives are processed. Directives look like this:

```
<%@ someDirective attribute="value" %>
```

There are three directive types: `page`, `include`, and `taglib`.

14.3.1 page Directive

Page directives are used to perform certain tasks before the page is loaded. Table 14.1 shows the attributes and accompanying descriptions for the `page` directive:

TABLE 14.1 Directive Properties

ATTRIBUTE	DESCRIPTION
`import`	Specify packages to import, just as in Java programming.
`errorPage`	Relative URL for the `errorPage` for this page.
`extends`	Java class name that this JSP will extend (rarely used).
`session`	Whether this page participates in a session. Possible values are `true` and `false`. Default is `true`.
`language`	Scripting language in use on the page. Java is the only currently supported value, though others could be implemented in the future.
`buffer`	Indicates the size of the output buffer. Appending `kb` (for kilobytes) is mandatory. Possible values are `none` or an integer.
`autoFlush`	Whether the buffer will be automatically flushed. Possible values are `true` or `false`. A value of `true` requires the `buffer` attribute to be set to a valid value.
`isThreadSafe`	Whether this page is thread safe or not. Possible values are `true` or `false`.

TABLE 14.1 Directive Properties (Continued)

ATTRIBUTE	DESCRIPTION
`info`	Arbitrary string text describing the page. Can be retrieved in the JSP using `servlet.getServletInfo()`.
`contentType`	Defines the character encoding used in this JSP and the MIME type for the response.
`pageEncoding`	Defines the character encoding for the JSP.
`isErrorPage`	Set to `true` if this page is an error page. This makes the `exception implicit` object available. By default this is `false`.

More than one attribute can be specified in a `page` directive:

```
<%@ page errorPage="errors/error.jsp" info="A neat page" %>
```

14.3.2 `include` Directive

This directive allows you to include the contents of another file at the specific location where the directive is called. It looks like this:

```
<%@ include file="some.jsp" %>
```

Note that this form of including an external file will first run the preprocessor, evaluating the contents of the included file and converting it to a servlet; only then are the contents included. See also the `<jsp:include>` tag, which does not preprocess the included file. The tag version acts more like a cut-and-paste kind of operation. That is, the `<jsp:include>` tag is more like the ColdFusion `<cfinclude>`.

14.3.3 `taglib` Directive

The `taglib` directive is used to specify the name of a custom tag library you want to import into your JSP. It looks like this:

```
<%@ taglib prefix="c" uri="http://java.sun.com/jstl/ea/core" %>
```

The above example indicates the `taglib` directive to use when importing the "Core" libraries from the JSP Standard Tag Library (JSTL). The URI provides a namespace for the library, and the prefix indicates the prefix name you want to use to call tags in the library on this page. So, for instance, once you've used the above `taglib` directive (and assuming you have the library and have added it to the deployment descriptor), you could do this later in the page:

```
<c:set var="fileName">
    <%= thePath + request.getParameter("file") + ".doc" %>
</c:set>
```

We will discuss tags in the JSTL and tag libraries in general later. The above tag just sets a variable called `fileName` to whatever string the expression evaluates to.

14.4 Actions

To begin with, there are few JSP tags with XML-compatible syntax. These most closely resemble ColdFusion tags and take this form:

```
<jsp:tagname attribute="value" />
```

A commonly used JSP tag that takes this form has a direct counterpart in ColdFusion's `<cfinclude>` tag: `<jsp:include/>`, which looks like this:

```
<jsp:include page="header.jsp" />
```

Calling this tag includes the content of `header.jsp` directly in the calling page.

You notice a couple of things here. First, there is a colon separating "jsp" and the name of the tag. This syntax allows developers to create coherent names for their own custom tags. For instance, you might write a custom tag to handle the checkout process for a user's shopping cart. It might look like this:

```
<ecommerce:cart action="checkout"/>
```

We'll address custom actions later. The second thing we notice about the tag is that, because it is XML-compatible, it is closed with a trailing slash, indicating that there is no separate closing tag.

Now let's look at the tags themselves and then see how they work in some examples. Much of what you know in working with ColdFusion Web application design will be useful in working with JSPs.

14.4.1 <jsp:forward>

This action is used to end the execution of the current template and forward the request to another URL. The specified URL can be another JSP, an HTML page, a servlet, or other Web resource. The resource is specified as relative to the root of the current application.

Usage:

```
<jsp:forward page="/javaforcf/secure.jsp" />
```

We have seen the forwarding mechanism at work already, in our servlet example. While we used the `forward()` method of the `servlet request` object in that case, that is what is happening under the hood here. Notice too that method is available in ColdFusion MX.

You can also use the `<jsp:param>` action to forward request parameters to the specified page:

```
<jsp:forward page = "/javaforcf/secure.jsp">
  <jsp:param name="userid" value="007" />
</jsp:forward>
```

The `</jsp:forward>` action attribute is shown in Table 14.2.

TABLE 14.2 `<jsp:forward>` Action Attribute

ATTRIBUTE	DESCRIPTION	NOTES
`page`	Page location	(required) Specifies the location of the page to forward to, relative to the root of the application.

The `<jsp:forward>` tag works like `<cflocation>`.

14.4.2 <jsp:include>

This action is used to include a static or dynamically referenced file at run time. Because of when the file is included, files included using the `<jsp:include>` action do not share `page` or `request`-scoped variables with the calling page. For this reason, files included with the action cannot process directives. This is in distinction to the `page` include directive we saw previously in this chapter.

Usage:

```
<jsp:include file="header.jsp" flush="true" />
```

The `<jsp:include>` action attributes are shown in Table 14.3.

TABLE 14.3 <jsp:include> Action Attributes

ATTRIBUTE	DESCRIPTION	NOTES
`page`	Page location	(required) Specifies location of the file to be included.
`flush`	Flush buffer	(optional) Specifies whether or not to flush the output buffer before including the file. Default value is `false`.

Note that the `page` attribute can be the result of a runtime expression; that is, it can be dynamically specified. In JSP 1.1, the flush attribute was required, and its only possible value was `true`.

Use the `<jsp:include>` action when you would use `<cfinclude>`. It is perfect for including headers, navigation bars, and footers, for instance. Also, you can append parameters to the original request with the `<jsp:param>` action. If the parameter already exists, the new value overwrites it. Multiple parameters can be specified in a comma-separated list.

14.4.3 <jsp:param>

This action allows you to pass parameters in the `request` scope. It is used within the bodies of `<jsp:forward>`, `<jsp:include>`, or `<jsp:plugin>`.

Usage:

```
<jsp:param name="userid"
   value='<%=request.getParameter(\"userid\")%>" />
```

The `<jsp:param>` action attributes are shown in Table 14.4.

TABLE 14.4 <jsp:param> Action Attributes

ATTRIBUTE	DESCRIPTION	NOTES
`name`	Parameter name	(required) Name of the parameter.
`value`	Parameter value	(required) Value of the parameter.

14.4.4 <jsp:params>

The <jsp:params> action wraps multiple <jsp:param> actions for passing to an applet.

Usage:

```
<jsp:params>
  <jsp:param name="Dept" value="Engineering" />
  <jsp:param name="Emp" value="Dilbert" />
</jsp:params>
```

14.4.5 <jsp:plugin>

The <jsp:plugin> action allows you to embed an applet or JavaBeans component directly in the JSP returned to the browser. It automatically generates the <embed> or <object> tags for you.

Usage:

```
<jsp:plugin
  type = "applet"
  code = "somClass.class"
  codebase = "intranet"
  width = "300"
  height = "400"
/>
```

The <jsp:plugin> action attributes are shown in Table 14.5.

TABLE 14.5 <jsp:plugin> Action Attributes

ATTRIBUTE	DESCRIPTION	NOTES
align	Alignment	(optional) Specifies alignment of applet area.
archive	Applet classes	(optional) Additional classes or resources, specified by URL, that must be loaded.
code	Class name	(required) Specifies name of the class containing the applet or bean.
codebase	Class location	(required) Specifies relative URL location of the class specified in the code attribute.

(Continued)

TABLE 14.5 `<jsp:plugin>` Action Attributes (Continued)

ATTRIBUTE	DESCRIPTION	NOTES
`height`	Height in pixels	(optional) Specifies height of the applet area.
`hspace`	Horizontal border in pixels	(optional) Specifies number of pixels wide the border on the side of the applet should be.
`iepluginurl`	URL for IE plugin	(optional) Location of the Java plugin for Internet Explorer.
`jreversion`	JRE version	(optional) Specifies minimum requirement for the Java Runtime Engine version. Default is 1.1.
`name`	Applet name	(optional) A name for the applet to keep it distinguished from other applets or beans on the page.
`nspluginurl`	URL for Netscape plugin	(optional) Location of the Java plugin for Netscape.
`title`	Label	(optional) A text description for the applet, which can appear in mouseover.
`type`	Object type	(optional) Whether the attribute is an applet or bean.
`vspace`	Vertical border in pixels	(optional) Defines a pixel border above and below the applet.
`width`	Width in pixels	(optional) Width of the applet.

That covers all of the tags in the JavaServer Pages specification—except for three. The remaining tags all have to do with JavaBeans, and we cover that in its own section, so those tags will be introduced at that point.

What we quickly notice is that there is no `<jsp:query>` action, no `<jsp:file>` action. That means that much of what developers are used to writing in JSP is with JavaBeans. We've seen in this section a few different methods that you use with beans—`useBean`, `setProperty`, and `getProperty`. We will examine beans more later in this chapter. For now, you can think of them as being like ColdFusion Components.

14.5 Model-View-Controller

A chief goal of the JSP architecture was to keep presentation and application business logic separate. By offloading the real work of your page into a bean, you can help ensure that your JSPs are mostly HTML and then simple, readable variable references. You may hear developers talking about the Model 2 architecture or the Model-View-Controller architecture. This is simply a fancy way of saying that presentation and business logic separation is important, and that you can achieve this using a proven design pattern. That pattern is as follows: The model holds the data. The view retrieves the data and presents it to the viewer. The controller acts as a broker or router, delegating responsibilities to the model and the view.

Not to equate the two, but if you have used the Fusebox methodology with ColdFusion, you should be familiar with this concept. In Fusebox, you've got a central switch that is never viewed itself, but routes responsibilities to the different "fuses" in the application, and then everything is `<cfinclude>`ed.

Generally, a JavaBean represents the model, a JSP the view, and a servlet acts as the controller. Think back to the security example. We weren't using beans, but we had a `DBUtil` class that held the data, the JSP to show the dynamic information, and the servlet that controlled request routing.

When you use this architecture, you often don't need more tags than this. Now, I must seriously qualify that statement. Clients want the same kinds of things over and over. Everyone likes to upload a file, for instance, or update their job listings. It is therefore important to be able to quickly add functionality to disparate applications. It would be really nice if we had the convenience of a `<jsp:file>` tag in JSP. But we don't. We have to write it ourselves as a custom tag or bean, or find it somewhere else. Of course, as with custom ColdFusion tags one might need to modify the source in order to tailor it to specific needs.

14.6 Implicit Objects

There are several useful objects that are available implicitly to a JSP. Some of these will be familiar from ColdFusion, chiefly the `request`, `session`, and `application` objects that correspond to the ColdFusion scopes.

These consist of the following:

- `page`
- `request`
- `response`
- `out`

- `config`
- `exception`
- `pageContext`
- `session`
- `application`

In the Java chapters earlier we talked about fashioning our Java code to represent things in the world. The implicit JSP objects each represent different aspects of the application in its various interactions with the client. These are defined in the following sections.

> **NOTE** Remember that servlets and JSPs are part of the Java 2 Enterprise Edition. While your container (such as ColdFusion MX or Tomcat 4) will have an appropriate run time, you will not find these classes referenced in the regular Standard Edition API we have used throughout this book; you need to look at the J2EE 1.3.1 API. Currently, this URL is *http://java.sun.com/j2ee/sdk_1.3/techdocs/api/*.

14.6.1 `page` Object

This object represents an instance of the current page. You can think of the `page` object as being similiar to the `this` reference of a regular Java object. The `page` object is of type `javax.lang.Object`.

14.6.2 `request` Object

The `request` object represents an HTTP client request. You can think of this object as being very much like the `request` scope that you may have used in ColdFusion. Placing variables into the `request` scope in ColdFusion exposes them to the entire HTTP request, including custom tags (which have their own "black box"). The JSP `request` object is commonly used to access variables passed from one page to another. JSP does not make a distinction between `form` and `URL` scopes the way ColdFusion does. You use the `request` scope in both cases in JSP. The `request` object is of type `javax.servlet.ServletRequest`.

For example, here is how you would use the `request` scope's `getParameter()` method to retrieve parameters passed from one page into another, whether they come from a URL or an HTML form:

```
String name = request.getParameter("name");
```

NOTE What's often hard for ColdFusion developers to remember at first about this is that we're used to referencing the variable without any quotation marks so that ColdFusion evaluates it, like this: `<cfoutput>#URL.name# </cfoutput>`. In JSP we let the `getParameter()` method handle the evaluation, so we need to put double quotes around the name of the parameter.

You can also retrieve all of the parameters in the request as an enumeration object:

```
...
Enumeration e = request.getParameterNames();
while (e.hasMoreElements) {
    String s = e.nextElement()
    // do something here
}
...
```

NOTE All parameters must be strings and are returned as `java.lang.-Strings`.

Here is how to get values of `request` parameters using a `String` array:

```
String [] s = request.getParameterValues("someFormField");
```

Finally, you can use the `request` object to gather information from the HTTP headers in the request. These include the content type, content length, character encoding, security, and so forth. Here are some methods you will perhaps find useful:

- `getHeader(String name)` returns the specified header as a string.
- `getPathInfo()` returns extra path information associated with the URL.
- `getQueryString()` returns the `query` string contained in the path.
- `getSession()` returns the `HttpSession` object associated with this client.

Here is an example of using the `request` object to see how these work.

14.6.3 objects.jsp

```
<%@page contentType="text/html"%>
<html>
<head><title>request demo</title></head>
<body>
```

```
<html>

Your browser: <%= request.getHeader("User-Agent") %>
<br>
Remote user: <%= request.getRemoteUser() %>
<br>
Remote address: <%= request.getRemoteAddr() %>
<br>
Remote host: <%= request.getRemoteHost() %>
<br>
Request URI: <%= request.getRequestURI() %>
<br>
Request protocol: <%= request.getProtocol() %>
<br>
Servlet path: <%= request.getServletPath() %>
<br>
Path info: <%= request.getPathInfo() %>
<br>
Path translated: <%= request.getPathTranslated() %>
<br>
Query string: <%= request.getQueryString() %>
<br>
Server name: <%= request.getServerName() %>
</body>
</html>
```

The result of running this page should be an output of information roughly equivalent to the CGI variables you're used to using in ColdFusion:

```
Your browser: Mozilla/4.0 (compatible; MSIE 6.0; Windows NT 5.1)
Remote user: null
Remote address: 127.0.0.1
Remote host: localhost
Request URI: /javaforcf/chp14/objects.jsp
Request protocol: HTTP/1.1
Servlet path: /chp14/objects.jsp
Path info: null
Path translated: null
Query string: name=eben
Server name: localhost
```

14.6.4 response Object

This object, familiar to ASP developers but less familiar to ColdFusion developers, represents the server's generated HTTP response. JSP uses an instance of the JspWriter class (the out object) to allow developers direct access to write out to the response.

The response is an object of type javax.servlet.ServletResponse. The response object is primarily useful when writing to the client is necessary inside, for example, a custom tag, or when you want to set information into the HTTP headers. For example:

```
setHeader(String name, Object value);
```

and

```
addCookie(Cookie cookie);
```

are sometimes useful.

14.6.5 out Object

The out object represents the character output stream for this page. The out object is of type javax.servlet.jsp.JspWriter. Its function is essentially to allow you to print out to the browser in a convenient manner. Note that this requires a scriptlet call, which is generally something you want to avoid when possible:

```
<% out.println("<h1>Hello, " + name + "!") %>
```

14.6.6 config Object

The config object is of type javax.servlet.ServletConfig. It allows you to gain information regarding the servlet underlying the JSP, such as the name of the servlet instance and any initialization parameters used.

14.6.7 exception Object

The exception object, as we saw in the last chapter, is only available on a specifically declared error page. An error page, like an error page in ColdFusion, is a custom error page to be sent to the browser instead of that used by default by the container. Each custom error page is associated with a certain HTTP status response in the container's configuration (such as the web.xml file) and can access this object. The exception object is of type javax.lang.Throwable.

It defines a `getMessage()` method, which is generally used on such pages to print the error message. The `printStackTrace()` method outputs the stack trace. ColdFusion's custom error pages offer similiar functionality.

14.6.8 `pageContext` Object

This implicit object contains a reference to the `javax.servlet.jsp.PageContext` object for the JSP currently being processed. It affords the developer a way to explicitly gain references to some of the following objects:

- `getOut()` is of the type `JspWriter`.
- `getPage()` is of the type `Object`.
- `getRequest()` is of the type `ServletRequest`.
- `getResponse()` is of the type `ServletResponse`.
- `getServletConfig()` is of the type `ServletConfig`.
- `getServletContext()` is of the type `ServletContext`.

14.6.9 `session` Object

The `session` object, like its ColdFusion counterpart, maintains client-specific information. It is an object of type `javax.servlet.http.HttpSession`. In ColdFusion, you set variables into the session by simply prefixing the name of the session to the variable:

```
<cfset session.username = FORM.user>
```

In JSP, you use the `setAttribute()` and `getAttribute()` methods:

```
<% session.setAttribute("username",
       request.getParameter("user") %>
```

Recall from the last chapter that ColdFusion MX allows you to share variables between its Application and Session scopes and that of JSP.

14.6.10 `application` Object

The `application` object is of type `javax.servlet.ServletContext`. You can use the JSP `application` object to gain information regarding the servlet container. Especially useful are the logging methods. You can also set values into this scope that you want to be shared across an entire application. This object is not generally explicitly used as often as its ColdFusion counterpart, though developers will often set utility JavaBeans into the application scope.

14.7 Error Pages

You can specify a custom error page to use with your JSPs just as you can in ColdFusion. In order to use an error page in ColdFusion, you need to specify its name in the `<cferror>` tag in the `application.cfm` file, like this:

```
<cferror type="request" template = "myRequestErrorPage.cfm">
```

On this page you can then use certain built-in ColdFusion error objects; for instance, you can reference `ERROR.diagnostics` in order to output information about the bad request.

It seems we are starting to see a number of ways in which the `application.cfm` file can be thought of as similiar to the `web.xml` file. It contains startup and initialization parameters and controls what happens in the application.

Anyway, in JSP, you can tell the application what error page to use for different HTTP error codes in the `web.xml` file. Add this entry:

```
<error-page>
   <error-code>404</error-code>
   <location>/chp14/error404.jsp</location>
</error-page>
```

The `<location>` tag requires a path relative to the root of the application that points to the location of the file you want to use. This is the equivalent to our `<cferror>` code above. However, in one thing that is different about the three types of messages ColdFusion limits us to, you can specify a different error page for each different kind of HTTP error returned by the request.

14.7.1 error404.jsp

```
<%--
    File: error404.jsp
    Purpose: display a custom error message
--%>

<%@ page isErrorPage = "true" %>

<!DOCTYPE HTML PUBLIC "-//W3C//DTD HTML 4.01 Transitional//
   EN">
<HTML>
```

```
<HEAD>
<TITLE>page not found (404)</TITLE>
</HEAD>
<BODY BGCOLOR="#FFFFFF">

<CENTER>

<table cellpadding="5" border="0" width="500" align="center"
valign="middle">
<tr>
<td>
<font face="arial, helvetica, sans-serif" size="3"
color="#000000">
<blockquote>
<b>The page you requested:</b>
<br>
<%=request.getRequestURL() %>
<br>
<b>is not available on this server.</b>
<br>
<b>Please check the address and try again.
<br>
<br>If you continue to receive this message, and feel you have
received it in error,<br>
please <a href="mailto:webmaster@mysite.com">contact the
Webmaster</a> for this server.</b>
</blockquote>
</font>
</td>
</tr>
</table>

</center>
</BODY>
</HTML>
```

Another kind of error page, that is, one for a different HTTP status code, could include exception object methods, which are the rough equivalent of the ColdFusion `ERROR.diagnostics` message:

```
<%= e.getMessage() %>
```

and

```
<%= e.printStackTrace() %> // like CF's ERROR.TagContext
```

TIP Remember that you must specify the elements in your `web.xml` file in a certain order. For instance, you must put the `<error-page>` element *after* any `<servlet>` element. The end of this chapter contains the complete list of possible values for this file and the order in which they must appear.

So now our `web.xml` file, if you kept adding to the same one from the previous chapter, looks like this:

```
<?xml version="1.0" encoding="ISO-8859-1"?>

<!DOCTYPE web-app
    PUBLIC "-//Sun Microsystems, Inc.//DTD Web Application
     2.3//EN"
    "http://java.sun.com/dtd/web-app_2_3.dtd">
<web-app>

  <servlet>
      <servlet-name>Login</servlet-name>
   <servlet-class>com.javaforcf.utils.Login</servlet-class>
  </servlet>

  <servlet-mapping>
      <servlet-name>Login</servlet-name>
      <url-pattern>*.jfcf</url-pattern>
   </servlet-mapping>

   <error-page>
      <error-code>404</error-code>
      <location>/chp14/error404.jsp</location>
   </error-page>

</web-app>
```

If we now reference some file within the purview of the `javaforcf` Web application that does not exist, then we should be redirected to the custom error page we have defined, as shown in Figure 14.1.

As with ColdFusion or IIS or other custom error pages, these make more than a lovely decorative finish to your applications they allow you to appear more professional and truly offer some help to your users. *Microsoft.com* has a very helpful error page, for instance—it offers you a search form and displays a complete site map.

FIGURE 14.1 Our custom error page is displayed when an HTTP 404 is returned to the client.

14.8 JavaBeans

A JavaBean is a regular Java class that has its member variables (its properties) available to `set` methods, which update their values, and `get` methods, which retrieve their values. They are simple, easy-to-write repositories for information that must define a method to get and another method to set each of their elements.

JavaBeans are actually carried over from Swing, where they have a rather different meaning. In the Swing world, JavaBeans create reusable components, often for making Java IDEs. There are several truths (or at least conventions) that your JavaBeans for JSP must uphold:

- The Java class that defines your bean should be named `ClassNameBean`. That is, your descriptive name should be appended with "Bean." So, a bean whose purpose is to track orders in an e-commerce site should be called `OrderBean`.
- JavaBeans optionally implement the serializable interface. This is primarily for use with Enterprise JavaBeans, however—another subject altogether.
- A JavaBean must define a no-argument constructor. Typically, member variables are initialized in this constructor.
- Every bean property generally consists of a member variable, a `getVar()` method, and a `setVar()` method. The methods should be named accord-

ingly, though an exception is made for boolean variables, which can use the "is" prefix; for example, `isCurrent()`.

- The naming of the variables and methods is as follows: their initial letter should be lowercase, and subsequent words in the identifier should have initial caps—for instance, `getManagerBonus()` and `setManagerBonus()`. The method names should match their variable names. That is, using the above methods, you should have a `managerBonus` variable in your bean.

14.8.1 <jsp:useBean>

The `<jsp:useBean>` action checks for an instance of a bean in the given class and scope. If one is found, it is referenced with the `id` attribute. If an instance is not found, it instantiates the bean. The bean is then available for processing by referencing the `id` and scope.

Usage:

```
<jsp:useBean id="myBean" class="com.packageName.className">
```

Table 14.6 shows the `<jsp:useBean>` action attributes.

TABLE 14.6 `<jsp:useBean>` Action Attributes

ATTRIBUTE	DESCRIPTION	NOTES
`beanName`	Bean name	(optional) Specifies name of the bean component you are using to instantiate the bean. This is the same as the name of the bean in the `instantiate()` method of `java.beans.Beans`.
`class`	Class name	(optional) Used to specify class of the bean you are instantiating.
`id`	Bean reference	(required) Specifies name by which you will reference the bean being instantiated.
`type`	Variable type	(optional) Sets the type of scripting variable to be used as a bean, defined by the `id` attribute—the class that the bean gets cast to.

14.8.2 <jsp:setProperty>

The <jsp:setProperty> action sets the value of a property inside a JavaBean.

Usage:
The action performs somewhat differently depending on how it is called.

```
<jsp:setProperty name="counter" property="count" param="count">
```

Table 14.7 shows the <jsp:setProperty> action attributes.

TABLE 14.7 <jsp:setProperty> Action Attributes

ATTRIBUTE	DESCRIPTION	NOTES
`name`	Bean name	(required) Name of the bean containing the property to be set.
`param`	Request parameter	(optional) Specifies the request parameter whose value will be set to the bean property value. Use of this attribute obviates use of the `value` attribute.
`property`	Bean property	(required) Specifies the property to be set.
`value`	Set value	(optional) Sets the value of the specified property. Can be any runtime expression that evaluates to a string.

14.8.3 <jsp:getProperty>

This action is used to retrieve the specified property value from a JavaBean; the output value is a string. The specified bean must first be instantiated with the <jsp:useBean> action.

Usage:

```
<jsp:getProperty name="cart" property = "orderid" />
```

Table 14.8 shows the <jsp:getProperty> action attributes.

TABLE 14.8 `<jsp:getProperty>` Action Attributes

ATTRIBUTE	DESCRIPTION	NOTES
`name`	Name of bean	(required) Specifies name of a bean, already instantiated in any scope.
`property`	Property of bean	(required) Specifies the bean property to retrieve the value of.

Let's look at a quick example to demonstrate the typical usage of a bean. Below is a simple bean example that defines a counter.

14.8.4 testCounterBean.jsp

```
<%-- File: testCounterBean.jsp
     Purpose: show JSP using a JavaBean
--%>

<%@page contentType="text/html"%>

<html>
<head><title>session hit counter</title></head>
<body>

<%-- instantiate the counter bean, this is
     usually at or near the top of a page --%>

<jsp:useBean id="counter" scope="session"
class="beans.ACounterBean" />

<%-- set the property --%>

    <jsp:setProperty name= "counter" property="count"
       param="count"/>

<%-- retrieve the property --%>

The count: <jsp:getProperty name="counter" property="count" />

</body>
</html>
```

Below is the Java class that this JSP uses to handle the counting business. Note one thing about working with beans: You cannot simply write this bean and compile it into the same directory as the JSP. Java classes used for beans and custom tags and objects in Web applications should reside under the `WEB-INF/classes` directory. So, this bean is compiled into `<TOMCAT_HOME>/webapps/javaforcf/WEB-INF/classes/beans`. The JSP, however, is in the `<TOMCAT_HOME>/webapps//javaforcf/chp14` directory. The container knows where to find your classes.

14.8.5 ACounterBean.java

```
/* File: CounterBean.java
 * Purpose: demo beans by creating a simple counter
 */

package beans;

public class ACounterBean {

    int count = 0;

        // no-arg constructor
    public ACounterBean() {
    }
        // getter method
    public int getCount() {
        // increment on each request
        count++;
        return this.count;
    }

        // set the count for this instance
    public void setCount(int count) {
        this.count = count;
    }
}
```

Closing the browser and opening it again will restart the count, because the bean operates in the session. JSP automatically handles the initiating of sessions for you.

In the following section, we will look at a somewhat more interesting example, though the same simple principles are still clearly at work. Note that an advantage of using beans is that they do not require any special deployment parameters.

14.9 Sample Bean Application: Writing Dynamic XML

This example application uses what we know about beans to query a database and write out its result set as an XML file. You can then transform the resulting XML file for presentation to a WAP client or an HTTP client.

To run this application, you need to download the Xalan XML parser from *http://xml.apache.org*. Once you've got it, install it in Tomcat's `WEB-INF/lib` directory, and restart Tomcat to make it available to the application.

14.9.1 `writeNews.jsp`

```
<%--File: writeNews.jsp
    Purpose: call the writeNewsXMLBean, which does a query to
    get News events and writes out the result as an XML file.
    --%>

<jsp:useBean id="newsQ2xml"
    class = "javaforcf.writeXMLNewsBean" />

<% newsQ2xml.writeXMLNews(); %>

<h1>The files were written.</h1>
```

The purpose of `writeNews.jsp` is to call the `writeNewsBean` bean to handle all the work of the application.

14.9.2 `writeNewsBean.java`

```
/* Purpose: query a database and write out an XML document
   representing the dataset.
   This can then be read into a Flash movie, or consumed by
   any other kind of client.
 */
package javaforcf;
```

```
import java.io.*;
import java.sql.*;
import java.util.*;

public class writeXMLNewsBean  {

        public void writeXMLNews()
        {
            // delete old file
            File oldFile = new File("/usr/tomcat4/webapps/
                 javaforcf/xmlout/news.xml");
            boolean fileDeleted = oldFile.delete();

            if (fileDeleted) {

// declare a file output object
                FileOutputStream out;
// declare a print stream object
                PrintStream p;
// holds News items from db
                int cols;
                String thexml, url, sql, colName, path;


            try
                {
            // connect to the database
url = "jdbc:mysql:///
cybertrailscomdb?user=eben&password=secret";

                    // query
                sql = "SELECT itemName, itemText from items
                       WHERE isCurrent = 1";

                    // use mysql database
                Class.forName("org.gjt.mm.mysql.Driver");
  Connection conn = DriverManager.getConnection(url, "", "");
                Statement stmt = conn.createStatement();
                ResultSet rset = stmt.executeQuery(sql);
                ResultSetMetaData rsmd = rset.getMetaData();

                cols = rsmd.getColumnCount();

                // set the query into an xml string
                thexml = "<?xml version=\"1.0\"?>";
                thexml += "<dataset>";
```

```
                while (rset.next()) {
    thexml += "<row>";

                    for(int i=1; i<=cols; i++) {

                    colName = rsmd.getColumnLabel(i);
                    thexml += "<" +colName.toLowerCase()+ ">" +
cleanseData(rset.getString(i)) +
"</" + colName.toLowerCase() + ">";
    }
        thexml += "</row>";
                }
                thexml += "</dataset>";

                        // Create a new file output stream
                        // connect

path = "/usr/tomcat4/webapps/javaforcf/xmlout/news.xml";
                out = new FileOutputStream( path );

                // Connect print stream to the output stream
                        p = new PrintStream( out );

                        // write the file data
                        p.println (thexml);

                        // close the connection
                        p.close();
                }
                catch (Exception e) {
                 System.err.println ("Error writing to file");
                }
            }
        }

        public String cleanseData(String data) {

//String to hold the cleansed text
                String cleantext = "";

/*
    Object to break down the string into tokens delimited by
                < and >
 */
StringTokenizer breakdown = new StringTokenizer(data, "<>");
```

```
                    //Stop holds the original amount of tokens
                    int stop = breakdown.countTokens();

 /*
 Loop to go over the tokens, discarding the 'br' which
 is in the middle of < and > so that only the text gets
 taken into the cleantext variable and written out to xml
 */
                    for(int x = 0; breakdown.hasMoreTokens(); x++)
                    {
                        cleantext = cleantext +
breakdown.nextToken();

/*
 stop/2 + 1 is the last time the loop will run
 so that only 1 token will be taken the last time
 so that the tokenizer never throws an exception
 */
                            if(x != stop - (stop/2 + 1))
                            {
                            breakdown.nextToken();
                            }
                    }
                    return cleantext;
                }
}
```

First the bean hits the database, then it deletes a file that might exist and writes out a new XML file containing elements corresponding to the column names.

Below is the XML file that is produced by the bean. If the file already exists, it is overwritten:

14.9.3 News.xml

```
<?xml version="1.0"?>
<dataset>
<row>
<itemname>My Special Headline</itemname>
<itemtext>This is the text from the database. This is an
important article. blah blah blah.
</itemtext>
</row>
</dataset>
```

```
<dataset>
<row>
<itemname>Some Other Title</itemname>
<itemtext>Another bit of text. This could go on for a while.
Yadda yadda yadda.
</itemtext>
</row>
</dataset>
```

One thing to note about the above XML file is that it has been reformatted here; when the bean writes out the file, it will be all on one line. You can add a line break, but it is not necessary and may make it more difficult to parse. Unless humans are going to read your XML file, there's probably little benefit to adding breaks.

A good reason to write out your data to XML in this manner is so that you can pass it into another application, a Flash client, a WAP client, or transform it using XSLT.

> **NOTE** If you are very interested in this kind of flexibility, ColdFusion has made working with XML much easier with CFMX's `<cfxml>` tag. But XML parsing is also native to the JDK 1.4, and you can find numerous extensions for XML to use in conjunction with Java. One such application that is still rather new but popular is Cocoon. Cocoon, XML parsers, XSL transformers, and many other fine applications are available for download from *http://xml.apache.org*.

14.10 What's Next?

The next chapter will demonstrate how to extend the power of JSP using custom actions (JSP jargon for custom tags). Custom actions are perhaps more important in JSP than they are in ColdFusion, because JSP has fewer core tags.

When JSP was first introduced, there was a proliferation of JSP tags loaded with scriptlets. This is not good design, because it does not encourage separation of the logic and presentation layers. Beans made huge strides toward this end, but they still often require scriptlets to iterate over their results. Custom tags can make working with any kind of data or return value easier for Web designers to deal with. They help the portability of your code between applications and allow you to share your work easily with others.

Like beans, custom actions are essentially special Java classes. That means the primary challenge facing custom action developers is getting their tags deployed. They require some setup on the server, and we'll cover that, write some example tags, and have a good time.

15

JSP Custom Tags

This chapter introduces custom tags. We start off looking at how to write a simple custom tag and deploy it. Then we'll see how you can use custom tags in your JavaServer Pages. We also will look at how you can import JSP tag libraries into ColdFusion MX templates for use in these applications.

In JavaServer Pages you can write your own tags as you can in ColdFusion. Like beans, JSP custom tags are regular Java classes; the chief distinguishing characteristic of these classes is that they extend one of a few API classes that support custom tag evaluation.

Writing custom JSP tags allows developers to distribute tag libraries, or collections of tags that have a uniform purpose or overarching theme. Tag libraries consist of one or more tags that have something in common. Sometimes the commonality is simply that they are from the same company. This is the case with the JRun tag library, which comes with Macromedia JRun. There are a number of tags in this library that make it very easy to work with JRun. These tags include some for querying databases, working with XML, and performing iterative loops.

The introduction of the JavaServer Pages Standard Tag Library by the Apache Software Foundation marks a new stage in JSP development. The standard tag library, which we will look at in this chapter, consists of many different tags, including those for iteration and logic, database access, internationalization, and formatting.

15.1 Getting Started with Custom Tags

Tag libraries are fairly complex. In ColdFusion, it is very easy to start writing CFML custom tags. It isn't in JSP. That is, unless you know a little Java. Then you realize that all that is happening is that you're extending a certain set of classes and then describing the tag in an XML format. With everything we now know about Java you should find it much easier to get started writing custom tags than would a Web developer with little or no Java knowledge. This accounts somewhat for the structure of this book. Custom tags are simply much more important in JSP than they are in ColdFusion. That's because ColdFusion already has 90 tags for you to work with right out of the box. JSP doesn't. So in this section we will see how to write custom tags.

15.1.1 Beans and Tags

There are distinct differences between writing a custom tag and a bean, though they share certain goals. We will look briefly at these so that you can wisely choose when to write a tag and when to write a bean.

First of all, it is generally easier to write and deploy a bean than a tag. All you have to do is define your class and call `<jsp:useBean/>`. This may come down to who is on your development team, what their roles are, and what the life of the application will be like. For example, if you work in a job shop and plan on reusing your e-commerce application for a number of different clients, then using tags is a great choice because of the simplicity and familiarity they afford designers.

A major difference is that tags can manipulate content and beans cannot. You can define tags devoted to HTML output or formatting, for instance.

Beans can add flexibility within an application. That's because they can be defined in one servlet or JSP and then used in a different one. Custom tags, on the other hand, can add flexibility across multiple applications. Their work assignments often make them self-contained. Because of the different kinds of work beans and tags are often assigned, it can be easier to port tag libraries. Developers often make their tag libraries available for free download or for sale; one doesn't generally see "bean libraries."

15.1.2 Custom Tag Syntax

The syntax of a custom tag is exactly like the syntax of the predefined JSP actions. It consists of a prefix, followed by the name of the tag. The prefix is the name of the tag library you define.

```
<prefix:tagname />
```

In practice this syntax looks like this:

```
<jsp:include page="some.jsp"/>
```

When you write custom tags, they follow the same form:

```
<ecommerce:cart action="addItem" itemID="5" />
```

Here we reference a tag called `cart` in the ecommerce tag library. It has two attributes, `action`, which defines what specific thing we want to do in the cart, and `itemID`, which specifies the product to work with in the tag.

15.1.3 Defining Custom Tags

There are a few things necessary to make custom tags work. It is not like in ColdFusion where you can write a file with a certain name and then reference it directly without having to even restart your server.

> **NOTE** JRun 4 now has "hot deployment"; Tomcat, however, requires that you restart it every time you make any change to Java classes. The basic rule is this: If you modify only the code, such as scriptlet code, in a JSP, then you can simply restart the page to see your change; if you modify a bean, a custom tag class, or any regular Java helper class, you need to restart Tomcat for the change to take effect.

To begin with, you need a *tag library*. These are all of the classes that make up the Java program the custom tags call. The second thing you need is the `taglib` directive. You write this into your JSP to signify that you will be using this library; the directive also specifies the prefix name you will use to reference your library. Third, you need a *tag library descriptor*, or TLD. This is an XML document that describes the library. In the following sections, we'll discuss these in more detail. Finally, we need to tell Tomcat's `web.xml` file (or other corresponding file in a different container) that we will use this tag library.

15.1.4 Tag Handlers

The tag handler is responsible for evaluating tag actions during execution of the calling JSP. Every tag library must support one of the tag handler classes, which allow passing information between the tag and the caller. These handlers are `javax.servlet.jsp.tagext.TagSupport` and `javax.servlet.jsp.tagext.BodyTagSupport`. These utility classes provide the basic built-in functionality to make custom tags work. As their names imply, these classes serve a different kind of tag writing. If you want to make a tag that does not need to evaluate any body content (anything between the opening and closing tags), then you can extend `javax.servlet.jsp.tagext.TagSupport`. Tags in different languages that do not need to evaluate any body content include the following:

```
<br>

<cfset name="value>

<jsp:forward page="some.jsp"/>

<cart:view />
```

> **NOTE** The API reference included with this book contains the complete listing of `javax.servlet.jsp` classes and their methods and constants. It is a good idea to read over this so that you know what functionality is built into the API.

> **NOTE** Because they are XML-compliant, regular JSP tags and custom tags must include a trailing slash if they do not have a separate closing tag.

The `TagSupport` class has a number of methods that are useful. These include the following:

- `doStartTag()` defines processing for the beginning tag. It corresponds to `ThisTag.ExecutionMode = "start"` in ColdFusion.
- `doEndTag()` performs the work designated in the closing tag. It corresponds to `ThisTag.ExecutionMode = "end"` in ColdFusion.
- `release()` releases tag state.
- `setPageContext(PageContext pageContext)` returns `void`, setting the `pageContext` for the current JSP.
- `getParent()` returns the parent tag.

> **NOTE** Remember, custom tags and all things JSP and servlet are not part of the J2SE—they are in the J2EE, and so you won't find information about their classes or methods in the API we've been using for most of this book. This API is currently available at *http://java.sun.com/j2ee/sdk_1.3/techdocs/api/*.

The doStartTag() method is executed as soon as the tag is instantiated. The doEndTag() is executed the moment doStartTag() completes. These methods both return int values in the guise of readable text messages (Java constants) such as SKIP_BODY or EVAL_BODY. The container decides what action it needs to take next based on the value returned.

Here are the int values that doStartTag() returns:

- EVAL_BODY_INCLUDE indicates that the body between the opening and closing tags should be included in the output stream. A tag returning this value must extend TagSupport and cannot process the body content (though it can be included in the output stream).
- EVAL_BODY_TAG indicates that a new BodyContent object should be created and the body of the tag should be processed. Only tags extending BodyTagSupport can return this value.
- SKIP_BODY indicates that a body should not be processed if one exists.

The doEndTag() method can return either of the two following values:

- EVAL_PAGE indicates that the container should continue processing the remainder of the JSP.
- SKIP_PAGE indicates that the container should *not* continue processing the remainder of the JSP.

15.1.5 The taglib Directive

The taglib directive ties the JSP page to the TLD and sets the namespace prefix for the tag to use on the page. Its job is to import the tag library to make it available for use on this JSP.

It looks like this:

```
<%@taglib uri="/WEB-INF/tlds/myTaglib.tld"
          prefix="ecommerce" %>
```

Call this at the top of your JSP to make your tag library available. The uri must reference a custom XML-based description of the tags in the library called a TLD. The prefix is what you use as a prefix to reference the tag on the JSP caller.

15.1.6 The Tag Library Descriptor

The Tag Library Descriptor (TLD) serves two purposes. First, it contains all of the information required by the runtime to know what to execute during JSP translation. Second, it contains information to assist JSP authoring tools in understanding and displaying this information.

When the JSP is translated into a servlet at runtime, the TLD for each of the libraries associated with the page is loaded. Next, the TLD is parsed and the information contained in it is offloaded to helper classes. Then it waits. When the runtime encounters a reference to a tag in the JSP, it visits the data stored in the helper classes and validates the tag's syntax. Finally, it creates a stub for the tag (which is why you see a `stubs` directory in CFMX).

An example of a TLD follows. We'll use an expanded version of this listing in the next chapter.

15.1.7 example.tld

```
<?xml version="1.0" encoding="ISO-8859-1" ?>
<!DOCTYPE taglib PUBLIC
    "-//Sun Microsystems, Inc.//DTD JSP Tag Library 1.2//EN"
    "http://java.sun.com/dtd/web-jsptaglibrary_1_2.dtd">

<taglib>
    <tlib-version>1.0</tlib-version>
    <jsp-version>1.2</jsp-version>
    <short-name>ecommerce shopping cart libary</short-name>
    <description>a shopping cart</description>
    <tag>
        <name>message</name>
        <tag-class>com.javaforcf.store.tags.MessageTest
        </tag-class>
        <body-content>empty</body-content>
        <description>test: show a message</description>
        <attribute>
            <name>message</name>
            <required>true</required>
            <rtexprvalue>false</rtexprvalue>
            <type>java.lang.String</type>
        </attribute>
    </tag>
</taglib>
```

In the above TLD, a number of things happen. First, we declare that this is an XML document and declare its namespace.

NOTE The TLD must be syntactically valid. If it is not, your custom tag will not work, and Tomcat will tell you the problem on startup. That means that you must take care of typical XML things, such as making sure that the XML declaration begins at the very first column of the document.

Then we write a top-level `<taglib>` element, specifying the version of the library and the version of JSP used. The short name and description tags are arbitrary strings describing the tag library. Next, each tag in the library must have its own `<tag>` element. In the above example, only one tag is declared; more would be annexed in just this way. Any attributes must be declared, and you must specify whether or not they are required.

15.2 Writing a Simple Custom Tag

In this section we walk through the entire process of writing and deploying a custom tag. We'll start with the tag definition itself, `Message.java`, which just prints a message to the browser.

15.2.1 `Message.java`

```
/*
 * File: Message.java
 * Purpose: demo simple custom tag by displaying message
 * passed in custom tag attribute.
 */
package javaforcf.ch15;

import javax.servlet.jsp.*;
import javax.servlet.jsp.tagext.*;

public class MessageTest extends TagSupport {
    private String message="";

    public void setMessage(String m) {
        this.message = m;
    }
    public String getMessage() {
        return message;
    }
    public int doStartTag() throws JspException {
```

```
        try {
            pageContext.getOut().print("Hello" +
               this.getMessage());
        }

        catch (Exception ioException ) {
            System.err.print(ioException.toString());
            throw new JspException(ioException );
        }

        return SKIP_BODY;
    }
}
```

This is a very simple custom tag. In order to call the tag, we have to write a TLD for it, which looks like this:

15.2.2 cart.tld

```
<?xml version="1.0" encoding="ISO-8859-1" ?>
<!DOCTYPE taglib PUBLIC
    "-//Sun Microsystems, Inc.//DTD JSP Tag Library 1.2//EN"
    "http://java.sun.com/dtd/web-jsptaglibrary_1_2.dtd">

<taglib>
    <tlib-version>1.0</tlib-version>
    <jsp-version>1.2</jsp-version>
    <short-name>a simple demo tag</short-name>
    <description>displays a pleasant greeting</description>
    <tag>
        <name>message</name>
        <tag-class>javaforcf.chp15.MessageTest
        </tag-class>
        <body-content>empty</body-content>
        <description>test: show a message</description>
        <attribute>
            <name>message</name>
            <required>true</required>
            <rtexprvalue>false</rtexprvalue>
            <type>java.lang.String</type>
        </attribute>
    </tag>
</taglib>
```

This TLD first declares that we require version 1.2 of JSP (though there is nothing really in the tag that requires it). We give it a short name and a description, both of which are arbitrary text strings for human readers. Then we write the `<tag>` element, which will hold all of the information that the container is interested in regarding this tag.

First we give it a name, and then we tell the container where it can find the tag handler class file. We specify the body content as empty, which means that we will extend `TagSupport`, not `BodyTagSupport`. Because our tag has an attribute, we need to specify what the attribute is called and specify whether it is required. Then we specify whether this tag has a return expression value and what type the attribute accepts, and we're done.

Once you have written and compiled the tag handler and written the TLD, you then need to write a JSP that imports the TLD and calls the tag. That JSP might look like this:

15.2.3 MessageCaller.jsp

```
<%-- File: simpletag.jsp
     Purpose: call a custom tag
 --%>

<%@page contentType="text/html"%>
<%@ taglib prefix="cart" uri="/WEB-INF/cart.tld" %>

<html>
<body>
<%-- call the tag--%>
<h1><cart:message message="I am a custom tag."/></h1>

</body>
</html>
```

The tag prefixes the output with "Hello" and prints it to the browser. The important part of the code is shown here:

```
        try {
            pageContext.getOut().print("Hello" +
               this.getMessage());
                  }
```

The output is shown in Figure 15.1.

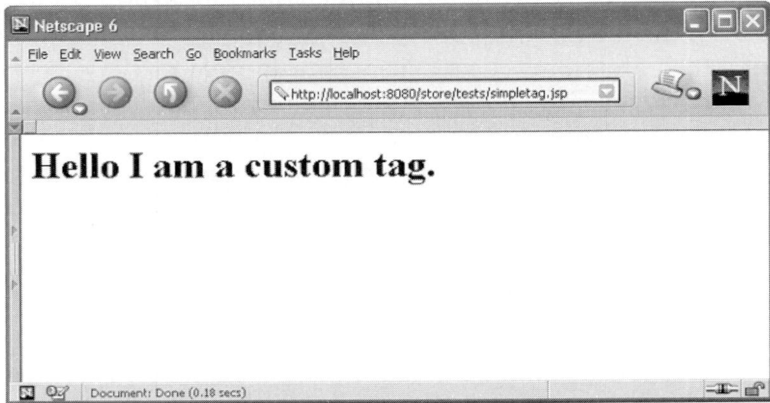

FIGURE 15.1 Custom tag display.

This also demonstrates use of JSP's `PageContext` class, which we'll put to work in the next chapter. Its purpose is to offer one point of reference for many of the attributes of a page. The `pageContext` variable stores the value of the `PageContext` object for the current page. Note that CFMX makes use of the `PageContext` variable for its `forward()` and `include()` methods.

To deploy the tag, mention the library in your `web.xml` file, put the TLD in the directory specified in `web.xml`, put the class file in the directory specified in the TLD, write a JSP that calls it, restart Tomcat, and you're in business.

15.3 Importing a JSP Library in CFMX

ColdFusion MX introduced the ability for developers to import JSP tag libraries into their own applications. This is very simple and requires the use of a new CFMX tag, `<cfimport>`. In this section, we'll briefly see how to use it. Let's do that by contrasting how a JSP imports a tag library for use:

In JSP:

```
<%@ taglib uri="mylibrary.tld" prefix="ecommerce" %>
```

In CFMX:

```
<CFIMPORT taglib="/WEB-INF/lib/mytags.jar" prefix="ecommerce">
```

It is very easy to use JSP tag libraries in ColdFusion this way. All you have to do is download your tag library, place the `.jar` file in the `WEB-INF/lib` directory as you would in Tomcat, write your `<cfimport>` tag, and reference the tag on that CFML page. However, there are a couple of things to look out for:

- You cannot call the `<cfimport>` tag in your `application.cfm` file as a shortcut to make it available to all of your CFML pages.
- You cannot define the library in a CFML page other than the one in which you use it; that is, you cannot `<cfinclude>` it.
- With regular CFMX tags, there is a central location where you can store custom tags and have them available to the entire server. This is not the case with imported JSP tag libraries. You must deploy it separately with each application.

That's all there is to it.

15.4 Working with the JSTL

The JavaServer Pages Standard Tag Library has been under development for some time (more than two years to arrive at version 1.0). It answers many of the concerns you may have had upon learning that JSP had only a few core tags. The purpose of the JSTL is to provide standard iteration, conditional evaluation, XML processing, database access, and expression-language tags.

While there sadly is not world enough and time to go into the JSTL in detail, you're a ColdFusion developer, so I don't think we'll need to. What you need to know is how to get it and install it. Once you've got it, it is very easy to poke around and start using it. But you need to do these things to start using JSTL:

1. Download the JSTL from *http://jakarta.apache.org/taglibs/doc/standard-doc/intro.html*.
2. Make the JSTL classes available to the server. This is easily done by placing them in your Web application's `WEB-INF/lib` directory.
3. Put the TLD files into your `WEB-INF` directory or a subdirectory thereof.
4. Download and install an XML parser. The JSTL requires this, and JSP 1.2 does not. That means that you may not have one of these installed on your system, and you'll need to get one that supports both SAX and DOM. It is a good idea for portability's sake that you include this parser with your Web application distribution. It is easy and free to use the Apache Xerces-J parser, which can be downloaded from *http://xml.apache.org/xerces-j*.

Once you have downloaded and installed the JSTL, it is a good idea to look at the source and read the included docs to see what is available to you. There are tags for setting variables (instead of `<cfset var="value">`, you can use `<c:set var="Value"/>`), and instead of `<cfswitch>` and `<cfcase>`, you use `<c:choose>` and `<c:when>`.

Let's look at an example now. The following code takes a parameter that defines an XSL file to be used. When the value of that parameter is determined, then the appropriate XML document is selected. This setup, while it may seem backwards, allows us to easily use partial views of the same XML document set for getting the specific content we want. Once we have both the XML and XSL files, we transform them using the JSTL `<x:transform>` tag in the following listing, `makeContent.jsp`.

15.4.1 xmlTransformerSwitch.jsp

```
<%--File: xmlTransformerSwitch.jsp
    Purpose: switch against url param xsl. Use this as the
        value of the xsl file for the transformation of
        content. Certain xsl files go with the few xml files,
        so those couplings are coded into the same cases. The
        benefit here is that you can add a touch of JSP code to
        check for the client and use a different XSL sheet to
        transform the content into WAP/WML output, for instance
--%>

<% //set the path to the files for reuse
   String xmlPath = "webapps/mycontext/WEB-INF/xmlcontent/";
   String xslPath = xmlPath + "xslt/";
%>

    <c:set var="theXSL">
       <%= xslPath + request.getParameter("style") + ".xsl" %>
    </c:set>

    <c:choose>
        <c:when test="${param.xsl == 'contactus'}">
            <c:set var="theXML">
                <%= xmlPath + "company.xml" %>
            </c:set>
        </c:when>
        <c:when test="${param.xsl == 'aboutus'}">
            <c:set var="theXML">
                <%= xmlPath + "company.xml" %>
            </c:set>
        </c:when>
```

```
        <c:otherwise>
            <c:set var="theXML">
                <%= xmlPath + "products.xml" %>
            </c:set>
        </c:otherwise>
    </c:choose>
```

This code performs a switch against the value passed in the `style` parameter. Once the parameter value is determined, it sets a path to a different XML file that will be transformed. This file is called by the `makeContent.jsp`, shown below.

15.4.2 makeContent.jsp

```
<%--File: makeContent.jsp
    Parameters: ?style=somexsldoc
    Use: page displays middle content area. xml data is
       transformed into html via documents stored under
       WEB-INF/xmlcontent.
    Purpose: to support display of data on multiple devices.
--%>

<%@ page language="java" contentType="text/html" %>
<%@ page errorPage="errorsgalore.jsp" %>

<!--get JSTL core library-->
<%@ taglib prefix="c" uri="http://java.sun.com/jstl/ea/core" %>

<!--get JSTL for XML -->
<%@ taglib prefix="x" uri="http://java.sun.com/jstl/ea/xml" %>

<jsp:include page = "header.jsp" />

<tr>
    <td width="25"><img src="images/spacer.gif" width="25"/>
    </td>
    <td valign="top" width="400">
     <span class="txt">

        <%--switch determines what xml and xsl file to use--%>
    <%@ include file="xmlTransformerSwitch.jsp" %>

        <%--perform transformation--%>
    <x:transform xmlUrl="${theXML}" xsltUrl="${theXSL}" />
```

```
      </span>
    </td>
  </tr>
<jsp:include page="footer.jsp" />
```

This file calls the JSTL `<x:transform>` tag to run an XML source and an XSLT file through the transformer together, to output an HTML result. A different XML file is used depending on the value of the XSL `"style"` param determined in the `xmlTransformerSwitch.jsp` above.

A sample XSL file that serves as the blueprint for the transformation is shown here. This simple file is `aboutus.xsl` and finds corresponding elements in an XML document to match and apply the style to.

15.4.3 aboutus.xsl

```
<?xml version="1.0" encoding="UTF-8"?>
<xsl:stylesheet version="1.0" xmlns:xsl="http://www.w3.org/
1999/XSL/Transform">
<!--ABOUTUS.xsl-->

<!-- import global variables-->
<xsl:import href="globals.xsl" />

<xsl:output method="xhtml"indent="yes" encoding="iso-8859-1"/>

<!--match root. select aboutus text only-->
<xsl:template match="/">
    <xsl:copy>
        <xsl:apply-templates select="/company/aboutus" />
    </xsl:copy>
</xsl:template>

<!-- header and text-->
<xsl:template match="aboutus">
    <img src="images/aboutUsHeader.gif" alt="about us" />
    <p><span class="greytext"><xsl:apply-templates /></span>
    </p>
</xsl:template>

</xsl:stylesheet>
```

These examples demonstrate how easy it can be to start doing sophisticated things with the JSTL—especially if you are a seasoned ColdFusion developer.

15.4.4 `taglib` for the JSTL

Here is a sample description used in a `web.xml` for the JSTL.

```
...
<!--JSP Standard Tag Library 1.0-->
<taglib>
  <taglib-uri>http://java.sun.com/jstl/ea/core</taglib-uri>
  <taglib-location>/WEB-INF/jstl10/tld/c.tld</taglib-location>
  </taglib>
  <taglib>
  <taglib-uri>http://java.sun.com/jstl/ea/core-rt</taglib-uri>
  <taglib-location>/WEB-INF/jstl10/tld/c-rt.tld
  </taglib-location>
  </taglib>
  <taglib>
    <taglib-uri>http://java.sun.com/jstl/ea/xml</taglib-uri>
    <taglib-location>/WEB-INF/jstl10/tld/x.tld
    </taglib-location>
  </taglib>
  <taglib>
    <taglib-uri>http://java.sun.com/jstl/ea/xml-rt</taglib-uri>
    <taglib-location>/WEB-INF/jstl10/tld/x-rt.tld</taglib-
location>
  </taglib>
  <taglib>
    <taglib-uri>http://java.sun.com/jstl/ea/fmt</taglib-uri>
    <taglib-location>/WEB-INF/jstl10/tld/fmt.tld</taglib-
location>
  </taglib>
  <taglib>
    <taglib-uri>http://java.sun.com/jstl/ea/fmt-rt
</taglib-uri>
    <taglib-location>/WEB-INF/jstl10/tld/fmt-rt.tld
</taglib-location>
  </taglib>
  <taglib>
    <taglib-uri>http://java.sun.com/jstl/ea/sql</taglib-uri>
    <taglib-location>/WEB-INF/jstl10/tld/sql.tld
</taglib-location>
  </taglib>
```

```
  <taglib>
    <taglib-uri>http://java.sun.com/jstl/ea/sql-rt
</taglib-uri>
    <taglib-location>/WEB-INF/jstl10/tld/sql-rt.tld
</taglib-location>
  </taglib>
  <taglib>
    <taglib-uri>/jstl-examples-taglib</taglib-uri>
    <taglib-location>/WEB-INF/jstl10/tld/jstl-examples.tld
</taglib-location>
  </taglib>
  <taglib>
    <taglib-uri>http://jakarta.apache.org/taglibs/standard/
          scriptfree</taglib-uri>
    <taglib-location>/WEB-INF/jstl10/tld/scriptfree.tld
</taglib-location>
  </taglib>
  <taglib>
    <taglib-uri>http://jakarta.apache.org/taglibs/standard/
          permittedTaglibs</taglib-uri>
    <taglib-location>/WEB-INF/jstl10/tld/
          permittedTaglibs.tld</taglib-location>
  </taglib>
</web-app>
```

The folder name jstl10 is arbitrary: It's the name you use when you unzip the JSTL download from Apache.

15.5 The `web.xml` File

It can be useful to know the structure of a `web.xml` document, as Tomcat expects the elements in the document to come in a certain order and will not function properly otherwise. In this section, we will outline the order of a complete `web.xml` document. It is not complete, but almost complete, and defines most of the elements you are likely to use without stepping into Enterprise JavaBeans. Remember that you don't need to use any of these elements inside the `<web-app>` element, but if you do, they must be in this order.

```
<?xml version="1.0" encoding="ISO-8859-1"?>
<!DOCTYPE web-app PUBLIC
 "-//Sun Microsystems, Inc.//DTD Web Application 2.3//EN"
"http://java.sun.com/j2ee/dtd/web-app_2_3.dtd">
```

```
<web-app>

<!--meta information that GUI tools or IDEs might use
    to represent this app -->
<icon>
    <small-icon>/images/AppRepresentationSM.gif</small-icon>
    <large-icon>/images/AppRepresentationLG.gif</large-icon>
</icon>

<display-name>Java for CF</display-name>

<description>my application description</description>

<!-- filter -->
<filter>
    <filter-name>SomeFilter</filter-name>
    <filter-class>com.mysite.SomeFilter</filter-class>
</filter>

<!-- make a mapping for this filter -->
<filter-mapping>
    <filter-name>SomeFilter</filter-name>
    <url-pattern>*.jsp</url-pattern>
</filter-mapping>

<!-- define a servlet -->
<servlet>
    <servlet-name>Login</servlet-name>
    <servlet-class>com.somesite.Login</servlet-class>
    <init-param>
        <param-name>paramName</param-name>
        <param-value>paramValue</param-value>
    </init-param>
    <load-on-startup>1</load-on-startup>
</servlet>

<!-- mapping for another servlet -->
<servlet-mapping>
    <servlet-name>DBController</servlet-name>
    <url-pattern>*.jfcf</url-pattern>
</servlet-mapping>

<!--set default session timeout in minutes -->
<session-config>
    <session-timeout>45</session-timeout>
</session-config>
```

```
<!-- set MIME mapping -->
<mime-mapping>
    <extension>doo</extension>
    <mime-type>application/x-something</mime-type>
</mime-mapping>

<!--default welcome file list -->
<welcome-file-list>
<welcome-file>login.jsp</welcome-file>
</welcome-file-list>

<!-- error page -->
<error-page>
    <error-code>404</error-code>
    <location>/errors/a404.jsp</location>
</error-page>

<!-- define tag library -->
<taglib>
    <taglib-uri>/store</taglib-uri>
    <taglib-location>/WEB-INF/tlds/mylibrary.tld
    </taglib-location>
</taglib>

<!-- define a container level security constraint -->
<security-constraint>
    <web-resource-collection>
       <web-resource-name>Java for CF app</web-resource-name>
         <url-pattern>/*</url-pattern>
       </web-resource-collection>
    <auth-constraint>
       <role-name>javaforcfusers</role-name>
    </auth-constraint>
</security-constraint>

<!-- define login configuration -->
<login-config>
    <auth-method>BASIC</auth-method>
    <realm-name>My App</realm-name>
</login-config>

</web-app>
```

15.6 JSP Satellite Developments

By early 2003, JSP 1.3 should be released. A number of features will be added to this release. In the meantime, there are a number of important developments in the world of JSP that can help developers get the job done, working in conjunction with JSP. In the following sections, we will introduce these so that you have enough information to look into them yourself.

15.6.1 Struts

Struts, began by developer Craig McClanahan, is the name of an open-source product by the Jakarta project at Apache. Struts is a very large application framework that defines numerous custom tags. Its purpose is to provide an open-source framework for working with servlets and JSPs.

Struts is based on the Model-View-Controller design pattern, discussed in the previous chapter. Model components (the data objects) are not included with Struts. These must be defined as custom business logic by the developer implementing the Struts framework. View components include many JSP tags that mimic and extend the behavior of regular HTML tags. Here is an example of a Struts view tag at work:

```
<%@taglib uri="/WEB-INF/struts-html.tld" prefix="html"%>
<html:form action="userLoginAction.do" name="loginForm"
          type = "javafocf.LoginForm>
   Username: <html:text property="username"><br/>
   Password: <html:password property="password"></br>
<html:submit/>
</html:form>
```

The custom `<html>` JSP tags in this snippet look familiar. They are very much like their true HTML counterparts, with an important difference: They have a `property` attribute. This names a unique attribute present in the `ActionForm` bean defined for this form. The object created by the `LoginForm` will have the properties referenced set to the field values.

The Controller component included with Struts is its central, pivotal member. A servlet called `ActionServlet` takes requests from the client and forwards control of the request to a user-defined `Action` class. It is mapped to a set of URLs in the `web.xml` file; often the mapping is to `.do`, as in the above example. There is a servlet configuration process that uses a number of initialization parameters in a file that is generally called `struts-config.xml`. This file defines how the application will respond to and route requests. Such mappings are defined as ActionMappings; objects of this class map a given Action subclass to a given request.

You write Controller components to do the work of your application by writing classes that extend org.apache.struts.action.Action class. The actual work of your component you write inside the perform() method, which looks like this:

```
public ActionForward perform(ActionMapping mapping,
     ActionForm form,
     HttpServletRequest req,
     HttpServletResponse, res)
          throws IOException, ServletException
```

An ActionForward object names the view component to which the request should be forwarded once processing is complete. ActionForward objects map JSPs to logical names in the struts-config.xml file.

An ActionForm subclass is a JavaBean that provides structured access to the request parameters coming in from the form, and can store them as session or request values and perform validation, forwarding the view back to the form page for correction if necessary. Struts also defines error message classes for this purpose (ActionError and ActionErrors).

Struts was developed beginning in May of 2000, so it predates the JSTL. That means that there is a bit of overlap in their functionality, particularly with the formatting tags.

> **Note** If you are interested in Struts, its homepage is at *http://jakarta.apache.org/struts/*. You can download the framework and find out more about it here.

15.6.2 JavaServer Faces

JavaServer Faces offers a way for developers to work with a standard framework for creating GUI components. The design goals of JSF as defined in JSR 127 read as follows:

1. Create a standard GUI component framework that can be leveraged by development tools to make it easier for tool users to both create high-quality GUIs and manage the GUIs' connections to application behavior.

2. Define a set of simple lightweight Java base classes for GUI components, component state, and input events. These classes will address GUI lifecycle issues, notably managing a component's persistent state for the lifetime of its page.
3. Provide a set of common GUI components, including the standard HTML form input elements. These components will be derived from the simple set of base classes (outlined in #1) that can be used to define new components.
4. Provide a JavaBeans model for dispatching events from client-side GUI controls to server-side application behavior.
5. Define APIs for input validation, including support for client-side validation.
6. Specify a model for internationalization and localization of the GUI.
7. Automatic generation of appropriate output for the target client, taking into account all available client configuration data, such as browser version, etc.
8. Automatic generation of output containing required hooks for supporting accessibility.

> **Note** As mentioned in the previous chapter, new Java technologies are put forward with Java Specification Request documents created by the Java Community Process. JavaServer Faces is JSR 127, and you can investigate its homepage here at *www.jcp.org/jsr/detail/127.jsp*.

As you can see, there is some overlap with Struts; this is generally viewed as a strength, however, as the two may likely converge the best of both worlds.

15.6.3 Cocoon

Cocoon, sponsored by Apache, began in 1999 as a project of Stefano Mazzocchi. It is at heart a dynamic content generation tool, kind of the way JSP and ColdFusion are. Cocoon is entirely XML-based, however. Every request passed through Cocoon statically or dynamically produces XML, and then transforms it and formats it for the response. Cocoon makes it fun to generate output suited for all different kinds of devices, including HTML, WML, PostScript, or SVG.

Cocoon is essentially a servlet that receives requests. It generates a stream of XML events to be fed through a pipeline and uses the SAX events model to process the source. Finally, a serializer creates output from the processing in the form of HTML, WML, text, XML, SVG, etc. Commonly an XSLT transformer is wedged in here, running an XSL stylesheet against the source document to transform the display.

You can find out more about Cocoon at *http://xml.apache.org/cocoon*.

15.6.4 Log4J

This is another open-source project sponsored by Apache Software Foundation. It was founded by Ceki Gulcu, whose vision was to offer a simple but powerful way for Java developers to integrate logging into their applications. To follow the latest developments of Log4J, visit *http:jakarta.apache.org/log4j*.

15.7 What's Next?

The next chapter consists entirely of an e-commerce case study. The case study takes you start to finish through the building process of a complete online store. In the process, we'll write regular Java classes to represent objects in our store (such as the products) and use JavaBeans to unify working with the catalog. We also keep an eye on separating presentation from business by writing custom tags to handle shopping cart interaction. Finally, we'll incorporate a number of different tags from the JSTL to see how they interoperate.

What the store example affords is a number of things: we get to see all of the different aspects of JSP mentioned above, as well as directives, scriptlets, expressions, and request and session variables, interacting in a complete application. It also highlights exactly how you can write a fairly portable and flexible JSP application that allows you to reuse components and change entirely the look and feel of the site for your own use.

16

J2EE Case Study: An E-commerce Site

This chapter contains all of the code for a complete Java e-commerce application. It puts to work a lot of the things we've learned throughout the book, including Java classes, JavaBeans, custom tags, JDBC, JSPs, and the JSTL.

The primary purpose is to show you how all of the elements can come together in a working application that you can test and deploy. Auxiliary purposes include demonstrating a pretty good division of labor, and how to separate presentation and business logic using these varied aspects of J2EE technology.

16.1 Application Overview

Our example will be a complete store, by which I mean it has a catalog with categories and subcategories of products. Products in this store can have options associated with them. For instance, a clothing item could have size and color, while a computer can have hard drive size and RAM. This is a feature that is often required by real e-commerce sites, but it is rarely demonstrated. The relational database handles the work in join tables for defining option sets, each of which have a number of options. There is some extra work required in the checkout and order retrieval process to handle the options facet of the application.

An `ArrayList` stores the items in a user's cart in the session object. The checkout process includes forms for billing and shipping. The shipping form prepopulates with the information passed from the billing form, because they are often the same. Then the user is shown everything in his or her cart and the shipping and billing info, and he or she provides credit card information. The complete order is sent to the database. It is then retrieved by the merchant using a JSP that you can put in a password-protected administration area.

The application runs off of Tomcat 4 and uses a MySQL 3.2 database, but it could be easily ported to other platforms.

I am grateful for the work of Vic Miller—he contributed in myriad ways to this application.

16.1.1 ColdFusion Modeling

Because it can be tedious writing a database application of much complexity in Java, it is not a bad idea to demo the application in ColdFusion before writing it in Java. This has a couple of benefits. First, it means you can ensure that your database works, and it allows you to tweak it easily. Then you can start getting data out of the database from your ColdFusion templates. Then, once you've got everything just as you like it, you can still use a good portion of the SQL queries you've written. This process assumes somewhat that you are on a small team and have a lot of the responsibility for putting up the app. If you have a different person to design the database, write the queries, do the JSP, and write the Java classes, then performing a demo before writing probably is of little benefit.

16.2 Database

In order to make the store work, create a database in MySQL that follows the table description indicated below. You can use another database with little modification. I have not used a username and password in the code below for simplicity's sake. The database in the code is called "storecybertrailscomtest." The tables look like this:

16.2.1 `Categories` Table

```
catid int(11)   PRI  NULL  auto_increment
catname varchar(100)
```

16.2.2 `Subcategories` Table

```
subcatid int(11)  PRI  NULL  auto_increment
subcatname varchar(75)
```

16.2.3 ProductsCategories Table

```
productid int(11)     0
catid int(11)         0
subcatid int(11)      0
```

16.2.4 Products Table

```
productid int(11)  PRI  NULL  auto_increment
name varchar(150)  YES  NULL
price float  YES   NULL
shortdescription varchar(200)  YES  NULL
longdescription text  YES  NULL
smimage varchar(75)  YES  NULL
lgimage varchar(75)  YES  NULL
ships tinyint(1)  0
isfeatured tinyint(1) 0
```

16.2.5 OptionSets Table

```
optionsetid int(11)PRINULLauto_increment
optionsetname varchar(50)
```

16.2.6 Options Table

```
optionidint(11)  PRI   NULL  auto_increment
optionname varchar(50)
optionsetid int(11) 0
priceadd float YES  NULL
```

16.2.7 ProductsOptionSets Table

```
productid int(11)    0
optionsetid int(11)  0
```

16.2.8 Orders Table

```
orderidint(11) PRI  NULL  auto_increment
customeridint(11)0
shipinfoidint(11)0
subtotal float 0
shipping float 0
tax float 0
grandtotal float 0
orderdate varchar(50)
isprocessed tinyint(1) 0
```

16.2.9 Customers Table

```
customerid int(11)  PRI  NULL  auto_increment
billaddress varchar(150) binary
billstate varchar(50)
billzipcode varchar (10)0
billcountry varchar(50)
billphone varchar(50)
billemail varchar(75)
creditnumber varchar(50)
creditname varchar(100)
creditexpdate varchar(50)
billname varchar(50)
billcity varchar(75) YES  NULL
```

16.2.10 ShippingInfo Table

```
shipinfoid int(11)  PRI  NULL  auto_increment
shipaddress varchar(150)
shipcity varchar(100)
shipstate varchar(75)
shipzipcode varchar(10)  YES  NULL
shipcountry varchar(75)  YES  NULL
shipemail varchar(75)  YES  NULL
shipname varchar(75)  YES  NULL
shipphone varchar(20)  YES  NULL
```

16.2.11 OrderProducts Table

```
ordersproductsid int(11) PRI  NULL  auto_increment
orderid int(11)   0
productid int(11)  0
qty int(11)        0
price varchar(10) YES  NULL
```

16.2.12 OrderProductOptionChoice Table

```
ordersproductsid int(11) YES  NULL
optionid int(11) YES  NULL
```

Once you have created this database, populate it with some test data. Then you just need a little setup and you're ready.

16.3 Setup

There are a few things you need to make sure are in place to get the app off the ground.

- Make sure the MYSQL database is set up.
- Create a new context in Tomcat to run it under Tomcat. To do this, copy a folder called `store` into `<TOMCAT_HOME>/webapps`. You must fill out four key items on the Context Addition if you are using Tomcat's Administrator Web app:
  1. Doc Base: `javaforcf`
  2. Path: `/javaforcf`
  3. Working Directory: `work\Standalone\localhost\javaforcf`
  4. SessionID Initializer: `org.apache.catalina.session.StandardManager`
- Then save and commit changes.
- Restart Tomcat.
- You must have the JSTL installed. Click taglibs and download the most recent stable version. I am using `jakarta-taglibs-standard-1.0.zip`. Extract it using `zip` or `jar` to your `WEB-INF` root in a folder called `jstl10`. The `web.xml` file is included in the listings below.

> **NOTE** If you are modifying files and think that your changes are not being reflected, you may need to delete the generated servlet files in the work directory and then restart. This forces Tomcat to recreate the servlets.

If you want to manually set up Tomcat for a new Web application, then you can do so like this:

Edit `tomcat4\conf\server.xml` file. Under the manager entry (look for `<!-- Tomcat Root Context -->`), add this entry:

```
<Context path="/store" docBase="store"
 debug="0" privileged="true"/>
```

Then, you need to write the following files into the directories as specified in the remainder of the chapter.

16.4 Root Application Files

The root of the application is the `<TOMCAT_HOME>webapps/store` folder. Individual files are prefixed with "Listing." Folder names are indicated in this chapter by top-level headers.

16.4.1 index.jsp

```
<%--
   template: index.jsp
   purpose: view default page
   use: called as index when site is requested. Just has link
     to the catalog.
--%>
<jsp:include page="header.jsp" flush="true" />
          <%-- begin middle content --%>
<tr>
<td align="center" valign="top" width="445">

<table cellpadding="0" cellspacing="0" border="0" width="445"
align="center">
<tr>
<td width="98"> </td>
<td><br>welcome to our online store.
<br>
<br>
<a href="viewCatalog.jsp">View the catalog</a>
</td>
</tr>
</table>
</td>
<td width="250" align="right" valign="top">

<%-- includes menu --%>
<jsp:include page="sideNav.jsp" flush="true" />

</td>
</tr>

<jsp:include page="footer.jsp" flush="true" />
```

The `index.jsp` file acts as the default file in the application. It simply includes header and footer files, as well as a side navigation bar. The main thing it does is show a link to `viewCatalog.jsp`, which is where the store application really begins. The application was set up this way so that you can define specials in the database and show them here, or use this as an informative page.

16.4.2 header.jsp

```
<%--
   template: header.jsp
   purpose: set html head info
   use:
--%>

<% String base = "http://localhost:8080/store/"; %>

<html>
<head>
    <title>ecommerce site</title>

    <link rel="stylesheet" type="text/css"
        href="styles/main.css" title="Store">
    <base href="<%= base %>">
</head>

<body topmargin="0" leftmargin="0" marginwidth="0"
    marginheight="0" background="images/bglines.gif">

<!--Main Table-->
<table cellpadding="0" cellspacing="0"
       border="0" width="764" align="left"
       background="images/spacer.gif">
<tr>
<td bgcolor="#FFFFFF" valign="top" width="763" align="left">
<table cellpadding="0" cellspacing="0" border="0" width="763">
            <!--Header And Navigation-->
<tr>
   <td colspan="3" align="left">
     <table cellpadding="0" cellspacing="0" border="0"
         width="100%">
         <tr>
            <td align="left" width="184">
               <a href="<%= base %>" border="0">
                  <img src="images/logo.gif" alt=""
                    width="184" height="59" border="0"></a>
```

```
                <td width="255" height="59">
                    <img src="images/spacer.gif"
                        width="225" height="59">
                </td>
                <td align="right" valign="bottom">
            <!-- links or images can go here -->
    <br>
    <a href="http://mysite.com">home</a>
    <br>
                   </td>
               </tr>
               <tr>
                  <td colspan="3" height="147">
                     <img src="images/trail.jpg" width="764"
                         height="102">
                     <br>
                     <img src="images/spacer.gif" width="50"
                         height="1">
                     <img src="images/storeHeader.gif">
                  </td>
               </tr>
             </table>
           </td>
         </tr>
```

The file header.jsp consists primarily of static HTML. We define a base link that you would need to change for production. All store pages will include this file—except for those in the checkout process, which use a slightly different header that includes JavaScript form validation.

16.4.3 sideNav.jsp

```
<%--
   template: index.jsp
   purpose: show default page
   use: called as index when site is requested.
--%>

<table border="0" width="200" height="300" cellspacing="5">
    <tr>
        <td valign="top" align="right">
            <a href="viewCart.jsp">view cart
              </a> <br>
```

```
            <br>
            <a href="viewCatalog.jsp">continue shopping
              </a> <br>

        </td>
    </tr>
</table>
```

This file is another static page that just allows you to define a separate navigation bar on the right-hand side of the screen. Its purpose is to give the user links to view the items in his or her cart and to return to the catalog to continue shopping after he or she has added an item.

16.4.4 footer.jsp

```
<%--
   template: footer.jsp
   purpose: include footer HTML
   use: included from index.jsp
--%>

    <tr>
        <td colspan="3" valign="bottom"
            valign="right"><br><br><br><br><br><br>
            <table cellpadding="0" cellspacing="0" border="0"
               width="763" align="center">
                <tr>
                    <td colspan="3" align="center">
                      <span class="greytext">
                        online store
                      </span>
                    </td>
                </tr>
                <tr>
                    <td width="34" bgcolor="#000000">
                        <img src="images/spacer.gif"
                             alt="" width="34"
                             height="15" border="0">
                    </td>
                    <td width="32" bgcolor="#666666">
                        <img src="images/spacer.gif"
                            alt="" width="32" height="15"
                            border="0">
                    </td>
```

```
                        <td width="32" bgcolor="#CC0000">
                            <img src="images/spacer.gif"
                                alt="" width="32" height="15"
                                border="0">
                        </td>
                    </tr>
                </table>
            </td>
        </tr>
        </table>
    </td>
    <td bgcolor="#000000" width="1" align="left">
        <img src="images/spacer.gif"
           alt="" width="1" border="0">
    </td>
    <td> </td>
    </tr>
    </table>
    </body>
    </html>
```

The `footer.jsp` file ends the display, and it consists exclusively of HTML design elements, all of which you'll want to replace when using your own design.

16.4.5 viewCatalog.jsp

```
<%--
   template: viewCatalog.jsp
   purpose: show categories, products in subcategories
        and product details.
        Allows user to add items to cart.
   use: called when user clicks link on index. This is the
        homepage of the store.
--%>

<%@ page import = "java.sql.ResultSet, java.util.*,
java.text.*" %>

<%--BEAN TO NAVIGATE CATALOG--%>
<jsp:useBean id="catalog"
     class = "com.cybertrails.store.beans.CatalogBean"
     scope="request"/>

<jsp:include page = "header.jsp" />
```

```
<tr>
    <td width="25"><img src="images/spacer.gif" width="25"/>
    </td>
    <td valign="top" width="487">
        <br> 
        <img src="images/bgspacertest.gif" width="487"
          height="1"/>

        Categories:<br>

<%-- This scriptlet connects to the database and gets the
categories. Then loop over the result and set name and id into
local variables to be output on the page --%>

         <%
            catalog.connect();
            ResultSet rs = catalog.getCategories();
            while (rs.next()) {
                  String catname = rs.getString("catname");
                  String catid = rs.getString("catid");
         %>

         <table width="400" border="0">
             <tr>
                <td align="left">
                    <span class="title1">
                    <a href="viewSubs.jsp?catid=<%= catid %>">
                       <%= catname %>
                  </a>
                    </span>
                    <br>
                </td>
             </tr>
         </table>

            <%--end while loop --%>
         <% }   %>

    </td>
    <td width="250" align="right" valign="top">
         <%-- includes menu --%>
         <jsp:include page="sideNav.jsp" flush="true" />
    </td>
   </tr>
<jsp:include page="footer.jsp" />
```

This page uses a JavaBean (defined in the source file `CatalogBean.java`) to connect to the database and get a result containing all of the category names. Once we've got this, we loop over them and output them. We also build the link dynamically so that we can pass the `categoryID` as a parameter. Our categories page is shown in Figure 16.1.

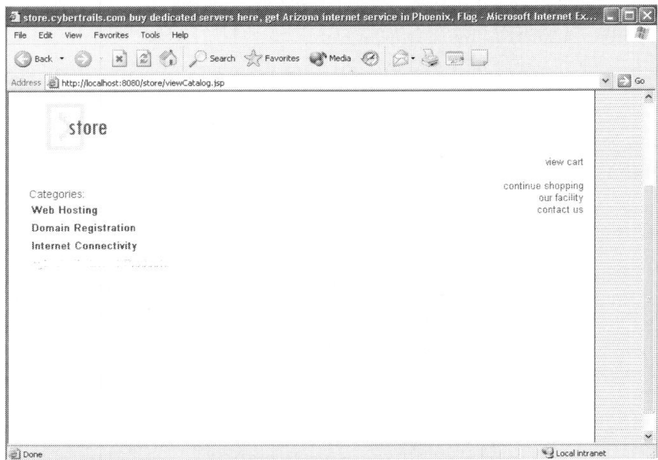

FIGURE 16.1 The categories page.

> **NOTE** One thing to note about these catalog files is that they reintroduce the bean and reconnect to the database each time. Refactoring this aspect of the code to make this process more efficient is left as an exercise for the reader.

16.4.6 viewSubs.jsp

```
<%--
   template: viewSubs.jsp
   purpose: show subcategories in chosen product category
   use: called when an ID param is passed from the
     viewCategory.jsp
--%>

<%@ page import = "java.sql.ResultSet, java.util.*,
java.text.*" %>

<%--BEAN TO NAVIGATE CATALOG--%>
<jsp:useBean id="catalog" class =
"com.cybertrails.store.beans.CatalogBean" scope="request"/>
```

```
<jsp:include page = "header.jsp" />

<tr>
    <td width="25"><img src="images/spacer.gif" width="25"/></
td>
    <td valign="top" width="487">
        <br> 
        <img src="images/bgspacertest.gif" width="487"
height="1"/>

        Subcategories:<br>

<%
catalog.connect();
ResultSet
rs = catalog.getSubCategories(request.getParameter("catid"));
while (rs.next()) {
   String subcatname = rs.getString("subcatname");
   String subcatid = rs.getString("subcatid");
%>

         <table width="400" border="0">
             <tr>
                <td align="left">
                    <span class="title1">

<a href="viewProducts.jsp?subcatid=<%= subcatid %>">
<%= subcatname %>
</a>
                    </span>
                    <br>
                </td>
             </tr>
         </table>
            <%--end while --%>
         <% }   %>

    </td>
    <td width="250" align="right" valign="top">
         <%-- includes menu --%>
         <jsp:include page="sideNav.jsp" flush="true" />
    </td>
   </tr>
<jsp:include page="footer.jsp" />
```

The viewSubs.jsp file is almost exactly like viewCategories.jsp. Its purpose is to show the subcategories in a particular category. For example, if you had defined a main category called "Drinks" and then clicked that link in viewCategory.jsp, you would now see all associated subcategories, which might include "Coffee," "Tea," and "Soda." Clicking on one of these subcategories will pass the subcategory ID to the next page, viewProducts.jsp.

16.4.7 viewProducts.jsp

```
<%--
   File: viewProducts.jsp
   Purpose: show products in a chosen subcategory
--%>

<%@ page import = "java.sql.ResultSet, java.util.*,
java.text.*" %>

<%@ taglib prefix="c" uri="http://java.sun.com/jstl/ea/core" %>

<%--BEAN TO NAVIGATE CATALOG--%>
<jsp:useBean id="catalog" class =
"com.cybertrails.store.beans.CatalogBean" scope="request"/>

<jsp:include page = "header.jsp" />

<tr>
    <td width="25"><img src="images/spacer.gif" width="25"/></
td>
    <td valign="top" width="487">
        <br> 
        <img src="images/bgspacertest.gif" width="487"
height="1"/>

        Products:<br>

         <%
            catalog.connect();
            ResultSet rs =
        catalog.getProducts(request.getParameter("subcatid"));
            while (rs.next()) {
                String name = rs.getString("name");
                String productid = rs.getString("productid");
                String price = rs.getString("price");
                String shortdescription =
                     rs.getString("shortdescription");
```

```
                String smimage = rs.getString("smimage");
        %>

        <table width="400" border="0">
            <tr>
                <td align="left">
                    <span class="title1">
<a href="viewProductDetail.jsp?productid=<%= productid %>">
<%= name %>
</a>
                    </span>
                    <span class="txt">
                    <br>price: $<%= price %>
                    <br>description: <%= shortdescription %>
                    <br>image: <%= smimage %>
                    </span>
                    <br>
                </td>
            </tr>
        </table>
           <%--end while --%>
        <% }   %>

    </td>

<td width="250" align="right" valign="top">

        <%-- includes menu --%>
        <jsp:include page="sideNav.jsp" flush="true" />

    </td>
   </tr>


<jsp:include page="footer.jsp" />
```

This file is very much like its predecessors. It shows you all of the products in a particular subcategory, as shown in Figure 16.2. The product links are also dynamically built in the same manner. Clicking on one of the product names takes you to a detail page for that product, `viewProductDetail.jsp`.

I don't have any images for these products, so in these product pages I have just output the name of the image stored as a path in the database. This is a very common way to deal with images that need to be referenced dynamically. The only adjustment you need to make is to output the value into the "src" attribute of an HTML `<img>` tag instead of printing it directly to the browser.

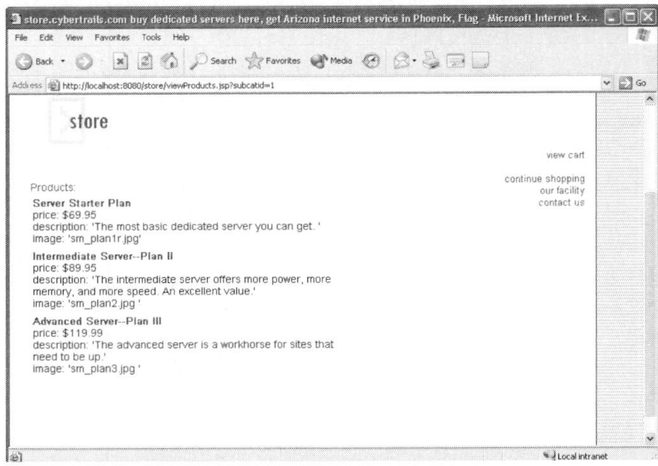

FIGURE 16.2 The list of products and their short descriptions in a given subcategory.

16.4.8 viewProductDetail.jsp

```
<%--
template: viewSubs.jsp
purpose: show subcategories in chosen product category
use: called when a param is passed from viewSubs.jsp
--%>

<%@ page import = "java.sql.ResultSet, java.util.*,
java.text.*" %>

<%--BEAN TO NAVIGATE CATALOG--%>
<jsp:useBean id="catalog" class =
"com.cybertrails.store.beans.CatalogBean" scope="request"/>

<jsp:include page = "header.jsp" />

<tr>
    <td width="25"><img src="images/spacer.gif" width="25"/>
</td>
    <td valign="top" width="487">
        <br> 
        <img src="images/bgspacertest.gif" width="487"
height="1"/>
<%
catalog.connect();
```

```
ResultSet rs =
catalog.getOneProduct(request.getParameter("productid"));

String productName = "";

while (rs.next()) {
    String productid = rs.getString("productid");
    productName = rs.getString("name");
    String price = rs.getString("price");
    String longdescription = rs.getString("longdescription");
    String lgimage = rs.getString("lgimage");
%>

         <table width="400" border="0">
             <tr>
                <td align="left">
                    <span class="title1"><%= productName %>
                    </span>
                    <br>price: $<%= price %>
                    <br>description: <%= longdescription %>
                    <br>image: <%= lgimage %>
                    <br>
                </td>
             </tr>
         </table>
            <%-- End While --%>
            <% } %>

         <form action="doCart.jsp" method="POST">

             <table width="400" border="0">

                <%-- get product option set --%>
<%
ResultSet ors =
catalog.getProductOptions(request.getParameter("productid"));
String currentOptionSet = "";
while (ors.next()) {
String optionsetid = ors.getString("optionsetid");
String optionsetname = ors.getString("optionsetname");
String optionid = ors.getString("optionid");
String optionname = ors.getString("optionname");
String optionpriceadd = ors.getString("priceadd");
```

```
%>

<tr>
  <td align="left">
<!--this acts like <cfquery group="">.
   without it, the option set name would be displayed next to
    every option-->

<% if(!(currentOptionSet.equals(optionsetname))) {
currentOptionSet = optionsetname;
%>
<br><b><%= optionsetname %></b><br>
<%
} %>

<input type = "radio" name="oset|<%= optionsetid %>"
value = "<%= optionname %>|<%= optionpriceadd %>|
<%= optionid %>">
<%= optionname %> (add:  $<%= optionpriceadd%>)

                </td>
             </tr>

            <%--end while --%>
         <% }   %>

         </table>
         <br>
         <table width="400" border="0">
             <tr>
                <td align="left">
<input type="hidden" name="productid"
     value="<%= request.getParameter("productid") %>">
<input type="hidden" name="productName"
     value="<%= productName %>">
<input type="hidden" name="action" value="add">

<input type="text" name="quantity" value="1"
      maxlength="2" size="2">
<input type="submit" name="submit" value="add to cart">
                    <br>
                </td>
             </tr>
         </table>
       </form>
    </td>
```

```
      <td width="250" align="right" valign="top">
           <%-- includes menu --%>
           <jsp:include page="sideNav.jsp" flush="true" />
      </td>
     </tr>
  <jsp:include page="footer.jsp" />
```

This is an important listing. Its job is to show detailed information about a product. Detail information in this case means a long description, a bigger picture, and the options associated with a product. Few demonstration stores will show how to successfully implement this aspect of online shopping, despite the fact that it is a prevalent part of real online shopping. Options represent choices the shopper should make about the product. For instance, a shirt would require at least two option sets: color and size. Within each of these option sets, you need to define the individual options that the user can choose from, such as red or blue, and S, M, L, or XL. This is all done in the database design, though it makes our checkout and completed order-retrieval page a touch trickier.

> **NOTE** Here is one thing you almost certainly want to change in this file if you implement this store in production: Right now, no options are checked by default. So a shopper could order an item without specifying any options if he or she wasn't paying attention. For instance, you could receive an order for a laptop with no hard drive size specified. Now, I know that users are conscientious, careful, savvy creatures who always read all of the instructions. But on some rare occasion, there is a slim chance of this happening. Because the options are output in a loop, you'd probably want to add some conditional logic to check against a MOD.

Note that the value of the option radio button gets dynamically set. The value includes a delimited list including the name of the option, the option set it is in, and the amount of money that choosing this option adds to the price of the current product. See Figure 16.3 for our product detail page.

This also affords a nice opportunity to show how to deal with nested query outputs. In ColdFusion, you can simply call another `<cfoutput>` and use its `group` attribute. Because JSP has no such built-in mechanism, we home grow it this way.

Once a shopper has viewed an item, he or she can add it to the cart with the link, or return to another page to continue shopping. The link hits `doCart.jsp`, the next listing.

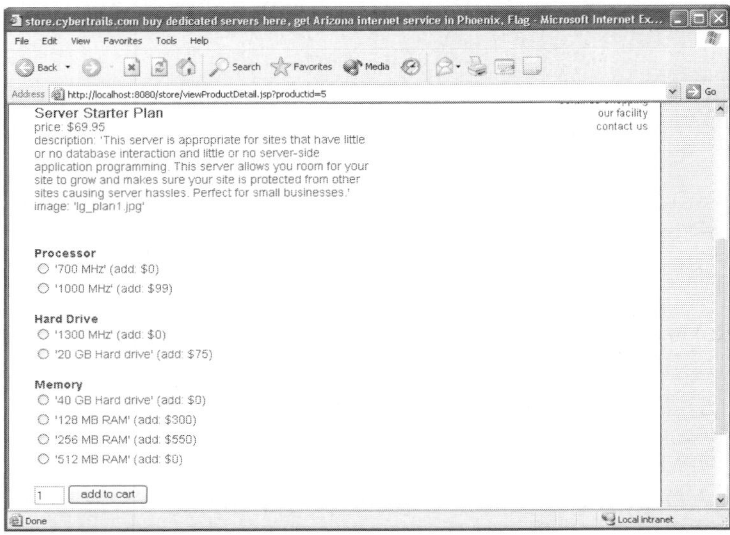

FIGURE 16.3 The product detail view.

16.4.9 doCart.jsp

```
<%--
   template: doCart.jsp CUSTOM TAG CALLER
   purpose: perform any necessary action in the cart and
      forward request to viewCart
   use:

ADD or REMOVE an item:
<cart:product action="add|remove" productid = "productid"/>

VIEW the contents of the cart:
<cart:product action="view"/>
--%>

<%@taglib prefix="cart" uri="/WEB-INF/cart.tld" %>
<%@taglib prefix="c" uri="http://java.sun.com/jstl/ea/core" %>

<% String productid = request.getParameter("productid"); %>

<c:choose>
  <c:when test="${param.action == 'add'}">
   <cart:product action="add" productid = "<%= productid %>"/>
```

```
  </c:when>
<c:when test="${param.action == 'remove'}">
<cart:product action="remove" productid = "<%= productid %>"/>
            </c:when>
            <c:otherwise>
                <cart:product action="view"/>
            </c:otherwise>
        </c:choose>

<%--now that processing is done,
    forward to the view page to see cart.
    like using <cflocation>--%>

<jsp:forward page="viewCart.jsp" />
```

This file uses the `when/otherwise` tags in the JSTL. These tags act like `<cfswitch>` and `<cfcase>` in some regards. Here they are used to determine whether or not the user wants to add or remove something from the cart. If the request parameter "action" was specified, then the `<c:when>` clause that matches it calls the product tag with the appropriate attribute values. The page then forwards control to `viewCart.jsp`, which shows the contents of the cart and gives the user the option to check out. The `viewCart` page is shown in Figure 16.4.

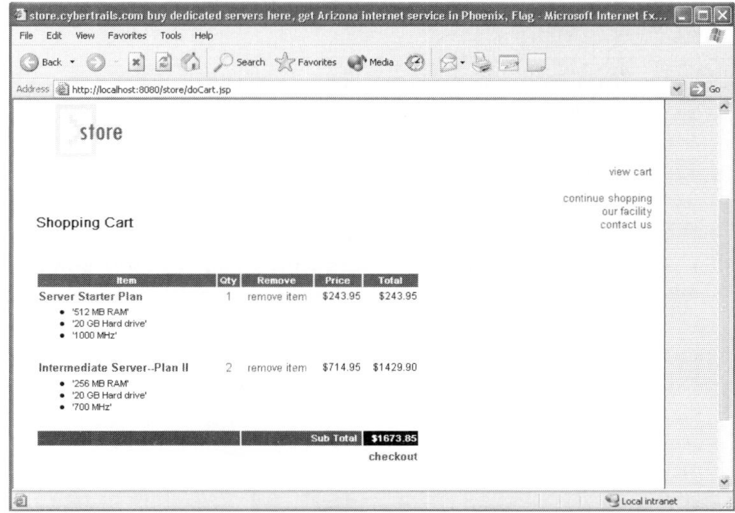

FIGURE 16.4 The `viewCart` page, showing the item and options selected, quantity, price, and subtotal. The user is given the option to remove the item or checkout.

16.4.10 viewCart.jsp

```
<%--
    File: viewCart.jsp
    Purpose: show the contents of the cart.
    Use: this page is called after every interaction with the
    cart so that the user can see the updates.
--%>

<%@ page import = "java.sql.ResultSet, java.util.*,
java.text.*" %>
<%@ taglib prefix="cart" uri="/WEB-INF/cart.tld" %>
<jsp:include page = "header.jsp" />

  <tr>
    <td width="25"><img src="images/spacer.gif" width="25"/>
    </td>
    <td valign="top" width="487">
        <br> 
        <img src="images/bgspacertest.gif" width="487"
              height="1"/>

        <h1>Shopping Cart</h1>

            <cart:view />

<%
ArrayList currentItems =
(ArrayList)session.getAttribute("currentItems");
    if (currentItems != null && currentItems.size() != 0 ) {
%>
            <table border="0" width="450">
                <tr>
                  <td bgcolor="white" align="right">
                    <a href="checkout.jsp"><b>checkout</b></a>
                  </td>
                </tr>
            </table>

        <% // close if
            } %>
        <br>
    </td>
    <td width="250" align="right" valign="top">
         <%-- includes menu --%>
```

```
        <jsp:include page="sideNav.jsp" flush="true" />
    </td>
   </tr>
<jsp:include page="footer.jsp" />
```

The bold font in the viewCart listing shows the call to the <cart:view> custom tag. This tag writes out the HTML table that displays the contents of the cart directly where it is called from. Then we check the size of the cart. If it is null, then it hasn't been created yet; if it has no items in it, then its size is 0. If either of these conditions is true, then we do not show the checkout link. If there is something in the user's cart, we show the link to checkout.jsp.

16.4.11 checkout.jsp

```
<%--
    File: checkout.jsp
    Purpose: this file starts the checkout process
    Use: we arrive here when the user clicks "checkout" on
      viewCart.jsp.
--%>
<%@ page import="java.util.*" %>

<%
    Enumeration ses = session.getAttributeNames();

    if (ses != null) {
    out.println("SESSION SCOPE: <br>");
    while(ses.hasMoreElements()) {
      out.println (ses.nextElement() + "<br>");
   }
}
    else out.println ("nothing in session");
%>

<jsp:forward page="viewBilling.jsp" />
```

NOTE Nothing actually happens in checkout.jsp. The file forwards to viewBilling.jsp, which shows the form to the user to enter billing information. What the file does do is enumerate over the session. I include it here because this was useful during development, and, after all, this is a case study. Because the request gets forwarded to viewBilling, nothing will actually print to the browser from checkout.jsp. In your own application, you would remove this page and forward directly to viewBilling—unless there was some logging or cleanup work that you wanted to do here.

Let's interject this little utility script right here. This scriptlet is not a necessary part of the e-commerce site, but you can use this scriptlet, which acts like a call to `<CFDUMP var=#session#>` by just printing out what's in the session:

```
<%@page import="java.util.*">
<%
Enumeration ses = session.getAttributeNames();
Object temp;
  if (ses != null) {
    out.println("SESSION SCOPE: <br>");
      while(ses.hasMoreElements()) {
        temp = ses.nextElement();
        out.println(temp.toString() + ": " +
        session.getAttribute(temp.toString()) + "<br>");
      }
  }
  else out.println("nothing in session");
%>
```

16.4.12 viewBilling.jsp

```
<%@page contentType="text/html"%>
<%@ taglib prefix="cart" uri="/WEB-INF/cart.tld" %>

<jsp:include page="headerWithValidation.jsp" flush="true"/>

  <tr>
    <td width="25"><img src="images/spacer.gif" width="25"/>
</td>
    <td valign="top" width="487">
        <br> 
        <img src="images/bgspacertest.gif" width="487"
height="1"/>

        <h1>Billing Info</h1>

<%-- show form for billing input--%>

<table width="450" border="0" cellspacing="0" cellpadding="0">
<tr>
<td colspan="2" valign="top">
Please take your time filling out the following information.
```

```
If you are placing an online order via credit card, your
billing information should appear as it does on your Credit
Card billing statements.
You will have opportunities to cancel your order after this
step.

<form name="Billing_Form" onSubmit="return
checkBillingForm(this)" action="doBilling.jsp" method="POST">

<table width="450" align="center" border="0">
<tr>
<td colspan="2" align="center" bgcolor="#CC0000"
class="cartHeaders2">Billing Information<br></td>
</tr>
<tr>
<td align="left" width="110">Name<br></td>
<td><INPUT TYPE="Text" NAME="bName" SIZE="25" MAXLENGTH="100"
onBlur="validfn(bName.value)"><br></td>
</tr>
<tr>
<td align="left" align="top">Address<br></td>
<td><textarea cols=23 rows=2 wrap="virtual" name="bAddress"
style="font-size: 11; font-family: arial, helvetica, sans-
serif; height: 40; width: 190;"></textarea><br></td>
</tr>
<tr>
<td align="left">City<br></td>
<td><INPUT TYPE="Text" NAME="bCity" SIZE="25"
MAXLENGTH="50"><br></td>
</tr>
<tr>
<td align="left">State<br></td>
<td>
<SELECT NAME="bState" SIZE="1">
    <jsp:include page="states.jsp" />
</SELECT>
<br>
</td>
</tr>
<tr>
<td align="left">Zip Code<br></td>
<td><INPUT TYPE="Text" NAME="bZipCode" SIZE="25" MAXLENGTH="10"
onClick="validZip(zip.value)"><br></td>
</tr>
```

```
<tr>
<td align="left">Country<br></td>
<td><INPUT TYPE="Text" NAME="bCountry" SIZE="25"
MAXLENGTH="100" VALUE="USA"><br></td>
</tr>
<tr>
<td align="left">Phone<br></td>
<td><INPUT TYPE="Text" NAME="bPhone" SIZE="25"
MAXLENGTH="50"><br></td>
</tr>
<tr>
<td align="left">E-mail<br></td>
<td><INPUT TYPE="Text" NAME="bEmail" SIZE="25"
MAXLENGTH="100"><br></td>
</tr>
<tr>
<td colspan="2"><hr width="100%" size="3" color="#666666"></td>
</tr>
<tr>
<td colspan="2" align="right">
<input type="submit" value="Go to the Next Step" style="font-
size: 11; font-family: Verdana; width: 180;"><br></td>
</tr>
</table>
</form>
</td>
</tr>
</table>

<br>
    </td>
<td width="250" align="right" valign="top">
         <%-- includes menu --%>
         <jsp:include page="sideNav.jsp" flush="true" />
    </td>
   </tr>
<jsp:include page="footer.jsp" flush="true"/>
```

This page is standard HTML for the most part; it appears as shown in Figure 16.5. The only two items of note are the following: First, we include the list of states to populate the form. Second, we use a different header, `headerWithValidation.jsp`. That header, shown below, includes some JavaScript to make sure that something is entered in the form.

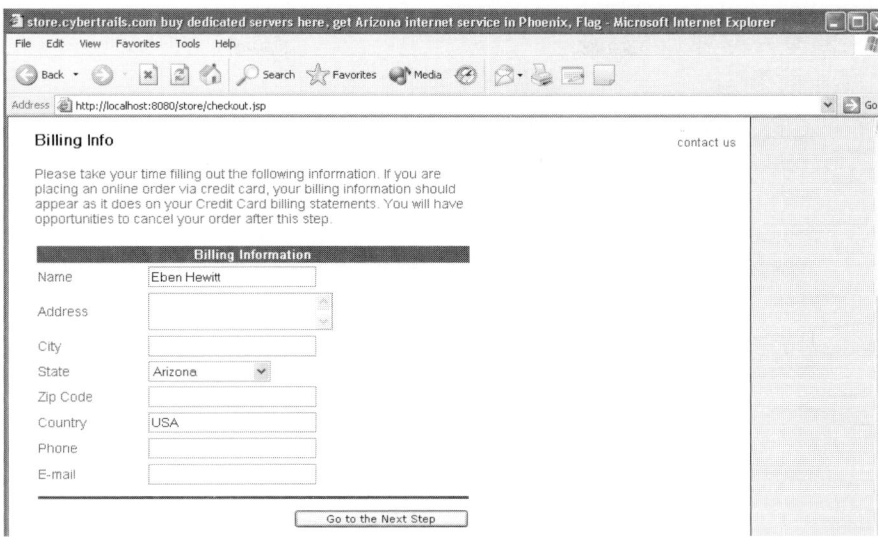

FIGURE 16.5 The billing information page.

16.4.13 headerWithValidation

```
<%--
Template: headerWithValidation.jsp

Purpose: included HTML header. The only
        difference between this and header.jsp
        is that this includes JS to validate form
        data entered by user.

Use: Called from shipping, billing, and confirm
        templates instead of the header.jsp
--%>

<% String base = "http://localhost:8080/store/"; %>

<html>
<head>
    <title>ecommerce site</title>
    <link rel="stylesheet" type="text/css" href="styles/
main.css" title="CyberTrails">
    <base href="<%= base %>">
```

```
<!-- validates form fields -->
<script language="JavaScript">
 function checkBillingForm(form) {

    var emailFilter=/^([\w-]+(?:\.[\w-]+)*)@((?:[\w-
]+\.)*\w[\w-]{0,66})\.([a-z]{2,6}(?:\.[a-z]{2})?)$/i

    if(form.bName.value == "") {
        alert("You must enter a billing name.")
        return false
    }
    else if(form.bAddress.value == "") {
        alert("You must enter a billing address.")
        return false
    }
    else if(form.bCity.value == "") {
        alert("You must enter a billing city.")
        return false
    }
    else if(form.bZipCode.value == "") {
        alert("You must enter a billing zipcode.")
        return false
    }
    else if(form.bCountry.value == "") {
        alert("You must enter a billing country.")
        return false
    }
    else if(!emailFilter.test(form.bEmail.value)) {
        alert("Please enter a valid email address")
        return false
    }

}

function checkShippingForm(form) {

    var emailFilter=/^([\w-]+(?:\.[\w-]+)*)@((?:[\w-
]+\.)*\w[\w-]{0,66})\.([a-z]{2,6}(?:\.[a-z]{2})?)$/i

    if(form.sName.value == "") {
        alert("You must enter a shipping name.")
        return false
```

```
    }
    else if(form.sAddress.value == "") {
        alert("You must enter a shipping address.")
        return false
    }
    else if(form.sCity.value == "") {
        alert("You must enter a shipping city.")
        return false
    }
    else if(form.sState.value == "") {
        alert("You must enter a shipping state.")
        return false
    }
    else if(form.sZipCode.value == "") {
        alert("You must enter a shipping zipcode.")
        return false
    }
    else if(form.sCountry.value == "") {
        alert("You must enter a shipping country.")
        return false
    }
    else if(!emailFilter.test(form.sEmail.value)) {
        alert("Please enter a valid email address")
        return false
    }
}

</script>

</head>

<body topmargin="0" leftmargin="0" marginwidth="0"
marginheight="0" background="images/bglines.gif">

//... rest of file omitted...
```

The JavaScript validation is the only item of interest here, and the rest of the file is just the same HTML from `header.jsp`. Once the form is submitted, it goes to `doBilling.jsp` to process the request.

16.4.14 states.jsp

```
<!-- list of states for inclusion
     in the select box for billing and shipping forms.
  -->
<OPTION VALUE="AL">Alabama</OPTION>
<OPTION VALUE="AK">Alaska</OPTION>
...// some states omitted
<OPTION VALUE="WY">Wyoming</OPTION>
<OPTION VALUE="INT">International</OPTION>
```

This file simply contains a list of all the state abbreviations and names. It is used to populate the form on `viewBilling.jsp`.

16.4.15 doBilling.jsp

```
<%--
    File: doBilling.jsp
    Purpose: this file accepts request params from the
    viewBilling page and calls the checkout tag.
    Control is then forwarded to the next step,
    which is shipping info (if info is different than billing)
    or payment info (if the same).
--%>

<%@ page contentType="text/html"%>
<%@ taglib prefix="cart" uri="/WEB-INF/cart.tld" %>

<html>
<head><title>ecommerce</title></head>
<body>

<%-- do the shipping insert action--%>

<cart:checkout action="billing" />

<%--forward to display page for next step--%>

<jsp:forward page="viewShipping.jsp" />

</body>
</html>
```

This file accepts request parameters from the `viewBilling` page and calls the checkout tag to add the parameters to the session object.

16.4.16 viewShipping.jsp

```
<%--
    File: viewShipping.jsp
    Purpose: enter shipping information. The data entered
    in billing is all spilled over into this form so that
    users don't have to re-enter if it is the same.
   --%>

<%@page contentType="text/html"%>
<%@ taglib prefix="cart" uri="/WEB-INF/cart.tld" %>

<jsp:include page="headerWithValidation.jsp" flush="true"/>

  <tr>
    <td width="25"><img src="images/spacer.gif" width="25"/></
td>
    <td valign="top" width="487">
        <br> 
        <img src="images/bgspacertest.gif" width="487"
height="1"/>

        <h1>Shipping/Setup Info</h1>

<%-- show form for shipping input--%>

<table width="450" border="0" cellspacing="0" cellpadding="0">
<tr>
<td colspan="2" valign="top">

If you have ordered <b>products</b>, they must be shipped to
you or someone else.
Please enter the correct shipping information below.<br>
<br>
If you have ordered <b>services</b> (such as Web hosting), they
do not require shipping, they require setup instead.<br> Please
make the appropriate selection at the bottom of this form.

<form name="Shipping_Form" onSubmit="return
checkShippingForm(this)" action="doShipping.jsp" method="POST">

<table width="450" align="center" border="0">
<tr>
<td colspan="2" align="center" bgcolor="#CC0000"
class="cartHeaders2">Shipping/Setup Information<br></td>
</tr>
```

```
<tr>
<td align="left" width="110">Name<br></td>
<td><INPUT TYPE="Text" NAME="sName" SIZE="25" MAXLENGTH="100"
value="<%= session.getAttribute("bName") %>"><br></td>
</tr>
<tr>
<td align="left" align="top">Address<br></td>
<td><textarea cols=23 rows=2 wrap="virtual" name="sAddress"
style="font-size: 11; font-family: arial, helvetica, sans-
serif; height: 40; width: 190;"><%=
session.getAttribute("bAddress") %></textarea><br></td>
</tr>
<tr>
<td align="left">City<br></td>
<td><INPUT TYPE="Text" NAME="sCity" SIZE="25" MAXLENGTH="50"
value="<%= session.getAttribute("bCity") %>"><br>
</td>
</tr>
<tr>
<td align="left">State<br></td>
<td>
<INPUT TYPE="Text" NAME="sState" SIZE="25" MAXLENGTH="10"
value="<%= session.getAttribute("bState") %>"><br>
<br>
</td>
</tr>
<tr>
<td align="left">Zip Code<br></td>
<td><INPUT TYPE="Text" NAME="sZipCode" SIZE="25" MAXLENGTH="10"
value="<%= session.getAttribute("bZipCode") %>"><br>
</td>
</tr>
<tr>
<td align="left">Country<br></td>
<td><INPUT TYPE="Text" NAME="sCountry" SIZE="25"
MAXLENGTH="100" value="<%= session.getAttribute("bCountry")
%>"><br>
</td>
</tr>
<tr>
<td align="left">Phone<br></td>
<td>
    <INPUT TYPE="Text" NAME="sPhone" SIZE="25" MAXLENGTH="50"
value="<%= session.getAttribute("bPhone") %>"><br>
```

```
</td>
</tr>
<tr>
<td align="left">E-mail<br></td>
<td>
    <INPUT TYPE="Text" NAME="sEmail" SIZE="25" MAXLENGTH="100"
value="<%= session.getAttribute("bEmail") %>"><br>
</td>
</tr>

<tr>
<td align="left" valign="top">Shipping Method<br></td>
<td>
    <input type="radio" name="ShipMethod" value="0"> Services
ONLY--no shipping<br>
    <input type="radio" name="ShipMethod" value="20" checked>
Ground (add $20)<br>
    <input type="radio" name="ShipMethod" value="27"> Express
(add $27.00)<br>
    <input type="radio" name="ShipMethod" value="45">
International (add $45)<br>
</td>
</tr>
<tr>
<td colspan="2"><hr width="100%" size="3" color="#666666"></td>
</tr>
<tr>
<td colspan="2" align="right">
    <input type="submit" value="Go to the Next Step"
style="font-size: 11; font-family: Verdana; width: 180;"><br></
td>
</tr>
</table>
</form>
</td>
</tr>
</table>
<br>
    </td>
<td width="250" align="right" valign="top">
        <%-- includes menu --%>
        <jsp:include page="sideNav.jsp" flush="true" />
    </td>
   </tr>
<jsp:include page="footer.jsp" flush="true"/>
```

This file makes use of the values passed from the billing form and set into the session scope. We prepopulate the form using these values so that if the shipping is the same as the billing, the user can simply hit Next and continue the checkout process. Either way, the values are added to the session and ultimately to the database.

16.4.17 doShipping.jsp

```
<%@page contentType="text/html"%>
<%@ taglib prefix="cart" uri="/WEB-INF/cart.tld" %>
<html>
<head><title>ecommerce</title></head>
<body>

<%-- do the shipping insert action--%>

<cart:checkout action="shipping" />

<%--forward to display page for next step--%>

<jsp:forward page="viewConfirm.jsp" />
</body>
</html>
```

The `doShipping` file, just like the `doBilling` file, adds the parameters passed from the request into the session.

> **NOTE** We don't add anything to the database until the very last possible minute. This helps make sure we don't have a lot of bad data in our database consisting of half-placed orders. Everything is kept in the session until the last step. We also don't pass anything sensitive, such as product price, as hidden form fields, because they are both easy to exploit and generally difficult to maintain.

16.4.18 viewConfirm.jsp

```
<%--
    File: viewConfirm.jsp
    Purpose: this file shows users what exactly they are
    purchasing and lets them enter credit card info if
    the order, billing, and shipping are all correct.
    Calls tag that calculates tax and adds everything
    for grand total.
```

```
    Submits to doConfirm.jsp which finalizes the order.
--%>

<%@page contentType="text/html"%>
<%@ page import="java.util.*" %>

<%@ taglib prefix="cart" uri="/WEB-INF/cart.tld" %>

<jsp:include page="header.jsp" flush="true"/>

  <tr>
    <td width="25"><img src="images/spacer.gif" width="25"/>
</td>
    <td valign="top" width="487">
        <br> 
        <img src="images/bgspacertest.gif" width="487"
height="1"/>

        <h1>Confirmation</h1>

<table width="450" border="0" cellspacing="0" cellpadding="0">
<tr>
<td width="141" rowspan="2" valign="TOP">

<form name="Confirm_form" method="post" action="doConfirm.jsp">

</td>
</tr>
<tr>
<td>
<p>Please verify that the following information is correct.
The billing information should appear exactly as shown on your
credit card.
Once you have double-checked that the following information is
correct, enter your credit card information and click "Submit
Order" to place your order.</p>
<table width="450" border="0" cellspacing="0" cellpadding="0">
<tr>
<td width="50%" bgcolor="#CC0000" class="cartHeaders2">Billing
Information<br></td>
<td width="50%" bgcolor="#CC0000" class="cartHeaders2">Shipping
Information<br></td>
</tr>
<tr>
<%-- output billing information--%>
<td valign="top">
```

```
<%= session.getAttribute("bName") %><br>
<%= session.getAttribute("bAddress") %><br>
<%= session.getAttribute("bCity") %>,
<%= session.getAttribute("bState") %>
<%= session.getAttribute("bZipCode") %><br>
<%= session.getAttribute("bCountry") %><br>
Phone: <%= session.getAttribute("bPhone") %><br>
</td>
<br><br>
</td>
<%--output shipping information--%>
<td valign="top">
<%= session.getAttribute("sName") %><br>
<%= session.getAttribute("sAddress") %><br>
<%= session.getAttribute("sCity") %>,
<%= session.getAttribute("sState") %>
<%= session.getAttribute("sZipCode") %><br>
<%= session.getAttribute("sCountry") %><br>
Phone: <%= session.getAttribute("sPhone") %><br>
</td>
</tr>
</table>

<%-- output the current items in the cart,
    along with chosen options and subtotal--%>

<cart:view />

<%--output shipping, tax, and grand total--%>

<table width="450" cellspacing="2" cellpadding="2" border="0">
<tr>
<td colspan="3" align="right" bgcolor="#666666"
class="cartHeaders">Shipping</td>
<td align="right" class="text">
$<%= request.getParameter("ShipMethod") %>
<br></td>
</tr>
<tr>

<%--calculate tax if business in this state--%>
<td colspan="3" align="right" bgcolor="#666666"
class="cartHeaders">Tax</td>
<td align="right" class="text">
$<cart:calculate item="tax"/>
```

```
<br></td>
</tr>
<tr>

<td colspan="3" align="right" bgcolor="#000000"
class="cartHeaders">Total</td>
<td align="right" class="text">
$<b><cart:calculate item="total"/></b>
<br>
</td>
</tr>
</table>

<br>
<table width="450" cellspacing="2" cellpadding="2" border="0">
<tr>
<td colspan="2" bgcolor="#CC0000" align="center"
class="cartHeaders2">Credit Card Information<br></td>
</tr>
<tr>
<td align="right">Name on card:<br></td>
<td><INPUT TYPE="Text" NAME="ccName" SIZE="30"><br></td>
</tr>
<tr>
<td align="right">Card number:<br></td>
<td><INPUT TYPE="Text" NAME="ccNumber" SIZE="30"><br></td>
</tr>
<tr>
<td align="right">Expiration date:<br></td>
<td><INPUT TYPE="Text" NAME="ccExpirationDate" SIZE="10"><br>
</td>
</tr>
</table>
<p>
<div align="right">
<input type="submit" value="Submit Order" style="font-size: x-
small; font-family: Verdana;">
</div>
</form>
</center>
</td>
</tr>
</table>
```

This file again makes use of the <cart:view> tag—the same one used during the shopping process. It is nice to reuse this tag because it makes this step easier, and it makes the app easier to maintain. We just output the shipping and billing information directly to allow the users to confirm what they typed and confirm their entire order. We also use the <cart:calculate> tag to calculate and output the tax and the grand total for the order.

16.4.19 doConfirm.jsp

```
<%--
    File: doConfirm.jsp
    Purpose: this file inserts the completed order,
    then redirects to the thank you page.
--%>

<%@page contentType="text/html"%>
<%@ taglib prefix="cart" uri="/WEB-INF/cart.tld" %>

<html>
<head><title>ecommerce</title></head>
<body>

<%-- do the shipping insert action--%>

<cart:checkout action="placeOrder"/>

<%--forward to display page for next step--%>

<jsp:forward page="viewThankyou.jsp" />

</body>
</html>
```

Once the user has confirmed his or her purchase, this page calls the <cart:checkout> tag once again, but this time the page passes it to the placeOrder value for the action attribute. This action will take everything in the session (shipping, billing, products ordered, and the options for each product) and distribute it with other miscellaneous order information (such as the tax and grand total) into the correct tables in the database. The confirmation page is shown in Figure 16.6.

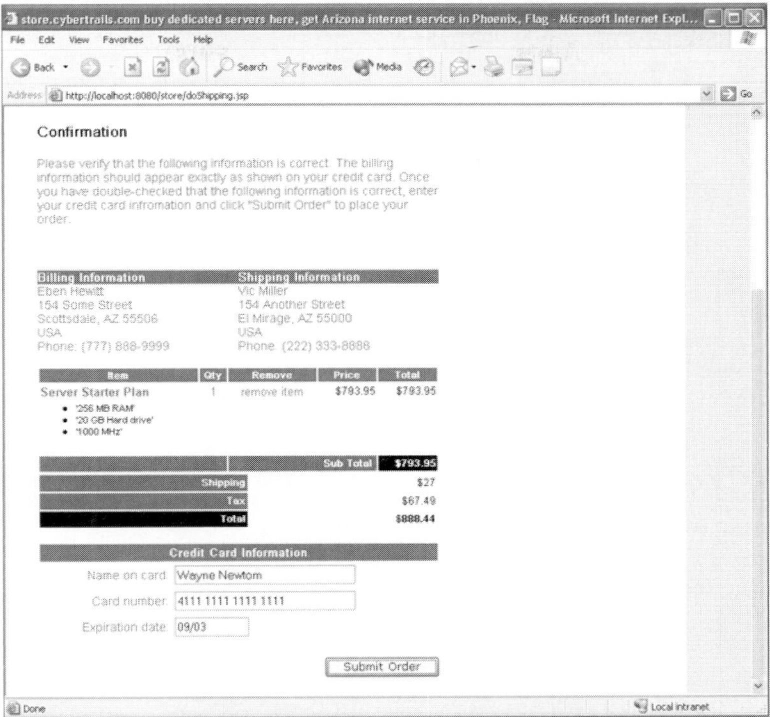

FIGURE 16.6 The confirmation page displaying the shipping and billing information and the complete order. The user enters credit card information here.

> **NOTE** No real-time credit card transaction happens here. You can easily add this functionality to the site because of the way this page is built. Simply add the appropriate account information and code to this page and then insert the order based on the return code. What happens here is that the credit card information is stored directly in the database, and when the order is retrieved, the credit card must be run manually. That poses a slight problem if the credit card fails.

16.4.20 viewThankyou.jsp

```
<%--File: viewThankyou.jsp
   Purpose: inform the viewers that they successfully checked
    out.
--%>
```

```
<jsp:include page = "header.jsp" />

  <tr>
    <td width="25"><img src="images/spacer.gif" width="25"/></
td>
    <td valign="top" width="487">
        <br> 
        <img src="images/bgspacertest.gif" width="487"
height="1"/>

        <h1>Thank you</h1>
<p align="center">
Thank you for placing an order with us. Your order is complete.
</p>
<p align="center">
Your order identification number is:
<%= session.getAttribute("orderid") %>
<br>
You may want to print this page or save the number for your
records.
</p>

<%
       // remove session from memory
    session.invalidate();
%>
        <br>
        <br>
    </td>
<td width="250" align="right" valign="top">
         <%-- includes menu --%>
         <jsp:include page="sideNav.jsp"/>
       </td>
   </tr>
<jsp:include page="footer.jsp" />
```

Once the user knows the transaction went through, we end the checkout process by destroying his or her session.

The following file, `viewCompletedOrder.jsp`, is not part of the e-commerce application that the user sees. It is what the merchant uses on the back end to retrieve orders that have been placed.

16.4.21 viewCompletedOrder.jsp

```
<%--
File: viewCompleteOrders.jsp
Purpose: show a list of all the orders in the database
Use: for the admin area of the store
Authors: Vic Miller, Eben Hewitt
comments:
--%>
<%@ page import="java.sql.*" %>
<%@ page import="java.util.*" %>

<jsp:include page = "header.jsp" />

<jsp:useBean id="CompleteOrder" scope="page"
       class="com.cybertrails.admin.GetOrderBean" />

<%
    //Variable Declarations
    ResultSet rs;
    String isProcessed = "";
    String currentOrderID = "0";
// Used to track when we change orders
    String currentOPID = "0";
//Used to track when we change products within one order

    //Get the complete order list from the database
    CompleteOrder.connect();

// if the form has been submitted then process
// the order in the db
        if (request.getParameter("orderid") != null) {
            isProcessed =
CompleteOrder.setIsProcessed(request.getParameter("orderid"));
    }

    rs = CompleteOrder.getNewOrders();

    CompleteOrder.disconnect();
%>

<tr>
<td align="center">
<h2><% if (isProcessed.length() > 1) { %>
    <%= isProcessed %>
<% } %>
```

```
</h2>
</td>
</tr>
    <td>
<%
//While loop over the result set to display the orders
while(rs.next()) {
    //Set the orderid into a string
    String orderid = rs.getString("orderid");
    //Test to if we have moved onto a new order
    if(!orderid.equals(currentOrderID)) {
    //Set the currentID to the ID that we are on
    currentOrderID = orderid;
%>
<br><br>
<table border="0" cellpadding="0" cellspacing="0" width="95%"
     align="center">
   <tr>
     <td bgcolor="#CC9900" align="left" width="50%"
         colspan="2">
         <b>   <font color="#ffffff">
Order ID:  <%= orderid %></font></b>
      </td>
   </tr>
    <tr>
      <td>
        <table width="95%" cellpadding="0" cellspacing="0"
               border="0" align="center">
          <tr>
            <td><b><i>Billing Information:</i></b></td>
          </tr>
          <tr>

<td>Name:  <%=rs.getString("billname")%></td>
          </tr>
          <tr>
<td>Address:  <%= rs.getString("billaddress") %>
</td>
          </tr>
          <tr>
<td>City:  <%=rs.getString("billcity")%></td>
          </tr>
          <tr>
<td>State:  <%=rs.getString("billstate")%></td>
          </tr>
```

```
            <tr>
            <td>Zip Code:  
<%= rs.getString("billzipcode") %></td>
            </tr>
            <tr>
<td>Phone:  <%=rs.getString("billphone")%></td>
            </tr>
            <tr>
<td>E-Mail:  <%=rs.getString("billemail")%></td>
            </tr>
          </table>
        </td>
        <td valign="top">
          <table width="95%" cellpadding="0" cellspacing="0"
             border="0" align="center">
                <tr>
                  <td><b><i>Shipping Information:</i></b></td>
                </tr>
                <tr>
<td>Name:  <%=rs.getString("shipname")%></td>
                </tr>
                <tr>
<td>Address:  <%= rs.getString("shipaddress") %>
</td>
                                        </tr>
                                        <tr>
<td>City:  <%=rs.getString("shipcity")%></td>
                    </tr>
                    <tr>

<td>State:  <%=rs.getString("shipstate")%></td>
                    </tr>
                    <tr>
<td>Zip Code:  <%= rs.getString("shipzipcode") %>
</td>
                    </tr>
                    <tr>
<td>E-Mail:  <%=rs.getString("shipemail")%></td>
                   </table>
                   </td>
                   </tr>
                  </table>
<%-- self-posting form --%>
```

```
<form name="orderprocessor" method="POST"
    action="<%= request.getRequestURL() %>">

<table border="0" width="95%" align="center">
   <tr>
     <td><br><b><i>Processing Information</i></b></td>
   </tr>
   <tr>
      <td>CC Number:  
<%= rs.getString("creditnumber") %></td>
    </tr>
    <tr>
     <td>CC Name:  <%= rs.getString("creditname") %>
     </td>
    </tr>
    <tr>
   <td>CC Exp:  <%= rs.getString("creditexpdate") %>
</td>
    </tr>
    <tr>
      <td>
   <input type="hidden" name="orderid" value="<%= orderid %>">
   <input type = "submit" name="process" value="process">
      </td>
     </tr>
     <tr>
       <td><hr width="50%" align="left"></td>
     </tr>
    </table>
  </form>

<table width="95%" border="0" cellpadding="0" cellspacing="0"
   align="center">
  <tr>
   <td><b><i>Product Information:</i></b></td>
  </tr>
</table>

<% } //End of same order if statement %>

<%
// do a check for each product - check currentOPID

if(!currentOPID.equals(rs.getString("ordersproductsid"))) {
  //Set the currentOPID to the current product
```

```
  currentOPID = rs.getString("ordersproductsid");
%>

<table width="95%" border="0" cellpadding="0" cellspacing="0"
   align="center">
   <tr>
     <td><br>
      Product Name:  <%= rs.getString("name") %>
     </td>
   </tr>
   <tr>
      <td>
      Product Price:  <%= rs.getString("price") %>
      </td>
   </tr>
   <tr>
     <td>
      Quantity Ordered:  <%= rs.getString("qty") %>
     </td>
   </tr>
   <tr>
     <td align="left"><b><i>Options</i></b></td>
   </tr>
  </table>
<% }// End the products if %>

<%
//Make sure the current optionid is not null then display it
   if(rs.getString("optionid") != null) {
%>
<table width="95%" border="0" cellpadding="0" cellspacing="0"
    align="center">
   <tr>
      <td>Option Chosen:  
         <%= rs.getString("optionname") %></td></td>
    </tr>
   </table>
  <% } //End of option if %>

<% }
   // End of the While Loop over the Entire Result Set
%>
    </td>
</tr>
<jsp:include page="footer.jsp" />
```

The `viewCompletedOrder.jsp` page gets all of the completed orders that have not yet been processed and outputs them on this page. This page is to be used by the merchant in a password-protected area (you can use the servlet we wrote earlier, perhaps). This page displays all of the information about each unprocessed order along with a `Process` button. This allows the merchant to view the order, take down the shipping information and product information, fulfill the order, and run the credit card. Then the merchant hits the Process button, which just sets the `isProcessed` bit in the database to 1 instead of 0. Then it refreshes the page (because it is a self-posting form) in case there are any other orders.

It would be a good idea to show a message if there are no orders initially and to hash all but the last four digits of the credit card.

16.5 Styles

This folder contains one file, `styles.css`, that we use to define the styles for the app. Most of it is omitted here, because you'll make your own style.

16.5.1 main.css

```
<style type="text/css">
<!--

td  {
font-family : Arial, Helvetica, Sans-Serif;font-size : 14px;
font-weight : normal; color : #666666;
 }
.cartHeaders      {
      font-family : Arial, Helvetica, Sans-Serif;
      font-size : 11px;
      font-weight : normal;
      color : #FFFFFF;
      font-weight : 600;
      }

.cartHeaders2    {
    font-family : Arial, Helvetica, Sans-Serif;
    font-size : 13px;
    font-weight : normal;
    color : #FFFFFF;
    font-weight : 600;
}
```

```
.text {
      font-family : Arial, Helvetica, Sans-Serif;
      font-size : 12px;
      font-weight : normal;
      color : #000000;
      font-weight : 400;
     }
.options {
      font-family : Arial, Helvetica, Sans-Serif;
      font-size : 11px;
      font-weight : normal;
      color : #000000;
      font-weight : 400;
     }
-->
</style>
```

16.6 WEB-INF

The `WEB-INF` folder contains classes, including beans and tags, as well as the `web.xml` file.

16.6.1 web.xml

```
<?xml version="1.0" encoding="ISO-8859-1"?>

<!DOCTYPE web-app
    PUBLIC "-//Sun Microsystems, Inc.//DTD Web Application
     2.3//EN"
     "http://java.sun.com/dtd/web-app_2_3.dtd">

<web-app>
  <description>an online store</description>

  <taglib>
    <taglib-uri>http://store.mysite.com/tags/cart</taglib-uri>
    <taglib-location>/WEB-INF/cart.tld</taglib-location>
  </taglib>

<!--JSP Standard Tag Library 1.0 Core tags-->
 <taglib>
  <taglib-uri>http://java.sun.com/jstl/ea/core</taglib-uri>
  <taglib-location>/WEB-INF/jstl10/tld/c.tld</taglib-location>
```

```
 </taglib>
</web-app>
```

In the `web.xml` file, we need to declare that we want to use the JSTL core tags, and we point to their TLD. We do the same for our custom tags. The only difference is that `c.tld` is defined by the Jakarta project, and we just need to put it in the right place, but we have to write our own `cart.tld`. So that is shown next.

16.6.2 `cart.tld`

```
<?xml version="1.0" encoding="ISO-8859-1" ?>
<!DOCTYPE taglib PUBLIC
    "-//Sun Microsystems, Inc.//DTD JSP Tag Library 1.2//EN"
    "http://java.sun.com/dtd/web-jsptaglibrary_1_2.dtd">

<taglib>
    <tlib-version>1.0</tlib-version>
    <jsp-version>1.2</jsp-version>
    <short-name>ecommerce shopping cart</short-name>
    <description>a shopping cart</description>
    <tag>
        <name>message</name>
        <tag-class>com.cybertrails.store.tags.MessageTest
        </tag-class>
        <body-content>empty</body-content>
        <description>test: show a message</description>
        <attribute>
            <name>message</name>
            <required>true</required>
            <rtexprvalue>false</rtexprvalue>
            <type>java.lang.String</type>
        </attribute>
    </tag>
    <tag>
        <name>view</name>
        <tag-class>com.cybertrails.store.tags.ViewCartTag
        </tag-class>
        <body-content>empty</body-content>
        <description>view contents of the shopping cart
        </description>
    </tag>

    <tag>
        <name>product</name>
```

```
        <tag-class>com.cybertrails.store.tags.ProductCartTag</
tag-class>
        <body-content>empty</body-content>
        <description>add items to a cart</description>
        <attribute>
            <name>action</name>
            <required>true</required>
            <rtexprvalue>false</rtexprvalue>
            <type>java.lang.String</type>
        </attribute>
        <attribute>
            <name>productid</name>
            <required>false</required>
            <rtexprvalue>false</rtexprvalue>
            <type>java.lang.String</type>
        </attribute>
    </tag>

    <tag>
        <name>checkout</name>
        <tag-class>com.cybertrails.store.tags.CheckoutTag
        </tag-class>
        <body-content>empty</body-content>
        <description>walk through checking out process
        </description>
        <attribute>
            <name>action</name>
            <required>true</required>
            <rtexprvalue>true</rtexprvalue>
            <type>java.lang.String</type>
        </attribute>
    </tag>

    <tag>
        <name>calculate</name>
        <tag-class>
          com.cybertrails.store.tags.CalculateCartTag
        </tag-class>
        <body-content>empty</body-content>
        <description>calculates shipping, tax, and total for
final checkout page</description>
        <attribute>
            <name>item</name>
            <required>true</required>
```

```
            <rtexprvalue>true</rtexprvalue>
            <type>java.lang.String</type>
        </attribute>
    </tag>
</taglib>
```

The TLD describes where the container can find the classes for custom tags and how they must be called.

16.7 WEB-INF/classes/com/cybertrails/store

Because we are keeping our tags in packages, we need to have the `Item.java` and `Order.java` listings in this folder. These two classes are not beans or tags. They are classes that stand in for the objects (items and orders) that appear in the real world. As we talked about in Chapter 5, it is generally good design practice to have classes representing the objects in the real world and then define methods for what can be done to and with those things.

Java on the Web still maintains the same principle, of course, but with the restrictions of HTML, such as with forms, things work a little differently. It's not really necessary, for instance, to create a "Customer" class. While a customer is an important (actually, necessary) part of the application, the Web allows us to just hit the database from the session, which is populated from the forms, and this would perhaps be more trouble than it is worth. We could have, I suppose, stored the billing information in an object instead of the session. But the shipping information is not necessarily part of the customer, and so we'd have to figure out something new to do at that stage. There's no point for this application to create an entire object to store customer information that will never be referenced by the application again (that's assuming that the back end order retrieval happens as part of another application).

16.7.1 Item.java

```
/*
 * Item.java
 */
package com.cybertrails.store;
import java.util.*;
import java.sql.*;

public class Item {
```

```
private String productID;
private String productName;
private String qty;
private String price;
private ArrayList options;
private ArrayList priceAdds;
private ArrayList optionIDs;
private int optionid;

private String error;
private Connection con;

/** CONSTRUCTOR */
public Item(String productID, String productName,
       ArrayList options, ArrayList priceAdds,
       ArrayList optionIDs,
       String q, String p) {

    this.productID = productID;
    this.productName = productName;
    this.options = options;
    this.priceAdds = priceAdds;
    this.optionIDs = optionIDs;
    this.qty = q;
    this.price = setPrice();

}

public void setProductID(String p) {
    this.productID = p;
}
public void setProductName(String n) {
    this.productName = n;
}
public void setQty(String q) {
    this.qty = q;
}
public void setOptions(ArrayList o) {
    this.options = o;
}
public void setPriceAdds(ArrayList p) {
    this.priceAdds = p;
}
public String getProductID() {
    return productID;
```

```
    }
    public String getProductName() {
        return productName;
    }

    public String getQuantity() {
        return qty;
    }

    public ArrayList getOptions() {
        return options;
    }
    public ArrayList getOptionIDs() {
        return optionIDs;
    }

    public double getAdjustedPrice(){
        double adjustedPrice = 0.0;

        for(int x = 0; x < priceAdds.size(); x++) {
            if (priceAdds.get(x) != null) {
                adjustedPrice +=
Double.parseDouble(priceAdds.get(x).toString());
            }
        }

        return (adjustedPrice + Double.parseDouble(price));
    }

    // get product total price
    // by multiplying quantity times adjusted price
    public double getFinalProductPrice(double x) {
        double p =  x * Integer.parseInt(getQuantity());
        return p;
    }

    // ******** setPrice()
    public String setPrice() {

        try {
            if (con == null) {
                connect();
            }
            ResultSet rs;
            PreparedStatement getPrice;
```

```
            String s = new String("SELECT price FROM products
                  WHERE productID = ?;");
            getPrice = con.prepareStatement(s);

            // in JDBC, the first ? is index 1 (not 0)
         getPrice.setInt(1, Integer.parseInt(getProductID()));
            rs = getPrice.executeQuery();
            while (rs.next()) {
                price = rs.getString("price");
            }

        }
        catch (SQLException sqle) {
            sqle.printStackTrace();

        }
        catch (Exception e) {
            e.printStackTrace();

        }
        return price;
    }   // end setPrice

    public String getPrice() {
        return price;
    }
    // ********** getPrice()
    public String getPricePriceAdds() {
        int adjustedPrice = 0;
        ResultSet ars = null;
        try {

            PreparedStatement getAdjustedPrice;
            String s = new String("SELECT priceadd FROM
                   options WHERE priceadd IS NOT NULL
                   AND optionid IN( ");
            for(int x = 0; x < options.size() - 1; x++) {
                s +=
Integer.parseInt(options.get(x).toString()) + ",";
            }
            s +=
Integer.parseInt(options.get(options.size()).toString());

            // end SQL statement
            s += ")";
            getAdjustedPrice = con.prepareStatement(s);
```

```
            ars = getAdjustedPrice.executeQuery();

            while(ars.next()){
                adjustedPrice +=
Integer.parseInt(ars.getString("priceadd"));
            }

            adjustedPrice += Double.parseDouble(getPrice());
            con.close();
        }
        catch (SQLException sqle) {
            sqle.printStackTrace();
        }
        catch (Exception e) {
            e.printStackTrace();
        }

        return Integer.toString(adjustedPrice);
    }   // end getPrice


    // *********** getOptionInfo()
    public ResultSet getOptionInfo(String productid) throws
SQLException, Exception {
        ResultSet rs = null;
        try {

            PreparedStatement getOptionInfo;
            String s = new String("SELECT * FROM options
                   WHERE optionid = ?;");
            getOptionInfo = con.prepareStatement(s);
            getOptionInfo.setInt(1, optionid);
            rs = getOptionInfo.executeQuery();

        }
        catch (SQLException sqle) {
            sqle.printStackTrace();

        }
        catch (Exception e) {
            e.printStackTrace();

        }
        return rs;
    }   // end getOptionInfo
```

```
    // ************ connect()
    public void connect() throws ClassNotFoundException,
SQLException, Exception {

        try {
            // load driver
            Class.forName("org.gjt.mm.mysql.Driver");
            // make connection
            con = DriverManager.getConnection("jdbc:mysql:///
storecybertrailscomtest","","");
        }
        catch (ClassNotFoundException cnfe) {
            error = "Class not found: can't find driver";
            throw new ClassNotFoundException(error);
        }
        catch (SQLException sqle) {
            sqle.printStackTrace();
        }
        catch (Exception e) {
            e.printStackTrace();
        }
    } //end connect

    //********* connect()
    public void disconnect() throws SQLException {
        try {
            if ( con != null ) {
                //close connection
                con.close();
            }
        }
        catch (SQLException sqle) {
            sqle.printStackTrace();
        }
    } // end disconnect()
}
```

We use these same connect and disconnect methods over again in other classes. It might be a good exercise for you to offload some of this work into a database utility object as we did with the Swing query app in Chapter 12.

16.7.2 Order.java

```
package com.cybertrails.store;

import java.util.*;
import java.sql.*;
import javax.servlet.http.*;
import javax.servlet.*;

public class Order {

    //variables
    private HttpSession session;
    private HttpServletRequest request;
    private Connection con;
    private String error;

    private String customerid, shipinfoid, orderid,
orderproductsid;

    private String bName, bAddress, bCity, bState,
      bZipCode, bCountry,
      bPhone, bEmail, creditnumber, creditname, creditexpdate;

    private String sName, sAddress, sCity, sState,
      sZipCode, sCountry, sPhone, sEmail;

    public Order(HttpSession ses) {
        session = ses;
    }

    public void dbController() {
        try{
                //Insert the customer into the database
            putCustomer();
                //Get the customer ID of the customer
                //just inserted
            getCustomerID();
                //Insert the shipping info into the database
            putShipInfo();
                //Get the shipinfo ID for the orders table
            getShipInfoID();
                // put the order in
            putOrder();
```

```
                //Get the orderid
            getOrderID();
                //Enter the order into the database
            putOrderProducts();

        }
        catch (SQLException sqle) {
                sqle.printStackTrace();
                error = "SQL Error:" + sqle;
                System.err.println(error);
        }
        catch (Exception e) {
                e.printStackTrace();
                error = "An unknown exception occured in
                    DBController";
                System.err.println(error);
        }
    }

    public void putCustomer() throws SQLException, Exception {

        bName = (String) session.getAttribute("bName");
        bAddress = (String)session.getAttribute("bAddress");
        bCity = (String)session.getAttribute("bCity");
        bState = (String)session.getAttribute("bState");
        bZipCode = (String)session.getAttribute("bZipCode");
        bCountry = (String)session.getAttribute("bCountry");
        bPhone = (String)session.getAttribute("bPhone");
        bEmail = (String)session.getAttribute("bEmail");
        creditnumber =
(String)session.getAttribute("creditnumber");
        creditname =
(String)session.getAttribute("creditname");
        creditexpdate =
(String)session.getAttribute("creditexpdate");

                String customerSQL;
                customerSQL = "INSERT into customers" +
                "(billname, billaddress, " +
                "billcity, billstate, billzipcode,
                billcountry, " +
                "billphone, billemail,creditnumber,
                creditname, " +
                "creditexpdate) VALUES ('" +
```

```
            bName + "', '" + bAddress + "', '" + bCity +
            "', '" + bState + "', " + bZipCode + ", '" +
            bCountry + "', '" + bPhone + "', '" + bEmail +
            "', '" + creditnumber + "', '" + creditname  +
            "', '" + creditexpdate + "');";

        try {

            Statement putOrder = con.createStatement();
            putOrder.executeUpdate(customerSQL);

        }
        catch (SQLException sqle) {
            sqle.printStackTrace();
            error = "SQL Error";
            throw new SQLException(error);
        }
        catch (Exception e) {
            e.printStackTrace();
            error = "An unknown exception occured";
            throw new Exception(error);
        }

  }

  ////////////getCustomerID()
  public void getCustomerID() throws SQLException, Exception
{
            ResultSet rs = null;
            String cidSQL;
            cidSQL = "SELECT max(customerid) AS customerid
                     from customers";
        try {

        Statement getCustomerID;
        getCustomerID = con.createStatement();
        rs = getCustomerID.executeQuery(cidSQL);

        while(rs.next()) {
                customerid = rs.getString("customerid");
            }

        }
        catch (SQLException sqle) {
            sqle.printStackTrace();
```

```
                error = "SQL Error";
                throw new SQLException(error);
            }
            catch (Exception e) {
                e.printStackTrace();
                error = "An unknown exception occured in
                         getCustomerID";
                throw new Exception(error);
            }
    }

            ////////////// PUT SHIP INFO
        public void putShipInfo() throws SQLException,
Exception {

            sName = (String)session.getAttribute("sName");
            sAddress =
(String)session.getAttribute("sAddress");
            sCity = (String)session.getAttribute("sCity");
            sState = (String)session.getAttribute("sState");
            sZipCode =
(String)session.getAttribute("sZipCode");
            sCountry =
(String)session.getAttribute("sCountry");
            sPhone = (String)session.getAttribute("sPhone");
          sEmail = (String)session.getAttribute("sEmail");

                String shipSQL;
                shipSQL = "INSERT into shippinginfo" +
                "(shipname, shipaddress, " +
                "shipcity, shipstate, shipzipcode,
                shipcountry, " +
                "shipphone, shipemail) VALUES ('" + sName +
                "', '"
                + sAddress + "', '" + sCity + "', '" + sState
                + "', " + sZipCode
                + ", '" + sCountry + "', '" + sPhone + "', '"
                + sEmail + "');";

            try {

                Statement putShipping = con.createStatement();
                putShipping.executeUpdate(shipSQL);
```

```
            }
            catch (SQLException sqle) {
                sqle.printStackTrace();
                error = "SQL Error";
                throw new SQLException(error);
            }
            catch (Exception e) {
                e.printStackTrace();
                error = "An unknown exception occured in put
                         shipping";
                throw new Exception(error);
            }
      } // end putShipInfo

      ////////////GET SHIP INFO ID
    public void getShipInfoID() throws SQLException, Exception
{
                ResultSet rs = null;
                String siidSQL;
                siidSQL = "SELECT max(shipinfoid) AS
                     shipinfoid from shippinginfo";
            try {

            Statement getShipInfoID;
            getShipInfoID = con.createStatement();
            rs = getShipInfoID.executeQuery(siidSQL);

            while(rs.next()) {
                    shipinfoid = rs.getString("shipinfoid");
                }
            }
            catch (SQLException sqle) {
                sqle.printStackTrace();
                error = "SQL Error";
                throw new SQLException(error);
            }
            catch (Exception e) {
                e.printStackTrace();
                error = "An unknown exception occured in
getShpInfoID";
                throw new Exception(error);
            }
    }
```

```
  public void putOrder() throws SQLException, Exception {
          // get stuff we need from session
String subtotal = (String) session.getAttribute("subTotal");
String tax = (String) session.getAttribute("tax");
String shipCost = (String) session.getAttribute("shipCost");
String total = (String) session.getAttribute("total");
          // order date
      java.util.Date orderDate = new java.util.Date();

              String oSQL;
              oSQL = "INSERT INTO Orders (customerid,
              shipinfoid, subtotal, " +
              "shipping, tax, grandtotal, orderdate,
              isprocessed) " +
              "VALUES (" + customerid + ", " + shipinfoid +
              ", " + subtotal + ", " +
              shipCost + " , " + tax + ", " + total + ", '"
              + orderDate + "',0);";

          try {

              PreparedStatement putOrder;
              putOrder = con.prepareStatement(oSQL);
              putOrder.executeUpdate();

          }
          catch (SQLException sqle) {
              sqle.printStackTrace();
              error = "SQL Error";
              throw new SQLException(error);
          }
          catch (Exception e) {
              e.printStackTrace();
              error = "An unknown exception occured in
                  putOrder";
              throw new Exception(error);
          }
  }

    ////////////get order id
  public void getOrderID() throws SQLException, Exception {
              ResultSet rs = null;
              String oidSQL;
```

```
                oidSQL = "SELECT max(orderid) AS orderid from
orders";
            try {

            Statement getOrderID;
            getOrderID = con.createStatement();
            rs = getOrderID.executeQuery(oidSQL);

            while(rs.next()) {
                    orderid = rs.getString("orderid");
                }
                // add to session so we can output it
                // on the Thankyou.jsp page
            session.setAttribute("orderid", orderid);
            }
            catch (SQLException sqle) {
                sqle.printStackTrace();
                error = "SQL Error";
                throw new SQLException(error);
            }
            catch (Exception e) {
                e.printStackTrace();
                error = "An unknown exception occured in
                        getOrderID";
                throw new Exception(error);
            }
    }

        //////// PUT ORDERPRODUCTS
    public void putOrderProducts() throws SQLException,
Exception {
            // get the cart
                ArrayList currentItems =
(ArrayList)session.getAttribute("currentItems");
                String poSQL;
                String productid;
                String qty;
                double adjPrice;

                // loop over
            for(int i = 0 ; i < currentItems.size(); i++) {
                   Item temp = (Item)currentItems.get(i);
                        productid = temp.getProductID();
                        qty = temp.getQuantity();
```

```
//This is the price plus the options the user chose
                 adjPrice = temp.getAdjustedPrice();

                   poSQL = "INSERT INTO OrdersProducts
                   (orderid, productid, qty, price )" +
                   "VALUES (" + orderid + ", " + productid +
                   ", " + qty + ", " + adjPrice + ");";

               try {
                   PreparedStatement putOrderProducts;
              putOrderProducts = con.prepareStatement(poSQL);
                   putOrderProducts.executeUpdate();
               }
               catch (SQLException sqle) {
                   sqle.printStackTrace();
                   error = "SQL Error";
                   throw new SQLException(error);
               }
               catch (Exception e) {
                   e.printStackTrace();
                   error = "An unknown exception occured in
                          putOrderProducts";
                   throw new Exception(error);
               }

               getOrderProductsID();
               putOrdersProductsOptionChoice(temp);

           }//end of loop over currentitems
    }

         ////////////GET OrderProductsID
    public void getOrderProductsID() throws SQLException,
                                     Exception {
               ResultSet rs = null;
               String opidSQL;
               opidSQL = "SELECT max(ordersproductsid) AS
               orderproductsid from ordersproducts";
           try {

           Statement getOrderProductsID;
           getOrderProductsID = con.createStatement();
           rs = getOrderProductsID.executeQuery(opidSQL);
```

```
            while(rs.next()) {
                    orderproductsid =
                       rs.getString("orderproductsid");
                }
            }
            catch (SQLException sqle) {
                sqle.printStackTrace();
                error = "SQL Error";
                throw new SQLException(error);
            }
            catch (Exception e) {
                e.printStackTrace();
                error = "An unknown exception occured in
                         getOrdersproductsID";
                throw new Exception(error);
            }
    }

       //////// PUT OrdersProductsOptionChoice
    public void putOrdersProductsOptionChoice(Item temp)
                          throws SQLException, Exception {
            // get the cart
                ArrayList optionIDs = temp.getOptionIDs();
                String opocSQL;
                String optionid;

                    // loop over
            for(int i = 0 ; i < optionIDs.size(); i++) {
                    optionid = (String)optionIDs.get(i);

                    opocSQL = "INSERT INTO
                    ordersproductoptionchoice
                    (ordersproductsid, optionid )" +
                    "VALUES (" + orderproductsid + ", " +
                    optionid + ");";

                try {
                    PreparedStatement
putOrdersProductsOptionChoice;
                    putOrdersProductsOptionChoice =
con.prepareStatement(opocSQL);

putOrdersProductsOptionChoice.executeUpdate();
                }
```

```
                catch (SQLException sqle) {
                    sqle.printStackTrace();
                    error = "SQL Error";
                    throw new SQLException(error);
                }
                catch (Exception e) {
                    e.printStackTrace();
                    error = "An unknown exception occured in
                             putOrdersProductsOptionChoice";
                    throw new Exception(error);
                }

            }// End of For Loop to enter all the optionID's

    }


// ************ CONNECT
    public void connect() throws ClassNotFoundException,
SQLException, Exception {

        try {
            // load driver
            Class.forName("org.gjt.mm.mysql.Driver");
            // make connection
            con = DriverManager.getConnection("jdbc:mysql:///
storecybertrailscomtest","","");
        }
        catch (ClassNotFoundException cnfe) {
            error = "Class not found: can't find driver";
            throw new ClassNotFoundException(error);
        }
        catch (SQLException sqle) {
            error = sqle.getMessage();
            throw new SQLException(error);
        }
        catch (Exception e) {
            error = "Exception: unknown";
            throw new Exception(error);
        }
    } //end connect

            //********* DISCONNECT
    public void disconnect() throws SQLException {
```

```
        try {
            if ( con != null )
            {
                //close connection
                con.close();
            }
        }
        catch (SQLException sqle) {
            error = ("SQLException: can't close connection");
            throw new SQLException(error);
        }
    } // end disconnect()

} // eoc
```

16.8 WEB-INF/classes/com/cybertrails/store/beans

This folder contains the CatalogBean class, which takes users through the products in the store, allowing them to view categories, subcategories, and products.

16.8.1 CatalogBean.java

```
/*
 * CatalogBean.java
 */

package com.cybertrails.store.beans;

import java.sql.*;
import java.util.*;

public class CatalogBean {
    String error;
    Connection con;

    public CatalogBean() {}

            //************GET CATEGORIES
    public ResultSet getCategories() throws SQLException,
                                             Exception {
            ResultSet rs = null;
        try {
```

```
            Statement getCategories;
            String s = new String("SELECT catid, catname
                  FROM categories;");
            getCategories = con.createStatement();
            rs = getCategories.executeQuery(s);

        }
        catch (SQLException sqle) {
            sqle.printStackTrace();
            error = "SQL Error:";
            throw new SQLException(error);
        }
        catch (Exception e) {
            e.printStackTrace();
            error = "An unknown exception occured while
                    executing query: getCategories";
            throw new Exception(error);
        }
        return rs;
    }   // end getCategories


                //********** GET SUB CATS
        public ResultSet getSubCategories(String catid) throws
                                SQLException, Exception {
            ResultSet rs = null;
        try {

            PreparedStatement getSubCategories;
            String s = new String("SELECT DISTINCT
                pc.subcatid, pc.catid,
                sc.subcatid, sc.subcatname " +
                "FROM productscategories pc " +
                "INNER JOIN subcategories sc " +
                "ON pc.subcatid = sc.subcatid " +
                "WHERE catid = ?;");
          getSubCategories = con.prepareStatement(s);

            // like referencing #url.catid# in CF
          getSubCategories.setInt(1, Integer.parseInt(catid));
          rs = getSubCategories.executeQuery();
```

```
        }
        catch (SQLException sqle) {
            sqle.printStackTrace();
            error = "SQL Error:";
            throw new SQLException(error);
        }
        catch (Exception e) {
            e.printStackTrace();
            error = "An unknown exception occured while
                    executing getsubCategories query";
            throw new Exception(error);
        }
        return rs;
    }   // end getSubCategories


            // g*********** GET PRODUCTS
    public ResultSet getProducts(String subcatid) throws
                            SQLException, Exception {
                ResultSet rs = null;
            try {

                PreparedStatement getProducts;
                String s = new String("SELECT pc.catid,
                       p.productid, p.name, p.price,
                       p.shortdescription, p.smimage " +
                    "FROM productscategories pc " +
                    "INNER JOIN products p " +
                    "ON pc.productid = p.productid " +
                    "WHERE subcatid = ?;");
                getProducts = con.prepareStatement(s);
                getProducts.setInt(1,
                   Integer.parseInt(subcatid));
                rs = getProducts.executeQuery();

            }
            catch (SQLException sqle) {
                sqle.printStackTrace();
                error = "SQL Error";
                throw new SQLException(error);
            }
            catch (Exception e) {
                e.printStackTrace();
                error = "An unknown exception occured in
```

```
                query: getProducts";
            throw new Exception(error);
        }
        return rs;
    }   // end getProducts

            // *********** GET ONE PRODUCT
public ResultSet getOneProduct(String productid) throws
                SQLException, Exception {
            ResultSet rs = null;
        try {

            PreparedStatement getOneProduct;
            String s = new String("SELECT *
                   FROM products WHERE productid = ?;");
            getOneProduct = con.prepareStatement(s);
            getOneProduct.setInt(1,
                  Integer.parseInt(productid));
            rs = getOneProduct.executeQuery();

        }
        catch (SQLException sqle) {
            sqle.printStackTrace();
            error = "SQL Error";
            throw new SQLException(error);
        }
        catch (Exception e) {
            e.printStackTrace();
            error = "An unknown exception occured in
                  getOneProduct";
            throw new Exception(error);
        }
        return rs;
    }   // end getOneProduct


            // *********** GET PRODUCT OPTIONS
public ResultSet getProductOptions(String productid)
                  throws SQLException, Exception {
        ResultSet rs = null;
        try {

            PreparedStatement getProductOptions;
```

```
                String s = new String("SELECT pos.productid,
                     pos.optionsetid, os.optionsetname,
                     o.optionid, o.optionname, o.priceadd " +
                    "FROM productsoptionsets pos " +
                    "LEFT JOIN optionsets os " +
                    "ON pos.optionsetid = os.optionsetid " +
                    "LEFT JOIN options o " +
                    "ON o.optionsetid = os.optionsetid " +
                    "WHERE pos.productid = ?;");

                getProductOptions = con.prepareStatement(s);
                getProductOptions.setInt(1,
                    Integer.parseInt(productid));
                rs = getProductOptions.executeQuery();

            }
            catch (SQLException sqle) {
                sqle.printStackTrace();
                error = "SQL Error";
                throw new SQLException(error);
            }
            catch (Exception e) {
                e.printStackTrace();
                error = "An unknown exception occured in
getProductOptions";
                throw new Exception(error);
            }
            return rs;
        }   // end getProductOptions

// ************ CONNECT
    public void connect() throws ClassNotFoundException,
                SQLException, Exception {

        try {
            // load driver
            Class.forName("org.gjt.mm.mysql.Driver");
            // make connection
con = DriverManager.getConnection("jdbc:mysql:///
storecybertrailscomtest","","");
        }
        catch (ClassNotFoundException cnfe) {
            error = "Class not found: can't find driver";
            throw new ClassNotFoundException(error);
```

```
        }
        catch (SQLException sqle) {
            error = sqle.getMessage();
            throw new SQLException(error);
        }
        catch (Exception e) {
            error = "Exception: unknown";
            throw new Exception(error);
        }
    } //end connect

            //********* DISCONNECT
    public void disconnect() throws SQLException {
        try {
            if ( con != null )
            {
                //close connection
                con.close();
            }
        }
        catch (SQLException sqle) {
            error = ("SQLException: can't close connection");
            throw new SQLException(error);
        }
    } // end disconnect()
}   // eof
```

16.9 WEB-INF/classes/com/cybertrails/store/tags

This folder contains the custom tags for the application. These tags allow you to add and remove items from the cart, view items in the cart, and calculate the sales tax and the order total. The `Checkout` custom tag checks to see what step in the checkout process the user is currently in. Possible values are "billing," "shipping," or "confirm." Other steps can be inserted as your application requires. The parameter value is passed from the previous JSP controller.

16.9.1 ProductCartTag.java

```
/*
   File: ProductCartTag.java
 * Purpose: add and remove products from the cart
 * Notes: if user closes browser, the session is automatically
 * destroyed.
```

```
 * PRODUCTID attrib is not required because the tag ACTION
 * defaults to VIEW.
 */
package com.cybertrails.store.tags;

import javax.servlet.*;
import javax.servlet.http.*;
import javax.servlet.jsp.JspWriter;
import javax.servlet.jsp.tagext.TagSupport;
import javax.servlet.jsp.JspException;
import javax.servlet.jsp.JspTagException;
import java.io.IOException;

import java.util.*;
import com.cybertrails.store.Item;

public class ProductCartTag extends TagSupport {

    private String action="";
    private String productid="";
    private String productName="";
    private String price="";

    public void setAction(String action) {
        this.action = action;
    }
    public String getAction() {
        return this.action;
    }
    public void setProductid(String p) {
        this.productid = p;
    }
    public void setProductName(String n) {
        this.productName = n;
    }
    public void setPrice(String price) {
        this.price = price;
    }


        // everything happens here
    public int doStartTag() throws JspException {
        try {
```

```
                // get out writer
            JspWriter out = pageContext.getOut();
                // get session
            HttpSession session = pageContext.getSession();

ArrayList currentItems =
(ArrayList)session.getAttribute("currentItems");

      if (currentItems == null) {
           currentItems = new ArrayList();
           session.setAttribute("currentItems", currentItems);
           session.setAttribute("price", price);
      }

      if (getAction() == "add") {

               String productid =
pageContext.getRequest().getParameter("productid");
               String productName =
pageContext.getRequest().getParameter("productName");
               String price =
pageContext.getRequest().getParameter("price");
               String qty =
pageContext.getRequest().getParameter("quantity");

               ArrayList options = new ArrayList();
               ArrayList priceAdds = new ArrayList();
               ArrayList optionIDs = new ArrayList();

               StringTokenizer token;
               StringTokenizer optionsToken;

               Enumeration e =
                 pageContext.getRequest().getParameterNames();

       while (e.hasMoreElements()) {
            String  optionSet = e.nextElement().toString();
            token = new StringTokenizer(optionSet, "|");
               String testAgainst = token.nextToken();

               if(testAgainst.equalsIgnoreCase("oset")) {
```

```
                    optionsToken = new
            StringTokenizer(pageContext.getRequest().getParameter
(optionSet), "|");
                        options.add(optionsToken.nextToken());
                        priceAdds.add(optionsToken.nextToken());
                        optionIDs.add(optionsToken.nextToken());
                       }
                   }

                   if (productid !=null) {
                       Item myItem = new Item(productid,
                                    productName, options,
                                    priceAdds, optionIDs, qty,
                                    price);

                    currentItems.add(myItem);
                    }
                } // end "add" action

                else if (getAction() == "remove") {

                  String itemToRemove =
pageContext.getRequest().getParameter("position");
                            // get an iterator
                  Iterator it  = currentItems.iterator();
                            // loop over collection to find
                            // this productid

                  for (int i = 0; i < currentItems.size(); i++) {
                     out.println("itemToRemove: " + itemToRemove);
                     out.println("i: " + i);
                     if (i == Integer.parseInt(itemToRemove)) {
                        currentItems.remove(i);
                     }
                  }
                 } // end "remove" action

               else if (getAction()=="view") {
                    out.print("VIEW ITEMS IN CART:<br>");
                        // No items in cart
                if (currentItems.size() == 0) {
                  out.println("There are no items in your cart.");
```

```
                }
                // loop over cart and show each item
               else {
                 int counter = 0;
                 for(int i = 0 ; i < currentItems.size(); i++) {
                    Item Temp = (Item)currentItems.get(i);
                    out.println(Temp.toString());
                    out.println("<br>
               <a href=\"doCart.jsp?action=remove&position=" +
                      counter + "\">remove item</a><br>");
                      counter++;
                      }
                  }
              } // end "view" action
          }
          catch(IOException ioe) {
              throw new JspException();
          }
          return SKIP_BODY;
      }
  }
```

16.9.2 ViewCartTag.java

```
/*
 * File: ViewCartTag
 * Purpose: custom tag to display items in shopping cart.
 * Authors: Eben Hewitt, Vic Miller,
 * June 28 02
 */

package com.cybertrails.store.tags;

import javax.servlet.*;
import javax.servlet.http.*;
import javax.servlet.jsp.JspWriter;
import javax.servlet.jsp.tagext.TagSupport;
import javax.servlet.jsp.JspException;
import javax.servlet.jsp.JspTagException;
import java.io.IOException;

import java.text.*;
import java.util.*;
import com.cybertrails.store.Item;
```

```
import java.sql.*;

public class ViewCartTag extends TagSupport {

   public int doStartTag() throws JspException {

     try{
              // make it easier to call a writer
          JspWriter out = pageContext.getOut();
              // get session
          HttpSession session = pageContext.getSession();
          ArrayList currentItems =
            (ArrayList)session.getAttribute("currentItems");

                  // there are no items in cart
    if (currentItems == null || currentItems.size() == 0 ) {
     out.println("<h1>There are no items in your cart.</h1>");

       }
          // display headers for cart.
          // then loop over cart and show each item
       else {
           out.println("<table width=\"450\" cellspacing=\"2\"
cellpadding=\"1\" border=\"0\">");
            out.println("<tr><td bgcolor=\"#CC0000\"
align=\"center\" class=\"cartHeaders\">Item<br></td>");
            out.println("<td bgcolor=\"#CC0000\"
align=\"center\" class=\"cartHeaders\">Qty<br></td>");
            out.println("<td bgcolor=\"#CC0000\"
align=\"center\" class=\"cartHeaders\">Remove<br></td>");
            out.println("<td bgcolor=\"#CC0000\"
align=\"center\" class=\"cartHeaders\">Price<br></td>");
            out.println("<td bgcolor=\"#CC0000\"
align=\"center\" class=\"cartHeaders\">Total<br></td></tr>");

             //Decimal Format object
DecimalFormat formatter = new DecimalFormat("0.00;-0.00");
             // counter for number of item rows
             int counter = 0;
             // adds all finalPrices together in the loop
double cartTotal = 0.0;
             // loop over cart and output values
             // for each item
```

```
for(int i = 0 ; i < currentItems.size(); i++) {
             Item Temp = (Item)currentItems.get(i);
             String productID = Temp.getProductID();
             String productName = Temp.getProductName();
             String qty = Temp.getQuantity();
             String price = Temp.getPrice();
             double adjPrice = Temp.getAdjustedPrice();
             double finalPrice =
                    Temp.getFinalProductPrice(adjPrice);

             ArrayList opts = Temp.getOptions();
             Iterator it = opts.iterator();

            out.println("<tr><td>
<a href=\"viewProductDetail.jsp?productid=" + productID +
                "\"><b>" + productName + "</b></a><br>
</td><br>");
            out.println("<td align=\"center\">" + qty + "<br></
td>");
            out.println("<td align=\"center\">
<a href=\"doCart.jsp?action=remove&position=" + counter +
            "\">remove item</a><br</td>");
                //Format the Adjusted price abdTotal
                String adjPriceFmt =
formatter.format(adjPrice);
                String finalPriceFmt =
formatter.format(finalPrice);

                //Put the final price into the session for use
with Confirm Order of viewConfirm

pageContext.getSession().setAttribute("subTotal",
finalPriceFmt);

                // "price" column
            out.println("<td align=\"right\" class=\"text\">$"
+ adjPriceFmt + "<br></td>");
                // "total" column
            out.println("<td align=\"right\" class=\"text\">$"
+ finalPriceFmt +"<br></td></tr>");

                // loop over options
            out.println("<tr><td class=\"options\"><ul>");
            for (int o = 0; it.hasNext(); o++){
```

```
            out.println("<li>" + it.next() + "</li>");
        }
        out.println("</ul><td colspan=\"4\"> </td>
            </tr>");

        cartTotal += finalPrice;
        counter++;
        } // end item row loop

        // format cartTotal so it's pretty
        String cartTotalFmt = formatter.format(cartTotal);

        out.println("<tr><td colspan=\"2\"
             bgcolor=\"#666666\"> </td>");

        out.println("<td colspan=\"2\" align=\"right\"
             bgcolor=\"#666666\" class=\"cartHeaders\">Sub
             Total <br></td>");
        out.println(" <td align=\"right\"
             bgcolor=\"#000000\" class=\"cartHeaders\">$"
             + cartTotalFmt + "<br></td></tr></table>");

            } // end else

      }
      catch(IOException ioe) {
         throw new JspException();
      }
      return SKIP_BODY;
   }
}
```

16.9.3 CheckoutTag.java

```
/*
 * File: CheckoutTag.java
 * Purpose: do the work for each step in the checkout process.
 */

package com.cybertrails.store.tags;

import javax.servlet.*;
import javax.servlet.http.*;
import javax.servlet.jsp.JspWriter;
```

```
import javax.servlet.jsp.tagext.TagSupport;
import javax.servlet.jsp.JspException;
import javax.servlet.jsp.JspTagException;
import java.io.IOException;
import com.cybertrails.store.Order;

import java.util.*;

public class CheckoutTag extends TagSupport {

    //action is "billing" (step one) or
    // "shipping" (optional step two) or
    // "confirm" (final step three)
    private String action;
    //Shorten the pagecontext request parameter retrieval method
    protected javax.servlet.ServletRequest request;

    public void setAction(String action) {
        this.action = action;
    }
    public String getAction() {
        return this.action;
    }

    // tag execution starts here
    public int doStartTag() throws JspException {
        try {
                // get out writer
            JspWriter out = pageContext.getOut();

                //get the session from the calling page
            HttpSession session = pageContext.getSession();

                //get the request from the calling page
            request = pageContext.getRequest();

         if (getAction() == "billing") {
//BILLING: set request attribs into session

                //Billing Name
               String bName = request.getParameter("bName");
               session.setAttribute("bName", bName);
```

```
                //Billing Address
               String bAddress =
               request.getParameter("bAddress");
               session.setAttribute("bAddress", bAddress);

                //City
               String bCity = request.getParameter("bCity");
               session.setAttribute("bCity", bCity);

                //State
               String bState = request.getParameter("bState");
               session.setAttribute("bState", bState);

                //Zip Code
               String bZipCode =
               request.getParameter("bZipCode");
               session.setAttribute("bZipCode", bZipCode);

                //Country
               String bCountry =
               request.getParameter("bCountry");
               session.setAttribute("bCountry", bCountry);

                //Phone
               String bPhone = request.getParameter("bPhone");
               session.setAttribute("bPhone", bPhone);

                //E-Mail
               String bEmail = request.getParameter("bEmail");
               session.setAttribute("bEmail", bEmail);

            }
            else if (getAction() == "shipping") {
// SHIPPING

                //Ship Name
               String sName = request.getParameter("sName");
               session.setAttribute("sName", sName);

                //Ship Address
               String sAddress =
               request.getParameter("sAddress");
               session.setAttribute("sAddress", sAddress);
```

```
     //Ship city
    String sCity = request.getParameter("sCity");
    session.setAttribute("sCity", sCity);

     //Ship State
    String sState = request.getParameter("sState");
    session.setAttribute("sState", sState);

     //Ship Zip Code
    String sZipCode =
    request.getParameter("sZipCode");
    session.setAttribute("sZipCode", sZipCode);

     //Ship Country
    String sCountry =
    request.getParameter("sCountry");
    session.setAttribute("sCountry", sCountry);

     // Ship Phone
    String sPhone = request.getParameter("sPhone");
    session.setAttribute("sPhone", sPhone);

     //E-Mail
    String sEmail = request.getParameter("sEmail");
    session.setAttribute("sEmail", sEmail);

     //ShippingMethod
    String ShippingMethod =
    request.getParameter("ShippingMethod");
    session.setAttribute("ShippingMethod",
    ShippingMethod);

     } // end else
 else if (getAction() == "placeOrder") {

 //Set the credit card info into the session scope
     session.setAttribute("creditname",
     request.getParameter("ccName"));
     session.setAttribute("creditnumber",
     request.getParameter("ccNumber"));

     session.setAttribute("creditexpdate",
     request.getParameter("ccExpirationDate"));
```

```
                Order order = new Order(session);
                order.connect();
                order.dbController();
                order.disconnect();
            }

        }
        catch(IOException ioe) {
            System.err.println("IOE: " + ioe.getMessage());
        }
        catch(Exception e) {
            System.err.println("E: " + e.toString());
            e.printStackTrace();
        }
        return SKIP_BODY;
    }
}
```

16.9.4 CalculateCartTag.java

```
/*
 * File: ViewCartTag
 * Purpose: custom tag to calculate sales tax, total.
 * Authors: eben.hewitt, vic.miller
 */

package com.cybertrails.store.tags;

import javax.servlet.*;
import javax.servlet.http.*;
import javax.servlet.jsp.JspWriter;
import javax.servlet.jsp.tagext.TagSupport;
import javax.servlet.jsp.JspException;
import javax.servlet.jsp.JspTagException;
import java.io.IOException;
import java.text.*;
import java.util.*;
import java.sql.*;

public class CalculateCartTag extends TagSupport {

        // what action to perform
        // possible values are item = "tax"
        // or item = "total"
```

```
    private String item;
                    // variables to use in calculations
    double total;
    double s;


    double tax;

    public void setItem(String item) {
        this.item = item;
    }
    public String getItem() {
        return this.item;
    }

    public void setTax(double tax) {

        this.tax = tax;
    }
    public double getTax() {
        return this.tax;
    }

    public int doStartTag() throws JspException {

         try{
                // get a formatter object to format the tax
    DecimalFormat formatter = new DecimalFormat("0.00;-0.00");
                // get session
            HttpSession session = pageContext.getSession();
                // get request
            ServletRequest request = pageContext.getRequest();
                // make it easier to call a writer
            JspWriter out = pageContext.getOut();

            ArrayList currentItems =
(ArrayList)session.getAttribute("currentItems");

            // change this depending on your state

if (session.getAttribute("bState").toString().equals("AZ")){
s =
Double.parseDouble(session.getAttribute("subTotal").toString()
);
```

```
double taxRate = 0.085;
setTax(s * taxRate);
                }
                else {
                    setTax(0.00);
                }

               // there are no items in cart
            if (getItem() == "tax") {
                out.println(formatter.format(getTax()));
            }
            else if (getItem() == "total") {
                double subTotal =
Double.parseDouble(session.getAttribute("subTotal").toString()
);
                double shipCost =
Double.parseDouble(request.getParameter("ShipMethod"));
                session.setAttribute("shipCost",
Double.toString(shipCost));
                total = (getTax() + subTotal + shipCost);
                session.setAttribute("total",
formatter.format(total));
                session.setAttribute("tax",
formatter.format(getTax()));
                out.println(formatter.format(total));
            }

            else {
                out.println("Error: no item specified in
<cart:calculate>");
            } // end else
         }
         catch(IOException ioe) {
            throw new JspException();
         }
         return SKIP_BODY;
    }
}
```

16.10 WEB-INF/classes/com/cybertrails/admin

This folder contains the GetOrderBean, which allows the site merchant or administrator (in conjunction with the viewCompletedOrder JSP) to view all of the orders that have been placed but not yet processed. This allows the merchant to charge the card and fulfill the order.

16.10.1 GetOrderBean.java

```
package com.cybertrails.admin;

import java.util.*;
import java.sql.*;
import javax.servlet.http.*;
import javax.servlet.*;

public class GetOrderBean {

    //variables
    private Connection con;
    private String error;

        // constructor
    public GetOrderBean() {
    }

    public ResultSet getNewOrders() throws SQLException,
Exception {
                ResultSet rs = null;
                String SQL;
                SQL = "SELECT o.orderid, o.customerid,
o.shipinfoid, o.subtotal, " +
"o.shipping, o.tax, o.grandtotal, o.orderdate, " +
"op.ordersproductsid, op.productid, op.qty, op.price, " +
"p.productid, p.name, " +
"opt.optionname, opt.optionid, " +
"c.billname, c.billaddress, c.billcity, c.billstate, " +
"c.billzipcode, c.billcountry, c.billphone, c.billemail, " +
"c.creditnumber, c.creditname, c.creditexpdate, " +
"s.shipname, s.shipaddress, s.shipcity, s.shipstate, " +
"s.shipzipcode, s.shipcountry, s.shipemail " +
"FROM orders o " +
"INNER JOIN customers c ON c.customerid = o.customerid " +
```

```
"INNER JOIN shippinginfo s ON s.shipinfoid = o.shipinfoid " +
"INNER JOIN products p ON p.productid = op.productid " +
"INNER JOIN  ordersproducts op ON o.orderid = op.orderid " +
"LEFT OUTER JOIN ordersproductoptionchoice opoc " +
"ON opoc.ordersproductsid = op.ordersproductsid " +
"LEFT OUTER  JOIN options opt ON opt.optionid = opoc.optionid"
+ "WHERE o.isprocessed = 0;";

    try {

      Statement getNewOrders;
      getNewOrders = con.createStatement();
      rs = getNewOrders.executeQuery(SQL);

    }
    catch (SQLException sqle) {
      sqle.printStackTrace();
        error = "SQL Error";
           throw new SQLException(error);
     }
     catch (Exception e) {
           e.printStackTrace();
           error = "An unknown exception occured in
                  getNewOrders";
           throw new Exception(error);
     }

     return rs;
    }

//////// setIsProcessed()
    public String setIsProcessed(String orderID) throws
                                 SQLException, Exception {
       String SQL;
       String isProcessed = "The order has been processed.";
       SQL = "Update orders SET isProcessed = 1
                WHERE orderid = " + orderID + ";";

        try {

           Statement getNewOrders;
           getNewOrders = con.createStatement();
           getNewOrders.executeQuery(SQL);
```

```
            }
            catch (SQLException sqle) {
                sqle.printStackTrace();
                error = "SQL Error";
                throw new SQLException(error);
            }
            catch (Exception e) {
                e.printStackTrace();
                error = "An unknown exception occured in
                                 getNewOrders";
                throw new Exception(error);
            }
      return isProcessed;
    }

// ************ CONNECT
    public void connect() throws SQLException, Exception {

        try {
            // load driver
            Class.forName("org.gjt.mm.mysql.Driver");
            // make connection
con = DriverManager.getConnection("jdbc:mysql:///
storecybertrailscomtest","","");
        }
        catch (SQLException sqle) {
            error = sqle.getMessage();
            throw new SQLException(error);
        }
        catch (Exception e) {
            error = "Exception: unknown";
            throw new Exception(error);
        }
    } //end connect

 //********* DISCONNECT
    public void disconnect() throws SQLException {
        try {
            if ( con != null )
            {
                //close connection
                con.close();
            }
        }
```

```
            catch (SQLException sqle) {
                error = ("SQLException: can't close connection");
                throw new SQLException(error);
            }
        } // end disconnect()
    } // eof
```

16.11 WEB-INF/lib

This folder contains `.jar` files that you want to make available to the application. In our case, that must include those for the JSTL.

16.12 WEB-INF/jstl10

This folder contains the JSP Standard Tag Library. You must download this from *http://jakarta.apache.org* and expand it here.

16.13 What's Next?

The remainder of the book contains appendices that you may find useful. The first of these is a JSP tag reference. It is followed by the API for servlets and JSPs, so you know what methods and constants are available to you. These will be very useful, especially for filling out things we were only able to touch on.

It also includes a couple of things that I hope will be handy as you start doing your own developing. Appendix C is a glossary that quickly defines key Java terms, because it can sometimes be difficult to keep abstract classes and interfaces straight. Appendix D is a very short list of Java bookmarks—places on the Internet where you can download code, read articles, and keep up-to-date. The book concludes with Appendix E, a Quick Reference that shows you how to do important Java functions with no fluff. This is useful when it's hard to remember something, but it is also helpful for things we didn't get to cover much. For instance, it shows you how to use the `.jar` utility to pack up and unpack an application.

A

JSP 1.2 Reference

This appendix serves as a reference for the syntax of comments, directives, and standard actions for JSP 1.2, in alphabetical order.

A.1 Comments

JSP 1.2 allows two kinds of comments: JSP comments and HTML comments.

JSP comments are written as follows:

```
<%-- This is a JSP comment. It is not visible in the source
returned to the client. -->
```

HTML comments are written as follows:

```
<!-- An HTML comment is visible in the source code returned to
the client. -->
```

Although you already know how to write HTML comments, they are included here for two specific reasons. First, it may be necessary to make the distinction that you can in fact write HTML comments from within JSP. Second, it is useful on occasion to utilize JSP from within an HTML comment, which is legal.

For instance, you can write the name of the current template and return it in the viewable source. This is done as follows:

```
<!-- The current template is<%= request.getRequestURI() %>.
Today is <% Date today = new Date();
DateFormat formatter;
```

```
formatter = DateFormat.getDateInstance(DateFormat.SHORT,
Locale.US);%>
<%= formatter.format(today) %>
-->
```

The above HTML comment would look something like this when the page source is viewed on the client:

```
<!-- The current template is /javaforcf/comment.jsp.
Today is 7/30/02 -->
```

A.2 Directives

JSP directives send instructions to the JSP container regarding page properties, tag libraries, and include files. Directives are specified with this opening JSP tag: <%@. There are three directives for use within a JSP: `include`, `page`, and `taglib`.

A.2.1 The `include` Directive

The `include` directive allows you to include a separate text file within the current page. The `include` directive processes any JSP within the included file *at run time*. This manner of processing is distinct from the `jsp:include` action.

The `include` directive has one attribute: `file`, which indicates the file to be included.

Usage:

```
<%@ include file='header.jsp' @%>
```

NOTE In JSP, you use the `include` directive when you would use the ColdFusion tag `<cfinclude template = "header.cfm">` in ColdFusion.

TABLE A.1 `include` Directive Attributes

ATTRIBUTE	DESCRIPTION	NOTES
`file`	File location	(required) Specifies the file to be included. The root directory is the root of the page's application.

The implication of the `include` directive processing the included file content when it does is that inserted variables reside in the local page scope; all code is included as if it had originally been written directly in the calling template.

A.2.2 The page Directive

The page directive specifies attributes for the page and how it should load. You may have one or more page attributes within a given template. All attributes are optional. Default values are specified for many of the attributes.

Usage:

```
<%@ page language = 'java' session = 'true'
import = 'java.util.*' %>
```

TABLE A.2 page Directive Attributes

ATTRIBUTES	DESCRIPTION	NOTES
`autoFlush`	Toggles the buffer flush	Boolean value determines whether the buffer will be automatically flushed or flushed via programmatic control. Default is true.
`buffer`	Buffer size in kB	Defines buffer size in format 16 kB. Default is 16 kB.
`contentType`	Page MIME type	MIME type and character set of the page to use in response. Default is text/html; charset=ISO-8859-1.
`errorPage`	Error page to use	Defines relative URL to forward processing to if an error occurs.
`extends`	Class the page extends	States the Java class this JSP extends.
`import`	Packages to import	Allows you to import Java packages, which are separated by commas.
`info`	Page information	Allows you to set information about the page that can be retrieved with the `getServletInfo()` method.

(Continued)

TABLE A.2 page Directive Attributes (Continued)

ATTRIBUTES	DESCRIPTION	NOTES
isErrorpage	Error page flag	Set this value to true if the current page is an error page so that it has access to the Exception object. Default is false.
isThreadSafe	Threads	Define how the current JSP handles threads. If true, the page handles all requests with a single instance to maintain session information. Default is true.
language	Script language	Specifies which scripting language the page uses. Possible values are Java or JavaScript. Default is Java.
session	Session management	Specifies whether the page can access session information. Default is true.

A.2.3 The taglib Directive

The taglib directive defines a library namespace for the page. It maps the URI of the tag library descriptor to a prefix that can be used to reference tags from that library within the page.

The taglib directive has two attributes: url and prefix. The url attribute specifies the location of the tag library descriptor, and the prefix attribute specifies the prefix the custom actions use.

Usage:

```
<%@ taglib uri='javaforcftags' prefix='javaforcf' %>
```

A.3 Standard Actions

The JSP 1.2 specification provides several XML-compliant actions in the form of tags that allow you to include external pages, forward control to another page, or use a JavaBean or the Java plugin. This section describes these actions.

TABLE A.3 taglib Directive Attributes

ATTRIBUTE	DESCRIPTION	NOTES
prefix	Tag prefix	(required) Defines the prefix you will use to call the custom tags.
uri	Library location	(required) Specifies location of the tag library namespace.

A.3.1 <jsp:forward>

This action is used to end the execution of the current template and forward the request to another URL. The specified URL can be another JSP, an HTML page, a servlet, or other Web resources. The resource is specified as relative to the root of the current application.

Usage:

```
<jsp:forward page='/javaforcf/secret.jsp' />
```

You can also use the <jsp:param> action to forward request parameters to the specified page:

```
<jsp:forward page = '/javaforcf/secret.jsp'>
<jsp:param name='userid' value='admin' />

</jsp:forward>
```

TABLE A.4 <jsp:forward> Action Attributes

ATTRIBUTE	DESCRIPTION	NOTES
page	Page location	(required) Specifies the location of the page to forward to, relative to the root of the application.

A.3.2 <jsp:getProperty>

This action is used to output the specified property value from a JavaBean. The output value is a string. The specified bean must first be instantiated with the <jsp:useBean> action.

Usage:

```
<jsp:getProperty name='cart' property = 'orderid' />
```

TABLE A.5 <jsp:getProperty> Action Attributes

ATTRIBUTE	DESCRIPTION	NOTES
`name`	Name of bean	(required) Specifies name of a bean, which is already instantiated in any scope.
`property`	Property of bean	(required) Specifies the bean property to retrieve the value of.

A.3.3 <jsp:include>

This action is used to include a static or dynamically referenced file at run time. Because of when the file is included, files included using the `<jsp:include>` action do not share page or request-scoped variables with the calling page. For this reason, files included with the action cannot process directives. This is in distinction to the `include` directive.

Usage:

```
<jsp:include file='header.jsp' flush='true' />
```

TABLE A.6 <jsp:include> Action Attributes

ATTRIBUTE	DESCRIPTION	NOTES
`flush`	Flush buffer	(optional) Specifies whether or not to flush the output buffer before including the file. Default value is false.
`page`	Page location	(required) Specifies location of the file to be included.

Note that the page attribute can be the result of a runtime expression; that is, it can be dynamically specified. In JSP 1.1, the `flush` attribute was required, and its only possible value was true.

Also, you can append parameters to the original request with the `<jsp:param>` action. If the parameter already exists, the new value overwrites it. Multiple parameters can be specified in a comma-separated list.

A.3.4 `<jsp:param>`

This action allows you to pass parameters in the request scope. It is used within the bodies of `<jsp:forward>`, `<jsp:include>`, or `<jsp:plugin>`.

Usage:

```
<jsp:param name='userid'
 value='<%=request.getParameter(\'userid\')%>' />
```

TABLE A.7 `<jsp:param>` Action Attributes

ATTRIBUTE	DESCRIPTION	NOTES
`name`	Parameter name	(required) Name of the parameter.
`value`	Parameter value	(required) Value of the parameter.

A.3.5 `<jsp:params>`

The `<jsp:params>` action wraps multiple `<jsp:param>` actions for passing to an applet.

Usage:

```
<jsp:params>
<jsp:param name='Dept' value='Engineering' />
<jsp:param name='Emp' value='Dilbert' />
</jsp:params>
```

TABLE A.8 `<jsp:params>` Action Attributes

ATTRIBUTE	DESCRIPTION	NOTES
`name`	Parameter name	(required) Name of the parameter.
`value`	Parameter value	(required) Value of the parameter.

A.3.6 <jsp:plugin>

The <jsp:plugin> action allows you to embed an applet or a JavaBeans component directly in the JSP returned to the browser. It automatically generates the <embed> or <object> tags for you.

Usage:

```
<jsp:plugin
type = 'applet'
code = 'productivityChart.class'
codebase = 'intranet'
width = '300'
height = '400'
/>
```

TABLE A.9 <jsp:plugin> Action Attributes

ATTRIBUTE	DESCRIPTION	NOTES
align	Alignment	(optional) Specifies alignment of applet area.
archive	Applet classes	(optional) Additional classes or resources, specified by URL, that must be loaded.
code	Class name	(required) Specifies name of the class containing the applet or bean.
codebase	Class location	(required) Specifies relative URL location of the class specified in the code attribute.
height	Height in pixels	(optional) Specifies height of the applet area.
hspace	Horizontal border in pixels	(optional) Specifies number of pixels wide the border on the side of the applet should be.
iepluginurl	URL for IE plugin	(optional) Location of the Java plugin for MS Internet Explorer.
jreversion	JRE version	(optional) Specifies minimum requirement for the Java Runtime Engine version. Default is 1.1.

TABLE A.9 `<jsp:plugin>` Action Attributes (Continued)

ATTRIBUTE	DESCRIPTION	NOTES
`name`	Applet name	(optional) A name for the applet to keep it distinguished from other applets or beans on the page.
`nspluginurl`	URL for Netscape plugin	(optional) Location of the Java plugin for Netscape.
`title`	Label	(optional) A text description for the applet, which can appear in mouseover.
`type`	Object type	(optional) Whether the attribute is an applet or a bean.
`vspace`	Vertical border in pixels	(optional) Defines a pixel border above and below the applet.
`width`	Width in pixels	(optional) Width of the applet.

Many of these attributes correspond exactly to their HTML counterparts.

A.3.7 `<jsp:setProperty>`

The `<jsp:params>` action wraps multiple `<jsp:param>` actions for passing to an applet.

Usage:

```
<jsp:setProperty name='thisBook'
     property='author'
     value='JiminyChristmas'
     />
```

Note that this is equivalent to the following scriptlet:

```
<% thisBook.setAuthor('JiminyChristmas'); %>
```

TABLE A.10 `<jsp:setProperty>` Action Attributes

ATTRIBUTE	DESCRIPTION	NOTES
`name`	Bean name	(required) Name of the bean containing the property to be set.
`param`	Request parameter	(optional) Specifies the request parameter whose value will be set to the bean property value. Use of this attribute obviates use of the `value` attribute.
`property`	Bean property	(required) Specifies the property to be set.
`value`	Set value	(optional) Sets the value of the specified property. Can be any runtime expression that evaluates to a String.

A.3.8 <jsp:useBean>

The `<jsp:useBean>` action checks for an instance of a bean in the given class and scope. If one is found, it is referenced with the `id` attribute. If an instance is not found, it instantiates the bean. The bean is then available for processing by referencing the `id` and `scope`.

Usage:

```
<jsp:useBean id='myBean'>
```

TABLE A.11 `<jsp:useBean>` Action Attributes

ATTRIBUTE	DESCRIPTION	NOTES
`beanName`	Bean name	(optional) Specifies name of the bean component you are using to instantiate the bean. The same as the name of the bean in the `instantiate()` method of `java.beans.Beans`.
`class`	Class name	(optional) Used to specify class of the bean you are instantiating.

TABLE A.11 `<jsp:useBean>` Action Attributes (Continued)

ATTRIBUTE	DESCRIPTION	NOTES
`id`	Bean reference	(required) Specifies name by which you will reference the bean being instantiated.
`type`	Variable type	(optional) Sets the type of scripting variable to be used as a bean and is defined by the `id` attribute. The class that the bean gets cast to.

B

API Reference

This reference outlines the classes and interfaces in the JSP 1.2 and Servlet 2.3 specifications, per the September 25, 2001, final release. There are four packages that contain them:

1. **javax.servlet** Classes and interfaces to support servlets
2. **javax.servlet.http** Classes and interfaces for using servlets with HTTP
3. **javax.servlet.jsp** Classes and interfaces to support JSP
4. **javax.servlet.jsp.tagext** Classes and interfaces for creating custom actions (tag extensions) in JSP

The reference contains a list of the methods for the interfaces, classes, and exceptions in each package.

B.1 `javax.servlet` Interfaces, Classes, and Exceptions

B.1.1 Package `javax.servlet`

- `Filter`
- `FilterChain`
- `FilterConfig`
- `GenericServlet`
- `RequestDispatcher`
- `Servlet`
- `ServletConfig`
- `ServletContext`

- ServletContextAttributeEvent
- ServletContextAttributesListener
- ServletContextEvent
- ServletContextListener
- ServletException
- ServletInputStream
- ServletOutputStream
- ServletRequest
- ServletRequestWrapper
- ServletResponse
- ServletResponseWrapper
- SingleThreadModel
- UnavailableException

B.1.2 Package javax.servlet.http

- Cookie
- HttpServlet
- HttpServletRequest
- HttpServletRequestWrapper
- HttpServletResponse
- HttpServletResponseWrapper
- HttpSession
- HttpSessionActivationListener
- HttpSessionAttributesListener
- HttpSessionBindingEvent
- HttpSessionBindingListener
- HttpSessionContext
- HttpSessionEvent
- HttpSessionListener
- HttpUtils

B.2 JSP API for `javax.servlet.jsp` and `java.servlet.jsp.tagext`

B.2.1 Package `javax.servlet.jsp`

- `HttpJspPage`
- `JspEngineInfo`
- `JspException`
- `JspFactory`
- `JspPage`
- `JspTagException`
- `JspWriter`
- `PageContext`

B.2.2 Package `javax.servlet.jsp.tagext`

- `BodyContent`
- `BodyTag`
- `BodyTagSupport`
- `IterationTag`
- `PageData`
- `Tag`
- `TagAttributeInfo`
- `TagData`
- `TagExtraInfo`
- `TagInfo`
- `TagLibraryInfo`
- `TagLibraryValidator`
- `TagSupport`
- `TagVariableInfo`
- `TryCatchFinally`
- `VariableInfo`

B.3 `javax.servlet`

This package contains classes and interfaces required for writing servlets. This package includes the `Servlet` interface, which is implemented by all servlets.

B.3.1 `javax.servlet` Interfaces

B.3.1.1 `Filter`

A filter object performs filtering on requests and resources. It can also filter the response from a resource. The `Filter` interface has three methods. Every `Filter` object has access to a `FilterConfig` object for receiving initialization parameters.

```
public void init(FilterConfig filterConfig)
throws ServletException
```

`init()` is called by the Web container when the filter is instantiated. It is passed to a `FilterConfig` object containing configuration information about the filter's environment.

```
public void destroy()
```

`destroy()` is called when the filter is taken out of service.

```
public void doFilter(ServletRequest request,
ServletResponse response,
FilterChain chain)

throws java.io.IOException, ServletException
```

`doFilter()` is called by the container each time a client request for which this filter is registered gets received. The `FilterChain` passed in to this method allows the filter to pass the request and response to the next entity in the chain.

B.3.1.2 `FilterChain`

`FilterChain` is an object provided by the servlet container that represents a series of filters to be invoked in a filtered resource request. Filters use the next filter in the chain to invoke the resource at the end of the chain. If this is the last filter in the chain, the filtered resource itself is invoked.

```
public interface FilterChain
```

The `FilterChain` interface has one method, `doFilter()`.

```
public void doFilter(ServletRequest request,
ServletResponse response)

throws java.io.IOException, ServletException
```

B.3.1.3 FilterConfig

```
public interface FilterConfig
```

A `FilterConfig` object gets used by the container to pass configuration information to a filter while it is being initialized.

```
public String getFilterName()
```

`getFilterName()` returns the name of the filter, which corresponds to the definition in the deployment descriptor (web.xml).

```
public String getInitParameter(String param)
```

`getInitParameter()` returns a string containing the named initialization parameter. It returns null if there is no initialization parameter.

```
public java.util.Enumeration getInitParameterNames()
```

`getInitParameterNames()` returns an enumeration of the names of the initialization parameters.

```
getServletContext()
```

`getServletContext()` returns the servlet context in which this filter is running.

```
public ServletContext getServletContext()
```

`getServletContext()` returns a reference to the servlet context in which the caller is executing.

B.3.1.4 RequestDispatcher

The `RequestDispatcher` defines an object that receives client requests and passes them to another server resource. Though it was intended to wrap servlets, this resource can be an HTML page, a JSP, or a servlet.

```
public void forward(ServletRequest request,
ServletResponse response)

throws ServletException, java.io.IOException
```

`forward()` forwards one request to another resource on the server. In this way, one resource can handle preliminary processing and another can return a response.

`forward()` must be called before the response is generated for the client; that is, before the response output is flushed. Otherwise, an IllegalStateException will be thrown.

The request and response must be either the same objects as were passed to the calling servlet's `service()` method, or be subclasses of the `ServletRequestWrapper` or `ServletResponseWrapper` classes that wrap them.

```
public void include(ServletRequest resuest,
ServletResponse response)

throws ServletException, java.IO.IOException
```

`include()` includes the content of another resource in the response. The resource may be an HTML page, another servlet, or a JSP.

An included servlet cannot change the response status code or change headers. Attempts to do so are ignored.

The request and response must be either the same objects as were passed to the calling servlet's `service()` method, or be subclasses of the `ServletRequestWrapper` or `ServletResponseWrapper` classes that wrap them.

B.3.1.5 `Servlet`

```
public interface Servlet
```

All servlets must implement the `Servlet` interface. This interface defines the "life cycle" methods for servlets; that is, the methods that initialize a servlet, let it service requests, and then remove it.

When writing a servlet, these methods are called in the following order:

1. The servlet is constructed. It is initialized with the `init` method.
2. Client calls to the `service()` method are handled.
3. The servlet is removed from service. It is destroyed, garbage collected, and finalized.

There are two methods defined that are not life cycle methods. One is the `getServletConfig()` method. The servlet can use this method to discover initialization parameters. The other is the `getServletInfo()` method, with which the servlet exposes information about itself such as author and version.

```
public void init(ServletConfig config)
throws ServletException
```

`init()` is called by the container to indicate that the servlet is being put into service.

```
public ServletConfig getServletConfig()
```

`getServletConfig()` returns a `ServletConfig` object containing the servlet's initialization parameters.

```
public void service(ServletRequest request,
ServletResponse response)

throws ServletException, java.io.IOException
```

`service()` gets called by the servlet container to allow the servlet to respond to a request. This method gets called only after the `init()` method is successfully completed. The code that represents the actual work of the servlet is placed inside the `service()` method.

```
public String getServletInfo()
```

`getServletInfo()` returns a string containing servlet information such as the author, copyright, and version.

```
public void destroy()
```

`destroy()` is called by the container when the servlet is to be removed from service. This allows the servlet to release associated resources.

B.3.1.6 `ServletConfig`

```
public abstract interface ServletConfig
```

The `ServletConfig` object is used to pass initialization parameters to a servlet.

```
public String getInitParameter(String name)
```

`getInitParameter()` returns a string containing the value of the named parameter. It returns `null` if the parameter does not exist.

```
public java.util.Enumeration getInitParameterNames()
```

`getInitParameterNames()` returns an enumeration of `String` objects containing the names of all of the servlet's initialization parameters.

```
public ServletContext getServletContext()
```

`getServletContext()` returns the ServletContext associated with the calling servlet. This object contains environment information.

```
public String getServletName()
```

`getServletName()` returns the name of the current servlet instance. If unnamed, the method returns the servlet's class name.

B.3.1.7 **`ServletContext`**

```
public abstract interface ServletContext
```

The `ServletContext` interface declares methods that a servlet uses to communicate with its servlet container. One `ServletContext` per Web application per JVM exists. If a Web application's deployment descriptor describes it as "distributed," then there will be one context per JVM.

```
public Object getAttribute(String name)
```

`getAttriubte()` returns the servlet container attribute with the specified name. If none exists, it returns `null`.

```
public java.util.Enumeration getAttributeNames()
```

`getAttributeNames()` returns an `Enumeration` object containing the available attribute names within this servlet context.

```
public ServletContext getContext(String uripath)
```

`getContext()` returns the `ServletContext` object for the resource at the specified URL.

```
public String getInitParameter(String name)
```

`getInitParameter()` returns a string with the value of the specified initialization parameter. It returns `null` if the parameter does not exist.

```
public java.util.Enumeration getInitParameterNames()
```

`getInitParameterNames()` returns an enumeration of `String` objects containing the names of the context's initialization parameters. If no initialization parameters exists, it returns `null`.

```
public int getMajorVersion()
```

`getMajorVersion()` returns the version of the Java servlet API supported by this container. For Servlet version 2.3 supporting containers, this method returns `2`.

```
public String getMimeType(java.lang.String file)
```

`getMimeType()` returns the MIME type of the specified file. If the MIME type is not known, it returns `null`.

```
public int getMinorVersion()
```

`getMinorVersion()` returns the minor version of the Java servlet API supported by this container. For Servlet version 2.3, it returns `3`.

```
public RequestDispatcher getNamedDispatcher(String name)
```

`getNamedDispatcher()` returns a `RequestDispatcher` object that acts as a wrapper for the servlet.

```
public String getRealPath(String path)
```

`getRealPath()` returns the real path as a string for the specified virtual path.

```
public RequestDispatcher getRequestDispatcher(String path)
```

`getRequestDispatcher()` returns a `RequestDispatcher` object that acts as a wrapper for the resource at the specified path.

```
public java.net.URL getResource(String path)
```

`getResource()` returns a URL object to the resource mapped to the specified path. It returns `null` if there is no resource mapped to the path. The path must begin with a /. The path is interpreted as relative to the current context root.

```
public java.io.InputStream getResourceAsStream(String path)
```

`getResourceAsStream()` returns the resource mapped to the specified path as an `InputStream` object.

```
public java.util.Set getResourcePaths(String path)
```

`getResourcePaths()` returns all of the paths to resources in the specified subdirectory of the Web application as `String` prepended with a /.

```
public String getServerInfo()
```

`getServerInfo()` returns a `String` object containing the name and version number of the servlet container in which the servlet is running.

```
public Servlet getServlet(String name)
```

Deprecated; it is defined to retrieve a servlet from a servlet context.

```
public String getServletContextName()
```

`getServletContextName()` returns the name of the Web application as specified in the Web application's deployment descriptor in the "display-name" element.

```
public java.util.Enumeration getServletNames()
```

Deprecated; it is defined to return an enumeration of all known servlet names in this context.

```
public java.util.Enumeration getServlets()
```

Deprecated; it is defined to return an enumeration of all known servlets in this context.

```
public void log(Exception e, String message)
```

Deprecated; it is defined to write an exception's stack trace and a message to the servlet log file, and it is replaced with `log(String message, Throwable throwable)`.

```
public void log(String message, Throwable throwable)
```

`log()` writes the specified message to the servlet log file. This is generally an event log.

```
public void removeAttribute(String name)
```

`removeAttribute()` removes the attribute corresponding to the specified name from the servlet context.

```
public void setAttribute(String name, Object object)
```

`setAttribute()` binds an object to the specified attribute name in the current servlet context.

B.3.1.8 ServletContextAttributeListener

Objects that implement the `ServletContextAttributeListener` interface can receive notifications that their attribute lists have changed. In order to receive such notifications, a servlet must be configured in the Web application's deployment descriptor.

```
public void attributeAdded(ServletContextAttributeEvent scab)
```

`attributeAdded()` should be called after the attribute is added to the servlet context to make notification that the new event was added.

```
public void attributeRemoved(ServletContextAttributeEvent scab)
```

`attributeRemoved()` should be called after the attribute is removed from the servlet context. The specified `ServletContextAttributeEvent` contains information about the event.

```
public void attributeReplaced()
```

`attributeReplaced()` should be called after the attribute is replaced in the servlet context. The specified `ServletContextAttributeEvent` contains information about the event.

B.3.1.9 ServletContextListener

An object that implements the `ServletContextListener` interface receives notifications about changes to the servlet context of the Web application in which they reside. In order to receive notification events, the implementation class must be configured in the Web application's deployment descriptor.

```
public void contextDestroyed(ServletContextEvent sce)
```

`contextDestroyed()` represents notification that a Web application is about to be destroyed.

```
public void contextInitialized(ServletContextEvent sce)
```

`contextInitialized()` represents notification that a Web application has been initialized and can process requests.

B.3.1.10 ServletRequest

The `ServletRequest` interface contains numerous methods that are useful in providing client request information to a servlet. The servlet container creates a `ServletRequest` object and passes it as an argument to the servlet's `service` method.

```
public java.lang.Object getAttribute(String name)
```

`getAttribute()` returns the value of the specified attribute as an `Object`. It returns `null` if none exists.

```
public java.util.Enumeration getAttributeNames()
```

`getAttributeNames()` returns an `Enumeration` object containing the names of the attributes available to the invoking servlet request.

```
public String getCharacterEncoding()
```

`getCharacterEncoding()` returns the name of the character encoding type used for this request.

```
public int getContentLength()
```

`getContentLength()` returns the length in bytes of the input stream request body. If the length is not known, it returns `-1`.

```
public String getContentType()
```

`getContentType()` returns the MIME type of the request. It returns `null` if the type is not known.

```
public ServletInputStream getInputStream()
throws java.io.IOException
```

`getInputStream()` returns the body of the request as a `ServletInputStream` object containing binary data.

```
public java.util.Locale getLocale()
```

`getLocale()` returns the client's preferred `Locale` for content acceptance. This value is based on the Accept-Language header returned by the browser.

```
public java.util.Locale getLocales()
```

`getLocales()` returns an enumeration of acceptable locales in descending order of preference.

```
public String getParameter(String name)
```

`getParameter()` returns a `String` value of the specified request parameter. It returns `null` if the parameter does not exist.

```
public java.util.Map getParameterMap(String name)
```

`getParameterMap()` returns a `java.util.Map` of the current request's parameters.

```
public java.util.Enumeration getParameterNames()
```

`getParameterNames()` returns an enumeration of strings containing the parameter names in the current request.

```
public java.lang.String[] getParameterValues(String name)
```

`getParameterValues()` returns an array of strings containing all of the values of the specified parameter in the current request. It returns `null` if the parameter does not exist.

```
public String getProtocol()
```

`getProtocol()` returns the name as a string of the protocol used in the current request in this form: *protocol/majorversion/minorversion*. `HTTP/1.1` is an example.

```
public java.io.BufferedReader getReader()
throws java.io.IOException
```

`getReader()` returns a `BufferedReader` object that can read the body of the request as character data.

```
public String getRealPath(String path)
```

Deprecated; use `ServletContext.getRealPath` instead.

```
public String getRemoteAddr()
```

`getRemoteAddr()` returns the IP address of the client who sent the request.

```
public String getRemoteHost()
```

`getRemoteHost()` returns the fully qualified name of the client who sent the request.

```
public getRequestDispatcher(String path)
```

`getRequestDispatcher()` returns a `RequestDispatcher` object that acts as a wrapper for the resource at the specified path.

```
public String getScheme()
```

`getScheme()` returns the name of the scheme used for the current request. `http`, `https`, or `ftp` are examples.

```
public String getServerName()
```

`getServerName()` returns the name of the server processing the request.

```
public int getServerPort()
```

`getServerPort()` returns the port number of the server processing the request.

```
public boolean isSecure()
```

`isSecure()` returns a `boolean` indicating whether this request was made via a secure channel such as HTTPS.

```
public void removeAttribute(String name)
```

`removeAttribute` removes an attribute from the current request.

```
public void setAttribute(String name, Object obj)
```

`setAttribute()` binds a value to the specified attribute name. Once the request has been processed, the attribute is reset.

```
public void setCharacterEncoding(String enc)
throws java.io.UnsupportedEncodingException
```

`setCharacterEncoding()` overrides the character encoding used in the body of the current request.

B.3.1.11 ServletResponse

```
public void flushBuffer()
```

`flushBuffer()` forces any content in the buffer to be written to the client.

```
public int getBufferSize()
```

`getBufferSize()` returns the actual buffer size used in the response.

```
public String getCharacterEncoding()
```

`getCharacterEncoding()` returns the charset of the MIME type used in the response body. Default is "ISO-8859-1," which corresponds to Latin-1.

```
public java.util.Locale getLocale()
```

`getLocale()` returns the locale assigned to the response.

```
public ServletOutputStream getOutputStream()
throws java.io.IOException
```

`getOutputStream()` returns a `ServletOutputStream` suitable for writing binary data in the response.

```
public java.io.PrintWriter getWriter()
```

`getWriter()` returns a `PrintWriter` object that can be used to return character text to the client.

```
public boolean isCommitted()
```

`isCommitted()` returns a `boolean` value indicating whether or not the response has been committed.

```
public void reset()
```

`reset()` clears all data in the buffer, status codes, and header.

```
public void resetBuffer()
```

`resetBuffer()` clears the content of the underlying buffer in the response without clearing headers or status code.

```
public void setBufferSize()
```

`setBufferSize()` sets the buffer size for the response body.

```
public void setContentLength()
```

`setContentLength()` sets the length of the content body in the response. It also sets the `Content-Length` HTTP header when HTTP is used.

```
public void setContentType(String type)
```

`setContentType()` sets the content type for the response returned to the client. The MIME type is specified in the string passed to the method. It may also include the character encoding type, such as `text/plain; charset=ISO-8869-1`.

```
public void setLocale(java.util.Locale loc)
```

`setLocale()` sets the locale for the response by setting the HTTP headers. It will modify the Content-Type's charset.

B.3.1.12 SingleThreadModel

```
public interface SingleThreadModel
```

The `SingleThreadModel` interface declares no methods. This interface ensures that a servlet processes only one request at a time (that is, no two threads can execute its `service()` method concurrently). This can happen in one of two ways: first, by synchronizing access to a single servlet instance, and second, by assigning a free servlet instance from a pool of instances to each new request.

B.3.2 javax.servlet Classes

B.3.2.1 GenericServlet

```
public abstract class GenericServlet
extends Object
implements Servlet, ServletConfig, java.io.Serializable
```

The `GenericServlet` class defines a generic, protocol-independent servlet. To use a servlet for the Web, extend `HTTPServlet`. `GenericServlet` provides an implementation of the interfaces defined in `Servlet` and `ServletConfig`. In order to write a generic servlet, you extend the abstract `service` method.

```
public void destroy()
```

`destroy()` is called by the servlet container to indicate that the servlet is being removed from service.

```
public String getInitParameter(String name)
```

`getInitParameter()` returns a string containing the value of the specified initialization parameter. It returns `null` if the parameter does not exist.

```
public java.util.Enumeration getInitParameterNames()
```

`getInitParameterNames()` returns an enumeration of strings containing the names of the servlet's initialization parameters. It returns an empty enumeration if none exist.

```
public ServletConfig getServletConfig()
```

`getServletConfig()` returns the current servlet's `ServletConfig` object, which contains the initialization parameters for the servlet.

```
public ServletContext getServletContext()
```

`getServletContext()` returns a `ServletContext` object reference for the context in which the current servlet is running.

```
public String getServletInfo()
```

`getServletInfo()` returns a string containing information about the servlet, including author, copyright, and version.

```
public String getServletName()
```

`getServletName()` returns the name of this servlet instance.

```
public void init(ServletConfig config)
throws ServletException
public void init()
throws ServletException
```

`init()` should get called when a servlet is first loaded. By overriding `init()`, you obviate calling `super.init(config)`. `init(ServletConfig config)` is called by the servlet container to indicate that a servlet is being placed into servlet.

```
public void log(String msg)
```

`log()` writes the specified message to the servlet's log file. The message is prepended with the name of the servlet.

```
public void log(String msg, java.lang.Throwable thr)
```

`log()` writes the specified message to the servlet's log file and a stack trace for the specified `Throwable` exception.

```
public abstract void service(ServletRequest req,
ServletResponse res)
```

`service()` is called by the servlet container to allow the servlet to process a request. The code representing what the servlet actually does is written inside this method. As this method is abstract, a concrete subclass of `GenericServlet` must be implemented.

B.3.2.2 ServletContextAttributeEvent

```
public class ServletContextAttributeEvent
extends ServletContextEvent
```

A `ServletContextEvent` is the event class for notifications that an attribute has been added to, removed from, or replaced in the `ServletContext` of a Web application.

```
public ServletContextAttributeEvent(ServletContext source,
String name, Object value)
```

The constructor accepts values for the `ServletContext` in which the event took place and for the name and value of the attribute.

```
public String getName()
```

`getName()` returns the name of the new, replaced, or removed attribute from the `ServletContext`.

```
public java.lang.Object getValue()
```

`getValue()` returns the value of the new, replaced, or removed attribute from the `ServletContext`.

B.3.2.3 ServletContextEvent

```
public class ServletContextEvent
extends java.util.EventObject
```

A `ServletContextEvent` is the event object used for notifications regarding changes to the servlet context of a Web application.

```
public ServletContextEvent(ServletContext source)
```

The constructor constructs a `ServletContextEvent` from the specified context.

```
public ServletContext getServletContext()
```

`getServletContext()` returns the `ServletContext` in which the event took place.

B.3.2.4 `ServletInputStream`

`ServletInputStream` provides an input stream to read binary data from a client request and can be used to read data sent from the client when `HTTP POST` and `PUT` methods are used. It provides one method other than those in `InputStream` and `readLine`, which read the data line by line.

```
protected ServletInputStream()
```

The constructor does nothing, as `ServletInputStream` is never directly created because it is an abstract class. Subclasses of this class must implement `java.io.InputStream.read()`.

```
public int readLine(byte[ ] b, int off, int len)
throws java.io.IOException
```

`readline()` reads data one line at a time. It starts at the specified offset and reads bytes into an array until it reads a certain number of bytes (as specified in `len`) or reaches a newline character. The newline character is also stored in the byte array. The method returns `-1` if the end-of-file is reached before the maximum number of bytes is read.

B.3.2.5 `ServletOutputStream`

`ServletOutputStream` provides an output stream to send binary data to the client and also provides overloaded versions of the `print()` and `println()` methods used for handling primitive and `String` datatypes.

```
protected ServletOutputStream()
```

The constructor does nothing, as `ServletOutputStream` is never directly created because it is an abstract class.

```
public abstract class ServletOutputStream
extends java.io.OutputStream
```

```
public void print(boolean b)
throws java.io.IOException
public void print(char c)
throws java.io.IOException
public void print(double d)
throws java.io.IOException
public void print(float f)
throws java.io.IOException
public void print(long l)
throws java.io.IOException
public void print(int i)
throws java.io.IOException
public void print(String s)
throws java.io.IOException
```

`print()` prints the specified primitive type (or string) to the client, without appending a carriage return/line return.

```
public void println(boolean b)
throws java.io.IOException
public void println(char c)
throws java.io.IOException
public void println(double d)
throws java.io.IOException
public void println(float f)
throws java.io.IOException
public void println(long l)
throws java.io.IOException
public void println(int i)
throws java.io.IOException
public void println(String s)
throws java.io.IOException
```

`println()` prints the specified primitive type (or string) to the client, appending a carriage return/line return.

The no argument version of `println()` writes only a carriage return/line feed to the client.

B.3.2.6 `ServletRequestWrapper`

```
public class ServletRequestWrapper
extends Object
implements ServletRequest
```

The `ServletRequestWrapper` provides an implementation of the `ServletRequest` interface that can be subclassed in order to adapt the request to a servlet. It implements the `Wrapper` or `Decorator` pattern.

```
public ServletRequestWrapper(ServletRequest req)
```

The constructor creates a `ServletRequest` adapter that wraps the specified request object.

```
public ServletRequest getRequest()
```

`getRequest()` returns the wrapped `ServletRequest`.

```
public void setRequest(ServletRequest req)
```

`setRequest()` sets the `ServletRequest` to be wrapped.

```
public Object getAttribute(String name)

public java.util.Enumeration getAttributeNames()

public String getCharacterEncoding()

public int getContentLength()

public String getContentType()

public ServletInputStream getInputStream()
throws java.io.IOException

public java.util.Locale getLocale()

public java.util.Enumeration getLocales()

public String getParameter(String name)

public java.util.Map getParameterMap()

public java.util.Enumeration getParameterNames()
```

```
public String[] getParameterValues()

public String getProtocol()

public java.io.BufferedReader getReader()
throws java.io.IOException

public String getRealPath(String path)

public String getRemoteAddr()

public String getRemoteHost()

public RequestDispatcher getRequestDispatcher(String path)

public String getScheme()

public String getServerName()

public int getServerPort()

public boolean isSecure()

public void removeAttribute(String name)

public void setAttribute(String name, Object obj)

public void setCharacterEncoding(String enc)
throws java.io.UnsupportedEncodingException
```

B.3.2.7 ServletResponseWrapper

```
public class ServletResponseWrapper
extends Object
implements ServletResponse
```

ServletResponseWrapper provides an implementation of the Servlet-Response interface that can be subclassed in order to adapt the response from a servlet. Its methods call the same methods on the wrapped response object.

```
public ServletResponseWrapper(ServletResponse response)
```

The `ServletResponseWrapper` constructor creates a wrapper around the specified `ServletResponse` object.

```
public ServletResponseWrapper getResponse()
```

`getResponse()` returns the wrapped `ServletResponse`.

```
public void setResponse(ServletResponse response)
```

`setResponse()` sets the `ServletResponse` to be wrapped.

```
public void flushBuffer()
throws java.io.IOException

public void getBufferSize()

public String getCharacterEncoding()

public java.util.Locale getLocale()

public ServletOutputStream getOutputStream()
throws java.io.IOException

public java.io.PrintWriter getWriter()
throws java.io.IOException

public boolean isCommitted()

public void reset()

public void resetBuffer()

public void setContentLength(int len)

public void setContentType(String type)

public void setLocale(java.util.Locale loc)
```

B.3.3 javax.servlet Exceptions

```
public class ServletException
extends Exception
```

ServletException is a general exception thrown by servlets when processing has become ambiguous or difficult.

```
public ServletException()
public ServletException(String message)
public ServletException(String message, java.lang.Thowable
rootCause)
public ServletException(java.lang.Throwable rootCause)
```

These constructors allow a String message and/or a Throwable that represents the rootCause of the difficulty encountered.

```
public Throwable getRootCause()
```

getRootCause() returns the Throwable that caused the servlet exception.

B.3.3.1 UnavailableException

```
public class UnavailableException
extends ServletException
```

UnavailableException is thrown by a servlet to indicate that it is permanently or temporarily unavailable.

```
public UnavailableException(String message)
```

This constructor indicates that the servlet is permanently unavailable. The String parameter is a message describing the problem.

```
public UnavailableException(String message, int seconds)
```

This constructor indicates that the servlet is temporarily unavailable. It accepts a string that describes the problem and an estimate in seconds of how long the servlet will be available. Passing 0 or a negative number indicates the length of unavailability is unknown.

```
public boolean isPermanent()
```

isPermanent() returns true if the servlet is unavailable permanently.

```
public int getUnavailableSeconds()
```

`getUnavailableSeconds()` returns the estimated number of seconds that the servlet will be unavailable.

B.4 javax.servlet.http Interfaces and Classes

The `javax.servlet.http` package allows a convenient way for developers to create servlets that are to be used specifically for the HTTP protocol. Session tracking, access to cookies, and methods for processing a variety of HTTP request types are made available here.

B.4.1 javax.servlet.http Interfaces

B.4.1.1 HttpServletRequest

```
public abstract interface HttpServletRequest
extends Servlet
```

`HttpServletRequest` extends the `ServletRequest` interface to provide information to servlets regarding HTTP requests. The servlet container creates an `HttpServletRequest` object and passes it as an argument to the servlet's service methods, such as `doGet()` and `doPost()`.

The following fields are made available; each is a `String` identifier for Basic authentication:

```
public static final java.lang.String BASIC_AUTH
public static final java.lang.String CLIENT_CERT_AUTH
public static final java.lang.String FORM_AUTH
public static final java.lang.String DIGEST_AUTH
```

```
public String getAuthType()
```

`getAuthType()` returns the name of the authentication scheme in use for this resource, and it returns `null` if no scheme is in use. This is the same as the CGI variable `AUTH_TYPE`.

```
public String getContextPath()
```

`getContextPath()` returns the portion of the request URI that indicates the request context.

Returns `""` for servlets in the root context.

```
public Cookie[] getCookies()
```

getCookies() returns an array of all Cookie objects sent by the client with this request. It returns null if no cookies were sent.

```
public long getDateHeader(String name)
throws java.lang.IllegalArgumentException
```

getDateHeader() returns a long representing a Date object of the request header of headers that contain dates. The Date is returned as the number of milliseconds since January 1, 1970. If the request did not have an available Date header as specified, it returns -1.

```
public String getHeader(String name)
```

getHeader() returns the value of the specified header name as a String object. It returns null if the specified header does not exist.

```
public Enumeration getHeaders(String name)
```

getHeaders() returns an enumeration of strings of the specified header. It returns an empty enumeration if the request did not include any headers of the specified name.

```
public Enumeration getHeaderNames()
```

getHeaderNames() returns an enumeration of all header names in this request. If your servlet container does not allow this method, it returns null.

```
public int getIntHeader(String name)
throws NumberFormatException
```

getIntHeader() returns the value of the specified header as an int. It throws NumberFormatException if the header cannot be converted to an int, and it returns -1 if the request does not have a header of the name specified.

```
public String getMethod()
```

getMethod() returns the name of the HTTP method used to make the current request (for instance, GET, POST, PUT, or DELETE).

```
public String getPathInfo()
```

`getPathInfo()` returns any extra path information associated with the URL sent by the client when the request was made. This information precedes the query string and follows the servlet path. It returns `null` if there is no extra path information and is the same as calling the CGI variable `PATH_INFO`.

```
public String getPathTranslated()
```

`getPathTranslated()` returns any extra path information associated with the URL sent by the client when the request was made, and translates it to a real path. It returns `null` if there is no extra path information and is the same as the CGI variable `PATH_TRANSLATED`.

```
public String getQueryString()
```

`getQueryString()` returns the query string in the URL of the current request following the path. It returns `null` if the URL contains no query string and returns the same information as the CGI variable `QUERY_STRING`.

```
public String getRemoteUser()
```

`getRemoteUser()` returns the login of the requesting user if that user has been authenticated. It returns `null` otherwise and is the same as the value of the CGI variable `REMOTE_USER`.

```
public String getRequestSessionId()
```

`getRequestSessionId()` returns the session ID specified by the client, which may not be the same as the ID of the actual session in use. It returns `null` if the request does not specify a session ID.

```
public String getRequestURI()
```

`getRequestURI()` returns the part of the URL from the protocol name up to the query string.

```
public StringBuffer getRequestURL()
```

`getRequestURL()` returns a `StringBuffer` object of the URL requested by the client without the query string.

```
public String getServletPath()
```

`getServletPath()` returns the part of the URL containing the servlet call. It includes the servlet name or path to the servlet and does not include any query string. It is the same as the CGI variable `SCRIPT_NAME`.

```
public HttpSession getSession()
```

`getSession()` gets the current session associated with this request. It creates a session if none is so associated.

```
public HttpSession getSession(boolean create)
```

`getSession()` gets the current session associated with this request. If there is no current session so associated and create is `true`, it returns a new session. If there is no valid session associated with the request and create is `false`, it returns `null`.

```
public java.security.Principal getUserPrincipal()
```

`getUserPrincipal()` returns the name of the current authenticated user as a `Principal` object. It returns `null` if the user is not authenticated.

```
public boolean isRequestedSessionIdFromCookie()
```

`isRequestedSessionIdFromCookie()` checks whether the requested session ID came from a cookie.

```
public boolean isRequestedSessionIdFromUrl()
```

Deprecated; use `isRequestedSessionIdFromURL()` instead.

```
public boolean isRequestedSessionIdFromURL()
```

`isRequestedSessionIdFromURL()` checks whether the requested session ID came in as part of the URL.

```
public boolean isRequestedSessionIdValid()
```

`isRequestedSessionIdValid()` checks whether the requested session ID is still valid.

```
public boolean isUserInRole(String role)
```

`isUserInRole()` returns a boolean indicating whether the authenticated user is allowed in the specified logical role. Roles and membership therein can be described using deployment descriptors. It returns `false` if the user has not been authenticated.

B.4.1.2 `HttpServletResponse`

```
public interface HttpServletResponse
extends ServletResponse
```

The `HttpServletResponse` interface extends the funtionality of the `ServletReponse` interface by providing methods for accessing HTTP-specific features. Such features include headers and cookies.

The servlet container creates an `HttpServletRequest` object and passes it as an argument to the servlet's service methods, such as `doGet` and `doPost`.

The following constants represent status codes defined in the HTTP specification. Each status code is followed by its numeric value and its meaning in HTTP.

```
public static final int SC_CONTINUE
```

100. The client should continue with his or her request.

```
public static final int SC_SWITCHING_PROTOCOLS
```

101. The server understands the client's request for a change in application protocol.

```
public static final int SC_OK
```

200. Success. The server's response contains the requested data.

```
public static final int SC_CREATED
```

201. A new resource has been created.

```
public static final int SC_ACCEPTED
```

202. The request has been accepted but not entirely processed.

```
public static final int SC_NON_AUTHORITATIVE_INFORMATION
```

203. Information returned in the entity header is not definitive. It comes from a copy.

`public static final int SC_NO_CONTENT`

204. The server has fulfilled the request, but it needn't return an entity body.

`public static final int SC_RESET_CONTENT`

205. The browser should clear the form that caused the request.

`public static final int SC_PARTIAL_CONTENT`

206. The server has carried out a partial `GET` request.

`public static final int SC_MULTIPLE_CHOICES`

300. The requested resource corresponds to any one of a set of representations.

`public static final int SC_MOVED_PERMANENTLY`

301. The requested resource has been moved permanently.

`public static final int SC_MOVED_TEMPORARILY`

302. The requested resource resides temporarily in another location.

`public static final int SC_SEE_OTHER`

303. The response to the request can be found at another location, as specified in the header.

`public static final int SC_NOT_MODIFIED`

304. The client has performed a conditional `GET` request, but the document is unchanged.

`public static final int SC_USE_PROXY`

305. The requested resource must be accessed through the proxy given in the Location field.

`public static final int SC_BAD_REQUEST`

400. The request contained malformed syntax and could not be understood.

`public static final int SC_UNAUTHORIZED`

401. The request lacks proper authorization to access the specified resource.

`public static final int SC_PAYMENT_REQUIRED`

402. The request is reserved for future use.

```
public static final int SC_FORBIDDEN
```

403. The server understood the request, but it refuses to fulfill it.

```
public static final int SC_NOT_FOUND
```

404. The server does not have a resource matching the one requested.

```
public static final int SC_METHOD_NOT_ALLOWED
```

405. The method specified in the request line is not allowed for the resource that has been identified.

```
public static final int SC_NOT_ACCEPTABLE
```

406. This resource can only generate incompatible responses for these request headers.

```
public static final int SC_PROXY_AUTHENTICATION_REQUIRED
```

407. The client must first authenticate itself with the proxy.

```
public static final int SC_REQUEST_TIMEOUT
```

408. The client did not produce a request within the server's time limit.

```
public static final int SC_CONFLICT
```

409. The request could not be completed because of a conflict with the resource.

```
public static final int SC_GONE
```

410. The resource is not available at this address and no forwarding information is known.

```
public static final int SC_LENGTH_REQUIRED
```

411. The server refuses to accept the request without a defined `Content-Length`.

```
public static final int SC_PRECONDITION_FAILED
```

412. The precondition given in one or more of the IF request-header fields evaluated to false.

```
public static final int SC_REQUEST_ENTITY_TOO_LARGE
```

413. The request entity is larger than the server can or will process.

```
public static final int SC_REQUEST_URI_TOO_LONG
```

414. The request URI is longer than the server will interpret.

```
public static final int SC_UNSUPPORTED_MEDIA_TYPE
```

415. The entity body of the request is in an unsupported format.

```
public static final int SC_REQUESTED_RANGE_NOT_SATISFIABLE
```

416. The server cannot serve the requested byte range.

```
public static final int SC_EXPECTATION_FAILED
```

417. The server could not meet the expectation given in the Expectation header.

```
public static final int SC_INTERNAL_SERVER_ERROR
```

500. The server encountered an error that prevented it from fulfilling the request.

```
public static final int SC_NOT_IMPLEMENTED
```

501. The server does not support the functionality required to fulfill the request.

```
public static final int SC_BAD_GATEWAY
```

502. The server received an invalid response from a server it consulted as a proxy.

```
public static final int SC_SERVICE_UNAVAILABLE
```

503. The server cannot handle the request because of temporary overloading or maintenance.

```
public static final int SC_GATEWAY_TIMEOUT
```

504. The server did not receive a response from the upstream server while acting as proxy.

```
public static final int SC_HTTP_VERSION_NOT_SUPPORTED
```

505. The server does not support the request version of HTTP.

```
public void addCookie(Cookie cookie)
```

addCookie() adds the specified cookie to the response. Multiple cookies can be added.

```
public void addDateHeader(String name, long date)
```

addDateHeader() adds a response header with the given name and date value.

```
public void addHeader(String name, String value)
```

addHeader() adds a response header with the given name and value.

```
addIntHeader(String name, int value)
```

addIntHeader() adds a response header with the given name and int value.

```
public boolean containsHeader(String name)
```

containsHeader() returns true if the response header includes the specified header name. It can be used before calling a set() method to determine if the value has already been set.

```
public String encodeRedirectURL(String url)
```

encodeRedirectURL() encodes the specified URL by including the session ID in it. If encoding is not necessary, it returns the URL unchanged.

```
public String encodeURL(String url)
```

encodeURL() encodes the specified URL by including the session ID in it. If encoding is not necessary, it returns the URL unchanged.

```
public void sendError(int sc, String msg)
```

sendError() sends an error response to the client with the specified status code. It clears the buffer.

```
public void sendRedirect(String location)
```

sendRedirect() sends a temporary redirect response to the client using the specified location.

```
public void setDateHeader(String name, long date)
```

`setDateHeader()` sets a response header with the given name and date value.

```
public void setIntHeader(String name, int value)
```

`setIntHeader()` sets a response header with the given name and integer value.

```
public void setStatus(int sc)
```

`setStatus()` sets the status code for this response.

B.4.1.3 HttpSession

The `HttpSession` interface provides a way to identify a user across mulitple requests and to store information about that user. The information can be maintained by using cookies or by rewriting URLs. The `HttpSession` interface allows servlets to read and manipulate session information (such as the session identifier, creation time, and last accessed time). It also allows servlets to bind objects to sessions so that user information persists across multiple requests. Session information is scoped only to the current Web application (ServletContext), so information is not shared between them.

```
public Object getAttribute(String name)
```

`getAttribute()` returns the object bound with the specified name in this session. If none is found, it returns `null`.

```
public java.util.Enumeration getAttributeNames()
```

`getAttributeNames()` returns an enumeration of `String` objects containing the names of all of the objects bound to this session.

```
public long getCreationTime()
```

`getCreationTime()` returns a long of the time this session was created. It is represented as the number of milliseconds since midnight, January 1, 1970.

```
public String getID()
```

`getID()` returns a string containing this session's unique identifier.

```
public long getLastAccessedTime()
```

`getLastAccessedTime()` returns a `long` containing the last time the client sent a request associated with this session. It is represented as the number of milliseconds since midnight, January 1, 1970, and it is marked by the time the container received the request.

```
public int getMaxInactiveInterval()
```

`getMaxInactiveInterval()` returns the maximum time interval (in seconds) that the container will keep the session open between requests.

```
public ServletContext getServletContext()
```

`getServletContext()` returns the servlet context to which this session belongs.

```
public void invalidate()
```

`invalidate()` invalidates the current session and unbinds any associated objects.

```
public boolean isNew()
```

`isNew()` returns a `boolean` indicating whether the client has joined the session yet.

```
public void removeAttribute(String)
```

`removeAttribute()` removes the object bound with the name specified from this session.

```
public void setAttribute(String name, Object value)
```

`setAtrribute()` binds an object to the session using the specified name.

```
public void setMaxInactiveInterval(int interval)
```

`setMaxInactiveInterval()` specifies the time in seconds between client requests before the container will invalidate the session.

B.4.1.4 HttpSessionActivationListener

```
public abstract interface HttpSessionActivationListener
extends java.util.EventListener
```

An object bound to a session that implements this interface can be registered to receive notification regarding when its session will be passivated and activated. A container that migrates a session, for example, to another Virtual Machine must make such notification.

```
public void sessionDidActivate(HttpSessionEvent hse)
```

`sessionDidActivate()` is called when the session has just successfully been activated.

```
public void sessionWillPassivate(HttpSessionEvent hse)
```

`sessionWillPassivate()` is called when the session is about to be passivated.

B.4.1.5 HttpSessionAttributeListener

```
public interface HttpSessionAttributeListener
extends java.util.EventListener
```

An object that implements this interface can receive notifications of changes to the attribute lists of sessions within this Web application.

```
public void attributeAdded(HttpSessionBindingEvent sbe)
```

`attributeAdded()` is called when an attribute has been added to the session.

```
public void attributeRemoved(HttpSessionBindingEvent sbe)
```

`attributeRemoved()` is called when an attribute has been removed from the session.

```
public void attributeReplaced(HttpSessionBindingEvent sbe)
```

`attributeReplaced()` is called when an attribute in a session is replaced.

B.4.1.6 `HttpSessionBindingListener`

```
public interface HttpSessionBindingListener
extends java.util.EventListener
```

`HttpSessionBindingListener` causes an object to be notified when it is bound to or unbound from a session. This is typically the result of a session timing out or a session being invalidated.

```
public void valueBound(HttpSessionBindingEvent event)
```

`valueBound()` is called when an object is bound to a session.

```
public void valueUnbound(HttpSessionBindingEvent event)
```

`valueUnbound()` is called when the object is being unbound from a session.

B.4.1.7 `HttpSessionListener`

```
public interface HttpSessionListener
```

An object that implements this interface can be registered to receive notification when an `HttpSession` is created or destroyed.

```
public void sessionCreated(HttpSessionEvent se)
```

`sessionCreated()` is called when a session is created. It receives an `HttpSessionEvent` that contains information regarding the event.

```
public void sessionDestroyed(HttpSessionEvent se)
```

`sessionDestroyed()` is called when a session is destroyed. It receives an `HttpSessionEvent` that contains information about the event.

B.4.2 `javax.servlet.http` Classes

B.4.2.1 `Cookie`

```
public class Cookie
extends java.lang.Object
implements java.lang.Cloneable
```

`Cookie` creates a cookie object. Because cookies can uniquely identify clients, they are commonly used for session management. A cookie consists of a name, a single value, and some other optional information such as a comment, a path and domain qualifier, a maximum age, and a version number. The maximum age acts as an expiration date. If no date is supplied, the cookie is deleted when the session ends.

A cookie is sent to the browser by a servlet using the `HttpServletResponse.addCookie()` method. Browsers are expected to support 20 cookies for each Web server—300 cookies total—and to impose a limit of 4 kB to each cookie.

Cookies can be retrieved from the request header using the `HttpServletRequest.getCookies()` method.

Note that this class does not support HTTP 1.1 cache control. It does support version 0 (defined by Netscape) and version 1 (defined by RFC 2109) cookie specifications. The default is version 0.

```
public Cookie(String name, String value)
```

This constructor creates a cookie with the name and value specified.

```
public Object clone()
```

`clone()` overrides the standard cloning method as available in `java.lang.Object.clone`. It returns a copy of the current cookie.

```
public String getComment()
```

`getComment()` returns the comment describing this cookie's purpose. If no comment is present, it returns `null`.

```
public String getDomain()
```

`getDomain()` returns this cookie's domain name.

```
public int getMaxAge()
```

`getMaxAge()` returns the length of time in seconds that the cookie will persist on the client. Its value is `-1` by default, indicating that it will persist until the browser is closed.

```
public String getPath()
```

`getPath()` returns the server path to which the browser returns the current `Cookie` object.

```
public boolean getSecure()
```

`getSecure()` returns `true` if the browser is sending cookies only over a secure protocol. It returns `false` if the browser can send cookies via any protocol.

```
public String getValue()
```

`getValue()` returns the value of the cookie.

```
public int getVersion()
```

`getVersion()` returns the version of the protocol this cookie complies with.

```
public void setComment(String purpose)
```

`setComment()` updates or sets the comment associated with the cookie. The comment is generally used to describe the purpose of the cookie.

```
public void setDomain(String pattern)
```

`setDomain()` specifies the domain within which this cookie should be visible.

```
public void setMaxAge(int expr)
```

`setMaxAge()` sets the maximum age of the cookie in seconds.

```
public void setPath(String uri)
```

`setPath()` specifies the path on the server to which the browser should return the cookie object. The cookie will be available to this directory as well as all subdirectories of the specified path.

```
public void setSecure(boolean flag)
```

`setSecure()` indicates to the browser whether the cookie should only be set using a secure protocol such as HTTPS.

```
public void setValue(String newValue)
```

`setValue()` assigns a new value to the cookie after it has been created.

```
public void setVersion(int ver)
```

`setVersion()` sets the version number of the cookie protocol with which this cookie complies.

B.4.2.2 HttpServlet

```
public abstract class HttpServlet
extends GenericServlet
implements java.io.Serializable
```

`HttpServlet` provides an abstract class, the concrete classes of which must override at least one of the methods defined in `HttpServlet` or `GenericServlet` classes. The `doGet()`, `doPost()`, `doDelete()`, and `doPut()` are the methods most frequently overridden.

```
public HttpServlet()
```

`HttpServlet()` is the constructor. However, it does nothing, as this is an abstract class.

```
protected doDelete(HttpServletRequest req, HttpServletResponse
res)
throws ServletException, java.io.IOException
```

`doDelete()` is called by the server via the `service()` method to handle an HTTP `DELETE` request.

```
protected void doGet(HttpServletRequest req,
HttpServletResponse res)
throws ServletException, java.io.IOException
```

`doGet()` is called by the server via the `service()` method to handle an HTTP `GET` request.

```
protected void doHead(HttpServletRequest req,
HttpServletResponse res)
throws ServletException, java.io.IOException
```

`doHead()` is called by the server via the `service()` method to handle an HTTP `HEAD` request.

```
protected void doOptions(HttpServletRequest req,
HttpServletResponse res)
throws ServletException, java.io.IOException
```

`doOptions()` is called by the server via the `service()` method to handle an HTTP `OPTIONS` request.

```
protected void doPost(HttpServletRequest req,
HttpServletResponse res)
throws ServletException, java.io.IOException
```

`doPost()` is called by the server via the `service()` method to handle an HTTP `POST` request.

```
protected void doPut(HttpServletRequest req,
HttpServletResponse res)
throws ServletException, java.io.IOException
```

`doPut()` is called by the server via the `service()` method to handle an HTTP `PUT` request.

```
protected void doTrace(HttpServletRequest req,
HttpServletResponse res)
throws ServletException, java.io.IOException
```

`doTrace()` is called by the server via the `service()` method to handle an HTTP `TRACE` request. This is not generally overridden.

```
protected void getLastModified(HttpServletRequest req)
throws ServletException, java.io.IOException
```

`getLastModified()` returns the time, in milliseconds since midnight, January 1, 1970, that the resource was last modified.

```
protected void service(HttpServletRequest req,
HttpServletResponse res)
throws ServletException, java.io.IOException

public void service(HttpServletRequest req, HttpServletResponse
res)
throws ServletException, java.io.IOException
```

The `service()` methods both receive HTTP requests and send them to the appropriate `do()` method. These are not generally overridden.

B.4.2.3 HttpServletRequestWrapper

```
public class HttpServletRequestWrapper
extends ServletRequestWrapper
implements HttpServletRequest
```

HttpServletRequestWrapper provides an implementation of HttpServletRequest that can be subclassed when the programmer needs to adapt the request to a servlet. Methods default to calling through to the wrapped request object.

```
public HttpServletRequestWrapper(HttpServletRequest req)
```

This constructor creates an HttpServletRequestWrapper around the specified HttpServletRequest object.

Unless they are overridden in a subclass, the following methods of HttpServletResponseWrapper call the equivalent method on the wrapped HttpServletResponse:

```
public String getAuthType()
public String getContextPath()
public Cookie[] getCookies()
public long getDateHeader()
public java.util.Enumeration getHeaderNames()
public java.util.Enumeration getHeaders()
public int getIntHeader()
public String getPathInfo()
public String getPathTranslated()
public String getQueryString()
public String getRemoteUser()
public String getRequestedSessionId()
public String getRequestURI()
public StringBuffer getRequestURL()
public String getServletPath()
public HttpSession getSession()
public HttpSession getSession(boolean create)
public java.security.Principal getUserPrincipal()
public boolean isRequestedSessionIdFromCookie()
public boolean isRequestedSessionIdFromUrl()
public boolean isRequestedSessionIdFromURL()
public boolean isRequestedSessionIdValid()
public boolean isUserInRole(String role)
```

B.4.2.4 HttpServletResponseWrapper

```
public class HttpServletResponseWrapper
extends ServletResponseWrapper
implements HttpServletResponse
```

HttpServletResponseWrapper provides an implementation of HttpServletResponse that can be subclassed when the programmer needs to adapt the response to a servlet. Methods default to calling through to the wrapped request object.

```
public HttpServletResponseWrapper(HttpServletResponse res)
```

This constructor creates an HttpServletResponseWrapper around the specified HttpServletResponse object.

Unless they are overridden in a subclass, the following methods of HttpServletResponseWrapper call the equivalent method on the wrapped HttpServletResponse:

```
public void addCookie(Cookie cookie)
public void addDateHeader(String name, long date)
public void addHeader(String name, String value)
public void addIntHeader(String name, int value)
public boolean constainsHeader()
public String encodeRedirectUrl(String url)
public String encodeRedirectURL(String url)
public String encodeUrl(String url)
public String encodeURL(String url)
public void sendError(int sc)
public void sendError(int sc, String msg)
public void sendRedirect(String location)
public void setDateHeader(String name, long date)
public void setHeader(String name, String value)
public void setIntHeader(String name, int value)
public void setStatus(int sc)
public void setStatus(int sc, String sm)
```

B.4.2.5 HttpSessionBindingEvent

```
public class HttpSessionBindingEvent
extends HttpSessionEvent
```

An HttpSessionBindingEvent is the type of event that is sent to an object implementing HttpSessionBindingListener when it is bound or unbound from a session or to an HttpSessionAttributeListener that has been configured in the deployment descriptor when any attribute is bound, unbound, or updated in a session.

```
HttpSessionBindingEvent(HttpSession session, String name)
```

```
HttpSessionBindingEvent(HttpSession session, String name,
Object value)
```

The constructors create an HttpSessionBindingEvent object. The session and name are the parameters to which the object is bound or unbound.

B.4.2.6 HttpSessionEvent

```
public class HttpSessionEvent
extends java.util.EventObject
```

An HttpSessionEvent represents event notifications for changes to a session.

```
HttpSessionEvent(HttpSession source)
```

HttpSessionEvent constructs a given session. It must be passed from a reference to the HttpSession to which the event relates.

```
public HttpSession getSession()
```

getSession() returns the session associated with this event.

B.4.3 javax.servlet.jsp Interfaces

The javax.servlet.jsp package contains interfaces and classes of the JavaServer Pages specification. Many of these are intended for use by the JSP engine—not within an actual JSP.

B.4.3.1 HttpJspPage

```
public interface HttpJspPage
extends JspPage
```

This interface provides two methods that initialize and destroy a JSP; this class is generated by the processor and must satisfy them both. It extends JspPage and defines one method.

_jspService() is an implementation of the service() method specific to the HTTP protocol.

```
public void _jspService(
javax.servlet.http.HttpServletRequest request,
javax.servlet.http.HttpServletResponse response)
throws javax.servlet.ServletException,
java.io.IOException
```

_jspService() method corresponds to the body of the JSP page. The JSP processor defines this automatically. It returns no value.

B.4.3.2 JspPage

```
public interface JspPage
extends javax.servlet.Servlet
```

This interface must be implemented by a class generated by the JSP processor.

```
public void jspDestroy()
```

jspDetroy() is invoked when the JSP page is about to be removed. It corresponds to a servlet's destroy() method.

```
public void jspInit()
```

jspInit() is called when the JSP page is created, and can initialize the JspPage. It corresponds to a servlet's init() method.

B.4.4 javax.servlet.jsp Classes

B.4.4.1 JspEngineInfo

```
public abstract class JspEngineInfo
```

This is an abstract class that obtains information regarding the JSP engine.

```
public abstract String getSpecificationVersion()
```

getSpecificationVersion() returns a string containing the version number of the JSP specification supported by the engine; for example, 1.2. If the version is unknown, it returns null.

```
public JspEngineInfo()
```

`JspEngineInfo()` is the default constructor. Because this class is abstract, only subclasses call this constructor.

B.4.4.2 JspFactory

```
public abstract class JspFactory
extends java.lang.Object
```

`JspFactory` is an abstract class that allows for the creation of instances of classes and interfaces required to support the JSP implementation.

```
public JspFactory()
```

`JspFactory()` is the default constructor. Because this class is abstract, only subclasses call this constructor.

```
public static JspFactory getDefaultFactory()
```

`getDefaultFactory()` returns the default factory object reference for this implementation.

```
public abstract PageContext getPageContext(Servlet servlet,
ServletRequest request,
ServletResponse response,
String errorpageurl,
boolean needsSession,
int buffer,
boolean autoflush)
```

`getPageContext()` returns a `javax.servlet.jsp.PageContext` object for the calling servlet and pending request and response to be processed.

```
public abstract void releasePageContext(PageContext pc)
```

`releasePageContext()` releases the specified, previously allocated `javax.servlet.jsp.PageContext` object. This results in a call to the `PageContext.release()` method.

```
public static void setDefaultFactory(JspFactory dflt)
```

`setDefaultFactory()` sets the default JSP factory object for this JSP implementation. Only the JSP engine runtime may call this method.

B.4.4.3 JspWriter

```
public abstract class JspWriter
extends java.io.Writer
```

The `JspWriter` class is abstract and provides a character output stream usable by a JSP object. It is similar to `java.io.PrintWriter` in functionality.

```
public static final int DEFAULT_BUFFER
public static NO_BUFFER
public static final int UNBOUNDED_BUFFER
```

The above constants define different buffer sizes passable to the `JspWriter`'s constructor.

```
protected int bufferSize
protected boolean autoFlush
```

These fields indicate the `Writer` buffer size and whether the buffer will be automatically flushed, repsectively.

```
protected JspWriter(int bufferSize, boolean autoFlush)
```

This is a protected constructor that can be used by subclasses of `JspWriter`.

```
public abstract void clear()
throws java.io.IOException
```

`clear()` clears the buffer. If data has been written to the output stream prior to the method call, an exception is thrown.

```
public abstract void clearBuffer()
throws java.io.IOException
```

`clearBuffer()` clears the buffer. It does not throw an exception if data has been written to the output stream prior to the method call.

```
public void close()
throws java.io.IOException
```

`close()` flushes and then closes the stream. Once closed, any `write()` or `flush()` invocations will throw a `java.io.IOException`.

```
public abstract void flush()
throws java.io.IOException
```

`flush()` flushes the output buffer, writing any data in the buffer to their intended destination. If the intended destination is another data stream, it too is flushed. In this manner, all buffers in a chain of writers and output streams will be flushed.

```
public int getBufferSize()
throws java.io.IOException
```

`getBufferSize()` returns the buffer size in bytes (as in `int`). It returns 0 if there is no buffer.

```
public int getRemaining()
throws java.io.IOException
```

`getRemaining()` returns the number of bytes that are still left unused in the buffer.

```
public boolean isAutoFlush()
```

`isAutoFlush()` returns true if the buffer flushes automatically.

```
public abstract void newLine()
throws java.io.IOException
```

`newLine()` writes a new line character to the output stream. The line separator is defined by `line.separator` and, as such, may not be a single new line character.

```
public abstract void print(boolean b)
throws java.io.IOException
public abstract void print(char c)
throws java.io.IOException
public abstract void print(int i)
throws java.io.IOException
public abstract void print(long l)
throws java.io.IOException
public abstract void print(float f)
throws java.io.IOException
public abstract void print(double d)
throws java.io.IOException
public abstract void print(char[] ca)
```

```
throws java.io.IOException
public abstract void print(String s)
throws java.io.IOException
public abstract void print(Object o)
throws java.io.IOException
```

`print()` prints the primitive, object, or string as specified to the client without a new line character (`\n`). When an object is passed as the argument, it is converted to a string using `String.valueOf()`.

```
public abstract void println()
throws java.io.IOException
public abstract void println(boolean b)
throws java.io.IOException
public abstract void println(char c)
throws java.io.IOException
public abstract void println(int i)
throws java.io.IOException
public abstract void println(long l)
throws java.io.IOException
public abstract void println(float f)
throws java.io.IOException
public abstract void println(double d)
throws java.io.IOException
public abstract void println(char[] ca)
throws java.io.IOException
public abstract void println(String s)
throws java.io.IOException
public abstract void println(Object o)
throws java.io.IOException
```

`println()` prints the primitive, `Object`, or `String` as specified to the client with a carriage return/new line character (`\n`). When no argument is passed to the method, a carriage return/line feed is written. When an object is passed as the argument, it is converted to a `String` using `String.valueOf()`.

B.4.4.4 `PageContext`

```
public abstract class PageContext
extends java.lang.Object
```

`PageContext` is an abstract class to be extended for providing access to the various JSP scopes, as well as JSP utility methods. These utilities include convenience APIs for public objects, a JspWriter mechanism, session management, a way to include or forward pages, and errorpage exception processing.

```
public static final int APPLICATION_SCOPE
public static final int PAGE_SCOPE
public static final int REQUEST_SCOPE
public static final int SESSION_SCOPE
```

The above constants represent the JSP accessible scopes.

```
public static final String APPLICATION
public static final String CONFIG
publis static final String EXCEPTION
public static final String OUT
public static final String PAGE
public static final String PAGECONTEXT
public static final String REQUEST
public static final String RESPONSE
```

PageContext uses the above constants in an internal table.

```
public PageContext()
```

PageContext() is an empty default constructor. Because it is abstract, it can be used by subclasses of PageContext.

```
public abstract Object findAttribute(String name)
```

findAttribute() looks for the specified attribute in the page, request, session, and application scopes (in that order). It returns the value as an object or returns null if the attribute name is not found.

```
public abstract void forward(String relativeURLPath)
throws javax.servlet.ServletException, java.io.IOException
```

forward() redirects the current ServletRequest and ServletResponse to the application component at the specified URL.

```
getAttribute(String name)
throws NullPointerException
```

getAttribute() returns the object associated with the name in the page scope. It returns null if it is not found.

```
public abstract Object getAttribute(String name, int scope)
throws NullPointerException,
java.lang.IllegalArgumenttException
```

getAttribute() returns the object associated with the name in the specified scope and returns null if it is not found. The page scope is searched when no scope is specified. Use the constants defined for scope as the argument.

```
public abstract java.util.Enumeration
getAttributeNamesInScope(int scope)
```

getAttributeNamesInScope() returns an enumeration of names of all of the attributes in the specified scope.

```
public abstract int getAttributesScope(String name)
```

getAttributesScope() returns the scope of the specified attribute. 0 is returned if the attribute is not found.

```
public abstract java.lang.Exception getException()
```

getException() returns any exception passed to the method as an errorpage.

```
public abstract javax.servlet.jsp.JspWriter getOut()
```

getOut() returns the current JspWriter stream object used to generate the client response.

```
public abstract java.lang.Object getPage()
```

getPage() returns the Page implementation class instance associated with the current PageContext.

```
public abstract javax.servlet.ServletRequest getRequest()
```

getRequest() returns the ServletRequest object for the current PageContext.

```
public abstract javax.servlet.ServletResponse getResponse()
```

getResponse() returns the ServletResponse object for the current PageContext.

```
public abstract javax.servlet.ServletConfig getServletConfig()
```

getServletConfig() returns the ServletConfig object for the current PageContext.

```
public abstract javax.servlet.ServletContext
getServletContext()
```

getServletContext() returns the ServletConfig object for the current PageContext.

```
public abstract javax.servlet.http.HttpSession getSession()
```

getSession() returns the HttpSession object for the current PageContext. It returns null if no session is active in this context.

```
public abstract void handlePageException(java.lang.Exception e)
throws javax.servlet.ServletException,
java.io.IOException
```

handlePageException() processes exceptions at the page level. The exception can be redirected to the specified error page for this JSP or by performing an implementation-dependent action inside the method itself.

```
public abstract void include(java.lang.String relativeUrlPath)
throws javax.servlet.ServletException,
java.lang.SecurityException,
java.lang.IllegalArgumentException,
java.io.IOException
```

include() causes the specified resource at the relative URL to be included as part of the ServletRequest and ServletResponse. The current JspWriter "out" is flushed prior to processing the include.

```
public abstract void initialize(javax.servlet.Servlet servlet,
javax.servlet.ServletRequest req,
javax.servlet.ServletResponse res,
java.lang.String errorPageURL,
boolean needsSession,
throws java.io.IOException,
java.lang.IllegalStateException,
java.lang.IllegalArgumentException)
```

initialize() initializes an unitialized PageContext object. The errorPageURL represents the errorPageURL of this JSP. It can be set to null.

If the JSP is participating in a session, needsSession is true. This method is typically called by JspFactory.getPageContext() to initialize state.

```
public abstract JspWriter popBody()
```

popBody() returns the previous JspWriter "out" saved by a previous call to the corresponding pushBody(), and it updates the value of the "out" attribute in the page scope attribute namespace.

```
public abstract BodyJspWriter pushBody()
```

pushBody() returns a new BodyContent object, saves the current Jsp-Writer object, and updates the "out" attribute in the page scope attribute namespace.

```
public abstract void release()
```

release() resets the internal state of the PageContext by releasing all internal references and readying the PageContext for use. It is typically called from the releasePageContext() method of the JspFactory.

```
public abstract void removeAttribute(String name)
```

removeAttribute() removes the object reference associated with the specified name.

```
public abstract void removeAttribute(String name, int scope)
```

removeAttribute() removes the object reference associated with the specified name and in the specified scope.

```
public abstract void setAttribute(String name, Object attrib)
throws NullPointerException
```

setAttribute() stores the attribute name and associate object in the page scope.

```
public abstract void setAttribute(String name, Object obj, int
scope)
throws NullPointerException,
java.lang.IllegalArgumentException
```

setAttribute() stores the attribute name and associate object in the specified scope.

B.4.4.5 javax.servlet.jsp EXCEPTIONS

```
public class JspError extends JspException
public class JspError(String msg)
```

When caught, the JspError exception stops generation and forwards the exception to the errorpage.

```
public JspException()
public JspException(String msg)
public JspException(String msg, Throwable cause)
public JspException(Throwable cause)
```

JspException() is a constructor that returns no value.

B.4.5 javax.servlet.jsp.tagext Interfaces

javax.servlet.jsp.tagext is the package that provides classes and interfaces to support definition of JSP tag libraries.

B.4.5.1 Tag

```
public interface Tag
```

Tag is the interface to be implemented by a Tag handler class. It provides life cycle methods.

```
public int doEndTag()
throws JspException
```

doEndTag() processes the custom tag's end tag. It returns EVAL_PAGE to continue processing or SKIP_PAGE to skip processing the remainder of the page.

```
public int doStartTag()
throws JspException
```

doStartTag() processes the custom tag's start tag. It returns EVAL_BODY_INCLUDE or BodyTag.

```
public static final int EVAL_BODY_INCLUDE
```

EVAL_BODY_INCLUDE indicates that the tag body should be evaluated into the output stream.

```
public static final int EVAL_PAGE
```

EVAL_PAGE indicates that the evaluation of the page should continue.

```
public tag getParent()
```

getParent() returns the parent tag of the current tag.

```
public void release()
```

release() releases the tag handler once it has been used.

```
public void setPageContext(PageContext pc)
```

setPageContext() specifies the current PageContext. It is called before calling doStartTag().

```
public void setParent(Tag t)
```

setParent() specifies the parent Tag of the current Tag.

```
public static final int SKIP_BODY
```

SKIP_BODY indicates that the tag body should not be evaluated into the output stream.

```
public static final int SKIP_PAGE
```

SKIP_PAGE indicates that the remainder of the page should be skipped and not processed.

B.4.5.2 IterationTag

```
public interface IterationTag
extends Tag
```

IterationTag is the interface to be implemented by the Tag handler class when creating an iteration tag.

```
public static final int EVAL_BODY_AGAIN
```

EVAL_BODY_AGAIN indicates that the tag body should be evaluated again.

```
public int doAfterBody()
throws JspException
```

doAfterBody() gets called after the content of the tag body has been processed. It returns EVAL_BODY_AGAIN to submit another evaluation of the tag body and SKIP_BODY to submit that no further processing of the tag body should occur.

B.4.5.3 **BodyTag**

```
public interface BodyTag
extends IterationTag
```

public static final int EVAL_BODY_BUFFERED indicates that a new BodyContent object should be created for evaluation of the body content.

```
public void doInitBody()
throws JspException
```

doInitBody() is called before evaluation of the tag's body to initialize it.

```
public void setBodyContent(BodyContent b)
```

setBodyContent() sets the BodyContent object to be used with the evaluation of the tag's body.

B.4.5.4 **TryCatchFinally**

```
public interface TryCatchFinally
```

TryCatchFinally is implemented by a tag handler requiring extra exception handling.

```
public void doCatch(Throwable t)
throws Throwable
```

doCatch() is called if a Throwable exception occurs within a tag body or in any of the following methods: Tag.doStartTag(), Tag.doEndTag(), IterationTag.doAfterBody(), or BodyTag.doInitBody().

```
public void doFinally()
```

doFinally() is invoked after every invocation of doEndTag() for any tag handler class that implements Tag, IterationTag, or BodyTag.

B.4.6 javax.servlet.jsp.tagext Classes

B.4.6.1 BodyContent

```
public abstract class BodyContent
extends JspWriter
```

BodyContent extends the ability of JspWriter, allowing body evaluations to be processed and accessed.

```
protected BodyContent(JspWriter e)
```

This constructor is called by the generated servlet.

```
public void clearBody()
```

clearBody() clears the body associated with the invoking BodyContent object.

```
public void flush()
throws java.io.IOException
```

flush() overrides JspWriter's flush() method; no BodyContent object may flush.

```
public JspWriter getEnclosingWriter()
```

getEnclosingWriter() returns the JspWriter that encloses this BodyContent object.

```
public abstract java.io.Reader getReader()
```

getReader() returns the result of the body evaluation as a java.io.Reader.

```
public abstract void writeOut(java.io.Writer out)
throws java.io.IOException
```

writeOut() writes the body content to the "out" stream specified.

B.4.6.2 BodyTagSupport

```
public class BodyTagSupport
extends TagSupport
implements BodyTag
```

`BodyTag` extends `TagSupport`, providing a base class for body tag handlers.

```
protected BodyContent bodyContent
```

`bodyContent` references the current `BodyContent` object.

```
public BodyTagSupport()
```

The `BodyTagSupport()` constructor creates a `BodyTagSupport` object. Subclasses of `BodyTagSupport` must provide a no-arg constructor that calls this constructor.

```
public int doAfterBody()
throws JspException
```

`doAfterBody()` returns `SKIP_BODY`. It should be overridden if necessary.

```
public in doEndTag()
throws JspException
```

`doEndTag()` returns `EVAL_PAGE`. It should be overridden if necessary.

```
public void doInitBody()
```

`doInitBody()` does nothing. It should be overridden if necessary.

```
public int doStartTag()
throws JspException
```

`doStartTag()` returns `EVAL_BODY_BUFFERED`. It should be overriden if necessary.

```
public BodyContent getBodyContent()
```

`getBodyContent()` returns the `BodyContent` object for this tag handler.

```
public JspWriter getPreviousOut()
```

`getPreviousOut()` returns the enclosing `JspWriter` object.

```
public void release()
```

`release()` resets the tag handler's state.

```
public void setBodyContent(BodyContent b)
```

`setBodyContent()` stores the `BodyContent` object to be used in conjunction with the tag body's evaluation.

B.4.6.3 `BodyJspWriter`

```
public abstract class BodyJspWriter
extends JspWriter
```

`BodyJspWriter` is a subclass of `JspWriter`, and it can be used for processing body evaluations.

```
protected BodyJspWriter(int buffersize, boolean autoflush)
```

B.4.6.4 `PageData`

```
public abstract class PageData
extends java.lang.Object
```

A `PageData` object contains translation-time information about a JSP's XML document form.

```
public PageData()
```

A `PageData()` constructor takes no arguments.

```
public abstract java.io.InputStream getInputStream()
```

`getInputStream()` returns an `InputStream` that can make the XML document form of the JSP accessible.

B.4.6.5 TagAttributeInfo

```
public class TagAttributeInfo
extends java.lang.Object
```

A TagAttributeInfo object represents a tag attribute at translation time.

```
public static final String ID
```

ID represents the ID.

```
public TagAttributeInfo(String name,
boolean required, String type, boolean reqTime)
```

TagAttributeInfo() creates a TagAttributeInfo object. reqTime returns true if the attribute can be a request-time attribute.

```
public boolean canBeRequestTime()
```

canBeRequestTime() returns true if the attribute can hold a request-time value.

```
public static TagAttributeInfo
getIdAttribute(TagAttributeInfo[] a)
```

getIdAttribute() is a convenience method that retrieves the ID from an array of TagAttributeInfo objects.

```
public String getName()
```

getName() returns the attribute name.

```
public String getTypeName()
```

getTypeName() returns the name of the attribute type.

```
public boolean isRequired()
```

isRequired() returns true if the attribute is required.

```
public String toString()
```

toString() returns a String representation of the TagAttributeInfo object.

B.4.6.6 `TagData`

```
public class TagData
extends Object
implements Cloneable
```

A `TagData` object contains the name-value pairs of the attributes associated with a tag at translation time.

```
public Object getAttribute(String attrName)
```

`getAttribute()` returns the value of the specified attribute.

```
public java.util.Enumeration getAttributes()
```

`getAttributes()` returns an enumeration containing all the attributes of this tag.

```
public String getAttributeString()
```

`getAttirbuteString()` returns the value of the specified attribute as a `String`.

```
public String getId()
```

`getId()` returns the value of the `id` attribute. If it does not exist, it returns `null`.

```
public static final Object REQUEST_TIME_VALUE
```

`REQUEST_TIME_VALUE` represents an attribute value that is a runtime expression. It is therefore not known at translation time.

```
public void setAttribute(String attName, Object value)
```

`setAttribute()` sets the value of the attribute specified.

```
public TagData(Object[][] attrs)
public TagData(java.util.Hashtable attrs)
```

`TagData()` creates a `TagData` object. The name-value pairs representing the attributes of the `TagData` can be provided as a two-dimensional `Object` array or as a `Hashtable`.

B.4.6.7 TagExtraInfo

```
public abstract class TagExtraInfo
extends Object
```

A TagExtraInfo object contains extra information regarding a custom tag.

```
public TagExtraInfo()
```

This class is abstract. Subclasses may call this constructor.

```
public final TagInfo getTagInfo()
```

getTagInfo() returns the TagInfo object associated with the TagExtraInfo object.

```
public VariableInfo[] getVariableInfo(TagData data)
```

getVariableInfo() returns an array of VariableInfo objects containing information on scripting variables defined by the tag.

```
public boolean isValid(TagData data)
```

isValid() returns true if the attributes associated with the specified TagData object are valid at translation time. Request-time attributes are indicated.

```
public final void setTagInfo(TagInfo tagInfo)
```

setTagInfo() sets the TagInfo object that is associated with the invoking TagExtraInfo object.

B.4.6.8 TagInfo

```
public class TagInfo
extends java.lang.Object
```

A TagInfo object contains any information associated with a custom tag.

```
public static final String BODY_CONTENT_JSP
public static final String BODY_CONTENT_TAG_DEPENDENT
public static final String BODY_CONTENT_EMPTY
```

The above constants denote JSP, tag dependent, or empty tag body content.

```
public TagInfo(String tagName, String tagClassName, String
bodyContent,
String infoString, TagLibraryInfo taglib, TagExtraInfo,
tagExtraInfo,
TagAttributeInfo[] attribInfo, String displayName,
String smallIcon, String largeIcon,
TagVariableInfo[] tvi)
```

`TagInfo` creates a `TagInfo` object from the information contained in a JSP 1.2 format TLD. Another signature is used for creating the object from a JSP 1.1 format TLD (that signature is the same, except without all of the arguments following `attributeInfo`). The `tagName` is the name of the tag, `tagClass` is the name of the tag handler class, the `bodyContent` has information about the body content in the form of one of the constants, and `infoString` is optional.

```
public String getTagName()
```

`getTagName()` returns the tag name.

```
public TagAttributeInfo[] getAttributes()
```

`getAttributes()` returns an array of `TagAttributeInfo` objects that contain information on the tag's attributes.

```
public VariableInfo[] getVariableInfo(TagData data)
```

`getVariableInfo()` returns an array of `VariableInfo` objects that contain information on the scripting objects that are created by the tag at runtime.

```
public boolean isValid(TagData data)
```

`isValid()` returns `true` if the attributes associated with the specified `TagData` object are valid at translation time.

```
public void setTagExtraInfo(TagExtraInfo tei)
```

`setTagExtraInfo()` sets extra information for the tag.

```
public TagExtraInfo getTagExtraInfo()
```

`getTagExtraInfo()` returns the `TagExtraInfo` object associated with the tag.

```
public String getTagClassName()
```

`getTagClassName()` returns the name of the tag handler class.

```
public String getBodyContent()
```

`getBodyContent()` returns a string of information regarding the body content.

```
public String getInfoString()
```

`getInfoString()` returns the information string associated with the tag.

```
public void setTagLibrary(TagLibraryInfo tl)
```

`setTagLibrary()` sets the `TagLibraryInfo` object associated with the tag.

```
public TagLibraryInfo getTagLibrary()
```

`getTagLibrary()` returns the `TagLibraryInfo` object associated with the tag.

```
public String getDisplayName()
```

`getDisplayName()` returns the display name of the tag.

```
public String getSmallIcon()
```

`getSmallIcon()` returns the path to the tag's small icon.

```
public String getLargeIcon()
```

`getLargeIcon()` returns the path to the tag's large icon.

```
public TagVariableInfo[] getTagVariableInfos()
```

`getTagVariableInfos()` returns the array of `TagVariableInfo` objects associated with the tag.

```
public String toString()
```

`toString()` returns a `String` representation of the invoking `TagInfo` object.

B.4.6.9 TagLibraryInfo

```
public abstract class TagLibraryInfo
extends Object
```

A TagLibraryInfo object contains information about the tag library associated with a tag.

```
protected String prefix
protected String uri
protected TagInfo[] tags
protected String tlibversion
protected String jspversion
protected String shortname
protected String urn
protected String info
```

These instance variables hold information regarding the tag library.

```
protected TagLibraryInfo(String prefix, String uri)
```

This creates a TagLibraryInfo object.

```
public String getURI()
```

getURI() returns a string containing the URI as shown in the taglib directive for this library.

```
public String getShortName()
```

getShortName() returns the short name for this library.

```
public String getReliableURN()
```

getReliableURN() returns a reliable URN for this library.

```
public String getInfoString()
```

getInfoString() returns the information string associated with this library.

```
public String getRequiredVersion()
```

getRequiredVersion() returns the required version of the JSP container.

```
public TagInfo[] getTags()
```

getTags() returns an array of TagInfo objects containing information about all of the tags in the library.

```
public TagInfo getTag(String shortname)
```

getTag() returns a TagInfo object for the tag specified by its short name.

B.4.6.10 TagLibraryValidator

```
public abstract class TagLibraryValidator
extends Object
```

A TagLibraryValidator performs translation-time validation for a tag library.

```
public TagLibraryValidator()
```

This is an abstract class, so this constructor is not generally directly called.

```
public void setInitParameters(java.util.Map map)
```

setInitParameters() sets the initialization parameters for the TagLibraryValidator.

```
public java.util.Map getInitParameters()
```

getInitParameters() returns the initialization parameters for the TagLibraryValidator.

```
public String validate(String prefix, String uri, PageData
page)
```

validate() validates a JSP. It returns an error message; if there were no errors, it returns null.

```
public void release()
```

release() releases any data held by the TagLibraryValidator.

B.4.6.11 TagSupport

```
public class TagSupport
extends Object
implements IterationTag, java.io.Serializable
```

The `TagSupport` class provides a convenient implementation of the `IterationTag` interface.

```
protected String id
protected PageContext pageContext
```

`TagSupport` uses these instance variables to store the `id` and `PageContext` associated with this tag.

```
public TagSupport()
```

This creates a `TagSupport` object. Subclasses must provide a no-arg constructor that calls this constructor.

```
public static final Tag findAncestorWithClass(Tag from, Class c)
```

`findAncestorWithClass()` uses `Tag`'s `getParent()` method to find the instance of a given tag class that is closest to this tag.

```
public int doStartTag()
throws JspException
```

`doStartTag()` returns `SKIP_BODY`. It should be overridden if necessary.

```
public int doEndTag()
throwsJspException
```

`doEndTag()` returns `EVAL_PAGE`. It should be overridden if necessary.

```
public int doAfterBody()
throws JspException
```

`doAfterBody()` does nothing. It should be overridden if necessary.

```
public void release()
```

`release()` resets the tag state.

```
public void setParent(Tag t)
```

`setParent()` sets the parent tag of this tag.

```
public Tag getParent()
```

`getParent()` returns the parent tag of this tag.

```
public void setId(String id)
```

`setId()` sets the value of the `id` attribute to `String`.

```
public String getId()
```

`getId()` returns the value of the `id` attribute.

```
public void setPageContext(PageContext pc)
```

`setPageContext()` specifies the `PageContext` object associated with the tag.

```
public void setValue(String k, Object o)
```

`setValue()` sets the value of the attribute specified.

```
public Object getValue(String k)
```

`getValue()` returns the value of the attribute specified.

```
public void removeValue(String k)
```

`removeValue()` removes the specified attribute from the tag.

```
public java.util.Enumeration getValues()
```

`getValues()` returns an enumeration of all tag attributes.

B.4.6.12 TagVariableInfo

```
public class TagVariableInfo
extends Object
```

A `TagVariableInfo` object holds translation-time variable information, which it accesses from the Tag Library Descriptor (TLD).

```
public TagVariableInfo(String nameGiven,
String nameFromAttribute,
String className,
boolean declare,
int scope)
```

The constructor creates a `TagVariableInfo` object based on the TLD.

```
pubic String getNameGiven()
```

`getNameGiven()` returns the value of the `<name-given>` element in the TLD.

```
public String getNameFromAttribute()
```

`getNameFromAttribute()` returns the value of the `<name-from-attribute>` element of the TLD.

```
public String getClassName()
```

`getClassName()` returns the value of the `<variable-class>` element of the TLD.

```
public boolean getDeclare()
```

`getDeclare()` returns the value of the `<declare>` element of the TLD.

```
public int getScope()
```

`getScope()` returns the value of the `<scope>` element of the TLD.

B.4.6.13 `VariableInfo`

```
public class VariableInfo
extends Object
```

At runtime, a tag creates certain scripting variables. The `VariableInfo` object holds this data.

```
public static final int NESTED
public static final int AT_BEGIN
public static final int AT_END
```

The above constants define scopes available to scripting variables. NESTED defines a variable as visible within the start and end tags. AT_BEGIN defines a variable as visible after the start tag. AT_END defines a variable as visible after the end tag.

```
public VariableInfo(String varName,
String className,
boolean declare,
int scope)
```

This creates a VariableInfo object. If the variable is new, it may require declaration, which is indicated by setting the declare parameter to true.

```
public String getVarName()
```

getVarName() returns the scripting variable name.

```
public String getClassName()
```

getClassName() returns the scripting variable class name.

```
public boolean getDeclare()
```

getDeclare() returns true if the variable is new, as it may then need a declaration.

```
public int getScope()
```

getScope() returns the scripting variable scope.

C

Glossary of Terms

...with ruder terms, such as my wit affords, and over-joy of heart doth minister.

—William Shakespeare, *Henry VI*, pt. 2, 1.1

This section describes key terms associated with the Java programming language, object-oriented development, and programming in general. It is intended as reference material for use as you are getting started. Where appropriate, I have made distinctions with respect to ColdFusion terminology.

100% Pure Java A guide developed by Sun Microsystems to ensure that applications written in Java conform to a strict specification. The guide covers not only the writing of programs, but also their marketing. No application can use this trademark unless it meets all of the requirements as prescribed by Sun.

A

Abstract A keyword used in the Java programming language to specify a class that cannot be instantiated itself, or a method without implementation.

Abstract class A class that cannot itself be instantiated. Subclasses may inherit from an abstract class; that is, *extend* it.

Abstract method An abstract method has no implementation. The presence of an abstract method renders the class abstract.

Abstract Window Toolkit (AWT) Package of graphical user interface classes implemented in native platform component versions. AWT classes allow for the creation of buttons, frames, event handlers, and text in application interfaces. AWT's popularity has ebbed recently in favor of the newer Swing.

API Application programming interface. The specification that dictates how a programmer must write to access the state and behavior of objects and classes.

Applet A (generally small) program written in Java and capable of executing in a Web browser or other devices that support the applet model. Applets aided in Java's early popularity as a language, because they allow programs to be dynamically downloaded and securely executed. Applets are simply Java classes that extend `java.applet`. Applets can be viewed from the command line with appletviewer, part of the standard JDK. Alternatively, applets can be viewed in a Web page by referencing the applet with either the `<object>` or `<applet>` tags, both part of standard HTML.

Argument An argument is an item of data passed to a method. An argument may be an expression, a variable, or a literal. Many functions in ColdFusion are passed arguments.

Array An ordered set of data items, all of which must be of the same type. Each item in the array can be referenced by its integer position. Java arrays start at 0, not 1 as in ColdFusion.

ASCII American Standard Code for Information Interchange. An ASCII code is the 7-bit numerical representation of a character, which many different computing platforms can understand.

B

Bean A reusable Java software component. Beans are standard Java classes that conform to certain design and naming conventions.

Binary operator An operator with two arguments.

Bit Contracted form of "binary digit," the smallest unit of information in a computer. A bit is capable of holding one of two possible values: on or off, commonly represented as true or false, or 0 or 1.

Bitwise operator An operator that manipulates individual bits within a byte, generally by comparison or by shifting the bits to the left or right.

Block Any Java code between curly braces; for instance: { `int i = 0;` }

Boolean Named for English mathematician George Boole, refers to an expression or variable that may have only a true or false value. `boolean` is a primitive Java type.

Bounding box The smallest rectangle enclosing a geometric shape; used in GUI programming.

`break` A keyword in Java, `break` is used to resume program execution at the statement immediately following the current statement. In this regard, it functions like the `break` keyword in `<cfscript>`. If a label is in use, `break` returns to the label.

Byte Eight bits. Byte is also a type in the Java programming language. A byte is treated by Java as a signed integer.

Bytecode Generated by the Java compiler and executed by the Java interpreter, bytecode is machine-independent. Byte code can then be converted to native machine instructions on the fly by a JIT (Just-In-Time) compiler. `.class` files consist of bytecodes, serving as input to the Java Virtual Machine.

C

`case` A keyword in the Java programming language, used within a "switch" block to define a set of statements to be executed in the event that the specified `case` value matches the `switch` value.

Cast To explicitly convert one data type to another; for example, { `double d = 2.3; d= (int) d;` }

`catch` A keyword in the Java programming language used to declare a block of statements to be executed in the event that an exception occurs in a preceeding "try" block.

`char` A keyword used to declare a variable of type `char`, used to represent Unicode characters. `chars` are considered 16-bit integer primitives. Java allows simple conversion between `char` and other primitive integers.

Class In object-oriented programming, defines how a particular type of object can be implemented. A class defines instance and class variables and methods, specifies the interface the class implements, and defines the immediate superclass of the class (which it extends). In Java, all behavior within a program is defined by classes, and all classes inherit from the class `Object`. The `java.lang.Class` class reveals the runtime type of any object.

Class file A `.class` file is created when Java source code is compiled. The name of the file will match the name of the class. For instance, the file `Shirt.java`, which defines the Shirt class, will produce a bytecode file named `Shirt.class`.

Class method A method invoked without reference to any specific object. This method affects the class, but not a particular instance of a class (an object). Class methods are specified using the keyword `static`. The `java.lang.Math` class, for instance, defines only static (class) methods.

Class path An environmental variable that holds the location of class libraries used by the Java Virtual Machine.

Class variable A variable defined at the class level, not any specific instance of a class (an object). Class variables are specified within the class definition using the keyword `static`.

Codebase Used within the `code` attribute of the `<applet>` tag to specify the location (URL of the directory) of the main applet class file.

Comment Explanatory text ignored by the compiler. Java comments are the same as standard SQL and CFScript comments that ColdFusion developers should be familiar with: // specifies a single-line comment, /* marks the beginning of a multiline comment, and */ marks the end.

Compiler A program that translates source code in a `.java` file into the bytecode of a `.class` file. The compiler is part of the JDK; it is executed at the command line with the command `javac`.

Constructor A special method used only for the creation of objects. Constructors have the same name as their class, and they are invoked using the `new` keyword. A Java class may have zero or more constructor methods. If no constructor is specified, the superclass constructor is invoked. If more than one constructor is specified, each must have a unique argument list.

Container An item that provides lifecycle management, security, deployment, and runtime services to components. Additionally, every different container type provides its own services. Container types are applet, application client, EJB, JSP, servlet, and Web.

Context attribute An object bound with a servlet's context.

`continue` A Java keyword used within loops that causes execution to resume at the end of the current loop. In this regard, it functions like the `continue` keyword in `<cfscript>`. If a label is used, execution resumes at the label.

Core class A public class that is a standard member of the Java platform. A core class is therefore available on any operating system in which the Java platform runs.

D

Declaration A statement that establishes an identifier and associates attributes with it. It may or may not reserve memory space (for data declarations) or provide the implementation (for method declarations).

`default` A Java keyword used after all `case` conditions within a `switch` block to indicate the set of statements to execute in the default case (that is, if the `switch` value does not match any of the explicit `case` values).

Deployment descriptor An XML file describing how an application should be deployed. It includes specific instructions for the deployment tool regarding container options and required configuration. `web.xml`, used within Web applications for JSPs and servlets, is one such file.

Distributed application An application composed of two or more distinct components, running in separate runtimes, often on different platforms.

`do` A keyword used to declare a loop that iterates a set of statements. It functions similarly to a "do" loop in ColdFusion script.

DOM Document Object Model; a W3C specification for representing a document as a tree of objects with interfaces for traversing the tree. It must be representable as XML.

`double`, double precision `double` is a Java keyword used to define a variable of type `double`. A double precision variable is an IEEE standard 64-bit floating-point primitive capable of representing numbers in the range 1.8×10^{308} to 4.9×10^{-324} approximately.

DTD Document Type Definition. A `.dtd` file describes the structure and properties of one or more XML documents.

E

`else` A Java keyword used to specify a block of statements to be executed in the event that the condition of a previous `if` or `else if` statement evaluates to `false`.

Encapsulation Forming the data and behavior within an object so that the implementation and structure are hidden. In this way, encapsulation allows objects to be interacted with as black boxes that provide services within an application. Code encapsulation increases portability and ease of use of code.

Error class `Java.lang.Error` is a subclass of `Throwable`. It is the parent of all Java error classes. An error is a state from which a program cannot recover.

Exception An exception is a programmatic state that prevents the program from executing normally. An exception can often be "handled"—that is, anticipated and caught by the program.

Exception handler A block of code that consists of statements that react to an exception of a certain type. Java uses `throwable`, `try`, and `catch` in a manner syntactically similar to how ColdFusion implements these keywords. Exception handling in Java, however, also incorporates the `finally` keyword.

Extends One class extends another by adding functionality in the form of additional fields or methods or by overriding its methods. The extending class is referred to as a subclass of the extended class.

F

Field A data member of a class; that is, a variable defining a certain characteristic of a class.

`final` A keyword in Java, `final` indicates an entity that cannot be changed or derived from after having been established. A `final` class cannot be subclassed. A `final` method cannot be overridden. A `final` variable can have no value other than that with which it was initialized.

`finally` A Java keyword that executes a statement block regardless of whether or not an exception was encountered in a previously defined `try` block.

`float`, Float class A Java keyword defining a 32-bit floating-point primitive type number variable. The Float class defines a number of important constants such as `NaN` (Not a Number), `MAX_VALUE`, and `POSITIVE_INFINITY`.

`for` A Java keyword used to declare a loop type that iterates statements until a specified condition is met. It takes the form `(statement;exit condition; increment)` and is syntactically similar to a `for` loop inside a `<cfscript>` block.

G

Garbage collection The process by which the JVM frees memory resources that are no longer being referenced by the program. Programmers therefore never have to explicitly free objects, as other languages without this feature require.

GUI Graphical user interface. In Java, these components are created using AWT and Swing.

H

Hexadecimal Base 16 numbering system in which 0-9 and A-F represent the numbers 0 through 15. Java hexadecimals are prefixed with 0x.

I

Identifier An item within a Java program.

`implements` A Java keyword used to specify one or more interfaces implemented by the class. It is used in the class declaration; multiple interfaces are separated by commas.

`import` A Java keyword used to set package or individual class names to be referenced without these prefixes in a source code file. Only `java.lang` is imported automatically.

Inheritance The concept in object-oriented programming that a class automatically contains the variables and methods defined in the parent class. The parent class is also referred to as the superclass, in which case the class inheriting from it is refered to as the subclass.

Initialization parameter A variable that intializes a servlet's context.

Instance An object of a given class; that is, a particular instance of the class. An object is created using the `new` keyword.

Instance method A function that operates on the currect object. Instance methods are distinct from static methods, which operate at the class level.

Instance variable A data item associated with a particular class. Each time an object of the class is created, a new copy of an instance variable is created. Instance variables therefore stand in contrast to class level (static) variables.

`instanceof` A Java operator that tests whether a reference is of a particular type. It returns `true` if the reference passed can legally be cast to the reference type passed.

`int` A Java keyword that defines a 32-bit primitive integer type in the range of -214783648 to 2147483647. `int`s in Java are always treated as signed.

`interface` A Java keyword used to define a collection of method definitions and constants. Once defined, an interface can be implemented by other classes with the `implements` keyword.

Interpreter Reads, decodes, and executes bytecode for the Java Virtual Machine. See also Java Virtual Machine.

J

J2 platform A Java platform edition consists of a standard set of functionality across different markets, or optimized for different devices. Each edition of a platform is comprised of core (essential) packages and optional packages.

J2EE Java 2 Enterprise Edition. It provides functionality targeted at enterprises for use in multi-tier, multi-server environments.

J2ME Java 2 Micro Edition; for use with small devices, Smart Cards, set-top boxes, handhelds, and others.

J2SE Java 2 Standard Edition; for general-purpose application development.

JAR files Java Archive File is a file format used to aggregate a number of files into one. It uses the same compression algorithm as `.zip` files, and it can subsequently be opened with `.zip` utilities.

Java RMI For distributed environments; allows the methods of remote objects in a Java program to be executed from virtual machines residing on a different host.

Java Virtual Machine (JVM) As part of the Java Runtime Environment, the JVM is the software engine that interprets Java bytecode and executes it. Different specifications for JVMs include one for Smart Cards with only 512 bytes of RAM.

JAX A set of Java-based APIs for handling XML data. It supports XML parsing, RPC, UDDI repositories, and more.

JDBC Java database connectivity. It provides database-independent connectivity between Java and data-bases. The `java.sql` package of interfaces must be imported to use JDBC.

JDK Java Development Kit. It is the software development environment for creating Java applications and includes a utilities package, documentation, and a class library.

JFC Java Foundation Classes. This is a graphical user interface extension that adds to AWT for advanced functionality. It includes Accessibility, Application, Java 2D, Drag & Drop, and Swing.

JIT compiler Just-in-Time compiler. This replaces the Java bytecode interpreter and converts bytecode into native machine code on the fly as the program is run. The result is faster execution time.

JMS Java Message Service provides APIs for enterprise messaging systems.

JNDI Java Naming and Directory Interface; a set of APIs to interface with naming and directory services. `<cfldap>` would serve a similar, though more limited, purpose in ColdFusion.

JNI Java Native Interface; standard for interaction between Java and native code.

JRE Java Runtime Environment; the Java Virtual Machine, Java core classes, and other files. As a subset of the JDK, it enables the execution of Java programs. It is specified for end users and developers and does not include the compiler or its classes.

JSP JavaServer Pages; technology to return dynamic content (typically HTML or XML) to a client (typically a Web browser). It is an alternative to ColdFusion that often takes longer to write, but it can also be more powerful because Java code can be written directly in a JSP. See the JSP tag reference in this book for definitions of JSP-specific terms.

JVM See *Java Virtual Machine.*

K

Keyword Words reserved by the Java language that are therefore not available for naming variables or methods.

L

Local variable A data item declared inside a code block that is inaccessible from outside the block.

Long Wrapper class for 64-bit signed primitive long types ranging from -9223372036854775808 to 9223372036854775807.

M

Member A method, field, or inner class declared as part of a class.

Method A function defined within a class.

Method declaration The method header followed by the method body. The method body consists of the block of statements inside curly braces.

Modulus Operator represented as `%` in Java that returns the remainder of a division operation. It is represented in ColdFusion as `MOD`.

Multiple inheritance Allowed in other languages, it refers to the practice of subclassing more than one class. In Java this is not legal.

Multithreaded A program that executes code concurrently.

N

NaN Not a number. A floating-point constant that represents the results of an incorrect mathematical operation, such as attempting to divide by zero. Only the `isNaN()` method can determine whether a result is NaN.

`new` Java keyword used to create (instantiate) a new object (instance) of a class. It is also used to create a new array.

`null` `null` represents the absence of a value. It is represented in Java by the ASCII literal `null`.

O

Object In object-oriented programming, an object is the basic building block of applications. An object is a particular instance of a class. It holds data (fields) and provides methods with which to operate on that data.

OOP Object-oriented programming.

Overloading Using one identifier to refer to multiple items in the same scope. That is, a class may define multiple methods with the same name, provided that their parameter lists differ. This allows the class to be instantiated in different ways.

Overriding In a subclass, creating a different implementation of a method defined in the superclass. To do this, the overriding method must have the same return type and the same signature as the method in the superclass.

P

`package` A group of classes declared with the Java keyword `package`.

POSIX Portable Operating System for UNIX. It is a standard that defines a small language interface between the UNIX operating system and application programs.

`private` A Java keyword used to describe the access level (visibility) of a method or variable. Only other elements of the same class may access a private method or variable.

Process A space in a virtual addressing system that contains one or more threads.

Property Objects contain properties; that is, characteristics that can be set by the user.

`protected` A Java keyword used in the variable or method declaration to signify that the method or variable can only be accessed by elements residing in the current class, its subclasses, or any class in the same package.

`public` A Java keyword used in the variable or method declaration to signify that the method or variable can be accessed by elements in any other class.

R

Reference A data element whose value is an address.

`return` A Java keyword to finish the execution of a method, possibly followed by a value required by the method definition. In ColdFusion, user-defined functions employ the `return` keyword in a similar fashion.

RMI Remote method invocation; a distributed object model in which methods of remote objects written in Java can be invoked from other Java Virtual Machines.

RPC Remote procedure call; invokes a method (makes a procedure call) on an object residing at a remote host.

Runtime system The environment wherein programs compiled for the Java Virtual Machine can run. This includes any code necessary to load programs written in Java, manage its memory, handle exceptions, and more. It also includes an implementation of the Java Virtual Machine and is often referred to as a "Java runtime."

S

Sandbox Ensures that an untrusted application cannot gain access to system resources. In ColdFusion, a sandbox refers to the developer-specific rules set within the ColdFusion Administrator. While the concept is similar, in Java, a sandbox refers more specifically to a varied set of system components such as security managers and security measures built into both the Java language and the JVM.

SAX Simple API for XML. An alternative to the Document Object Model, the SAX interface is an event-driven access mechanism for working with XML documents. SAX is supported by virtually every Java XML parser. To write a SAX application in Java, you need to install additional SAX classes, such as `org.xml.sax.Parser`.

Scope Used to designate where an indentifier may be used. Class scope and local scope are the most commonly employed.

Servlet A Java program that extends the `javax.servlet` class. Servlets extend the functionality of the Web server (as ColdFusion does).

Servlet container A container that provides protocol services for processing requests and formatting responses.

Servlet context A servlet's context defines how a servlet sees the Web application in which it runs. This object can log events and set and store attributes that other servlets also in the context can access.

Servlet mapping Defines an association between a servlet and a URL pattern. When a request URL matches the pattern, the request is passed to the servlet for processing.

Session A set of HTTP requests associated with a particular user within a distinct time span.

`short` 16-bit integer primitive type in the range of –32768 to 32767, always treated as signed.

Signature A method's name, and the type and order of its parameter list.

Single precision A floating point number capable of data precision to 32 bits.

SOAP Simple Object Access Protocol. It incorporates a structure for data based on XML that relies on HTTP for its transport layer in order to invoke methods on objects in diverse, distributed locations on the Internet.

`static` A Java keyword used to define a variable or method as residing at the class level. Therefore, `static` variables refer to variables for which there is only one copy, regardless of how many instances of the class there are. By the same token, class methods are invoked by the class, not a specific instance of the class. Class methods may only operate on class variables.

Static field Another term for a class-level variable.

Static method Another term for a class-level method.

Stream Data read as a sequence (stream) of bytes from a sender to a receiver. The `java.io` package (for input/output) defines two abstract classes to send and receive data streams: `InputStream` and `OutputStream`.

String literal A sequence of characters contained within double quotes.

Subclass A class that directly or indirectly extends another class. All Java classes are subclasses of Object.

`super` Java keyword used to refer to parent class constructors, methods, or variables.

Superclass A class from which a given class is derived. All Java classes have the superclass Object.

Swing A set of advanced GUI components that run uniformly on any native platform that supports the Java virtual machine. It was created as an optional add-on for Java 1.1, and Swing components became part of the standard extensions in Java 2.

`switch` Java keyword used to evaluate a variable that can match a value within a `case` statement in order to execute the statements therein. It works much as it does in ColdFusion.

`synchronized` A Java keyword that guarantees that at most one thread at a time executes the code in its purview.

T

`this` A Java keyword that can represent an instance of the current class. It can be used to access class level variables and methods.

Thread A basic unit of program execution. One process may have multiple threads running concurrently, each of which performs a different, related function. Once a thread has completed its job, it is destroyed or suspended. The `java.lang.Thread` class defines the behavior of a single thread of control inside the Java Virtual Machine.

`throw` A Java keyword that allows the programmer to specify that a given class can throw an exception. It must have an associated `throwable` object.

Throwable The `java.lang.Throwable` class is the parent of every Java error and exception class.

`throws` A Java keyword used in method declarations that specify which exceptions are passed into the next higher level of the program.

`transient` A modifier that indicates that a field is not part of the persistent state of the object and should not be serialized with the object.

`try` A statement that specifies a block of code as one in which an exception may occur. One or more `catch` clauses, which perform some exception handling, must follow the `try` statement.

Type An object's interface. A distinction is created between class and type in OOP when an interface is separated from its implementation.

U

UDDI Unverisal Description, Discovery and Integration. This project provides a public XML-based registry for businesses to register their Web services.

Unary Operators affecting a single operand. For instance, the + and – are used to indicate the positive or negative value of an integer.

Unicode A 16-bit character set defined by the ISO 10646. All Java source code is written in Unicode, which eases global use. Arabic, Chinese, and Japanese are examples of languages that require 16 bits to represent characters. ColdFusion uses an 8-bit standard character set. It is possible to represent 16-bit data in ColdFusion, but it requires some effort.

URL A Uniform Resource Locator in Java is represented by the `java.net.URL` class. Using this class generates an InputStream to read the remote resource. It is used when you might use `<cfhttp>` to read a Web page.

V

Vector Defined as `java.util.Vector`, a vector class object holds an extensible array of Object references.

Virtual Machine The Java Virtual Machine is the interpreter for Java bytecodes, consisting of a bytecode instruction set, a set of registers, a stack, a heap, and an area for storing methods.

Visibility The level of access granted to other classes. For instance, the `protected` keyword can be used to define variables and methods that can be accessed by methods of classes in the same package or by methods of classes derived from that class.

`void` Java keyword used to indicate that a given method does not return a value. Such methods are run by the Java interpreter one by one until the end of the method is reached, at which point the method returns implicitly.

`volatile` A modifier that indicates that a field can be accessed by unsynchronized threads.

W

Web services A Web service is a self-contained application that can be described, published, and subscribed to over a network. Web services enable application-to-application interaction without the overhead of human intervention.

`while` A kind of loop common to Java and ColdFusion wherein the expression inside the `while` is evaluated; if the expression evaluates to `true`, the body of the loop is executed and tested again. This process continues until the expression evaluates to `false`.

Widening conversion Name for the conversion that occurs when a value of one type is converted to a wider type; that is, a type that has a larger range of possible values. Widening coversions are performed automatically by Java when, for instance, you assign an `int` literal to a `double` variable.

Wrapper Applied to Java classes in the `java.lang` package that correspond to the eight primitive variable types (boolean, byte, character, integer, etc.). These classes perform three functions: utility functions, constants, and object encapsulation of primitive values. Wrappers are objects that encapsulate and delegate to other objects in order to modify their behavior.

Writer The `java.io.Writer` class is the abstract base class used by classes to write data in a 16-bit character stream.

WSDL Web Services Description Language. An XML-based language used to describe a Web service, and specify how it can be communicated with.

Define, define, well-educated infant.

—William Shakespeare, *Love's Labour's Lost*, 1.2

D

Java Bookmarks

And now I will unclasp a secret book/And to your quick-conceiving discontents I'll read you matter deep and dangerous.

—William Shakespeare, *Henry IV*, pt I, 3.1

This appendix contains a list of Internet resources and brief descriptions that may be useful to you as you continue learning Java and its attendant technologies. They are listed here by topic and subtopic for easy reference. Some of the bookmarks may refer to specific sections of the same Web site.

D.1 General Java

D.1.1 Java 1.4 API Reference

http://java.sun.com/j2se/1.4/docs/api/index.html
This site contains online documentation for Java 1.4 Standard Edition.

D.1.2 Sun.com Forums

http://forums.java.sun.com
This site contains approximately 70 different forums related to specific aspects of Java technology.

D.1.3 JavaBoutique

http://javaboutique.internet.com/tutorials
This site contains numerous tutorials, many of which are beginner-level, on using applets and JSP.

D.1.4 Java Skyline

www.javaskyline.com

This site contains a number of Java-related news items, introductory articles, tutorials, and examples.

D.1.5 Java Developer's Journal

www.sys-con.com/java

The site for the Java Developer's Journal has forums, an archive of articles, and information regarding Java events.

D.1.6 JavaWorld

www.javaworld.com

This site contains a good deal of code, a newsletter, forums, reviews, and news.

D.1.7 Developer.com

www.developer.com

This site contains articles, tests, software, and more.

D.1.8 IBM alphaWorks

www.alphaworks.ibm.com/java

Software, downloads, articles, and information on Web services, wireless, systems management, and more can be found at this site.

D.1.9 ASCII Table

www.asciitable.com

This site contains a handy table of the ASCII character codes.

D.1.10 SitePoint

www.webmasterbase.com/subcats/47

You'll find articles on J2EE and web development at this site.

D.1.11 JavaCode.com

www.javacode.com

This site contains links and information on applets, newsgroups, games, and magazines.

D.1.12 Javalobby

www.javalobby.com

Links and information on applets, newsgroups, games, and magazines can be found here.

D.1.13 JADCentral

www.jadcentral.com

This site contains forums, code downloads, and information regarding JUGs (Java User Groups).

D.1.14 ONJava.com

www.onjava.com

O'Reilly's site is dedicated largely to selling its books, but it also contains a good deal of useful information.

D.2 JSP and Servlets

D.2.1 Apache Jakarta Project

http://jakarta.apache.org

This is Apache Software Foundation's site for the Jakarta project (Tomcat).

D.2.2 JSR 53 Java Servlet and JSP Specifications

http://jcp.org/aboutJava/communityprocess/first/jsr053/index.html

This site contains the servlet and JSP Java Specification Request at the Java Community Process section of the Sun site.

D.2.3 JSP Insider

www.jspinsider.com

This is a Web site for JSP tutorials, articles, code, and links.

D.2.4 Stardeveloper

http://stardeveloper.com

You'll find jobs and articles from authors at this site.

D.2.5 Model-View-Control Architecture

http://java.sun.com/blueprints/patterns/j2ee_patterns/model_view_controller

This site shows the MVC design pattern in the Java BluePrints section of the Sun site.

E

Quick Reference

Therefore, for God's sake, entertain good comfort/And cheer his grace with quick and merry words.

—William Shakespeare, *Richard III*, I.3

This appendix serves as a quick reference. It provides information for beginners on compiling and running Java files, primitive data types, variables, visibility, methods, importing, exceptions, and so forth.

E.1 Checking Environment Variables

You may need to check your environment settings to determine if a particular environment variable has been set or what its value is.

Steps:

1. Open a command prompt
2. Type `set`
3. The current environment variables display

E.2 Setting `CLASSPATH`

`CLASSPATH` tells the Java Virtual Machine where to find class libraries. Use the `set` command to set the `CLASSPATH` environment variable.

The path to a `.jar` or `.zip` file ends with the file name; the path to a `.class` file ends with the directory name.

Example:

1. Open a command prompt
2. `set CLASSPATH=.;C:\java\MyClasses;C:\java\My.jar`

Note that setting CLASSPATH in this manner will only sustain the variable for the current command prompt session. Closing the prompt and opening a new one resets the variable.

E.3 Setting JAVA_HOME

The environment variable JAVA_HOME tells the compiler where to find the home directory of your Java installation.

Example on Windows XP:

1. Navigate to Start > Control Panel > System
2. Choose the Advanced tab
3. Click Environment Variables
4. In the System Variables pane, click New
5. For Variable Name, type JAVA_HOME
6. For Variable Value type, C:\j2sdk1.4.0 for a default installation of SDK 1.4. You may need to adjust your value based on your installation.

Follow the same instructions for related environment variables such as TOMCAT_HOME.

E.4 Setting the PATH

The PATH environment variable tells the compiler where to find the java, javac, jar, and other executables. This enables you to compile Java classes, run your programs, make .jar files, and so forth, from any directory on your computer.

1. Navigate to Start > Control Panel > System
2. Choose the Advanced tab
3. Click Environment Variables
4. In the System Variables pane, double click the PATH variable
5. Scroll to the end of the list of variables, and add the following text (for default installation of SDK 1.4.0): C:\j2sdk1.4.0\bin

E.5 Checking Current Version

It is not uncommon to have many different JREs running on the same machine at the same time. These can be installed manually or by associated programs (such as IDEs). To check the current version, do the following:

1. Open a command prompt
2. Type `java -version`
3. You will see output similar to this:

```
Java(TM) 2 Runtime Environment, Standard Edition (build 1.4.0-
b92)
Java HotSpot(TM) Client VM (build 1.4.0-b92, mixed mode)
```

E.6 Compiling and Running Programs

1. Open a command prompt
2. `cd` to directory where the `.java` file you want to compile is stored
3. To compile: `javac myClass.java`
4. To run: `javac myClass`

E.7 Primitive Data Types

`boolean` true or false
`byte` 8 bits
`char` 16 bits, Unicode
`double` 64 bits
`float` 32 bits
`int` 32 bits
`long` 64 bits
`short` 16 bits

E.8 Declaring and Initializing Variables

E.8.1 Primitives

```
boolean isAuthorized = true;
char size = 'm';
int age = 30;
long ProductID = 01928493;
```

E.8.2 Arrays

Arrays can be created and populated as shown below. Remember that Cold-Fusion arrays starts at 1; Java arrays start at 0.

In this example, an array of length 3 that will hold `ints` is declared. The first two cells are then populated with the values 1 and 2, respectively.

```
int[] numbers = new int[3];
numbers[0] = 1;
numbers[1] = 2;
```

In this example, an `int` array is created and populated at the same time.

```
int[] numbers = {1,2,3};
```

Arrays can also be populated in loops.

E.8.3 Objects

```
String name;
String name = ''Zoe'';
String name = new String();

Button saveButton = new Button(''save'');
```

E.9 Class Definition

```
public class myClass {
// class definition here
}
```

E.10 Constructors

Constructors are invoked when an object is created. Constructors have the same name as the class and do not return a value.

```
class myClass {
    myClass() {
    // constructor
    }
}
```

E.11 Declaring Methods

This example declares a method called `setQuantity` that accepts a variable called `qty` of type `int`.

```
public void setQuantity(int qty);
```

This example declares a method called `getQuantity` that returns a variable of type `int`.

```
public int getQuantity();
```

E.12 Calling Methods

Methods are called using dot notation against the object that defines the method.

```
Car myCar = new Car();
myCar.honk();
```

E.13 Overloading Methods

Overloading a method means defining multiple methods in the same class, each with the same name, each of which accepts a different parameter list. In this example the `Vehicle` class extends the `Car` class. Let us assume that by default, the `honk()` method will make a honking sound one time.

```
class Car extends Vehicle {
    void honk() {
    // honk code goes here
    }
    void honk(int numberOfHonks) {
    // honk int number of times
    }
}
```

E.14 Overriding Methods

Overriding a method means defining a method in a subclass that has the same signature as the method of the same signature in the superclass.

```
class Car extends Vehicle {
    // override the move method defined in superclass
```

```
        void move() {
        // define move specific only to Car
        }
    }
```

E.15 package

A package is a logical and physical grouping of Java classes and interfaces that minimizes name conflicts. A package is declared using the `package` keyword as shown:

```
package JavaForCF.Loops

// class definition here...
```

E.16 import

The `import` command allows you to reference a class in the imported package only by its class name. For instance, the package `java.lang.String` is the complete `package` name for the `String` class. Since `java.lang` is always imported automatically, we are free to refer to a string without using the `package` name.

To import all of the classes in a package, use a wildcard:

```
import java.sql.*;
// now you can refer to any class in the java.sql package by
// class name only:

Statement stmt = con.createStatement();

class myClass {
    void make
}
```

E.17 Inheritance

The following example shows how to create a subclass using the `extends` keyword. In this example, `Vehicle` is the superclass, and `Car` is the subclass that inherits all of `Vehicle`'s behavior. `Car` then will define behavior specific only to `Car`s.

```
class Vehicle {}
class Car extends Vehicle {}
```

E.18 Defining and Implementing an Interface

An interface is a set of requirements to which classes must conform if they want to use the service provided by the interface. To implement an interface, first declare that your class will implement the given interface; second, define the methods in the interface.

`java.util.Collection` has an interface that defines, among other methods, an `add()` method. This ensures that any implementation of `java.util.Collection` will support its methods.

An interface is defined as follows:

```
public interface Collection {
public abstract boolean add(A o)
...
}
```

An interface is implemented as follows:

```
public class myClass implements Collection {
// code here. can write, for instance, add() since add() is a /
/ method of java.util.Collection
...
}
```

E.19 Exceptions

Declare an exception to be thrown as shown below:

```
public void someMethod() throws Exception {
    if(somethingBad) {
    throw new Exception();
    }
}
```

Catch an exception as shown below:

```
public void someMethod() {
    // code for an operation that could cause an exception...
    try {
    // ...some code
    }
    catch(Exception e) {
    // exception handling code here
```

```
        }
        finally {
        // this code executes whether an exception was
        // thrown or not
        }
    }
```

E.20 Creating a .jar File

A .jar file (Java Archive) uses the same algorithm as a Zip utility does to compress numerous documents into one archive document. The benefit of a .jar file is that the developer can combine HTML, applets, class files, images, sounds, and everything else that makes up an application and put them all into a .jar to facilitate easy distribution of the application. The .jar tool is a Java application tool, regularly available with the SDK.

To create a new .jar:

1. Navigate to the directory in which you want to create the .jar
2. Type at the command line: `jar cf myJar *.class`

To add all of the files in a particular directory to the .jar:

1. Navigate to the directory in which you want to create the .jar
2. Type at the command line: `jar cvf myApp.jar`

E.21 Creating the Proper Directory Structure for a Web Application

The proper directory structure for a Web application is as follows:

```
WEB-INF
WEB-INF\web.xml
WEB-INF\classes
WEB-INF\lib
```

E.22 The Simplest Possible web.xml File

The code for the simplest possible web.xml file is as follows:

```
<?xml version="1.0" encoding="ISO-8859-1"?>

<!DOCTYPE web-app
    PUBLIC "-//Sun Microsystems, Inc.//DTD Web Application 2.3/
/EN"
```

```
    "http://java.sun.com/dtd/web-app_2_3.dtd">

<web-app>
</web-app>
```

E.23 Creating a .war File

Web application archives (.wars) are similar to .jars, but they contain Web applications that might include classes, beans, HTML, JSP, images, and applets.

If you have manually created the proper directory structure for a Web application, follow these steps to create your .war for deployment using the jar tool distributed with the J2SE:

1. Navigate to the top-level directory of the application
2. Type at the command line: `jar cvf myWebApp.war`

Note that you can also create a .war file by calling the .war task of the ant build tool (available from *www.apache.org*). A third way to create a .war file is to use the packager tool distributed with the J2EE.

Index